ASIAN ECONOMIC INTEGRATION REPORT 2024

DECARBONIZING GLOBAL VALUE CHAINS

FEBRUARY 2024

ASIAN DEVELOPMENT BANK

CONTENTS

TABLES, FIGURES, AND BOXES

TABLES

FIGURES

BOXES

FOREWORD

Asia and the Pacific continues its recovery from the disruptions caused by the coronavirus disease (COVID-19) pandemic and other recent global economic headwinds. Growth—and the drivers behind that growth—vary by economy and subregion. Overall, domestic demand has been healthy. Inward remittances have seen a strong rebound. And industries such as tourism are recovering to close to their pre-pandemic levels. Inflation has largely moderated. Nonetheless, the impact from higher global interest rates, increasing geopolitical tensions, selected supply disruptions—including food supplies—and softer demand from advanced economies create a challenging backdrop for sustaining the region's relatively strong growth trajectory.

The Asian Economic Integration Report (AEIR) 2024 analyzes how these economic forces are affecting cross-border flows of goods and services and the movement of people, and the extent to which regional economies are responding to economic and geopolitical challenges by deepening economic interrelationships across Asia and the Pacific and its subregions. Economic integration in Asia and the Pacific now ranks close to that of the European Union (EU) in terms of regional value chains and social integration. One major driver has been the ongoing rapid digital transformation in many economies, particularly since the pandemic. Digitalization boosts connectivity and makes cross-border economic activity more efficient. Still, rising protectionism and the risks of global fragmentation mean cooperation through regional and subregional dialogues must deepen to help mitigate problems and find solutions that benefit all.

This year's AEIR theme chapter tackles the growing challenge of decarbonizing global value chains (GVCs). At each stage of the value chain, from raw material extraction to production of intermediate goods to assembly and ultimate market distribution, carbon dioxide (CO_2) emissions are produced and embedded in the process. GVCs' increasing share in total CO_2 emissions calls for renewed attention and commitment by policymakers to minimize the carbon footprints of GVC activities while realizing the economic benefits of globalization and global production networks. CO_2 emissions in developing Asia have increased despite a rapid reduction in CO_2 intensity during production through better technology and improved efficiency—due to rapid economic growth and industrialization. The chapter analyzes the many forces at play and estimates the economic and environmental effects of new initiatives like the EU's Carbon Border Adjustment Mechanism for Asian subregions. It suggests that domestic and global efforts to minimize environmental damage from GVCs use carbon pricing, accounting mechanisms for embedded emissions, increased trade cooperation, upgraded technology, and international cooperation for technology transfer to reduce CO_2 emissions.

I hope this report will encourage more dialogue and discussion on how deeper regional cooperation and economic integration and sound policy choices can limit climate damage from GVCs; make production, trade, and investment more efficient and cleaner; and help promote green, more inclusive, and sustainable development.

Albert Park
Chief Economist and Director General
Economic Research and Development Impact Department
Asian Development Bank

ACKNOWLEDGMENTS

The Asian Economic Integration Report (AEIR) 2024 was prepared by the Regional Cooperation and Integration Division (ERCI) of the Asian Development Bank's (ADB) Economic Research and Development Impact Department (ERDI), under the overall supervision of ERCI Director Jong Woo Kang. Kijin Kim coordinated the overall production, assisted by Mara Tayag. ERCI consultants under Technical Assistance 10136: Asian Economic Integration: Building Knowledge for Policy Dialogue, 2023–2025 (Subproject 3) contributed to data compilation, research, and analysis.

Contributing authors include Sanchita Basu-Das, Rolando Avendano, Lovely Ann Tolin, and Rainiel Aquino (Chapter 1: The Crucial Role of Regional Cooperation); Neil Foster-McGregor, Pramila Crivelli, Joshua Anthony Gapay, Carlos Cabaero, Pia Medrano, and Gerald Gracius Yee Pascua (Chapter 2: Trade and the Global Value Chains); Rolando Avendano, Clemence Fatima Cruz, and Lovely Ann Tolin (Chapter 3: Cross-Border Investment); Alexander Raabe and Ana Kristel Lapid, with data support from Marie Ann Cagas and Clemence Fatima Cruz (Chapter 4: Financial Integration); and Kijin Kim, Sanchita Basu-Das, Ma. Concepcion Latoja, and Ma. Veronica Domingo with data support from Pilar Dayag and Zemma Ardaniel (Chapter 5: Movement of People).

The section on Regional Cooperation Initiatives in Asia in Chapter 1 was consolidated by Paulo Rodelio Halili based on contributions by regional departments in ADB: Lyaziza G. Sabyrova, Xinglan Hu, Dorothea Lazaro, and Reneli Gloria (consultant) of the Central and West Asia Department; Thiam Hee Ng, Kanya Sasradipoera, Pia Reyes, Esnerjames Fernandez, and Leticia De Leon (consultant) of the South Asia Department; Alfredo Perdiguero, Maria Josephine Duque-Comia, Gary Krishnan, Jason Rush, Asadullah Sumbal, and Pamela C. Asis-Layugan (consultant) of the Southeast Asia Department; and Rosalind Mckenzie, Maria Carina Tinio, and Remrick Patagan (former staff) of the Pacific Department.

Neil Foster-McGregor coordinated and contributed to the production of the theme chapter, Decarbonizing Global Value Chains, with support from Rainiel Aquino, Joshua Anthony Gapay, Pia Medrano, and Mara Tayag. Background papers were provided by Emma Aisbett, Rolando Avendano, Justin Borevitz, Saule Burkitbayeva, Joseph Francois, Christopher Jackson, Jinerva McQueen, Oscar Pearce, Lovely Ann Tolin, and Lee White. The theme chapter benefited from comments and suggestions provided by the participants of the following workshops and seminars: AEIR 2024 Workshop: Decarbonizing Global Value Chains held on 16–17 October 2023 and Economists' Forum Session 1A: Greening Global Value Chains held on 18 January 2024. Helpful comments were also provided by ADB's regional departments. The overall guidance and comments of ADB Chief Economist Albert Park on the theme chapter are gratefully acknowledged.

Guy Sacerdoti and James Unwin edited the manuscript. Joseph Manglicmot typeset and produced the layout. Erickson Mercado created the cover design and assisted in typesetting. Tuesday Soriano proofread the report. Clemence Fatima Cruz, Carlos Cabaero, Clarisa Flaminiano, Rainiel Aquino, Pia Medrano, and Carol Ongchangco assisted in proofreading and page proof checking. Support for AEIR 2024 printing and publishing was provided by the Printing Services Unit of ADB's Corporate Services Department and by the Publishing and Dissemination Unit of the Department of Communications and Knowledge Management. Carol Ongchangco, Amiel Bryan Esperanza, Angel Love Roque, and Nanette Lozano provided administrative and secretarial support and helped organize the AEIR workshops, launch events, and other AEIR-related webinars and briefings. Terje Langeland, with support from Lean Alfred Santos, of the Department of Communications and Knowledge Management coordinated the dissemination of AEIR 2024.

ABBREVIATIONS

ADB	Asian Development Bank
ARCII	Asia-Pacific Regional Cooperation and Integration Index
ASEAN	Association of Southeast Asian Nations (Brunei Darussalam, Cambodia, Indonesia, the Lao People's Democratic Republic, Malaysia, Myanmar, the Philippines, Singapore, Thailand, and Viet Nam)
BCA	border carbon adjustment
BIMP-EAGA	Brunei Darussalam–Indonesia–Malaysia–Philippines East ASEAN Growth Area
BIMSTEC	Bay of Bengal Initiative for Multisectoral Technical and Economic Cooperation
CAREC	Central Asia Regional Economic Cooperation
CBAM	Carbon Border Adjustment Mechanism
CBDR	common but differentiated responsibilities
CGE	computable general equilibrium
CMIM	Chiang Mai Initiative Multilateralization
COVID-19	coronavirus disease
CO_2	carbon dioxide
DI	Diversification Index
EEF	embedded emissions accounting framework
ETS	emissions trading system
EU	European Union (Austria, Belgium, Bulgaria, Croatia, Cyprus, Czech Republic, Denmark, Estonia, Finland, France, Germany, Greece, Hungary, Ireland, Italy, Latvia, Lithuania, Luxembourg, Malta, the Netherlands, Poland, Portugal, Romania, Slovak Republic, Slovenia, Spain, and Sweden)
EVI	Economic Vulnerability Index
FAO	Food and Agriculture Organization
FDI	foreign direct investment
FTA	free trade agreement
GDP	gross domestic product
GHG	greenhouse gas
GMS	Greater Mekong Subregion
GVC	global value chain
HS	Harmonized System
IMT-GT	Indonesia–Malaysia–Thailand Growth Triangle

IPCC	Intergovernmental Panel on Climate Change
IPEF	Indo-Pacific Economic Framework
IRA	Inflation Reduction Act
OECD	Organisation for Economic Co-operation and Development
PIF	Pacific Islands Forum
PRC	People's Republic of China
PTA	preferential trade agreement
RVC	regional value chain
SAARC	South Asian Association for Regional Cooperation
SASEC	South Asia Subregional Economic Cooperation
SMEs	small and medium-sized enterprises
UK	United Kingdom
UNFCCC	United Nations Framework Convention on Climate Change
US	United States
WTO	World Trade Organization

HIGHLIGHTS

- **Regional integration has grown steadily since the mid-2000s with variations across dimensions and subregions.** Based on the Asia-Pacific Regional Cooperation and Integration Index (ARCII), the region shows integration comparable to the European Union (EU) in regional value chains, along with people and social integration. The most significant progress is observed in Asia and the Pacific's technology and digital connectivity dimension, driven by adoption of digital transformation policies by many economies, the pace of which went up during the coronavirus disease (COVID-19) pandemic. However, integration in trade and investment has slowed somewhat since 2019. While intrasubregional integration grew faster than intersubregional integration in Southeast Asia, East Asia, and Central Asia, South Asia showed deeper integration with other subregions within Asia as of 2021. Regional integration has become a crucial buffer against global shocks and helps mitigate their negative effects. While rising protectionism and the risks of global fragmentation compound economic challenges, increased cooperation and investment in connectivity—both "soft" (regulatory) and "hard" infrastructure—can strengthen economic resilience and provide mutual benefits. Closer dialogue and discussion on regional policies will help Asian economies better meet the challenges and risks of supply chain vulnerability and climate change.

Trade and Global Value Chains

- **A drop in external demand and the risk of global fragmentation have weakened Asia's trade environment.** After a strong rebound in global demand in 2021, Asia's trade began losing steam in 2022, with merchandise trade volume falling by 0.3%. Stagnant trade growth persisted in 2023 with tighter global monetary policy to contain inflation, geopolitical tensions, and a downturn in the semiconductor cycle. Nevertheless, the overall picture masks divergent trends across economies. For example, negative trade growth in 2022 came largely from the People's Republic of China (PRC) and Hong Kong, China; while the economies of the Association of Southeast Asian Nations (ASEAN), Japan, and the Republic of Korea saw trade expand. Given the lackluster growth forecast for the world economy in 2024, the region's economies must try to reinvigorate trade growth momentum through more liberal and freer trade regimes while forging economic cooperation with trade partners both within and outside the region. Developing new trading partners and diversifying the range of imported products can boost an economy's resilience to local shocks and intraregional and international supply disruptions, allowing greater flexibility in sourcing raw materials and intermediate goods.

- **Asia's participation in global value chains (GVCs) rebounded relatively strongly, with a reorientation toward more regional value chains.** In 2020, as the COVID-19 pandemic spread, Asia experienced a larger decline in GVC activity (–5.8%) than the rest of the world (–4.8%), with backward linkages more strongly affected. While the 2021 recovery was similar for Asia and the world generally, GVC activity in 2022 grew more strongly in Asia (10.7%) than the rest of the world (7.7%), with backward GVC linkages growing stronger. Historically, Asia's backward GVC linkages outpaced forward linkages, given the region's prominent role as an assembler along the supply chain, particularly in medium- to high-tech sectors. However, with Asia's backward linkages less diversified than in other regions—with diversification levels falling since the pandemic—there is the risk that any disruption in upstream supply chains could hamper GVC production and resilience. Conversely, Asia's forward GVC linkages have diversified since the pandemic. Recently, Asia's GVC integration has become more regional, especially in forward linkages. On the other hand, there are few signs of reshoring in the region. There is little evidence of increased sourcing of intermediates domestically or an increasing share of domestic value-added serving domestic demand.

- **Asia's trade policy landscape is evolving rapidly, embracing broad, modern trade and digital agreements, although trade restrictions persist.** In 2023, the region saw five agreements entering into force and 17 new agreements signed. These included strategic trade partnerships and initiatives reflecting the changing dynamics of international trade cooperation. Nonetheless, restrictive measures in response to global events, particularly those affecting energy and food, remain a concern. Asia plays a significant role in global agricultural and food trade, accounting for nearly 25% of world exports and 27% of world imports. However, economic uncertainties and geopolitical tensions continue to threaten food security in the region. Economies heavily reliant on food imports and lacking diversity in trading partners and imported food products are particularly vulnerable to external and global shocks. This supply chain vulnerability extends to several of Asia's least developed economies, especially in critical commodities such as sugar, rice, milk, onions, garlic, and pork, among others. Trade cooperation between importing economies and prospective regional exporters remains limited, and restrictive trade measures—including tariffs, quotas, and bans—led by regional economies affect approximately 2.7% of all food trade in Asia from 2021 to 2023. Efforts to deepen trade relationships and enhance regional cooperation on food security should be accompanied by measures aiming to eliminate these restrictions.

Cross-Border Investment

- **Despite sluggish global investment in 2022, foreign direct investment (FDI) inflows to Asia were relatively robust.** Global cross-border investment inflows slid by 12% from $1.5 trillion in 2021 to $1.3 trillion in 2022, with a similar decline in global outflows. Geopolitical tensions, high interest rates, and inward-looking industrial policies in strategic sectors weighed on cross-border investment. Despite weaker global trends, FDI to and from Asia remained resilient, as inflows grew by 8% with outflows rising by 18%. Firm-level data show a mixed landscape, with greenfield investment expanding almost 80%—driven by megaproject investments above $1 billion—in semiconductors and renewable energy—while mergers and acquisitions (M&As) fell by 30%. By sector, tertiary industries attracted almost three-fifths of Asia's total inbound FDI. Significant greenfield outlays for renewable energy projects— including solar, electric power, and e-transport—highlight the dynamism of climate-related investments in Asia. Information and communication technology-related sectors, such as data processing and hosting services, were prominent for M&As. Meanwhile, as the network of investment treaties gradually modernizes, international investment agreements signed in Asia since 2020 featured stronger provisions to safeguard an economy's right to regulate issues on the environment and labor standards, and transparency in investor–state arbitration.

- **More fragmented FDI poses both risks and opportunities for Asian economies.** Global investment activity is showing signs of fragmentation, as the pandemic highlighted the need for more diversified and resilient supply chains and production bases. Ambitious industrial policies in developed economies have also contributed to the relocation of foreign investment, notably in strategic sectors—including semiconductors, telecommunications and 5G, equipment for green energy transition, pharmaceutical ingredients, and critical minerals. Globally and in Asia, the average FDI in strategic sectors from 2010–2014 to 2020–2022 doubled, with target destinations expanding from East Asia to Southeast Asia, South Asia, and the Pacific and Oceania. Decarbonization policies are driving investments supporting the green energy transition, while semiconductor investments have become prominent in the region and tripled over the same period. Efficiency-seeking FDI in Asia, mostly concentrated in medium- and high-tech manufacturing, has been key to the region's GVC participation, contributing to job creation and knowledge transfer. To maximize the potential for industrial development, economies should adopt market-friendly FDI policies that enforce investment protection, support technology transfer and innovation, and target high productivity sectors, particularly in technology-related manufacturing and services. While the risk of global fragmentation cloud the FDI landscape, the region can improve the environment for market-seeking FDI by building on its growing purchasing power, strengthened by rising income levels and an expanding middle class.

Financial Integration

- **Asia's global financial integration has advanced steadily, increasing its exposure to financial shocks.** The region's financial integration with the world economy increased access to foreign capital, supplemented domestic investment, and smoothed consumption. It also improved finance sector competitiveness and the development of regional capital markets. However, the region's financial openness also makes the region prone to external shocks and capital flow volatility, notably emanating from the United States (US) and the EU. In 2022, the start of monetary policy tightening led to an increase in capital outflows from the region, partially recovering in 2023. Over 2014–2022, cross-border assets and liabilities as a share of regional gross domestic product increased by 16 and 5 percentage points, respectively. Asia's equity and bond markets are already more sensitive to global financial factors than regional ones, with regional bond market sensitivity to global factors on the rise since 2021. Regional financial integration also advanced, with the share of the intraregional inward portfolio debt stock rising from 28% in 2021 to 30% in 2022, while the inward equity ratio rose from 21% to 22% over the same period.

- **US dollar funding shocks are behind much of Asia's capital flow volatility.** Asia's rising global financial integration makes the region prone to spillovers from the US financial system—in particular centered around the US dollar's key role as the leading global currency. Asia is especially susceptible to US dollar funding shocks due to its high US dollar dependence. About four-fifths of Asia's exports and imports, over half of bank assets and liabilities, half of issued debt, and two-thirds of foreign exchange reserves are denominated in US dollars. It is an exchange rate anchor for 18 Asian economies. Also, the US dollar dominates global payment and currency trades. High US dollar dependence puts capital flows to the region at risk, as it amplifies any reversals driven by US dollar funding shocks. An empirical analysis covering a broad sample of developing economies and emerging markets in Asia shows that a one standard deviation increase in US dollar funding costs raises medium-term portfolio debt outflows from the region as a share of gross domestic product by up to 0.25%. In addition, an economy with a one standard deviation higher US dollar dependence is likely to experience outflows up to 0.3 of a percentage point higher. Policies that help mitigate risks from Asia's exposure to US dollar funding shocks include (i) strengthening bank balance sheet resilience, (ii) developing local currency bond markets, (iii) implementing macroprudential policies and temporary capital flow management measures, and (iv) reinforcing the regional financial safety net.

Movement of People

- **Migration outflows from Asia are recovering as major host economies seek greater access to skilled labor in the wake of worker shortages.** The rebound in migrant outflows is also due in part to changes in migration policies of host economies such as Australia, Canada, Japan, New Zealand, the United Kingdom, and the US. They are designed to attract skilled workers to fill labor shortages and fuel the post-pandemic recovery. Increasing investment in human capital and strengthening international skills partnerships—along with bilateral labor arrangements—could help meet the growing needs of host economies, while ensuring long-term continuity of labor market access.

- **Remittance inflows to Asia remained strong.** In 2022, remittances totaled $356.0 billion, 10.7% higher than in 2021, and are estimated to rise by 4.4% to $371.5 billion in 2023. Except for East Asia, inflows to all subregions increased in 2022—with notable growth in Central Asia (69.4%) and a robust rise in inflows that continued well into 2023 for Oceania (17.4% and 21.2%) and South Asia (12.2% and 7.2%). They stemmed from large transfers out of the Russian Federation, higher oil incomes in major host economies in the Middle East, and a robust job market in the US. The average cost of sending $200 to Asia was 5.2% as of the first quarter (Q1) of 2023, down from 6.1% in Q1 2020 but still above the Sustainable Development Goal target of 3.0% by 2030. Digital remittances have accelerated since the pandemic, but remain less than 20% of the total, even though digital remittance channels cost just 4.4% in Asia and globally. Policies that would help expand migrant worker access to banking services and digital infrastructure include adopting mobile services, standardizing data collection and reporting, and removing barriers to cross-border payments such as non-interoperable payment systems and regulations. Such policies could help the region achieve higher digital remittance uptake and deepen financial inclusion.

- **International tourism in Asia is recovering, yet still lags when compared to other regions.** In 2023, Asia reached 73.2% of its pre-pandemic (2019) arrivals and 77.1% of its receipts. The recovery was much faster than in 2022, when tourist arrivals reached 28.8% and receipts 36.5% of 2019 levels. Yet, Asia's tourism recovery remains slower than other regions—the Middle East recovered 108.7% of its tourist arrivals while Europe earned 117.6% of pre-pandemic tourism receipts in 2023. There are several reasons for the gap: Asian economies implemented some of the tightest travel restrictions from 2020 to 2022; and high airfares along with global macroeconomic and political conditions made potential tourists think twice before traveling. Also, the anticipated boost in tourists from the PRC has, so far, only been partially realized.

- **Digital technology could help the tourism industry build back better; the region needs to embrace policies that unlock the great potential of the digital economy.** Governments in Asia have been setting policies that support digital technology use—to entice investments and induce behavioral changes that build resilience against future shocks. For example, the Philippines began using its eTravel system to digitize arrival cards in May 2023, Malaysia launched its Malaysia Digital Arrival Card, and Singapore now uses a biometrics system in place of traditional passports for its citizens to clear immigration. Some Asian economies formed partnerships with digital platforms to facilitate transactions between local merchants and international tourists. For instance, Malaysia and the PRC collaborated to allow Alipay+ supported wallets from seven economies to use PayNet's DuitNow QR codes in Malaysia. As Asia continues to leverage digital technology, closer regional cooperation can help narrow gaps in information and communication technology infrastructure and digital regulations. Enhancing digital skills among people and firms could ensure safe, seamless cross-border travel while helping make the region's tourism industry smarter, more resilient, and sustainable.

Theme Chapter: Decarbonizing Global Value Chains

- **The impact of human-induced climate change on the natural environment, economies, and societies will likely be wide and far-reaching, with Asian economies highly affected.** The list is long—higher temperatures, drought, water scarcity, severe fires, rising sea levels, ocean warming and acidification, flooding, storms, and declining biodiversity, among others. These will all have severe consequences for human health, food production, access to fresh water and ocean resources, productivity, and critical infrastructure. Developing economies in Asia and the Pacific are particularly vulnerable to the impact of climate change, despite having contributed less historically to greenhouse gas emissions. Climate change is expected to disproportionately affect the region's economies due to their exposure to natural hazards, extreme weather events, and limited resources for mitigation and adaptation.

- **Despite a slowdown in the rate of growth, anthropogenic greenhouse gas (GHG) emissions continue to rise, with Asian economies contributing substantially to the increase.** The primary cause of human-induced climate change is the burning of fossil fuels, which increases GHG concentrations in the atmosphere. Carbon dioxide (CO_2) emissions from fossil fuels and industry cause most of the increase. Developing Asia accounts for a large and growing share of CO_2 emissions as global production structures are influenced by the rise of GVCs, population dynamics, and technological change. Mitigating climate change requires a fundamental shift in human behavior and rapid decarbonization of production. Reducing CO_2 emissions associated with GVCs raises specific challenges, with the global nature of emissions making them difficult to regulate through domestic policies alone.

- **CO_2 emissions can be considered to reflect both a scale and an intensity effect, with developments in these two effects working in opposite directions in recent years.** CO_2 emissions in developing Asia increased rapidly during 1995–2018, with emissions increasing by 114% over the period. This was despite a significant reduction in CO_2 intensity of production, which was not large enough to offset the increase in CO_2 emissions resulting from the rapid expansion in the scale of production. CO_2 intensities vary widely across both economies and sectors. Across a broad range of sectors they fell rapidly during 1995–2018, reflecting technological advances, improved efficiency, and a reallocation of production within sectors through GVCs. Within developing Asia, structural change has played a limited role in lowering aggregate emissions intensities, with reductions primarily driven by changes within sectors rather than shifts toward less emissions-intensive sectors. GVCs have an important impact on both the scale and intensity of producing CO_2 emissions. While increases in the level of GVC production are associated with similar increases in CO_2 emissions, the share of CO_2 emissions due to GVCs tends to be larger than their share in value added—indicating that GVC activity plays an outsized role in emissions production. Sectors involved in GVCs tend to be relatively emissions-intensive, with a higher share of GVC activity shown to be positively associated with higher aggregate emissions intensities. These associations differ between developed and developing economies, with GVC activity in developing economies tending to be more emissions-intensive than in developed economies.

- **There is an intricate relationship between international trade, GVCs, and GHG emissions.** While international trade remains both an essential conduit linking global production networks and a significant source of GHG emissions, it also holds the potential to contribute to climate change mitigation and adaptation—by facilitating the exchange of low-emission goods, green technologies, and increasing production efficiency. Expanding GVCs are generally considered to offer opportunities for developing economies to integrate into the global economy and industrialize. But it also creates challenges for mitigating climate change. The decoupling of consumption from production within GVCs raises concerns about firms relocating production to areas with weaker environmental regulations (the pollution haven hypothesis), potentially leading to higher emissions. Policymakers are increasingly concerned over GVCs' carbon footprint and potential carbon leakage to regions with weaker regulations. Climate change mitigation requires a shift away from carbon-based production, posing a potential risk to the existing GVC model that has contributed to economic development in many economies, but also increased energy consumption, emissions, and waste.

- **The production of CO_2 emissions continues to grow rapidly, with GVCs in developing Asian economies responsible for an increasing share.** During 1995–2018, global CO_2 emissions increased by an average of 2.1% per year. While the growth rate after 2010 (1.8%) was lower than before (2.2%), emissions continue to grow rapidly. Domestic production for domestic consumption remains the largest contributor to emissions, accounting for almost two-thirds of emissions production—GVCs accounted for 14% of CO_2 emissions in 2018, up from 12% in 1995. While playing a relatively small role in overall emissions production, GVCs' increasing contribution to aggregate CO_2 emissions come from the rapid growth in their emissions production. The share of developing Asia in global GVC-related emissions significantly increased over 1995–2018, reaching 42% in 2018. While population growth is a factor, CO_2 emissions per capita have also increased across developing Asia, in contrast with other regions. The increasing role developing Asia plays in GVC-related emissions is partly due to GVC positioning, sectoral structure, and the technological level of its GVC integration. Developing Asia is now a net supplier, exporting more CO_2 emissions embodied in intermediates than it imports. In contrast, developed regions like North America, the EU plus the United Kingdom, and developed Asia import more embodied CO_2 emissions through intermediates than they export in GVCs.

- **International cooperation is crucial to effectively address the challenge of climate change.** Despite national and subnational efforts to implement carbon pricing, the climate crisis worldwide and increased economic interdependence call for increased global coordination. Enhanced global cooperation can create a more coherent and predictable policy environment, increase transparency, and mobilize financial and technical resources to overcome capacity constraints and promote the spread of green technologies, especially to developing and emerging economies. Nonetheless, global coordination in climate mitigation remains weak. Major challenges to global coordination in carbon pricing arise from issues of free-riding and fairness. The possibility of free-riding makes coordination difficult, as economies may choose not to participate in carbon pricing while still reaping the benefits of carbon production. The fairness issue stems from historical contributions to global emissions, with developed economies historically emitting more. The principle of common but differentiated responsibilities recognizes these differences but complicates finding a common global carbon price.

- **Carbon pricing is generally considered the key mechanism for addressing the problem of CO_2 and GHG emissions during production.** Carbon pricing, through either carbon taxes or emissions trading system (ETS), aims to internalize the social costs of emissions, encouraging firms to reduce carbon intensity and transition to cleaner production methods. Despite efforts in various jurisdictions to implement carbon pricing policies, concerns remain over the speed and extent of the global response to the climate crisis. While numerous carbon pricing policies have been adopted globally, just a small percentage of emissions are covered at levels deemed necessary to prevent a 2°C temperature increase, the upper end of the limit in the Paris Agreement. The fragmented nature of carbon pricing across different jurisdictions raises the risk of carbon leakage. To address this, border carbon adjustment (BCA) mechanism have been suggested as a way of leveling the playing field, ensuring that foreign producers face equivalent carbon prices in export markets. However, BCAs raise concerns over fairness and equity, potentially impacting exporters, particularly in GVC supplier economies and developing economies.

- **The EU's Carbon Border Adjustment Mechanism (CBAM) should reduce carbon leakage, but it will have a limited impact on global emission reductions while significantly reducing exports into the EU from some Asian subregions.** Concerns over competitiveness, carbon leakage, and shortcomings of the EU's ETS led to CBAM, the first border adjustment mechanism. Initially targeting carbon-intensive products like cement, steel, and aluminum, the EU sees CBAM as a tool to align global carbon prices and accelerate emission reductions worldwide. For developing Asian economies, with high CO_2 intensities in sectors like ferrous metals, CBAM can create challenges—for example, the value-added tax equivalent of a €100 per metric ton of CO_2 price ranges between 3% and 12%. Estimations using computable general equilibrium (CGE) modeling suggest CBAM might reduce carbon leakage by around half compared to an ETS scheme with a similar carbon price. While the EU's ETS and CBAM may have a limited direct impact on emissions—reducing emissions globally by around 1.3% at €100 per metric ton of CO_2 and by 2.2% at €200 per metric ton of CO_2—it could significantly affect exports to the EU. A shift to a €100 per metric ton of CO_2 price could lead to significant declines in exports for some Asian regions, particularly Central and West Asia, which has a relatively high share of CBAM-covered exports to the EU. At the same time, reductions in EU production from CBAM could spread to many sectors, such as computer, electric and optical equipment, and motor vehicles and parts within the EU through industrial input–output linkages.

- **Extending CBAM to regions outside the EU could significantly reduce CO_2 emissions.** Considering scenarios where other economies of the Organisation for Economic Co-operation and Development (OECD) and regional members of the Asian Development Bank (ADB) implement both ETS and BCA, modeling suggests that global CO_2 emissions could be reduced by around 8.7% at €100 per metric ton of CO_2 and by 15% at €200 per metric ton of CO_2. How much emissions are reduced depends on coverage and carbon price, emphasizing the need to carefully consider these factors in designing and implementing these mechanisms. Extending these policies is also predicted to lead to a significant decline in global trade, highlighting the potential trade-off between emissions reduction and global integration. Extending CBAM to cover other OECD economies, for example, is estimated to reduce average developing Asian exports by 1.9% at a €100 per metric ton of CO_2 price and by 3.7% at €200 per metric ton of CO_2. The expected distributional and negative economic impact on ADB developing members in the extended model (OECD plus ADB regional members) suggests the need for proper compensation mechanisms internationally to draw ADB developing members into carbon pricing and BCA structures.

- **Existing accounting frameworks that measure embodied emissions are underdeveloped, limiting the effectiveness of climate policies.** Accurately measuring emissions embodied in goods and services is crucial for an effective approach to the net-zero transition, such as carbon pricing and BCAs. Yet existing frameworks are underdeveloped, with the measurement challenge more pronounced when considering indirect emissions, such as Scope 2 and Scope 3 emissions. While estimates of an economy's CO_2 emissions are generally reliable, measuring emissions embedded in products is more complex and varies across economies, firms, and time. Public embedded emissions accounting frameworks (EEFs) can play a vital role in decarbonizing GVCs in both developed and developing economies. They facilitate measurement, reporting, verification, and regulation, and support efforts to avoid carbon leakage globally and domestically in the context of trade-related climate policies. To be successful, EEFs need to be carefully designed to align with domestic and international frameworks and those of major trading partners, as global cooperation is crucial to establish a basic, common approach. In doing this, it is important to avoid an overly complex regime that disadvantages smaller producers and resource-constrained economies.

- **Trade policies can play a crucial role in climate change mitigation and adaptation.** Trade and trade policy hold the potential to be a force for CO_2 emissions reductions. It can influence the global movement of climate-friendly products and services, facilitate the transfer of green technologies, encourage higher environmental standards, and act as an external force for regulatory enhancement. Current trade policies, however, often favor carbon-intensive imports, with lower barriers on high carbon-intensive goods. This bias, largely influenced by factors unrelated to trade policy, has been estimated to be equivalent to a negative carbon price of $90 per ton of CO_2, potentially hindering efforts to reduce global emissions. Preferential trade agreements (PTAs) can also help decarbonize GVCs, with the number and breadth of PTAs and the number of PTAs with environmental provisions increasing rapidly in recent years. Evidence suggests that the breadth of a PTA between economies is associated with slightly lower CO_2 emissions intensity traded in GVCs, while the scale effect of a PTA leads to greater overall CO_2 emissions. Including environmental provisions in PTAs, especially provisions restricting trade in dirty goods, can lower emissions traded in PTAs. A one standard deviation increase in the share of trade restricting environmental provisions in PTAs is associated with a reduction in CO_2 emissions in GVCs of 1.2%, with the scale effect accounting for 0.34 percentage points and the intensity effect 0.90 percentage points.

- **Beyond carbon pricing and regional integration, a variety of other steps can be taken to decarbonize GVCs.** The decreasing cost of green technologies, especially in energy production, can promote their widespread adoption. With recent policy initiatives, including the US Inflation Reduction Act and the EU's mission-oriented approach to innovation, further encouraging research and development in renewable energy, opportunities for enhanced competition in green technologies and for providing new climate-related technologies are strong. For maximum impact on emissions reductions, these technologies need to be diffused widely, especially from developed to developing economies. Technology diffusion to developing economies can be facilitated by GVCs and multinational enterprises, potentially enabling these economies to leapfrog into green technologies while avoiding carbon-based production. Technology and technology diffusion can potentially remove any trade-off that exists between CO_2 reduction efforts and GVC production, reducing emissions while encouraging production, trade, and GVCs. Multilateral development banks can play an important role by supporting green infrastructure and technology diffusion while facilitating sustainable investments along value chains, and ensuring transparency and traceability of CO_2 emissions in GVCs.

1 The Crucial Role of Regional Cooperation

Shared Risks

Amid growing protectionism and risks of global fragmentation, regional cooperation and integration remain crucial to address shared challenges and to foster growth across the economies of Asia and the Pacific.[1]

Merchandise trade has been adversely affected by growing nontariff measures over the past 10 years. About 40% of the total nontariff measures in the region are related to sanitary and phytosanitary measures, while 43% are technical barriers to trade (Figure 1.1). Other notable measures such as antidumping and quantitative restrictions have recorded significant increases, ranging from 500 to 1,000 per year since 2012.

Services trade barriers have marginally increased, both globally and in Asia, since 2014. According to the Organisation for Economic Co-operation and Development (OECD) Services Trade Restrictiveness Index, most of the barriers are restrictions on foreign entry (Figure 1.2). Cross-border movement of persons also remains regulated, with restrictions taking the form of limitations on stay, nationality or residency requirements, and lack of recognition of professional qualifications across borders. Air transport, legal, and accounting services were the most restrictive sectors in 2022 (Figure 1.3).

Figure 1.1: Number of Nontariff Measures—Asia and the Pacific ('000)

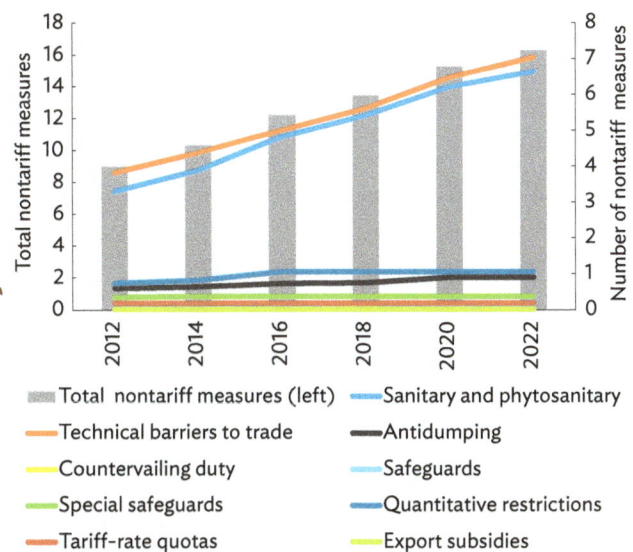

Note: Based on the cumulative number of measures in force at the end of each year.

Source: ADB calculations using data from the World Trade Organization. Integrated Trade Intelligence Portal. http://i-tip.wto.org (accessed May 2023).

Geopolitical risks are prompting policymakers to adopt nationalistic strategies for building resilient supply chains. Major disruptions due to the COVID-19 pandemic and the Russian invasion of Ukraine have underscored the vulnerabilities associated with supply chain disruption, which in turn have encouraged economies to diversify and reevaluate markets for exports and imports.

---

[1]   Asia and the Pacific, or Asia, consists of the 49 regional member economies of the Asian Development Bank (ADB). The composition of economies for Central Asia, East Asia, the Pacific and Oceania, South Asia, and Southeast Asia are outlined in ADB. Asia Regional Integration Center. Economy Groupings. https://aric.adb.org/integrationindicators/groupings.

Figure 1.2: Services Trade Restrictiveness Index—World and Asia and the Pacific (average)

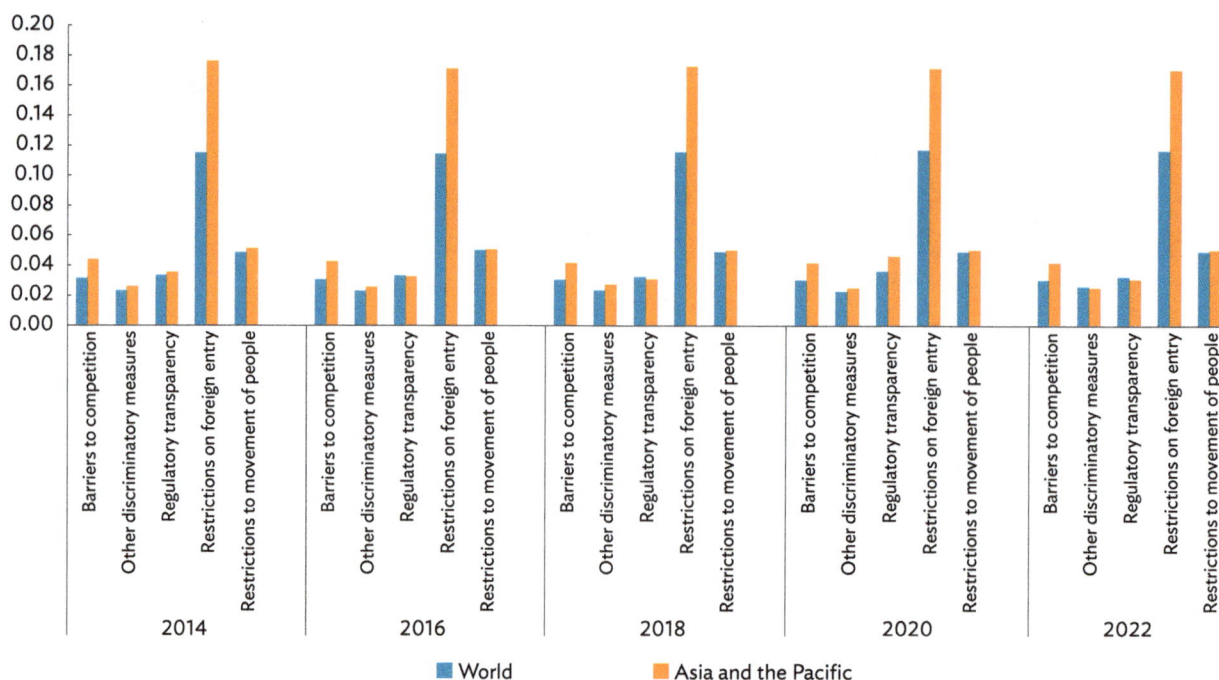

Notes: The index takes the value from 0 (completely open) to 1 (completely closed). The sample includes 50 economies, 12 of which are in Asia and the Pacific: Australia, India, Indonesia, Japan, Kazakhstan, Malaysia, New Zealand, the People's Republic of China, the Republic of Korea, Singapore, Thailand, and Viet Nam.

Source: ADB calculations using data from Organisation for Economic Co-operation and Development. OECDStat: Services Trade Restrictiveness Index. https://stats.oecd.org/Index.aspx?DataSetCode=STRI (accessed May 2023).

Figure 1.3: Services Trade Restrictiveness Index by Sector—World Average, 2022

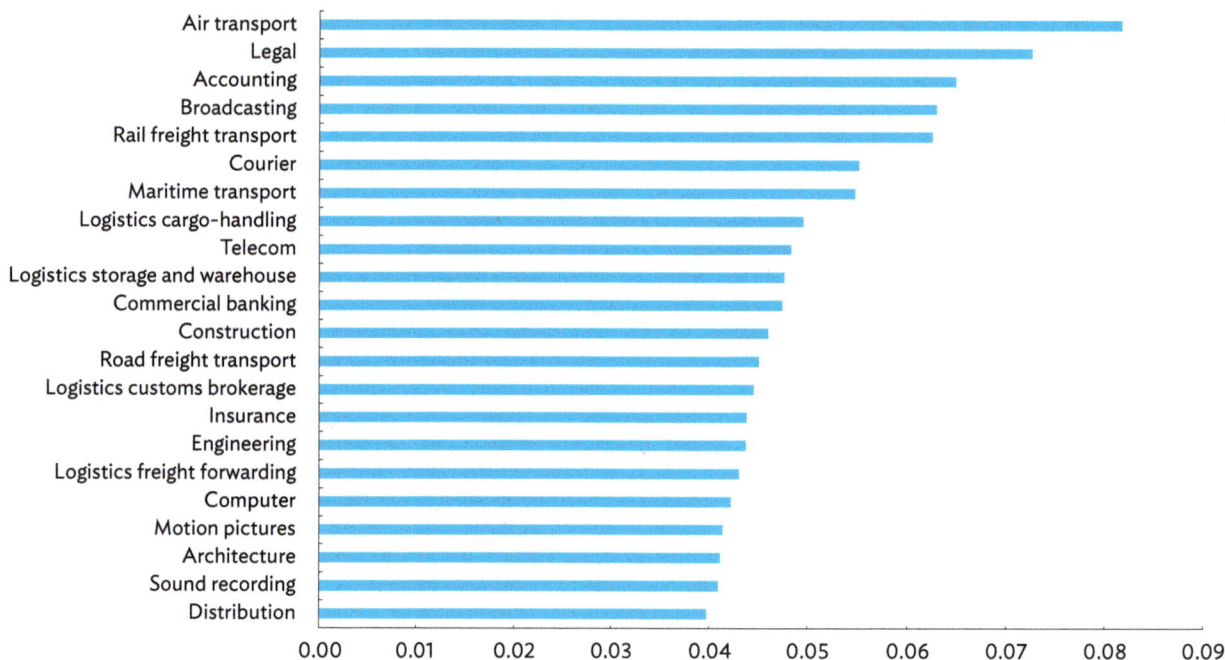

Notes: The index takes the value from 0 (completely open) to 1 (completely closed). The sample includes 50 economies, 12 of which are in Asia and the Pacific: Australia, India, Indonesia, Japan, Kazakhstan, Malaysia, New Zealand, the People's Republic of China, the Republic of Korea, Singapore, Thailand, and Viet Nam.

Source: ADB calculations using data from Organisation for Economic Co-operation and Development. OECDStat: Services Trade Restrictiveness Index. https://stats.oecd.org/Index.aspx?DataSetCode=STRI (accessed May 2023).

Excessive dependence on a single market make importing economies susceptible to external shocks. To improve resilience across supply chains, economies follow policies that strengthen domestic manufacturing, particularly in strategic sectors, while maintaining technological advantage. For instance, the United States (US) in 2022 and the European Union (EU) in 2023 signed laws institutionalizing efforts to bolster their semiconductor industries. The US is investing $280 billion over 10 years while EU support features a $47 billion plan to boost the semiconductor supply chain. Accordingly, multinational corporations' interest in moving production back home (reshoring) or to economies with aligned strategic interests (friend-shoring) has increased sharply in recent years (IMF 2023, also refer to Chapter 2: Trade and Global Value Chains). Meanwhile, restrictive trade interventions in Asian economies include import and export restrictions, additional licensing requirements, and nontariff measures, particularly on essential raw materials and goods (Table 1.1).

Many existing international cooperation measures need to be advanced to address new issues and improve efforts for implementation. The multilateral World Trade Organization (WTO) system, for example, needs significant reform to strengthen its rules to reduce risks from rising protectionism and geoeconomic fragmentation (IMF 2023). Meantime, two megaregional trade agreements, the Regional Comprehensive Economic Partnership and the Comprehensive and Progressive Transpacific Partnership, have provided ways to strengthen supply chains within Asia and need to ensure effective implementation. The proposed Indo-Pacific Economic Framework provides opportunities to enhance international cooperation in areas of trade; supply chains; clean energy, infrastructure and decarbonization; and tax and anti-corruption. The framework needs to expedite negotiation and lay out action plans for participating economies to undertake domestic reforms. The 14 economies recently

Table 1.1: Restrictive Export Measures by Selected Asian Economies, January 2022–November 2023

Economy	Type of Intervention	Affected Jurisdiction
Bangladesh	Export restriction on rice bran oil	1 economy
	Import restriction on onions	3 economies
Bhutan	Import restriction on vehicles	2 economies
Georgia	Export restriction on wheat and barley	Not listed
India	Export restriction on broken rice	40 economies
	Export restriction on wheat	14 economies
	Temporary export control in de-oiled rice bran	15 economies
	Export restriction on non-basmati white rice	96 economies
	Export control on wheat flour	20 economies
	Temporary export restriction on sugar	49 economies
Indonesia	Export restriction on cooking oil and its raw materials	106 economies
	Export ban on bauxite	1 economy
Malaysia	Export restriction on chicken	5 economies
	Import restriction on mixed waste and scraps of miscellaneous paper or paperboard	19 economies
Nepal	Temporary import restriction on more motorcycles and mobile phones	4 economies
Pakistan	Export restriction on sugar	Not listed
PRC	Export and import control on basic organic chemicals	94 economies
	Export control measures for gallium and germanium	44 economies
Thailand	Temporary export restriction on live swine	4 economies
Viet Nam	Import restriction for reexport of medical masks, gloves, and protective suits	55 economies

PRC = People's Republic of China.

Source: ADB compilation based on Global Trade Alert Database. https://www.globaltradealert.org/data_extraction (accessed November 2023).

announced substantial completion of negotiations to strengthen supply chain resilience for critical goods such as semiconductors and medicines, marking the initiative's first tangible outcome since its May 2022 inception.[2]

Despite the challenges, regional cooperation among Asian economies will remain relevant to tackle global risks and common problems to deliver improved outcomes for people. Trade and investment promotion will continue to remain a key agenda of regional cooperation, though greater attention will be paid on people-centric initiatives. Cooperation initiatives will be driven by expanding the range of beneficiaries to address deep inequities exposed by the pandemic. Hence, cooperation measures will be discussed for improved health care services, skills development or education, and food security to improve accessibility for low-income households and vulnerable populations. Given that regional cooperation will be sought to reap the benefits of digital transformation, it will become more important for economies to address key regulatory, infrastructural, and capacity challenges across borders. Finally, regional cooperation is vital to tackle climate change risks. Collective action, especially on a regional basis, is necessary for establishing a climate change strategy to curb coal utilization, encourage power sector decarbonization, and scale up renewable energy resources. Further, international cooperation remains essential in securing financial assistance for climate change adaptation in the region's vulnerable emerging markets.

Regional Integration in Asia Is Progressing Steadily, Though Variations Remain

The Asia-Pacific Regional Cooperation and Integration Index (ARCII) remained relatively stable between 2006 and 2021 (ADB 2022a). ADB's ARCII, a

multidimensional index to measure the pace and nature of regional integration, which tracks how Asia fares against other regions, shows the EU continues to lead (Figure 1.4). Across eight ARCII dimensions—trade and investment, money and finance, regional value chain (RVC), infrastructure and connectivity, people and social integration, institutional arrangements, technology and digital connectivity, and environmental cooperation—results reveal variation among regions. While the EU excels in the intensity of cross-border flows in some dimensions, Asia is not far behind. In fact, Asia stands at the same level of integration for RVC and people and social integration and leads in technology and digital connectivity. Asia's digital connectivity is driven by dynamic trade in information and communication technology goods and enhanced access and quality of internet services throughout the region (Figure 1.5).

Figure 1.4: Overall Intraregional Integration, by Region

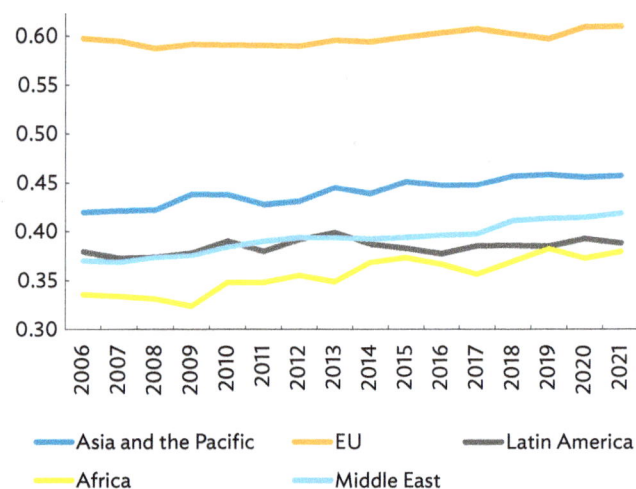

EU = European Union (27 members).

Notes: Based on ADB's Asia-Pacific Regional Cooperation and Integration Index estimates. Higher index estimates denote greater regional integration.

Source: ADB. Asia-Pacific Regional Cooperation and Integration Index Database. https://aric.adb.org/database/arcii (accessed November 2023).

[2]   The 14 economies are Australia, Brunei Darussalam, Fiji, India, Indonesia, Japan, Malaysia, New Zealand, the Philippines, the Republic of Korea, Singapore, Thailand, the United States, and Viet Nam.

Figure 1.5: Intraregional Integration by Dimension, 2021

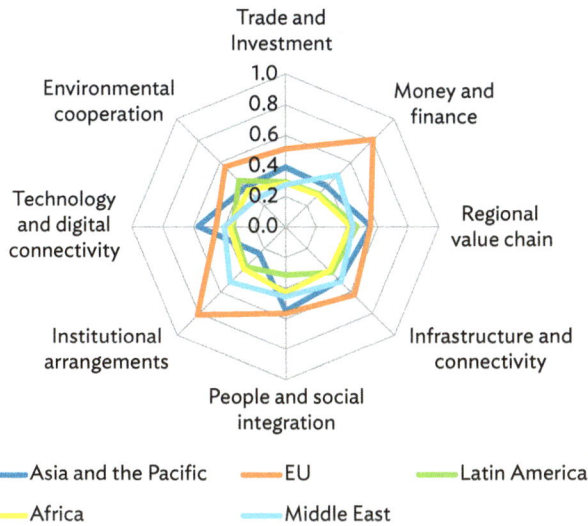

EU = European Union (27 members).

Notes: Based on ADB's Asia-Pacific Regional Cooperation and Integration Index estimates. Higher index estimates denote greater regional integration.

Source: ADB. Asia-Pacific Regional Cooperation and Integration Index Database. https://aric.adb.org/database/arcii (accessed November 2023).

Figure 1.6: Intraregional Integration in Asia and the Pacific, by Dimension

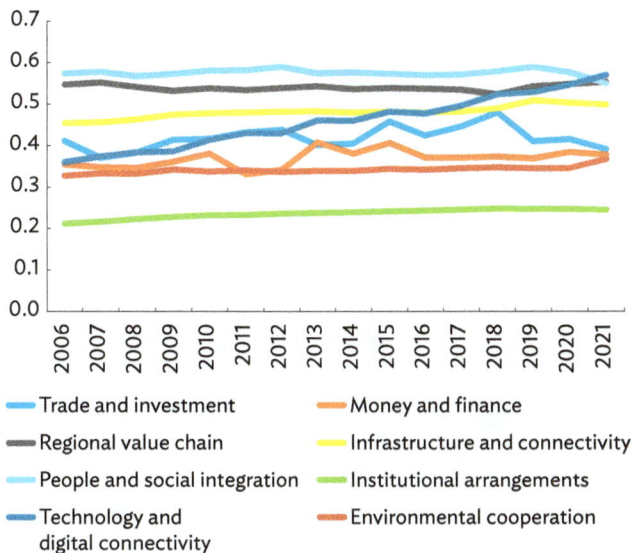

Notes: Based on ADB's Asia-Pacific Regional Cooperation and Integration Index estimates. Higher index estimates denote greater regional integration.

Source: ADB. Asia-Pacific Regional Cooperation and Integration Index Database. https://aric.adb.org/database/arcii (accessed November 2023).

ARCII dimensions show a varied pace and level of integration for the Asian region.

While the people and social integration dimension shows a lot of cross-border activity and is driven by international tourism (though this came to a halt during the pandemic), technology and digital connectivity experienced a rapid surge with economies embracing digital transformation initiatives over the past decade and the pace accelerating during the pandemic. Trade and investment integration in Asia, however, slowed from 2019 amid the US and the People's Republic of China (PRC) trade dispute and supply chain disruptions. This trend is also reflected in the RVC dimension, which showed modest improvement (Figure 1.6).

Most subregions showed stronger integration among their members between 2006 and 2021, with varying trends by dimension.

In 2021, East Asia led estimates for intraregional integration for five dimensions, including infrastructure and connectivity, RVC, trade and investment, environmental cooperation, and technology (Figure 1.8a). Southeast Asia and Central Asia followed (Figure 1.7 a-d). Southeast Asia has achieved notable integration in various areas of connectivity (institution and infrastructure), RVC, and money and finance.

In terms of intersubregional integration—an economy's integration with Asian economies outside its own subregion—South Asia has performed strongly.

In 2021, estimates for South Asia exhibited the deepest integration in RVC, infrastructure, and technology (Figure 1.8b). For economies in the Southeast Asia subregion, their own integration overtook their integration with the rest of Asia around RVC and trade and investment. This reflected the subregion's growing emphasis on establishing the ASEAN Economic Community (AEC) in 2015. The subregion particularly showed greater cross-border activities in people and social integration across Asia, driven by international tourism and technology and digital connectivity. Intersubregional

Figure 1.7: Subregional Integration Estimates—Asia and the Pacific

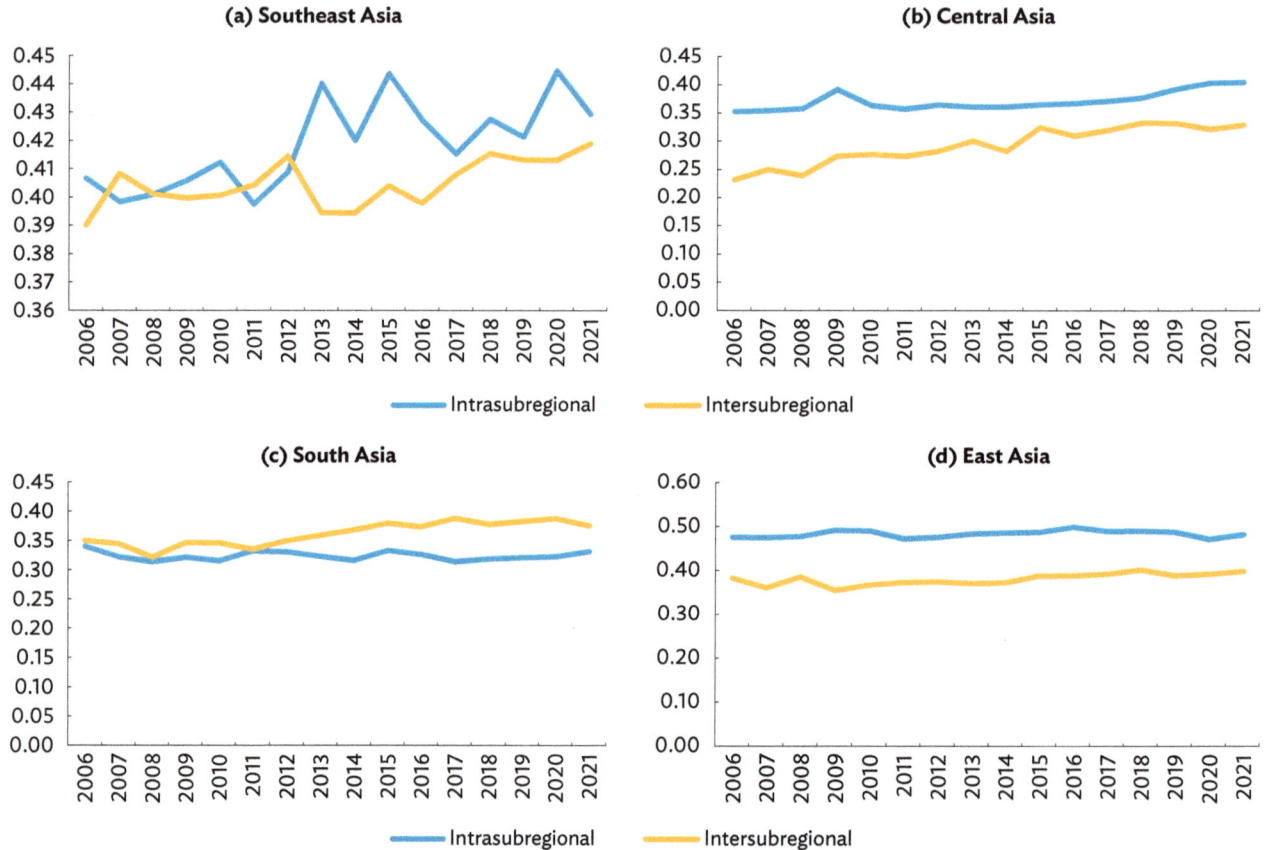

(a) Southeast Asia

(b) Central Asia

(c) South Asia

(d) East Asia

— Intrasubregional   — Intersubregional

Notes: Based on ADB's Asia-Pacific Regional Cooperation and Integration Index estimates. Higher index estimates denote greater regional integration. Intrasubregional integration is measured within members of the same subregion. Intersubregional integration is measured with other Asian economies outside each subregion.

Source: ADB. Asia-Pacific Regional Cooperation and Integration Index Database. https://aric.adb.org/database/arcii (accessed November 2023).

Figure 1.8: Subregional Integration Estimates by Dimension—Asia and the Pacific, 2021

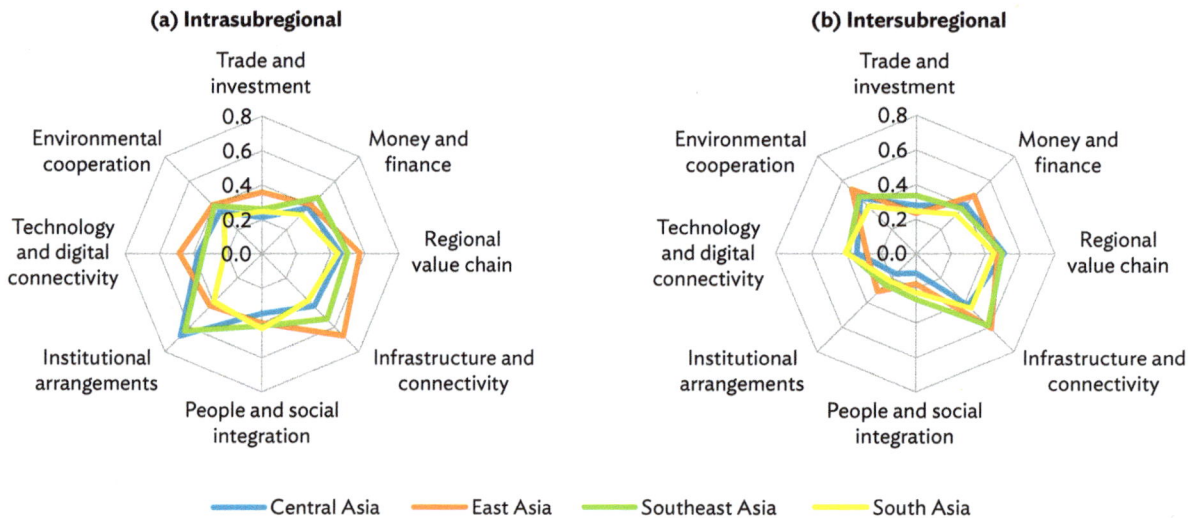

(a) Intrasubregional

(b) Intersubregional

— Central Asia   — East Asia   — Southeast Asia   — South Asia

Notes: Based on ADB's Asia-Pacific Regional Cooperation and Integration Index estimates. Higher index estimates denote greater regional integration. Intrasubregional integration is measured within members of the same subregion. Intersubregional integration is measured with other Asian economies outside each subregion.

Source: ADB. Asia-Pacific Regional Cooperation and Integration Index Database. https://aric.adb.org/database/arcii (accessed November 2023).

cooperation in East Asia and Central Asia progressed well in parallel with intrasubregional activities. In 2021, while East Asia showed greater intersubregional integration in institution building and connectivity, reflecting economic cooperation through connectivity initiatives and regional trade agreements, Central Asia was ahead in RVC (Figure 1.8b).

Integration within the Pacific economies remains low. While data availability is a challenge to measure the pace of integration among the Pacific economies, preliminary estimates suggest intrasubregional integration has slightly improved and peaked in 2018 (Figure 1.9). The subregion consists of small island developing states that have gradually integrated with economies outside their subregion, especially with developed markets such as Australia and New Zealand. From 2006 to 2021, the Pacific has become more integrated in infrastructure and connectivity, and in trade and investment.

Figure 1.9: Subregional Integration Estimates—The Pacific

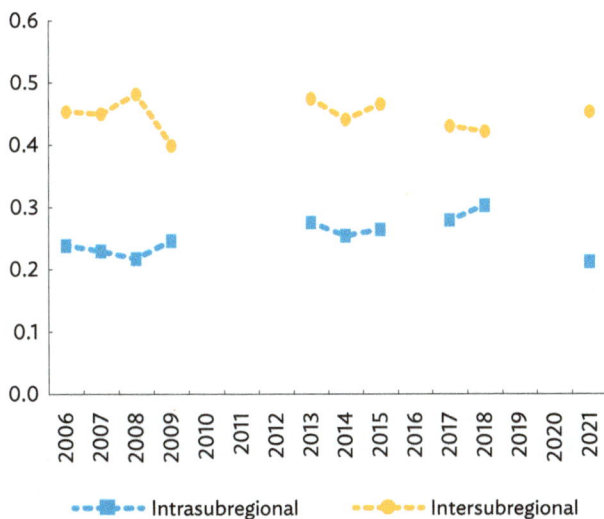

Notes: Based on ADB's Asia-Pacific Regional Cooperation and Integration Index estimates. Higher index estimates denote greater regional integration. Intrasubregional integration is measured within members of the same subregion. Intersubregional integration is measured with other Asian economies outside each subregion. Results are at a preliminary stage. A more comprehensive analysis for the Pacific region is currently under development.

Source: ADB. Asia-Pacific Regional Cooperation and Integration Index Database. https://aric.adb.org/database/arcii (accessed November 2023).

Regional Cooperation Initiatives in Asia

Regional initiatives have made progress, though challenges remain limiting the capacity to implement them. ADB takes a three-pillar approach to regional initiatives: (i) greater and higher quality connectivity between economies; (ii) expanded global and regional trade and investment opportunities; and (iii) increased and diversified regional public goods—to support economies in their efforts of regional cooperation (ADB 2019). Using the same pillars, this section looks at cooperation initiatives in the Asian subregions. It highlights their progress, outlines ADB support, and discusses challenges. Policy recommendations are provided as a way forward. It should be noted that the discussion in this section does not reflect progress in the ARCII, which assesses regional cooperation in a way that goes beyond ADB-supported subregional initiatives.

ARCII estimates for subregional initiatives showed steady progress over time, though the pace varies based on a subregion's macroeconomic and social context, available resources, and capabilities.

Figures 1.10 to 1.12 show cross-border activities among the members of the subregional initiatives and between the subregional initiative and the rest of Asia. Looking at Southeast Asian initiatives, constituent members of the Greater Mekong Subregion (GMS) achieved greater integration with each other than with the rest of Asia, though the pace of this intrasubregional integration has been consistent in recent years. In the South Asia subregion, the Bay of Bengal Initiative for Multisectoral Technical and Economic Cooperation (BIMSTEC) shows greater integration through 2006–2021 than South Asia Subregional Economic Cooperation (SASEC), for both intrasubregional and intersubregional activities. The gap between the two initiatives has narrowed for intersubregional

Figure 1.10: Subregional Initiatives—Southeast Asia, 2006–2021

(a) Intrasubregional

(b) Intersubregional

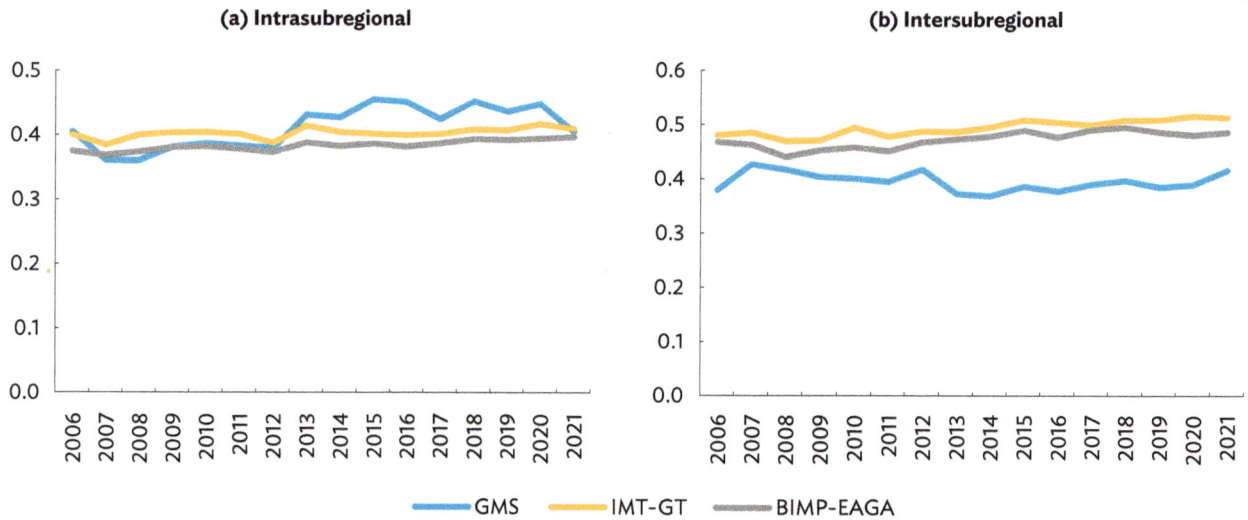

BIMP-EAGA = Brunei Darussalam–Indonesia–Malaysia–Philippines East ASEAN Growth Area, BIMSTEC = Bay of Bengal Initiative for Multi-Sectoral Technical and Economic Cooperation, GMS = Greater Mekong Subregion, IMT-GT = Indonesia-Malaysia-Thailand Growth Triangle.

Notes: Based on ADB's Asia-Pacific Regional Cooperation and Integration Index estimates. Higher index estimates denote greater regional integration. Intrasubregional integration is measured within members of the same subregional initiative. Intersubregional integration is measured with other Asian economies outside each subregional initiative.

Source: ADB. Asia-Pacific Regional Cooperation and Integration Index Database. https://aric.adb.org/database/arcii (accessed November 2023).

Figure 1.11: Subregional Initiatives—South Asia, 2006–2021

(a) Intrasubregional

(b) Intersubregional

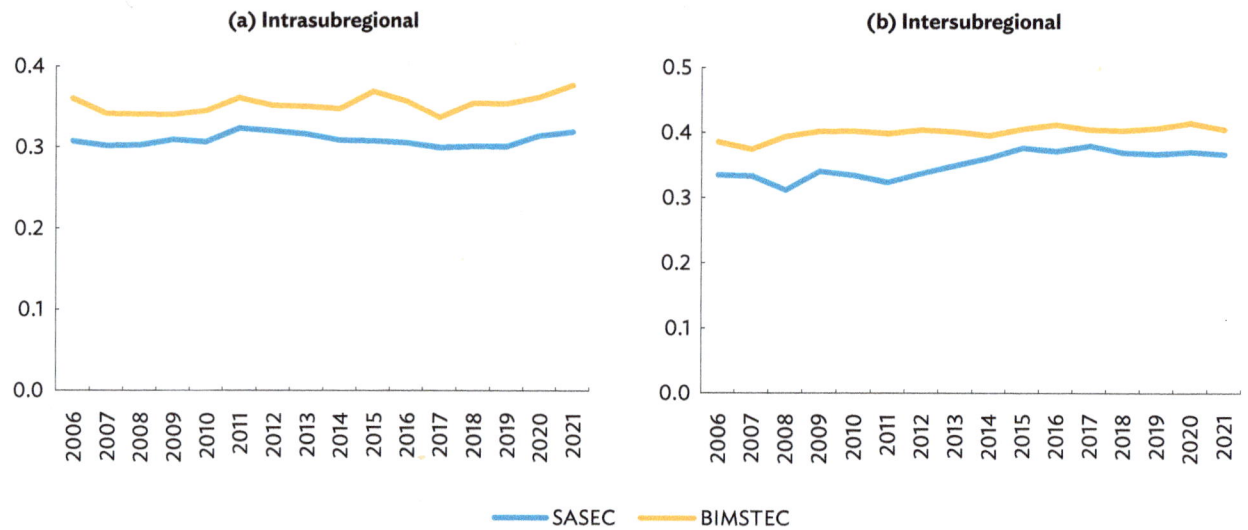

BIMSTEC = Bay of Bengal Initiative for Multi-Sectoral Technical and Economic Cooperation, SASEC = South Asia Subregional Economic Cooperation.

Notes: Based on ADB's Asia-Pacific Regional Cooperation and Integration Index estimates. Higher index estimates denote greater regional integration. Intrasubregional integration is measured within members of the same subregional initiative. Intersubregional integration is measured with other Asian economies outside each subregional initiative.

Source: ADB. Asia-Pacific Regional Cooperation and Integration Index Database. https://aric.adb.org/database/arcii (accessed November 2023).

cross-border activities in recent years. For the Central Asia Regional Economic Cooperation (CAREC) initiative, higher intrasubregional integration is driven by institutional arrangements and people and social integration, underscoring potential for member economies to deepen integration based on these pillars.

Figure 1.12 Central Asia Regional Economic Cooperation Program Integration, 2006–2021

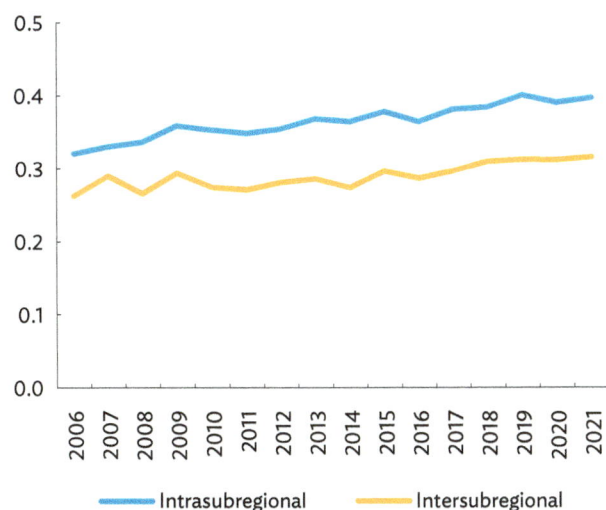

Notes: Based on ADB's Asia-Pacific Regional Cooperation and Integration Index estimates. Higher index estimates denote greater regional integration. Intrasubregional integration is measured within members of the same subregional initiative. Intersubregional integration is measured with other Asian economies outside each subregional initiative.

Source: ADB. Asia-Pacific Regional Cooperation and Integration Index Database. https://aric.adb.org/database/arcii (accessed November 2023).

Southeast Asia

Southeast Asian economies' regional cooperation is discussed through their participation in three ADB-supported subregional initiatives: the GMS, Indonesia–Malaysia–Thailand Growth Triangle (IMT-GT), and the Brunei Darussalam–Indonesia–Malaysia–Philippines East ASEAN Growth Area (BIMP-EAGA).[3] These programs complement each other and aim to strengthen the regional cooperation agenda of the bigger Association of Southeast Asian Nations (ASEAN) regional initiative.

GMS, BIMP-EAGA, and IMT-GT have made notable progress over the years. A summary of developments in each initiative is provided in Table 1.2.

ADB provides broad-based support to all three subregional programs. It provides overall secretariat support to the GMS program while serving as a Regional Development Advisor to BIMP-EAGA and Regional Development Partner to IMT-GT. ADB supports these subregional programs in promoting cross-border infrastructure and economic integration, and in strengthening climate action and other regional public goods (ADB 2023a).

Greater Mekong Subregion

In recent years, the GMS program has achieved notable progress, particularly in preparing subregion-wide guiding documents. These include (i) the new GMS Economic Cooperation Program Strategic Framework 2030 (GMS-2030), which sets the strategic directions and priorities of the program in the medium term and beyond; (ii) the GMS COVID-19 Response and Recovery Plan 2021–2023, which identifies some achievable initiatives to support the subregion's economy during the COVID-19 pandemic and beyond, facilitate economic recovery, and help prepare the GMS for any further similar health crises; and (iii) the GMS Gender Strategy, which provides entry points to mainstream gender across GMS operations, while complementing and adding value to GMS-2030, GMS sector strategies, and GMS economy-level efforts to achieve gender equality.

Altogether, during 2020–2023, the GMS program mobilized $5.9 billion for 21 projects across sectors including agriculture and natural resources, wind power, health, industry and trade, tourism, and transportation. Of this, ADB provided $4.2 billion of the financing and mobilized $1.2 billion from development partners/private sector while GMS governments contributed $500 million for these projects.[4]

---

[3]   The GMS was initiated in 1992 among six economies including Cambodia, the PRC (specifically Yunnan Province and Guangxi Zhuang Autonomous Region), the Lao People's Democratic Republic (Lao PDR), Myanmar, Thailand, and Viet Nam. Established in 1994, BIMP-EAGA aimed to accelerate socioeconomic development of Brunei Darussalam, Indonesia, Malaysia, and the Philippines through regional cooperation. IMT-GT was created to improve welfare and economic growth in less developed states and provinces in Indonesia, Malaysia, and Thailand.

[4]   GMS Secretariat figures.

Table 1.2: Selected Projects in Greater Mekong Subregion, Indonesia–Malaysia–Thailand Growth Triangle, and Brunei Darussalam–Indonesia–Malaysia–Philippines East ASEAN Growth Area

Connectivity	Trade	Regional Public Goods
Makassar-Parepare railway—connects two major port cities and serves five districts in South Sulawesi province of Indonesia (BIMP-EAGA 2023a).	**Tourism Recovery Communications Plan and Toolkit 2022–2024**—jointly prepared by BIMP-EAGA and IMT-GT to boost the tourism industry in the subregion (BIMP-EAGA 2022c).	**Nuclear Technology for Controlling Plastic Pollution Project**—aims to increase the volume of recycled plastic and convert more plastic waste into reusable resources, particularly for the production of industrial goods (BIMP-EAGA 2023b).
ASEAN-EU Comprehensive Air Transport Agreement—first region-to-region air transport agreement which aims to strengthen air transport services, connecting people, cultures, and businesses across continents (BIMP-EAGA 2022a).	**The Lao PDR–Thailand–Malaysia–Singapore Power Integration Project**—serves as ASEAN's pilot project in addressing technical, legal, and financial issues of multilateral electricity trade (BIMP-EAGA 2022b).	**ASEAN Regional Action Plan for Combating Marine Debris in the ASEAN Member States (2021–2025)**—provides a scalable, solution-focused joint strategy to tackle marine plastic pollution (BIMP-EAGA 2021).
The PRC–Lao PDR railway freight transit yard—aims to bolster the transport of goods and further improve the efficiency of international transportation between the PRC and ASEAN economies (GMS 2022a).	**Trans-Borneo Power Grid Sarawak–West Kalimantan Interconnection Project**—a flagship project that provides interconnection for the transmission and sale of electricity between Indonesia and Malaysia (BIMP-EAGA 2022b).	**GMS Cross-Border Livestock Health and Value Chains Improvement Project**—aims to enhance productivity and resilience of the livestock subsector by reducing risks from transboundary animal diseases, zoonoses, and antimicrobial resistance; expanding animal health monitoring and service delivery; enhancing food safety; and promoting subregional cooperation in GMS.[b]
Some of the completed infrastructure projects in economic corridors are the following (BIMP-EAGA 2019): • Expansion of the Adi Soemarmo International Airport in Indonesia; • Construction of the Pan Borneo Highway Sarawak Package 1 from Teluk Melano to Sematan in Malaysia; • Upgrade of the General Santos City International Airport in the Philippines; • Expansion of the Zamboanga Port in the Philippines; and • Construction of roads in the Western Mindanao Development Corridor in the Philippines.	**Two-way energy trade between the PRC and the Lao PDR**—aims to facilitate the power trade agreement between the two economies (GMS 2022b). **Monsoon Wind Power Project**—a 600-megawatt wind-power project in the Lao PDR that will export and sell electricity to Viet Nam. It will be the first cross-border wind power project in the Lao PDR and the largest in Southeast Asia. It will provide a substantial source of clean renewable energy supply to Viet Nam.[a]	**Green City Action Plan (GCAP)**—under the IMT-GT program, the GCAPs of Medan and Batam Island in Indonesia, Melaka in Malaysia and Hat Yai and Songkhla in Thailand develop sustainable and equitable urban development plans for cities through a pipeline of immediate, mid-term, and long-term infrastructure projects. GCAPs were also prepared for Kendari, Kota Kinabalu, and General Santos under BIMP-EAGA (IMT-GT; BIMP-EAGA).

ASEAN = Association of Southeast Asian Nations, BIMP-EAGA = Brunei Darussalam–Indonesia–Malaysia–Philippines East ASEAN Growth Area, GMS = Greater Mekong Subregion, IMT-GT = Indonesia–Malaysia–Thailand Growth Triangle, Lao PDR = Lao People's Democratic Republic, PRC = People's Republic of China.

[a] ADB. Lao People's Democratic Republic: Monsoon Wind Power Project. https://www.adb.org/projects/55205-001/main.
[b] ADB. Cambodia: Greater Mekong Subregion Cross-Border Livestock Health and Value Chains Improvement Project. https://www.adb.org/projects/53240-003/main.

Sources: ADB compilation based on the ADB, BIMP-EAGA, and GMS websites.

The GMS program's notable achievements in select sectors include the following:

- Completion of major transport infrastructure projects such as the PRC–Lao PDR (Kunming–Vientiane) Highspeed Rail Project, the Thailand GMS Highway Expansion Phase 2 Project, and Cambodia Phnom Penh–Sihanoukville Expressway Project. Other key projects are in advanced stages of construction, including the Viet Nam Ha Noi–Lang Son Expressway Project.

- In trade and investment, a GMS Task Force on Trade and Investment was established to explore, identify, and initiate collaborative actions and programs to boost trade and investment in the GMS.

- In energy, the GMS Energy Transition Task Force replaced the GMS Regional Power Trade Coordination Committee to effectively address the need for sustainable energy. The task force will facilitate the ongoing energy transition in the GMS, with the strong promotion of renewable energy, energy efficiency, and green financing for energy projects.

- In the health sector, the "One Health" approach was adopted and pursued under the GMS COVID-19 Response and Recovery Plan 2021–2023. One Health provides an integrated, unifying approach that aims to sustainably balance and optimize the health of people, animals, and ecosystems. This approach established a Regional One Health Working Group and continued to support regional technical assistance linked to existing One Health networks and resources.

Brunei Darussalam–Indonesia–Malaysia–Philippines East ASEAN Growth Area

As of 2023, ADB approved over $3.5 billion worth of loan to invest in 14 projects in BIMP-EAGA. Amid the COVID-19 pandemic, ADB helped prepare the Joint BIMP-EAGA and IMT-GT Tourism Recovery Communications Plan and Toolkit 2022–2024 as well as capacity-building support. ADB also prepared special economic zone studies for BIMP-EAGA and IMT-GT, proposing strategic measures to make the zones more competitive. A joint BIMP-EAGA and IMT-GT blue economy strategy is underway to help bolster enabling conditions for blue economy growth, particularly in terms of attracting greater investments. A study on BIMP-EAGA economic corridors expansion and reconfiguration is ongoing, which provides strategic approaches for enhanced trade, tourism, and investments flows in the subregion. In the Philippines alone, about $380 million is allocated to improving 280 kilometers of sustainable roads and bridges in Mindanao to enhance commerce and connectivity. The loan also includes provision for knowledge support. Meanwhile, a green city action plan has been developed for General Santos City.

Indonesia-Malaysia-Thailand Growth Triangle

Integrated solutions to sustain regional cooperation and integration (RCI) projects in IMT-GT include developing knowledge products such as green city action plans and integrated green transportation plans. Potential "green projects" are being structured, and innovative financing models will be piloted under the ASEAN Catalytic Green Finance Facility financed by ASEAN Infrastructure Fund. As of 2023, ADB has supported 16 technical assistance projects amounting $33.98 million (with co-funding) to develop smart and livable cities, improve transport connectivity, enhance urban planning, build capacities of the developing member economies in managing RCI, support trade facilitation aligned with ASEAN agreements, promote health security, and encourage clean energy transition. Of these, seven remaining active technical assistance projects are providing support to (i) strengthen institutional capacities; (ii) transition to a cleaner energy future; (iii) help developing member economies to prepare and/or implement COVID-19 vaccination roll out and expand in the delivery of ADB procured vaccines; (iv) support sustainable tourism facility initiatives; (v) enhance trade facilitation in IMT-GT; (vi) promote action on plastic pollution; and (vii) support plans to develop livable cities that are smart, inclusive, environmentally sustainable, resilient, and competitive.

The Pacific

ADB contributes substantial and comprehensive support to the Pacific Islands Forum (PIF), a key regional cooperation initiative of the Pacific economies.[5] The PIF is guided by the *2050 Strategy for the Blue Pacific Continent* which outlines the following thematic areas: (i) political leadership and regionalism; (ii) people-centered development; (iii) peace and security; (iv) resource and economic development; (v) climate change and disasters; (vi) ocean and environment; and (vii) technology and connectivity. The strategy guides PIF economies in navigating challenges in these thematic areas, leveraging their collective strengths in creating a sustainable future in the region (PIFS 2022). A sample of ADB- and non-ADB-supported projects that focused on enhancing connectivity, boosting trade in goods and services, and strengthening adaptation and resilience to climate change in the Pacific are found in Table 1.3.

---

[5] The Pacific Islands Forum comprises 18 economies: Australia, Cook Islands, the Federated States of Micronesia, Fiji, French Polynesia, Kiribati, the Marshall Islands, Nauru, New Caledonia, New Zealand, Niue, Palau, Papua New Guinea, Samoa, Solomon Islands, Tonga, Tuvalu, and Vanuatu.

Table 1.3: Selected Projects in the Pacific, 2020–2023

Connectivity	Trade	Regional Public Goods
Smart Islands Project—adopts an innovative approach to deliver connectivity and sustainable services to disadvantaged island communities (ITU 2021).	**Pacific Regional E-commerce Strategy and Roadmap**—outlines the Pacific consensus on the priority regional measures to boost e-commerce readiness in the region (UNCTAD 2022).	**Framework for Resilient Development in the Pacific**—provides a strategic guidance on how to enhance resilience to climate change and disasters (SPC 2016).
East Micronesia Cable Project—aims to provide faster, higher quality, and more reliable communications to more than 100,000 people across the Federated States of Micronesia, Kiribati, and Nauru (AIFFP).	**Pacific Quality Infrastructure**—aims to strengthen a demand-oriented quality infrastructure and access to services that enhance trade competitiveness in the Pacific region (PIFS 2020a).	**Declaration on Preserving Maritime Zones in the Face of Climate Change-related Sea-level Rise**—sets out the region's collective position on the rules on maritime zones with regard to climate change-related sea-level rise (PIFS 2021).
Nauru airport upgrade—includes resurfacing of the runway and upgrade of some critical air traffic control equipment to ensure the airport continues to operate safely and meet international standards (AIFFP 2022b).	**Pacific Ecotourism Recovery Initiative**—aims to assess the potential of ecotourism experiences as a diversification strategy for the region's tourism sector (SPTO 2022).	**Pacific Regional Framework on Climate Mobility**—aims to guide governments in addressing legal, policy, and practical issues that arise on climate mobility (PIFS 2023).
Papua New Guinea maritime port infrastructure upgrade—aims to increase the capacity of critical maritime infrastructure to accommodate larger ships, which will improve trade and connectivity (AIFFP 2022a).		**Pacific Climate Change Finance Assessment Framework**—provides guidance on the assessment of the Pacific economies' ability to access and manage climate change resources (PIFS 2013).
		Pacific Humanitarian Pathway on COVID-19—COVID-19 pandemic emergency response that enabled the movement of medical and humanitarian supplies across the region (PIFS 2020b).

Sources: ADB compilation based on information from the Australian Infrastructure Financing Facility for the Pacific, International Telecommunication Union, Secretariat of the Pacific Community, Pacific Islands Forum Secretariat, South Pacific Tourism Organization, and United Nations Conference on Trade and Development.

ADB takes a systematic approach to support the integration of Pacific economies, guiding investments and technical assistance in connectivity infrastructure, regional public goods, and capacity-building.

The Pacific Approach 2021–2025 lays down ADB's operational regional strategy in the Pacific and focuses on three critical development challenges: vulnerability to shocks, weak service delivery, and slow growth. ADB's regional investments in the Pacific, which increased by 45.3% (year-on-year) in 2023, seek to support connectivity, trade facilitation, and resilience to shocks (Figure 1.13). For instance, the rehabilitation and expansion of Nuku'alofa Port in Tonga involves strengthening its operations and management, and so promotes resilient connectivity and merchandise trade. Other ADB efforts to enhance trade promotion and facilitation in Tonga include establishment

of an authorized economic operator program to streamline procedures for accredited exporters and the implementation of an electronic phytosanitary certification system to facilitate agricultural exports. ADB is also helping to enhance digital connectivity in Samoa by establishing policies on digital identification and providing digital financial services; and domestic shipping in Tuvalu, which will also benefit intraregional connectivity by providing safe and reliable transport for people and trade to other subregional destinations such as Fiji and Kiribati.

In addition, a national reference laboratory is being built in Papua New Guinea to enhance and improve regional health surveillance capacity through specialized diagnostics services to detect, diagnose, and manage communicable disease and pathogens. Regional training programs for medical personnel will also build technical capacity and create knowledge and experience-sharing opportunities across the Pacific.

Figure 1.13: ADB Regional Investment in the Pacific: Loans and Grants, 2010–2023

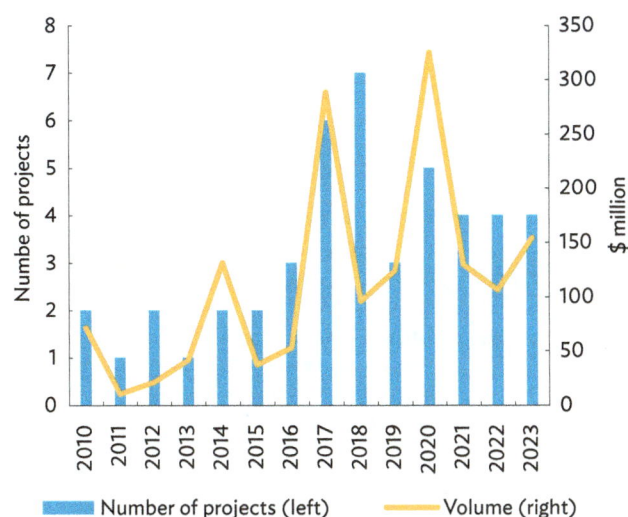

Source: ADB. Pacific Program Portfolio. Unpublished.

Further, ADB approved the fourth phase of the Pacific Disaster Resilience Program to provide another round of financing for Kiribati, Samoa, Solomon Islands, and Tonga to mitigate the adverse impacts of climate change and disasters from physical hazards. The program focuses on strengthening policy, institutional frameworks, and tools for risk management, and on improving public financial management and risk financing.

Regional technical assistance projects in 2023 focused on accelerating the transition to renewable energy, improving regional financial systems and knowledge, education, information and communication technology knowledge solutions, and capacity building.

South Asia

South Asian economies have been at the forefront of regional cooperation over the past decade. The South Asian Association for Regional Cooperation (SAARC) since 1985 has been promoting economic, social, and cultural development among its eight member states: Afghanistan, Bangladesh, Bhutan, India, Maldives, Nepal, Pakistan, and Sri Lanka (ADB 2023a).[6] The Bay of Bengal Initiative for Multisectoral Technical and Economic Cooperation (BIMSTEC), established in 1997, strives to increase cross-border investment and tourism and to promote technical cooperation among its seven member states: Bangladesh, Bhutan, India, Nepal, Sri Lanka, Myanmar, and Thailand.[7] Transport connectivity is a key area of cooperation, with BIMSTEC acting as a bridge linking South and Southeast Asia (ADB 2022b).

To build further momentum in regional cooperation, ADB initiated the South Asia Subregional Economic Cooperation (SASEC) in 2001. The seven member economies in SASEC (Bangladesh, Bhutan, India, Maldives, Myanmar, Nepal, and Sri Lanka) aim to promote regional prosperity by improving cross-border connectivity, facilitating faster and less costly trade, and tackling development challenges in the subregion. In 2016, the SASEC economies approved the SASEC Operational Plan 2016–2025, a 10-year strategic road map which expands the program's focus beyond intraregional cooperation to developing linkages with Southeast Asia and East Asia, widening the scope of transport, trade facilitation, and energy cooperation (ADB 2016).

ADB has been supporting the South Asian economies' participation in regional cooperation mechanisms.

ADB is the Secretariat and lead financier for the SASEC program and also a development and knowledge partner for BIMSTEC and SAARC. ADB and the SAARC Secretariat signed a memorandum of understanding in 2004 to establish a cooperative relationship for promoting regional cooperation among the SAARC member states (ADB 2023a). In 2022, ADB and BIMSTEC signed a memorandum of understanding that formalized their partnership in five areas of cooperation: transport connectivity and financing, energy connectivity and trade, trade facilitation, tourism promotion, and economic corridor development.

---

6   ADB placed on hold its regular assistance to Afghanistan effective 15 August 2021.

7   Effective 1 February 2021, ADB placed a temporary hold on sovereign project disbursements and new contracts in Myanmar.

Subregional programs such as SASEC, BIMSTEC, and SAARC have made progress with projects and knowledge activities (Table 1.4).

ADB'S investments supporting RCI in South Asia increased by $1.77 billion in 2023. The financing was committed to support seven projects with a total investment cost of $2.13 billion.[8] As of 31 December 2023, the SASEC portfolio consists of 86 committed

Table 1.4: Selected Projects in South Asian Association for Regional Cooperation, Bay of Bengal Initiative for Multisectoral Technical and Economic Cooperation, and South Asia Subregional Economic Cooperation, 2020–2023

Connectivity	Trade	Regional Public Goods
Cross-Border energy, trade, and transit deals—signed by India and Nepal to trade electricity and develop hydropower as well as a revised treaty of transit that would improve trade through rail and waterways (SASEC 2023c). **BIMSTEC Masterplan for Transport Connectivity**—approved in 2022, workshops organized in 2023 shared updates on implementation progress (ADB 2022b). **SASEC Chittagong-Cox's Bazar Railway Project**—aims to boost tourism in Bangladesh and facilitate access for population and products to subregional markets and trade.[a] **Land port at Dawki, Meghalay**—helped to strengthen trade and facilitate easier travel between Bangladesh and India (SASEC 2023b). **Nepal's Gautam Buddha International Airport**—started operations expanding tourism and trade; and improving international air transport access in Lumbini (SASEC 2022). **India's Eastern Grid Waterway Network**—sets link waterways among Bangladesh, Bhutan, India, and Nepal, boosting regional integration (SASEC 2023d).	**BIMSTEC Trade Facilitation Strategic Framework 2030**—approved in 2022, training program organized in 2023 to facilitate its implementation (ADB 2022c). **Agreement on the Movement of Traffic (Goods) in Transit**—signed allowing Bhutan's imports and exports to pass through Bangladesh, including exiting through the seaports (SASEC 2023a). **118MW Nikachhu Hydropower Plant**—construction has been completed in 2023 and is expected to increase export of clean energy from Bhutan to India.[b] **SASEC Customs Reform and Modernization for Trade Facilitation Program**—supported simplification, harmonization, and modernization of Nepal's trade processes to meet international standards and boost international trade. This was completed in 2020.[c] **SASEC Power Transmission and Distribution System Strengthening Project**—enables excess power from Kathmandu in Nepal to be traded with neighboring economies.[d] **Policy-Based Loan for Subprogram 1 Nepal: South Asia Subregional Economic Cooperation Customs and Logistics Reforms Program**— approved in June 2023, the program will support continuing reforms in customs by implementing the Customs Reform and Modernization Plan, 2021–2026 and improving trade logistics through the preparation and implementation of a new Trade Logistics Policy 2022 in Nepal.[e]	**Responsive COVID-19 Vaccines for Recovery Project under the Asia Pacific Vaccine Access Facility**—provides support for vaccination programs to prevent the spread of the COVID-19 virus. ADB provided support to Bhutan and Maldives in 2022, and Bangladesh, India, Nepal, and Sri Lanka in 2021 (ADB 2020b). **SASEC Customs Resiliency Action Plan**—adopted by all SASEC customs administrations to be used as guidelines for maintaining trade flows during unforeseen future trade disruption events. **SAARC**—has been conducting capacity-building workshops, knowledge-sharing events, and policy dialogues on climate change and energy trade. The SAARC finance ministers meeting in 2023 discussed leveraging RCI for greater participation in global value chains.

BIMSTEC = Bay of Bengal Initiative for Multi-Sectoral Technical and Economic Cooperation, COVID-19 = coronavirus disease, MW = megawatt, SAARC = South Asian Association for Regional Cooperation, SASEC = South Asia Subregional Economic Cooperation.

[a] ADB. Bangladesh: South Asia Subregional Economic Cooperation Chittagong-Cox's Bazar Railway Project, Phase 1. https://www.adb.org/projects/46452-002/main.
[b] ADB. Bhutan: Second Green Power Development Project. https://www.adb.org/projects/44444-013/main.
[c] ADB. Nepal: South Asia Subregional Economic Cooperation Customs Reform and Modernization for Trade Facilitation Program. https://www.adb.org/projects/50254-001/main.
[d] ADB. Nepal: South Asia Subregional Economic Cooperation Power Transmission and Distribution System Strengthening Project. https://www.adb.org/projects/50059-003/main.
[e] ADB. Programmatic Approach and Policy-Based Loan for Subprogram 1 Nepal: South Asia Subregional Economic Cooperation Customs and Logistics Reforms Program (Subprogram 1). https://www.adb.org/projects/54402-001/main.

Source: ADB compilation based on media releases from SASEC. https://www.sasec.asia/.

---

[8]   In 2023, seven projects include three on transport connectivity, two on economic corridor development, one on trade facilitation, and one on health.

projects with a cumulative cost of $20.54 billion (Figure 1.14). Since 2001, ADB has funded about $12.63 billion in total. The transport sector accounts for the greatest number of projects, followed by energy, economic corridor development, trade facilitation, health, and information and communication technology (ICT). ADB also provided $222.53 million in 154 technical assistance grants.

Between 2022 and 2023, ADB's regional investments in South Asia continued to promote improving connectivity between economies, expanding regional trade and investment opportunities, and supporting implementation of policy reforms on customs and trade facilitation.

ADB is investing in improving transport connectivity along priority routes within South Asia and supporting trade logistics policy reforms needed to accelerate industrialization and trade.

The SASEC Chittagong–Cox's Bazar Railway Project will support the Government of Bangladesh in upgrading the railway corridor that is part of the Trans-Asia Railway network. This will boost the economy through further development of Cox's Bazar into a major tourist destination and facilitating access of population and products to subregional markets and trade. The SASEC Highway Enhancement Project in Nepal is part of the SASEC priority corridor linking Kathmandu via Kakarbhitta to Chattogram and Mongla ports in Bangladesh. It is expected to boost border trade and logistics by reducing transport costs. Tranche 2 of the multitranche financing facility for the Visakhapatnam–Chennai Industrial Corridor (VCIC) Development Program in India will boost economic competitiveness to create more jobs and stronger climate resilience along the VCIC, which aligns with the Bay of Bengal Highway connecting to Cox's Bazaar to Thootuikudi and is one of the SASEC priority corridors.

ADB also provides support for policy reforms needed to speed up industrialization and expand subregional trade and commerce. The SASEC Integrated Trade Facilitation Sector Development Program in Bangladesh will introduce policy reforms to help the economy comply with the WTO Trade Facilitation Agreement and complement these with upgraded infrastructure at border crossing points. Meanwhile, the SASEC Customs and Logistics Reforms Program (Subprogram 1) in Nepal will support the preparation and implementation

Figure 1.14: South Asia Subregional Economic Cooperation Investments (cumulative, $ million)

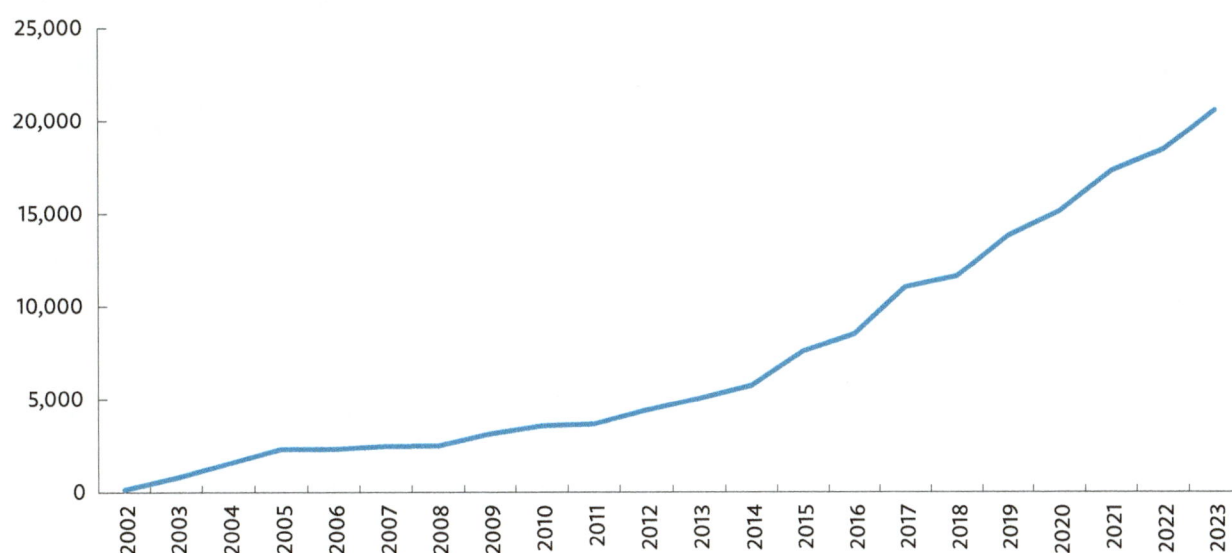

Source: ADB. SASEC Program Portfolio. Unpublished.

of a new trade logistics policy to sustain reforms implemented under the SASEC Customs Reform and Modernization for Trade Facilitation Program. The Strengthening Multimodal and Integrated Logistics Ecosystem (SMILE) program will also support the Government of India undertake reforms in the logistics sector, strengthen institutional and policy frameworks for interministerial coordination and engage the private sector, improve external trade logistics, and encourage the use of smart and automated systems for improved service delivery.

ADB is implementing technical assistance to support the implementation of regional initiatives through BIMSTEC and SAARC.

ADB has financed the preparation of the BIMSTEC Master Plan for Transport Connectivity, the BIMSTEC Grid Interconnection Master Plan, the Leveraging Thematic Circuits for BIMSTEC Tourism Development, the financing transport connectivity projects for BIMSTEC; the updating of the SAARC Regional Multimodal Transport Study, and the harmonization of 8-digit Harmonized System tariff lines of SAARC member economies. These studies are expected to support agreement on subregional priorities to improve regional interconnectivity for movement of goods and people as well as facilitate intraregional trade, including cross-border energy trade.

Central and West Asia, East Asia, and the Caucasus

ADB has been supporting the economies of Central and West Asia, East Asia, and the Caucasus in their participation in international platforms and regional cooperation mechanisms,[9] primarily the Central Asia Regional Economic Cooperation (CAREC) program. CAREC is a partnership of 11 member economies (Afghanistan, Azerbaijan, Georgia, Kazakhstan, the Kyrgyz Republic, Mongolia, Pakistan, the PRC, Tajikistan,

Turkmenistan, and Uzbekistan), that work together with development partners to promote development, accelerate growth, and reduce poverty in the subregion (ADB 2023e).

The CAREC program has made substantial progress in areas of regional connectivity and global and regional trade.

CAREC 2030 provides the long-term strategic framework for the program leading to 2030. It is anchored on a broader mission to connect people, policies, and projects for shared and sustainable development, serving as the premier economic cooperation platform for the region (ADB 2017). It is embarking on new areas to promote regional public goods including on regional heath security and a cross-cutting vision on climate change. Table 1.5 lists selected and notable projects from the past 3 years.

Figure 1.15: Central Asia Regional Economic Cooperation Investment Projects by Sector ($ million)

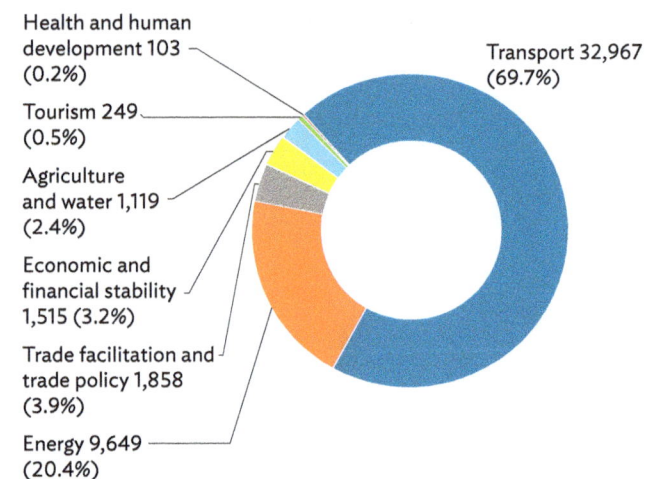

- Health and human development 103 (0.2%)
- Tourism 249 (0.5%)
- Agriculture and water 1,119 (2.4%)
- Economic and financial stability 1,515 (3.2%)
- Trade facilitation and trade policy 1,858 (3.9%)
- Energy 9,649 (20.4%)
- Transport 32,967 (69.7%)

Note: Data show Central Asia Regional Economic Cooperation (CAREC) investment by sector as of 30 June 2023.

Source: ADB. CAREC Program Portfolio. Unpublished.

From 2001 to June 2023, CAREC investments reached almost $47.27 billion covering 257 regional projects. Of that, more than $16.53 billion was financed by ADB,

---

9   The economies of Central and West Asia, East Asia, and the Caucasus participate in the Shanghai Cooperation Organization (SCO), the Eurasian Economic Union (EAEU), cooperation agreements with the EU, and the Investment Framework Agreement with the United States.

Table 1.5: Selected Projects and Initiatives in Central Asia Regional Economic Cooperation, 2020–2023

Connectivity	Trade	Regional Public Goods
Modernization of Eastern Uzbekistan Railway Network—helps to stimulate economic growth in Eastern Uzbekistan and improve trade and regional connectivity (ADB 2020a).	**Regional Improvement of Border Services Project**—aims to upgrade the participating economies, cross border facilities and modernize customs and trade systems (CAREC 2022).	**CAREC Post Pandemic Framework for a Green, Sustainable, and Inclusive Recovery**—aims to boost the region's recovery from the economic impacts of the pandemic and geopolitical conflicts, among other shocks (CAREC 2022b).
Toll-Road Concession Project in Kazakhstan—aims to reduce congestion in Almaty and to create a by-pass for commercial vehicles following the "Western PRC–Western Europe" transnational highway (IsDB 2020).	**Border Efficiency for Sustainable Trade Project**—aims to upgrade facilities and systems to support economic diversification, trade efficiency, health security and resilience at the borders.[a]	**CAREC Green Energy Alliance**—the first financing vehicle specifically for renewable energy and energy efficiency in the region (ADB 2022e).
Azerbaijan Railway and Logistics Modernization Program—aims to improve the railway and freight logistics (CAREC 2022).	**Developing the Economic Cooperation Zone project and Inner Mongolia Sustainable Cross-Border Development Investment Program**—parallel investments to support economic cooperation zone between Mongolia and the PRC.[b]	**Almaty–Bishkek Economic Corridor Real Time Air Quality Data**—helps identify local sources of pollution, inform which mitigation measures are most effective, and compare their costs with health impacts (CAREC 2021a).
The PRC's National Transport Planning Outline 2021–2035—aims to boost innovation through a reformation of the rail supply sector and better integrate rail with other transport modes (CAREC 2022).	**Pilot Initiatives to Improve Sanitary and Phytosanitary Measures**—aims to enhance market access and horticultural value chain development of national plant protection organizations of Kazakhstan, the Kyrgyz Republic, Tajikistan, Turkmenistan, and Uzbekistan (CAREC 2021b).	**CAREC Health Strategy 2030 (approved in 2021)**—aims to enhance health security through regional cooperation, benefiting the CAREC region's population (migrants and vulnerable groups) and health systems improvement (ADB 2022d).
Extension of Georgia's Kutaisi International Airport—aims to increase the airport's capacity and improve its services (CAREC 2022).		
Pakistan's Logistics and Freight Policy—aims to enhance the domestic and international supply chains through seamless integration of logistics through road, rail, marine, inland waterways, and aviation (CAREC 2022).	**CAREC Advanced Transit System and Information Common Exchange Pilot Project**— provides a harmonized electronic system for goods in transit to help trade flow more smoothly and efficiently across the borders (CAREC 2021b).	**Regional Action on Climate Change: A Vision for CAREC (endorsed in 2023)**—develops principles and identifies priority areas for investments, explicitly providing climate change as a crosscutting priority area under the CAREC 2030 Strategy, and proposes steps and institutional arrangements to achieve more sustainable and climate-resilient growth (ADB 2023b).
Kazakhstan, Turkmenistan, and Iran Railway Freight Corridor—aims to help promote seamless transport connectivity through enhanced railroad cooperation among the three economies (CAREC 2022).	**Cooperation Framework for Agricultural Development and Food Security in the CAREC Region**—focuses on international cooperation to modernize agriculture, strengthen policies, and develop food value chains (CAREC 2022c).	
Marakand–Karshi Railway Electrification Project—aims to support the development of Uzbekistan's railway system and strengthen trade cooperation with neighboring economies (CAREC 2022).		

CAREC = Central Asia Regional Economic Cooperation, PRC = People's Republic of China.

[a] ADB. Mongolia: Border Efficiency for Sustainable Trade Project. https://www.adb.org/projects/55044-002/main.
[b] ADB. People's Republic of China: Inner Mongolia Sustainable Cross-Border Development Investment Program. https://www.adb.org/projects/51192-001/main.

Sources: ADB compilation based on media releases from ADB, Central Asia Regional Economic Cooperation, the Islamic Development Bank, and the European Bank for Reconstruction and Development.

$20.94 billion by other development partners, and $9.8 billion by CAREC governments. Although the biggest chunk focuses on traditional sectors of transport, energy and trade connectivity, investment is diversifying into more sectors, including agriculture and tourism (Figure 1.15). Green development and climate adaptation and mitigation are also increasingly getting attention.

Common Regional Cooperation Challenges

Many of the challenges for regional cooperation derive from domestic socioeconomic conditions of member economies (e.g., macroeconomic environment, limited resources, different policy priorities). There are concerns at the regional level as well, including financing gaps for regional projects. Discussion turns to common challenges across all subregions that are hindering progress in regional cooperation.

Almost all regional cooperation initiatives came under pressure post-COVID-19 as constituent economies embarked on recovery and adjusted to challenging global conditions. High inflation, rising interest rates, supply chain disruptions, the risk of recession, food insecurity, energy instability, and rising global debt weighed on their progress.

Some subregions lack economic incentives to undertake regional cooperation. A case in point is South Asia, where intraregional trade accounted for just 4.6% of the subregion's total trade in 2022. Despite the formation of the South Asia Free Trade Area (SAFTA) in 2004, the reluctance of participating members to reduce tariffs has limited the success of regional integration (Salsabeel 2022). In addition, nontariff barriers to trade persist, including inadequate infrastructure and lack of modern border clearance procedures. Similarly, Central Asia's intraregional trade was 7.3% of its total trade in 2022. The presence of barriers pertaining to trade policy, transport, and transit systems in the region, amid geopolitical conflicts, are among factors holding back merchandise trade performance in Central Asia.

Implementation of regional initiatives remains a critical challenge across all subregional initiatives. Whereas there is high political willingness to undertake regional cooperation, there is often insufficient alignment between regional measures and domestic reforms. Member economies also lack the financial and human resources to understand the technicalities of projects they commit to, while budgetary deficiencies often delay developments substantially. These challenges are aggravated by inequality, financing gaps, and the impacts of climate change.

Inequality within economies and across a subregion continues to be a significant issue. For example, widening gaps between and within Southeast Asian economies in income, human capital, technology adoption, and infrastructure threaten economic

competitiveness, a key objective behind the establishment of the ASEAN Economic Community. The growing digital divide—reflected by gaps in the use of digital technologies, internet speed and usage, and technology production—remains a concern (Ing and Markus 2023).

Subregional cooperation initiatives have been challenged by the vulnerability of participating economies to climate change. Many subregion geographic features and socioeconomic conditions (such as in Southeast Asia, the Pacific, and South Asia) expose populations to climate-related risks such as rising temperatures, increased frequency of heat waves and large storms, widening variability in precipitation, and sea level rise (ADB 2023a). An example of the implications comes from Southeast Asia, where it is estimated the subregion's economy could shrink by 11% by the end of the century if climate change is not tackled since it takes a toll on key sectors such as agriculture, tourism, and fisheries (ADB 2015b). Similarly, severe droughts and heat waves are affecting agricultural yields in Central Asia, putting food security at risk especially given that the water resources of Central Asia are limited (ADB 2023e). Many times, these push member governments to address climate change concerns rather than build physical and social infrastructure.

Almost all subregions are challenged by the widening infrastructure financing gap. Besides macroeconomic challenges, the COVID-19 pandemic and adverse impacts of climate change have exacerbated the demand for and cost of developing sustainable infrastructure. According to ADB (2023d), the total infrastructure investment need for the Southeast Asia subregion is estimated at between $2.8 trillion (the baseline estimate) and $3.1 trillion (climate-adjusted), placing the annual investment need at a $184 billion baseline and $210 billion adjusted for climate investments. Similarly, South Asian economies need an estimated $ 6.4 trillion infrastructure investment (climate-adjusted) during 2016–2030. The issue is particularly severe in the Pacific subregion, where damages from extreme weather raise the cost of investment in transport infrastructure, which hampers the implementation of many cross-border projects for regional integration.

Some subregional cooperations, such as initiatives in the Pacific and Central Asia, face challenge from small size and difficult geography. The Pacific economies suffer from small size and geographic remoteness that limit economies of scale. For instance, Kiribati has a territory of 811 square kilometers, consisting of 33 coral atolls spread over 3.5 million square kilometers of ocean (World Bank 2021b). Such wide dispersal and remoteness makes investment expensive and raises transaction costs, which is an increasing challenge for regional cooperation (ADB 2015a). The Central Asia subregion is dominated by landlocked economies with limited (or no) direct access to the sea (trading gateways). Transportation in economies such as Tajikistan, where mountains cover 87% of the economy's geography, and the Kyrgyz Republic, where 94% of the economy's geography is mountainous (FAO 2016), is a challenge as routes may be indirect or hazardous. Fragmented supply chains combined with inadequately structured transit procedures have led to high transportation costs and unpredicted transit times for international shipments, undermining competitiveness of the region's products. All these make regional cooperation initiatives, particularly for improving cross-border connectivity, expensive.

Policy Recommendations

Regional cooperation will continue to play a vital role in fostering the post-pandemic economic recovery in Asia as well as addressing the region's weaknesses and vulnerabilities.

Amid rising protectionism and geopolitical risks, regional (and subregional) cooperation remains critical to addressing shared challenges, specifically in the dimensions of institutional arrangements and environment cooperation (as observed from discussion on the ARCII). Governments in the region should invest in economic cooperation initiatives to improve connectivity through regulatory coherence and infrastructure, undertaking digital transformation and accelerating climate change adaptation and resilience.

Each of the subregions has its own set of common challenges which require cooperation measures that are more suitable for the region.

For example, Central Asia faces complex challenges due to its landlocked geography, climate change vulnerability, disruption in transport and transit routes, weak institutions, and others. These challenges are deeply intertwined and cannot be addressed effectively by a single economy, thereby strengthening the rationale for regional cooperation. Though the intraregional trade share is low in the South Asian subregion, initiatives such as SASEC in South Asia are crucial for enhancing cooperation among member economies, providing frameworks that improve aspects of development in critical sectors such as trade, transport, and energy (Salsabeel 2022). Given the region's major challenges such as low intraregional trade, climate change vulnerability, lack of infrastructural and logistical resources, taking collective regional and subregional actions is more likely to develop solutions to such issues and challenges over the long term (World Bank 2021a).

Enhancing regional cooperation is vital in mitigating the risks to economic growth posed by growing protectionism.

Amid creeping protectionist sentiments and geopolitical tensions, Asia should continue its momentum in forging trade partnerships within and beyond the region. In this regard, while the mega-regionals, the Regional Comprehensive Economic Partnership and the Comprehensive and Progressive Transpacific Partnership, and the proposed Indo-Pacific Economic Framework will enhance market access, reduce trade barriers, and raise supply chain resilience, they should be implemented with greater integrity. In addition, regional rules and initiatives should be designed and implemented in line with the multilateral framework of the WTO and remaining economies at the minimum must complete their WTO accession process. Currently, several operational aspects of the WTO multilateral trading system are in need of significant reform to keep pace with the changing nature of international trade. These include the dispute settlement body and the scope and coverage of operational agendas.

Supply chain resilience should be strengthened through trade facilitation and regional cooperation.

A series of shocks, including the COVID-19 pandemic and the Russian invasion of Ukraine, have brought to the fore the vulnerabilities in global supply chains. Policymakers should pay greater attention to identify supply chain risks and forge regional cooperation to diversify trading partners and transport and transit routes. Within subregional pacts, economies should prioritize their digital infrastructures to modernize supply chain infrastructure. Paperless trade or digitally driven trade facilitation can advance trade at lower cost. Customs automation, pre-arrival data processing, port call optimization, and other digital solutions can substantially speed up port handling and customs operations, a desired outcome particularly during the times of crisis (UNCTAD 2022).

Climate change policy needs urgent attention by all economies.

In this regard, establishing a carbon pricing mechanism is one of many important policy tools to lower greenhouse gas emissions (ADB 2023a). In Asia, economies have started instituting their carbon pricing mechanisms, though much work is still to be done. As of April 2023, two carbon taxes (Japan and Singapore) and five economy-level emissions trading system (Indonesia, Kazakhstan, New Zealand, the PRC, and the Republic of Korea) are in operation, and several economies (Brunei Darussalam, India, Pakistan, the Philippines, Thailand, and Viet Nam) are planning to implement them. Besides the adoption of carbon pricing schemes, policymakers should explore the development of bilateral and/or regional carbon market linkages. Linking creates a larger carbon market, which adds liquidity and increases price competition, and so reduces the overall cost of emissions reduction and generating economic efficiencies (ADB 2023a). Moreover, a mechanism for sharing knowledge among economies should be explored as such collaboration would facilitate policy and technical dialogue among economies, improving the possibility of cooperation toward developing an integrated carbon market in Asia (ADB 2016). Regional-level action is also needed. A good start was made with the November 2023 endorsement of the Regional Action on Climate Change: A Vision for CAREC to guide and promote cooperation in tackling the effects of climate change.

Innovative finance mechanisms to mobilize increased capital investment should be explored to narrow the infrastructure financing gap.

Innovative finance mechanisms as an alternative to commercial debt finance can attract private and institutional capital, along with public funds, for developmental activities (ADB 2023f). More important, innovative finance is focused on the delivery of positive social and environmental outcomes through market-based financing instruments. For innovative finance to succeed, effective action and collaboration among all stakeholders in the infrastructure project life cycle is critical. Asian economies should institute the development of policy frameworks and build capacity to promote innovative finance options. Business models supported by digital platforms should be considered since they contribute to increased efficiency and transparency, thus creating an enabling environment for sustainable infrastructure investment in the region.

Economies should harness opportunities from digital transformation through greater regional cooperation.

Regional cooperation will play a critical role in developing a coherent, innovative, secure, and inclusive digital ecosystem. With the rise of e-commerce, digital payments, online work, cloud storage, and other digitally enabled services highlighting that digital transformation has penetrated deeply into many socioeconomic systems, there is still a significant disparity in access to technology among and within Asia. In this regard, the ASEAN Digital Economic Framework Agreement, which will serve as ASEAN's means to create a seamless digital trade ecosystem across Southeast Asia, forms a good starting point toward narrowing the digital divide in the region. Moreover, regional collective action is needed to resolve digitalization challenges by improving the quality of key digital enablers to achieve digital technology adoption, enhance domestic preparedness for digital transformation, upskill the workforce, and improve the quality of privacy and competition (Ing and Markus 2023).

References

Asian Development Bank (ADB). https://www.adb.org/trade-supply-chain-finance-program/supply-chain-finance (accessed January 2024).

———. 2015a. *Pacific Opportunities Leveraging Asia's Growth*. Manila.

———. 2015b. *Southeast Asia and the Economics of Global Climate Stabilization*. Manila.

———. 2016. *South Asia Subregional Economic Cooperation Operational Plan 2016–2025*. Manila.

———. 2017. *CAREC 2030: Connecting the Region for Shared and Sustainable Development*. Manila.

———. 2019. *Strategy 2030 Operational Plan for Priority 7 Fostering Regional Cooperation and Integration, 2019–2024*. Manila.

———. 2020a. *ADB Approves $121 Million Loan to Complete Modernization of Eastern Uzbekistan Railway Network*. Manila.

———. 2020b. *ADB's Support to Enhance COVID-19 Vaccine Access*. Manila.

———. 2022a. *Asia-Pacific Regional Cooperation and Integration Index Database*. https://aric.adb.org/database/arcii (accessed November 2023).

———. 2022b. *BIMSTEC Master Plan for Transport Connectivity*. Manila.

———. 2022c. *BIMSTEC Trade Facilitation Strategic Framework*. Manila.

———. 2022d. *CAREC Health Strategy 2030*. Manila.

———. 2023a. *Asian Economic Integration Report 2023: Trade, Investment, and Climate Change in Asia and the Pacific*. Manila.

———. 2023b. *CAREC Countries Endorse New Vision to Fight Climate Change Together*. News Release. 30 November. Tbilisi. https://www.adb.org/news/carec-countries-endorse-new-vision-fight-climate-change-together (accessed December 2023).

———. *CAREC Program Portfolio*. Unpublished.

———. *Pacific Program Portfolio*. Unpublished.

———. 2023e. *Q&A: Addressing Intertwined Challenges in Central Asia and the Caucasus through Regional Cooperation*. Manila.

———. 2023f. *Reinvigorating Financing Approaches for Sustainable and Resilient Infrastructure in ASEAN+3*. Manila.

Australian Infrastructure Financing Facility for the Pacific (AIFFP). Connecting the Federated States of Micronesia, Kiribati and Nauru to the Internet via Submarine Cable. https://www.aiffp.gov.au/investments/investment-list/connecting-the-federated-states-of-micronesia-kiribati-and-nauru-to-the-internet-via-submarine-cable (accessed January 2024).

———. 2022a. *Growing Together: Further Maritime Support for PNG*. News. 1 December. https://www.aiffp.gov.au/news/growing-together-further-maritime-support-png (accessed December 2023).

———. 2022b. *Nauru Airport Refurbishment*. News. 3 March. https://www.aiffp.gov.au/news/nauru-airport-refurbishment (accessed December 2023).

Brunei Darussalam–Indonesia–Malaysia–Philippines East ASEAN Growth Area (BIMP-EAGA). *The Green Cities Initiative for BIMP-EAGA*. Manila.

———. 2019. BIMP-EAGA Tops Project Completion Targets. Sabah. https://bimp-eaga.asia/article/bimp-eaga-tops-project-completion-targets (accessed January 2024).

———. 2021. Southeast Asia Takes Action against Plastic Pollution. 3 June. Sabah. https://bimp-eaga.asia/article/southeast-asia-takes-action-against-plastic-pollution (accessed December 2023).

———. 2022a. ASEAN, EU Ink World's First Region-to-Region Air Transport Deal. Sabah. 11 November. https://bimp-eaga.asia/article/asean-eu-ink-worlds-first-region-region-air-transport-deal (accessed December 2023).

———. 2022b. *Building the ASEAN Power Grid: Opportunities and Challenges*. Sabah. https://bimp-eaga.asia/article/building-asean-power-grid-opportunities-and-challenges (accessed December 2023).

———. 2022c. *Joint BIMP-EAGA and IMT-GT Tourism Recovery Communications Plan and Toolkit 2022–2024*. Sabah.

———. 2023a. *Building Sulawesi's First Railway*. Sabah. https://bimp-eaga.asia/index.php/article/building-sulawesis-first-railway (accessed December 2023).

———. 2023b. *Four Southeast Asian Countries Pilot the Use of Nuclear Technology in Plastics Recycling*. https://bimp-eaga.asia/article/four-southeast-asian-countries-pilot-use-nuclear-technology-plastics-recycling (accessed November 2023).

Central Asia Regional Economic Cooperation (CAREC) Program. 2021a. *ADB, Kyrgyz Republic Presented Air Quality Data Available Online*. Manila.

———. 2021b. Trade Sector Progress Report and Work Plan. Manila.

———. 2022a. *2021–2022 Country Highlights*. Manila. https://www.carecprogram.org/?page_id=18721 (accessed December 2023).

———. 2022b. *CAREC Post-Pandemic Framework for a Green, Sustainable, and Inclusive Recovery*. Manila.

———. 2022c. *Cooperation Framework for Agricultural Development and Food Security in the CAREC Region*. Manila.

———. 2023. *Georgia: Model Law on Electronic Transferable Records (MLETR) Capacity Building*. 20 April. https://www.carecprogram.org/?event=georgia-model-law-on-electronic-transferable-records-mletr-capacity-building (accessed January 2024).

Food and Agriculture Organization (FAO). 2016. AQUASTAT Database. In International Transport Forum (ITF). 2019. Enhancing Connectivity and Freight in Central Asia. Paris.

Global Trade Alert Database. https://www.globaltradealert.org/data_extraction (accessed November 2023).

Greater Mekong Subregion (GMS). 2022a. PRC-Lao PDR Railway Launches Freight Transit Yard to Boost Transshipment of Goods to Thailand. News. 5 August. Manila. https://greatermekong.org/taxonomy/term/1922 (accessed December 2023).

———. 2022b. PRC, Lao PDR Achieve Two-way Energy Trade. News. 5 August. Manila. https://greatermekong.org/g/prc-lao-pdr-achieve-two-way-energy-trade (accessed December 2023).

Indonesia-Malaysia-Thailand Growth Triangle (IMT-GT). *Green Cities Initiative*. Putrajaya.

Ing, L. Y. and I. Markus. 2023. ASEAN Digital Community 2040. *Policy Brief*. No. 2022-11. Jakarta: Economic Research Institute for ASEAN and East Asia.

International Telecommunication Union (ITU). 2021. Smart Islands: Boosting Connectivity to Unlock Pacific Potential. News. 25 Nov. https://www.itu.int/hub/2021/11/smart-islands-boosting-connectivity-to-unlock-pacific-potential/ (accessed December 2023).

International Monetary Fund (IMF). 2023. *World Economic Outlook: A Rocky Recovery.* Washington, DC.

Islamic Development Bank (IsDB). 2020. IsDB Finances the First Public-Private Partnership Toll-Road Concession in Kazakhstan. News. 6 August. https://www.isdb.org/news/isdb-finances-the-first-public-private-partnership-toll-road-concession-in-kazakhstan (accessed December 2023).

Organisation for Economic Co-operation and Development (OECD). OECD Services Trade Restrictiveness Index database. https://stats.oecd.org/Index.aspx?DataSetCode=STRI (accessed May 2023).

Pacific Islands Forum Secretariat (PIFS). 2013. *Pacific Climate Change Finance Assessment Framework.* Final Report. Suva.

———. 2020a. *Pacific Quality Infrastructure (PQI).* Suva.

———. 2020b. Pacific Humanitarian Pathway on COVID-19 Continues Delivery of Medical Supplies. Media Release. 30 June. https://www.forumsec.org/2020/06/30/pacific-humanitarian-pathway-on-covid-19-continues-delivery-of-medical-supplies/ (accessed December 2023).

———. 2021. *Declaration on Preserving Maritime Zones in the Face of Climate Change-related Sea-Level Rise.* Suva.

———. 2022. *2050 Strategy for the Blue Pacific Continent.* Suva.

———. 2023. *Pacific Regional Framework on Climate Mobility.* Suva.

Salsabeel, N. 2022. Revisiting Bounties of Sub-Regional Cooperation: The Case of South Asia. Commentary. *South Asia Journal.* 6 July. https://southasiajournal.net/revisiting-bounties-of-sub-regional-cooperation-the-case-of-south-asia/ (accessed December 2023).

Secretariat of the Pacific Community (SPC). 2016. *Framework for Resilient Development in the Pacific: An Integrated Approach to Address Climate Change and Disaster Risk Management (FRDP) 2017–2030.* Suva.

South Asia Subregional Economic Cooperation (SASEC). 2022. *Action Plan for SASEC Initiatives 2022–2024.* Manila.

———. 2022. Prime Minister Inaugurates Nepal's Second International Airport. News. 16 May. Manila. https://www.sasec.asia/index.php?page=news&nid=1395&url=nep-pm-2nd-intl-airport (accessed December 2023).

———. 2023a. Bangladesh and Bhutan Sign Agreement on the Movement of Traffic-in-Transit and Protocol. News. 22 March. Manila. https://www.sasec.asia/index.php?page=news&nid=1472&url=ban-bhu-sign-transit-agreement (accessed December 2023).

———. 2023b. Bangladesh-India Land Port at Dawki, Meghalaya Inaugurated. Manila. https://www.sasec.asia/index.php?page=news&nid=1497&url=ban-ind-land-port-dawki (accessed December 2023).

———. 2023c. India and Nepal Sign Cross-Border Energy, Trade and Transit Deals. News. 2 June. Manila. https://www.sasec.asia/index.php?page=news&nid=1510&url=india-nepal-sign-cross-border-energy-trade-transit (accessed December 2023).

———. 2023d. India to Develop Eastern Grid Waterway Network. News. 17 June. Manila.https://www.sasec.asia/index.php?page=news&nid=1517&url=india-eastern-grid (accessed December 2023).

South Pacific Tourism Organization (SPTO). 2022. Pacific Geoparks Initiative. https://southpacificislands.travel/projects/pacific-geoparks-initiative/ (accessed December 2023).

United Nations Conference on Trade and Development
(UNCTAD). 2022. Pacific Islands Forum Joins
UNCTAD-Led eTrade for All Initiative. News.
3 November. https://unctad.org/news/pacific-
islands-forum-joins-unctad-led-etrade-all-
initiative (accessed December 2023).

World Bank. 2021a. *Climate Change Action Plan 2021–
2025 South Asia Roadmap.* Washington, DC.

———. 2021b. *Kiribati Digital Government Project.*
Washington, DC.

World Trade Organization (WTO). Integrated Trade
Intelligence Portal. http://i-tip.wto.org/goods/
Default.aspx (accessed May 2023).

2

Trade and Global Value Chains

Introduction

Globalization and especially the development of global value chains (GVCs) over the past 3 decades have been linked with improvements in efficiency and productivity and to developing and emerging economies increasing their participation in global production. However, concerns have been raised about the costs and risks of integration into global production networks, particularly of disruption in GVCs. The interconnected nature of GVCs makes their interruption particularly damaging, with the coronavirus disease (COVID-19) pandemic an example of how disruptions can percolate across economies.

Besides the direct impact on production, the pandemic highlighted the challenges caused by interruptions to GVC linkages through border closures and lockdowns as well as breakdowns in the international transport network connecting different nodes in GVCs (Brenton, Ferrantino, and Maliszewska 2022), while the negative demand shock associated with the pandemic had further spillover effects within GVCs (Pahl et al. 2021). Disruptions have been more challenging for sectors strongly integrated into GVCs (e.g., electronics and automobiles) and those further downstream (Malacrino, Mohommad, and Presbitero 2022).

Supply disruptions that followed the COVID-19 pandemic affected various sectors and products, with the widespread shortages of critical medical equipment (e.g., respirators) and critical inputs into several manufacturing subsectors (e.g., semiconductors) representing two specific examples. Such disruptions are not new, however, with earlier disruptions associated

with the 2008 global financial crisis as well as more localized disasters, such as those in Japan and Thailand, percolating across economies. Disruptions since the pandemic include the Russian invasion of Ukraine and lingering global inflation, which have been felt hard in the food and agriculture sectors.

GVCs have been shown to be resilient to disruptions that occurred both during and after the COVID-19 pandemic, especially for economies more deeply integrated into GVCs.

Brenton, Ferrantino, and Maliszewska (2022) show that economies well integrated into GVCs were able to recover more quickly. GVCs were also crucial in dealing with some of the disruptions that occurred during the pandemic (e.g., the provision of personal protective equipment). Despite this resilience, concerns around the risk of GVC disruptions have only increased with the COVID-19 pandemic, with debate raging over the extent to which global integration can expose domestic production to shocks from abroad. Concerns also abound over the risk of being dependent on a small number of suppliers and of relying on global production networks for products that are considered essential.

Such concerns build upon earlier discussions on the need to engage in reshoring and nearshoring for diverse reasons, including those related to job creation, the rise of new technologies, and the increasing concentration of GVC activity, with the most recent discussions emphasizing the need for strategic autonomy by the European Union (EU), the United States (US), and others (see, for example, European Parliament 2021).[10]

---

[10]   Recent evidence from the International Monetary Fund (IMF) suggests that severe geopolitical fragmentation could reduce global gross domestic product by up to 7% through its impact on trade, technology, and capital flows (IMF 2023).

In respect to strategic autonomy, the supply chain security of key industries has become of concern to various economies, reflected in the trade conflict between the People's Republic of China (PRC) and the US and recent policy announcements by the US and the EU, among others, involving efforts to move away from reliance on production in the PRC—the so-called de-risking of value chains. Beyond the PRC, concerns have been expressed about the diverse set of causes of supply chain disruptions (Grossman, Helpman, and Lhuillier 2021) and over both the frequency of supply chain disruptions and the link between disruptions and the geographic footprint of a sector (McKinsey Global Institute 2020). A typical response to supply chain disruption risk is to suggest bringing the different production stages of a value chain closer to home, either through reshoring or nearshoring, and that supply chains should become shorter.

In certain cases, notably in the food sector, policies such as export bans have been suggested and implemented, with the intention of developing autonomy in critical sectors. Modeling from Brenton, Ferrantino, and Maliszewska (2022) and IMF (2022), among others, provides a contrast to the increased calls for reshoring and nearshoring; however, these modeling exercises tend to support the view that increased, rather than diminished, GVC integration is needed to make economies more resilient to external shocks. This conclusion further suggests that diversification— specifically regarding suppliers in GVCs—is a more viable strategy to create resilience than reshoring and nearshoring, given that latter approaches reduce vulnerability to global shocks but leave economies at risk of economy-specific shocks.

Besides presenting the latest trends in trade and GVC outcomes and trade policy developments, this chapter turns the focus on the properties of an economy's GVC integration, and it delves into food sector resilience, which is a trade issue of great importance for Asia and the Pacific.[11]

Considering recent discussions on risk and resilience in GVCs, the chapter examines the extent to which economies are diversified within GVCs, how this has changed in recent years, and the dynamics of regionalism within GVCs. The analysis indicates that strategies associated with generating resilience in GVCs—including reshoring, nearshoring, and the diversification of partners in GVCs—do not seem to have played much of a role in the recent dynamics of Asia's GVC integration. Diversification trends vary significantly, while the evidence of increased regionalism in supplier networks (that is, backward linkages) in Asian GVCs is limited. The issue of food resilience remains a concern for many Asian economies, however, with diversification efforts, the creation and expansion of free trade agreements (FTAs), and the digitization of trade procedures means of achieving resilience.

Recent Growth Trends in Asia's Trade

Amid global shocks and rising prices, and despite services trade continuing to recover, Asia's growth slowed in 2022 as its merchandise trade contracted.

The gross domestic product (GDP) growth in the world and Asia slowed in 2022 amid geopolitical tensions and escalating inflation. In the aftermath of the COVID-19 pandemic in 2021, global inflation surged as the world simultaneously experienced energy and food crises brought about by global supply chain disruptions from the COVID-19 pandemic, the Russian invasion of Ukraine, and effects of climate change on the energy and agriculture sectors. In comparison to the robust growth of more than 6% in 2021, even as growth was driven by unprecedented fiscal and monetary stimulus enacted to bolster economic recovery from the pandemic, growth rates in Asian economies and the world shrank by 3 percentage points in 2022 (Figure 2.1).

---

[11]   Asia and the Pacific, or Asia, consists of the 49 regional member economies of the Asian Development Bank (ADB). The composition of economies for Central Asia, East Asia, the Pacific and Oceania, South Asia, and Southeast Asia are outlined in ADB. Asia Regional Integration Center. Economy Groupings. https://aric.adb.org/integrationindicators/groupings.

Figure 2.1: Merchandise and Services Trade Volume and Real Output Growth—Asia and the Pacific, and the World

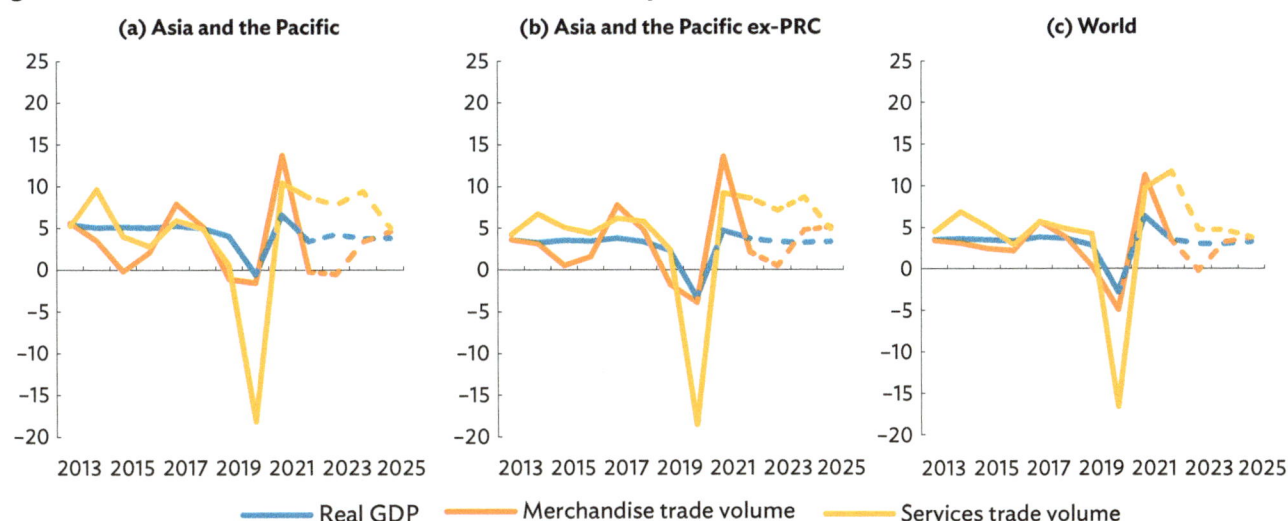

GDP = gross domestic product, PRC = People's Republic of China.

Sources: ADB calculations using data from International Monetary Fund (IMF). World Economic Outlook October 2023 Database. https://www.imf.org/en/Publications/WEO/weo-database/2023/October; IMF. Direction of Trade Statistics. https://data.imf.org/dot; and WTO-Organisation for Economic Cooperation and Development (OECD) Balanced Trade in Services Dataset (BaTIS)—BPM6. https://www.wto.org/english/res_e/statis_e/trade_datasets_e.htm (all accessed November 2023).

Driven by a substantial downturn in merchandise trade in the PRC, Asia's merchandise trade contracted in 2022. World and Asian trade recovered strongly in 2021 with the jump in demand supported by various monetary and fiscal stimuli and the easing of pandemic-related restrictions. However, 2022 saw a marked downturn in the growth of global merchandise trade amid escalating inflationary pressures, geopolitical tensions, and renewed lockdown measures in response to emerging variants of the coronavirus disease. While world merchandise trade grew by 3.4% in 2022 (down from 11.2% in 2021), merchandise trade in Asia contracted by 0.3%, a sharp drop from a 13.6% growth rate in the previous year.

The overall growth rate of −0.3% for Asia masks divergent economy-level developments, with merchandise trade dropping (by 5.6% overall) in 10 Asian economies in 2022 but increasing (by 5.4%) in the remaining 43 economies. Of those economies witnessing a decline in merchandise trade, 96% of the total reduction in merchandise trade emanated from just two economies, the PRC (53%) and Hong Kong, China (43%). Of the increases observed in the 43 remaining economies, the Association of Southeast Asian Nations (ASEAN) member economies collectively contributed 34% to the increase, while Japan was the largest single-economy contributor at 22%, with the Republic of Korea accounting for 12% and India 11% of the total increase.

This divergent performance in merchandise trade between the PRC and other Asian economies highlights the dominant role of the PRC in driving overall regional trends, but further suggests that trade performance in most Asian economies was positive in 2022 (Figure 2.1b). This further underscores the potential for these economies to develop parallel global supply chains even as major economies explore strategies for de-risking from the PRC through dual or multiple sourcing strategies.

In contrast to merchandise trade and despite being more severely impacted during the COVID-19 pandemic, services trade maintained its robust recovery in 2022. Global services trade increased by 11.6%, up by 2.0 percentage points from the previous year. Meanwhile, Asia's services trade expanded by 8.6%, although at a rate that was slightly lower than in 2021.

These divergent trends between merchandise and services trade may be explained by the fact that global shocks in 2022 primarily impacted goods production and global supply chains. In contrast, the growing digitalization of services trade has provided significant resilience against global supply chain-related issues, while the relaxation of border restrictions has spurred recovery in the travel and tourism sectors.

Slow Growth in Asia's Trade for 2023 Amid Lingering Pressures

Asian trade in 2023 remains below 2022 levels, with growth through 2023 likely to be slow amid ongoing challenges. After robust growth from mid-2020 to mid-2021, followed by a prolonged downturn through 2022 due to surging inflation, renewed lockdowns and geopolitical disruptions, Asian trade has been stagnant in 2023. Total trade volume in the region bottomed out in February 2023, before something of an uneven recovery in the following months, in part supported by easing inflation, the reopening of the PRC, and the World Health Organization's downgrade of COVID-19 from a global health emergency in May 2023 (Figure 2.2). Nevertheless, global trade growth is expected to remain slow amid monetary tightening and ongoing geopolitical tensions (United Nations 2023a).

While inflation has eased in 2023, monetary tightening is likely to constrain trade expansion in the near term (Figure 2.1). Global inflation is projected to decline from

8.7% in 2022 to 6.8% in 2023 as a result of lower food and energy prices and reduced global demand (IMF 2023). Despite evidence of falling global food prices, domestic food inflation remains high in many economies because of continuing high import costs, food export bans, local supply disruptions, and market imperfections (United Nations 2023b). While Asia's trade prospects remain subdued, its growth is expected to benefit from improved demand in the US and the EU, economic recovery in the PRC, and strong growth in India, which is set to be the fastest growing major economy in 2023 (IMF 2023; United Nations 2023b).

Trade Structure Changes

Associated with the pandemic-induced global supply chain crisis, there has been something of a shift of merchandise trade in Asia toward intraregional partners.

In the past 3 decades, the focus of Asian merchandise trade shifted from traditional Western economic partners toward the PRC and other global regions.

Figure 2.2: Monthly Trade by Value and Volume—Asia and Pacific

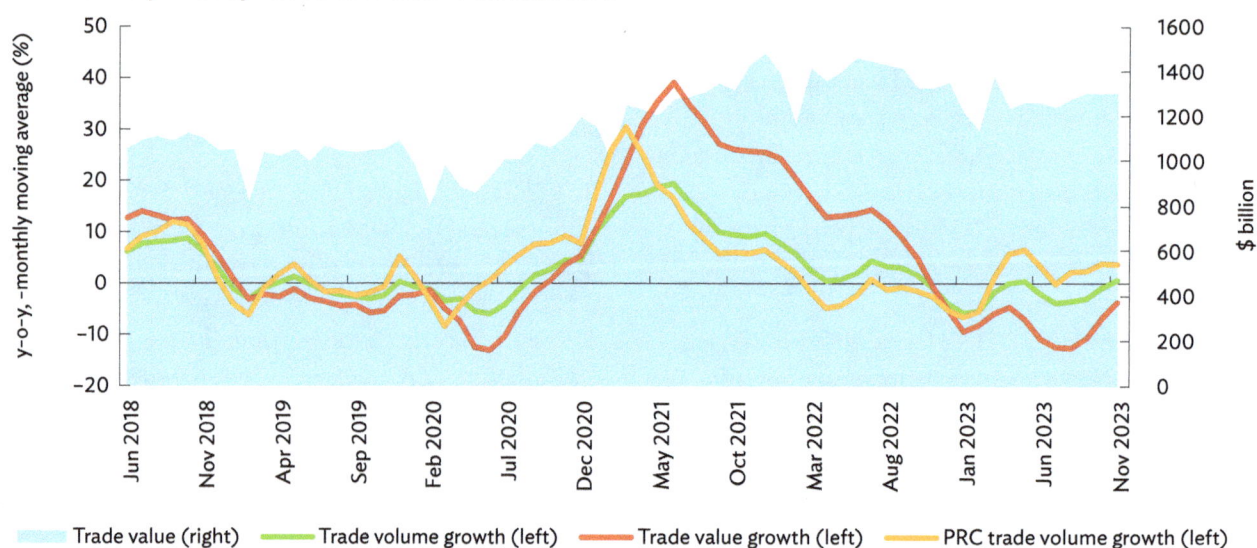

PRC = People's Republic of China, y-o-y = year-on-year.

Notes: Trade volume growth rates were computed as the 3-month moving average year-on-year growth using volume indexes. For each period and trade flow type (i.e., imports and exports), available data include indexes for the PRC and Japan, and aggregate indexes for selected economies in Asia and the Pacific: (i) advanced economies excluding Japan (Hong Kong, China; the Republic of Korea; Singapore; and Taipei,China); and (ii) emerging economies excluding the PRC (India, Indonesia, Malaysia, Pakistan, the Philippines, Thailand, and Viet Nam). The aggregate index for Asia and the Pacific was computed using trade values as weights.

Sources: ADB calculations using data from CEIC Data Company; and CPB Netherlands Bureau for Economic Policy Analysis. World Trade Monitor. https://www.cpb.nl/en/world-trade-monitor-november-2023 (both accessed February 2024).

By 2010, Asia's merchandise trade with the PRC surpassed that with the EU and North America, with the PRC establishing itself as Asia's most important single-economy trade partner for goods (Figure 2.3).

Accompanying the 2021–2023 global supply chain crisis, Asia's trade patterns have also restructured. Something of a reorientation of Asian trade has taken place between 2020 and 2023, with increased shares for intraregional trade and trade with other global regions at the expense of trade shares with the PRC, North America, and Europe (Figure 2.3), the latter continuing something of a longer-term trend. The share of Asian merchandise trade with the PRC dropped from 17% in 2020 to 15% in 2022, while that of the EU plus the United Kingdom (EU+UK) dropped from 12.6% to 11.9% and North America from 13.6% to 13.2%. In contrast, the share of intraregional trade within Asia, excluding the PRC, rose from 41.5% to 42.0%, while the share of Asia's trade with the rest of the world increased from 15.3% to 17.8%.

Trade in services is less regionally integrated within Asia, though enhancing services trade may be a means of

strengthening supply chain resilience. Figure 2.3 shows that Asia has a higher degree of regional integration in merchandise trade than in services trade. In 2022, 57.1% of its trade in goods occurred within the region, whereas less than half (46.2%) of its services trade was intraregional. Over the past 2 decades, Asia's trade pattern in services has remained relatively stable. The EU+UK has traditionally been its most significant partner, accounting for a 22.5% share in 2021, followed by North America at 16.7%, and other global regions at 14.5%. In contrast, intraregional services trade with the PRC stood at 10.7%. The stability of Asia's services trade structure amid global supply chain disruptions, combined with the relatively strong growth of services trade in the most recent period (Figure 2.1), suggests the sector is relatively resilient to post-pandemic shocks. Improving trade in services can therefore strengthen economies' resilience to global supply chain disruptions by diversifying into a sector with supply chain dynamics distinct from merchandise trade. Furthermore, physical supply chains can benefit from increased flexibility, reduced transportation dependency, and optimization facilitated by digital service-based tools and strategies.

Figure 2.3: Merchandise and Services Trade of Asia and the Pacific, by Partner (%)

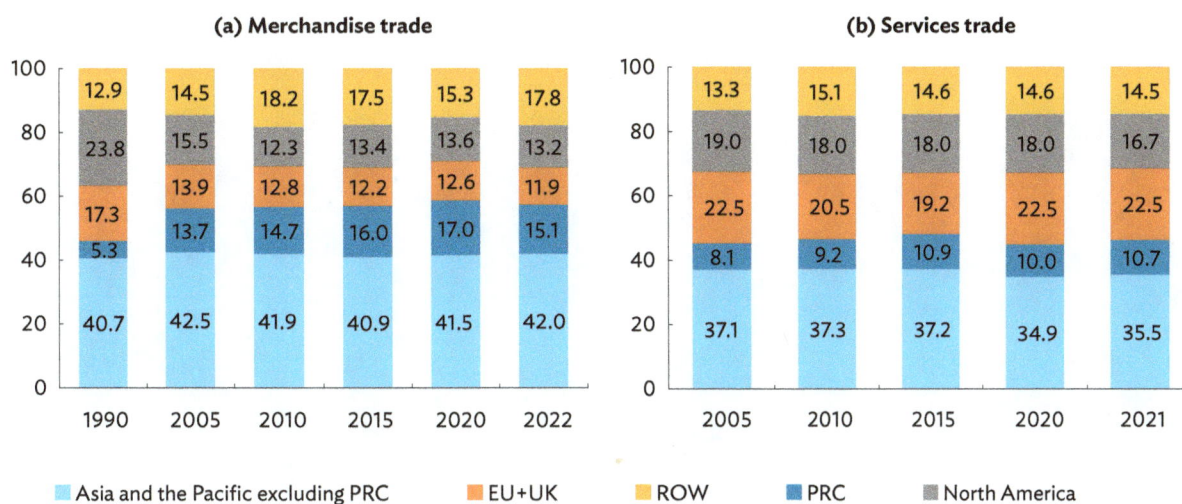

EU = European Union (27 members), PRC = People's Republic of China, ROW = rest of the world, UK = United Kingdom.

Notes: Values expressed as percentage of the region's total merchandise trade value (sum of exports and imports). North America covers Canada, Mexico, and the United States.

Sources: ADB calculations using data from International Monetary Fund. Direction of Trade Statistics. https://data.imf.org/dot; and WTO-OECD Balanced Trade in Services Dataset (BaTIS)—BPM6. https://www.wto.org/english/res_e/statis_e/trade_datasets_e.htm (both accessed November 2023).

Asia's Global Value Chain Growth Reinforces Downstream Role

The decline in overall GVC activity during the COVID-19 pandemic in 2020 was larger in Asia (–5.8%) than the rest of the world (–4.8%), although not as large (–5.1%) when excluding PRC data (Figure 2.4).

Trends differ notably for forward and backward linkages in GVCs. Whereas the –8.3% drop in backward GVC linkages in Asia was much larger than the –3.5% drop in the rest of the world, the reverse was the case for forward GVC linkages (–2.6% in Asia and –5.9% in the rest of the world). Recovery in overall GVC rates in 2021 was similar for Asia and the rest of the world, with growth of 10.7%, though the rate for Asia was larger when excluding the PRC (13.4%). Robust growth of overall GVC activity continued in 2022, with the rate being larger in Asia (10.7%) than the rest of the world (7.7%). The growth rate of backward linkages in Asia since 2020 has been larger than that for forward linkages, especially when excluding PRC data.

The relatively rapid growth of backward GVC linkages in Asia in the aftermath of the COVID-19 pandemic has further increased the gap between Asia's backward and forward GVC integration, a gap that had diminished at the onset of the pandemic. Such dynamics highlight the traditional role of Asia as a downstream assembler in GVCs, with the response of GVCs in Asia following the pandemic reinforcing that role. This is seen in Figure 2.5, which reports an indicator of GVC positioning and highlights the stronger backward GVC participation in Asia compared with other regions. The figure further highlights the increase in Asia's relative backward linkages since the pandemic. It is also notable that Asia's relative backward linkages in GVCs are lower when excluding the PRC (Figure 2.5a), highlighting the significant role of the PRC in downstream production in GVCs within Asia, though the values including and excluding the PRC have converged since the pandemic. The increase in Asia's relative backward linkages since the pandemic has been driven by relatively higher backward linkages in medium to high tech sectors (Figure 2.5b).

Figure 2.4: Overall, Backward, and Forward Global Value Chain Participation Rates

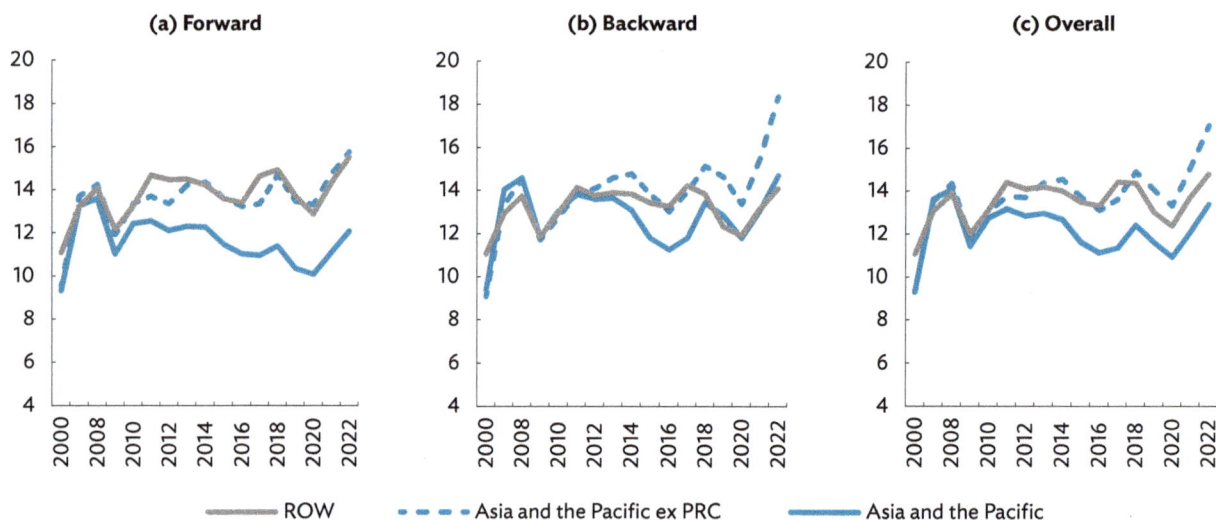

PRC = People's Republic of China, ROW = rest of the world.

Note: Participation rates are calculated as the share of forward global value chain activity in total value-added in the case of forward linkages and as the share of backward global value chain activity in final production in the case of backward linkages.

Sources: ADB calculations using data from ADB Multiregional Input–Output Database; and methodology by Wang et al. (2017).

Figure 2.5: Global Value Chain Position Index

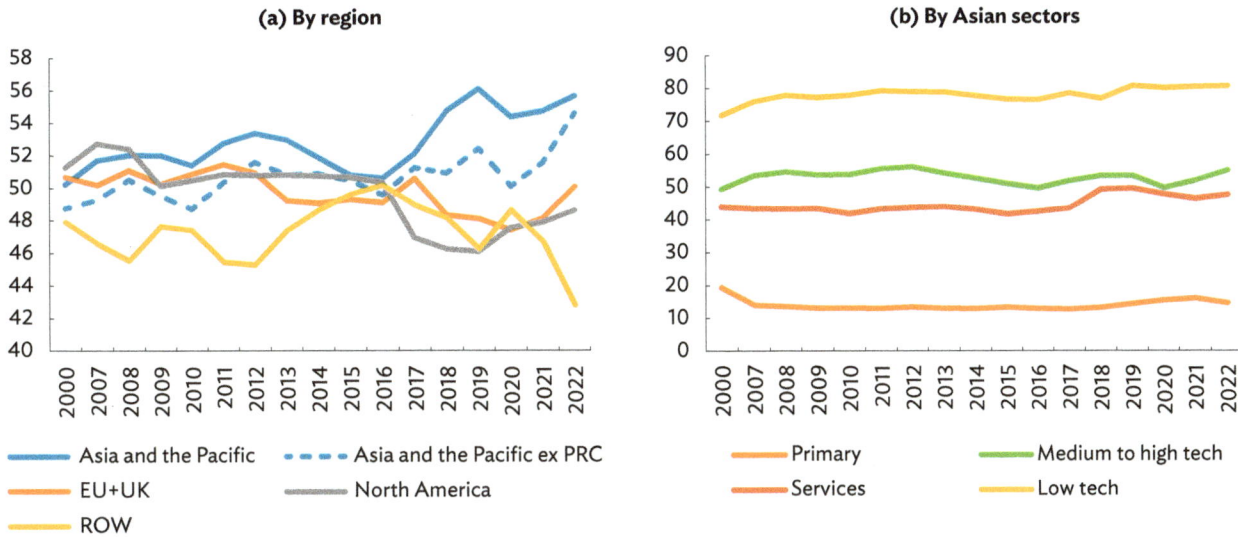

(a) By region

(b) By Asian sectors

EU = European Union (27 members), PRC = People's Republic of China, ROW = rest of the world, UK = United Kingdom.

Note: Global value chain (GVC) position index is calculated as backward GVC activity divided by the sum of forward and backward GVC activities, then multiplied by 100.

Sources: ADB calculations using data from ADB Multiregional Input–Output Database; and methodology by Wang et al. (2017).

Figure 2.6: Global Value Chain of Asia and the Pacific, by Selected Sectors

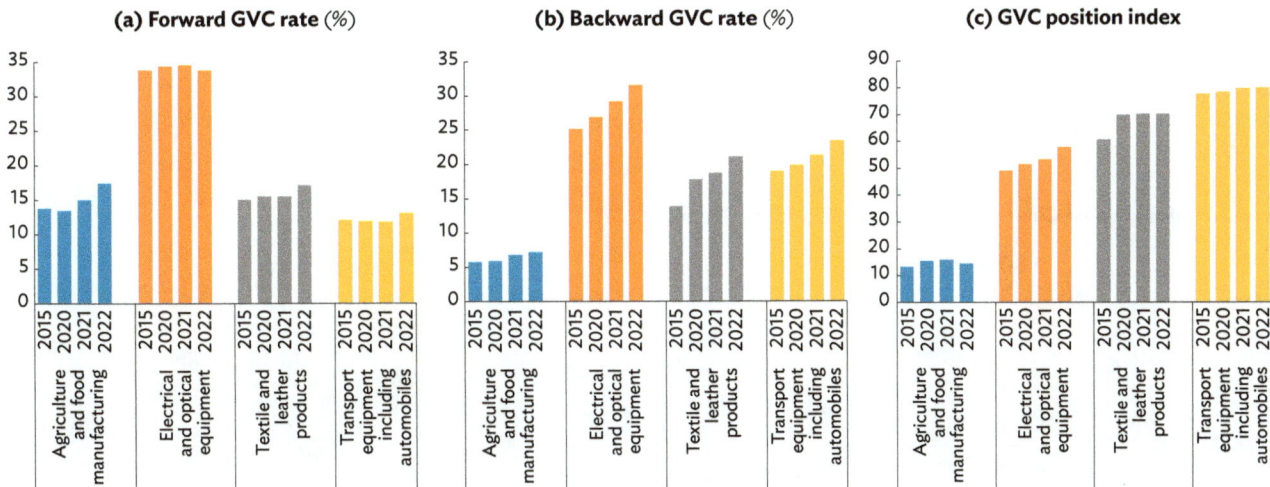

(a) Forward GVC rate (%)

(b) Backward GVC rate (%)

(c) GVC position index

GVC = global value chain.

Notes: Participation rates are calculated as the share of forward GVC activity in total value-added in the case of forward linkages and as the share of backward GVC activity in final production in the case of backward linkages. Global value chain position index is calculated as backward GVC activity divided by the sum of forward and backward GVC activities, then multiplied by 100.

Sources: ADB calculations using data from ADB. Multiregional Input–Output Database; and methodology by Wang et al. (2017).

Focusing on a set of traditional GVC sectors, Figure 2.6 illustrates that while forward GVC linkages in Asia have remained stable over time, though with some increases in agriculture and food manufacturing, textile and leather products, and transport equipment in the most recent period, backward linkages are on a more persistent upward trend, especially for electrical and optical equipment. Combined, these dynamics point to an increase in relative backward linkages and to more downstream production within the major GVC sectors in Asia.

Developments in the Structure of Asia's Global Value Chain Participation

During and after the COVID-19 pandemic, Asia's GVC integration has shown signs of becoming more regional, though regionalization of backward linkages has not been as great as for forward linkages.

The supply chain disruptions associated with the COVID-19 pandemic heightened calls to bring suppliers in value chains closer to home through nearshoring. Examining the share of forward and backward GVC linkages that are regional suggests that while forward linkages in GVCs have become more regional since the onset of the pandemic, the regionalization of backward linkages has been less substantial (Figure 2.7). The share of value-added in GVCs due to forward linkages within Asia has increased since 2015, from 38.5% in 2015 to 50.5% in 2022, with the shares increasing in East Asia (from 21% to 27.4%) and to a lesser extent in Southeast Asia (6.9% to 10.2%) and other Asia (3.3% to 6.0%). Regional shares of Asia's backward GVC linkages also increased between 2015 and 2022, but to a much lesser

extent (from 37.3% to 41.9%, with the share for East Asia increasing from 16.1% to 18.9%). As such, data indicate some evidence of the geographic shortening of GVCs in Asia, with this trend being stronger when considering forward linkages within GVCs.

Asian economies have a less diversified range of GVC partners compared to other regions, and the diversification has narrowed since the COVID-19 pandemic.

Asia's diversification of partners through backward linkages in GVCs is low when compared with EU+UK and the rest of the world (Figure 2.8a). While diversification levels increased rapidly from 2015 onward in Asia since the onset of the COVID-19 pandemic diversification levels have diminished again. This drop in diversification is consistent with trends in other regions, though the drop in Asia has been larger than other regions. Relatively high levels of specialization of supplier economies in Asian GVCs present a risk to the resilience of Asia's GVC production. At the subregional level, diversification of backward GVC linkages has remained low in South Asia (Figure 2.8b). Conversely, diversification has increased over time in Central Asia and East Asia, although with declines since the pandemic.

Figure 2.7: Global Value Chain of Asia and the Pacific, by Partner

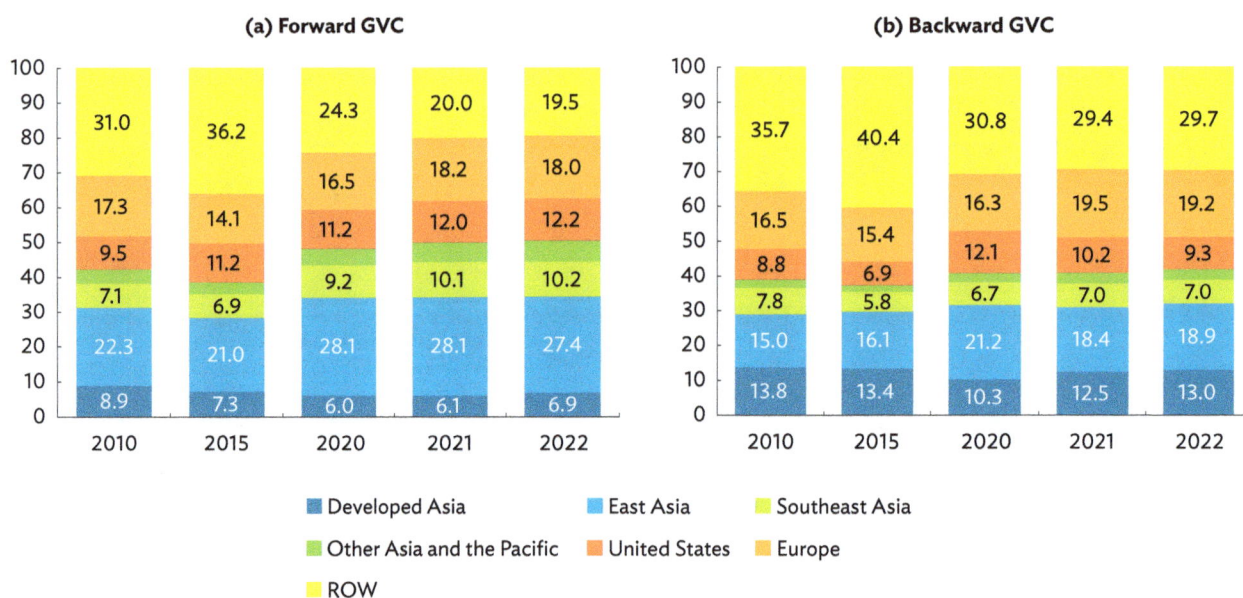

GVC = global value chain, ROW = rest of the world.

Sources: ADB calculations using data from ADB Multiregional Input–Output Database; and methodology by Wang et al. (2017).

Figure 2.8: Diversification Index by Region and Asian Subregions—Backward Global Value Chain Linkages

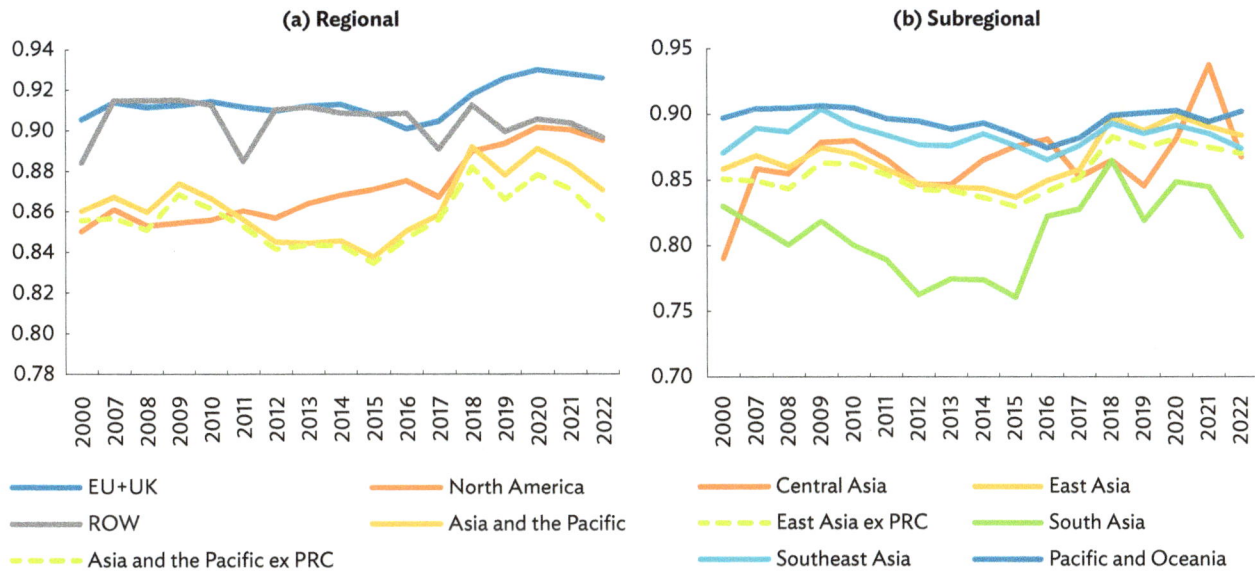

(a) Regional

(b) Subregional

EU = European Union (27 members), GVC = global value chain, PRC = People's Republic of China, ROW = rest of the world, UK = United Kingdom.

Note: The Diversification Index is constructed as the inverse Herfindahl–Hirschman Index using shares of partner economies in backward linkages.

Sources: ADB calculations using data from ADB. Multiregional Input–Output Database; and methodology by Wang et al. (2017).

Figure 2.9: Diversification Index, by Region and Asian Subregions—Forward Global Value Chain Linkages

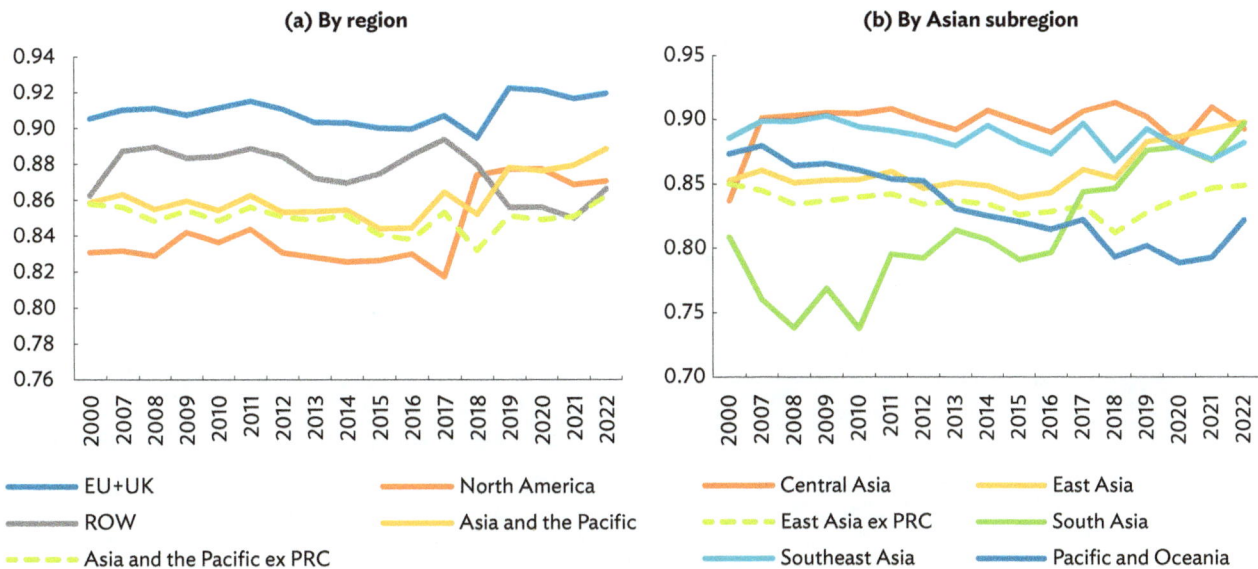

(a) By region

(b) By Asian subregion

EU = European Union (27 members), GVC = global value chain, PRC = People's Republic of China, ROW = rest of the world, UK = United Kingdom.

Note: The Diversification Index is constructed as the inverse Herfindahl-Hirschmann Index (HHI) using shares of partner economies in forward linkages.

Sources: ADB calculations using data from ADB. Multiregional Input–Output Database; and methodology by Wang et al. (2017).

The diversification of partners through forward GVC linkages in Asia is narrower than that of the EU+UK, but wider than in North America (Figure 2.9a), and in contrast to the backward linkages, has continued the upward trend, which began in the mid-2010s. The PRC has played a prominent role: measures of diversification in Asia when excluding the PRC are below those when the PRC is included. At the subregional level, the dynamics of diversification through forward linkages have been heterogeneous (Figure 2.9b). While South Asia and East Asia have seen increases in diversification over the period 2007–2022, with a relatively large increase in South Asia, diversification in the other regions has either been static or has declined.

There is little evidence of reshoring activity in Asia when using indicators of the extent to which domestic consumption is met by domestic production.

Discussions around reshoring often focus on increasing the share of inputs from domestic sources, with Krenz and Strulik (2021) using such arguments to develop an indicator of reshoring using multiregional input-output tables to measure the change in the ratio of domestic to foreign inputs. Adopting this approach, Figure 2.10a shows that whereas the change in domestic to foreign inputs in Asia has been positive for much of the period, indicating an increasing share of domestic inputs, since 2019 it has been negative. This trend is quite different for North America and the EU+UK, where the change in the domestic to foreign input ratio has been negative for most of the period. As such, the indicator suggests that in the aggregate reshoring of input purchases is not happening in major Western markets and the rising domestic share in Asia has also turned negative. The decreasing share of domestic to foreign inputs in the most recent period

Figure 2.10: Reshoring Indexes by Region and Asian Subregion

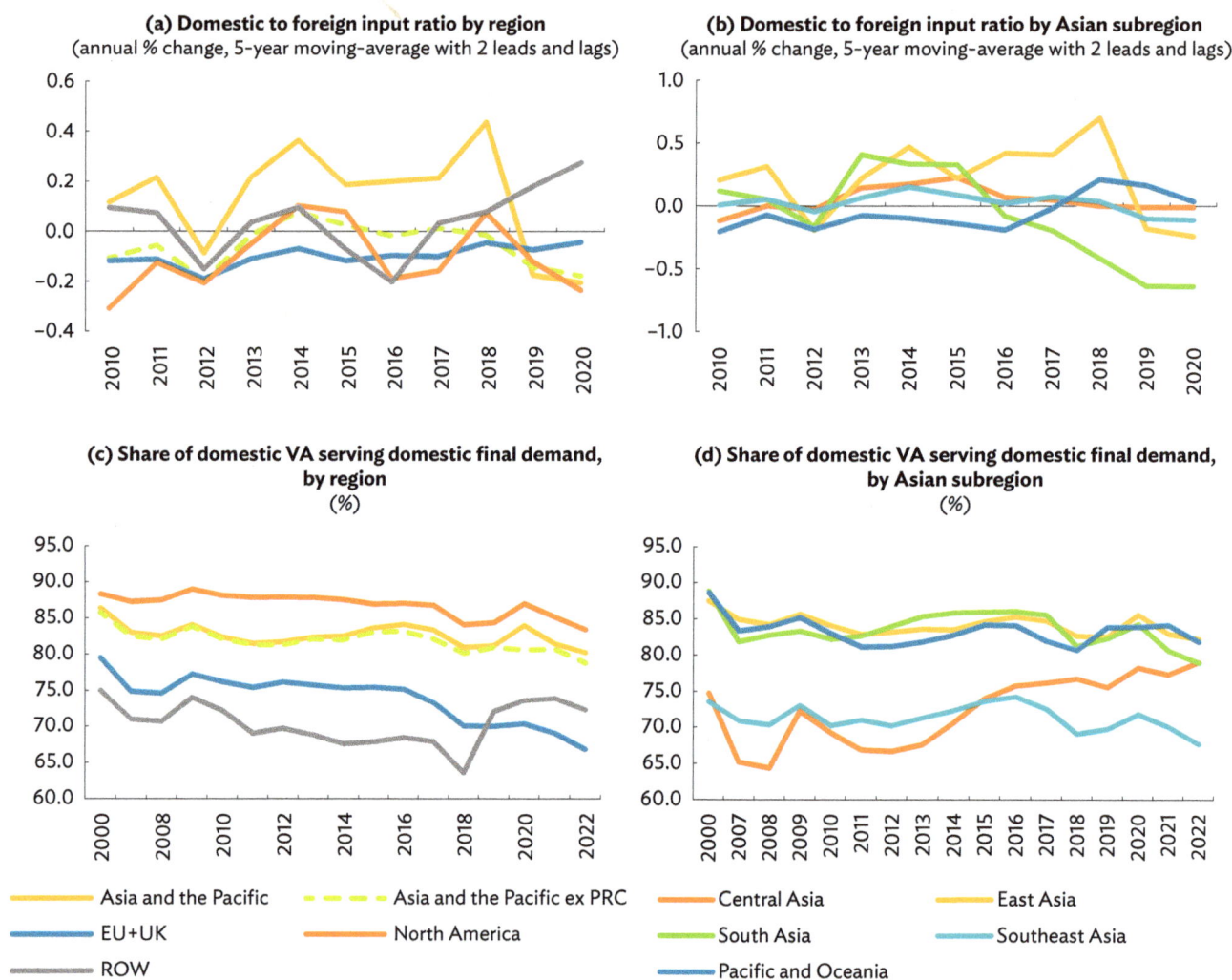

(a) Domestic to foreign input ratio by region
(annual % change, 5-year moving-average with 2 leads and lags)

(b) Domestic to foreign input ratio by Asian subregion
(annual % change, 5-year moving-average with 2 leads and lags)

(c) Share of domestic VA serving domestic final demand, by region
(%)

(d) Share of domestic VA serving domestic final demand, by Asian subregion
(%)

Legend: Asia and the Pacific, Asia and the Pacific ex PRC, Central Asia, East Asia, EU+UK, North America, South Asia, Southeast Asia, ROW, Pacific and Oceania

EU = European Union (27 members), PRC = People's Republic of China, ROW = rest of the world, UK = United Kingdom, VA = value-added.

Source: ADB calculations using data from ADB Multiregional Input–Output Database.

is observed in most subregions (Figure 2.10b), and represents a longer trend in South Asia.

An alternative view on reshoring that has been emphasized in recent policy discussions, including discussions on strategic autonomy, is the need to increase domestic production capacity to serve domestic demand. Multiregional input–output tables make it possible to identify the sources of value-added that serve domestic final demand. This alternative concept of reshoring provides little evidence of a rising share of domestic value-added serving domestic final demand (Figure 2.10c). Except for a brief time toward the end of the 2010s, notably for the rest of the world when the domestic share of value-added serving domestic final demand increased, the trend has been toward an increasing foreign share of value-added serving domestic final demand. This is also true for the subregions besides Central Asia, which began from a low level (Figure 2.10d).

Trade Policy Developments

The trade landscape in Asia is moving fast and forward. Newer, nontraditional forms of strategic trade partnerships and initiatives continue to develop (Figure 2.11).

Five trade agreements including at least one Asian economy entered into force in 2023 (Table 2.1). The Indonesia–Republic of Korea Comprehensive Economic Partnership Agreement (CEPA) took effect 2 years after it was signed in December 2020. Indonesia also signed an agreement with Iran, its second bilateral agreement in the Middle East after the Indonesia–United Arab Emirates CEPA, which entered into force in July 2022. Uzbekistan enforced separate bilateral agreements with Pakistan and Türkiye, in a move to expand its trade partnerships outside Central Asia.

The UK has signed three agreements since leaving the EU, all with Asian economies. Agreements with Australia (signed in 2021) and New Zealand (signed in 2022) both took effect in May 2023. They featured chapters on nontraditional disciplines such as digital trade, consumer

protection, development cooperation, gender in support of women's economic empowerment, labor, small and medium-sized enterprises, transparency and anti-corruption, and advanced provisions on environment including climate change.

In July 2023, the UK signed the Protocol of Accession to join the Comprehensive and Progressive Agreement for Trans-Pacific Partnership or the CPTPP (Table 2.2). New Zealand also signed a free trade agreement with the EU, which is expected to enter into force in the first half of 2024.

Thailand is stepping up its economic cooperation with the PRC by signing a mini-FTA with the coastal city of Shenzhen in Guangdong province in March and with Yunnan province in August (Government of Thailand, Ministry of Foreign Affairs 2023; Government of the People's Republic of China, State Council of the PRC 2023). A total of eight mini-FTAs have been inked between Thailand and its trading partners, including the Hainan Island and Gansu province of the PRC, Kofu of Japan, Telangana of India, and Busan and Gyeonggi of the Republic of Korea. The agreements aim to boost information exchange, promote business linkages, appoint trade representatives, and expand investment opportunities.

A year after launch, the Indo-Pacific Economic Framework (IPEF) concluded negotiations for a supply chain agreement (Table 2.3). The US-led initiative includes Australia, Brunei Darussalam, Fiji, India, Indonesia, Japan, the Republic of Korea, Malaysia, New Zealand, the Philippines, Singapore, Thailand, and Viet Nam, covering 40% of global GDP and 28% of global trade (USTR 2023a). While this is not a free trade agreement since it does not include market access provisions for goods or services, it is regarded as a modern regional arrangement to build cooperation and economic integration.

The IPEF Supply Chain Agreement would, among other achievements: create an IPEF Supply Chain Council to oversee the development of sector-specific action plans designed to build resilience and competitiveness in critical supply chain sectors; create an IPEF Supply Chain Crisis Response Network that can serve as an emergency communications channel; and establish an

Figure 2.11: Newly Effective Free Trade Agreements—Asia and the Pacific

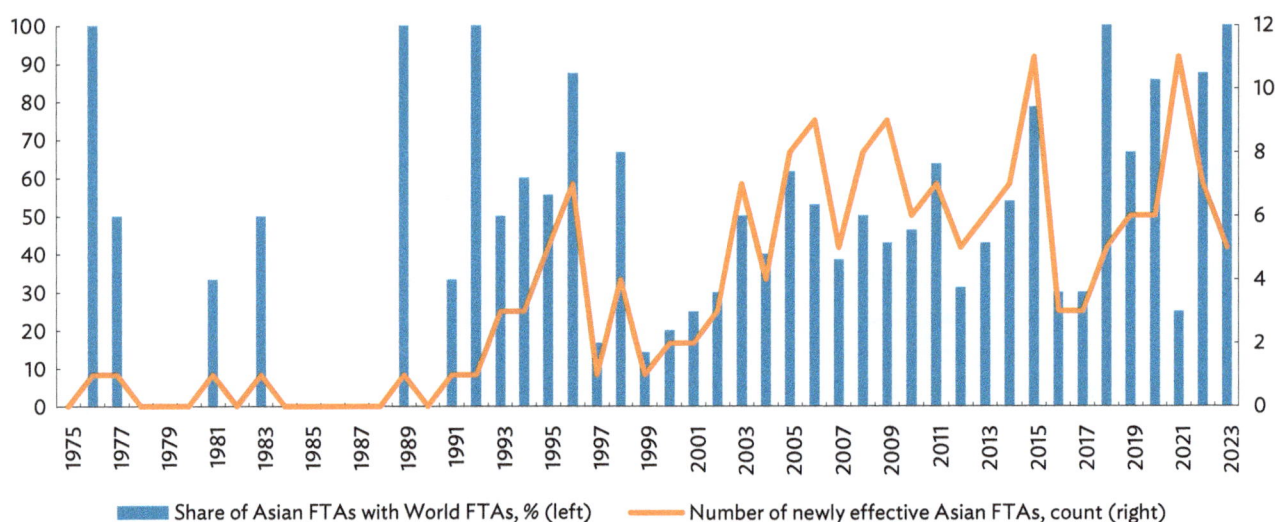

FTA = free trade agreement.

Notes: Trends for 1975–2022 derived using the World Trade Organization's Regional Trade Agreement Information System. The number of FTAs in 2023 derived using the Asia Regional Integration Center FTA Database and various sources. The share of Asian FTAs is the ratio between the number of newly effective FTAs including at least one Asian economy and the total number of newly effective FTAs.

Sources: ADB calculations using data from ADB. Asia Regional Integration Center FTA Database. https://aric.adb.org/database/fta; and World Trade Organization. Regional Trade Agreement Information System. http://rtais.wto.org (both accessed December 2023).

Table 2.1: New Regional Trade Agreements in Asia and the Pacific, January 2023–December 2023

Name	Type	Status (Date)
Intraregional		
Indonesia–Republic of Korea	CEPA	In force (1 January 2023)
Azerbaijan–Türkiye–Turkmenistan Trade and Economic Cooperation Agreement	FTA	Signed (4 February 2023)
Uzbekistan–Pakistan	FTA	In force (13 March 2023)
Philippines–Republic of Korea	FTA	Signed (7 September 2023)
Interregional		
Ecuador–People's Republic of China	FTA	Signed (11 May 2023)
Australia–United Kingdom	FTA	In force (31 May 2023)
New Zealand–United Kingdom	FTA	In force (31 May 2023)
Indonesia–Iran	FTA	Signed (23 May 2023)
Uzbekistan–Türkiye	FTA	In force (1 July 2023)
Cambodia–United Arab Emirates	CEPA	Signed (8 June 2023)
New Zealand–European Union	FTA	Signed (9 July 2023)
Israel–Viet Nam	FTA	Signed (25 July 2023)
People's Republic of China–Nicaragua	FTA	Signed (31 August 2023)
Pakistan-Gulf Cooperation Council	FTA	Signed (28 September 2023)
Georgia-United Arab Emirates	CEPA	Signed (10 October 2023)
Republic of Korea-Ecuador Strategic Economic Cooperation Agreement	FTA	Signed (11 October 2023)
Republic of Korea-United Arab Emirates	FTA	Signed (14 October 2023)
People's Republic of China-Serbia	FTA	Signed (17 October 2023)
Singapore-MERCOSUR	FTA	Signed (7 December 2023)
Eurasian Economic Union-Iran	FTA	Signed (25 December 2023)
Republic of Korea-Gulf Cooperation Council	FTA	Signed (28 December 2023)

CEPA = comprehensive economic partnership agreement, FTA = free trade agreement, MERCOSUR = Mercado Común del Sur (Southern Common Market).

Note: All agreements cover both goods and services.

Source: ADB compilation based on information available as of December 2023.

Table 2.2: Recently Upgraded/Expanded Trade Agreements—Asia and the Pacific, January–December 2023

Trade Agreement	Entry into Force	Recent Update	Remarks
People's Republic of China–Singapore FTA	12 November 2018	1 April 2023	Announced the substantive completion of the FTA upgrade. This first agreement that the People's Republic of China has adopted the negative list approach to services and investment. The upgrade further improved existing commitments, added a telecommunications chapter, and incorporated high-level economic and trade rules on transparency and digital economy.
CPTPP	30 December 2018	16 July 2023	The United Kingdom signs treaty of accession.

CPTPP = Comprehensive and Progressive Agreement for Trans-Pacific Partnership, FTA = free trade agreement.

Sources: ADB compilation based on information available as of December 2023, including announcements from parties to the agreements.

Table 2.3: Newer Forms of Cooperation and Partnerships—Asia and the Pacific, January–December 2023

Trade Agreement	Recent Update	Remarks
Korea– Singapore Digital Partnership Agreement (KSDPA)	14 January 2023	Entry into force of the KSDPA. Both economies also signed three MOUs to implement the Korea–Singapore Digital Economy Dialogue, facilitate the electronic exchange of data and enhance cooperation in artificial intelligence.
Malaysia–Singapore cooperation agreements	30 January 2023	Malaysia and Singapore signed green economy and digital economy framework agreements, as well as MOU personal data protection, and cybersecurity.
Indo-Pacific Economic Framework for Prosperity	27 May 2023	Conclusion of negotiations on supply chain agreement.
Digital Economy Partnership Agreement (DEPA)	8 June 2023	Conclusion of accession discussions with the Republic of Korea. Besides the Republic of Korea, the People's Republic of China, Canada, Costa Rica, and Peru have submitted formal requests to accede to the DEPA.

MOU = memorandum of understanding.

Source: ADB compilation based on information available as of December 2023, including announcements from parties to the agreements.

innovative tripartite IPEF Labor Rights Advisory Board to help identify areas where labor rights concerns pose risks to the resilience and competitiveness of partners' supply chains. Strengthening supply chains is one of four pillars for negotiation under the IPEF. The others are in the areas of trade, clean economy, and fair economy. Since the IPEF is designed to be flexible, partners are not required to join all pillars (Government of the United States, Department of Commerce 2023).

Most recently, the US and Taipei,China concluded negotiations on a 21st century trade initiative in May 2023, covering customs administration and trade facilitation, good regulatory practices, services domestic regulation, anticorruption, and small and medium-sized enterprises (Liang 2023).

Building Resilience in Asia's Food Sector

As Asia continues to be a significant player in global agriculture and food trade, the region's reliance on food imports and lack of diversification makes it vulnerable to external shocks and trade restrictions.

While trade agreements in the region are becoming broader, more modern and digital in scope, and contributing more to global sustainability efforts, restrictive measures in response to various economic and geopolitical developments (including the Russian invasion of Ukraine) continue to negatively impact essential sectors such as energy and food. To this end, high reliance on food imports and the lack of diversification can pose supply risks in some economies.

Figure 2.12: Share of World Food Products Exports and Imports, by Asian Subregion

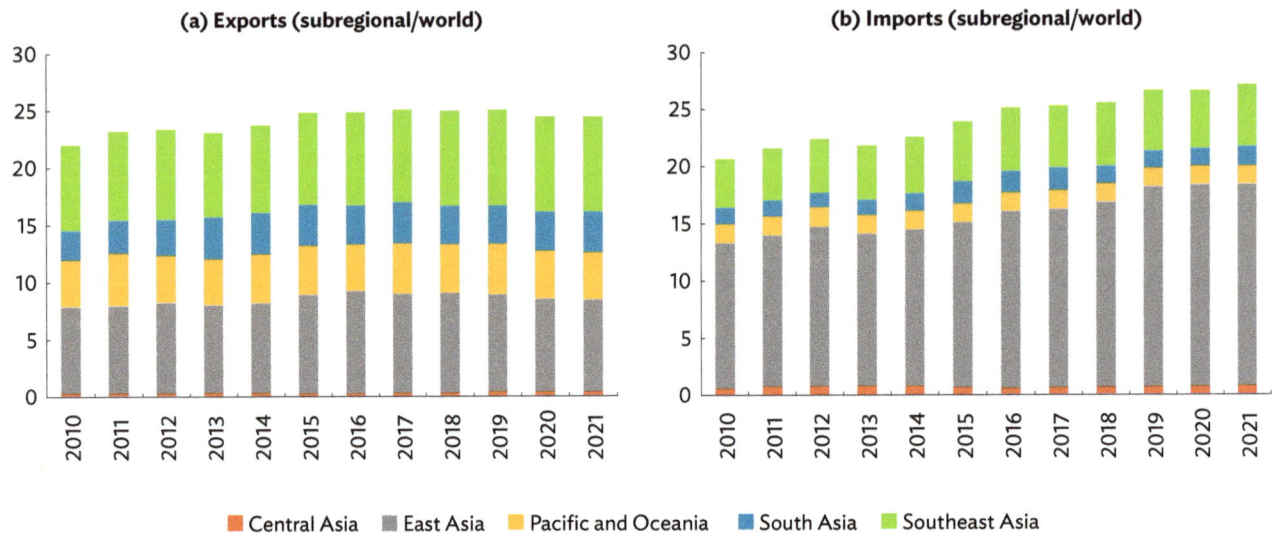

(a) Exports (subregional/world)

(b) Imports (subregional/world)

■ Central Asia   ■ East Asia   ■ Pacific and Oceania   ■ South Asia   ■ Southeast Asia

Note: Units are in percentage share to total world food exports and imports.

Source: ADB calculations using data from UN Commodity Trade Database. https://comtrade.un.org/ (accessed November 2023).

Over the past decade, the region's share in global food exports has increased from 22% to about 25% while imports rose from 21% to 27%. East Asia and Southeast Asia account for the largest shares of food exports. East Asia also dominated the region's food imports, increasing by about 5 percentage points (Figure 2.12). The Pacific and Oceania, South Asia, and Southeast Asia are net exporters, while East Asia and Central Asia have been consistent net importers of food products for the past decade (Figure 2.13).

Resilient Food Supply Chains Are Crucial to Ensure a Steady Stock of Food

Economies can leverage on trade and regional integration to help achieve an ample and stable supply of food in their domestic markets and weather external food supply shocks.

The 1996 World Food Summit defines food security as "when all people, at all times, have physical and economic access to sufficient safe and nutritious food that meets their dietary needs and food preferences for an active and healthy life" (FAO 2006). Four

Figure 2.13: Trade Balance of Food Products (Exports/Imports) by Asian Subregion

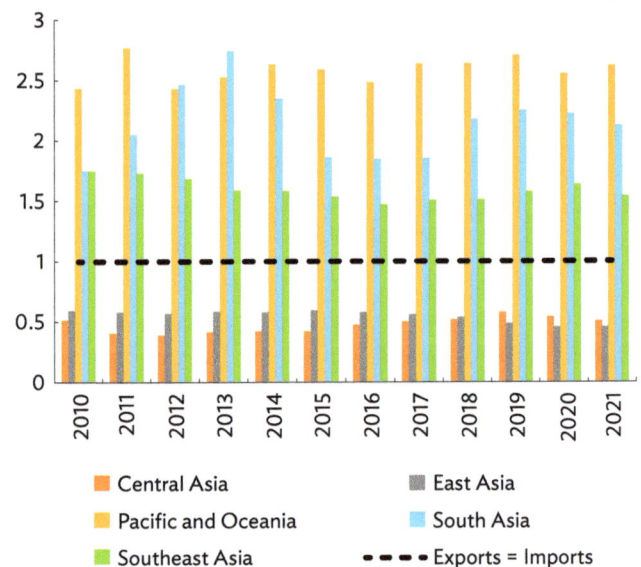

■ Central Asia   ■ East Asia
■ Pacific and Oceania   ■ South Asia
■ Southeast Asia   - - - Exports = Imports

Notes: Units represent subregional exports/imports. Values above 1, represented by the checkered black line would represent net exporters, while values below 1 are net importers.

Source: ADB calculations using data from UN Commodity Trade Database. https://comtrade.un.org/ (accessed November 2023).

dimensions crucial to food security were identified: physical availability of food; economic and physical access to food; food utilization; and stability. Trade is closely linked to the first dimension, particularly in augmenting the supply side and complementing domestic food production.

Global food trade has enabled many regions to secure food supply and overcome local limits of growth set by scarce natural resources or less developed farming practices (Porkka et al. 2017). Greater access to international markets and keeping trade-related costs as low as possible allows economies to more freely use imports to augment domestic food production, which helps ensure food is in ample supply. Likewise, greater trade also aids in bringing down food prices for greater accessibility, and offers a bigger menu of food commodities for people to choose (Thow 2009; Thow and Hawkes 2009; Kearney 2010). This ensures the food system is resilient in times of crisis and when local conditions are difficult (Seekell et al. 2017).

Conversely, highly interconnected food systems may pose risks caused by synchronous shocks across regions and sectors (Suweis et al. 2015; Gephart et al. 2017; Cottrell et al. 2019). McKinsey reports that about 40% of global trade is concentrated, meaning that importing economies rely on three or fewer nations for this share of global trade, even when global supply options have become more diversified. Over the past 5 years, the largest economies have not systematically diversified the origins of their imports (McKinsey Global Institute 2020). Import dependence leaves economies vulnerable to issues of food adequacy and accessibility when various shocks affect their partners' ability to export. Successfully navigating this dual effect requires a nuanced understanding of an economy's trade situation and a well-balanced, strategic trade policy.

The succeeding analysis in this chapter focuses on trade-related aspects of food security, and how strategic and proactive trade policy can help build resilient and stable food supply in the region. A multistep filtering process was employed to identify food products most at risk from trade-related supply disruptions. A brief outline of the filtering methodology is reported here:

(1) **Filter 1—Domestic production to consumption ratio:** Using data from the ADB Multiregional Input–Output Database (MRIOD),[12] economies with lower than regional average shares of domestic food production with respect to domestic food consumption were identified. Economies with lower shares of domestic food production have an increased reliance on trade to supplement their local food supply, resulting in increased vulnerability to external and global food shocks. Adopting a conservative approach, economies without MRIOD data are automatically included.

(2) **Filter 2—Diversification:** Focusing on the region's 20 most consumed food commodities identified from the Food and Agriculture Organization (FAO) database (Table 2.4),[13] two diversification indexes were computed for each economy capturing diversification in terms of trading partners and imported food products. Economies were identified as less diversified when both the trading partners and imported products diversification indexes were below the regional average. In addition, economies that exhibit decreasing diversification indexes and a shrinking share of domestic food production through time are also retained in the list. Having a small range of trading partners and imported products may be a disadvantage in the face of international food trade disruptions.

(3) **Product-level analysis and alternative suppliers:** After identifying the shortlist of economies, a product-level analysis was developed to gain a better understanding of the possible vulnerabilities to supply chain disruptions of selected products. For each economy, the top 20 imported HS4 commodities were identified and matched with the region's top 20 consumed HS4 commodities

---

[12]   Shares of domestic food production to domestic food consumption were derived from disaggregated output data from each economy's agriculture, fishery, food, and beverage sectors using the ADB MRIOD. The share is calculated as the ratio of the total domestic production of domestically consumed food to the total domestic consumption of food (including import-sourced domestic food consumption).

[13]   The FAO Supply Utilization Accounts Database compiles data on food availability of over 400 food and agriculture product groups as proxy for the average food consumption at the economy level (Gheri et al. 2020). The region's basket of most consumed food commodities, in terms of quantity, include meat products, milk, eggs, several varieties of fruits and vegetables, rice, flour, sugar, and malt beer. The top 20 commodities listed in Table 2.4 comprise more than 80% of the region's total food consumption in 2021.

using the FAO database. Food items that are common to both the "most imported" and "most consumed" lists are considered the most vulnerable to food trade shocks. In exploring the potential of trade diversification to build resilience, the analysis also identifies alternative regional suppliers for vulnerable food products.

Notwithstanding the importance of international food supply chains, food security is a complex, multidimensional issue that goes far beyond trade and trade policy.

Other factors (macroeconomic, geographic, institutional, political, etc.) can influence food supply, thereby affecting the economy's food resiliency and vulnerability. Utilization and nutritional value of consumed

Table 2.4: List of Top 20 Consumed HS4 Food Commodities in Asia and the Pacific, by Quantity, 2021 (Arranged by HS Code)

HS4 Code	FAO Commodity	HS4 code	FAO Commodity
0203	Meat of pig boneless, fresh or chilled		Yams
	Meat of pig with the bone, fresh or chilled	0714	Cassava, dry
0207	Meat of ducks, fresh or chilled		Sweet potatoes
	Meat of chickens, fresh or chilled	0803	Plantains and cooking bananas
	Edible offals and liver of chickens and guinea fowl, fresh, chilled or frozen		Tangerines, mandarins, clementines
	Meat of turkeys, fresh or chilled	0805	Other citrus fruit, nec
0401	Skim milk of cows		Oranges
	Raw milk of goats		Pomelos and grapefruits
0407	Eggs from other birds in shell, fresh, nec		Lemons and limes
0701	Potatoes	0807	Papayas
			Cantaloupes and other melons
0702	Tomatoes		Watermelons
0703	Leeks and other alliaceous vegetables	0808	Apples
	Onions and shallots, green		Pears
	Green garlic		Rice, broken
0704	Cabbages	1006	Husked rice
	Cauliflowers and broccoli		Rice, milled
0707	Cucumbers and gherkins		Rice
0708	Peas, green	1103	Flour of cereals nec
	Other beans, green		Cane sugar, non-centrifugal
	Broad beans and horse beans, green	1701	Refined sugar
0709	Asparagus		Raw cane or beet sugar (centrifugal only)
	Artichokes	2203	Beer of barley, malted
	Chilies and peppers, green (Capsicum spp. and Pimenta spp.)		
	Mushrooms and truffles		
	Eggplants (aubergines)		
	Spinach		

FAO = Food and Agriculture Organization, HS = Harmonized System, nec = not elsewhere classified.

Notes: The data are generated by matching data from the Food and Agriculture Organization database with their corresponding HS4 equivalent. The 20 HS4 products with the highest quantity consumed were selected.

Source: ADB calculations using data from Food and Agriculture Organization. Supply Utilization Accounts Database. https://www.fao.org/faostat/en/#data/SCL (accessed November 2023).

products are also issues to further investigate. These considerations, while relevant, are outside the scope of the analyses.

As an initial step, economies with below regional average shares of domestic production with respect to domestic consumption were identified (Figure 2.14). Economies with lower relative capacity for domestic food production face potential supply risk issues by relying more on imports to meet food consumption needs. However, it must be pointed out that economies with higher relative domestic production shares may still face structural food supply risks, though not necessarily trade related.

Diversity in Trading Partners Is Key to Food Trade Resilience

Reliance on imports is not inherently a vulnerability; however, complications may arise when economies lack a diverse set of trading partners and import a limited range of food commodities.

The extent of dependence on imports in an economy's food supply becomes more palpable when disruptions impede the production and export capabilities of an economy's trading partners. Thus, as a next step, the analysis computes the Diversification Index (DI) to determine the level of import diversification in terms of trading partners and of imported food products.

Figure 2.14: Shares of Domestic Food Production to Domestic Food Consumption—Asia and the Pacific, 2010–2022 Average

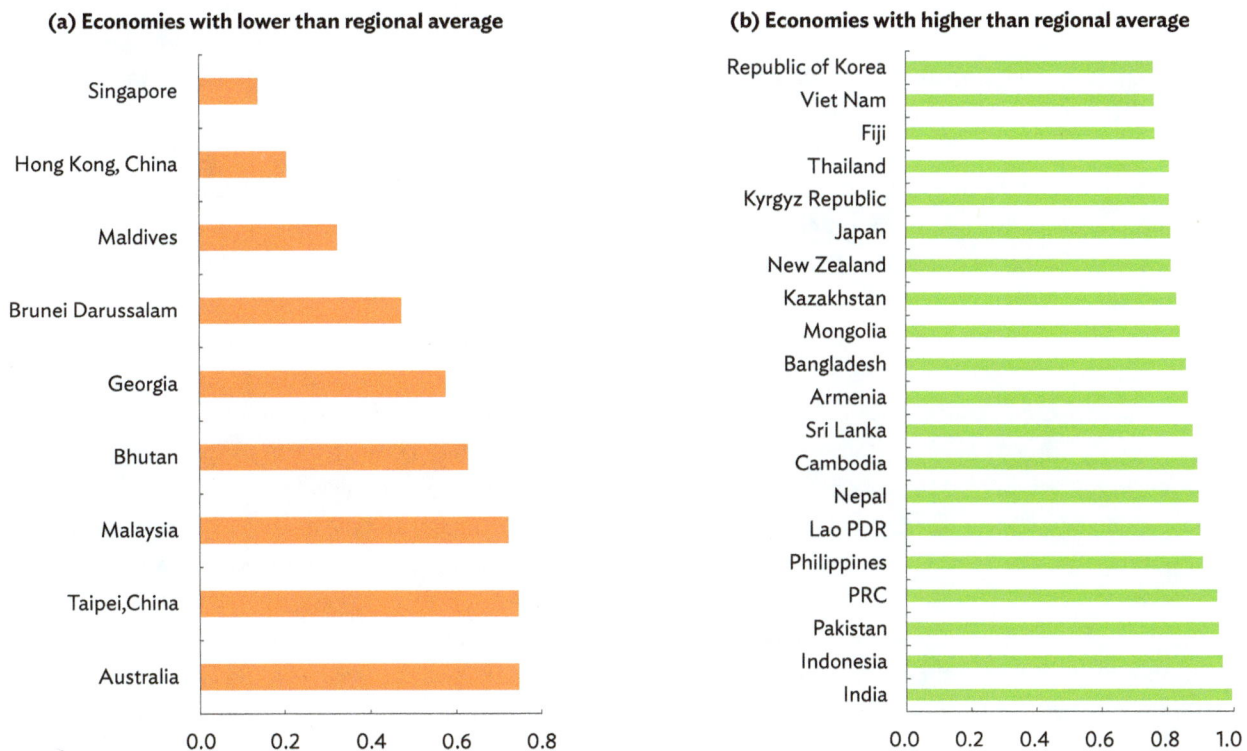

(a) Economies with lower than regional average

(b) Economies with higher than regional average

Lao PDR = Lao People's Democratic Republic, PRC = People's Republic of China.

Notes: The domestic share of consumption is derived as the share of domestically consumed food that is domestically produced. Figures are divided into groups based on the economy's share of domestic production to domestic consumption, in descending order. These groups are determined based on the average domestic share of 0.75. The figure covers 29 Asian economies, for which data are available in ADB Multiregional Input–Output Database.

Source: ADB calculations using data from ADB Multiregional Input-Output Database (accessed December 2023).

A higher trading partner DI value suggests that an economy sources its food products from a greater number of trading partners, thus making the economy more resilient to supply chain disruptions when some of its partners experience shocks. Likewise, a high DI for imported commodities indicates a more diverse selection of imported food products. A wider basket of imported food products affords greater flexibility and substitutability. A more diverse set of food imports also increases the variety of food available in an economy's domestic food market. To avoid the inclusion of products that do not constitute a particular threat to food availability, or highly specific goods produced only in one economy (i.e., no partner diversification), the analysis focuses on the top 20 consumed products in the region that are considered most relevant for identifying food trade vulnerabilities (Table 2.4).

Subregional trends show that Central Asia has the lowest diversification by partner but has the most diversified food import basket.

Central Asia's partner DI has taken a downward trend, from 0.9 in 2010 to 0.8 in 2021. The subregion imported more than 50% of its food commodities from three economies—the Russian Federation, Kazakhstan, and the Kyrgyz Republic—in 2021. This import concentration is intense compared to other subregions that have an average share of just 30% of their food commodities sourced from their top three trading partners over the same period. Central Asia's reliance on a small number of sourcing economies can affect its resilience to food supply disruptions. This has been exacerbated in recent years by the various economic sanctions on the Russian Federation, which supplies 43% of Central Asia's food product imports.

East Asia and South Asia have relatively low product diversification, suggesting that the regions' imports are concentrated on a limited group of food products. About 63% of South Asia's imports come from fruits, vegetables, and coffee, while about 56% of East Asia's food imports are meat, fish, and fruits. Although this can reflect preferences or domestic demand, such a pattern poses risks especially if the commodities of interest experience a shock to production or exports.

The filtering method not only looks at average levels of domestic production and diversification indexes, but also how these indicators change over time. This is to account for the possibility that economies move toward greater import dependence and decreased diversification across the years, even though the indicators do not suggest imminent risk. The averages for each indicator were computed for 2010 to 2015 and for 2016 to 2021, and the differences between the two 6-year periods were reported. Economies that exhibit decreasing diversification indexes and a decreasing share of domestic food production through time are retained in the list. Table 2.5 summarizes the results of the filtering methods. Economies highlighted in yellow (from Table 2.5) indicate cases with relatively lower shares of domestic production and decreasing diversification indexes by partner and by product.

Focusing on the shortlisted economies, a product-level analysis was employed to identify which food items are most vulnerable to trade shocks. The top 20 food imports were identified for each economy and matched with the region's top 20 consumed commodities using the FAO database (Table 2.6). Food items that are common to both the "most imported" and "most consumed" lists are considered the most vulnerable to trade shocks.

The product-level analysis shows numerous basic food commodities are at most risk. Sugar (Harmonized System [HS] 1701) has been identified as vulnerable among all shortlisted economies. Rice (HS 1006), a chief agriculture commodity in the region, is vulnerable for most listed economies. Milk (HS 0401), onion and garlic (HS 0703), and pig meat (HS 0203) are vulnerable for at least half of the economies in the shortlist. Other such food items include eggs, citrus fruits, apples and pears, bananas, tomatoes, other vegetable varieties (in Bhutan), and fowl meat (in the Federated States of Micronesia).

Food availability risks and supply chain vulnerability can be mitigated by engaging with alternative suppliers within the region.

Table 2.5: Share of Domestic Production to Consumption and the Diversification Index, by Asian Economy

Economy	Value (2010–2021 Average)			Difference 2016–2021 and 2010–2015 Averages		
	DP/DC Ratio	Partner DI	Product DI	DP/DC Ratio	Partner DI	Product DI
Regional average	0.75	0.68	0.72			
India	0.99	0.65	0.52	0.01	0.00	0.04
Indonesia	0.96	0.79	0.67	0.01	-0.04	-0.11
Pakistan	0.95	0.69	0.71	0.00	0.02	-0.17
China, People's Republic of	0.95	0.89	0.81	-0.02	0.07	0.08
Philippines	0.91	0.78	0.70	-0.02	0.01	0.04
Lao PDR	0.90	0.39	0.66	-0.06	-0.08	-0.13
Nepal	0.89	0.27	0.56	-0.03	-0.05	-0.03
Cambodia	0.89	0.62	0.66	-0.09	0.07	0.10
Sri Lanka	0.88	0.68	0.57	0.02	-0.03	0.05
Armenia	0.86	0.81	0.79	-0.02	0.07	-0.02
Bangladesh	0.86	0.66	0.60	0.09	0.03	0.05
Mongolia	0.84	0.81	0.84	0.04	0.09	0.08
Kazakhstan	0.83	0.85	0.82	0.02	-0.04	-0.01
New Zealand	0.81	0.89	0.84	-0.02	0.07	0.01
Japan	0.81	0.91	0.76	-0.05	0.02	0.01
Kyrgyz Republic	0.80	0.82	0.81	0.10	0.02	0.06
Thailand	0.80	0.71	0.79	-0.18	0.09	-0.05
Fiji	0.76	0.79	0.76	-0.06	0.00	0.02
Viet Nam	0.76	0.82	0.81	-0.17	0.04	0.03
Korea, Republic of	0.76	0.89	0.78	-0.08	0.00	0.13
Australia	0.75	0.89	0.73	-0.03	0.01	0.02
Taipei,China	0.75	0.91	0.84	-0.06	0.01	0.01
Malaysia	0.72	0.86	0.78	-0.03	0.00	0.02
Bhutan	0.63	0.02	0.58	0.02	-0.02	-0.03
Georgia	0.58	0.84	0.80	0.07	0.06	0.04
Brunei Darussalam	0.47	0.76	0.77	0.18	0.13	0.15
Maldives	0.33	0.76	0.90	-0.08	0.00	0.00
Hong Kong, China	0.21	0.85	0.88	0.15	-0.01	-0.01
Singapore	0.14	0.90	0.90	-0.02	0.01	0.01
Azerbaijan		0.67	0.59		0.30	0.02
Cook Islands		0.25	0.76		0.20	0.19
Kiribati		0.72	0.55		0.13	0.17
Marshall Islands		0.65	0.76		0.27	0.26
Micronesia, Federated States of		0.45	0.70		0.26	0.25
Nauru		0.51	0.87		0.10	0.09
Niue		0.15	0.73		-0.10	-0.12
Palau		0.47	0.77		0.21	0.25
Papua New Guinea		0.70	0.51		-0.01	0.02
Samoa		0.78	0.76		0.03	0.03
Solomon Islands		0.55	0.50		0.20	0.08

continued on next page

Table 2.5 *continued*

Economy	Value (2010–2021 Average)			Difference 2016–2021 and 2010–2015 Averages		
	DP/DC Ratio	Partner DI	Product DI	DP/DC Ratio	Partner DI	Product DI
Tajikistan		0.80	0.62		-0.02	0.20
Timor-Leste		0.66	0.56		0.16	0.16
Tonga		0.67	0.81		-0.29	-0.11
Turkmenistan		0.76	0.69		0.00	0.06
Tuvalu		0.70	0.77		-0.02	0.02
Uzbekistan		0.74	0.46		-0.19	0.26
Vanuatu		0.76	0.73		-0.08	-0.01

DC = domestic consumption, DI = Diversification Index, DP = domestic production, Lao PDR = Lao People's Democratic Republic.

Notes:

(i) The domestic share of consumption is derived as the share of domestically consumed food that is domestically produced. Values marked in orange denote shares that are below the regional average of the data (a DI score of 0.75), while values marked in green are above the average. Negative differences between the periods 2016–2021 and 2010–2015 are marked in orange, positive differences in green.

(ii) The figure covers 29 Asian economies for which data are available in the ADB Multiregional Input–Output Database. Economies not available in the database were automatically forwarded to filtering by DI scores.

(iii) Partner/Product DI scores are calculated as 1 minus the sum of the squared shares of imports from a partner/product to total imports from all partners/products. The index value ranges from 0 to 1, with higher values illustrating higher diversification of partners/products. Values in green denote DIs above the regional average and values in orange denote values below average.

(iv) Economies in the table are arranged in descending order based on their share of domestic production to domestic consumption. Cells in yellow indicate economies fulfilling the conditions set in the methodology.

Sources: ADB calculations using data from ADB Multiregional Input-Output Database; United Nations Commodity Trade Database. https://comtrade.un.org/; and Food and Agriculture Organization (FAO) Supply Utilization Accounts Database. https://www.fao.org/faostat/en/#data/SCL (all accessed November 2023).

Table 2.6: Import Shares (% > Regional Average) of Highly Consumed HS4 Commodities in Selected Asian Economies, 2021

Product (HS4)	Economy (DP/DC, Partner DI and Product DI < Regional Average)									
	Azerbaijan	Bhutan	Lao PDR	Federated States of Micronesia	Nepal	Papua New Guinea	Solomon Islands	Timor-Leste	Tonga	Vanuatu
Sugar (1701)	12.3%	4.6%	10.4%	5.0%	4.1%	5.8%	13.5%	6.0%	4.9%	6.9%
Rice (1006)	2.7%	21.8%	4.6%	16.0%	27.5%	27.9%	22.2%	36.4%		22.1%
Milk and cream (0401)		4.5%		2.5%		1.9%	1.1%	3.0%	9.6%	3.7%
Onion, garlic, leeks, etc. (0703)		2.0%	2.0%		2.6%		1.7%	1.4%	1.3%	1.3%
Meat of swine (0203)		1.7%		3.0%		2.4%		1.4%	0.3%	
Bird's eggs (0407)				3.4%			1.0%	2.4%	1.7%	1.2%
Citrus fruit (0805)	2.8%		1.0%		1.2%				2.3%	
Apple, pears, and quinces (0808)					4.1%			1.1%	2.7%	1.1%
Bananas and plantains (0803)	3.1%				1.1%					
Tomatoes (0702)		1.0%								
Other vegetables (0709)				3.8%						

DC = domestic consumption, DI = Diversification Index, DP = domestic production, HS = Harmonized System, Lao PDR = Lao People's Democratic Republic.

Notes:

(i) List of products consists of the common food products found by matching the top 20 most consumed food products in Asia and the Pacific and the top 20 most imported food products, excluding malt beer, per listed economy. Cells in orange indicate that an economy is vulnerable to disruption in the supply of a particular product based on its low share of domestic production out of domestic consumption, and its limited diversification of suppliers and imported products.

(ii) Import shares inside the orange cells pertain to shares of an economy's HS4 product import to its total food imports.

Sources: ADB calculations using data from United Nations Commodity Trade Database. https://comtrade.un.org/; and Food and Agriculture Organization (FAO) Supply Utilization Accounts Database. https://www.fao.org/faostat/en/#data/SCL (both accessed December 2023).

Table 2.7 charts the top exporters of vulnerable food items depicted in Table 2.6. Establishing or enhancing trade partnerships with these exporters allows economies to more freely leverage on imports to augment their domestic food production and better ensure food supply.

Interestingly, the list of economies showing at least one food product potentially vulnerable to trade disruptions comprises 5 of the 11 economies in Asia categorized as least developed economies. In the 2023 triennial review by the Committee for Development Policy, four of these economies—Bangladesh, Bhutan,[14] the Lao People's Democratic Republic (Lao PDR), and Nepal—exhibited a relatively low Economic Vulnerability Index (EVI), below the 2021 least developed economy inclusion and graduation thresholds (United Nations Economic and Social Council 2023). Our analysis, however, identifies food resilience risks for these economies. This can be explained by the export focus of EVI; out of the eight EVI indicators, two relate to trade: merchandise exports concentration and instability of goods and services. The analysis therefore suggests that import-side vulnerabilities should not be overlooked in contributing to food trade resilience.

Analysis of existing trade partnerships reveals missed opportunities. In the case of sugar, for example, only the Lao PDR has a trade agreement with the multiple key exporters in the region (Table 2.8). Meat importers have trade agreements with only one exporter, while a significant number of rice importers have none. Current FTAs are notably formed between economies in geographic proximity, with partnerships across subregions less common. By diversifying its partners and expanding trade linkages to other subregions, an economy can enhance its resilience to localized shocks and intraregional disruptions.

Furthermore, trade restricting measures were observed to be imposed on sugar, rice, onions, and garlic. Restrictive policy interventions in the form of tariffs, quotas, and bans, among others, are additional significant obstacles to enhancing food availability among import-reliant domestic markets. Thus, arduous negotiations to ease or lift such restrictive interventions should be prioritized toward the mutual economic benefit of potential trading partners.

Table 2.7: List of Alternative Regional Suppliers for Selected Products, 2021

HS4 Code	Description	Alternative Supplier in Asia and the Pacific				
1701	Cane or beet sugar and chemically pure sucrose, in solid form	India	Thailand	Australia	Indonesia	Malaysia
1006	Rice	India	Thailand	Viet Nam	Pakistan	PRC
0401	Milk and cream; not concentrated nor containing added sugar or other sweetening matter	New Zealand	Australia	Thailand	PRC	Hong Kong, China
0703	Onions, shallots, garlic, leeks and other alliaceous vegetables; fresh or chilled	PRC	India	Pakistan	New Zealand	Uzbekistan
0203	Meat of swine; fresh, chilled or frozen	Australia	PRC	Hong Kong, China	Singapore	Japan

HS = Harmonized System, PRC= People's Republic of China.

Notes: HS4 products were selected from the top five most commonly occurring highly consumed, highly traded commodities from the filtered economies. Alternative regional suppliers are the top five exporters of each HS4 product in Asia and the Pacific, as calculated by the economy's share in exports / total world exports of their respective HS4 commodity, as filtered through the Food and Agriculture Organization (FAO) database.

Sources: ADB calculations using data from United Nations Commodity Trade Database. https://comtrade.un.org/; and FAO Supply Utilization Accounts Database. https://www.fao.org/faostat/en/#data/SCL (both accessed November 2023).

[14] Bhutan is included in the list but graduated on 13 December 2023.

Table 2.8: Trade Partnerships and Trade Policy Restrictions between Top Importers and Top Regional Exporters of Selected Food Products in 2021

HS 1701: Cane or beet sugar and chemically pure sucrose, in solid form					
	India	Thailand	Australia	Indonesia	Malaysia
Azerbaijan	0	0	0	0	0
Bhutan	2	0	0	0	0
Lao PDR	0	0	0	0	0
FSM	0	0	0	0	0
Nepal	2	0	0	0	0
Papua New Guinea	0	0	0	0	0
Solomon Islands	0	0	0	0	0
Timor-Leste	2	0	0	0	0
Tonga	0	0	0	0	0
Vanuatu	0	0	0	0	0
HS 1006: Rice					
	India	Thailand	Viet Nam	Pakistan	PRC
Azerbaijan	0	0	0	0	0
Bhutan	4	0	0	0	0
Lao PDR	0	0	0	0	0
FSM	0	0	0	0	0
Nepal	8	0	0	0	0
Papua New Guinea	4	0	0	0	0
Solomon Islands	0	0	0	0	0
Timor-Leste	0	0	0	0	0
Vanuatu	0	0	0	0	0
HS 0401: Milk and cream					
	New Zealand	Australia	Thailand	PRC	Hong Kong, China
Bhutan	0	0	0	0	0
FSM	0	0	0	0	0
Papua New Guinea	0	0	0	0	0
Solomon Islands	0	0	0	0	0
Timor-Leste	0	0	0	0	0
Tonga	0	0	0	0	0
Vanuatu	0	0	0	0	0
HS 0703: Onions, shallots, garlic, leeks and other alliaceous vegetables; fresh or chilled					
	PRC	India	Pakistan	New Zealand	Uzbekistan
Bhutan	0	1	0	0	0
Lao PDR	0	0	0	0	0
Nepal	1	2	0	0	0
Solomon Islands	0	0	0	0	0
Timor-Leste	0	0	0	0	0
Tonga	0	0	0	0	0
Vanuatu	0	0	0	0	0

continued on next page

Table 2.8 *continued*

	Australia	PRC	Hong Kong, China	Singapore	Japan
0203: Meat of swine; fresh, chilled or frozen					
Bhutan	0	0	0	0	0
FSM	0	0	0	0	0
Papua New Guinea	0	0	0	0	0
Timor-Leste	0	0	0	0	0
Tonga	0	0	0	0	0
Vanuatu	0	0	0	0	0

FSM = Federated States of Micronesia, HS = Harmonized System, Lao PDR = Lao People's Democratic Republic, PRC= People's Republic of China.

Notes: The color green denotes that the two economies are party to at least one bilateral or plurilateral free trade agreement or preferential trade agreement. The color orange denotes that the two economies are not part of the same trade agreement. Values on the table indicate the number of existing restrictive import or export interventions between each pair of economies. Trade restrictive interventions are counted per export policy from the alternative supplier or import policy from the importing economy.

Sources: ADB. Asia Regional Integration Center FTA Database. https://aric.adb.org/database/fta; and Global Trade Alert Database. https://www.globaltradealert.org (accessed November 2023).

Restrictive Trade Policies Are Roadblocks to Resilience

Efforts in deepening trade and enhancing regional integration should go hand in hand with efforts to eliminate restrictive food trade policies.

Restrictive trade interventions impede the potential to build resilient and stable regional food supply (Figure 2.15). This disproportionately impacts economies with lower diversification of trade partners or trade products as they face greater supply risks and lack the diversity to compensate imports. Using recently available data from the Global Trade Alert database, the following discusses restrictive food trade policies in the region, and their implications on import-dependent economies.

Restrictive food trade measures have impacted Asia more significantly compared to other regions.

The share of Asia's food trade covered by restrictive interventions has increased from about 1% in 2019 to approximately 2.7% from 2021 to 2023(Figure 2.16). Up until 2022, the largest share of restrictive interventions in Asia was implemented by economies within the region. Conversely, the share of Asia's food trade covered by

liberalizing interventions also increased, reaching up to 6% of the region's total food trade in 2022.

Food trade interventions have not had the same effect across Asian subregions.

Among subregions in Asia, Central Asia, East Asia, and Southeast Asia have the greatest share of total food trade subject to restrictive interventions in 2023 (Figure 2.16). On average, South Asia and the Pacific and Oceania are largely covered by restrictive measures imposed by Asian economies. Conversely, Central Asia is dominated by restrictive measures imposed by the rest of the world. The Pacific and Oceania has the highest share of food trade covered by liberalizing measures in 2023, followed by South Asia and Southeast Asia. A significant amount of liberalizing interventions in the Pacific and Oceania, Southeast Asia, and South Asia were implemented from within the region.

As discussed earlier, restrictive import and export policies present significant roadblocks to trade between economies. Economies with a lower diversification of trade partners or trade products also face greater risks, as they lack the diversity to compensate imports when a major partner implements a trade restrictive intervention. Notably, a significant number of economies that were highlighted by this section's three-stage filtering belong to Central Asia, which heavily relies on

Figure 2.15: Shares of Food Trade Affected by Trade Interventions, by Region

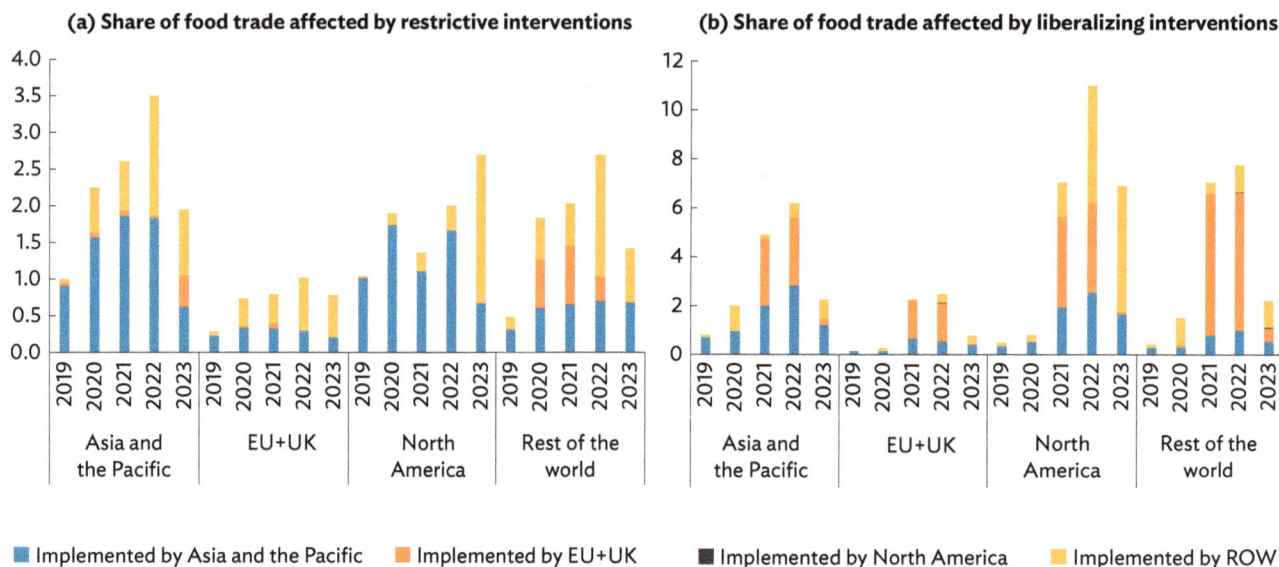

(a) Share of food trade affected by restrictive interventions

(b) Share of food trade affected by liberalizing interventions

■ Implemented by Asia and the Pacific   ■ Implemented by EU+UK   ■ Implemented by North America   ■ Implemented by ROW

EU = European Union (27 members), ROW = rest of the world, UK = United Kingdom.

Sources: ADB calculations using data from Global Trade Alert Database. https://www.globaltradealert.org; and United Nations Commodity Trade Database. https://comtrade.un.org/ (accessed December 2023).

Figure 2.16: Shares of Trade Affected by Trade Interventions, by Asian Subregion

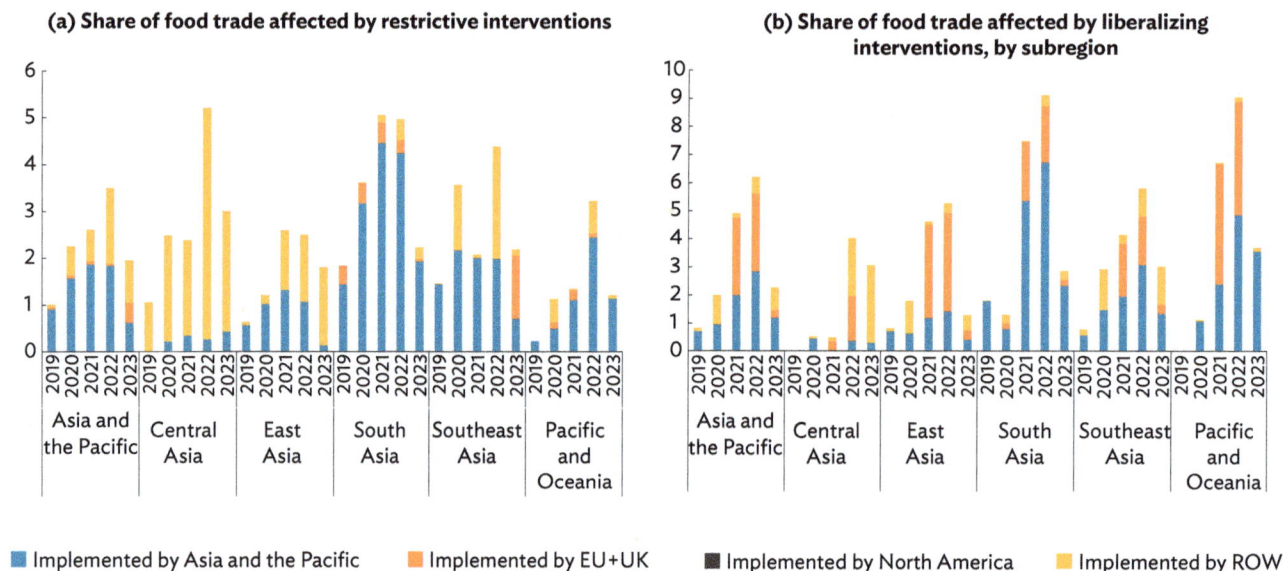

(a) Share of food trade affected by restrictive interventions

(b) Share of food trade affected by liberalizing interventions, by subregion

■ Implemented by Asia and the Pacific   ■ Implemented by EU+UK   ■ Implemented by North America   ■ Implemented by ROW

EU = European Union (27 members), ROW = rest of the world, UK = United Kingdom.

Sources: ADB calculations using data from Global Trade Alert Database. https://www.globaltradealert.org; and United Nations Commodity Trade Database. https://comtrade.un.org/ (accessed December 2023).

trade from the Russian Federation. Therefore, these economies are more vulnerable to supply availability issues, especially amid economic sanctions in response to the Russian invasion of Ukraine.

Presented with both opportunities and risks, trade and regional cooperation plays a crucial role in achieving resilient food systems in a manner that is inclusive and sustainable.

Diversifying trading partners and traded food commodities are key to building domestic absorptive capacity to supply shocks. Economies are, therefore, encouraged to eliminate or reduce trade restricting measures that prevent or constrain trade in food, and should refrain from introducing them in times of crisis. Policy responses and actions that jeopardize the food supply chain resilience in other economies should also be avoided. The effectiveness of well-connected, regional and global food chains crucially rests on continued collaboration and commitment between economies and the international community to keep markets open. With food security as one of the most complex global challenges of the 21st century, concerted efforts and strong cooperation at the multilateral, regional, and bilateral level is strongly needed to build resilient food supply chains.

Reducing trade barriers through means such as digitalization of trade procedures (e.g., accepting electronic phytosanitary and veterinary certificates), improved transparency in trade policies, and strengthened international governance and coordination mechanisms prevent trade policies from being used for restrictive purposes. Instead, policymakers should implement complementary policies catering to potentially disadvantaged sectors. For example, implementing social protection measures to complement trade liberalization and to compensate those harmed by import competition, and investing in rural infrastructure and in agriculture knowledge and innovation, with a view to building and improving domestic productivity and competitiveness.

References

Asian Development Bank (ADB). Asia Regional Integration Center. Economy Groupings. https://aric.adb.org/integrationindicators/groupings.

____. Asia Regional Integration Center. Free Trade Agreements. https://aric.adb.org/fta (accessed November 2023).

Brenton, P., M. J. Ferrantino, and M. Maliszewska. 2022. *Reshaping Global Value Chains in Light of COVID-19: Implications for Trade and Poverty Reduction in Developing Countries*. Washington, DC: The World Bank.

Cottrell, R., K. Nash, B. Halpern, T. Remenyi, S. Corney, A. Fleming, E. Fulton, S. Hornborg, A. Johne, R. Watson, and J. Blanchard. 2019. Food Production Shocks Across Land and Sea. *Nature Sustainability*. 2. pp. 130–137.

CPB Netherlands Bureau for Economic Policy Analysis. World Trade Monitor. https://www.cpb.nl/en/world-trade-monitor-august-2023 (accessed October 2023).

European Parliament. 2021. *Post COVID-19 Value Chains: Options for Reshoring Production Back to Europe in a Globalised Economy*. Brussels.

Food and Agriculture Organization (FAO). Supply Utilization Accounts. https://www.fao.org/faostat/en/#data/SCL (accessed November 2023).

____. 2006. Food Security. *FAO Policy Brief*. Issue 2. June. Rome.

Gephart, J., L. Deutsch, M. Pace, M. Troell, and D. A. Seekell. 2017. Shocks to Fish Production: Identification, Trends, and Consequences. *Global Environmental Change*. 42. pp. 24–32.

Gheri, F., C. Alvarez-Sanchez, A. Moltedo, S. Tayyib, T. Filipczuk, and C. Cafiero. 2020. Global and Regional Food Availability from 2000 to 2017: An Analysis Based on Supply Utilization Accounts Data. *FAO Statistics Working Paper Series*. 20-19. Rome: Food and Agriculture Organization.

Global Trade Alert. Database. https://www.globaltradealert.org/ (accessed November 2023).

Government of the People's Republic of China, State Council of the PRC. 2023. Thailand, China to Expand Trade Cooperations via Chinese Entrepreneurs Convention, Mini FTAs. News release. 23 February. https://english.www.gov.cn/news/internationalexchanges/202302/23/content_WS63f72e6bc6d0a757729e7221.html.

Government of Thailand, Ministry of Foreign Affairs. 2023. Director-General of the Department of East Asian Affairs Co-chaired the Seventh Thailand - Yunnan Cooperation Working Group Meeting in Kunming. News release. 13 September. https://www.gov.uk/government/news/uk-signs-treaty-to-join-vast-indo-pacific-trade-group-as-new-data-shows-major-economic-benefits.

Government of the United States, Department of Commerce. 2023. Substantial Conclusion of Negotiations on Landmark IPEF Supply Chain Agreement. News release. 27 May. https://www.commerce.gov/news/press-releases/2023/05/substantial-conclusion-negotiations-landmark-ipef-supply-chain.

Grossman, G., E. Helpman, and H. Lhuillier. 2021. Supply Chain Resilience: Should Policy Promote Diversification or Reshoring? *NBER Working Paper* No. 29330. Cambridge, MA: National Bureau of Economic Research.

International Monetary Fund (IMF). 2022. *World Economic Outlook, Global Trade and Value Chains During the Pandemic*. April 2022. Washington, DC.

_____. 2023. *World Economic Outlook Update, July 2023*. Washington, DC.

_____. Direction of Trade Statistics. https://data.imf.org/dot (accessed November 2023).

_____. World Economic Outlook October 2023 Database. https://www.imf.org/en/Publications/WEO/weo-database/2023/October (accessed November 2023).

Kearney, J. 2010. Food Consumption Trends and Drivers. *Philosophical Transactions of the Royal Society B: Biological Sciences*. 365 (1554). pp. 2793–2907.

Krenz, A., and H. Strulik. 2021. Quantifying Reshoring at the Macro Level: Measurement and Applications. *Growth and Change*. 52 (3). pp. 1200–1229.

Liang, A. 2023. *BBC*. 1 June. https://www.bbc.com/news/business-65773797.

Malacrino, D., A. Mohommad, and A. F. Presbitero. 2022. Global Trade Needs More Supply Diversity, Not Less. *IMF Blog*. 12 April. https://www.imf.org/en/Blogs/Articles/2022/04/12/blog041222-sm2022-weo-ch4.

McKinsey Global Institute. 2020. *Risk, Resilience, and Rebalancing in Global Value Chains*. Washington, DC. https://www.mckinsey.com/~/media/McKinsey/Business%20Functions/Operations/Our%20Insights/Risk%20resilience%20and%20rebalancing%20in%20global%20value%20chains/Risk-resilience-and-rebalancing-in-global-value-chains-full-report-vH.pdf.

Pahl, S., C. Brandi, J. Schwab, and F. Stender. 2021. Cling Together, Swing Together: The Contagious Effects of COVID-19 on Developing Countries through Global Value Chains. *The World Economy*. 45 (2). pp. 539–560.

Porkka, M., J. H. A. Guillaume, S. Siebert, S. Schaphoff, and M. Kummu. 2017. The Use of Food Imports to Overcome Local Limits to Growth. *Earth's Future*. 5 (4). pp. 393–407.

Seekell, D., J. Carr, J. Dell'Angelo, P. D'Odorico, M. Fader, J. Gephart, M. Kummu, N. Magliocca, M. Porkka, M. Puma, Z. Ratajczak, M. C. Rulli, S. Suweis, and A. Tavoni. 2017. Resilience in the Global Food System. *Environmental Research Letters*. 12 (2). pp. 1–10.

Suweis, S, J. Carr, A. Maritan, and P. D'Odorico. 2015. Resilience and Reactivity of Global Food Security. *Proceedings of the National Academy of Sciences of the United States of America*. 112 (22). pp. 6902–6907.

Thow, A. M. 2009. Trade Liberalisation and the Nutrition Transition: Mapping the Pathways for Public Health Nutritionists. *Public Health Nutrition*. 12 (11). pp. 2150–2158.

Thow, A. M. and C. Hawkes. 2009. The Implications of Trade Liberalization for Diet and Health: A Case Study from Central America. *Globalization and Health*. 5 (5).

United Nations. 2023a. World Economic Situation and Prospects: June 2023 Briefing. No. 172. 1 June. https://www.un.org/development/desa/dpad/publication/world-economic-situation-and-prospects-june-2023-briefing-no-172/.

_____. 2023b. World Economic Situation and Prospects: August 2023 Briefing. No. 174. 1 August. https://www.un.org/development/desa/dpad/publication/world-economic-situation-and-prospects-august-2023-briefing-no-174/.

_____. Commodity Trade Database. https://comtrade.un.org (accessed November 2023).

United Nations Economic and Social Council. 2023. *Committee for Development Policy Report on the Twenty-Fifth Session, 20–24 February 2023*. New York.

United States Trade Representative (USTR). 2023a. *Indo-Pacific Economic Framework for Prosperity (IPEF)*. https://ustr.gov/trade-agreements/agreements-under-negotiation/indo-pacific-economic-framework-prosperity-ipef.

Wang, Z., S-J. Wei, X. Yu, and K. Zhu. 2017. Measures of
      Participation in Global Value Chains and Global
      Business Cycles. *NBER Working Paper* No. 23222.
      Cambridge, MA: National Bureau of Economic
      Research.

World Trade Organization (WTO) and Organisation
      for Economic Co-operation and Development
      (OECD). Balanced Trade in Services Dataset
      (BaTIS)—BPM6. https://www.wto.org/english/
      res_e/statis_e/trade_datasets_e.htm (accessed
      November 2023).

____. Regional Trade Agreement Information System.
      http://rtais.wto.org (accessed November 2023).

3 Cross-Border Investment

Overview

Global investment activity tempered in 2022 against a backdrop of persistent global uncertainty. While global foreign direct investment (FDI) recovered in 2021, persistent pressures on the global landscape weighed against cross-border flows,[15] and global investment inflows in 2022 eased by 12% to $1.3 trillion.[16] Meanwhile global outflows dipped by 14% to $1.5 trillion after reaching a 5-year peak in 2021 (UNCTAD 2023). This easing is expected to continue, as global economic conditions remain lukewarm amid persistent geopolitical tensions, uncertain financial market conditions, and elevated interest rates.

In Asia and the Pacific, both inward and outward FDI continued to grow, though at a more tempered pace than the previous year.[17] Inward FDI into the region grew by 8% in 2022, while outward FDI rose by 18% in the same year, slightly down from 24.9% the year prior (Figure 3.1). As investment to and from non-Asian economies slid in 2022, Asia's share in global investment activity rose. Overall, investment to Asian economies accounted for 52% of global inflows, while investment from Asian economies comprised 48% of global outflows.

Regional Inward Investment in M&As Slowed Significantly

After 2 years of sustained growth, merger and acquisition (M&A) deal receipts in Asia slid in 2022. Both intraregional and extraregional M&As declined in value by roughly 30% each (Figure 3.2a). An uncertain economic environment, high prices, and increasing interest rates have exacerbated this trend. Meanwhile, greenfield investment expanded further in 2022, including from non-Asian sources, showing resilience despite the challenging investment environment. Greenfield projects in the region expanded by 79% in 2022, with intraregional greenfield investment growing by 54%. In 2022, another feature of inward investment was the considerable number of mega projects—projects above $1 billion in capital investment. A total of 41 were reported in Asia in 2022, mainly concentrated in high-tech manufacturing sectors such as semiconductors and in service sectors such as renewable energy.

---

[15] For discussions on recent FDI trends, this chapter analyzes standard balance of payments data along with firm-level data by mode of entry (greenfield investment and mergers and acquisitions).

[16] The United Nations Conference on Trade and Development World Investment Report excludes the Caribbean financial centers from its total estimate. These include Anguilla, Antigua and Barbuda, Aruba, the Bahamas, Barbados, British Virgin Islands, the Cayman Islands, Curaçao, Dominica, Grenada, Montserrat, Saint Kitts and Nevis, Saint Lucia, Saint Vincent and the Grenadines, Saint Maarten, and the Turks and Caicos Islands.

[17] Asia and the Pacific, or Asia, consists of 49 member economies of the Asian Development Bank (ADB). The composition of economies for Central Asia, East Asia, the Pacific and Oceania, South Asia, and Southeast Asia subregions are outlined in ADB. Asia Regional Integration Center. Economy Groupings. https://aric.adb.org/integrationindicators/groupings.

Figure 3.1: Global Foreign Direct Investment Inflows and Outflows, Balance of Payments

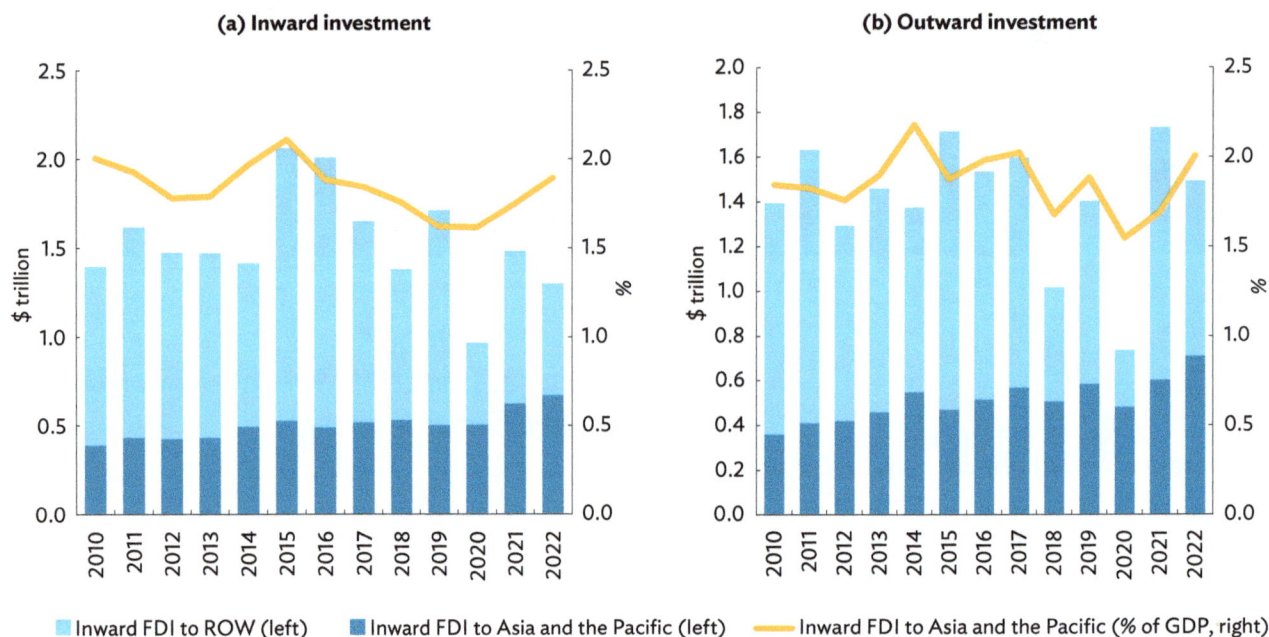

(a) Inward investment

(b) Outward investment

■ Inward FDI to ROW (left)   ■ Inward FDI to Asia and the Pacific (left)   — Inward FDI to Asia and the Pacific (% of GDP, right)

FDI = foreign direct investment, GDP = gross domestic product, ROW = rest of the world.

Notes: GDP estimates are obtained from the International Monetary Fund's *World Economic Outlook*. Estimates used are in current US dollars.

Sources: ADB calculations using data from ASEAN Secretariat. ASEANstats Data Portal. https://data.aseanstats.org (accessed July 2019); CEIC Data Company; Eurostat. Balance of Payments. https://ec.europa.eu/eurostat (accessed November 2023); International Monetary Fund. World Economic Outlook October 2023 database. https://www.imf.org/en/Publications/WEO/weo-database/2023/October (accessed October 2023); and United Nations Conference on Trade and Development. World Investment Report 2023 Statistical Annex Tables. https://unctad.org/topic/investment/world-investment-report (accessed July 2023).

Investment outflows from Asian companies rose by 32% in 2022, with investments to non-Asian economies driving this growth, largely heading towards the United Kingdom and the United States (US). Greenfield investments from Asian corporations grew by 89%, while M&As from the region slid by 5% (Figure 3.2b). Overall, Asia strengthened its external investment linkages through both entry modes, with greenfield projects to non-Asian economies doubling in 2022 and M&As to non-Asian economies expanding by 20%.

By major industry, firm-level investments to Asia continue to largely flow into the tertiary industries, which mostly involve services.

Global investments into Asia's tertiary industries accounted for 60% ($292 billion) of global flows in 2022, with 57% ($166 billion) of greenfield investments and 65% ($126 billion) of M&A receipts in Asia going to this industry (Figure 3.3). Manufacturing comprised the

second-largest share in both modes of entry in the same year, accounting for 39% ($114 billion) of greenfield investments and 29% ($56 billion) of M&As into Asia. Traditionally, greenfield projects in the region have focused on manufacturing, whereas M&As dominate in tertiary sectors. This trend persists, even in recent years.

Within the tertiary sector, wind electric power and other forms of renewable power generation amassed the largest greenfield investments in 2022. Major investments in energy transition, the digital economy, and reallocation of manufacturing are today driving forces of foreign direct investment (FDI). Foreign investments in renewable energy sectors continue to consolidate in the region. Wind electric power accounted for 11% of all greenfield investment in Asia's tertiary industry, while other forms of renewable power generation comprised roughly one-fourth of all greenfield investments in Asia's tertiary industry. Meanwhile, investments in digital sectors have been

Figure 3.2: Investment Flows for Asia and the Pacific by Mode of Entry

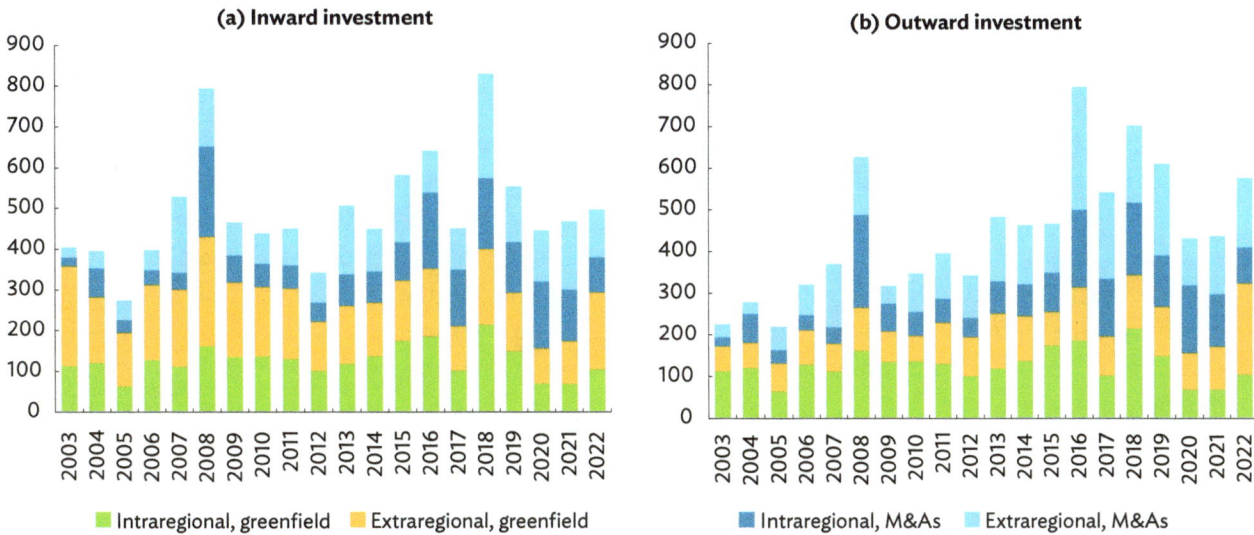

(a) Inward investment

(b) Outward investment

Intraregional, greenfield   Extraregional, greenfield

Intraregional, M&As   Extraregional, M&As

M&A = merger and acquisition.

Sources: ADB calculations using data from Bureau van Dijk. Zephyr M&A Database; and Financial Times. fDi Markets (both accessed April 2023).

Figure 3.3: Sectoral Composition of Firm-Level Investment in Asia and the Pacific—Global Investments, by Mode of Entry (%)

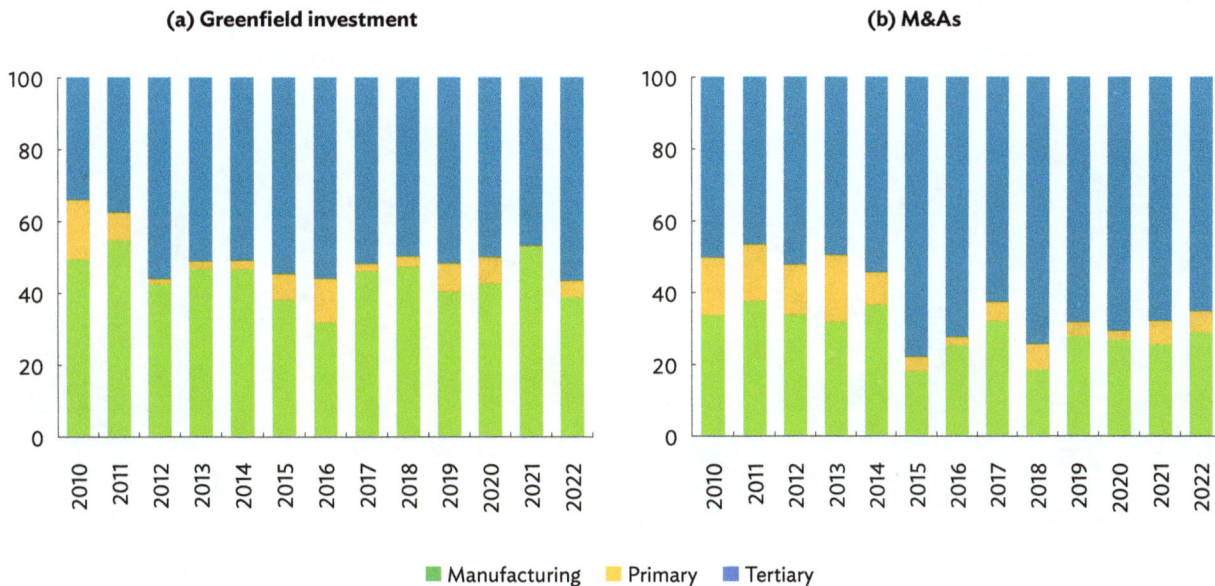

(a) Greenfield investment

(b) M&As

Manufacturing   Primary   Tertiary

M&A = merger and acquisition.

Sources: ADB calculations using data from Bureau van Dijk. Zephyr M&A Database; and Financial Times. fDi Markets (both accessed April 2023).

driving the region's FDI landscape for some time now. Data processing, hosting, and related services accounted for the largest portion of M&As in Asia's tertiary sector at 14%. As for the manufacturing industry, semiconductors accrued the largest share (34%) of manufacturing greenfield receipts in Asia, while computer and electronic product manufacturing garnered the highest share (27%) in M&As.

Asia Continues to Attract Investment, Led by Australia, India, and the People's Republic of China

Australia, India, Viet Nam, and the People's Republic of China (PRC) are the main recipients of foreign investment in the region. By economy, 2022 saw large greenfield projects flowing in Australia (mainly in the utilities and manufacturing sectors), India (in the manufacturing; and the professional, scientific, and technical services sectors) and Viet Nam (utilities and manufacturing). Meanwhile, large M&A receipts were logged in the PRC and in Australia in 2022 (Figure 3.4). In the PRC, large chunks of receipts were in the manufacturing and finance and insurance sectors, while in Australia, deal inflows were mostly in the information and utilities sector.

Intraregional linkages remain an important investment engine in the region.

Intraregional receipts through greenfield projects and M&As declined in 2022, though at a slower pace. The recovery in intraregional greenfield investment cushioned the fall in intraregional M&As, resulting in a more tempered 2% decline overall in 2022 compared with the previous year's sharp 16% fall. By Asian subregion, the Pacific and Oceania saw large greenfield investments from East Asia in 2022, with this subregion amassing about $41 billion, or roughly 40% of total intraregional greenfield receipts (Figure 3.5). The increase is partly explained by megadeals such as the Republic of Korea's POSCO project in Australia for nearly $40 billion to build a green steel production factory and green hydrogen manufacturing facility. Southeast Asia was the second-largest recipient subregion with about $30 billion—30% of intraregional

Figure 3.4: Investment in Asia and the Pacific by Mode of Entry and Destination, 2022

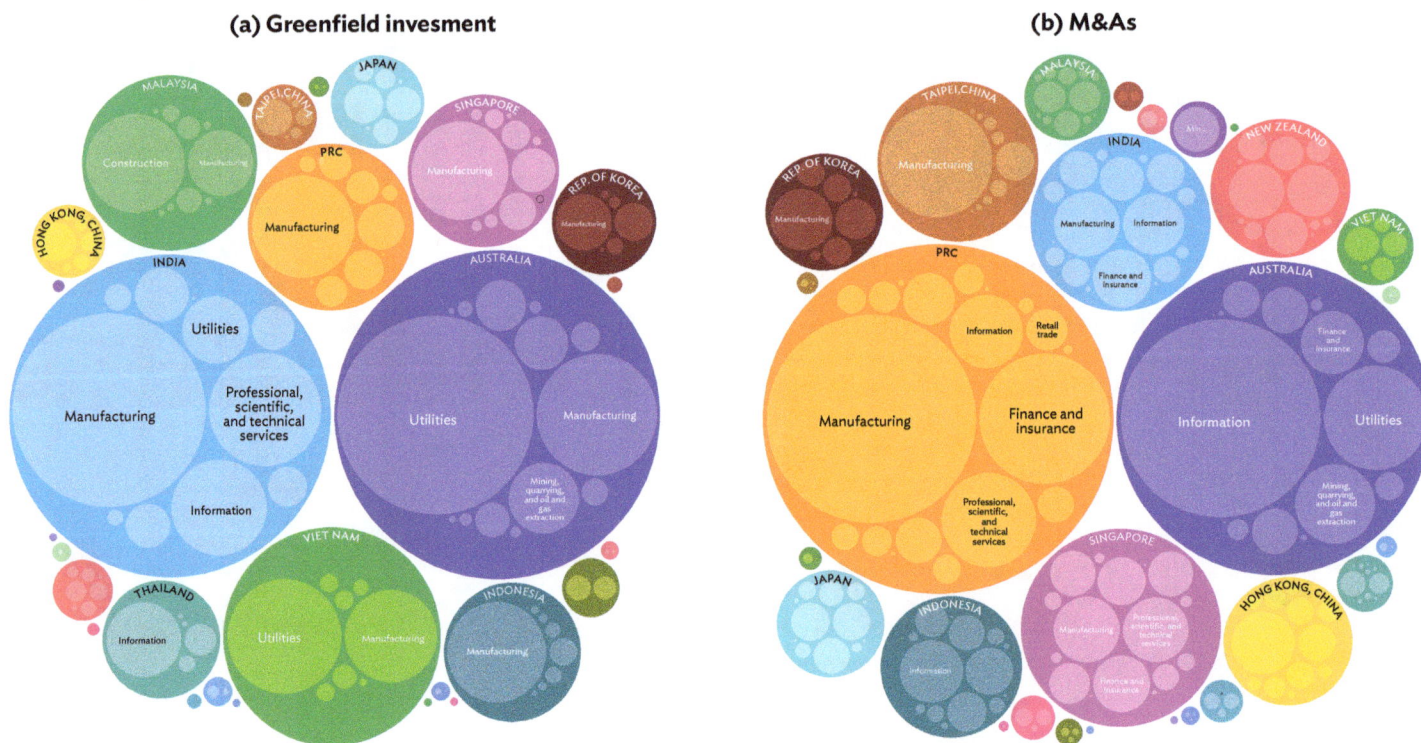

(a) Greenfield invesment

(b) M&As

M&A = merger and acquisition, PRC = People's Republic of China.

Notes: A bubble represents investment in US dollars received by each economy, and nested bubbles represent investment received in each sector. The size of the bubble is scaled using the amount of inflows.

Sources: ADB calculations using data from Bureau van Dijk. Zephyr M&A Database; and Financial Times. fDi Markets (both accessed April 2023).

Figure 3.5: Intraregional Linkages in Asia and the Pacific by Mode of Entry and Subregion, 2022 (% of total intraregional investment)

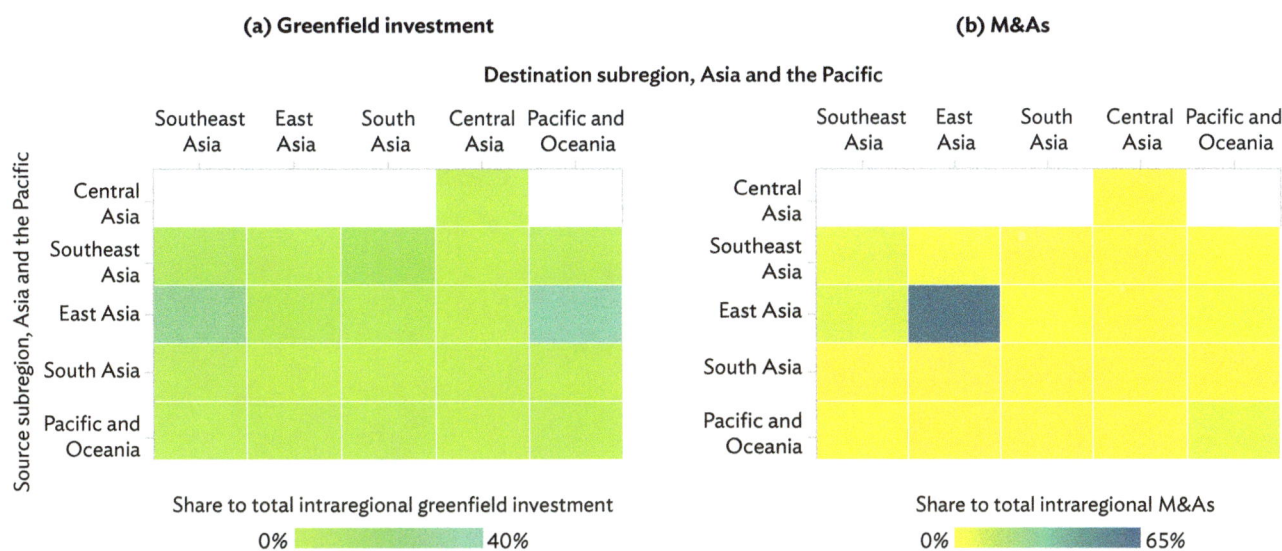

(a) Greenfield investment

(b) M&As

Destination subregion, Asia and the Pacific

Share to total intraregional greenfield investment
0% — 40%

Share to total intraregional M&As
0% — 65%

M&A = merger and acquisition.

Notes: Data used are shares to total intraregional investment, by mode of entry. Color scale and intensity are set with a maximum of 100% for consistency.

Sources: ADB calculations using data from Bureau van Dijk. Zephyr M&A Database; and Financial Times. fDi Markets (both accessed April 2023).

greenfield investment—from East Asia. Meanwhile, East Asia forged strong intrasubregional M&A linkages in 2022, with nearly $53 billion or 62% of total intraregional M&A transactions circulating within the subregion that year. Southeast Asia also reinforced linkages with East Asia, attracting $7 billion—8% of total intraregional M&A deals—in M&A deals from East Asia.

Greenfield Investments of Multinationals Shift to High-Tech and Green Energy Sectors

Greenfield investments are prioritizing a different range of activities in the operations of multinational enterprises. Investment by business activity, available for greenfield projects only, focuses on the actual function of the operation and allows the identification of upstream and downstream opportunities in the value chain where multinationals are investing more actively. Business activity data for Asia show continued dominance in manufacturing, attracting roughly half of the region's greenfield investment. However, 2022 saw a shift toward manufacturing activities in the semiconductors and other electronic components compared with large inflows in

basic chemicals in 2003 (Figure 3.6; Box 3.1). In line with global trends, the region saw an increase in investments in renewable energy, electric mobility, and other sustainability sectors in 2022 (IEA 2023).

After manufacturing, investment in electricity-related activities garnered the largest greenfield inflows, with wind and solar power dominating. This shift toward more sustainable practices is more visible with the fall in investment in extraction activities. In 2003, extraction activities pulled in the second-largest greenfield investment, whereas in 2022, there was a large drop in inflows for these activities. The regional trend is similar to other regions, as investments in renewable energy and sectors related to green energy transition continue to accelerate (ADB 2023a, 2023b; Financial Times 2023). While the trend for Asia is positive, evidence for 2023 suggests activity in the oil and gas sector has found its way back in other regions, particularly in the Middle East, due to a reshaping of energy investments after the Russian invasion of Ukraine. A new focus on energy security, investing in renewables while ensuring access to hydrocarbons for the energy transition has gained ground (Financial Times 2023).

Figure 3.6: Greenfield Investment in Asia and the Pacific, by Activity and Subsector

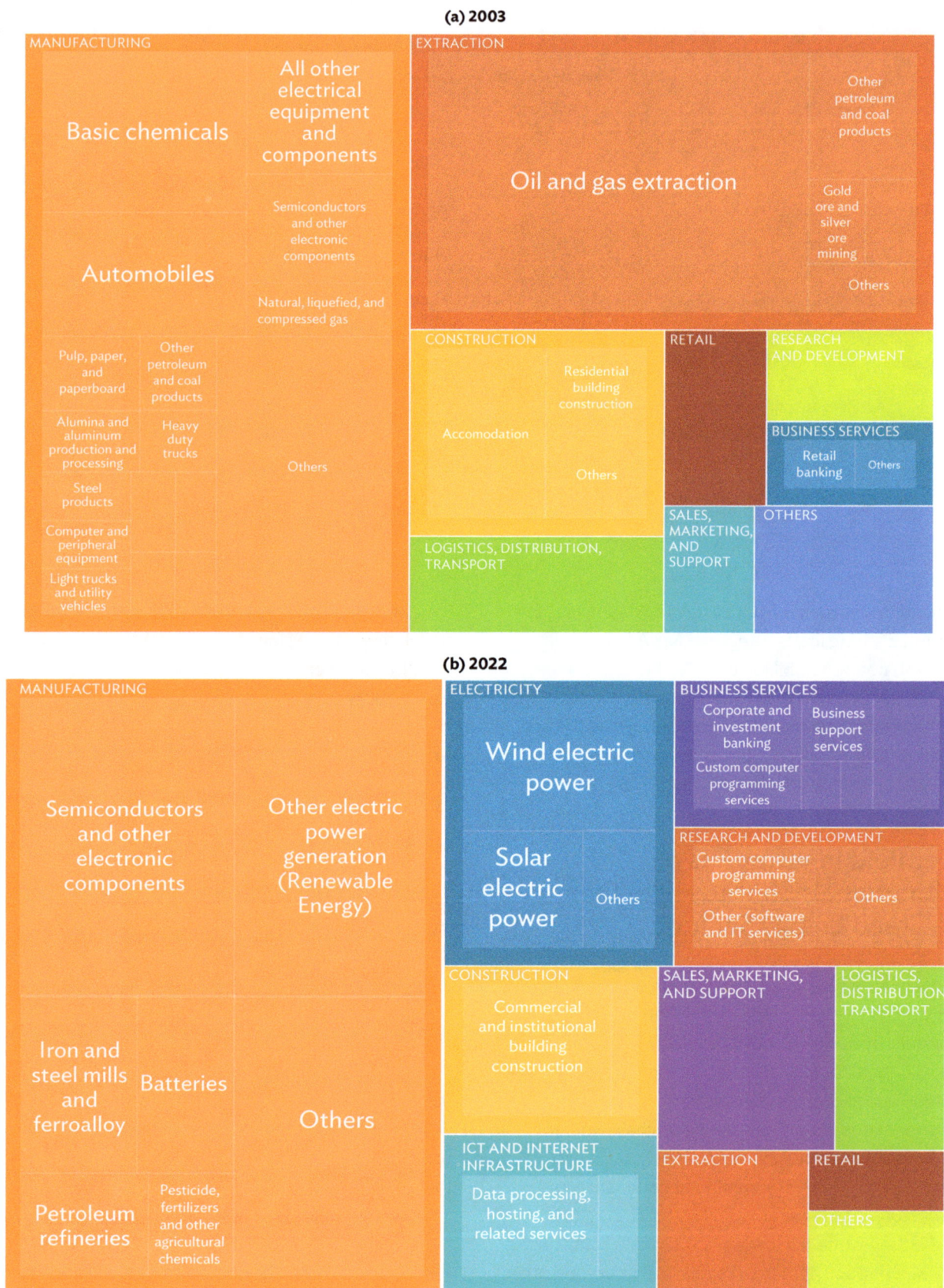

(a) 2003

(b) 2022

ICT = information and communications technology.

Sources: ADB calculations using data from Bureau van Dijk. Zephyr M&A Database; and Financial Times. fDi Markets (both accessed April 2023).

The general outlook for Asia's investment landscape remains cautious.

The year 2022 proved to be challenging for global economic activity, especially with the after-effects of the Russian invasion of Ukraine and persistent pressures from food inflation, high energy prices, looming recession, and debt sustainability issues in several economies. These factors have contributed to more volatile investment flows, especially to and from more developed economies. Despite the bleak backdrop, investment in Asia remained strong in 2022. Together with these developments, the landscape of international investment agreements continues to change in Asia.

New international investment agreements signed since 2020 include large regional agreements such as the European Union (EU)–PRC FTA and the Regional Comprehensive Economic Partnership (Box 3.1). The global landscape was still challenging in 2023 given ongoing geoeconomic tensions and volatile capital markets. As such, leveraging investments in and enacting enabling policies to attract efficiency-seeking investment—which is surmised to contribute to the ability to compete and participate in international markets, as well as allow for export diversification and advance in the value chain—may continue to support development in Asia.

Box 3.1: Recent Developments in International Investment Agreements

Since 2020, the landscape of international investment agreements (IIAs) in Asia and the Pacific has developed. IIAs include bilateral investment treaties (BITs), self-standing instruments to attract foreign direct investment and safeguard economic interests of host economies and foreign investors, as well as free trade agreements (FTAs) and other comprehensive cooperation agreements with an investment chapter or provisions. Based on ADB's International Investment Agreement Tool Kit, 16 new agreements have been signed in Asia since 2020, bringing the total number of concluded IIAs to 1,155 (box table). These new generation agreements reflect some changes in investment policies, particularly regarding environmental protection and investor–state dispute settlement (ISDS). In 2022, for the first time, the number of effective treaty terminations surpassed new agreements.

ADB's IIA Tool Kit provides granular information on IIAs by mapping 15 investment provisions and evaluating whether they grant extensive or circumscribed rights to the investor (ADB 2021). Since 2020, the most recent IIAs signed in the region suggest that treaties have introduced stronger provisions for safeguarding states' rights to regulate (box figure). For example, all IIAs signed since 2020 include environmental or climate related references in at least one provision. Likewise, more circumscribed provisions in the noneconomic standards and exception clause could indicate that states are gradually incorporating sustainability issues in their investment treaties. Recent investment chapters in FTAs, such as the Australia–United Kingdom agreement, include stronger environmental provisions or a dedicated chapter on environment.

Some reinforced provisions have been included in the ISDS since 2020. All IIAs include specific mechanisms for investor–state dispute settlement, which may include procedures for appointing arbitrators, obligations of contracting parties, enforcement of awards, and so on. Recent BITs in Asia grant more circumscribed rights to investors, whereas investment chapters in FTAs grant more extensive rights. Transparency in investor–state arbitration has substantially improved in new IIAs, denoting an effort to include, for example, stipulations on public arbitration hearings. The use of the umbrella clause, where a state agrees to meet specific undertakings toward foreign investors, is also less recurrent in recent agreements. The average umbrella clause in new IIAs is more circumscribed, both in BITs and FTAs indicating a more restrictive jurisdiction for application of the agreement, which in principle should limit the state responsibilities and offer investors less protection.

From the recent FTAs including investment provisions in the region since 2020, the Regional Comprehensive Economic Partnership (RCEP) is arguably the most visible. RCEP investment provisions cover investment liberalization, protection, and dispute settlement. It provides for most favored nation and national treatment, fair and equitable treatment before and after foreign investment is established and protection for the transfer of funds, expropriation, and compensation. Whereas provisions for the ISDS are not included, state-to-state dispute settlement provisions are. Overall, RCEP is expected to enhance investment through investment protection, market access and digital provisions, including in digital privacy and paperless trade.

continued on next page

Box 3.1: continued

Updates on Investment Treaties—Bilateral Investment Treaties and Free Trade Agreements

	Participating Economies	Date of Signature	Date Entered into Force
BIT	Japan–Morocco	2020	—
	Brazil–India	2020	—
	Côte d'Ivoire–Japan	2020	2021
	Hong Kong, China–Mexico	2020	2021
	Hungary–Kyrgyz Republic	2020	2022
	Georgia–Japan	2021	2021
	Indonesia–Switzerland	2022	—
FTA	Cambodia–PRC	2020	2022
	Japan–UK	2020	2021
	RCEP	2020	2022
	Indonesia–Republic of Korea	2020	2023
	Israel–Republic of Korea	2021	—
	Australia–UK	2021	—
	Pacific Alliance–Singapore	2022	—
	New Zealand–UK	2022	—
	PRC–EU	2021*	—

* = agreement in principle, BIT = bilateral investment treaty, EU = European Union (27 members), FTA = free trade agreement, PRC = People's Republic of China, RCEP = Regional Comprehensive Economic Partnership, UK = United Kingdom.

Source: ADB International Investment Agreement Database. https://aric.adb.org/database/iias (accessed November 2023).

Average Score for Provisions in Asia's International Investment Agreements

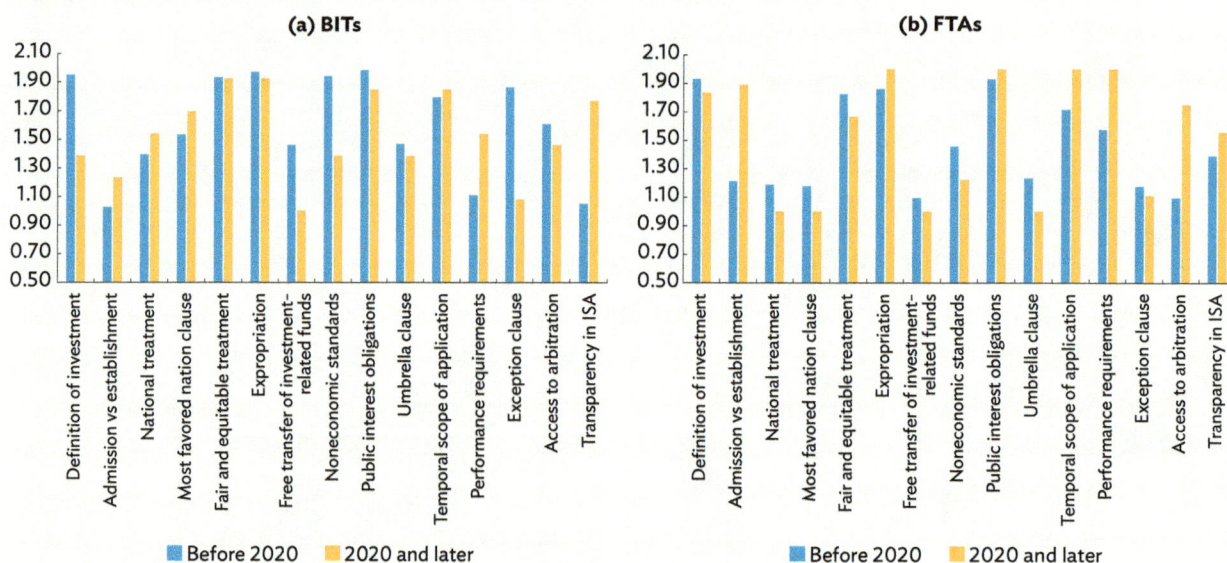

BIT = bilateral investment treaty, FTA = free trade agreement, ISA = investor–state arbitration.

Note: Provisions are scored depending on whether they grant circumscribed rights (score = 1) or extensive rights (score = 2) to the investor.

Source: ADB calculations using data from ADB International Investment Agreement Database. https://aric.adb.org/database/iias (accessed November 2023).

The increasing ambition in investment provisions in Asia also highlights the increasing use of FTAs and other regional cooperation agreements as an investment policy instrument. It also underlines the trend in Asian economies, particularly after COVID-19, to strike a balance between protecting their right to regulate investment while attracting and retaining new investment. Despite these positive developments, some important areas of IIA reform are still not part of new generation agreements, for example on investor obligations or investment facilitation.

Source: ADB, based on data from International Investment Agreement Database. https://aric.adb.org/database/iias (accessed November 2023).

Investment Policy

Over the past 5 years, global investment activity has shown signs of fragmentation and disruption. The COVID-19 pandemic highlighted the need for more resilient supply chains, which resulted in multinationals reassessing the need to bring production back home or diversify production bases. Besides logistical considerations, mounting geopolitical tensions have continued to drive the relocation of production and investment. In these developments, the investment criteria of multinational enterprises have moved beyond labor and input cost considerations. Other factors, including reshoring and friend-shoring strategies, targeted industrial policies, and an increasing geopolitical alignment are increasingly important to explain recent investment trends.

While some economies are benefiting from these trends, developing economies may be more vulnerable.

Emerging and developing economies, which typically rely on and benefit from cross-border investment, are also more exposed to the effects of investment reallocation (IMF 2023a). As geopolitical tensions continue to shape cross-border transactions in the region, multinational enterprises from industrialized economies have begun to implement de-risking investment strategies, particularly with regard to the PRC, which have contributed to a slowdown in investments since the latter half of 2022. In tandem, economies such as those in Southeast Asia are viewed as viable alternatives owing to a favorable investment climate and competitive labor and input costs. As such, it becomes important for them to define investment strategies that attract quality investment, with clear spillovers to host economies, and maximize development gains.

Supply Chain Disruptions, Geoeconomic Tensions Prompt Multinationals to Adjust Investments in Strategic Sectors

As supply chain disruptions and economic tensions intensify, multinationals have taken steps to adjust their investments, particularly in strategic sectors. Geopolitical alignment in foreign investment was brewing pre-pandemic and has accelerated in recent years. Trade tensions between the US and the PRC embody this trend and have resulted in both economies relocating production centers and future investment, with US and European multinationals reshoring investments or targeting other Asian economies. Meanwhile, the PRC has strived toward becoming more self-sufficient in semiconductor and high-tech production while strengthening economic relations with partners outside the region, including the Russian Federation (The Straits Times 2023). This shift is nowhere more visible than in strategic sectors, which generally include five main industries: semiconductors; telecommunications and 5G infrastructure; equipment for green energy transition; active pharmaceutical ingredients; and strategic and critical minerals (Atlantic Council 2022; IMF 2023a).

Industrialized economies have implemented ambitious policies targeting strategic sectors to bolster self-sufficiency and resilience in domestic industries.

The US' Creating Helpful Incentives to Produce Semiconductors (CHIPS) and Science Act, aims to boost research and development for the domestic production of semiconductors. CHIPS is a combined package of subsidies, tax credits, and domestic content rules for $52.7 billion. Its investment tax credits are contingent on recipients refraining from making new investments in PRC manufacturing facilities. Meanwhile, the US Inflation Reduction Act (IRA), introduced in August 2022, stepped up US efforts in addressing climate change and has been instrumental for encouraging large investments in green technologies (Government of the United States, The White House 2022, 2023). As in the CHIPS, the IRA foresees financial incentives, including tax credits on electric vehicles and investment in renewables conditional on domestic content requirements.[18] Thanks to IRA and similar policies, e-mobility technologies have become a strategic area of foreign investment. Meanwhile, the European Chips Act also aims to bolster production and investments in microelectronics and semiconductors (European Commission n.d.). The PRC is also taking similar strides, as the government announced a $143 billion package to strengthen its semiconductor industry (Reuters 2022).

The effects of domestic policies in strategic sectors implemented by developed economies are still to be seen. In the case of the IRA, by discriminating against products manufactured outside the United States–Mexico–Canada Agreement, the provisions are expected to adversely impact other economies via trade and relocation channels, including in Asia. These effects imply not only that investment will relocate toward the US to comply with domestic content requirements, but also a potential relocation of productivity gains from green investments. Estimated impacts from IRA for some Asian economies could be significant. In a conservative scenario, India, Japan, the PRC, and the Republic of Korea could lose up to 10% of their exports to North America in electrical and optical equipment. Relocation effects, captured through production, could also be large. IRA could entail production losses estimated at 1% to 5% for the PRC, 3% to 18% for Malaysia, and 2% to 13% for Viet Nam (Attinasi, Boeckelmann, and Meunier 2023).

While not always explicit, new industrial policies entail a form of investment policy tightening, including in strategic sectors.

Domestic investment policies in the region have in general remained favorable to foreign investment; however, less favorable measures to FDI still accounted for 30% of new policies enacted in 2022 (Figure 3.7a) (UNCTAD 2023). Furthermore, policy changes in strategic sectors, associated with innovation and research and development spillovers, information technologies, or energy security, have followed. After recently implemented measures, an uptick in overall FDI restrictiveness is reported since 2019, especially in non-Asian economies. FDI restrictions in strategic sectors outside of Asia, which are generally lower, have also tightened since 2018 (Figure 3.7b). Meanwhile, Asia's regulatory restrictions, which remain higher than other regions, remained stable in 2019 and 2020.

Foreign investments in strategic sectors continue to grow in Asia, with telecommunications and 5G infrastructure and green energy transition leading among these sectors.

Foreign investment in strategic sectors has increased in recent years, both globally and in Asia. Globally, they averaged almost $1 trillion between 2020 and 2022, roughly double the average flows to these sectors between 2010 and 2014. In Asia, strategic sector investments averaged $180 billion between 2020 and 2022, almost doubling in value from average investments in 2010–2014 (Figure 3.8). Trends in investment toward strategic sectors reflect global and regional priorities in production and investment. Decarbonization policies have made investments in strategic sectors under equipment for green energy transition increase considerably, with average investments reaching $368 billion globally from 2020 to 2022 (Box 3.2). Telecommunications continue to attract investments, with global investments averaging $367 billion in 2020–2022. Meanwhile, semiconductor investments have shifted significantly, tripling on average between 2010–2014 and 2020–2022. Foreign investment for sourcing critical minerals for e-mobility remains lower than in other strategic sectors, but it should increase in 2024 to match the increasing needs of the sector.

---

[18]   To qualify for tax credits for electric vehicles, final assembly and origin of components and minerals should take place in North America or economies where the US holds a free trade agreement. For investments in renewable energy, the IRA includes an additional tax credit of components produced in North America.

Figure 3.7: Restrictive and Facilitative Investment Measures in Asia and the Pacific

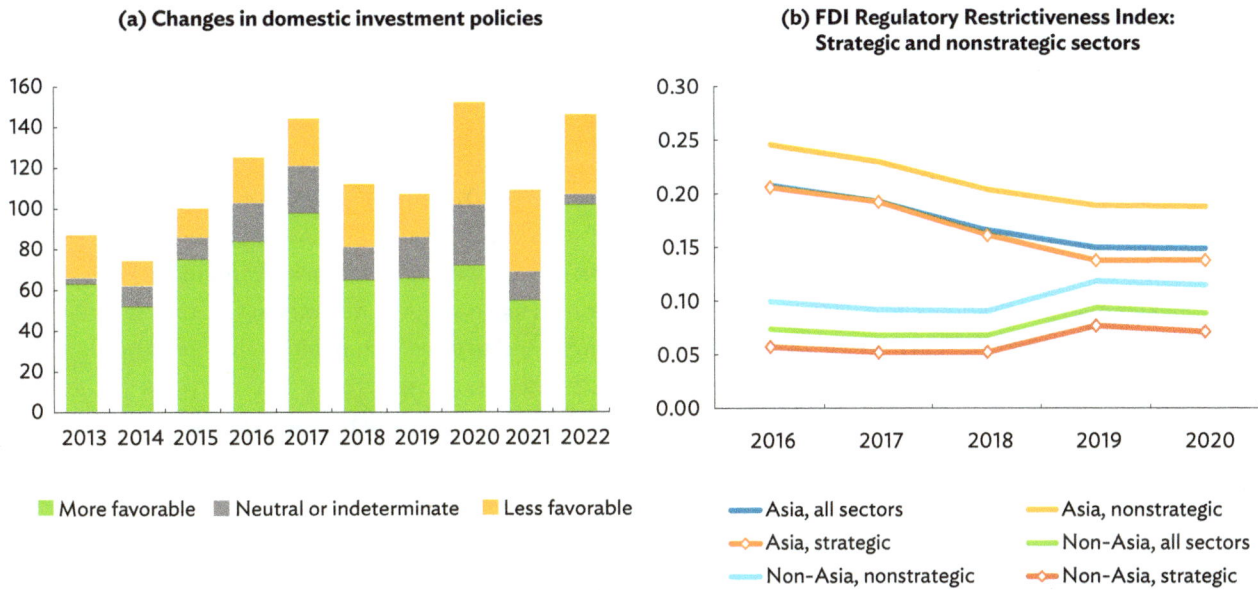

(a) Changes in domestic investment policies

■ More favorable   ■ Neutral or indeterminate   ■ Less favorable

(b) FDI Regulatory Restrictiveness Index: Strategic and nonstrategic sectors

— Asia, all sectors   — Asia, nonstrategic
—◇— Asia, strategic   — Non-Asia, all sectors
— Non-Asia, nonstrategic   —◇— Non-Asia, strategic

FDI = foreign direct investment.

Notes: Estimates for panel (a) are sourced from the *World Investment Report 2023* released by the United Nations Conference of Trade and Development. The FDI Regulatory Restrictiveness Index measures statutory restrictions on FDI in 22 sectors. The index examines restrictions in four main areas in FDI policy: foreign equity limitations, discriminatory screening or approval mechanisms, foreign employment restrictions in key positions, and other operation restrictions. Values range from 0 to 1, with 0 being more open and 1 being more closed.

Sources: ADB calculations using data from Organisation for Economic Co-operation and Development. FDI Regulatory Restrictiveness Index. https://stats.oecd.org/Index.aspx?datasetcode=FDIINDEX# (accessed September 2023); UNCTAD (2023); and methodology from Atlantic Council (2022); and International Monetary Fund (2023a).

Figure 3.8: Average Foreign Investment in Strategic Sectors—Total Firm-Level Activity, Greenfield Investments and M&As
($ billion)

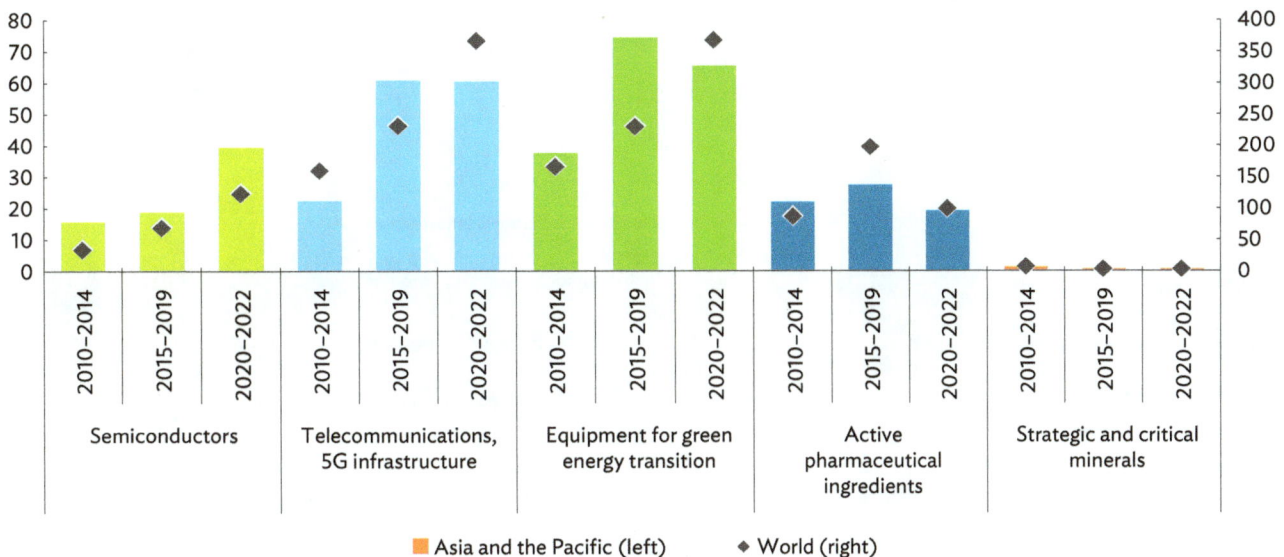

■ Asia and the Pacific (left)   ◆ World (right)

M&A = merger and acquisition.

Sources: ADB calculations using data from Bureau van Dijk. Zephyr M&A Database; and Financial Times. fDi Markets (both accessed April 2023); and methodology from Atlantic Council (2022); and International Monetary Fund (2023a).

Multinationals Have Consolidated Their Investments in Asia's Strategic Sectors

Some economies in the region are driving the growth in strategic sector investments (Figure 3.8). In India, inward FDI in strategic sectors has been led by large projects in semiconductors in 2022, including the Hon Hai semiconductor and display complex in Gujarat ($20 billion). Strategic inward FDI in the economies of the Association of Southeast Asian Nations (ASEAN) grew on average by 22% annually from 2003 to 2022, with technology firms, including Apple, Samsung, and Sony shifting portions of their supply chains to Viet Nam or Thailand. Overall, regional inflows to telecommunications ($60 billion on average in 2020–2022), green energy ($65 billion), and semiconductors ($39 billion) remained high, with greenfield investment as the prevalent mode of entry.

Although the pandemic did have a hand in slowing investments to the region, the slowdown may also hint at an effort toward diversifying FDI destinations.

Investments to strategic sectors in East Asian economies dwindled in 2022, particularly in semiconductors, as well as in telecommunications and 5G infrastructure. Meanwhile, investments to telecommunications and green energy transition in Southeast Asian economies—which stand to benefit from more diversified production bases—continued to increase in recent years (Figure 3.9). This is the case in economies like Viet Nam, Thailand, and Malaysia, which have become important recipients of FDI inflows in strategic sectors. Overall, while multinationals in strategic sectors have historically been more concentrated in East Asia—generally driven by the PRC—they show a more diversified landscape by destination.

Figure 3.9: Total Firm Investment in Strategic Sectors—by Asian Subregion ($ billion)

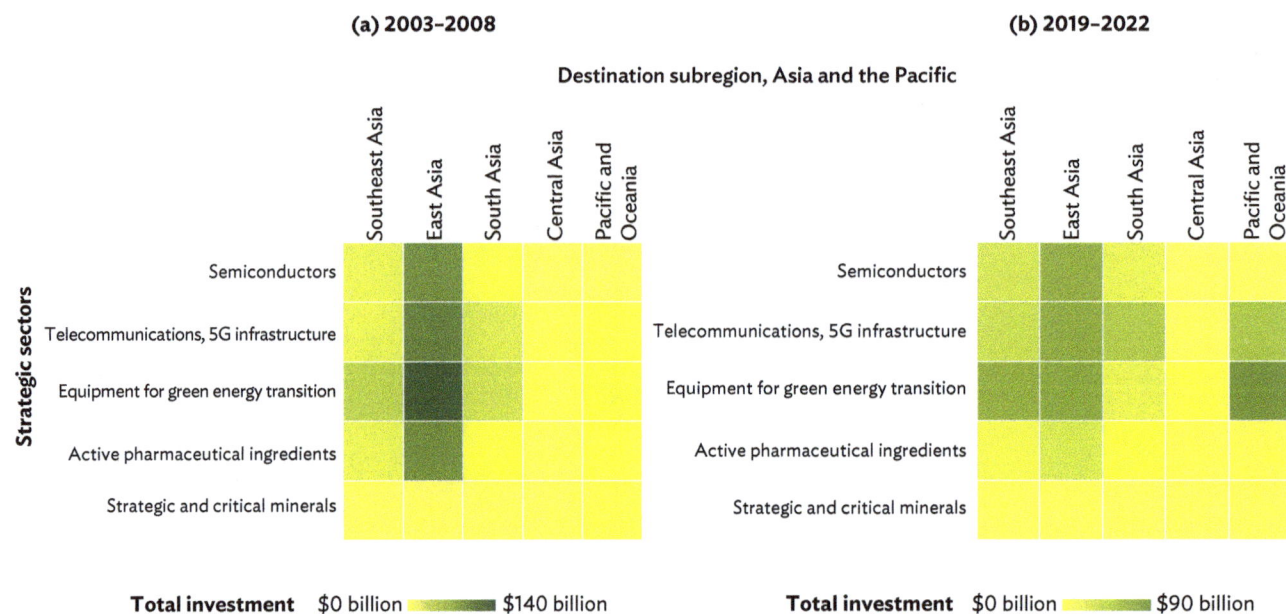

M&A = merger and acquisition.

Notes: Data used are total investment (greenfield plus M&As), by mode of entry. Color scale and intensity are set with respect to the minimum and maximum of the estimates for consistency.

Sources: ADB calculations using data from Bureau van Dijk. Zephyr M&A Database; and Financial Times. fDi Markets (both accessed April 2023); and methodology from Atlantic Council (2022); and International Monetary Fund (2023a).

Box 3.2: Green Investment—Recent Trends in Asia and the Pacific

As climate change policies gain traction and governments and businesses redefine their investment strategies, foreign direct investment (FDI) in related sectors has grown, both globally and in Asia and the Pacific (box figure, panel a). In 2022, green FDI, measured as the global investment by multinationals in environmental goods and services (EGS), represented $475 billion, about two-thirds higher than in 2021.

While receipts in EGS sectors accounted for only 4% of multinational investments in 2023, these sectors comprised nearly one-fifth of total investment in 2022. By region, most EGS investments were in the European Union plus the United Kingdom, with 40% of global investment, followed by Asia and the Middle East, which account for about one-fifth apiece. Similar to global trends, FDI in environmental goods and services in Asia has grown substantially in the past 2 decades, with inflows to the region growing by 60% in 2022, reaching $102 billion. Most of these inflows came by way of greenfield projects, comprising 68% of the region's investment in these sectors.

By subsector, FDI in environmental goods and services in Asia has seen changes in composition. Investment in power generation has gradually focused on clean energy sources (box figure, panel b). Solar power has been the predominant subsector, while interest in other forms of

renewable energy has recently increased. By business activity, much of greenfield investment in Asia's EGS sectors in 2022 are still in manufacturing, accounting for half of inflows. Electricity followed suit, with 45% of greenfield EGS investments under the said business activity. Apart from manufacturing and generation activities, research and development plays a key role in accelerating innovation in renewable energy. Despite its small share to total EGS inflows in Asia, investment in research and development in EGS sectors continued to grow in Asia, accelerating further by 8% in 2022.

While trends remain upbeat in investment in EGS sectors, there is much room for improvement, especially in targeting investment toward different needs in transitioning toward renewable energy sources. The bulk of EGS investment, particularly in Asia, remains in manufacturing and generation activities; however, more attention must be paid to other aspects of energy transition such as energy efficiency, infrastructure, and storage (UNCTAD 2023). While economies can start attending to these needs locally, foreign investment remains a key component for tackling climate issues and can catalyze the introduction of green technologies and business practices (ADB 2023b; UNCTAD 2023).

Investment Trends in Environmental Goods and Services, by Destination Region ($ billion)

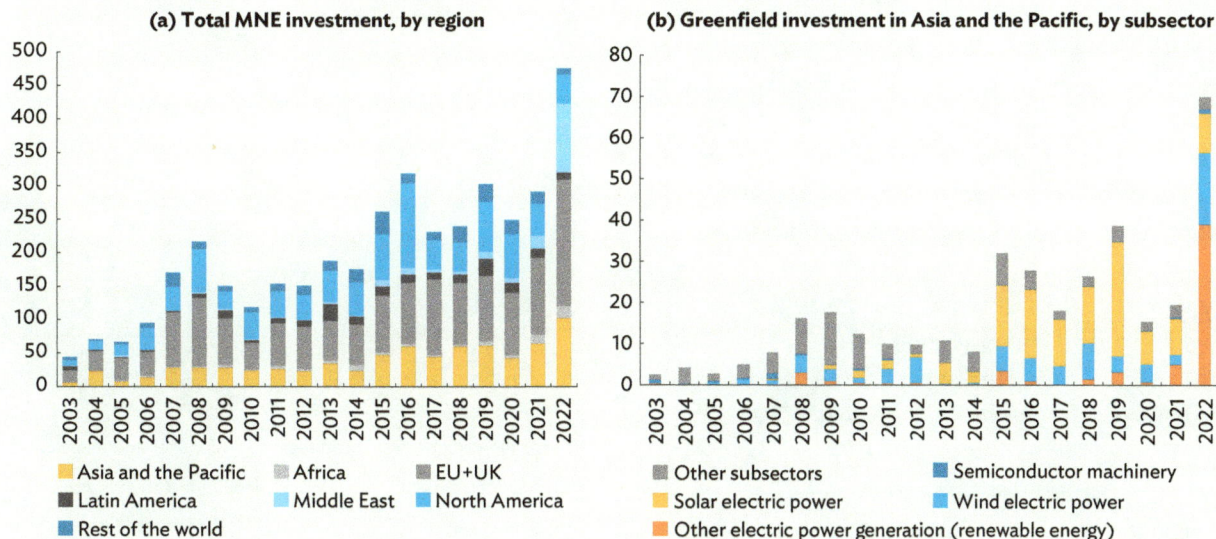

EU = European Union (27 members), M&A = merger and acquisition, MNE = multinational enterprise, UK = United Kingdom.

Sources: ADB calculations using data from Bureau van Dijk. Zephyr M&A Database; and Financial Times. fDi Markets (both accessed April 2023).

Source: ADB, based on ADB (2023b) and UNCTAD (2023).

While investment toward strategic sectors is likely to continue, the region should consider risks stemming from increasing fragmentation. Recent fragmentation of commodity markets has intensified as a result of geopolitical tensions, which could generate higher prices of critical minerals for the energy transition and disrupt investment plans. Price hikes in copper, lithium, cobalt, nickel, and other key materials could negatively impact investment on renewable energy generation and electric vehicles, with global net investment in these industries at risk of being 20% lower as a result of mineral market fragmentation (IMF 2023b).

A Changing Landscape: From Efficiency to Market-Seeking

Efficiency-seeking FDI has been instrumental in Asia's insertion in global value chains, job creation, and technological upgrading. As part of the expansion of global production networks, multinationals have typically structured their investments to capitalize on differences in factor prices, in particular labor costs, to access resources and to diversify risk. Such investments, generally defined as efficiency-seeking (or vertical) FDI, have helped leverage Asia's position in global value chains. Efficiency-seeking FDI is also associated with economic growth through the adoption of technologies for the production of intermediate goods (Ramondo, Rappoport, and Ruhl 2016). These technologies can enhance managerial expertise, productivity, and efficiency in local industries.

Steady growth in backward and forward linkages followed efficiency-seeking investments, prompting Asia's major role as an assembler in global value chains (GVCs).

To the extent that efficiency-seeking FDI generates linkages with domestic firms, improves quality of goods and services, enhances the "servicification" of exports, and favors technology transfer, it is useful to define a metric for this type of investment. To identify sectors that are more efficiency-seeking, an economy-level index

based on the ratio of total foreign firm exports over gross output is employed (Box 3.3). Intuitively, sectors where multinational presence is more prominent and products are exported abroad should reflect efficiency-seeking behavior.[19] Identifying efficiency-seeking FDI at the economy-level can also help improve policies to enhance this type of investment, which can include investment incentives (tax breaks, subsidies, or other financial incentives), infrastructure development, streamlined regulations, and technological and innovation support.

Efficiency-Seeking FDI in Asia Tends to Concentrate in Manufacturing

Based on these definitions, the main efficiency-seeking FDI sectors for selected Asian economies are generally concentrated in high-tech and medium-tech manufacturing, such as computer and electronic products, and chemicals (Figure 3.10). Economies in Southeast Asia have long been destinations for investment in medium-tech manufacturing to reduce

Figure 3.10: Efficiency-Seeking Investment in Asia and the Pacific—Total Firm-Level Investment ($ billion)

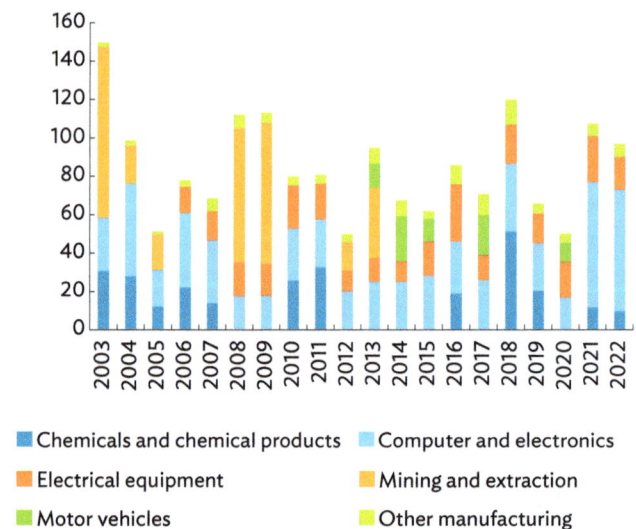

Sources: ADB calculations using data from Bureau van Dijk. Zephyr M&A Database; Financial Times. fDi Markets (both accessed April 2023); and classification based on Organisation for Economic Co-operation and Development. AMNE Database—Activity of Multinational Enterprises. https://www.oecd.org/sti/ind/amne.htm (accessed September 2023).

---

[19] Other definitions of efficiency-seeking sectors can be considered, based, for example, on the share of intermediate inputs from domestic and foreign suppliers in a given economy.

labor costs, while the PRC has concentrated investments in high-tech manufacturing. As economies like Malaysia, the Philippines, and Thailand become more competitive, they have attracted further investment in recent years.

The identification of efficiency-seeking sectors by economy also highlights the heterogeneity in production structure and the changing nature of efficiency-seeking investment in the region (Figure 3.11). These changes underscore a first phase of investment—broadly from 2000 to 2015—focused on resource and efficiency-seeking motives, and a second phase—starting in 2016 and up to 2023—hinting at market-seeking and strategic-seeking motives.

Figure 3.11: Efficiency-Seeking Investment in Selected Asian Economies—Total Firm-Level Investment ($ million)

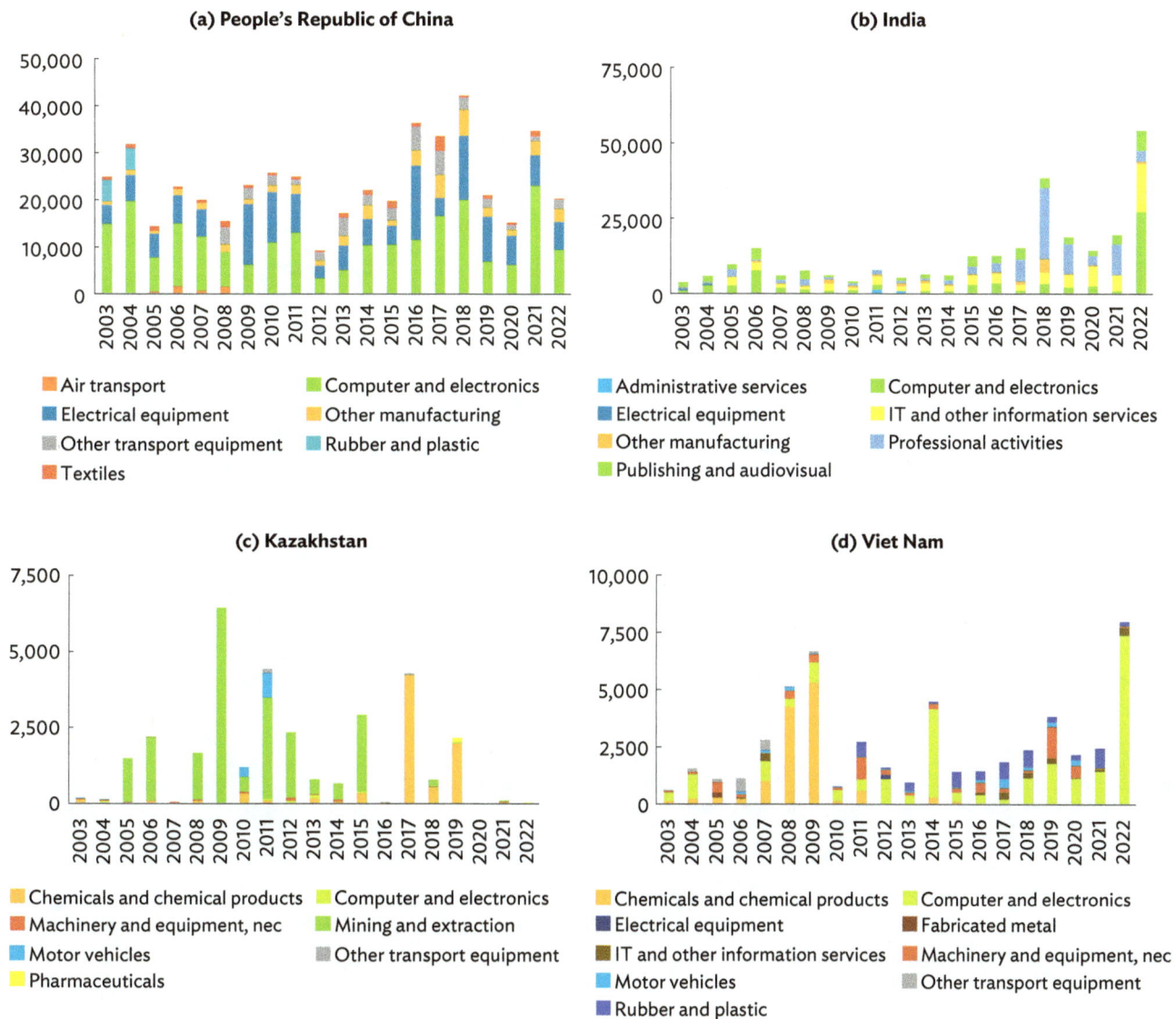

(a) People's Republic of China

Air transport | Computer and electronics
Electrical equipment | Other manufacturing
Other transport equipment | Rubber and plastic
Textiles

(b) India

Administrative services | Computer and electronics
Electrical equipment | IT and other information services
Other manufacturing | Professional activities
Publishing and audiovisual

(c) Kazakhstan

Chemicals and chemical products | Computer and electronics
Machinery and equipment, nec | Mining and extraction
Motor vehicles | Other transport equipment
Pharmaceuticals

(d) Viet Nam

Chemicals and chemical products | Computer and electronics
Electrical equipment | Fabricated metal
IT and other information services | Machinery and equipment, nec
Motor vehicles | Other transport equipment
Rubber and plastic

continued on next page

Figure 3.11 continued

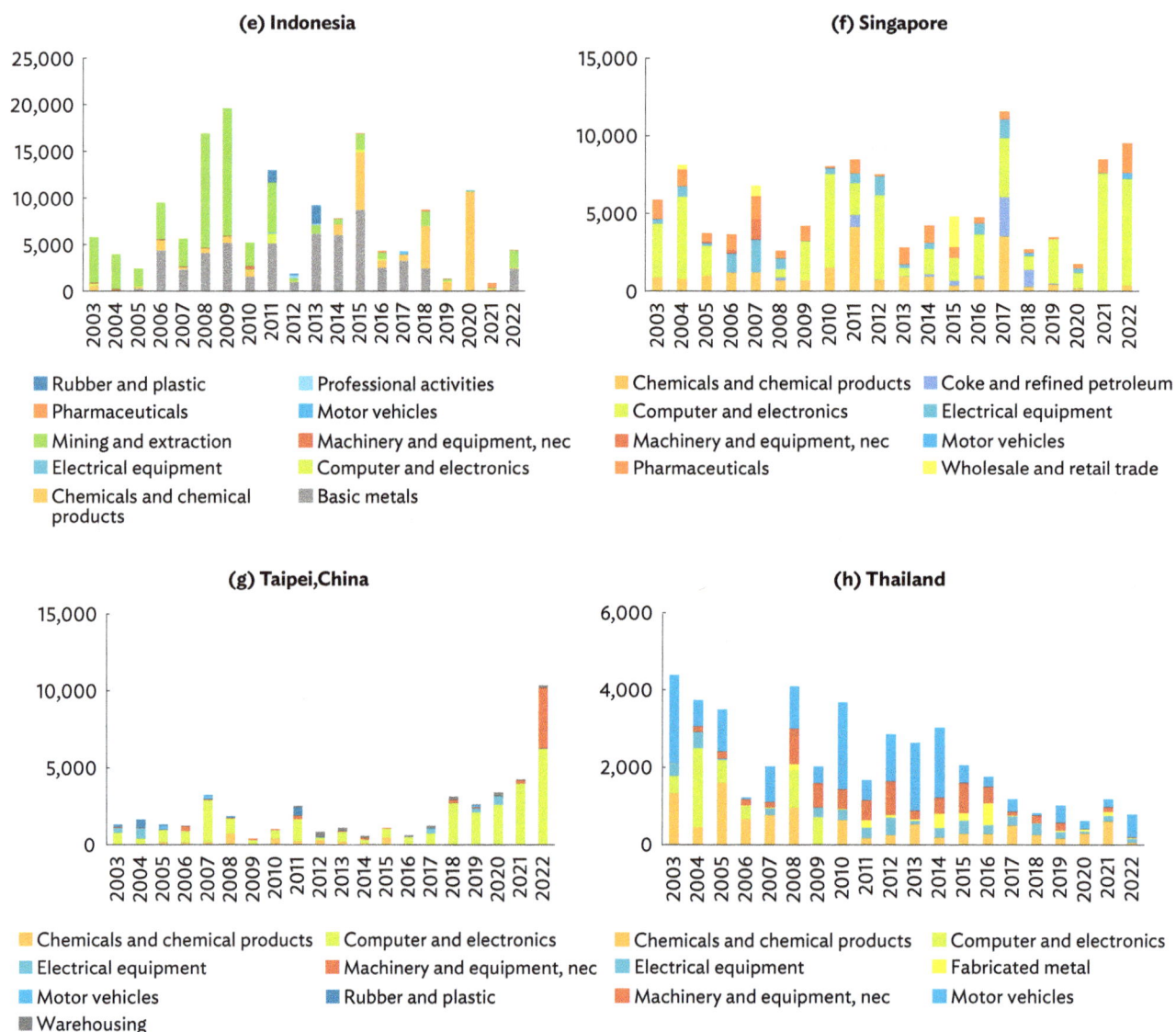

(e) Indonesia

Legend:
- Rubber and plastic
- Pharmaceuticals
- Mining and extraction
- Electrical equipment
- Chemicals and chemical products
- Professional activities
- Motor vehicles
- Machinery and equipment, nec
- Computer and electronics
- Basic metals

(f) Singapore

Legend:
- Chemicals and chemical products
- Computer and electronics
- Machinery and equipment, nec
- Pharmaceuticals
- Coke and refined petroleum
- Electrical equipment
- Motor vehicles
- Wholesale and retail trade

(g) Taipei,China

Legend:
- Chemicals and chemical products
- Electrical equipment
- Motor vehicles
- Warehousing
- Computer and electronics
- Machinery and equipment, nec
- Rubber and plastic

(h) Thailand

Legend:
- Chemicals and chemical products
- Electrical equipment
- Machinery and equipment, nec
- Computer and electronics
- Fabricated metal
- Motor vehicles

nec = not elsewhere classified.

Sources: ADB calculations using data from Bureau van Dijk. Zephyr M&A Database; Financial Times. fDi Markets (both accessed April 2023); and classification based on Organisation for Economic Co-operation and Development. AMNE Database—Activity of Multinational Enterprises. https://www.oecd.org/sti/ind/amne.htm (accessed September 2023).

Efficiency-seeking FDI has been driven by different sectors across Asian economies.

Results at the economy-level also underline some differences in efficiency-seeking behavior by multinationals. Computer and electronics is the main sector targeted for efficiency-seeking purposes in East Asian economies and Singapore. In some economies, they represent about half of efficiency-seeking FDI

investments and reflect important shifts in investments in the semiconductor industry, such as Viet Nam in 2022. For the PRC, efficiency-seeking investment mostly goes to high-tech manufacturing sectors (computer and electronics and electrical equipment). In India, information technology (IT) and information services have gained prominence in recent years, reflecting the economy's key role as an exporter of digital services. The increase in computer and electronics also reflect its ambition to expand its chip industry in 2022. Investments from Micron, Foxxcon, and AMD, among others, responded to government incentives to sustain FDI in these sectors since 2019 through its National Policy on Electronics. In Thailand, motor vehicles has been an important efficiency-seeking sector, although its importance has dwindled in recent years. While investments in primary sectors such as mining and extraction and metals were important in some Central Asian economies such as Kazakhstan, they have decelerated significantly in recent years.

Market-seeking FDI has allowed multinational firms to serve Asia's domestic and neighboring markets and ensure the provision of final goods and services.

Market-seeking factors have gradually become a motive among foreign investors in Asia as they identify and exploit new markets for final products. Foreign investment through a commercial presence (Mode 3) for the provision of services has been a common feature of foreign multinationals and represents an important share of Asia's overall inward investment. Companies pursuing

Box 3.3: Identifying Efficiency-Seeking and Market-Seeking Investment in Asia and the Pacific

Information from the Analytical Multinational Enterprise (AMNE) database by the Organisation of Economic Co-operation and Development (OECD) was employed to determine which sectors are efficiency-seeking and which are market-seeking (box figure).

The database presents detailed data on the activities of foreign affiliates in OECD economies (inward and outward activity of multinationals), including information on production, employment, value added, research and development, and exports. The database is based

Illustration of Intereconomy Input–Output Information by Firm Ownership

Source: Cadestin et al. (2018).

continued on next page

Box 3.3: continued

on annual surveys on activities of foreign-controlled enterprises and foreign affiliates abroad controlled by residents in OECD economies. The latest database covers the period 2000–2019 and includes a group of 76 economies, including 21 Asian economies and 41 industries. After determining the efficiency-seeking and market-seeking sectors, the database was merged with firm-level data from the fDi Markets database and Zephyr M&A Database at the industry level.

Based on the AMNE indicators, two indicators are developed for identifying efficiency-seeking and market-seeking FDI sectors:

- Proportion of exports from foreign firms over gross output (efficiency-seeking)
- Proportion of household final consumption expenditure from foreign firms over gross output (market-seeking)

A greater share of exports by foreign firms suggests that a specific sector in an economy is geared toward exports, a crucial feature of efficiency-seeking investment. Conversely, a higher percentage of household consumption from foreign firms signals robust demand for goods within a sector and economy, making it appealing for market-seeking investment.

To ensure the robustness of the findings, alternative definitions were explored, particularly on the identification of efficiency-seeking sectors. As an alternative approach, the analyis also involved the computation of the value-added embodied in exports. This approach seeks to assess the extent to which intermediate inputs from a host economy were utilized by foreign firms in their export production. Although the results did not exhibit significant differences, the first method was favored to account for the fact that foreign firms might not rely only on domestically sourced inputs in a host economy but also would import other materials for assembly.

Sources: ADB, based on Organisation for Economic Co-operation and Development. AMNE Database–Activity of Multinational Enterprises. https://www.oecd.org/sti/ind/amne.htm (accessed November 2023) and Cadestin et al. (2018).

market-seeking FDI motives usually consider domestic factors such as market size, growth, and market potential and penetration when allocating their investments. As in the previous case, identifying market-seeking FDI can help economies design better investment policies, from investment promotion to tariff reduction or market entry procedures. To identify market-seeking sectors in Asia, an index based on the economy's proportion of final consumption expenditure from foreign firms can shed light on the investor's motive.

Market-Seeking FDI Inflows in Asia Remain Concentrated in Services

Following the above definition, the main market-seeking FDI sectors for Asia are telecommunications, food and beverages, financial services, and pharmaceuticals. Consistent with the literature, services sectors tend to attract large amounts of market-seeking investment (Figure 3.12). Asia's large and evolving consumer markets, along with the growing presence of digital consumption and e-commerce, present promising opportunities for market-seeking investments (Google, Temasek, and Bain & Company 2023). The ASEAN region alone is projected to add about 140 million new consumers by 2030, representing 16% of the world's consumers.

Market-seeking investments also show significant sectoral variation across Asian economies (Figure 3.13). Telecommunications remains a targeted sector for market entry in India, the world's second-largest market with a subscriber base of 1.1 billion as of August 2023 (Government of India, Invest India 2023). Food products capture most of market-seeking FDI in the PRC, Kazakhstan, and Singapore. FDI in financial services is also noticeable in Viet Nam; Taipei,China; and Thailand. Notably, financial and insurance activities garner significant investment in many Asian economies, a trend influenced by digital technologies, and governments support policies for financial inclusion.

Figure 3.12: Market-Seeking Investment in Asia and the Pacific—Total Firm-Level Investment ($ billion)

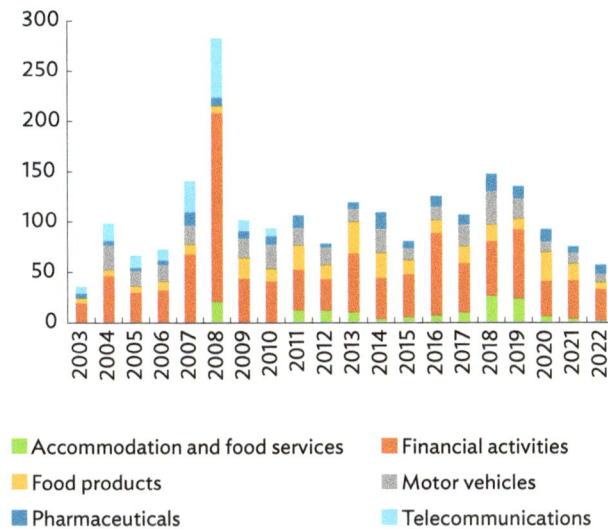

Legend:
- Accommodation and food services
- Food products
- Pharmaceuticals
- Financial activities
- Motor vehicles
- Telecommunications

Sources: ADB calculations using data from Bureau van Dijk. Zephyr M&A Database; Financial Times. fDi Markets (both accessed April 2023); and classification based on Organisation for Economic Co-operation and Development. AMNE Database—Activity of Multinational Enterprises. https://www.oecd.org/sti/ind/amne.htm (accessed September 2023).

For the PRC, the largest market-seeking investments remain in the motor vehicles sector. The PRC's large domestic vehicle market along with government incentives and subsidies to promote electric vehicles and eased foreign investment restrictions in commercial vehicle manufacturing, have aimed at making the economy an appealing destination for foreign firms (Financial Times 2021; Government of the US, International Trade Administration 2023). Recent policy adjustments, such as easing restrictions to new foreign entrants to access the PRC's passenger car market without mandatory partnerships with local brands, have further spurred foreign firms' interest in the economy. As a result, foreign car manufacturers still value their presence and ability to tap growing demand in the PRC and to establish regional hubs.

While the benefits from increased market-seeking FDI for host economies are less direct, economies in the region may aim at targeting this investment to meet their needs.

Economies might prioritize market-seeking FDI for several reasons. It can promote a more diversified industrial base. It often involves local operations which may create more employment than efficiency-seeking investment, typically more focused on technology and automated processes. It can also tailor technologies and management practices to market needs and promote long-term business relationships. For this purpose, identifying policies that create the conditions for attracting market-seeking FDI can be important. This involves, among other policies, expanding trade agreements and tariff reduction, enforcing consumer protection laws, regulations, and intellectual property protection, ensuring fair competition between domestic and foreign suppliers, and providing well-aligned sector incentives.

The allocation of foreign investment by motive underlines common strategies by foreign investors and regional differences in specialization and market potential.

Investment in primary production remains a purely efficiency-seeking activity in all regions, consistent with the notion that FDI in commodities and natural resource investments are mostly aimed at meeting foreign demand (Figure 3.14). This is also the case for high-tech manufacturing, which includes sectors such as semiconductors, pharmaceutical manufacturing, communications equipment, and aerospace. The picture for medium-tech manufacturing (e.g., plastic products, fabricated metals) and low-tech manufacturing (e.g., textiles, apparel, food) is more mixed, suggesting a combination of both efficiency-seeking and market-seeking motives in attracting investment. Services sectors are consistently more market-seeking in most regions, with some exceptions. In the EU, for example, sectors such as transport, telecommunications, and other market services tend to be exported rather than consumed domestically.

Figure 3.13: Market-Seeking Investment in Selected Asian Economies—Total Firm-Level Investment ($ million)

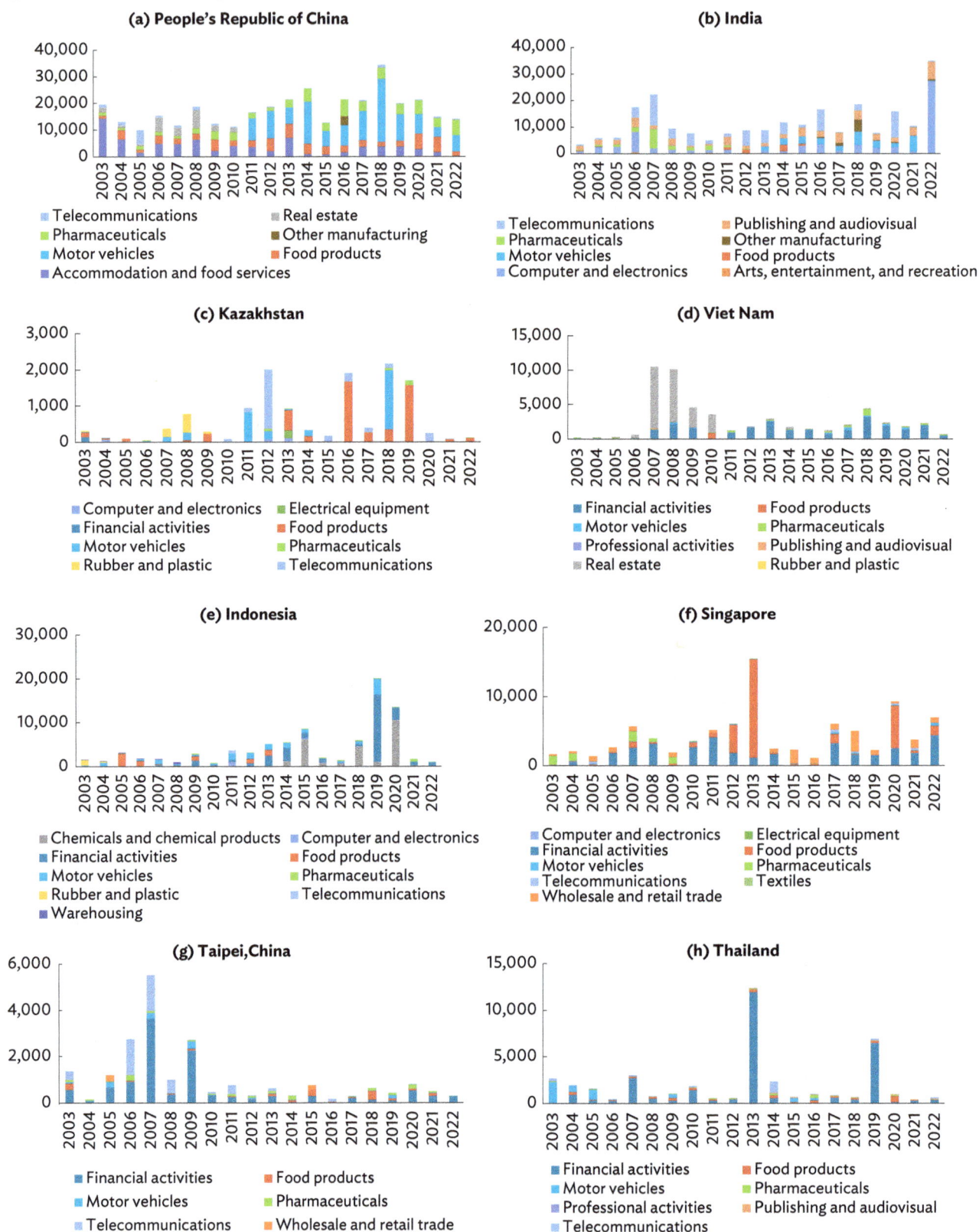

(a) People's Republic of China

Legend:
- Telecommunications
- Pharmaceuticals
- Motor vehicles
- Accommodation and food services
- Real estate
- Other manufacturing
- Food products

(b) India

Legend:
- Telecommunications
- Pharmaceuticals
- Motor vehicles
- Computer and electronics
- Publishing and audiovisual
- Other manufacturing
- Food products
- Arts, entertainment, and recreation

(c) Kazakhstan

Legend:
- Computer and electronics
- Financial activities
- Motor vehicles
- Rubber and plastic
- Electrical equipment
- Food products
- Pharmaceuticals
- Telecommunications

(d) Viet Nam

Legend:
- Financial activities
- Motor vehicles
- Professional activities
- Real estate
- Food products
- Pharmaceuticals
- Publishing and audiovisual
- Rubber and plastic

(e) Indonesia

Legend:
- Chemicals and chemical products
- Financial activities
- Motor vehicles
- Rubber and plastic
- Warehousing
- Computer and electronics
- Food products
- Pharmaceuticals
- Telecommunications

(f) Singapore

Legend:
- Computer and electronics
- Financial activities
- Motor vehicles
- Telecommunications
- Wholesale and retail trade
- Electrical equipment
- Food products
- Pharmaceuticals
- Textiles

(g) Taipei,China

Legend:
- Financial activities
- Motor vehicles
- Telecommunications
- Food products
- Pharmaceuticals
- Wholesale and retail trade

(h) Thailand

Legend:
- Financial activities
- Motor vehicles
- Professional activities
- Telecommunications
- Food products
- Pharmaceuticals
- Publishing and audiovisual

Sources: ADB calculations using data from Bureau van Dijk. Zephyr M&A Database; Financial Times. fDi Markets (both accessed April 2023); and classification based on Organisation for Economic Co-operation and Development. AMNE Database—Activity of Multinational Enterprises. https://www.oecd.org/sti/ind/amne.htm (accessed September 2023).

By subregion, investors tap both high-tech and medium-tech industries for efficiency motives, in line with Asia's role as a manufacturing hub. Noticeably, while most of Asia's investment in services is market-seeking, the efficiency-seeking motive is common in some services (i.e., publishing and audiovisual activities, professional scientific, and technical activities) in Southeast Asia, South Asia, and Central Asia. This underscores the potential of services FDI in these economies to generate outcomes in employment or technological upgrading.

Detailed results highlight the dominant sectors for efficiency-seeking investments in Asian subregions (Annex 3b.1). In East Asia and Southeast Asia, investments went to computer and electronics sectors, mainly in the PRC. Efficiency-seeking investment in South Asia is mostly focused in information and communication technology and professional activities, as the subregion is one of the largest exporters of IT and business process outsourcing services. In Central Asia and Oceania, the mining and extraction sector takes precedence, driven by their abundant mineral endowments. For market-seeking FDI, financial activities

Figure 3.14: Sectoral Concentration of Efficiency-Seeking and Market-Seeking FDI

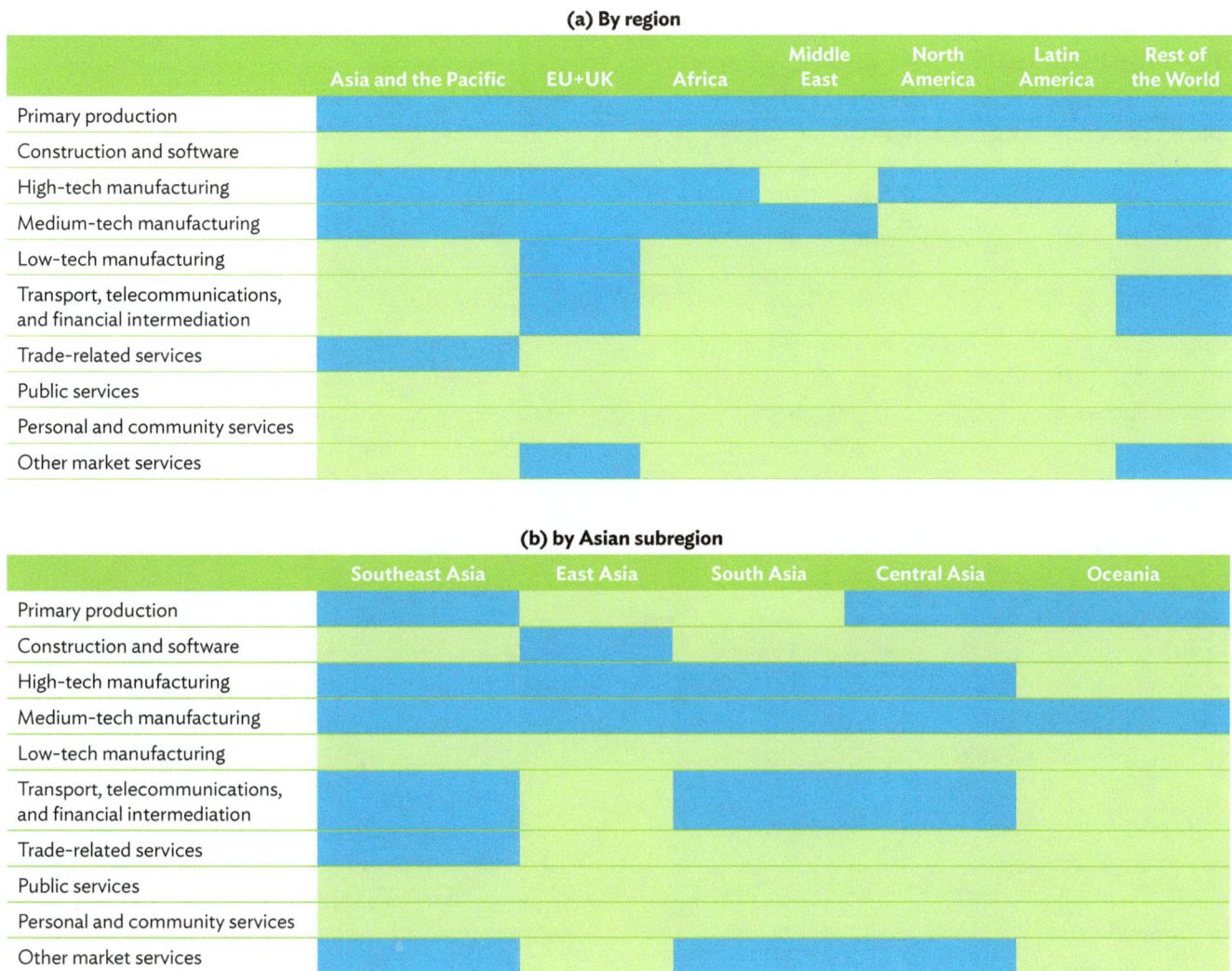

(a) By region

	Asia and the Pacific	EU+UK	Africa	Middle East	North America	Latin America	Rest of the World
Primary production	Blue	Blue	Blue	Blue	Blue	Blue	Blue
Construction and software	Green	Green	Green	Green	Green	Green	Green
High-tech manufacturing	Blue	Blue	Blue	Green	Blue	Blue	Blue
Medium-tech manufacturing	Blue	Blue	Blue	Blue	Green	Blue	Green
Low-tech manufacturing	Green	Blue	Green	Green	Green	Green	Green
Transport, telecommunications, and financial intermediation	Green	Green	Green	Green	Green	Green	Blue
Trade-related services	Blue	Green	Green	Green	Green	Green	Green
Public services	Green	Green	Green	Green	Green	Green	Green
Personal and community services	Green	Green	Green	Green	Green	Green	Green
Other market services	Green	Blue	Green	Green	Green	Green	Blue

(b) by Asian subregion

	Southeast Asia	East Asia	South Asia	Central Asia	Oceania
Primary production	Blue	Green	Green	Blue	Blue
Construction and software	Green	Blue	Green	Green	Green
High-tech manufacturing	Blue	Blue	Blue	Blue	Green
Medium-tech manufacturing	Blue	Blue	Blue	Blue	Blue
Low-tech manufacturing	Green	Green	Green	Green	Green
Transport, telecommunications, and financial intermediation	Blue	Green	Blue	Blue	Green
Trade-related services	Blue	Blue	Green	Green	Green
Public services	Green	Green	Green	Green	Green
Personal and community services	Green	Green	Green	Green	Green
Other market services	Blue	Green	Blue	Blue	Green

EU = European Union (27 members), FDI = foreign direct investment, UK = United Kingdom.

Notes: Blue color denotes predominantly efficiency-seeking sectors while green color denotes market-seeking sectors as defined in Box 3.3. Sectoral classification based on Annex 3a.

Sources: ADB calculations based on AMNE Database—Activity of Multinational Enterprises, Bureau van Dijk. Zephyr M&A Database; and Financial Times. fDi Markets.

is a major target in most subregions, especially in East Asia and Southeast Asia (Annex 3b.2). The rapid adoption of digital financial services by consumers, with digital payments now accounting over 50% of transactions in Southeast Asia, is one major factor of this expansion (Google, Temasek, and Bain & Company 2023). In South Asia, on the other hand, the large and fast-growing subscriber base has favored investment in telecommunications services. In Central Asia, the food industry receives a substantial amount of market-seeking investments.

Policy Recommendations

The current landscape brings uncertainty and poses challenges to policymakers for designing adequate policies to capitalize on the benefits of foreign investment. The distinction between efficiency-seeking and market-seeking FDI is relevant today in the context of FDI fragmentation. So far, fragmentation has had more visible impact in efficiency-seeking sectors, notably in semiconductors, which are more prone to be the target of policies aiming at reshoring production. Hampering investment measures in strategic sectors beyond semiconductors could follow, in particular critical minerals essential for the energy transition, with different levels of exposure and potential impact for Asian economies.

Risks stemming from FDI fragmentation are not unique to Asia, but given the important role of efficiency-seeking FDI in the region and the high share of multinational operations in strategic sectors, they should be considered. Even more so as increasing fragmentation is expected to cause larger economic costs in small, developing economies (IMF 2023a).

Economies in the region can prepare for this scenario through several strategies:

First, governments should be poised to support regional and global integration initiatives that facilitate multilateral cooperation in trade and investment. This implies enhancing World Trade Organization rules on export tariffs, discriminatory subsidies, local-content requirements, and equivalent provisions in international investment agreements. Multilateral cooperation in key industries for the region, including semiconductors, environmental goods and services, and automotive can be important to understand and assess the economic implications of reshoring, nearshoring, and other forms of industrial policy. For economies aiming to attract more market-seeking FDI, participation in trade agreements can also be crucial.

Second, governments should incorporate long-term investment plans to consider exposure to possible shocks in strategic sectors. Vulnerabilities in strategic sectors (semiconductors, telecommunications, green energy, critical minerals) could take place through inward FDI, if economies are hosting these investments, or through imports, if economies depend on these inputs for domestic production, the energy transition, or other objectives. The case of critical minerals is relevant given the increasing risks of fragmentation in commodity markets and potential implications for high-tech manufacturing and the green energy transition. At the same time, FDI relocation has unlocked opportunities for some economies in the region to attract investment in new sectors. Investment policy frameworks should assess potential risks and opportunities at the industry level. As stressed in the *Asian Economic Integration Report 2023*, diversification of investment sources beyond a few dominant investors or industries should remain a priority for several ADB's developing member economies where inbound FDI is highly concentrated (ADB 2023b).

Third, governments need to assess the role of foreign investors in supporting industrial development and technological upgrading. Evidence has shown that medium- and high-tech manufacturing has been tightly linked to foreign investment in some economies, particularly in the PRC. Seizing economic benefits of FDI in these sectors through market-oriented and competition-based policies remains important. Supporting research and development initiatives, innovation hubs, and technology transfer is critical, as is enforcing investment protection regarding intellectual property. Also, it is important for developing member economies to identify and support foreign investment in sectors with high potential, particularly technology-related services such as software development, data processing, and computer systems design.

Fourth, while FDI policies should target efficiency-seeking investment given its benefits for economic growth, productivity and technological upgrading, maximizing the potential of market-seeking FDI in Asia should also continue. Market-seeking FDI can improve spillovers in host economies through employment creation, transferring management skills, and adapting technologies and production to local needs. As economies become increasingly reliant on services, and market-seeking FDI targets these sectors, designing policies that maximize their potential remains important. For example, with the services content of manufacturing exports in Asia increasing, policies enhancing linkages between manufacturing and services could be further strengthened. Equally important is to invest in a skilled workforce and support innovation in services industries to enhance productivity, further liberalize trade in services, and strengthen streamline regulations in services industries.

References

Association of Southeast Asian Nations (ASEAN) Secretariat. ASEANstats Data Portal. https://data.aseanstats.org (accessed July 2019).

Asian Development Bank (ADB). 2021. *ADB International Investment Agreement Tool Kit: A Comparative Approach.* Manila.

____. 2023a. *Asian Development Outlook.* Manila.

____. 2023b. *Asian Economic Integration Report 2023: Trade, Investment, and Climate Change in Asia and the Pacific.* Manila.

____. ADB International Investment Agreement Database. https://aric.adb.org/database/iias (accessed November 2023).

Attinasi, M. G., L. Boeckelmann, and B. Meunier. 2023. Unfriendly Friends: Trade and Relocation Effects of the US Inflation Reduction Act. *VoxEU.* 3 July 2023. https://cepr.org/voxeu/columns/unfriendly-friends-trade-and-relocation-effects-us-inflation-reduction-act.

Atlantic Council. 2022. Our Guide to Friend-Shoring: Sectors to Watch. https://www.atlanticcouncil.org/in-depth-research-reports/issue-brief/our-guide-to-friend-shoring-sectors-to-watch/.

Cadestin, C., K. De Backer, I. Desnoyers-James, S. Miroudot, M. Ye, and D. Rigoi. 2018. Multinational Enterprises and Global Value Chains: New Insights on the Trade-Investment Nexus. *OECD Science, Technology and Industry Working Paper.* No. 2018/05. Paris: OECD Publishing.

European Commission. n.d. European Chips Act. https://commission.europa.eu/strategy-and-policy/priorities-2019-2024/europe-fit-digital-age/european-chips-act_en.

Eurostat. Balance of Payments. https://ec.europa.eu/eurostat (accessed July 2023).

Financial Times. 2021. China's Car Market Is Electrifying. *fDi Intelligence.* https://www.fdiintelligence.com/content/feature/chinas-car-market-is-electrifying-79655.

____. 2023. *The fDi Report 2023: Global Greenfield Investment Trends.* London.

Franco-Bedoya, S., Y. Li, and V. Mercer-Blackman. 2021. Data and Methodologies Used to Decipher the Contribution of Services to Growth in South Asia. Washington, DC: The World Bank.

Google, Temasek, and Bain & Company. 2023. *e-Conomy SEA 2023 Report.* Google, Temasek and Bain.

Government of Canada, Statistics Canada. Industry Classifications. https://www.statcan.gc.ca/en/concepts/industry.

Government of India, Invest India. 2023. Telecom Industry Scenario. https://www.investindia.gov.in/sector/telecom.

Government of the United States, Census Bureau. North American Industry Classification System. https://www.census.gov/naics/.

Government of the United States, The White House. 2022. Fact Sheet: CHIPS and Science Act Will Lower Costs, Create Jobs, Strengthen Supply Chains, and Counter China. https://www.whitehouse.gov/briefing-room/statements-releases/2022/08/09/fact-sheet-chips-and-science-act-will-lower-costs-create-jobs-strengthen-supply-chains-and-counter-china/.

_____. 2023. Building a Clean Energy Economy: A Guidebook to the Inflation Reduction Act's Investments in Clean Energy and Climate Action. https://www.whitehouse.gov/wp-content/uploads/2022/12/Inflation-Reduction-Act-Guidebook.pdf.

Government of the United States, International Trade Administration. 2023. China - Country Commercial Guide. https://www.trade.gov/country-commercial-guides/china-automotive-industry.

International Energy Agency (IEA). 2023. *World Energy Investment 2023*. Paris. https://www.iea.org/reports/world-energy-investment-2023.

International Monetary Fund (IMF). 2023a. Geoeconomic Fragmentation and Foreign Direct Investment. In IMF. *World Economic Outlook: A Rocky Recovery*. Washington, DC.

_____. 2023b. Fragmentation in Commodity Markets: Vulnerabilities and Risks. In IMF. *World Economic Outlook: Navigating Global Divergences*. Washington, DC.

_____. World Economic Outlook April 2023 Database. https://www.imf.org/en/Publications/WEO/weo-database/2023/April (accessed April 2023).

_____. FDI Regulatory Restrictiveness Index. https://stats.oecd.org/Index.aspx?datasetcode=FDIINDEX# (accessed September 2023).

Ramondo, N., V. Rappoport, and K. J. Ruhl. 2016. Intrafirm Trade and Vertical Fragmentation in U.S. Multinational Corporations. *Journal of International Economics*. 98. pp. 51–59.

Reuters. 2022. Exclusive: China Readying $143 Billion Package for Its Chip Firms in Face of U.S. Curbs. 14 December. https://www.reuters.com/technology/china-plans-over-143-bln-push-boost-domestic-chips-compete-with-us-sources-2022-12-13/.

The Straits Times. 2023. China Vows Deeper Trade, Investment with Russia despite Western Rebuke. 20 September. https://www.straitstimes.com/asia/east-asia/china-vows-deeper-trade-investment-with-russia-despite-western-rebuke.

United Nations Conference on Trade and Development (UNCTAD). 2023. *World Investment Report 2023: Investing in Sustainable Energy for All*. Geneva.

_____. World Investment Report 2023 Statistical Annex Tables. https://worldinvestmentreport.unctad.org/annex-tables/ (accessed July 2023).

Annex 3a: Analytical and Broad Sector Classification

Sector Code	Sector Label	Analytical Sector	Broad Sector
A01T03	Agriculture, forestry, and fishing	Primary production	Agriculture and natural resource extraction
B05T09	Mining and extraction of energy producing products	Primary production	Agriculture and natural resource extraction
C10T12	Food products, beverages, and tobacco	Low-tech manufacturing	Manufacturing
C13T15	Textiles, wearing apparel, leather, and related products	Low-tech manufacturing	Manufacturing
C16	Wood and products of wood and cork	Low-tech manufacturing	Manufacturing
C17T18	Paper products and printing	Low-tech manufacturing	Manufacturing
C19	Coke and refined petroleum products	Medium-tech manufacturing	Manufacturing
C20	Chemicals and chemical products	Medium-tech manufacturing	Manufacturing
C21	Pharmaceuticals, medicinal chemical, and botanical products	Medium-tech manufacturing	Manufacturing
C22	Rubber and plastic products	Medium-tech manufacturing	Manufacturing
C23	Other nonmetallic mineral products	Medium-tech manufacturing	Manufacturing
C24	Basic metals	Medium-tech manufacturing	Manufacturing
C25	Fabricated metal products	Medium-tech manufacturing	Manufacturing
C26	Computer, electronic and optical products	High-tech manufacturing	Manufacturing
C27	Electrical equipment	High-tech manufacturing	Manufacturing
C28	Machinery and equipment, nec	High-tech manufacturing	Manufacturing
C29	Motor vehicles, trailers and semi-trailers	High-tech manufacturing	Manufacturing
C30	Other transport equipment	High-tech manufacturing	Manufacturing
C31T33	Other manufacturing; repair and installation of machinery and equipment	High-tech manufacturing	Manufacturing
D35_E36T39	Electricity, gas, water supply; sewerage, waste and remediation services	Construction and infrastructure	Construction and utilities
F41T43	Construction	Construction and infrastructure	Construction and utilities
G45T47	Wholesale and retail trade; repair of motor vehicles	Trade-related services	Services
H49	Land transport and transport via pipelines	Transport, telecommunications, and financial intermediation	Services
H50	Water transport	Transport, telecommunications, and financial intermediation	Services
H51	Air transport	Transport, telecommunications, and financial intermediation	Services
H52	Warehousing and support activities for transportation	Transport, telecommunications, and financial intermediation	Services
H53	Postal and courier activities	Transport, telecommunications, and financial intermediation	Services
I55T56	Accommodation and food services	Other market services	Services
J58T60	Publishing, audiovisual, and broadcasting activities	Other market services	Services
J61	Telecommunications	Transport, telecommunications, and financial intermediation	Services
J62T63	IT and other information services	Transport, telecommunications, and financial intermediation	Services

continued on next page

Annex 3a continued

Sector Code	Sector Label	Analytical Sector	Broad Sector
K64T66	Financial and insurance activities	Transport, telecommunications, and financial intermediation	Services
L68	Real estate activities	Other market services	Services
M69T75	Professional, scientific, and technical activities	Other market services	Services
N77T82	Administrative and support services	Other market services	Services
O84	Public administration and defense; compulsory social security	Public services	Services
P85	Education	Public services	Services
Q86T88	Human health and social work	Public services	Services
R90T93	Arts, entertainment, and recreation	Personal and community services	Services
S94T96	Other service activities	Personal and community services	Services
T97T98	Private households with employed persons	Personal and community services	Services

IT = information technology, nec = not elsewhere classified.

Note: Analytical and broad sector group classifications are based on Franco-Bedoya, Li, and Mercer-Blackman (2021).

Source: ADB compilation based on Franco-Bedoya, Li, and Mercer-Blackman (2021).

Annex 3b: Efficiency-Seeking and Market-Seeking Investment by Asian Subregion

(1) Efficiency-Seeking Investment by Asian Subregion—Total Firm-Level Investment ($ million)

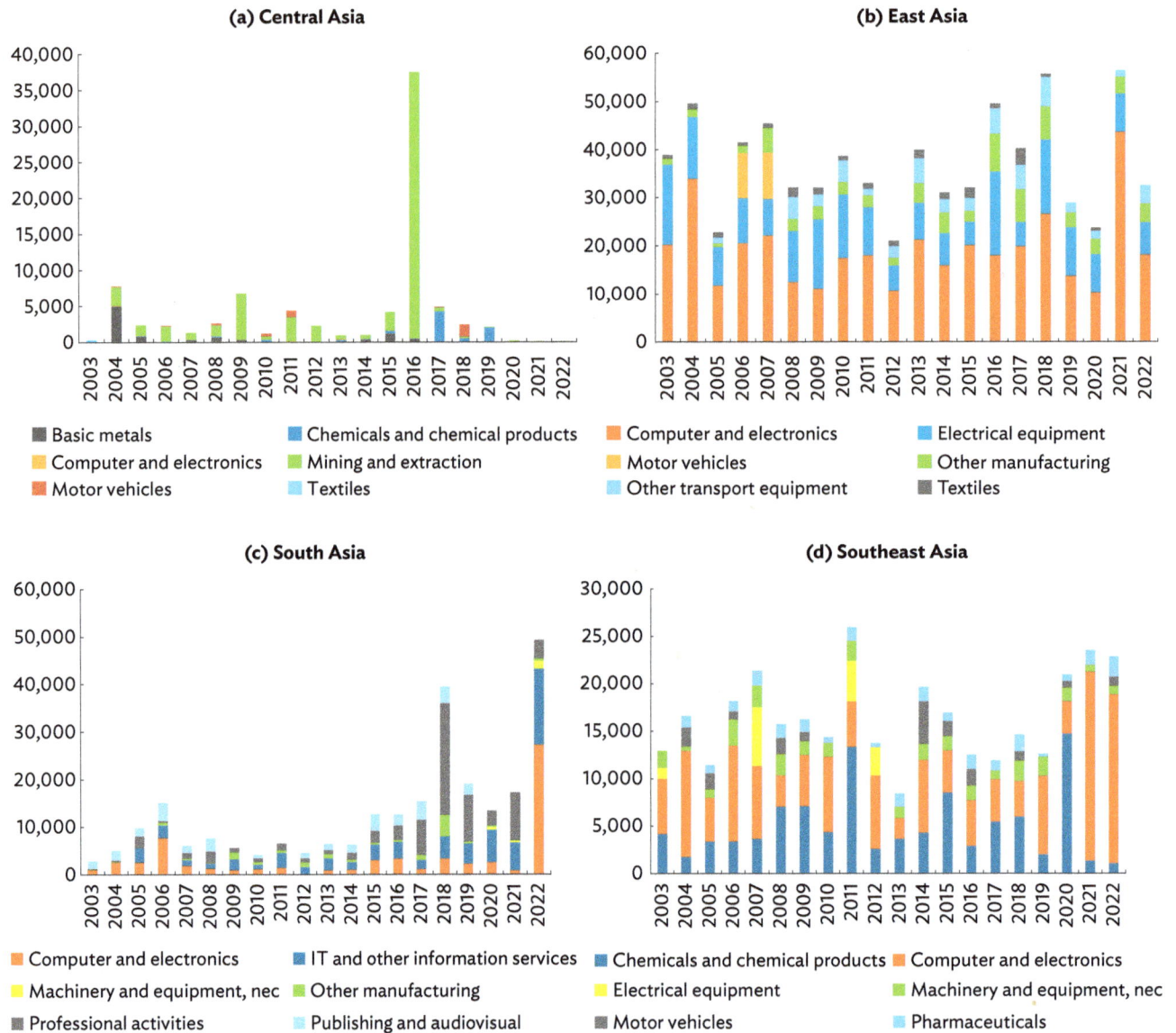

(a) Central Asia

Legend:
- Basic metals
- Computer and electronics
- Motor vehicles
- Chemicals and chemical products
- Mining and extraction
- Textiles

(b) East Asia

Legend:
- Computer and electronics
- Motor vehicles
- Other transport equipment
- Electrical equipment
- Other manufacturing
- Textiles

(c) South Asia

Legend:
- Computer and electronics
- Machinery and equipment, nec
- Professional activities
- IT and other information services
- Other manufacturing
- Publishing and audiovisual

(d) Southeast Asia

Legend:
- Chemicals and chemical products
- Electrical equipment
- Motor vehicles
- Computer and electronics
- Machinery and equipment, nec
- Pharmaceuticals

continued on next page

Annex 3b continued

(e) Oceania

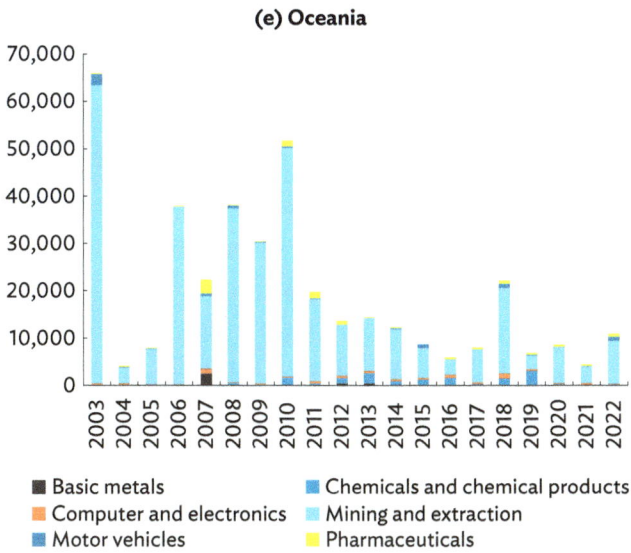

- Basic metals
- Chemicals and chemical products
- Computer and electronics
- Mining and extraction
- Motor vehicles
- Pharmaceuticals

(2) Market-Seeking Investment by Asian Subregion—Total Firm-Level Investment ($ million)

(a) Central Asia

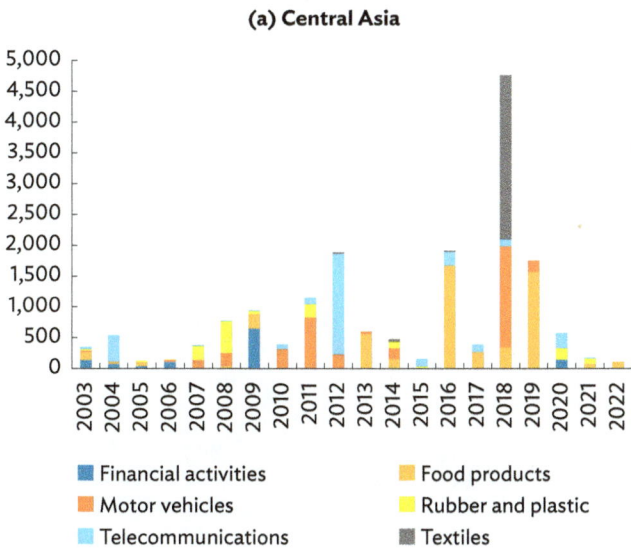

- Financial activities
- Food products
- Motor vehicles
- Rubber and plastic
- Telecommunications
- Textiles

(b) East Asia

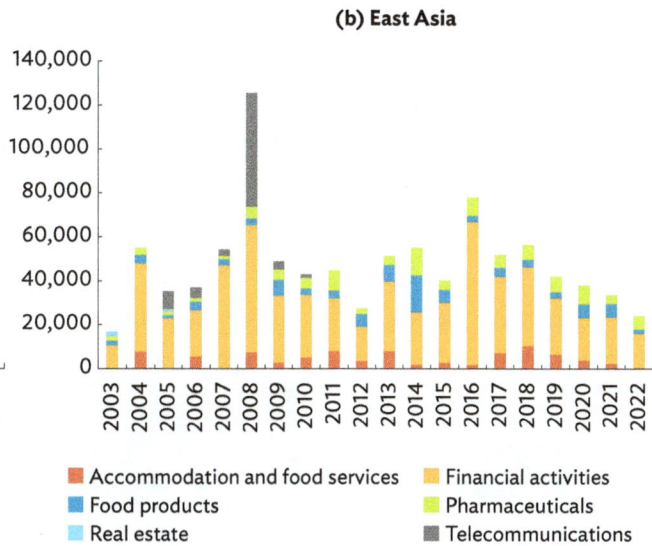

- Accommodation and food services
- Financial activities
- Food products
- Pharmaceuticals
- Real estate
- Telecommunications

continued on next page

Annex 3b continued

(c) South Asia

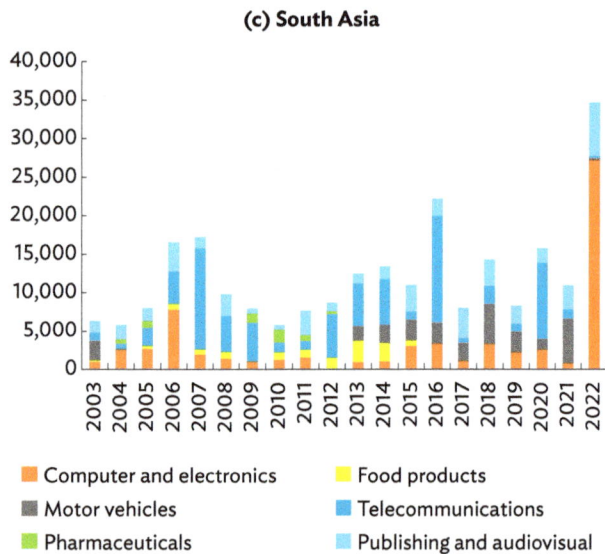

Legend:
- Computer and electronics
- Food products
- Motor vehicles
- Telecommunications
- Pharmaceuticals
- Publishing and audiovisual

(d) Southeast Asia

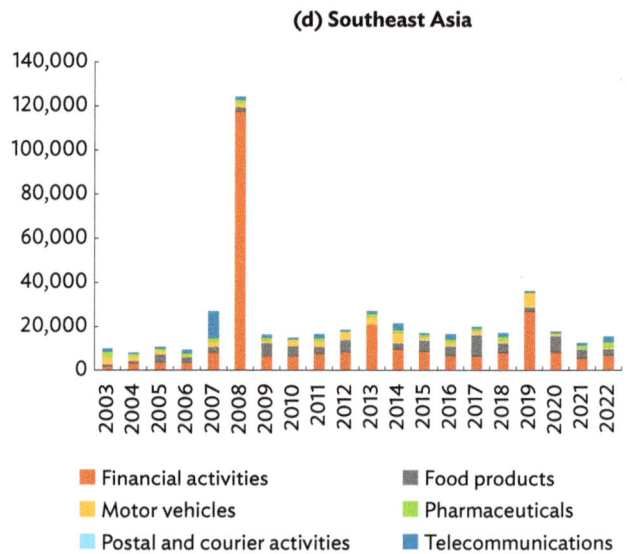

Legend:
- Financial activities
- Food products
- Motor vehicles
- Pharmaceuticals
- Postal and courier activities
- Telecommunications

(e) Oceania

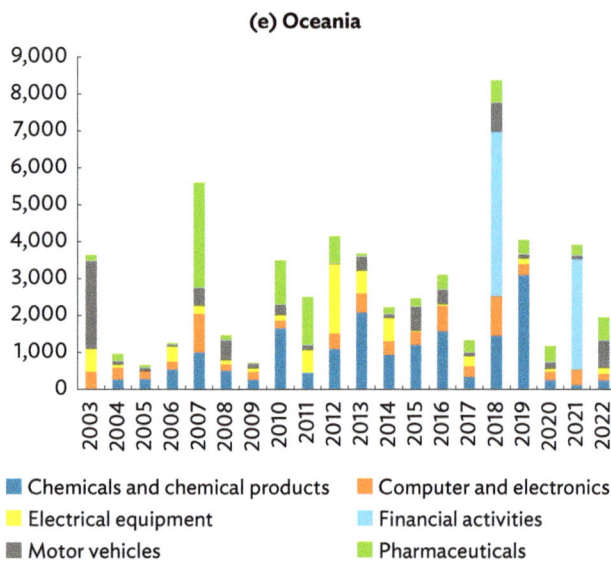

Legend:
- Chemicals and chemical products
- Computer and electronics
- Electrical equipment
- Financial activities
- Motor vehicles
- Pharmaceuticals

nec = not elsewhere classified.

Sources: ADB calculations using data from Bureau van Dijk. Zephyr M&A Database; Financial Times. fDi Markets (both accessed April 2023); and classification based on Organisation for Economic Co-operation and Development. AMNE Database—Activity of Multinational Enterprises. https://www.oecd.org/sti/ind/amne.htm (accessed September 2023).

4 Financial Integration

Opportunities and Risks of Financial Integration

Integration Has Made the Region More Vulnerable to Global Financial Shocks

Financial integration of economies in Asia and the Pacific has deepened significantly in recent decades, both within the region and outward globally.[20] A 34% increase in cross-border assets and 22% increase in liabilities as shares of regional gross domestic product (GDP) over 2010–2022 reflects the region's financial openness and the effectiveness of numerous policy initiatives to build more integrated capital markets. Progress in cross-border financial integration further attests to significant gains in harnessing the opportunities of financial openness, notably access to foreign capital in support of the region's development priorities, knowledge transfers aiding the development of regional capital markets, and risk sharing. In line with rising wealth, greater integration with international financial markets allows Asia's investors to better diversify risks.

Advances in financial integration bestow many benefits such as access to foreign capital to supplement domestic investment, consumption smoothing, and improved finance sector competitiveness. However, financial integration also makes the region more prone to external shocks, which increases the volatility of capital flows.

Large inflows and their sudden reversals entail significant risks such as sizable exchange rate movements and finance sector imbalances. Various policy initiatives such as the Asian Bond Market Initiative in support of local currency bond issuance strengthened regional economies' resilience to external shocks (Kim et al. 2023; Park, Shin, and Tian 2018). Nevertheless, the region remains vulnerable. This chapter focuses in particular on vulnerabilities arising from the region's dependence on external funding denominated in United States (US) dollars.

Global financial conditions remained tight in 2023, raising financial stability risks.

Advanced economy central banks aggressively tightened monetary policy in 2022 (Figure 4.1). The increase in the US policy rate was the steepest rate hiking cycle since the early 1980s, with restrictive monetary policy mirrored in the euro area, the United Kingdom (UK), and emerging markets. The significant tightening raised recession concerns given that a decade of low borrowing costs may have weakened balance sheets' resilience to financial stress. Financial conditions started to ease in the second half of 2022 as US monetary policy became less hawkish on account of slowing US inflation. This improvement continued in the first half of 2023, initially buoyed by the reopening of the People's Republic of China (PRC) after its pandemic lockdowns. The collapse of US regional banks and the globally systemically important bank Credit Suisse led to financial turmoil in the first quarter of 2023,

---

[20] Asia and the Pacific, or Asia, refers to the 49 regional members of the Asian Development Bank (ADB), which includes Japan and Oceania (Australia and New Zealand) in addition to 46 developing Asian economies. Subregional compositions for Central Asia, East Asia, the Pacific and Oceania, South Asia, and Southeast Asia are outlined in ADB. Asia Regional Integration Center. Economy Groupings. https://aric.adb.org/integrationindicators/groupings.

Figure 4.1: Monetary Policy Rates and Inflation—Selected Advanced Economies (%)

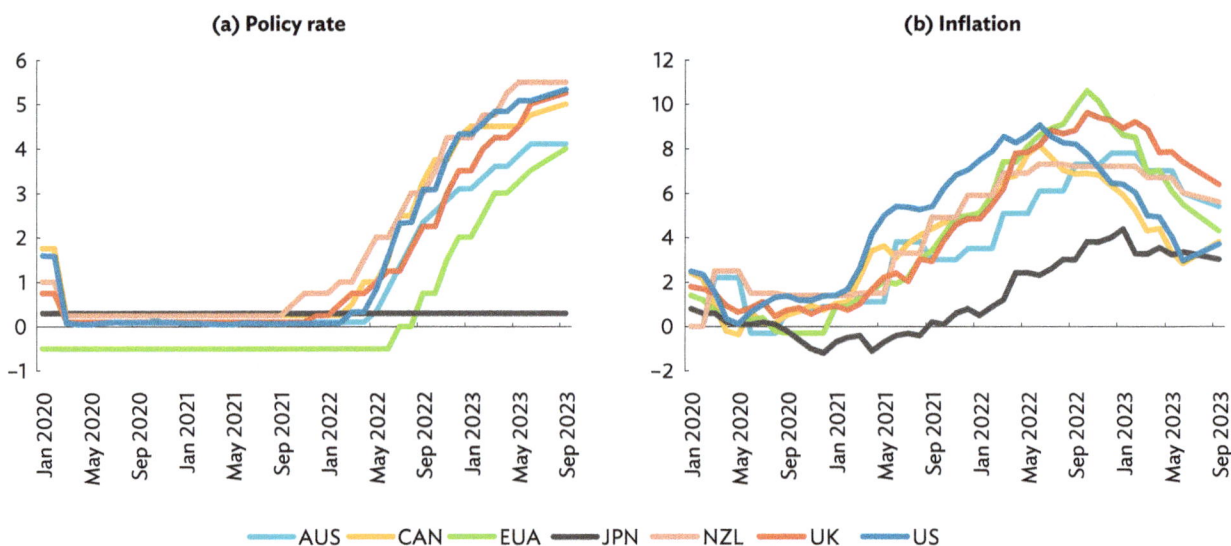

AUS = Australia, CAN = Canada, EUA = Euro area, JPN = Japan, NZL = New Zealand, UK = United Kingdom, US = United States.

Note: Inflation refers to the year-on-year change of the consumer price index.

Source: CEIC Data Company.

though it was quickly contained by decisive regulatory action. Global financial conditions are expected to remain tight and uncertainty high given the risk of financial stress from high interest rates for longer, potential negative spillovers from the PRC's growth slowdown, the continued Russian invasion of Ukraine, and geopolitical tensions.

Nonresident capital flows to Asia experienced significant outflows in 2022, with only partial recovery in the first half of 2023.

The abrupt advanced economy monetary policy tightening and associated unwinding of carry trades, as well as the PRC's growth slowdown due to its zero-COVID (coronavirus disease) policy, resulted in a reversal of capital inflows in the second half of 2022 (Figure 4.2). Capital inflows started to return gradually in 2023 as the slowing pace of US interest rate rises led investor sentiment to improve, with India, Japan, and the PRC's reopening leading the recovery, although the PRC's subsequent growth slowdown decelerated the recovery. As global financial conditions remain restrictive and uncertainty high, capital inflows are still below their pre-pandemic average and remain vulnerable to

renewed global financial stress triggering capital flow reversals from Asia.

Portfolio investment and other investment flows contributed most to the recovery of capital flows in 2023, accounting for around two-thirds of inflows into the region. As these capital flow types have been shown to be the most sensitive to global financial conditions (Eichengreen, Gupta, and Masetti 2018; Levy Yeyati and Zúñiga 2015), the region remains prone to capital flow reversals should global financial stress suddenly intensify. Foreign direct investment (FDI) is considered a less volatile source of inflows and accounted for one-third of inflows into the region (Figure 4.3).

Asset markets in Asia show signs of a moderate, but varied recovery relative to the end of 2022.

Following a broad-based depreciation of regional currencies against the US dollar following the 2022 US monetary policy tightening, regional local currencies only partially recovered against the US dollar from their trough in the second quarter of 2022 (Figure 4.4a).

Figure 4.2: Nonresident Capital Flows—Selected Asian Economies ($ billion)

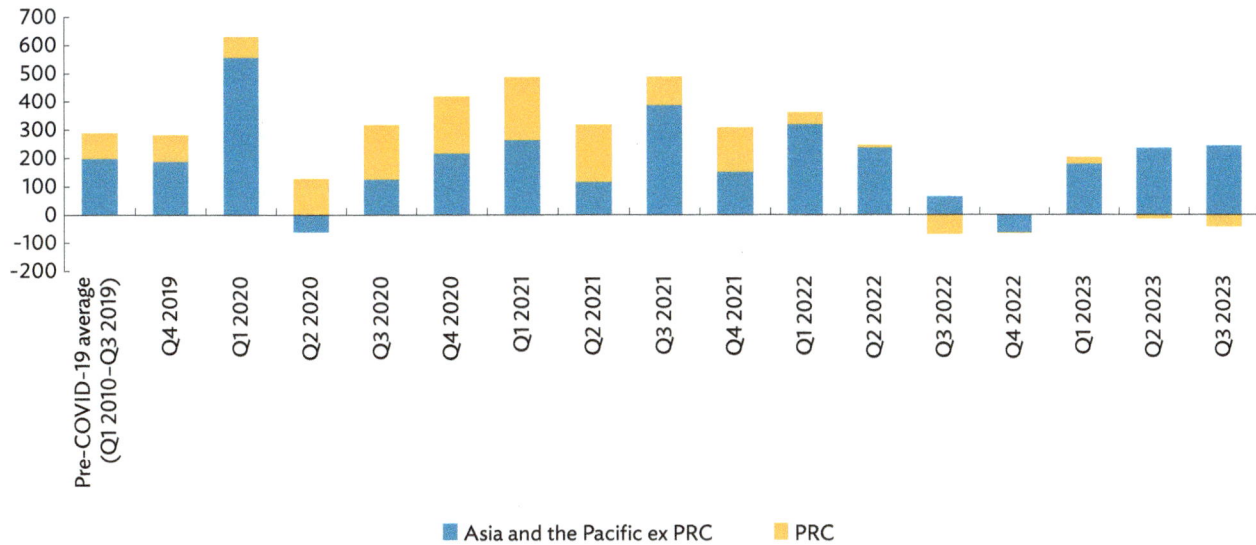

COVID-19 = coronavirus disease, PRC = People's Republic of China, Q = quarter.

Notes:
(i)   Nonresident net capital flows in the third quarter of 2022 amounted to $4 billion.
(ii) Positive values denote inflows, negative values denote outflows.
(iii) Selected Asian economies include Armenia; Azerbaijan; Bangladesh; Cambodia; Fiji; Georgia; Hong Kong, China; India; Indonesia; Japan; Kazakhstan; Malaysia; Pakistan; the PRC; the Philippines; the Republic of Korea; Samoa; Tajikistan; Taipei,China; Thailand; and Uzbekistan.

Source: ADB calculations using data from the International Monetary Fund. Balance of Payments and International Investment Position Statistics. Accessed from CEIC Data Company.

Figure 4.3: Nonresident Capital Flows by Type—Selected Asian Economies (% of total)

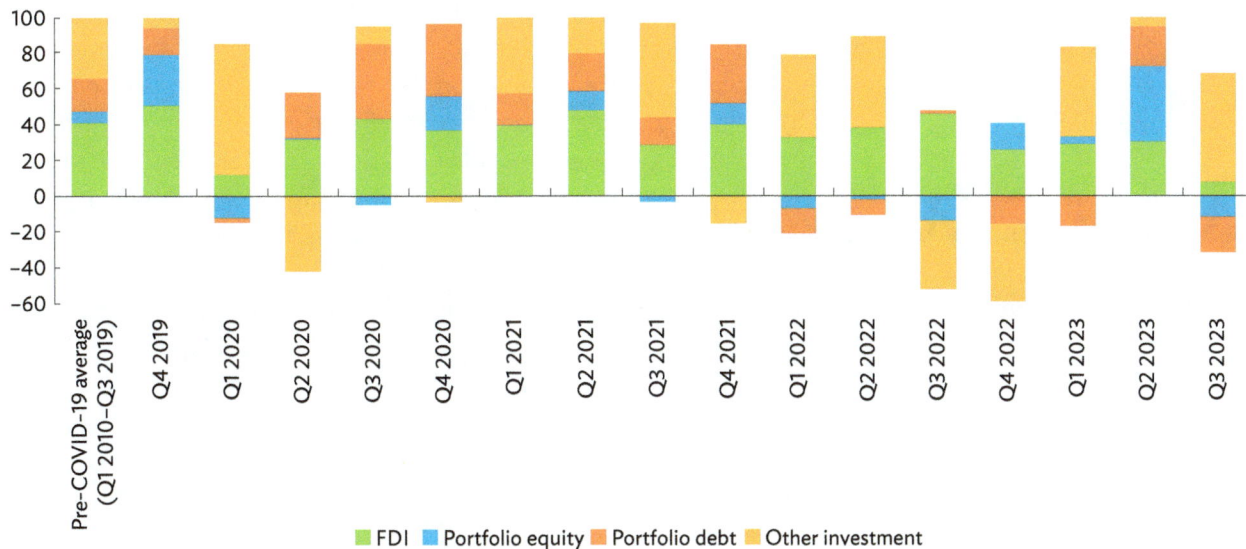

COVID-19 = coronavirus disease, FDI = foreign direct investment, Q = quarter.

Notes:
(i)   Selected Asian economies include Armenia; Azerbaijan; Bangladesh; Cambodia; Fiji; Georgia; Hong Kong, China; India; Indonesia; Japan; Kazakhstan; Malaysia; Pakistan; the People's Republic of China; the Philippines; the Republic of Korea; Samoa; Tajikistan; Taipei,China; Thailand; and Uzbekistan.
(ii) The "Other investment" category includes currency and deposits; insurance, pension, and standardized guaranteed schemes; loans; other accounts payable; other equity; special drawing rights; and trade credit and advances.

Source: ADB calculations using data from the International Monetary Fund. Balance of Payments and International Investment Position Statistics. Accessed from CEIC Data Company.

Figure 4.4: Year-to-Date Change—Selected Asian Economies (%, as of 18 December 2023)

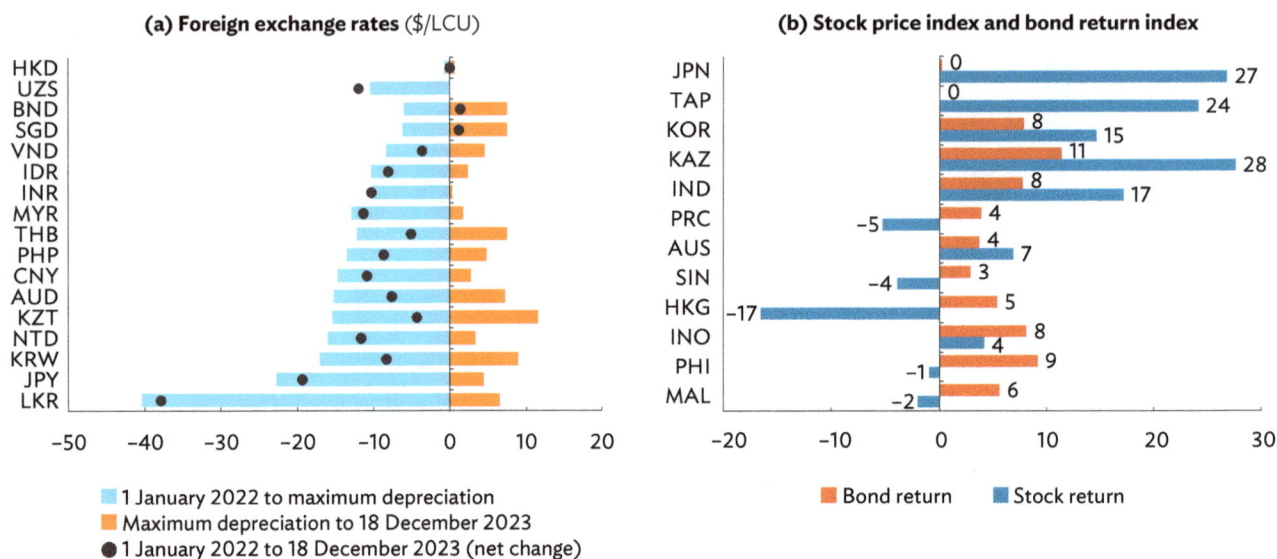

(a) Foreign exchange rates ($/LCU)

Legend:
- 1 January 2022 to maximum depreciation
- Maximum depreciation to 18 December 2023
- 1 January 2022 to 18 December 2023 (net change)

(b) Stock price index and bond return index

Legend:
- Bond return
- Stock return

AUD = Australian dollar; AUS = Australia; BND = Brunei Darussalam dollar; CNY = yuan; HKD = Hong Kong dollar; HKG = Hong Kong, China; IDR = Indonesian rupiah; IND = India; INO = Indonesia; INR = Indian rupee; JPN = Japan; JPY = Japanese yen; KAZ = Kazakhstan; KOR = Republic of Korea; KRW = Korean won; KZT = Kazakhstani tenge; LCU = local currency unit; LKR = Sri Lanka rupee; MAL = Malaysia; MYR = Malaysian ringgit; NTD = NT dollar; PHI = Philippines; PHP = Philippine peso; PRC = People's Republic of China; SGD = Singapore dollar; SIN = Singapore; SRI = Sri Lanka; TAP = Taipei,China; THA = Thailand; THB = Thai baht; UZB = Uzbekistan; UZS = Uzbekistani som; VIE = Viet Nam; VND = Vietnamese dong.

Note: The point in time at which local currencies reach maximum depreciation in Figure 4.4a is specific to each economy.

Source: Bloomberg L.P.

The still restrictive monetary policy stance in advanced economies is a key reason for the partial recovery (Figure 4.1a). Equity and bond markets in the region performed unevenly through most of 2023. Advanced Asian economies led the recovery (Figure 4.4b).

Asia's Financial Markets Are Increasingly Driven by Global Factors

Equity and bond markets are more sensitive to global than regional factors, indicating vulnerability to global financial shocks (Figure 4.5). The impact of global factors is particularly pronounced in crisis periods such as the onset of the coronavirus disease (COVID-19) pandemic. While equity markets are on average more exposed to global factors, bond markets have become more sensitive to global factors since 2021.

Asia's increased cross-border assets and liabilities imply heightened exposure to global shocks.

Asia's cross-border assets increased by 16 percentage points in 2014–2022, expressed as share of regional

GDP, but declined in 2020–2022 in line with the crises of the pandemic, the Russian invasion of Ukraine, and monetary policy tightening in advanced economies. Over the same period, Asian investors retrenched more from investments outside the region than from intraregional investments, leading intraregional shares to rise slightly for portfolio debt from 21% to 23%, and for equity from 21% to 22%. Meanwhile, shares for FDI remained stable at 51% (Figure 4.6). However, over 2014–2022, the intraregional share remained broadly unchanged across all of Asia's cross-border investment types.

The region's exposure to global shocks also increased on the liability side. Total cross-border liabilities in terms of regional GDP increased by about 5 percentage points over 2014–2022 while the intraregional share increased from 17% to 22% for portfolio equity liabilities, from 43% to 45% for bank liabilities, and from 29% to 30% for portfolio debt liabilities (Figure 4.7). Extraregional investors primarily from the European Union (EU) and the US account for Asia's increased borrowing (Figures 4.9 and 4.10).

Figure 4.5: Variance Decomposition of Equity and Bond Returns (%)

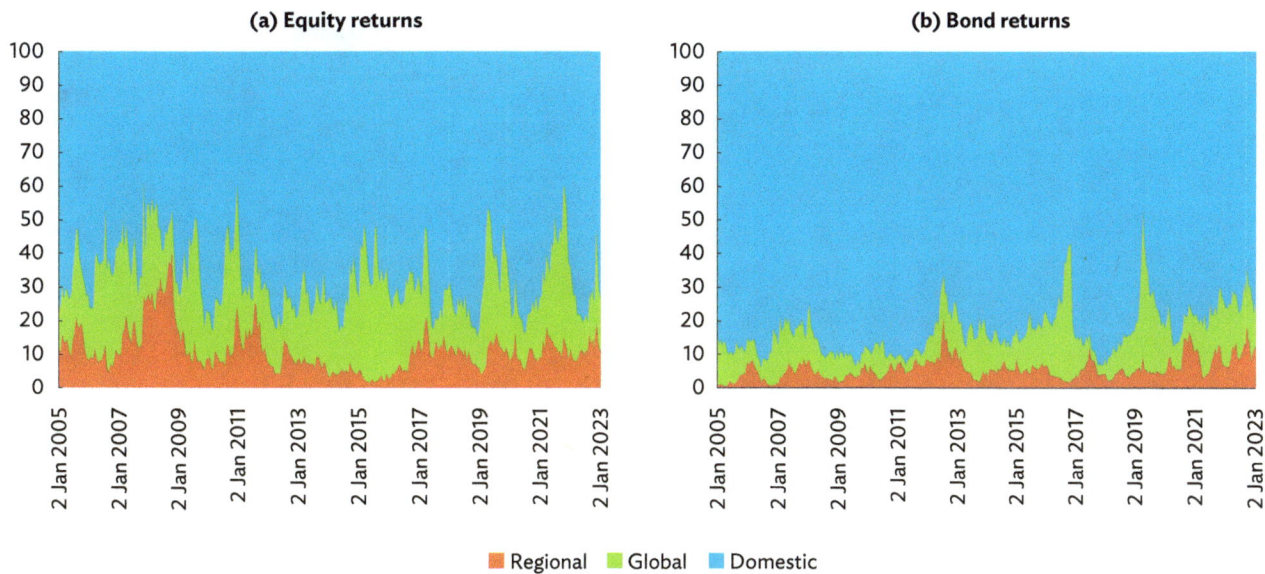

(a) Equity returns

(b) Bond returns

■ Regional ■ Global ■ Domestic

Notes: Asia includes Australia; Bangladesh (equities only); Cambodia (equities only); Georgia (equities only); Hong Kong, China; India; Indonesia; Japan; Kazakhstan; the Kyrgyz Republic (equities only); the Lao People's Democratic Republic (equities only); Malaysia; Mongolia (equities only); Nepal (equities only); New Zealand (equities only); Pakistan (equities only); the People's Republic of China; the Philippines; the Republic of Korea; Singapore; Sri Lanka (equities only); Taipei,China; Thailand; Uzbekistan (equities only); and Viet Nam.

Sources: ADB calculations using data from Bloomberg L.P.; CEIC Data Company; and methodology by Lee and Park (2011) using 1-year rolling window estimations.

Figure 4.6: Cross-Border Assets—Asia and the Pacific, by Type

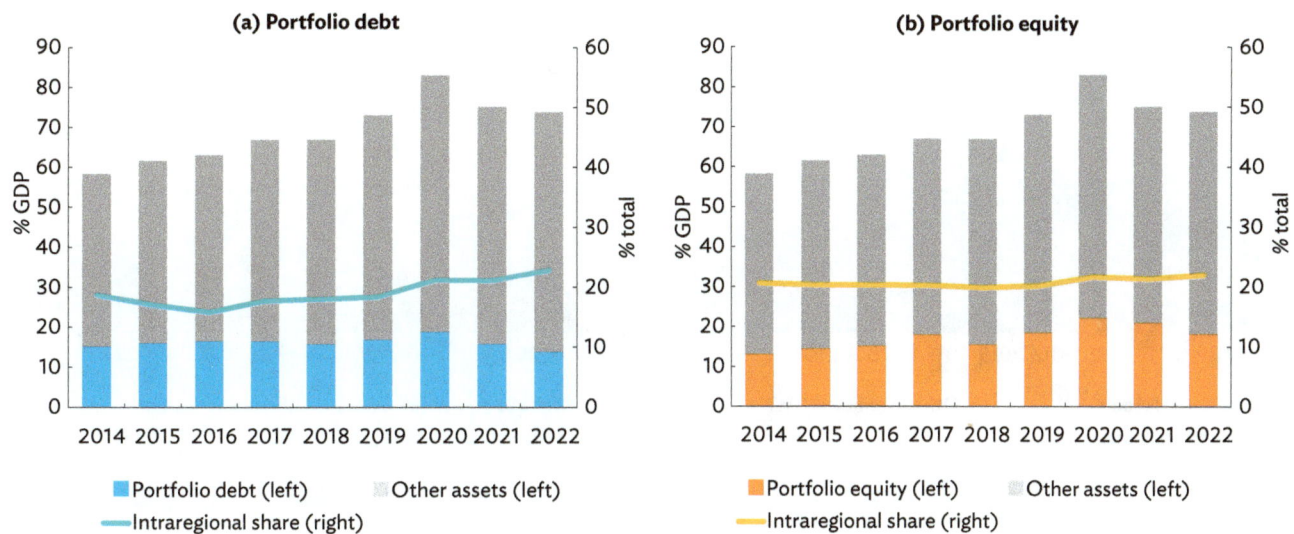

(a) Portfolio debt

(b) Portfolio equity

■ Portfolio debt (left)   ■ Other assets (left)
— Intraregional share (right)

■ Portfolio equity (left)   ■ Other assets (left)
— Intraregional share (right)

continued on next page

Figure 4.6 continued

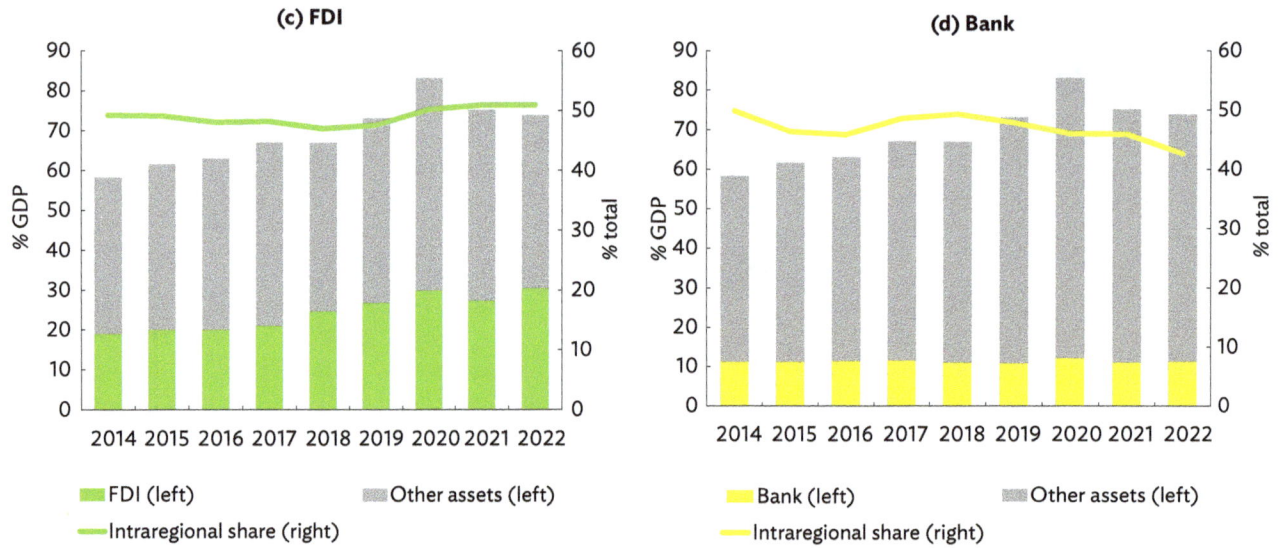

(c) FDI

(d) Bank

FDI = foreign direct investment, GDP = gross domestic product.

Notes: Estimates are as of the end of 2022 for bank, portfolio equity, and FDI. FDI assets refer to outward FDI holdings. Bank assets (claims) are limited to loans and deposits. Asia and the Pacific includes ADB regional members for which data are available.

Sources: ADB calculations using data from Bank for International Settlements. Locational Banking Statistics. https://stats.bis.org/statx/toc/LBS.html (accessed April 2023); International Monetary Fund (IMF). Coordinated Portfolio Investment Survey. https://data.imf.org/cpis (accessed September 2023); and IMF. Coordinated Direct Investment Survey. https://data.imf.org/cdis (accessed December 2022).

Figure 4.7: Cross-Border Liabilities—Asia and the Pacific, by Type

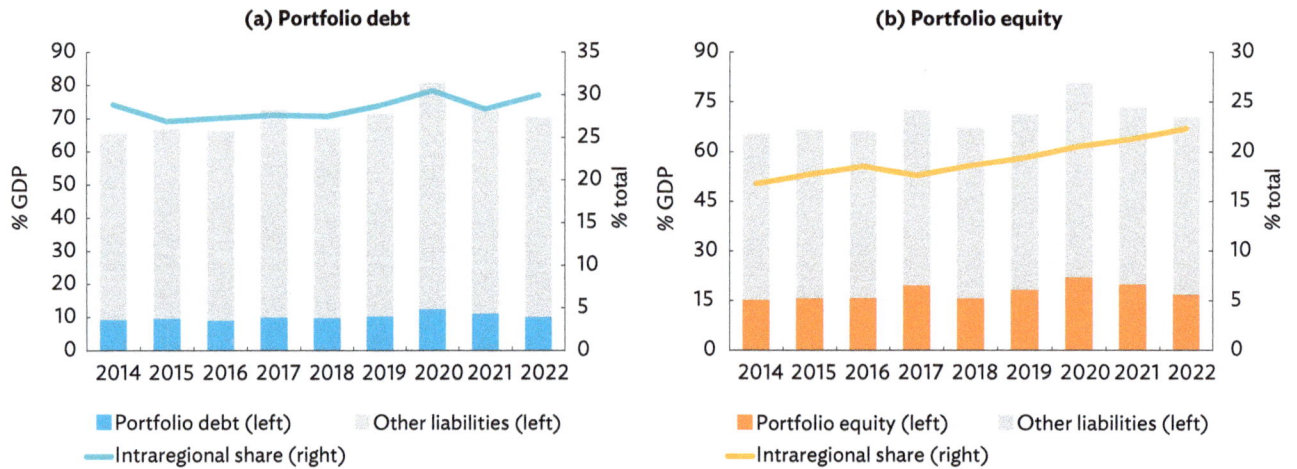

(a) Portfolio debt

(b) Portfolio equity

continued on next page

Figure 4.7 continued

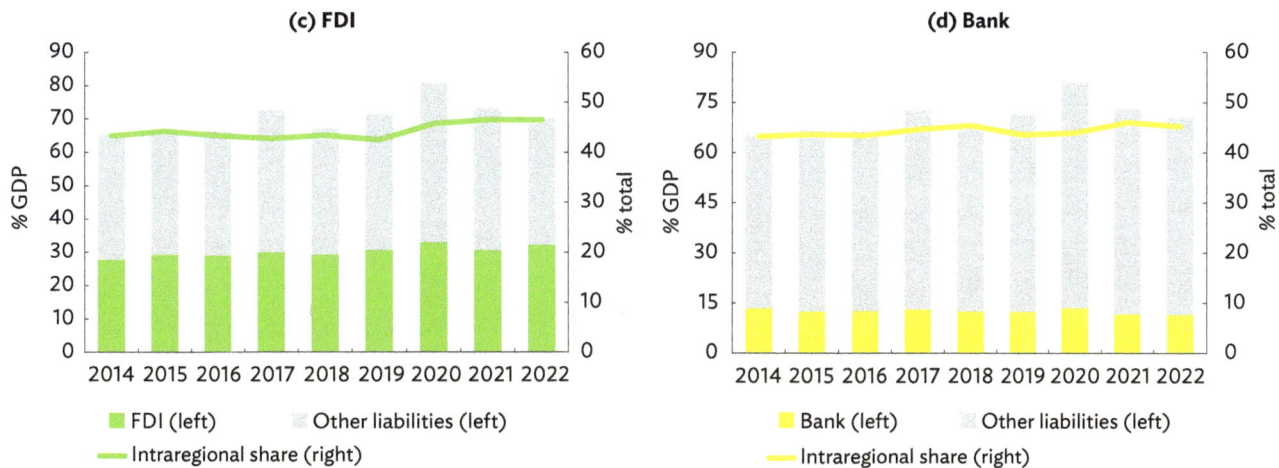

(c) FDI

FDI (left)   Other liabilities (left)
Intraregional share (right)

(d) Bank

Bank (left)   Other liabilities (left)
Intraregional share (right)

FDI = foreign direct investment, GDP = gross domestic product.

Notes: Estimates are as of the end of 2022 for bank, portfolio equity, and FDI. Bank liabilities are limited to loans and deposits. Asia and the Pacific includes ADB regional members for which data are available.

Sources: ADB calculations using data from Bank for International Settlements. Locational Banking Statistics. https://stats.bis.org/statx/toc/LBS.html (accessed April 2023); International Monetary Fund (IMF). Coordinated Portfolio Investment Survey. https://data.imf.org/cpis (accessed September 2023); and IMF. Coordinated Direct Investment Survey. https://data.imf.org/cdis (accessed December 2022).

Figure 4.8: Cross-Border Investment—Asia and the Pacific, by Type (% to total)

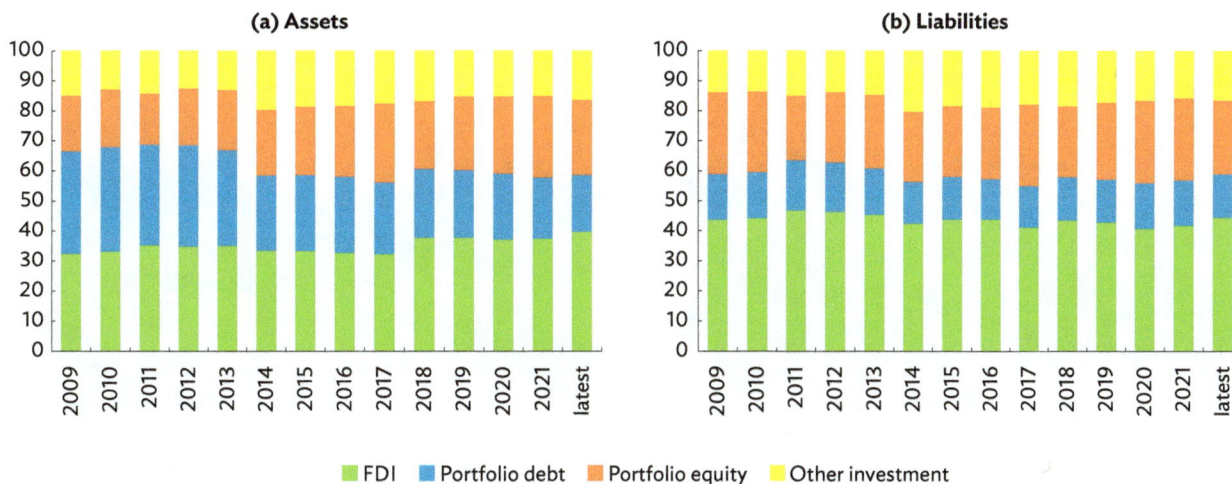

(a) Assets

(b) Liabilities

FDI   Portfolio debt   Portfolio equity   Other investment

FDI = foreign direct investment.

Notes: Estimates are as of the end of 2022 for bank, portfolio debt, and portfolio equity; and as of 2021 for FDI. FDI assets refer to outward FDI holdings. Bank assets (claims) are limited to loans and deposits. FDI liabilities refer to inward FDI holdings. Bank liabilities are limited to loans and deposits. Asia and the Pacific includes ADB regional members for which data are available.

Sources: ADB calculations using data from Bank for International Settlements. Locational Banking Statistics. https://stats.bis.org/statx/toc/LBS.html (accessed April 2023); International Monetary Fund (IMF). Coordinated Portfolio Investment Survey. https://data.imf.org/cpis (accessed September 2023); and IMF. Coordinated Direct Investment Survey. https://data.imf.org/cdis (accessed December 2022).

Whereas Asian investors have tended to allocate larger shares of foreign assets into FDI, mostly at the expense of equity portfolio investments, portfolio and bank claims still dominate investment portfolios, which exposes the region to asset repricing in foreign markets. The share of FDI investments grew from one-third of assets in 2009 to two-fifths in 2022 (Figure 4.8a). Similarly, Asia's liabilities depend on volatile sources, further exposing the region to external shocks. Since 2009, portfolio liabilities and bank liabilities have accounted for more than half of external investment in the region (Figure 4.8b).

The US and the EU are the largest extraregional investors in Asia, and thus likely sources of external shocks.

The US and the EU combined account for about two-fifths of Asia's inward portfolio debt investment, with some regional economies remaining significantly exposed (Figure 4.9). For instance, debt investment from the EU in Mongolia and Singapore account for about 10% of recipient economies' GDP. Thus, Asia is particularly vulnerable to economic and financial shocks from the US and the EU. Important financial centers like Singapore and Hong Kong, China maintain significant links across Asia, potentially transmitting shocks from the US and the EU.

The US and the EU were also the largest portfolio equity investors in the region, accounting for about half of total portfolio equity investment in Asia (Figure 4.10). Some regional economies display pronounced exposures: Hong Kong, China and Taipei,China received inward equity investments from the US worth about one-third of their respective GDP. The figure stands at about three-twentieths for Singapore. The Republic of Korea joined these three economies in being significantly exposed to the EU. In 2022, EU portfolio equity investments reached about 25% of destination economy GDP in Hong Kong, China; about 17% in Taipei,China; and about 10% in Singapore.

Figure 4.9: Inward Portfolio Debt Investment from Top 10 Sources (% of destination economy GDP)

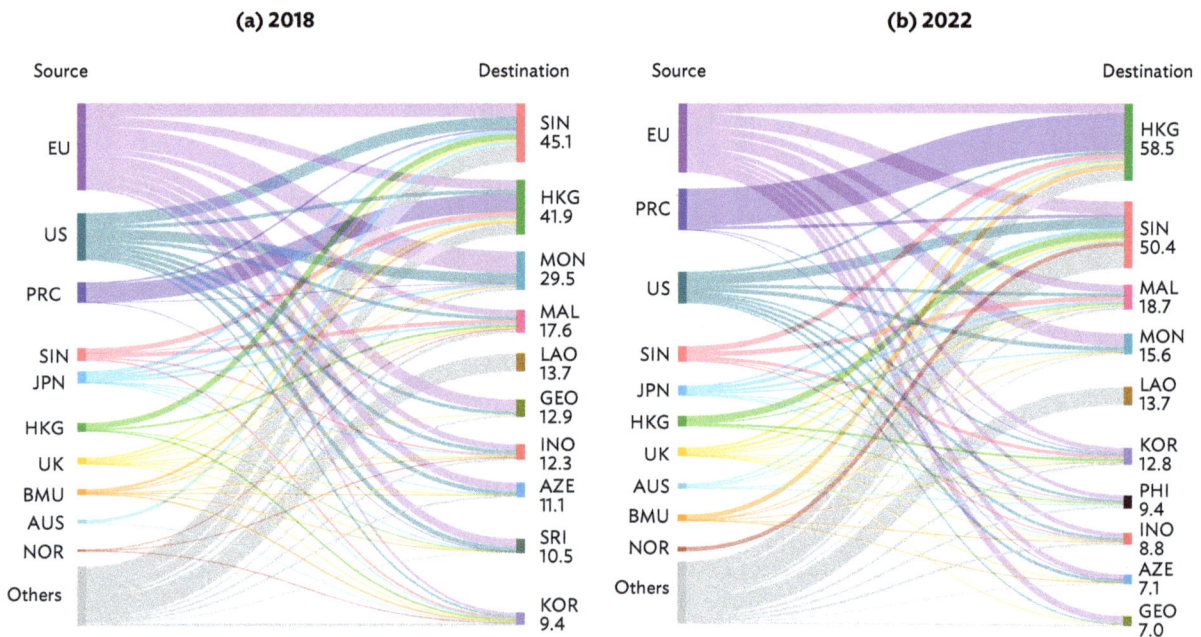

AUS = Australia; AZE = Azerbaijan; BMU = Bermuda; EU = European Union (27 members); GDP = gross domestic product; GEO = Georgia; HKG = Hong Kong, China; INO = Indonesia; JPN = Japan; KOR = Republic of Korea; LAO = Lao People's Democratic Republic; MAL = Malaysia; MON = Mongolia; NOR = Norway; PHI = Philippines; PRC = People's Republic of China; SIN = Singapore; SRI = Sri Lanka; UK = United Kingdom; US = United States.

Source: International Monetary Fund. Coordinated Portfolio Investment Survey. https://data.imf.org/cpis (accessed September 2023).

Figure 4.10: Inward Portfolio Equity Investment from Top 10 Sources (% of destination economy GDP)

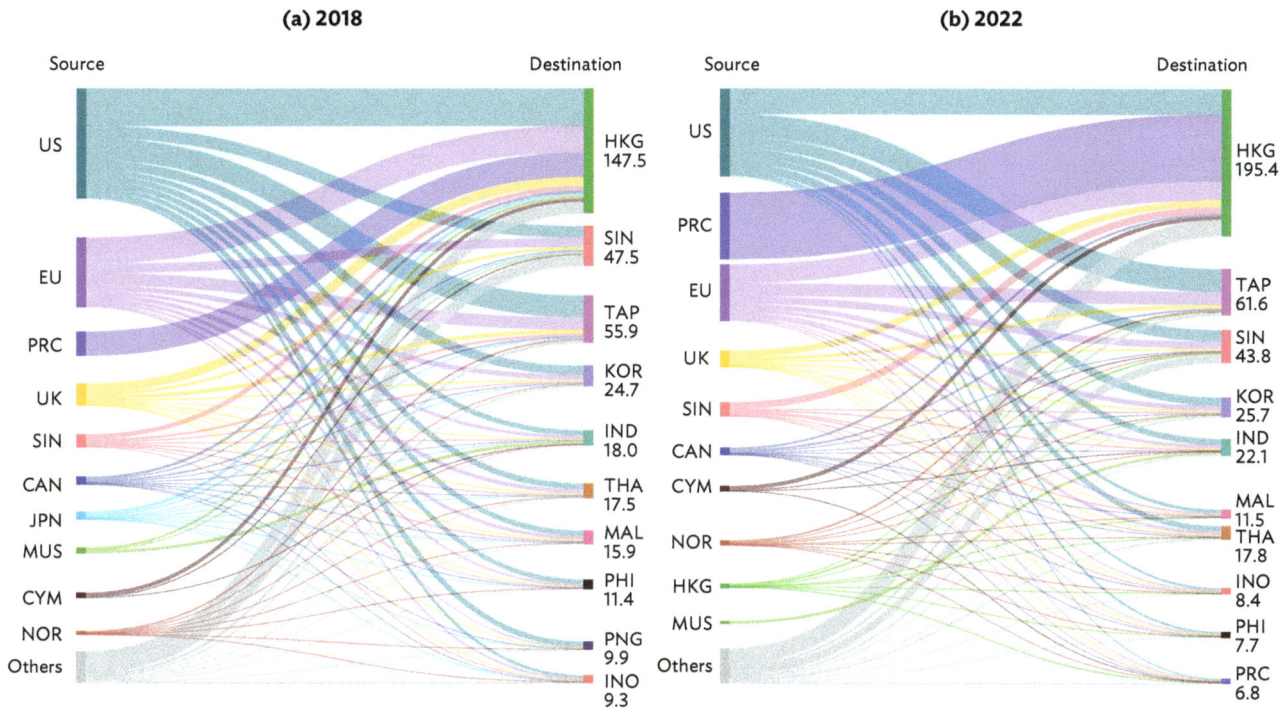

(a) 2018

(b) 2022

CAN = Canada; CYM = Cayman Islands; EU = European Union (27 members); GDP = gross domestic product; HKG = Hong Kong, China; IND = India; INO = Indonesia; JPN = Japan; KOR = Republic of Korea; MAL = Malaysia; MUS = Mauritius; NOR = Norway; PHI = Philippines; PNG = Papua New Guinea; PRC = People's Republic of China; SIN = Singapore; TAP = Taipei,China; THA = Thailand; UK = United Kingdom; US = United States.

Source: International Monetary Fund. Coordinated Portfolio Investment Survey. https://data.imf.org/cpis (accessed September 2023).

Drivers of Capital Flow Volatility in Asia

A Significant Rise in US Dollar Funding Costs Hit Global Financial Conditions in 2023

The previous section illustrated Asia's rising global financial integration. Consequently, the region is significantly exposed to spillovers from advanced economies, notably the US financial system. Together with global risk aversion, global liquidity, and commodity prices, US monetary policy and the US dollar exchange rate are key drivers of capital flows (BIS 2021a; Koepke 2019). Capital flows to Asia experienced significant volatility during US monetary policy tightening episodes like the 2013 taper tantrum and 2022 rate hiking cycle and declined sharply during US dollar funding stress episodes as exacerbated by rising trade tensions in 2019 and the COVID-19 pandemic (Figure 4.11).

With financial conditions tight amid elevated uncertainty and rising geoeconomic tensions, financial market turmoil in the US triggered global risk-off market moves in 2023. During such periods, the US dollar tends to appreciate against a broad basket of currencies, signaling increased demand for safe US dollar-denominated assets (Figure 4.11). This so-called broad US dollar exchange rate is a key gauge of global investor sentiment and reflects the US dollar as the ultimate safe asset as well as its pervasive role in trade finance and global payment systems (Avdjiev et al. 2017). This section highlights the key US dollar funding shocks exerting capital outflow pressure on Asia in 2023.

Recent aggressive US monetary policy tightening triggered large capital outflows from Asia.

Advanced economy central banks significantly raised monetary policy rates in 2022, likely to remain at historically high levels. Consequently, global investor

Figure 4.11: Aggregate Capital Inflows Timeline—Asia and the Pacific

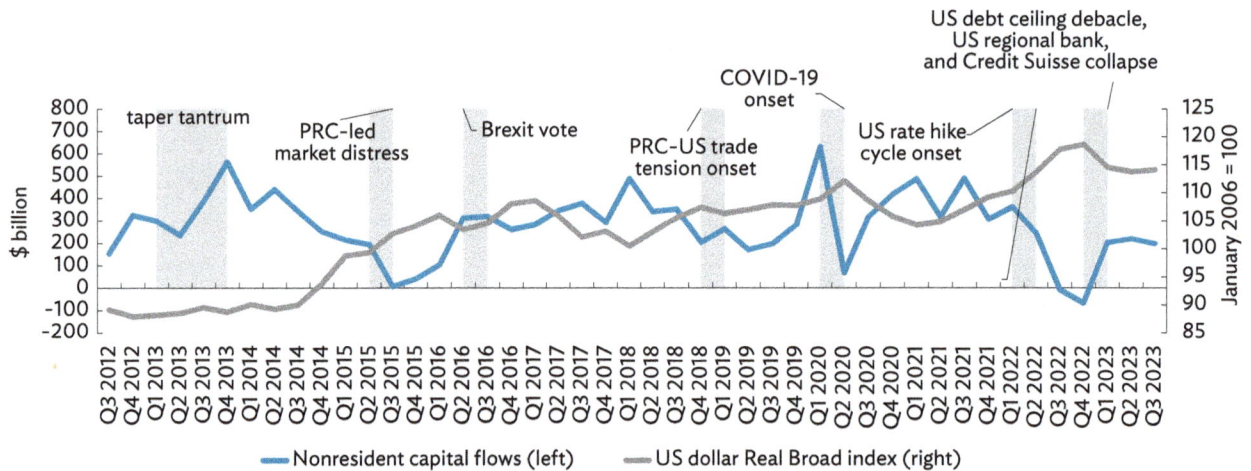

COVID-19 = coronavirus disease, PRC = People's Republic of China, Q = quarter, US = United States.

Note: The US dollar Real Broad index denotes the trade-weighted real effective US dollar exchange rate against a broad basket of 26 currencies.

Source: ADB calculations using data from CEIC Data Company.

Figure 4.12: Policy Rate Differential with the US Policy Rate—Selected Asian Economies (percentage points, as of July 2023)

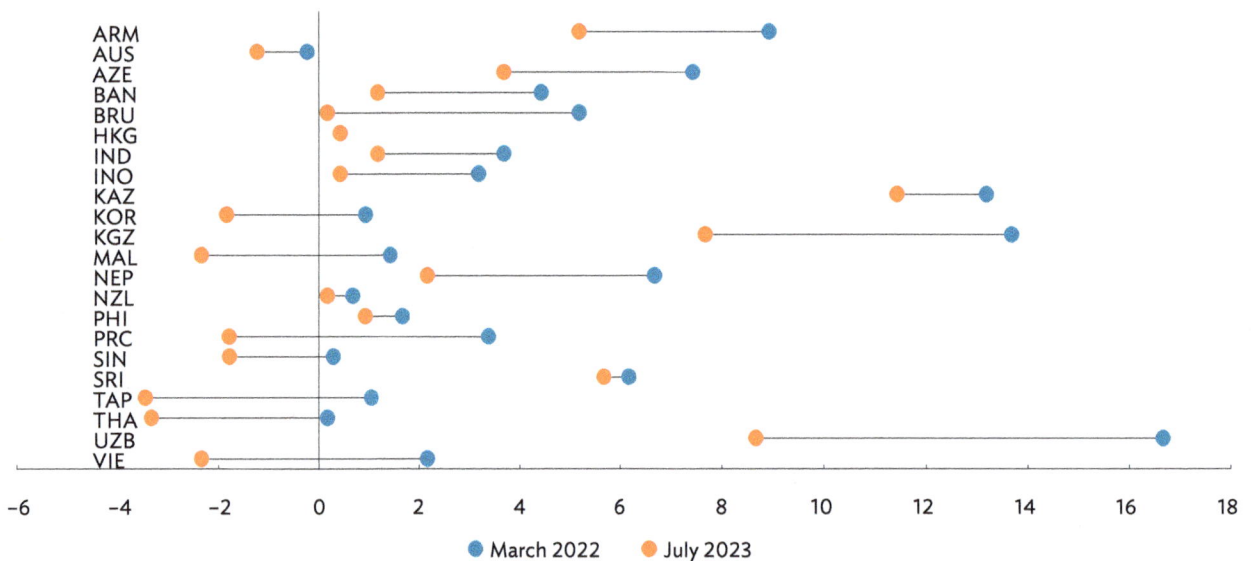

ARM = Armenia; AUS = Australia; AZE = Azerbaijan; BAN = Bangladesh; BRU = Brunei Darussalam; HKG = Hong Kong, China; IND = India; INO = Indonesia; KAZ = Kazakhstan; KOR = Republic of Korea; KGZ = Kyrgyz Republic; MAL = Malaysia; NEP = Nepal; NZL = New Zealand; PHI = Philippines; PRC = People's Republic of China; SIN = Singapore; SRI = Sri Lanka; TAP = Taipei,China; THA = Thailand; US = United States; UZB = Uzbekistan; VIE = Viet Nam.

Source: CEIC Data Company.

sentiment darkened and may decline further as the increase in borrowing costs raised the risk of financial stress. The US policy rate increases led to a narrowing of interest rate differentials between Asian economies and the US, triggering an unwinding of carry-trades and capital flow reversals from the region (Figures 4.11 and 4.12). While capital flows to Asia have partly recovered since late 2022 as discussed above, the recent rate hiking cycle underlines the US monetary policy as a key driver of capital flow volatility in the region.

Shifts in the geopolitical world order amplify capital flow volatility.

Trade tensions between the US and the PRC and the Russian invasion of Ukraine fostered fragmentation of the post-war geopolitical order across political, economic, financial, and technological spheres. The precedence of strategic competition and national security concerns over economic efficiency risks stalling global trade and investment as Asia's decades-long engine of growth. The number of economies introducing or expanding frictions to FDI such as investment screening related to national security concerns has nearly doubled since the onset of US–PRC trade tensions in 2019 (Figure 4.13). Continued geoeconomic fragmentation is also likely to harm trade through heightened uncertainty (Aiyar et al. 2023). The Russian invasion of Ukraine saw global uncertainty reach levels last seen during heightened US–PRC trade tensions in 2019 (Figure 4.14).

Spikes in trade tensions have been shown to increase capital flow volatility, as global investors reallocate portfolios and reduce cross-border credit (IMF 2023). This reversal of capital flows may increase borrowing costs in Asia and undermine financial stability through sudden corrections in asset prices. Moreover, borrowing costs may also rise because further geoeconomic fragmentation may raise demand for the US dollar as a safe asset, driving its price yet higher.

Figure 4.13: Number of Economies Introducing National Security-Related Investment Screening

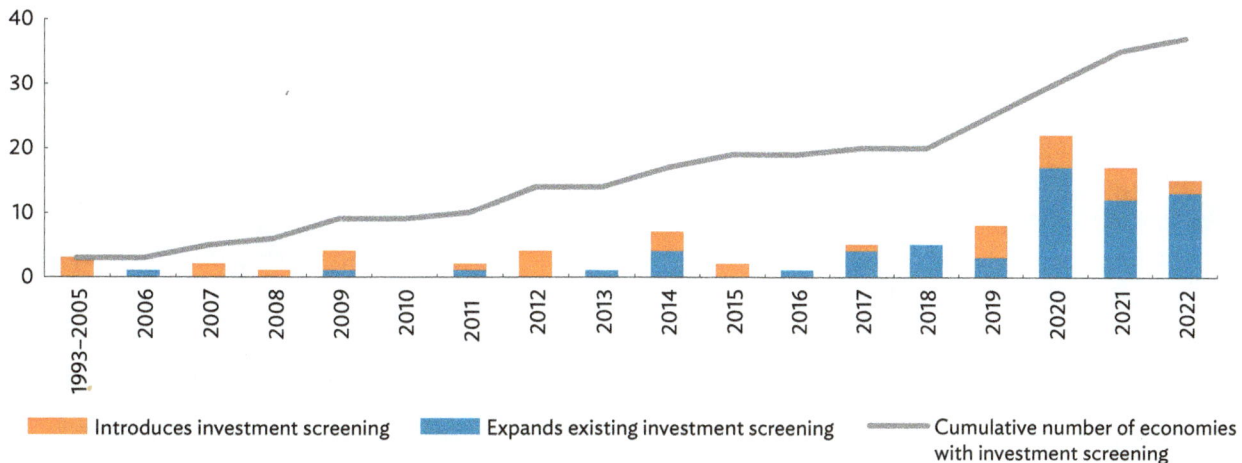

■ Introduces investment screening   ■ Expands existing investment screening   — Cumulative number of economies with investment screening

Source: UNCTAD (2023).

Figure 4.14: Global Uncertainty Measure—Asia and the Pacific (index)

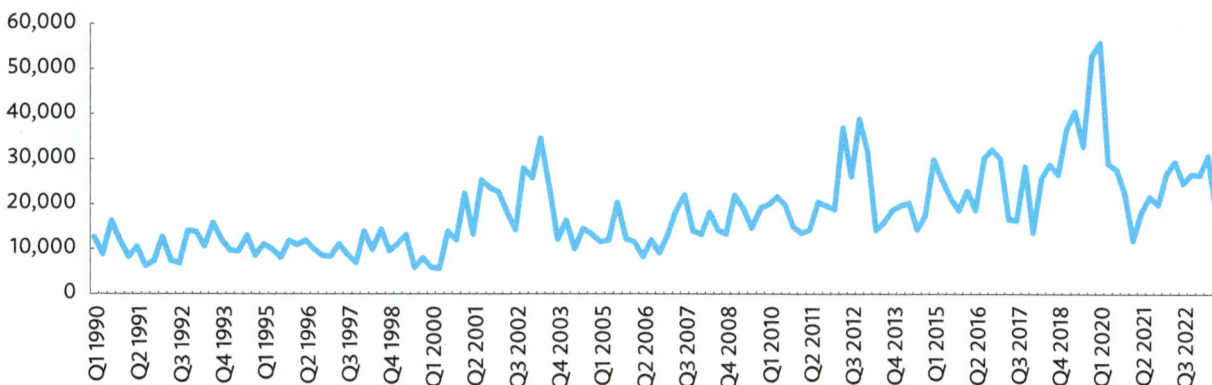

Q = quarter.

Notes: The World Uncertainty Index (WUI) is computed by counting the percentage that the word "uncertain" (or its variant) occurs in Economist Intelligence Unit (EIU) economy reports. The WUI is then rescaled by multiplying by 1,000,000. A higher number means higher uncertainty and vice versa. For example, an index of 200 corresponds to the word uncertainty accounting for 0.02% of all words, which—given the EIU reports are on average about 10,000 words long—means about two words per report.

Source: ADB calculations using data from Ahir, Bloom, and Furceri (2022).

Spillovers of US financial market gyrations add to Asia's capital flow volatility.

March 2023 bank runs caused the failure of two US regional banks, Silicon Valley Bank and Signature Bank of New York. Subsequent selling pressure on other US banks with similarly runnable assets forced the mid-sized First Republic Bank to be placed in receivership. The commensurate decline in market sentiment reverberated across the Atlantic leading to the collapse of Zurich-based Credit Suisse.

While the decisive action of regulators prevented a broader meltdown of global financial markets, the ensuing financial stress caused US dollar funding costs to rise globally (IMF 2023). This highlights that Asia remains vulnerable to US financial turmoil triggering sudden stops of capital flows, further accelerated by the rise of digital cross-border payment systems.

A near US default on federal debt in June 2023 highlighted the fragility of US dollar funding for Asia.

In January 2023, the US federal debt limit prevented the federal government from issuing debt and thus US dollar-denominated safe assets underpinning global financial stability. Uncertainty about the debt limit's political resolution saw US credit default swaps—a financial instrument protecting investors against a US sovereign default—rise to levels higher than during similar US debt ceiling discussions in 2011 (Figure 4.15).

While a default was narrowly averted, uncertainty lingers over the political process to resolve future debt limit debates. Coupled with declining US fiscal capacity to backstop US dollar-denominated debt, the episode led the rating agency Fitch to downgrade US debt in August 2023, the second downgrade after Standard & Poor's rating cut in 2011. A prospective US government shutdown in September 2023 further highlighted uncertainty about the process of US fiscal policymaking, leading the third big rating agency, Moody's, to issue a negative credit warning, later adding a negative outlook to the US credit rating. Volatility in short-term US dollar funding markets shot up in the wake of the debt debacle as markets expected an increased US debt issuance to replenish the US Treasury's cash buffers (BIS 2023). Such bouts of volatility in Asian financial institutions' core funding market suggests continued vulnerability to US dollar funding shocks.

Figure 4.15: US Dollar 1-Year Euro Credit Default Swap—United States (basis points)

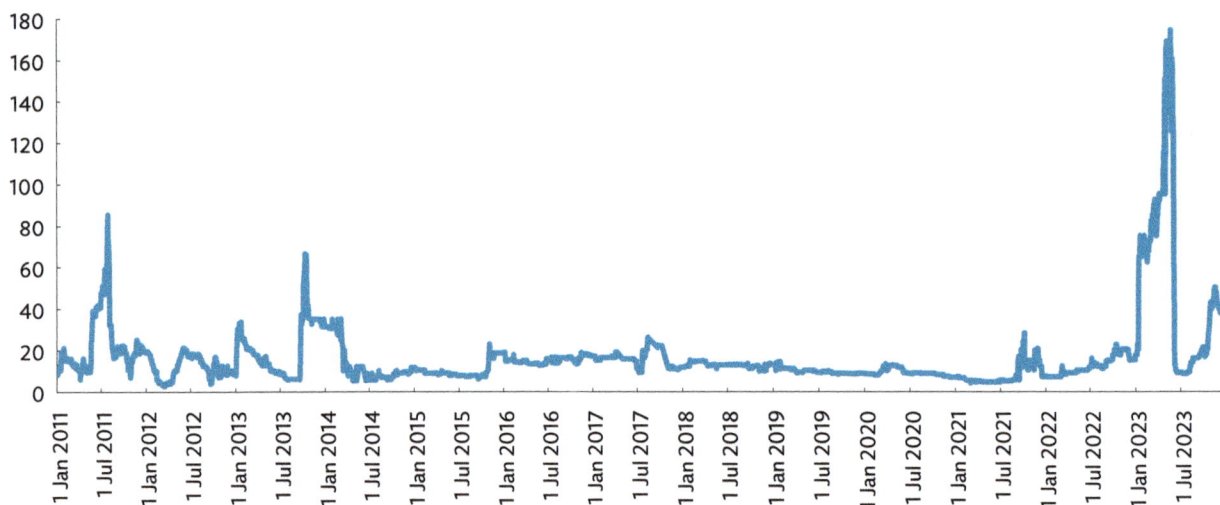

Source: Investing.com. https://www.investing.com/rates-bonds/united-states-cds-1-year-eur-historical-data (accessed 22 September 2023).

Risks of Entrenched US Dollar Dependence

Asia Is Prone to US Dollar Funding Shocks Due to High US Dollar Dependence

Asian economies are highly exposed to the US dollar, the globally dominant reserve currency over the past 60 years. The US dollar's central role fostered Asia's integration in global value chains, helping the region reap a growth dividend from globalization. On the flipside, high US dollar dependence injects a range of macrofinancial fragilities into the region. This section portrays stylized facts of US dollar dominance in Asia, and outlines its negative macroeconomic and financial repercussions for the region.

Most of Asian economies' trade is invoiced in US dollars, even when excluding the US as trading partner. Globally, one-third of exports and close to half of imports are invoiced in US dollars (Annex 4a, panels a and b). This contrasts with over four-fifths of exports and imports in Asia, with only Latin America and in part the Middle East posting higher US dollar invoicing shares (Annex 4b, panel a). The US dollar invoicing share in Asia stood between close to three and four times higher than the world average for exports over the past 2 decades, and about two times higher for imports, highlighting the outsized role of the US dollar for trade in Asia (Annex 4a, panels a and b). For both export and import trade invoicing, the US dollar is as important in Asia as the euro is in the euro area, where the euro is the common currency. This implies that the US dollar's role in Asia is akin to a common trade currency (Annex 4a, panels c and d).

Asian banks' balance sheets are skewed strongly toward the US dollar. As most of Asia's trade is invoiced in US dollars, bank trade financing for the region reflects the US dollar's heft. Coupled with demand from Asian investors for safe US dollar-denominated assets and banks' reliance on the depth and breadth of US dollar funding markets for short-term wholesale finance, Asian banks' balance sheets also strongly reflect use

of the US dollar. Globally, about two-fifths of banks' international assets and liabilities are denominated in US dollars (Annex 4a, panel e). In Asia, the share stands even higher at 55% in 2022, rising from 51% in 2001, and higher than in Africa and Europe (Annex 4b, panel b).

The US dollar constitutes the preferred currency for external debt issuances in Asia, accounting for about half of outstanding debt liabilities (Annex 4a, panel f). Only Latin America and North America excluding the US have a higher propensity to issue debt in US dollars (Annex 4b, panel c). Similarly, the US dollar plays a larger role in Asia for total external liabilities, with its share standing at 20% in Asia compared to 15% globally (Annex 4a, panel g). The US dollar has been the preferred currency for Asia's external debt issuances since at least 2010.

The US dollar remains the dominant store of value not only globally, but also in Asia. Two-thirds of disclosed official foreign exchange reserves in Asia are denominated in US dollars (Annex 4a, panel h). In line with Asian economies' buildup of self-insurance, this share increased from about half of total reserves at the time of the Asian financial crisis in the late 1990s. This contrasts with a decline of the US dollar's share in currency reserves globally from 71% in 2000 to 59% in 2023 (Annex 4a, panel h). The drop at the global level reflects central bank reserve managers' portfolio diversification (Arslanalp, Eichengreen, and Simpson-Bel 2022). Latest data suggest that US sanctions of the Russian Federation did not trigger a broad-based reallocation of reserves.

The US dollar is the key reference point for exchange rates of Asian economies. In line with the US dollar's historical role as anchor of the international monetary system, the US dollar serves as exchange rate anchor either exclusively or as part of a currency basket for 62 economies globally, of which 18 in Asia represent about one-fifth of global GDP including the PRC, and about 2% of global GDP if the PRC is excluded from that calculation (Annex 4a, panel i). This compares to 3.6% of world GDP for the Middle East, 1.5% for Latin America, and 0.4% for Africa. The use of the US dollar as anchor currency has increased over the past 2 decades, with economies using the US dollar as anchor, accounting for about one-quarter of world GDP (Ilzetzki, Reinhart, and Rogoff 2019). Moreover, the US dollar is the main reference point for crypto assets, as almost all stable coins are linked to the US dollar (Bertaut, von Beschwitz, and Curcuru 2023).

As a means of exchange, the US dollar ranks first in payments. Two-fifths of global payments are denominated in US dollars, followed by about one-third in euros, and the pound sterling accounting for less than 10% and the yen less than 5% (Annex 4a, panel j). The US dollar's share in global payments has increased by 10 percentage points over the past decade, largely at the expense of the euro and other smaller currencies. The US dollar's payments footprint in Asia could rise yet more if a US dollar-backed digital currency were to become widely used for payments in Asia.

The US dollar has the largest footprint in international currency trading. Reflecting US dollar liquidity needs for trade and cross-border finance as well as debt issuance, the US dollar takes the lead in international currency trading and was bought or sold in 44% of all international currency trades in 2022 (Annex 4a, panel k). Despite significant technological advances in international currency trading benefiting the trade of more currency pairs, the US dollar's share remained unchanged over the past 2 decades.

US dollar dominance could aggravate macroeconomic and financial fragilities in Asia.

The International Monetary and Financial System's high concentration in a handful of reserve currencies with the US dollar at its pinnacle led to global imbalances, excess capital flows, and liquidity shortages around the world, making the world dependent on the US Federal Reserve to act as lender of last resort. These repercussions are particularly pronounced in Asia given the region's high US dollar dependence, as evidenced repeatedly by excessive capital flow volatility during global financial stress. A large body of literature documents the drawbacks of US dollar dominance for developing economies, including in Asia.

A stronger US dollar reduces dollar-denominated cross-border capital flows and ultimately investment and GDP growth in recipient economies (Avdjiev et al. 2017, 2018; Di Giovanni and Rogers 2023; Hofmann, Shim, and Shin 2022). Export activity also falls (Hofmann and Park 2020). The subsequent decline in global economic activity affects the US economy relatively less, reinforcing the US dollar's appreciation and the negative repercussions of its rise (Akinci et al. 2022). Emerging Asia is particularly susceptible to declines in cross-border lending since such economies have limited ability to turn to other sources of US dollar borrowing, as few benefit from direct swap lines with the US Federal Reserve (Barajas et al. 2019).

The US dollar exchange rate is now a key conduit for US dollar funding conditions to Asia. Declines in cross-border credit growth and trade arise through the so-called "financial channel" of the exchange rate: a stronger US dollar lowers the US dollar value of local currency-denominated collateral of non-US borrowers, resulting in lower cross-border credit provision (Bruno and Shin 2015). Further, exports decline as a US dollar appreciation raises the cost of working capital of exporting firms (Bruno and Shin 2023). This financial channel of US dollar appreciations dominates the traditional "trade competitiveness channel" (Lee et al. 2021). The latter would suggest that a US dollar appreciation and commensurate local currency depreciation raises exports. The financial channel of the US dollar exchange rate compounds the effect of the "trade-invoicing channel," suggesting that an appreciation of the US dollar predicts a decline of global trade (Boz et al. 2020; Gopinath et al. 2020). This effect is increasing in the share of imports invoiced in US dollars (Ma, Schmidt-Eisenlohr, and Zhang 2020). In turn, the share of US dollar-denominated trade invoicing correlates positively with economies' participation in global value chains (GVCs) because of the strategic complementarity between price setting and integration in GVCs (Georgiadis et al. 2021; Mercado, Jacildo, and Basu Das 2023).

US dollar dominance in trade invoicing lowered Asia's resilience to external shocks, as flexible exchange rate regimes came to function less well as shock absorber

(Adler et al. 2020; Casas, Meleshchuk, and Timmer 2022). For instance, for a commodity-importing economy faced with rising commodity prices, a flexible exchange rate regime traditionally implies that a subsequent depreciation of the exchange rate automatically rebalances the external position. Under US dollar dominance in trade invoicing, such rebalancing requires large exchange rate adjustments. These may come with significant negative repercussions for fiscal and financial stability, especially given high US dollar-denominated debt.

Increased financial, nonfinancial corporate and sovereign stress may result from US dollar dominance. A US dollar appreciation can push firms in emerging markets with US dollar debt financing local currency assets into distress (Bruno and Shin 2018). Previously loose US dollar funding conditions incentivized firms to issue foreign-currency denominated bonds, increasing exchange rate mismatches and thus financial stability risks (Bacchetta, Cordonier, and Merrouche 2023). Rollover risks in currency hedges of Asian investors investing in US dollar-denominated assets abroad further fuel financial stability risks (McGuire et al. 2021). A US dollar appreciation also raises sovereign bond spreads, even for local currency sovereign bonds (Hofmann, Shim, and Shin 2017; Lee et al. 2021).

A high reliance on US dollar funding raises financial market stress. The COVID-19 induced US dollar funding squeeze sharply raised funding costs, capital outflows, and local currency depreciations, further aggravated by the pronounced US dollar funding dependence of globally active banks headquartered in high-income Asian economies (Pande and del Rosario 2020; Park, Rosenkranz, and Tayag 2020). This US dollar funding shortage highlighted the region's dependence on central bank swap lines offered by the US Federal Reserve. Global non-US banks' dependence on US dollar funding may also amplify the region-wide decline in asset prices when US dollar funding becomes more expensive (Ehlers, Hoffmann, and Raabe 2020).

US Dollar Dependence Puts Capital Flows at Risk

Capital inflows bring much-needed funding for investments, but can reverse quickly in response to factors unrelated to the recipient economy. Such reversals often destabilize the economy as a result of sudden asset price and growth declines (Calvo 1998; Forbes and Warnock 2012). As discussed above, US dollar funding shocks were a key driver of recent capital flow volatility. Asia relies heavily on the US dollar, and is thus particularly exposed to related shocks. This section presents empirical evidence how Asia's US dollar dependence culminates in heightened risk of capital flow reversals.

Capital flows to Asia tend to reverse in response to US dollar funding shocks.

An empirical analysis for a broad sample of developing economies and emerging markets in Asia shows that a one standard deviation increase in US dollar funding costs lowers medium-term portfolio debt flows into the region as a share of GDP by 0.2% to 0.25% and raises outflows by the same magnitude (Figure 4.16). US dollar funding costs are measured by the US short-term monetary policy rate known as federal funds rate, and by the US dollar Real Broad index measuring the trade-weighted real effective US dollar exchange rate against a broad basket of currencies. Other global factors commonly identified by the literature as global drivers of capital flows—notably global liquidity and investor sentiment—exert a smaller and statistically less significant effect on capital inflows. This emphasizes the US dollar's central role as predictor of capital flow reversals.

Dollar dependence amplifies capital flow reversals driven by US dollar funding shocks.

The analysis further reveals that the effect of more expensive US dollar funding costs on capital flows is increasing in economies' dependence on US dollar funding. The latter is defined as the need to refinance US dollar-denominated debt, measured by an economy's share of US dollar-denominated international debt.

Figure 4.16: Regression Coefficients of Capital Inflow Determinants

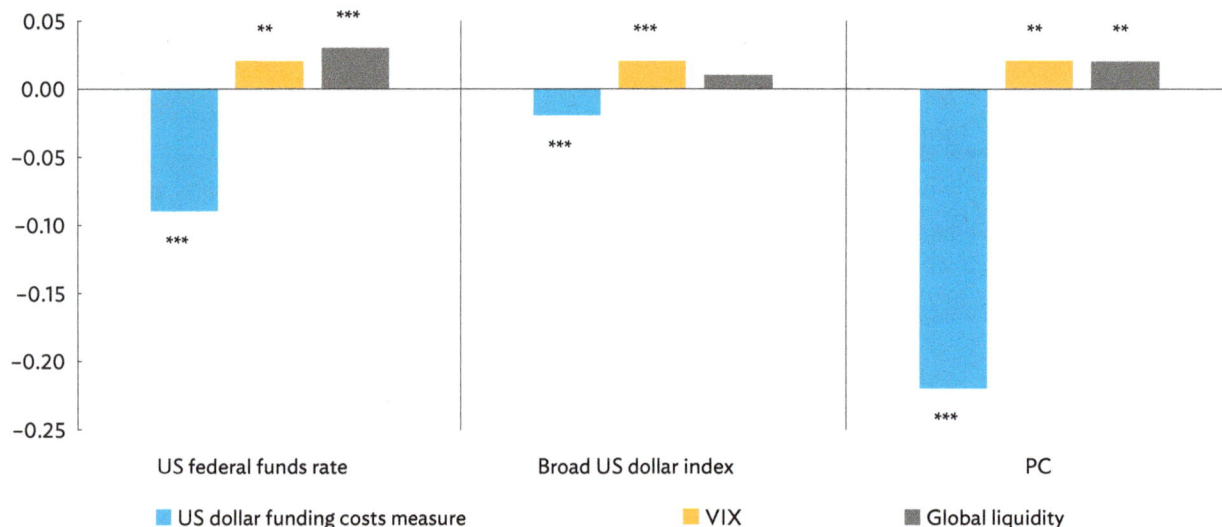

PC = first principal component of the US federal funds rate and the US dollar Real Broad index, US = United States, VIX = volatility index. Stars denote statistical significance levels: *** at 1%, ** at 5%, and * at 10%.

Note: See Box 4.1 for technical details.

Sources: ADB calculations using data from Bank for International Settlements (BIS). Global Liquidity Indicators. https://data.bis.org/topics/GLI; BIS. Effective Exchange Rate Indices. https://www.bis.org/statistics/eer.htm (both accessed August 2023); Bloomberg L.P.; and Haver Analytics.

The importance of US dollar dependence can be rationalized as follows: increased foreign funding costs weaken economies' debt sustainability, lowering their creditworthiness. Foreign creditors' lending capacity is also known to decline as funding costs increase, and a US dollar appreciation lowers the foreign credit to emerging market borrowers (Bruno and Shin 2015). Thus, rising US dollar funding costs are conjectured to reduce capital inflows more for economies with higher US dollar-denominated debt.

The results indicate that for a given level of US dollar funding costs measured by either the federal funds rate or the US dollar Real Broad index, an economy with a one standard deviation higher US dollar dependence experiences 0.05% to 0.3% lower capital inflows in addition to the direct effect of rising US dollar funding costs, and analogously, higher outflows by the same magnitude (Figure 4.17).

The response of capital flows to US dollar funding shocks varies by capital flow type and time horizon. Given a rise in US dollar funding costs, capital flow reversals due to higher US dollar dependence are most pronounced for portfolio debt and other investments. Higher US dollar dependence combined with an increase in US dollar funding costs can provoke portfolio debt outflows in both the short and long term. This effect rises over time, as the long-term effect is one-third larger than the short-term effect, suggesting that the effect of US dollar dependence takes time to become apparent. Results for a similar analysis using the effective US federal funds rate as a measure for dollar funding costs confirms US dollar dependence as a powerful vector in the international transmission of US dollar funding conditions (Annex 4c).

Figure 4.17: Regression Coefficients—International Debt Share and US Dollar Funding Costs

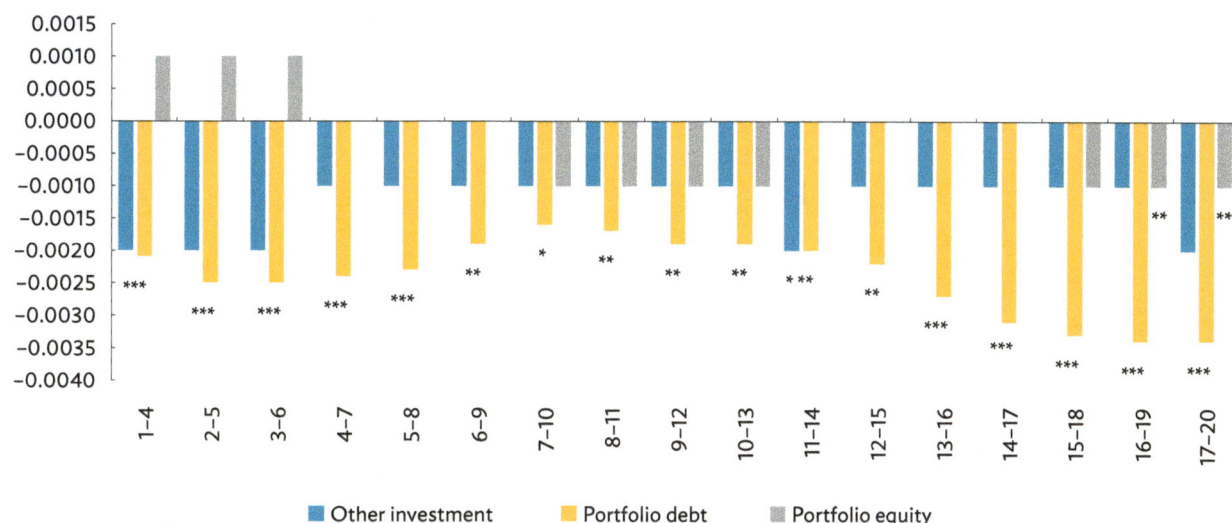

US = United States. X-axis shows 4-quarter long periods ahead. Stars denote significance levels: *** at 1%, ** at 5%, and * at 10%.

Note: See Box 4.1 for technical details.

Sources: ADB calculations using data from Bank for International Settlements (BIS). Global Liquidity Indicators. https://data.bis.org/topics/GLI; BIS. Effective Exchange Rate Indices. https://www.bis.org/statistics/eer.htm (both accessed August 2023); Bloomberg L.P.; and Haver Analytics.

Box 4.1: Methodological Note on the Determinants of Capital Inflows

This chapter discusses how the high dependence of Asia and the Pacific on the US dollar amplifies the risk of capital flow reversals from the region.

First, the chapter discusses how an increase in US dollar funding costs lowers medium-term portfolio debt flows into the region. The related evidence shown in Figure 4.16 relies on fixed effect panel regressions of capital inflows on US dollar funding costs, other global factors, and domestic economic conditions for a broad sample of developing and emerging market economies in Asia and the Pacific. The dependent variable is the 4-quarter average of gross portfolio debt inflows to individual economies scaled by gross domestic product (GDP) between 5 and 8 quarters ahead. US dollar funding costs are measured by (i) the effective US federal funds rate, (ii) the trade-weighted US real effective exchange rate against a broad basket of currencies (US dollar Real Broad index), and (iii) the first principal component of (i) and (ii). Other global factors comprise the S&P500 volatility index (VIX) and global liquidity measured by total international banks' claims on all sectors as scaled by global GDP. Domestic economic conditions include GDP per capita and the domestic monetary policy rate.

Second, this chapter shows that the effect of more expensive US dollar funding costs on capital flows is increasing in economies' dependence on US dollar funding. The results portrayed in Figure 4.17 are based on panel regressions of capital inflows on US dollar funding costs interacted with US dollar dependence and domestic economic conditions for a broad sample of emerging markets in Asia using economy and time fixed effects. The dependent variables are the 4-quarter average of capital inflows to individual economies scaled by GDP rolling forward over quarters 1 to 17 ahead, where capital inflows denote (i) portfolio debt inflows, (ii) portfolio equity inflows, or other investment inflows. US dollar funding costs are measured by (i) the effective US federal funds rate, and (ii) the trade-weighted US real effective exchange rate against a broad basket of currencies (US dollar Real Broad index). US dollar dependence corresponds to the share of US dollar-denominated international debt. Domestic economic conditions include GDP per capita, real GDP growth, the differential between the US and domestic monetary policy rate, a measure of capital account openness, and the ratio of external debt to foreign currency reserves. Results for the interaction between the international debt share and the federal funds rate as a measure of US dollar funding costs are available in Annex 4c.

Source: ADB.

Policy Options Can Mitigate Risks from US Dollar Exposure

Various policies aimed at lowering US dollar dependence may help prevent and mitigate its negative repercussions for capital flow volatility and financial stability.

First, it is important to strengthen the Asian banks' balance sheet resilience to US dollar funding shocks. Asian banks largely obtain US dollar funding through foreign exchange swap markets and indirectly through cross-border banking networks. These US dollar funding channels proved fragile during past global financial stress periods (Park, Rosenkranz, and Tayag 2020). Given the importance of bank-based finance in Asia, it is crucial to improve regulatory oversight of banks' foreign exchange liquidity risks and to broaden currency hedging mechanisms (BIS 2021b).

Second, expanding the depth and breadth of local currency bond markets remains a priority to reduce US dollar dependence. The Asian Bond Markets Initiative of the Association of Southeast Asian Nations Plus Three (ASEAN+3) has helped to significantly increase the issuance of and demand for local currency securities in long maturities, reducing short-term US dollar funding needs. Further efforts are being pursued to facilitate cross-border issuance, trading, and settlements for more integrated regional capital markets (Park 2017). However, local currency bond issuance only partially remedies capital flow reversal risk as a result of the transfer of currency mismatches to international investors (Hofmann, Shim, and Shin 2020). Given a small domestic investor base, regional economies' bond markets came to rely on these international investors. Their typically unhedged local currency bond holdings combined with obligations in their respective home economy currency and foreign currencies like the US dollar makes international investors prone to exchange rate shocks. International investors' losses from local currency depreciations lead to capital outflows further amplifying the depreciation. To avoid capital outflows resulting from such currency mismatches, it is important to broaden the domestic investor base.

Third, carefully calibrated policy interventions may help manage capital flow reversal risk. Sudden capital flow reversals are known to quickly tighten financial conditions, often leading to financial crises while also precipitating growth declines. In a first instance, to stem outflows, and where appropriate, central banks should raise monetary policy rates gradually. As this may give rise to increased financial vulnerabilities, and recognizing that flexible exchange rate regimes do not always fully insulate economies against external shocks, foreign exchange intervention and capital controls can improve policy trade-offs (IMF 2020). While Asian economies have successfully deployed macroprudential policies, capital flow management measures, and foreign exchange interventions, evidence points at the importance of the nature of shocks, economy characteristics, and initial conditions for the policies to be effective (Bergant et al. 2020; Eller et al. 2021; Frost, Ito, and van Stralen 2020; Gelos et al. 2019; Nier, Olafsson, and Rollinson 2020; Rebucci and Ma 2019). Importantly, these policy measures should not substitute for warranted macroeconomic, financial, and structural adjustments (IMF 2020).

Fourth, strengthening regional financial safety nets is imperative. Incorporating the lessons learned from the 1997 Asian financial crisis, the Chiang Mai Initiative Multilateralization's (CMIM) liquidity pool with a lending capacity of $240 billion allows ASEAN+3 economies (Japan, the PRC, and the Republic of Korea) to access liquidity by swapping local currency for US dollars or local currency of the swap provider. The CMIM is complemented by a precautionary credit line. The ASEAN+3 Macroeconomic Research Office (AMRO) supports the CMIM through macroeconomic surveillance and monitoring of CMIM funds, if deployed. Regional defenses against US dollar funding shocks can be strengthened by (i) increasing the CMIM's lending capacity such as through bond issuances backed by paid-in capital, (ii) widening its mandate to include the recapitalization of systematically important banks, and (iii) improving AMRO's surveillance capabilities for a timely and agile crisis response rooted in deep regional expertise.

References

Adler, G., C. Casas, L. Cubeddu, G. Gopinath, N. Li, S. Meleshchuk, C. O. Buitron, et al. 2020. Dominant Currencies and External Adjustment. *IMF Staff Discussion Note*. 2020/005. Washington, DC: International Monetary Fund.

Ahir, H., N. Bloom, and D. Furceri. 2022. The World Uncertainty Index. *NBER Working Paper*. 29763. Cambridge, MA: National Bureau of Economic Research.

Aiyar, S., J. Chen, C. Ebeke, R. Garcia-Saltos, T. Gudmundsson, A. Ilyina, A. Kangur, et al. 2023. Geoeconomic Fragmentation and the Future of Multilateralism. *IMF Staff Discussion Note*. 2023/001. Washington, DC: International Monetary Fund.

Akinci, O., G. Benigno, S. Pelin, and J. Turek. 2022. The Dollar's Imperial Circle. *Federal Reserve Bank of New York Staff Reports*. 1045. New York: Federal Reserve Bank of New York.

Arslanalp, S., B. Eichengreen, and C. Simpson-Bel. 2022. The Stealth Erosion of Dollar Dominance: Active Diversifiers and the Rise of Nontraditional Reserve Currencies. *IMF Working Paper*. WP/22/58. Washington, DC: International Monetary Fund.

Avdjiev, S., W. Du, C. Koch, and H. S. Shin. 2017. The Dollar, Bank Leverage and the Deviation from Covered Interest Parity. *BIS Working Papers*. 592. Basel: Bank for International Settlements.

Avdjiev, S., V. Bruno, C. Koch, and H. S. Shin. 2018. The Dollar Exchange Rate as a Global Risk Factor: Evidence from Investment. *BIS Working Papers*. 695. Basel: Bank for International Settlements.

Bacchetta, P., R. Cordonier, and O. Merrouche. 2023. The Rise in Foreign Currency Bonds: The Role of US Monetary Policy and Capital Controls. *Journal of International Economics*. 140. 103709.

Bergant, K., F. Grigoli, N. Hansen, and D. Sandri. 2020. Dampening Global Financial Shocks: Can Macroprudential Regulation Help (More than Capital Controls)? *IMF Working Paper*. 2020/16. Washington, DC: International Monetary Fund.

Bertaut, C., B. von Beschwitz, and S. Curcuru. 2023. The International Role of the U.S. Dollar. Post-COVID Edition. *FEDS Notes*. Washington, DC: Board of Governors of the Federal Reserve System.

Bank for International Settlements (BIS). 2021a. Changing Patterns of Capital Flows. *CGFS Papers*. 66. Basel.

———. 2021b. *BIS Quarterly Review: International Banking and Financial Market Developments*. Basel.

———. 2023. *BIS Quarterly Review: International Banking and Financial Market Developments*. Basel.

Barajas, A., J. Caparusso, Y. Chen, J. Cutura, A. Deghi, Z. K. Gan, O. Khadarina, et al. 2019. Banks' Dollar Funding: A Source of Financial Vulnerability. In *Global Financial Stability Report: Lower for Longer*. Washington, DC: International Monetary Fund.

Boz, E., C. Casas, G. Georgiadis, G. Gopinath, H. Le Mezo, A. Mehl, M. T. Nguyen. 2020. Patterns in Invoicing Currency in Global Trade. *IMF Working Paper*. 2020/126. Washington, DC: International Monetary Fund.

Bruno, V. and H. S. Shin. 2015. Capital Flows and the Risk-Taking Channel of Monetary Policy. *Journal of Monetary Economics*. 71. pp. 119–32.

———. 2018. Currency Depreciation and Emerging Market Corporate Distress. *BIS Working Papers*. 753. Basel: Bank for International Settlements.

———. 2023. Dollar Exchange Rate as a Credit Supply Factor—Evidence from Firm-Level Exports. *BIS Working Papers*. 819. Basel: Bank for International Settlements.

Calvo, G. 1998. Capital Flows and Capital-Market Crises: The Simple Economics of Sudden Stops. *Journal of Applied Economics*. 1. pp. 35–54.

Casas, C., S. Meleshchuk, and Y. Timmer. 2022. The Dominant Currency Financing Channel of External Adjustment. *International Finance Discussion Papers*. 1343. Washington, DC: Board of Governors of the Federal Reserve System.

Di Giovanni, J. and J. Rogers. 2023. The Impact of US Monetary Policy on Foreign Firms. *Federal Reserve Bank of New York Staff Reports*. 1039. New York: Federal Reserve Bank of New York.

Ehlers, T., M. Hoffmann, and A. Raabe. 2020. Non-US Global Banks and Dollar (Co-)dependence: How Housing Markets Became Internationally Synchronized. *BIS Working Papers*. 897. Basel: Bank for International Settlements.

Eichengreen, B., P. Gupta, and O. Masetti. 2018. Are Capital Flows Fickle? Increasingly? And Does the Answer Still Depend on Type? *Asian Economic Papers*. 17 (1). pp. 22–41.

Eller, M., N. Hauzenberger, F. Huber, H. Schuberth, and L. Vashold. 2021. The Impact of Macroprudential Policies on Capital Flows in CESEE. *SUERF Policy Brief*. 199. Vienna: SUERF—The European Money and Finance Forum.

Forbes, K. and F. Warnock. 2012. Capital Flow Waves: Surges, Stops, Flight, and Retrenchment. *Journal of International Economics*. 88 (2). pp. 235–251.

Frost, J., H. Ito, and R. van Stralen. 2020. The Effectiveness of Macroprudential Policies and Capital Controls Against Volatile Capital Inflows. *BIS Working Papers*. 867. Basel: Bank for International Settlements.

Gelos, G., L. Gornicka, R. Koepke, R. Sahay, and S. Sgherri. 2019. Capital Flows at Risk: Taming the Ebbs and Flows. *IMF Working Paper*. WP/19/279. Washington, DC: International Monetary Fund.

Georgiadis, G., A. Mehl, H. Le Mezo, and C. Tille. 2021. Fundamentals vs. Policies: Can the US Dollar's Dominance in Global Trade Be Dented? *ECB Working Paper*. 2021/25. Frankfurt: European Central Bank.

Gopinath, G., E. Boz, C. Casas, F. J. Díez, P. Gourinchas, and M. Plagborg-Møller. 2020. Dominant Currency Paradigm. *American Economic Review*. 110 (3). pp. 677–719.

Hofmann, B. and T. Park. 2020. The Broad Dollar Exchange Rate as an EME Risk Factor. *BIS Quarterly Review: International Banking and Financial Market Developments*. Basel: Bank for International Settlements.

Hofmann, B., I. Shim, and H. S. Shin. 2017. Sovereign Yields and the Risk-Taking Channel of Currency Appreciation. *BIS Working Papers*. 538. Basel: Bank for International Settlements.

Hofmann, B., I. Shim, and H. S. Shin. 2020. Emerging Market Economy Exchange Rates and Local Currency Bond Markets amid the COVID-19 Pandemic. *BIS Bulletin*. 5. Basel: Bank for International Settlements.

———. 2022. Risk Capacity, Portfolio Choice, and Exchange Rates. *BIS Working Papers*. 1031. Basel: Bank for International Settlements.

Ilzetzki, E., C. Reinhart, and K. Rogoff. 2019. Exchange Arrangements Entering the Twenty-First Century: Which Anchor Will Hold? *The Quarterly Journal of Economics*. 134 (2). pp. 599–646.

International Monetary Fund (IMF). 2020. Toward an Integrated Policy Framework. *IMF Policy Paper*. 2020/046. Washington, DC.

———. 2023. *Global Financial Stability Report: Safeguarding Financial Stability Amid High Inflation and Geopolitical Risks*. Washington, DC.

Kim, C., D. Park, J. Park, and S. Tian. 2023. Local Currency Bond Market Development and Currency Stability amid Market Turmoil. *ADB Economics Working Paper Series*. 688. Manila: Asian Development Bank.

Koepke, R. 2019. What Drives Capital Flows to Emerging Markets? A Survey of the Empirical Literature. *Journal of Economic Surveys*. 33 (2). pp. 516–40.

Lane, P. and J. C. Shambaugh. 2007. Financial Exchange Rates and International Currency Exposures. *NBER Working Paper*. 13433. Cambridge, MA: National Bureau of Economic Research.

Lee, J. W. and C. Y. Park. 2011. Financial Integration in Emerging Asia: Challenges and Prospects. *Asian Economic Policy Review*. 6 (2). pp. 176–98.

Lee, J., P. Rosenkranz, A. Ramayandi, and H. Pham. 2021. The Influence of US Dollar Funding Conditions on Asian Financial Markets. *ADB Economics Working Paper Series*. 634. Manila: Asian Development Bank.

Levy Yeyati, E. and J. Zuniga. 2015. Varieties of Capital Flows: What Do We Know? *CID Working Paper Series*. 2015.296. Cambridge: Harvard University.

Ma, S., T. Schmidt-Eisenlohr, and S. Zhang. 2020. The Causal Effect of the Dollar on Trade. *CESifo Working Paper*. 8727. Munich: Munich Society for the Promotion of Economic Research—CESifo GmbH.

McGuire, P., I. Shim, H. S. Shin, and V. Sushko. 2021. Outward Portfolio Investment and Dollar Funding in Emerging Asia. *BIS Quarterly Review: International Banking and Financial Market Developments*. Basel: Bank for International Settlements.

Mercado, R., R. Jacildo, and S. Basu Das. 2023. US Dollar Dominance in Asia's Trade Invoicing. *Centre for Applied Macroeconomic Analysis Working Paper*. 5/2023. Canberra: Australian National University.

Nier, E., T. T. Olafsson, and Y. G. Rollinson. 2020. Exchange Rates and Domestic Credit—Can Macroprudential Policy Reduce the Link?. *IMF Working Paper*. 2020/187. Washington, DC: International Monetary Fund.

Pande, P. and D. del Rosario. 2020. US Dollar Funding Stress in the ASEAN+3 Region. *AMRO Analytical Note*. https://amro-asia.org/download/29025/?tmstv=1685463382.

Park, C. Y. 2017. Developing Local Currency Bond Markets in Asia. *ADB Economics Working Paper Series*. 495. Manila: Asian Development Bank.

Park, C. Y., P. Rosenkranz, and M. C. Tayag. 2020. COVID-19 Exposes Asian Banks' Vulnerability to US Dollar Funding. *ADB Briefs*. 146. Manila: Asian Development Bank.

Park, D., K. Shin, and S. Tian. 2018. Do Local Currency Bond Markets Enhance Financial Stability? *ADB Economics Working Paper Series*. 563. Manila: Asian Development Bank.

Rebucci, A. and C. Ma. 2019. Capital Controls: A Survey of the New Literature. *NBER Working Paper Series*. 26558. Cambridge: National Bureau of Economic Research.

United Nations Conference on Trade and Development (UNCTAD). 2023. *World Investment Report 2023: Investing in Sustainable Energy for All*. Geneva.

Annex 4a: Currency Composition by International Currency Use (%)

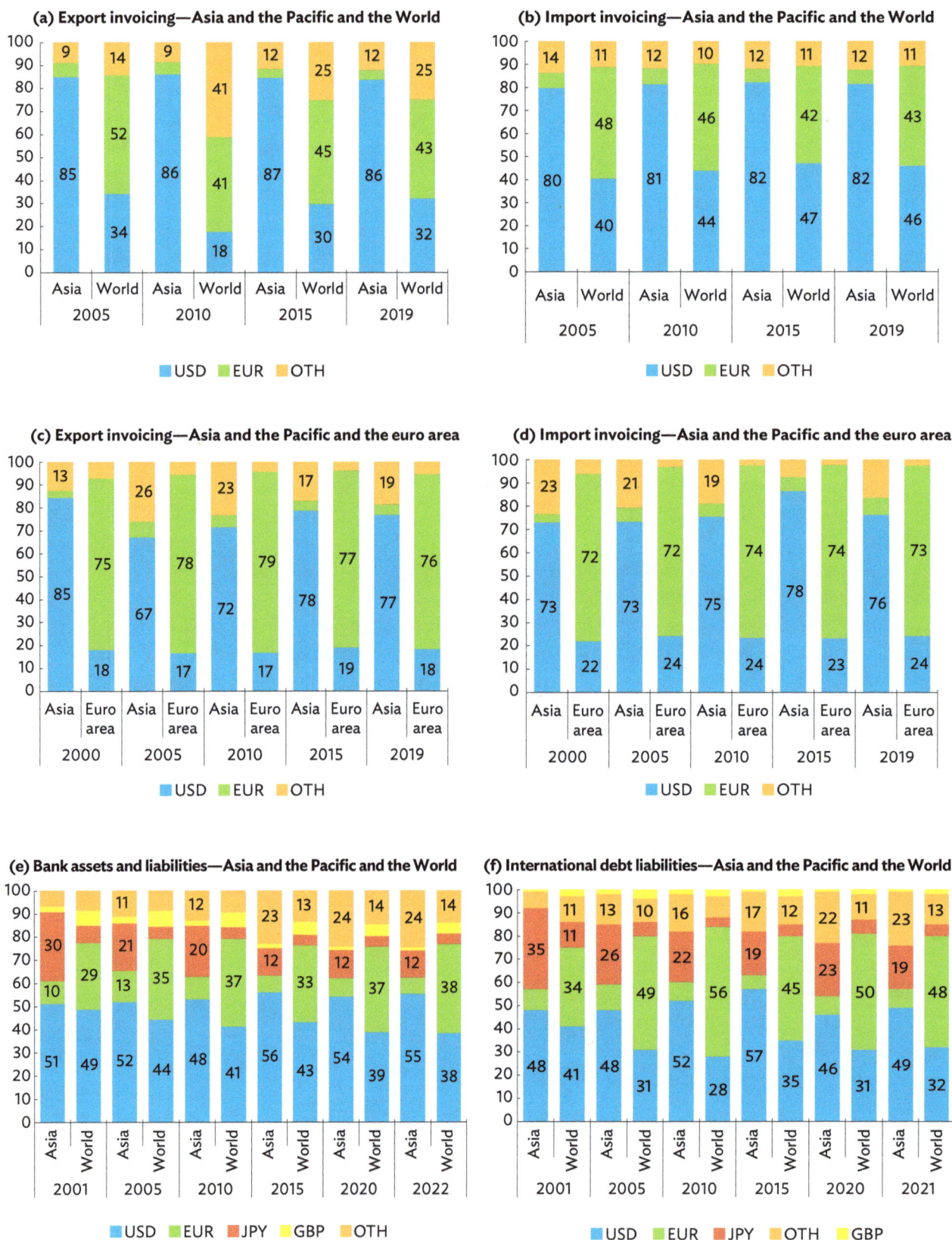

(a) Export invoicing—Asia and the Pacific and the World

	2005		2010		2015		2019	
	Asia	World	Asia	World	Asia	World	Asia	World
OTH	9	14	9	41	12	25	12	25
EUR	—	52	—	41	—	45	—	43
USD	85	34	86	18	87	30	86	32

USD ■ EUR ■ OTH

(b) Import invoicing—Asia and the Pacific and the World

	2005		2010		2015		2019	
	Asia	World	Asia	World	Asia	World	Asia	World
OTH	14	11	12	10	12	11	12	11
EUR	—	48	—	46	—	42	—	43
USD	80	40	81	44	82	47	82	46

USD ■ EUR ■ OTH

(c) Export invoicing—Asia and the Pacific and the euro area

	2000		2005		2010		2015		2019	
	Asia	Euro area	Asia	Euro area	Asia	Euro area	Asia	Euro area	Asia	Euro area
OTH	13	—	26	—	23	—	17	—	19	—
EUR	—	75	—	78	—	79	—	77	—	76
USD	85	18	67	17	72	17	78	19	77	18

USD ■ EUR ■ OTH

(d) Import invoicing—Asia and the Pacific and the euro area

	2000		2005		2010		2015		2019	
	Asia	Euro area	Asia	Euro area	Asia	Euro area	Asia	Euro area	Asia	Euro area
OTH	23	—	21	—	19	—	—	—	—	—
EUR	—	72	—	72	—	74	—	74	—	73
USD	73	22	73	24	75	24	78	23	76	24

USD ■ EUR ■ OTH

(e) Bank assets and liabilities—Asia and the Pacific and the World

	2001		2005		2010		2015		2020		2022	
	Asia	World	Asia	World	Asia	World	Asia	World	Asia	World	Asia	World
OTH	—	11	—	12	23	13	24	14	24	14		
JPY	30	21	20		12	12	12					
EUR	10	29	13	35	37	33	37	38				
USD	51	49	52	44	48	41	56	43	54	39	55	38

USD ■ EUR ■ JPY ■ GBP ■ OTH

(f) International debt liabilities—Asia and the Pacific and the World

	2001		2005		2010		2015		2020		2021	
	Asia	World	Asia	World	Asia	World	Asia	World	Asia	World	Asia	World
OTH	—	11	13	10	16	17	12	22	11	23	13	
JPY	35	11	26		22		19		23		19	
EUR	—	34	—	49	—	56	—	45	—	50	—	48
USD	48	41	48	31	52	28	57	35	46	31	49	32

USD ■ EUR ■ JPY ■ OTH ■ GBP

(g) International liabilities—Asia and the Pacific and the World

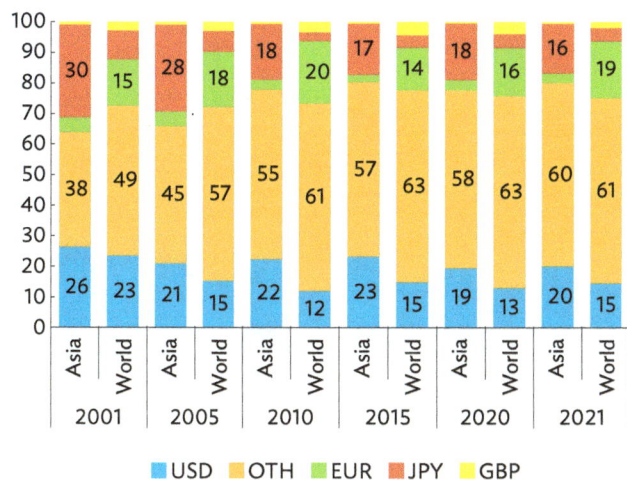

USD OTH EUR JPY GBP

(h) Official foreign exchange reserves—Asia and the Pacific and the World

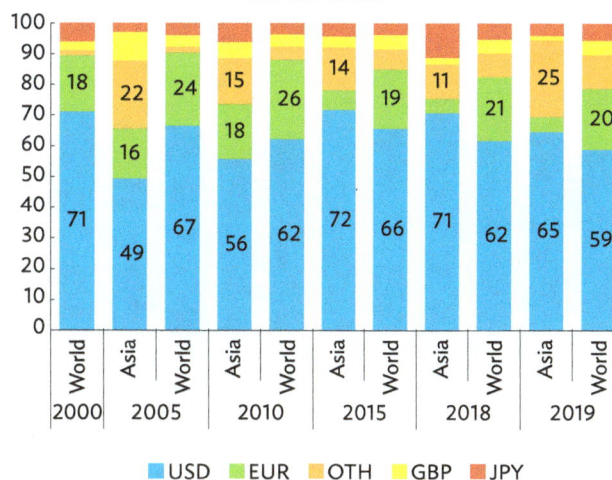

USD EUR OTH GBP JPY

(i) Currencies anchored to the US dollar (% of world GDP)

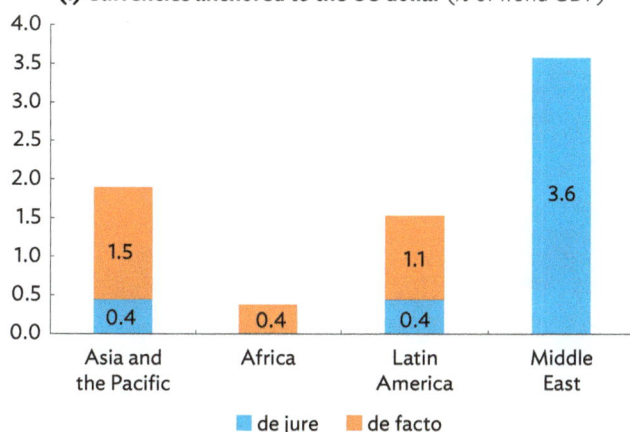

de jure   de facto

(j) Cross-border payments—World

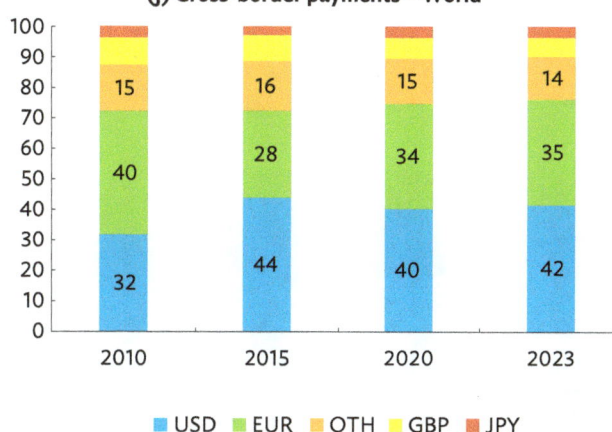

USD EUR OTH GBP JPY

(k) Foreign exchange turnover—World

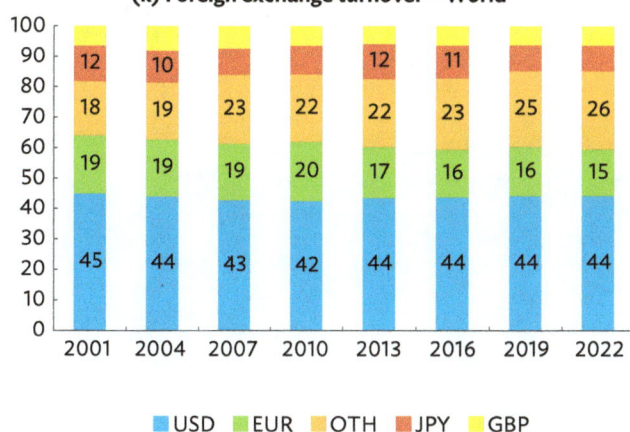

USD EUR OTH JPY GBP

EUR = euro, GBP = pound sterling, GDP = gross domestic product, JPY = yen, OTH = other currencies, USD = United States dollar.

Notes:

(i)   For panel f, the international debt liabilities category consists of portfolio debt liabilities and other debt liabilities from the International Monetary Fund's International Investment Position statistics, with the currency composition derived from Locational Banking Statistics of the Bank for International Settlements in line with Lane and Shambaugh (2007).

(ii) Panel i excludes the People's Republic of China.

Sources: ADB calculations using data from Bank for International Settlements. Locational Banking Statistics. https://stats.bis.org/statx/toc/LBS.html (accessed August 2023); Bloomberg L.P.; Boz et al. 2020; International Monetary Fund (2023); International Monetary Fund (IMF). Balance of Payments and International Investment Position Statistics. http://data.imf.org/IIP (accessed September 2023). IMF. Coordinated Direct Investment Survey. https://data.imf.org/cdis (accessed December 2022); IMF. Coordinated Portfolio Investment Survey. https://data.imf.org/cpis; IMF. Currency Composition of Official Foreign Exchange Reserves. https://data.imf.org/COFER; IMF. Direction of Trade Statistics. https://data.imf.org/dot; IMF. International Foreign Reserves and Foreign Currency Liquidity. https://data.imf.org/IRFCL; World Bank. World Bank Open Data. https://data.worldbank.org (all accessed September 2023); and national data sources; and methodology by Lane and Shambaugh (2007).

Annex 4b: Currency Composition by International Currency Use and by World Region (%)

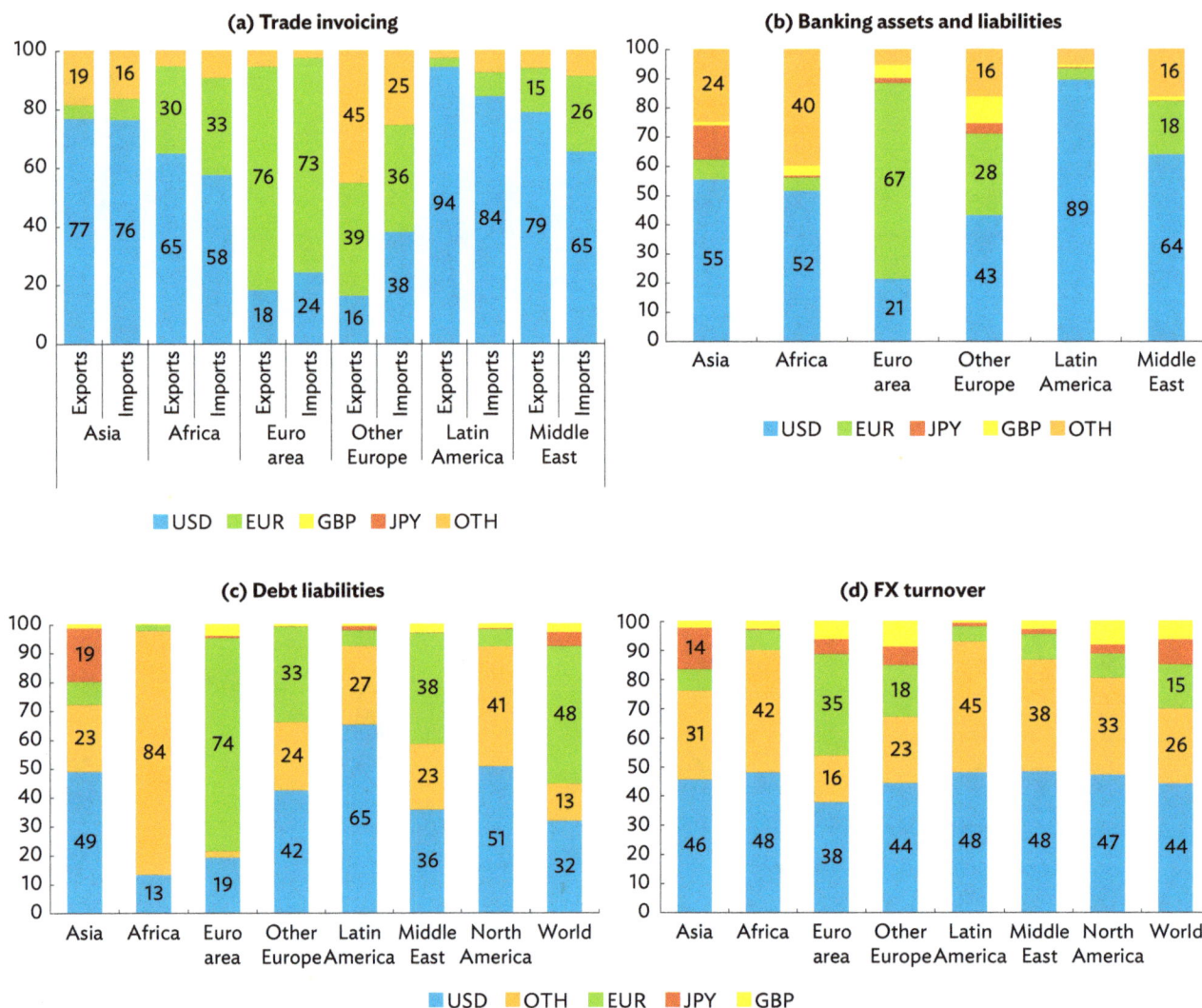

(a) Trade invoicing

Legend: USD, EUR, GBP, JPY, OTH

(b) Banking assets and liabilities

Legend: USD, EUR, JPY, GBP, OTH

(c) Debt liabilities

Legend: USD, OTH, EUR, JPY, GBP

(d) FX turnover

EUR = euro, FX = foreign exchange, GBP = pound sterling, JPY = yen, OTH = other currencies, USD = United States dollar.

Notes:
(i)   Data for trade invoicing are as of 2019, data for debt liabilities are as of 2021, and data for FX turnover are as of 2022.
(ii)   Asia and the Pacific includes Armenia; Australia; Azerbaijan; Bangladesh; Fiji; Georgia; Hong Kong, China; India; Indonesia; Japan; Kazakhstan; Kyrgyz Republic; Malaysia; Mongolia; Nepal; New Zealand; Pakistan; the People's Republic of China; the Philippines; the Republic of Korea; Singapore; Taipei,China; Thailand; and Timor-Leste; with heterogenous data availability.
(iii) Africa includes Angola, Botswana, Cabo Verde, Cote d'Ivoire, the Democratic Republic of Congo, Egypt, Eswatini, Ghana, Lesotho, Liberia, Malawi, Mauritius, Morocco, Mozambique, Namibia, the Niger, Nigeria, Rwanda, the Democratic Republic of São Tomé and Príncipe, Senegal, South Africa, Tanzania, Tunisia, and Zambia; with heterogenous data availability.
(iv)   The euro area includes Austria, Belgium, Croatia, Cyprus, Finland, France, Germany, Greece, Ireland, Italy, Latvia, Lithuania, Luxembourg, Malta, the Netherlands, Portugal, Slovak Republic, Slovenia, and Spain; with heterogenous data availability.
(v)   Other Europe includes Albania, Andorra, Belarus, Bosnia and Herzegovina, Bulgaria, the Czech Republic, Denmark, Hungary, Iceland, Moldova, Montenegro, North Macedonia, Norway, Poland, Romania, the Russian Federation, Serbia, Sweden, Switzerland, Ukraine, and the United Kingdom; with heterogenous data availability.
(vi)   Latin America includes Argentina, the Bahamas, Bolivia, Brazil, Chile, Colombia, Costa Rica, Ecuador, El Salvador, Honduras, Panama, Paraguay, Peru, Suriname, and Uruguay; with heterogenous data availability.
(vii) The Middle East includes Bahrain, Israel, Jordan, Saudi Arabia, Türkiye, the United Arab Emirates, and Yemen; with heterogenous data availability.
(viii) North America includes Canada and Mexico.

Sources: ADB calculations using data from Bank for International Settlements (BIS). BIS Triennial Central Bank Survey of Foreign Exchange and Over-the-counter (OTC) Derivatives Markets. https://www.bis.org/statistics/rpfx22.htm (accessed July 2023); BIS. Locational Banking Statistics. https://stats.bis.org/statx/toc/LBS.html (accessed August 2022); Boz et al. 2020; IMF. Balance of Payments and International Investment Position Statistics. http://data.imf.org/IIP (accessed September 2023). IMF. Coordinated Direct Investment Survey. https://data.imf.org/cdis (accessed December 2022); IMF. Coordinated Portfolio Investment Survey. https://data.imf.org/cpis; and IMF. Currency Composition of Official Foreign Exchange Reserves. https://data.imf.org/COFER (both accessed September 2023). IMF. Direction of Trade Statistics. https://data.imf.org/dot (accessed September 2023); and domestic sources.

Annex 4c: Regression Coefficients—International Debt Share and Federal Funds Rate

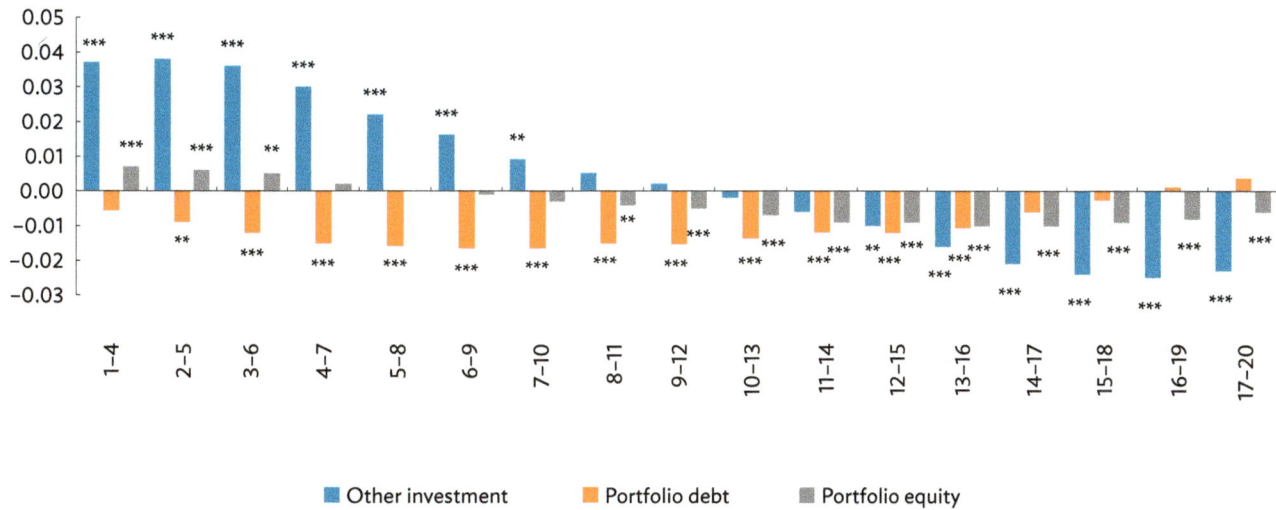

Other investment   ■ **Portfolio debt**   ■ **Portfolio equity**

US = United States. X-axis shows 4-quarter long periods ahead. Stars denote significance levels: *** at 1%, ** at 5%, and * at 10%.

Notes: Results are based on panel regressions of capital inflows on US dollar funding costs interacted with US dollar dependence and domestic economic conditions for a broad sample of emerging market economies in Asia and the Pacific using economy and time fixed effects. The dependent variables are the 4-quarter average of capital inflows to individual economies scaled by gross domestic product (GDP) rolling forward over quarters 1 to 17 ahead, where capital inflows denote (i) portfolio debt inflows, (ii) portfolio equity inflows, or other investment inflows. US dollar funding costs are measured by (i) the effective US federal funds rate, and (ii) the trade-weighted US real effective exchange rate against a broad basket of currencies (broad US dollar index). US dollar dependence corresponds to the share of US dollar-denominated international debt. Domestic economic conditions include GDP per capita, real GDP growth, the differential between the US and domestic monetary policy rate, a measure of capital account openness, and the ratio of external debt to foreign currency reserves.

Sources: ADB calculations using data from Bank for International Settlements (BIS). Global Liquidity Indicators. https://data.bis.org/topics/GLI/data; BIS. Effective Exchange Rate Indices. https://www.bis.org/statistics/eer.htm (both accessed August 2023); Bloomberg L.P.; and Haver Analytics.

5 Movement of People

Migration

Outflows from Asia and the Pacific Have Recovered, While Major Host Economies Have Broadened Access to Skilled Migrant Workers

Migration outflows from Asia and the Pacific have been recovering after the coronavirus disease (COVID-19) pandemic.[21] The pandemic saw a sharp dip in migrant outflows from major migrant source economies in Asia in 2020. Migrant workers from the region's top 10 sending economies account for 70.1% (65.2 million) of the 93 million Asian migrants across the world.[22] However, post-2020 figures indicate that the trend in migrant flows from traditional sending economies are recovering, but to varying degrees (Figure 5.1). For instance, outflows in 2022 have recovered from the pre-pandemic flows in 2019 for Bangladesh (162.2%), India (101.5%), Pakistan (133.0%), and Sri Lanka (147.8%). Meanwhile, outflows from Indonesia and the Philippines have risen but remain below the pre-pandemic level.

Figure 5.1: Outflow of Migrant Workers from Selected Asian Economies (2019 = 100)

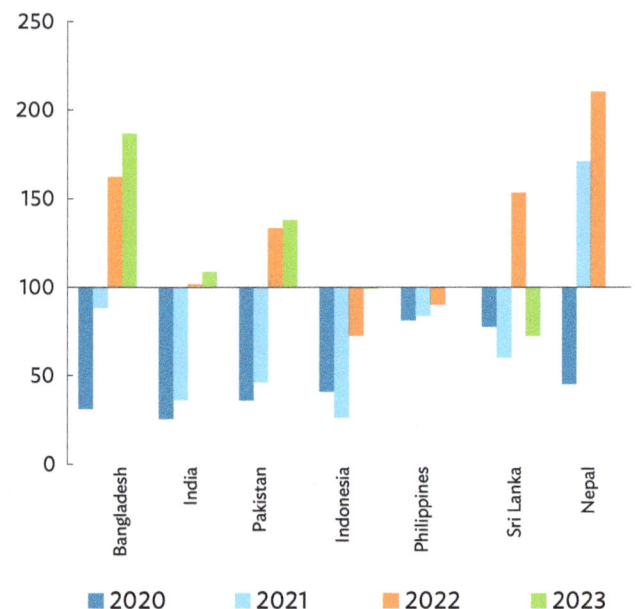

Note: The 2023 data are up to June for Sri Lanka.

Sources: Government of Bangladesh, Bureau of Manpower, Employment, and Training. http://www.old.bmet.gov.bd/BMET/stattisticalDataAction (accessed January 2024); Government of India, Ministry of External Affairs. Performance Smartboard. https://meadashboard.gov.in/ (accessed January 2024); Government of Malaysia, Migrant Worker Protection Agency (Badan Pelindungan Pekerja Migran Indonesia). https://bp2mi.go.id/ (accessed January 2024); Government of Nepal, Ministry of Labour, Employment and Social Security (2022); Government of Nepal, Department of Foreign Employment. https://dofe.gov.np/DetailPage.aspx/id/425/lan/ne-NP (accessed November 2022); Government of Pakistan, Bureau of Emigration and Overseas Employment. https://beoe.gov.pk/reports-and-statistics (accessed January 2024); Government of the Philippines, Philippine Statistical Authority (2020, 2021, 2022, 2023); and Government of Sri Lanka, Central Bank of Sri Lanka. https://www.cbsl.gov.lk/en/statistics/statistical-tables/external-sector (accessed January 2024).

---

[21] Asia and the Pacific, or Asia, consists of the 49 regional member economies of the Asian Development Bank (ADB). The composition of economies for Central Asia, East Asia, the Pacific and Oceania, South Asia, and Southeast Asia are outlined in ADB. Asia Regional Integration Center. Economy Groupings. https://aric.adb.org/integrationindicators/groupings.

[22] In 2020, the top 10 migrant-sending economies in Asia are India, the People's Republic of China, Bangladesh, Pakistan, the Philippines, Indonesia, Kazakhstan, Viet Nam, Nepal, and the Republic of Korea.

Pandemic-induced work-hour losses exacerbated labor shortages in developed economies, particularly in foreign labor-dependent sectors.

Lost work hours in 2020 were equivalent to 255 million full-time jobs, or $3.7 trillion in lost labor income (ILO 2021). This staggering figure highlights how persistent labor shortages could hinder recovery in major developed-economy migrant host economies.

In the United States (US), sectors with the highest percentage of migrant workers in 2019—such as hospitality, food services, and professional services—had significantly higher rates of unfilled jobs in 2021 (Figure 5.2a). Peri and Zaiour (2022) estimate that US sectors with 10% more migrant workers than another industry employing migrant labor in 2019 had a 3% increase in job vacancy rates in 2021. In 2022, foreign-born workers were more likely than native-born workers to be employed in service occupations; natural resources, construction, and maintenance occupations; and production, transportation, and material moving

occupations.[23] Similarly, job vacancy rates in Canada are particularly high in sectors connected to sales and services, trades and transport, health, and business finance and administration (Figure 5.2b).

Major migrant-host economies have expanded access to migrant workers to reduce skilled labor shortages.

As slow global growth continues its grip, many developed economies are relaxing their immigration policies to facilitate the higher inflow of foreign workers. Australia issued 38.4% more worker visas in 2022 than in 2021 under the Temporary Skilled Shortage program (Figure 5.3). It raised its permanent immigration intake by more than a fifth to 200,000 in 2022 to address labor shortage (Fildes 2022). Initiatives to accelerate visa processing are also in place for jobs in nursing, engineering, and technology and to boost the rural workforce. In early 2024, Australia will launch its new Pacific Engagement Visa category, allowing up to 3,000 nationals of Pacific island economies and Timor-Leste to migrate as permanent residents each year.[24]

Figure 5.2: Job Vacancies in the United States and Canada, by Sector

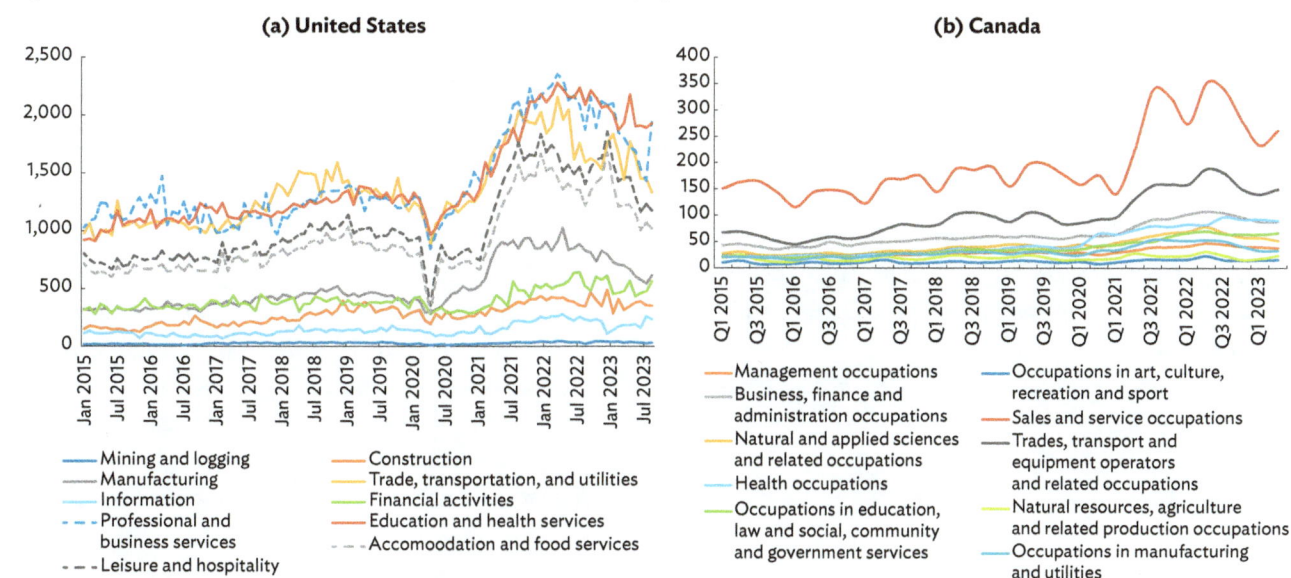

Q = quarter.

Sources: Government of the United States, Bureau of Labor Statistics. Job Openings and Labor Turnover Survey. https://www.bls.gov/jlt/ (accessed October 2023); Statistics Canada. Table 14-10-0356-01 Job Vacancies and Average Offered Hourly Wage by Occupation (Broad Occupational Category), Quarterly, Unadjusted for Seasonality. https://www150.statcan.gc.ca/t1/tbl1/en/tv.action?pid=1410035601.

[23] Government of the United States, Bureau of Labor Statistics. Job Openings and Labor Turnover Survey. https://www.bls.gov/jlt/ (accessed October 2023).

[24] Government of Australia, Department of Foreign Affairs and Trade. https://www.dfat.gov.au/geo/pacific/people-connections/people-connections-in-the-pacific/pacific-engagement-visa.

In New Zealand, 13 times more work visas were issued in 2022 (78,714) than in 2021 (5,778). By September 2023, that had doubled to 156,387. In October 2023, New Zealand rolled out the Skilled Migrant Category Resident Visa with a new points system for applicants.[25]

Canada released its 2023–2025 Immigration Levels Plan in November 2022, with targets to settle 465,000 permanent residents in 2023, rising to 485,000 in 2024 and 500,000 in 2025. The plan aimed to continue welcoming immigrants at a rate of about 1% of Canada's population a year, with a sharper focus on supporting economic resurgence and post-pandemic growth.

The United Kingdom (UK) saw a doubling of migrant worker inflows in 2022 from 2021. In August 2023, it introduced modifications to the Skilled Worker Route, including changes to the Shortage Occupation List. A job on the list makes it easier for licensed employers, including in the construction and fishing industries, to meet the points requirement to sponsor skilled workers.

In the US, the tripling of work visas issued in 2022 suggests a sharp deviation of migration policy from the previous administration's restrictive stance. For fiscal year 2024, the US has set its annual employment-based preference immigrants to least 140,000.[26] The People's Republic of China (PRC), India, and the Philippines were cited as having oversubscribed applications for certain types of employment-based visas, but visas for priority workers from these economies remain on track.

Japan's aging problem and low fertility rates are at the root of its labor shortage problem and led to the 2018 adoption of a law allowing 300,000 foreigners into the economy.[27] The Japan System for Special Highly Skilled Professionals (J-Skip) and the Japan System for Future Creation Individual Visa (J-Find) were rolled out in April 2023 to attract researchers, engineers, and high-level managers.

Figure 5.3: Work Visas Issued by Migrant Host Economy

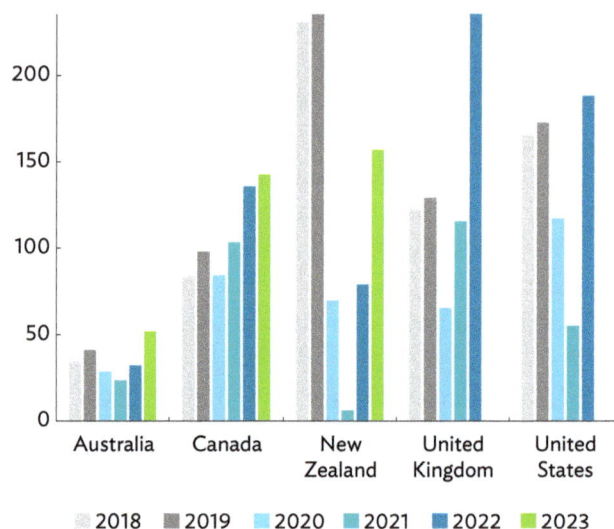

Note: In 2023, values for Canada and New Zealand refer to January to September data.

Sources: ADB calculations using data from Government of Australia, Department of Home Affairs. https://www.homeaffairs.gov.au/ (accessed October 2023); Government of Canada. Temporary Residents: Temporary Foreign Worker Program (TFWP) and International Mobility Program (IMP) Work Permit Holders – Monthly IRCC Updates. https://open.canada.ca/data/en/dataset/360024f2-17e9-4558-bfc1-3616485d65b9 (accessed November 2023); Government of the United States, Department of State, Bureau of Consular Affairs. https://travel.state.gov/content/travel/en/legal/visa-law0/visa-bulletin/2024/visa-bulletin-for-october-2023.html (accessed November 2023); and Government of the United Kingdom, Home Office. https://www.gov.uk/government/organisations/home-office (accessed October 2023).

Skilled migrants comprise a rising share of Asian migrant workers in developed host economies.

Migrant workers with background in science, technology, and mathematics are often employed in sectors that, besides being major drivers of innovation, research, and technical progress, also generate a job multiplier effect in the local economy. Figure 5.4 shows the share of highly skilled migrants has been increasing in the United Arab Emirates and the UK, two of the major destinations for Asian migrant workers, and more working migrants with a high degree of education has been observed in Australia,

---

[25]   According to Immigration New Zealand, these points can be made up from 3 to 6 points based on New Zealand occupational registration, qualifications, or income, and 1 point for each year having worked in New Zealand in a skilled job, up to a maximum of 3 points. Source: New Zealand Immigration. Skilled Migrant Category Resident Visa. https://www.immigration.govt.nz/new-zealand-visas/visas/visa/skilled-migrant-category-resident-visa.

[26]   Information of employment visa preferences is from Visa Bulletin for October 2023 of the US Department of State, Bureau of Consular Affairs. https://travel.state.gov/content/travel/en/legal/visa-law0/visa-bulletin/2024/visa-bulletin-for-october-2023.html.

[27]   The law creates two new visa categories under the Specified Skill Worker Program. Migrants in Type 1 are allowed in for up to 5 years if they have a certain level of skill and some proficiency in Japanese. Workers with higher skills would qualify for the Type 2 visa category for employment in construction and shipbuilding and ship machinery industries (Government of Japan, Ministry of Foreign Affairs. https://www.mofa.go.jp/mofaj/ca/fna/ssw/us/). As of February 2023, there were about 146,000 Type 1 holders and only 10 Type 2 holders.

Canada, France, and the US. While Organisation for Economic Co-operation and Development (OECD) economies make up only less than a fifth of the world's population, they host two-thirds of highly skilled migrants. About 70% of such workers are concentrated in four English-speaking economies—Australia, Canada, the UK, and the US with the US playing host to about half. As global competition for high-skilled human capital intensifies, other OECD economies, such as France, Germany, and Spain, have changed their skilled migrant policies.

Large outmigration challenges small economies like the Pacific islands with constrained working populations.

Australia and New Zealand have maintained immigration programs in the Pacific that are largely temporary and seasonal through various labor mobility schemes like the Seasonal Worker Program[28] and Pacific Labour Scheme[29] for Australia, and the Recognised Seasonal Employer[30] for New Zealand, mainly to relieve labor shortages in sectors with seasonal demand. The movement of workers began picking up in 2022, after a dip in 2021, and continued until 2023 (Figure 5.5). These labor mobility schemes aid the Pacific pandemic recovery through remittance inflows. The negative impact of worker outflows on domestic labor forces has intensified, especially for Pacific economies counting on the tourism revival to boost recovery. Fiji, for instance, has unprecedented need for foreign workers to fill tourism jobs left by Fijians who have moved mostly to Oceania.[31]

Figure 5.4: Employment Distribution of Migrants in Host Economies (% of total)

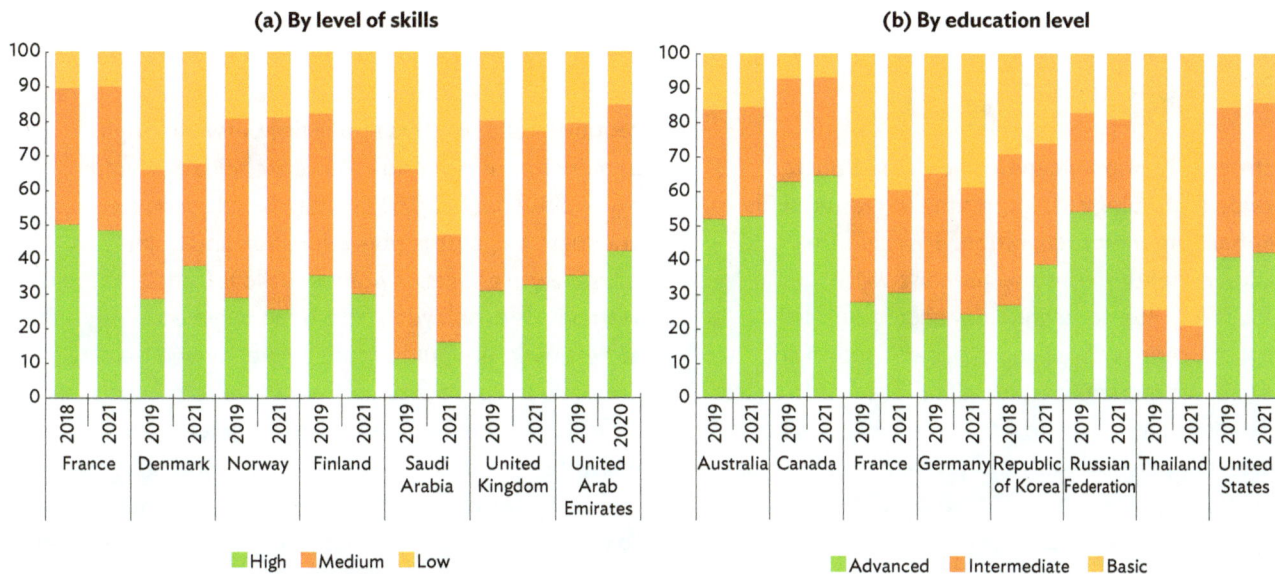

(a) By level of skills

(b) By education level

High   Medium   Low

Advanced   Intermediate   Basic

Notes: The International Standard Classification of Occupations defines skill level as a function of the complexity and range of tasks and duties needed in an occupation and is measured by considering any one of the following: (i) nature of work, (ii) level of formal education, and (iii) amount of informal on-the-job training and/or previous experience in a related occupation. High skill level refers to managers, professionals, and technicians and associate professionals. Medium skill level refers to clerical support workers; sales, and service workers; skilled agricultural, forestry, and fishery workers; crafts and related trades workers; and plant and machine operators and assemblers. Low skill level refers to elementary occupations.

Source: ADB calculations using data from International Labour Organization Statistical Database (ILOStat). https://ilostat.ilo.org/data/ and https://ilostat.ilo.org/resources/concepts-and-definitions/classification-occupation/ (accessed December 2023).

---

28 This program is now known as the short-term component of the Pacific Australia Labour Mobility scheme, filling labor gaps for up to 9 months. Eligible economies are Fiji, Kiribati, Nauru, Papua New Guinea, Samoa, Solomon Islands, Timor-Leste, Tonga, Tuvalu, and Vanuatu.

29 This program is now known as the long-term component of the Pacific Australia Labour Mobility scheme, allowing workers employment in Australia up to 4 years. Eligible economies are Fiji, Kiribati, Nauru, Papua New Guinea, Samoa, Solomon Islands, Timor-Leste, Tonga, Tuvalu, and Vanuatu.

30 The Recognised Seasonal Employer brings temporary workers from Fiji, Kiribati, Nauru, Papua New Guinea, Samoa, Solomon Islands, Tonga, Tuvalu, and Vanuatu to work in horticulture or viticulture.

31 From 2022 to October, around 50,000 Fijians have emigrated on employment and student visas (Tabureguci 2023).

Figure 5.5: Labor Mobility Scheme Workers in Australia and New Zealand ('000)

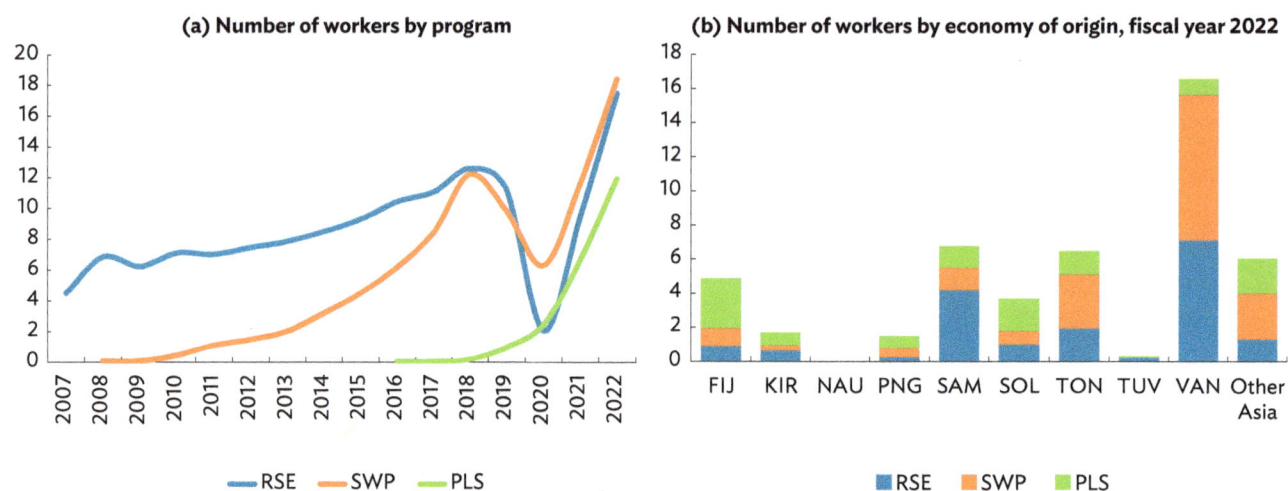

FIJ = Fiji, KIR = Kiribati, NAU = Nauru, PLS = Pacific Labour Scheme, PNG = Papua New Guinea, RSE = Recognised Seasonal Employer, SAM = Samoa, SWP = Seasonal Worker Program, TON = Tonga, TUV = Tuvalu, VAN = Vanuatu.

Notes: Values are based on fiscal year, which start in July and end in June of the following year (e.g., fiscal year 2007 refers to July 2007–June 2008). Other Asia in panel (b) refers to India; Indonesia; Malaysia; the Philippines; Taipei,China; Timor-Leste; and Viet Nam.

Source: Bedford (2023).

Policy Implications

Investments in human capital should be boosted alongside technology for improving migrants' skills and enhancing their recognition. To maximize migration benefits, prioritizing human capital development, internet technology access, and skills training is essential. Cross-regional certification and skills training programs are crucial for migrants to access opportunities and integrate into labor markets and host societies. Digitalized immigration systems or processes are significantly more efficient than paper-based ones and could support swift changes in policy.[32] Use of artificial intelligence has been gaining traction in border management, migration management, and asylum procedures (IOM 2020). Technology for migrants—such as apps for messaging, transportation and translation, and digital maps—could also help reduce vulnerabilities (ADBI, OECD, and ILO 2021).

Effective management of international labor migration requires collaborative strategies between origin and destination economies. Stakeholders should expand the pool of globally transferable skills through adequate and sustainable education and training to mitigate the effects of worker outflow. Consultations with private employers in both the origin economy and at destinations would ensure market-driven training.[33] Engaging the private sector is one way to mitigate the difficulties from a sudden spike in worker outflows. In many migrant-source economies, promoting higher education through private investment, especially related to emigrants' future occupations, is beneficial. Bilateral labor arrangements in several Asian economies align emigrant flow with destination economy industry needs, ensuring continuous labor market access.

---

[32] For example, within ASEAN, Mutual Recognition Arrangements and the ASEAN Qualifications Reference Framework form a framework for mutual skills recognition.

[33] For instance, Singapore plans to hire 4,000 more nurses by the end of 2023, registering Philippine nurses to deter their transfer to New Zealand, which offers residency to health workers (Philippine News Agency 2023). Thailand, a migration pathway for workers from economies within the Mekong subregion, has advanced to the second phase of its International Organization for Migration project, PROMISE, aiming by 2025 to aid 450,000 revolving or returning migrants across four economies through skills development for better employment, economic resilience, and poverty reduction (IOM Thailand 2022).

Remittances

Resilient Inflows to Asia Continue as the Main Source of External Finance for Development

Global remittance flows are estimated to climb 3% further to $860.3 billion in 2023 after rising 5.5% to $835.6 billion in 2022. Inflows to Asia totaled $356.0 billion, marking a 10.7% growth from 2021 and the highest since 2011 (Figure 5.6). These inflows were $34.5 billion greater than in 2021, and accounted for 79.5% of the total global increase of $43.4 billion in 2022. In 2023, inflows to the region are expected grow 4.4% to reach $371.5 billion. Remittances to the region were bolstered by robust employment rates in OECD economies, particularly the US, and a slowdown in inflation in high-income economies.   Large transfers from the Russian Federation to Central Asia, which raised remittance flows in 2022, are seen to have moderated in 2023.

Amid the global lockdown and shutdown caused by government-mandated COVID-19 control measures, global remittance inflows dipped only slightly by

1.4% in 2020 while flows to Asia slowed only by 1.9%. Remittances rebounded strongly in 2021 across major regions and the uptrend continued in 2022 (Figure 5.7). Across Asian subregions, inflows continued to rise in 2022 except in East Asia—with notable growth in Central Asia (69.4%) and robust rise in inflows that continued well into 2023 for Oceania (17.4% and 21.2%), and South Asia (12.2% and 7.2%). Even the Russian invasion of Ukraine did not dampen money transfers to Central Asia, which rose by 24.4% in 2021 and 69.4% in 2022.

India, the PRC, the Philippines, Pakistan, and Bangladesh were among the top 10 global recipients of remittances across all economies (Figure 5.8a). In several economies, remittance inflows account for a significant portion of gross domestic product, reaching as high as 40.6% in Tonga and 48.2% in Tajikistan in 2023 (Figure 5.8b). Central Asia received 80% of its remittances from the Russian Federation in 2021. In the months following the February 2022 Russian invasion of Ukraine, Central Asia experienced large money transfers from the Russian Federation as skilled workers and businesses relocated to the subregion (ADB 2023a, 2023b).

Since 2010, Asia has received about 43% of global remittances. However, with a greater number of Asian

Figure 5.6: Remittance Inflows to Asia and the Pacific, and the World

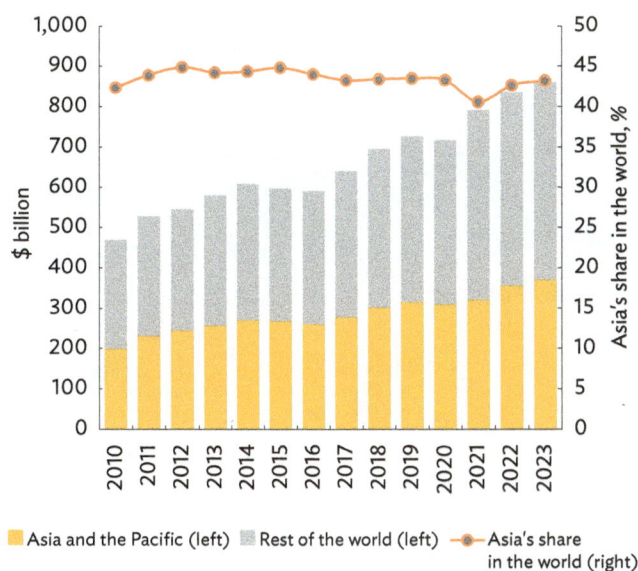

Source: ADB calculations using data from World Bank-KNOMAD (Global Knowledge Partnership on Migration and Development). http://www.knomad.org/data/remittances (accessed December 2023).

Figure 5.7: Inflows to Asia and the Pacific, by Subregion (2019 = 100)

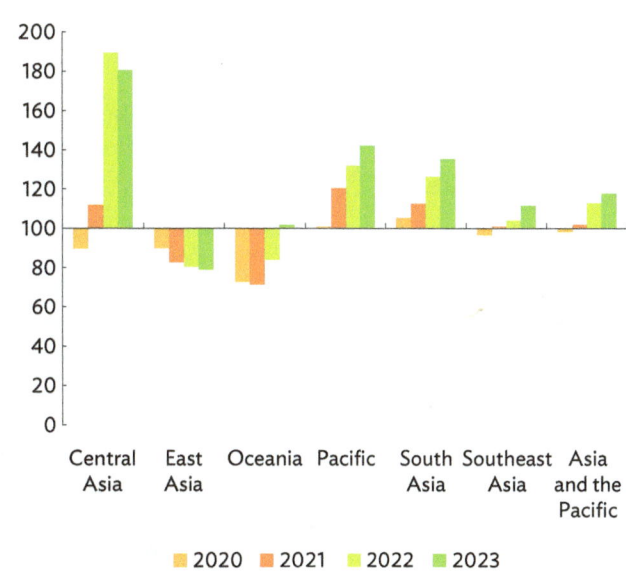

Source: ADB calculations using data from World Bank-KNOMAD (Global Knowledge Partnership on Migration and Development). http://www.knomad.org/data/remittances (accessed December 2023).

Figure 5.8: Top 10 Remittance Recipient Economies in Asia and the Pacific

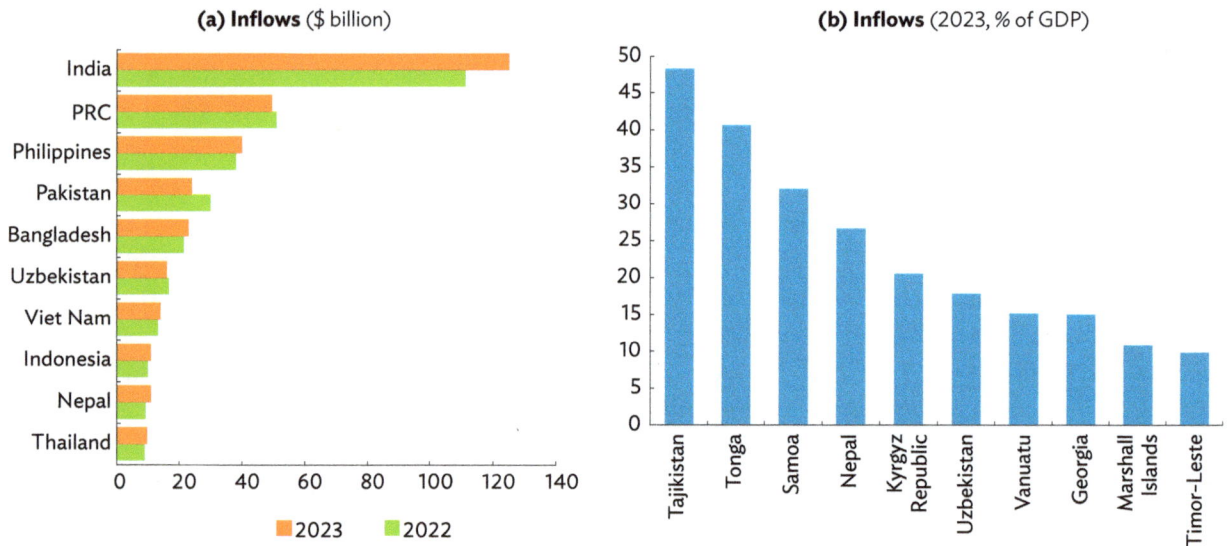

(a) **Inflows** ($ billion)

(b) **Inflows** (2023, % of GDP)

■ 2023 ■ 2022

PRC = People's Republic of China.

Source: ADB calculations using data from KNOMAD (Global Knowledge Partnership on Migration and Development. http://www.knomad.org/data/remittances (accessed December 2023).

migrants moving to non-Asian host economies in the past decade, it is no surprise that Asia's intraregional remittance shares have also fallen (Figure 5.9). For instance, in 2010, 33.2% of Asian remittance flows were from the region but this fell to 25.5% by 2021. Dependence on remittance between subregions varies (Figure 5.10). For example, Pacific economies received 81.6% more remittances from other Asian subregions between 2019 and 2021, while Southeast Asian economies received fewer remittances from the subregion and more from others. Studying the trend of intrasubregional dependence could help craft targeted initiatives to lower costs through different remittance corridors.

Digitalization Contributes to Resilience of Remittance Inflows, but Usage Remains Lower Than for Traditional Channels

The average cost of remittances remains high, significantly above the United Nations' Sustainable Development Goals target.

As of the first quarter of 2023, the average cost of sending $200 anywhere in the world was 6.3% of the remittance

Figure 5.9: Intraregional Remittance Share—Asia and the Pacific

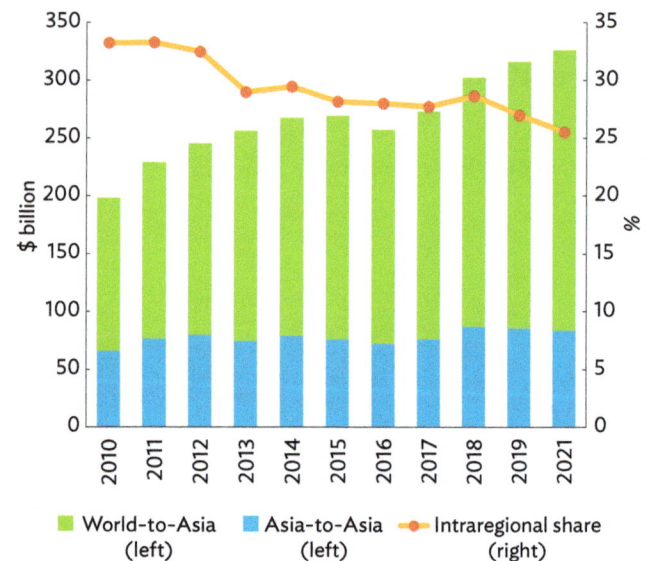

■ World-to-Asia (left) ■ Asia-to-Asia (left) ● Intraregional share (right)

Source: ADB calculations using data from World Bank-KNOMAD (Global Knowledge Partnership on Migration and Development. http://www.knomad.org/data/remittances (accessed December 2023).

amount, double the Sustainable Development Goal's 3.0% target (Figure 5.11a). In Asia, the rate had gone down to 5.2% in the first quarter of 2023 from 6.2% in the same period of 2020, with significant variations across regions. Costs in South Asia have been lower than other regions

Figure 5.10: Intraregional Profile of Remittance Sources of Asian Economies

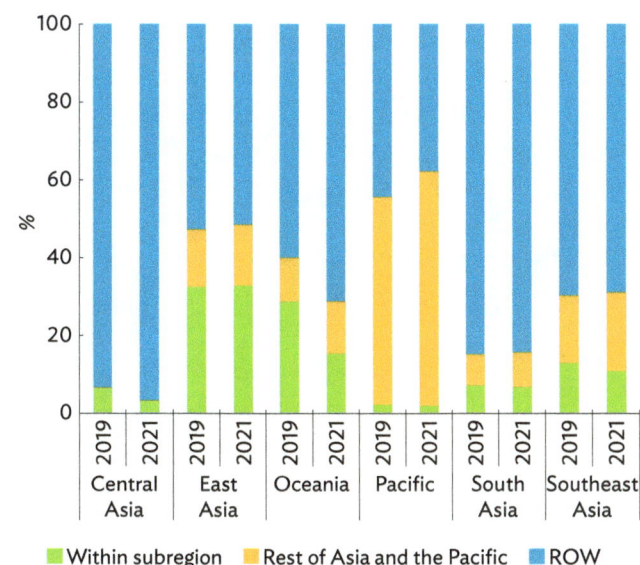

ROW = rest of the world.

Source: ADB calculations using data from World Bank-KNOMAD (Global Knowledge Partnership on Migration and Development. http://www.knomad.org/data/remittances (accessed December 2023)

due to the proliferation of remittance service providers. In the Pacific, rates historically are higher than both the global rates and the Asian average as its small market size prevents providers from scaling operations, leading to high transaction costs. The global trend of de-risking (that is, banks severing ties with high-risk financial institutions and clients to avoid potential liabilities) and enhanced regulatory pressures pushed correspondent banking relationships to shrink by 30% between 2011 and 2022—with a 60% decline for Pacific economies (Davies 2023). This raised Pacific banks' costs to service cross-border transactions and kept remittance fees high.

Especially relative to cash, digital remittances are among the most affordable payment instruments. Fees averaged 4.4% in Asia and globally as of the first quarter of 2023 (Figure 5.11b).

Digital remittances are typically sent digitally and received either in cash or digitally.

Digital remittances refer to "the electronic transfer of money from one person or entity to another, typically across international borders. The transfers are made through online platforms, mobile apps, and other digital channels that allow individuals to send and receive money quickly and securely."[34] The definition varies by institution, and the scope for estimating digital remittance volumes could vary as well (Table 5.1).

The pandemic accelerated the use of digital channels, notably in 2020, among emerging markets.

Efforts to digitalize remittances were under way before the pandemic. Lockdowns and social distancing rules in 2020 and 2021 boosted the use of digitalized remittance channels, and also lifted the capture of formal remittance data (ADB 2023a). Particularly in 2020, policy directions encouraged the use of digital channels for payments and remittances among emerging markets as did the use of digital banking and even digital fundraising for capitalization purposes (Cambridge Centre for Alternative Finance, World Bank, and World Economic Forum 2022).

Despite rapid growth, digital remittances remain limited, constituting less than 20% of total remittances. Publicly available estimates indicate that digital remittances grew at a rate of around 20% year-on-year from 2017 to 2023 (Figure 5.12). Yet the share of digital remittances to total remittances in 2023 was only around 18.5%. Transfers through online money transfer operators more than doubled to $135.2 billion in 2023 from $56 billion in 2017. Mobile money-enabled remittances increased sixfold from $3.8 billion in 2017 to $23.7 billion in 2023, thanks to the rise in internet and smartphone usage. Of the total usage of mobile money services, cross-border remittances accounted for only $15.9 billion or about 1% of global transaction volume in 2021, with usage in Asian economies

---

[34] This definition is from Statista. Digital Remittances - Worldwide. https://www.statista.com/outlook/dmo/fintech/digital-payments/digital-remittances/worldwide.

Figure 5.11: Average Total Cost of Remitting $200, as of Q1 2023

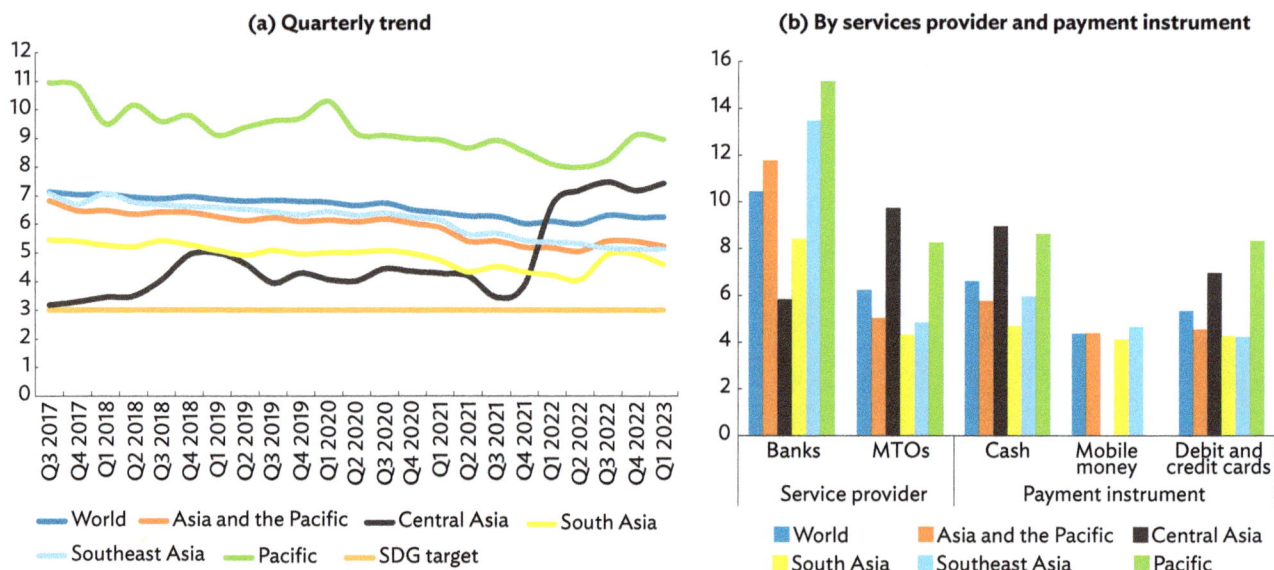

(a) Quarterly trend

(b) By services provider and payment instrument

World — Asia and the Pacific — Central Asia — South Asia — Southeast Asia — Pacific — SDG target

World — Asia and the Pacific — Central Asia — South Asia — Southeast Asia — Pacific

MTO = money transfer operator, Q = quarter, SDG = Sustainable Development Goal.

Note: Average cost is the simple and unweighted average of the total transaction costs of sending $200 in percentage.

Source: ADB calculations using data from World Bank. Remittance Prices Worldwide. https://remittanceprices.worldbank.org/ (accessed July 2023).

Table 5.1: Definition of Digital Remittances, by Institution

Source	Definition	Sending/Receiving Method	Transaction Estimate
World Bank	Digital remittances are sent online or self-assisted, received into accounts, like bank accounts, non-bank accounts, mobile money, or e-money	Sending digitally—receiving either in cash or digitally	–
International Organization for Migration	Digital remittances are made online using bank or money transfer operator apps or via bank card on bank or mobile operator websites	Sending digitally—receiving either in cash or digitally	–
Global System for Mobile Communications Association	Mobile money-enabled international remittances sent via mobile money to acquaintances	Sending digitally—receiving digitally	$21 billion in 2022
Visa Economic Empowerment Institute	Digital remittances are online transfers made via computer, mobile browser, or app, without in-person bank or money transfer operator visits	Sending digitally—receiving either in cash or digitally	34% as of second quarter 2022; 10% is digital end to end while 21% is digitally initiated
Statista	Online cross-border personal transfers, excluding payments for goods and domestic peer-to-peer transactions	Sending digitally—receiving either in cash or digitally; Does not include mobile money remittances	$200 billion in 2022

– = not available.

Sources: Global System for Mobile Communications Association (2023a); International Organization for Migration (2021); Statista Research Department. https://www.statista.com/ (accessed October 2023); Visa Economic Empowerment Institute (2022); and World Bank (2021).

Figure 5.12: Share of Digital Remittances in Total Remittances

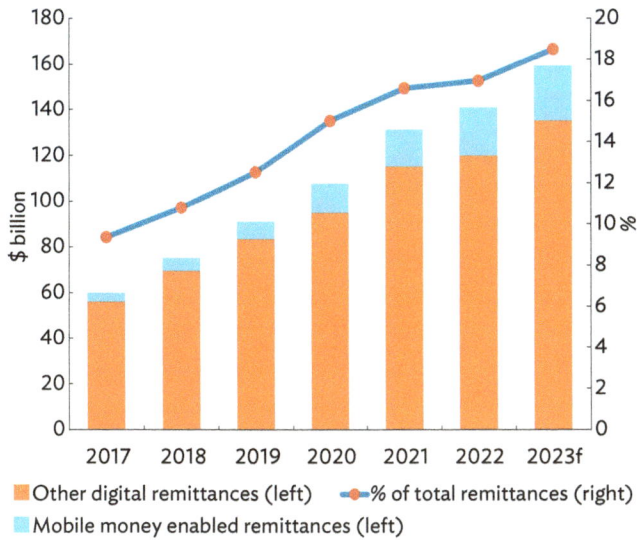

Other digital remittances (left) ●─ % of total remittances (right)
Mobile money enabled remittances (left)

Notes: Other digital remittances refer to the electronic transfer of money from one person or entity to another, typically across international borders. The transfers are made through online platforms, mobile apps, and other digital channels that allow individuals to send and receive money quickly and securely.

Sources: Global System for Mobile Communications Association (2023a), and Statista Research Department (2023a).

being much lower than in Africa (Figure 5.13; De Soyres et al. 2018; Mas and Radcliffe 2010; and Vodafone 2021). Meanwhile, Asia's usage of other digital remittances (20.4%) is the third largest globally, after Europe and North America (Figure 5.14).

The presence of a basic digital infrastructure is the minimum requirement for adoption of digital remittance.

The effective functioning of both hard and soft components of a foundational digital infrastructure is key to facilitating the widespread adoption of information and communication technologies, which has a notable impact on remittances (Gascon, Larramona, and Salvador 2023). Efficient and widespread internet connectivity, mobile phone ownership, improved mobile internet penetration, and affordable cost of using mobile internet are crucial elements to increase the utilization of mobile money for remittance transactions (Chokossa 2023). A well-functioning financial market facilitates the inflow of remittances through lower transaction costs (Bang, Mitra, and Wunnava 2013), provides access to financial services (Orozco and Yansura 2015), and creates options for sending and receiving remittances (Bare et al. 2022).

Figure 5.15 explores the relationship between digital remittances and factors including income, digital connectedness, and financial market development. This suggests a positive correlation between digital remittances and gross domestic product per capita, internet penetration as well as the Mobile Connectivity Index, which includes key enablers like infrastructure, affordability, readiness, and content and services.

Figure 5.13: Global Usage of Mobile Money Services, 2021

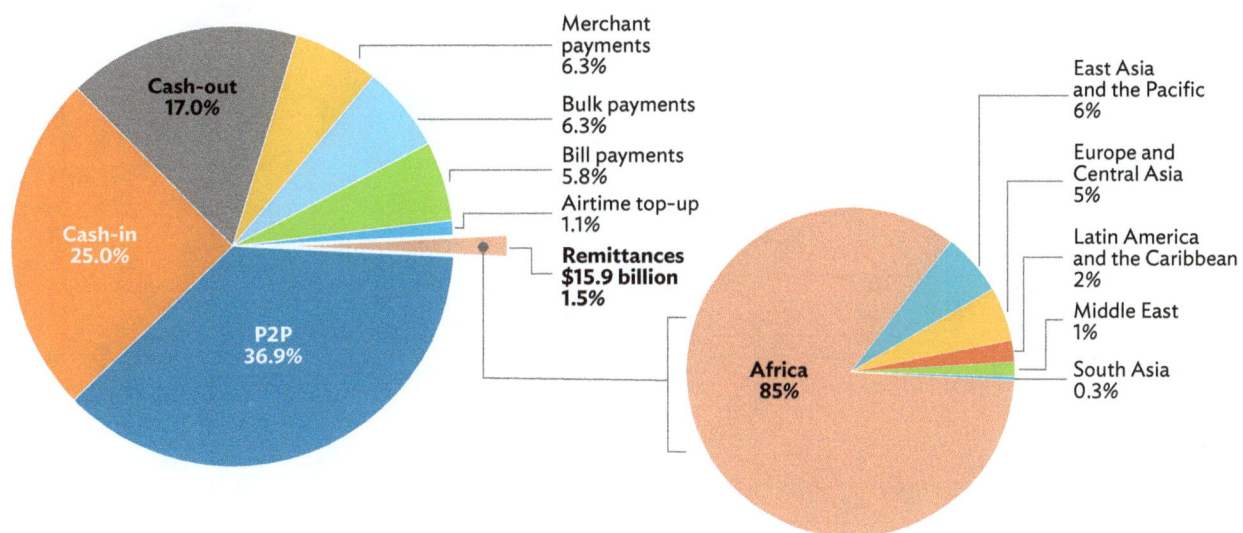

P2P = peer-to-peer.

Source: Global System for Mobile Communications Association (2021).

Digital remittance growth is limited by the digital ecosystem, infrastructural and regulatory challenges, and banking dominance.

Lack of a supportive ecosystem for digital payments limits the space for digital remittances to take root (Bank for International Settlements 2022). Especially in rural areas, information and communication technology infrastructure is weak and channels for receiving transfers digitally are limited (McKinsey & Company 2022). If funds received digitally must be converted to cash because many places do not accept digital payments, then cash remains more convenient. The cost of internet connectivity and phone ownership is also an issue for disadvantaged groups such as women-led households and rural communities.

Figure 5.14: Share of Other Digital Remittances by Sending Region, 2022

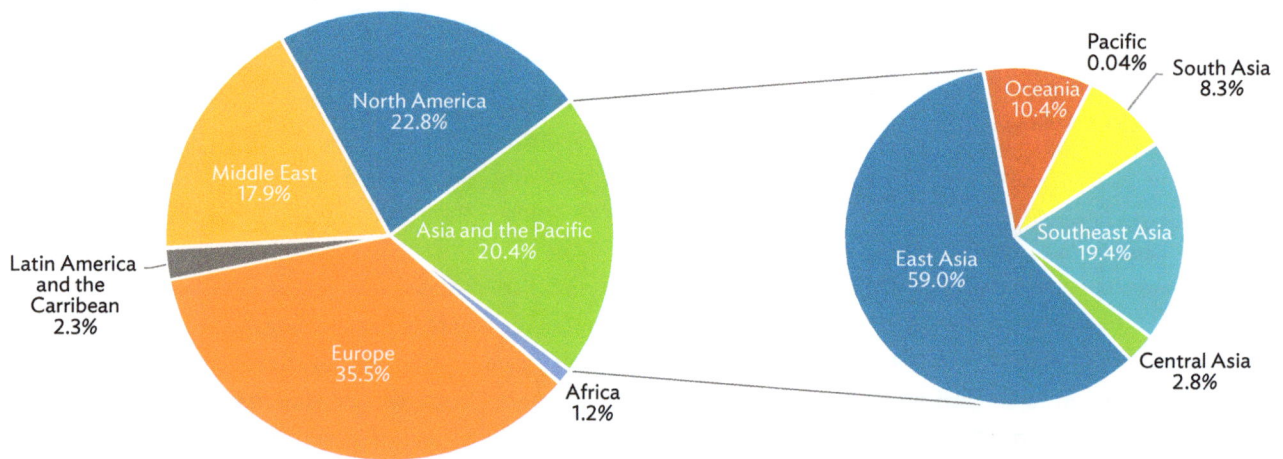

Notes: Other digital remittances refer to the electronic transfer of money from one person or entity to another, typically across international borders. The transfers are made through online platforms, mobile apps, and other digital channels that allow individuals to send and receive money quickly and securely.

Source: Statista Market Insights. https://www.statista.com/outlook/dmo/fintech/digital-payments/digital-remittances/worldwide?currency=usd (accessed November 2023).

Figure 5.15: Digital Remittances and Their Correlates—Asia and the Pacific, 2022

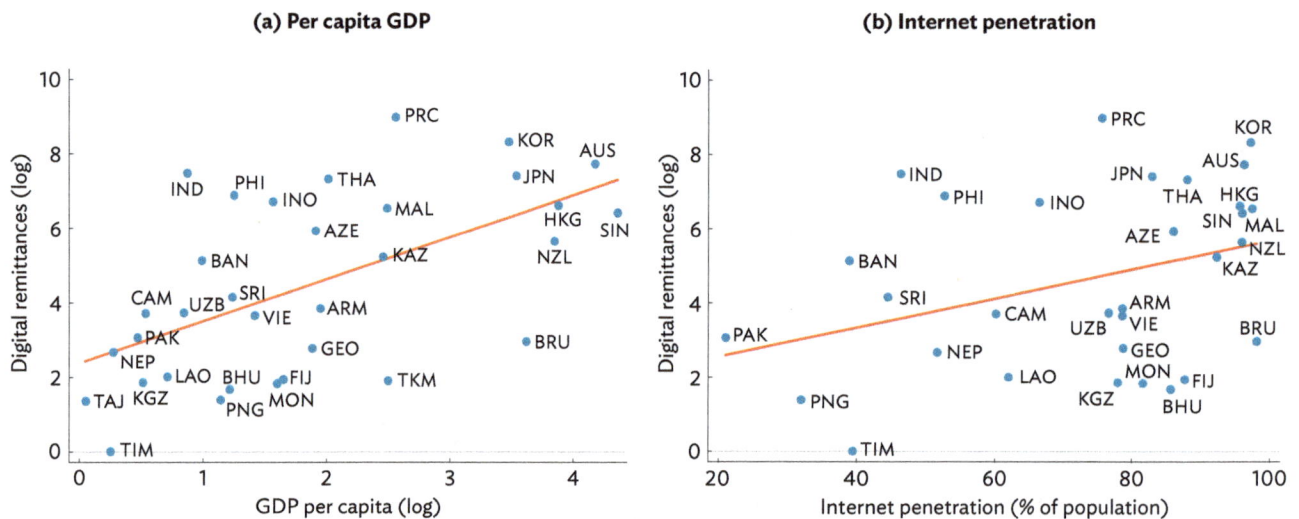

(a) Per capita GDP

(b) Internet penetration

continued on next page

Figure 5.15 continued

(c) Mobile connectivity

(d) Financial market development

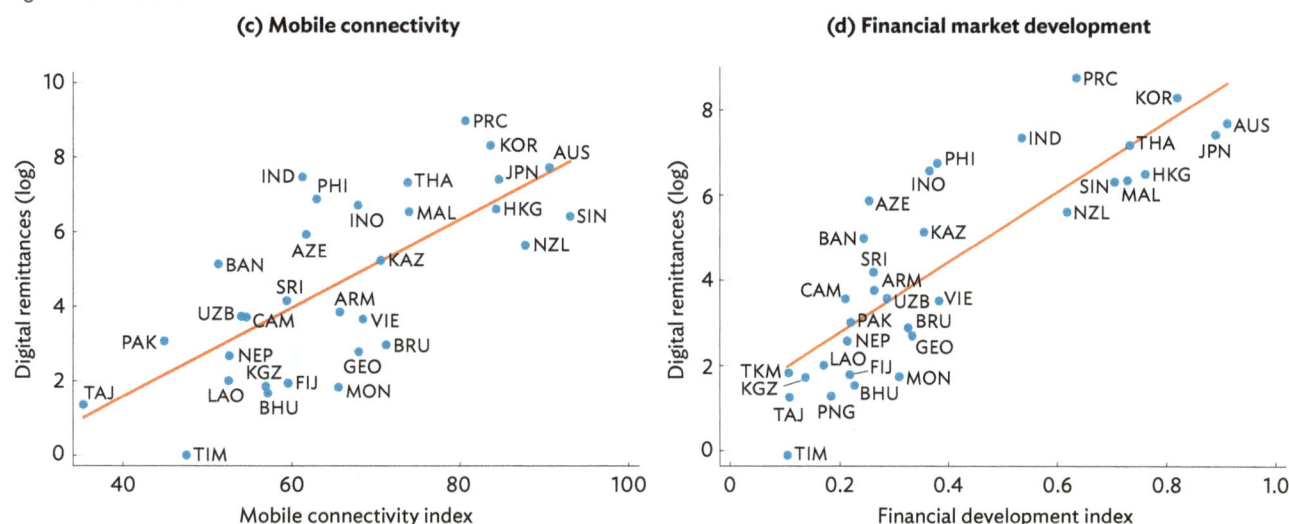

ARM = Armenia; AUS = Australia; AZE = Azerbaijan; BAN = Bangladesh; BHU = Bhutan; BRU = Brunei Darussalam; CAM = Cambodia; FIJ = Fiji; GDP = gross domestic product; GEO = Georgia; HKG = Hong Kong, China; IND = India; INO = Indonesia; JPN = Japan; KAZ = Kazakhstan; KOR = Republic of Korea; KGZ = Kyrgyz Republic; LAO = Lao People's Democratic Republic; MAL = Malaysia; MON = Mongolia; NEP = Nepal; NZL = New Zealand; PAK = Pakistan, PNG = Papua New Guinea; PRC = People's Republic of China; SIN = Singapore; SRI = Sri Lanka; TAJ = Tajikistan; THA = Thailand; TIM = Timor-Leste; UZB = Uzbekistan; VIE = Viet Nam.

Notes: For internet penetration, data refer to the year 2022 for GEO, HKG, INO, KAZ, KOR, MAL, PRC, SIN, THA, and VIE. For the rest of the economies, data refer to 2021.

Sources: ADB calculations using data from Statista Market Insights. https://www.statista.com/outlook/dmo/fintech/digital-payments/digital-remittances/worldwide?currency=usd (accessed November 2023); World Bank. World Development Indicators. https://databank.worldbank.org/ (accessed October 2023); Global System for Mobile Communications Association (2023a); and International Monetary Fund. Financial Development Index Database. https://data.imf.org/?sk=f8032e80-b36c-43b1-ac26-493c5b1cd33b (accessed October 2023).

Lack of access to financial services also limits both the number and access to transaction accounts. Many remittance sending and receiving households lack bank accounts, deposit-taking nonbank accounts, and mobile money for secure payment reception and value storage. This underscores the need to ramp up financial inclusion efforts.

Current and potential users of digital remittances have limited knowledge of digital products and tools, making cash the default and convenient option. Giving migrants more information about their options could also spillover to their beneficiary families.

The predominance of traditional banks in financial services can slow the pace of innovation even as the strongest recent advances have come from nonbank payment service providers.

The presence of foreign exchange controls could also make some consumers gravitate toward unregulated services, which offer greater convenience and even favorable exchange rates or require less documentation.

Fragmented Collection Methods for Digital Remittances Are a Major Challenge

According to the World Bank's Remittance Prices Worldwide, senders pay prominent online money transfer operators high service fees to transfer funds to bank accounts, credit cards, or debit cards, all accessed through the Internet. At the receiving end, cash is the most popular pick-up method, as observed in remittance corridors surveyed by the World Bank. Cash is followed by bank accounts, which are likely used for subsequent cash withdrawals. However, the share of direct cash pick-up declined to 30% to 40% in 2022 during the pandemic (Figure 5.16). Mobile wallets, which represent a completely digital transaction method, make up around 10%. This underscores the challenges of fully transitioning to digital transfers, especially at the receiver's end, where cash remains a favored option.

Figure 5.16: Trends of Pick-Up Methods for Remittances Sent Through Digital-Only Money Transfer Operators, Global Share (%)

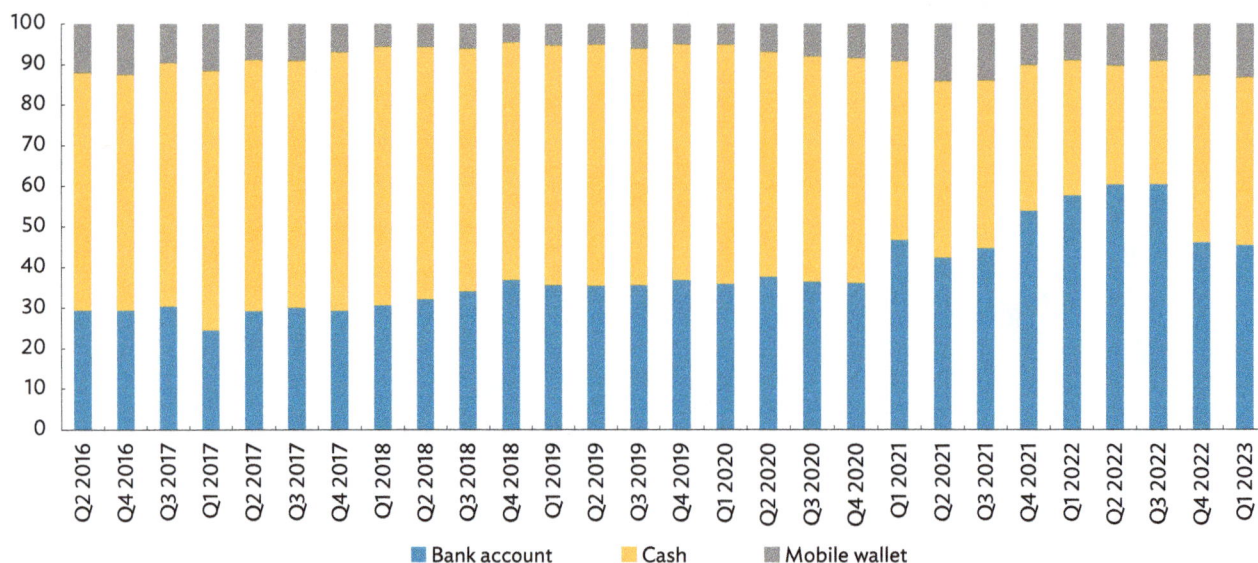

MTO = money transfer operator, Q = quarter.

Notes: Digital-only MTO includes five digital-only MTOs: Wise, Remitly, WorldRemit, InstaReM, and Xoom. The figures are based on the number of receiving channels available in the surveyed corridors. Sending is done through the internet only.

Source: ADB calculations using data from World Bank. Remittances Prices Worldwide. https://remittanceprices.worldbank.org/ (accessed July 2023).

Policy Implications

Expanding access to banking services could help hit the twin goals of greater financial inclusion and digital remittance uptake. Migrants and their families often lack access to banking services. Typically, their first interactions with the regulated finance sector come through remittance transactions. Digitalizing these can pave the way for financial inclusion and reduce remittance costs (Ardic et al. 2022). By transitioning to digital methods, like account-to-account transfers, policymakers and service providers can deepen financial inclusion and open entry point to financial services such as savings, insurance, and credit.

Enabling digital infrastructure is essential to transition successfully toward a more digitalized remittance market. Developing digital infrastructure for the remittance market requires governments to invest intensely in information technology infrastructure and human capital to build, manage, and deliver digital solutions. Governments can engage more private capital through public–private partnerships and incentives to keep capital flowing, and secure sufficient financial resources to keep data and technology expertise available.

Initiatives to standardize methods for collecting, processing, and reporting remittance data could optimize efforts to digitalize the remittance environment. Consolidating approaches toward collecting and compiling remittance data through internationally agreed standards and definitions is a step in the right direction. Strengthening bilateral remittance statistics would not only improve the flow analysis of remittance markets, but more timely remittance data could enhance evidence-based policymaking toward achieving remittance-related Sustainable Development Goals.

An enabling regulatory environment is crucial for wider mobile services adoption, potentially leading to increased use of remittances. A more facilitative regulatory environment is associated with greater mobile money usage, especially for women (Bahia, Sanchez-Vidal, and Taberner 2020). On the other hand, onerous regulations could stifle mobile money adoption (Evans and Pirchio 2015). The potential impact of favorable regulation on mobile adoption extends to enhanced financial inclusion and lower average transaction costs, while helping bridge the mobile gender divide (GSMA 2023b).

Increased international cooperation is essential for further reducing remittance costs and enhancing payment systems. While remittance costs have been lowered through the promotion of nonbanking payment systems, enhanced consumer financial literacy, and expanded market access for both providers and consumers, the role of shared commitments is becoming increasingly important. This shared focus includes improving cross-border payment infrastructure and arrangements. Key initiatives aim to reduce remittance transaction costs to below 3% and to eliminate high-cost corridors (Figure 5.17). Efforts are also being channeled into developing innovative payment systems for underserved groups, fostering digital inclusion, ensuring system interoperability, refining regulatory frameworks, and standardizing data and messaging protocols.

All remittance stakeholders can benefit from robust and widespread knowledge-sharing. The potential impact of digital remittances must be known not only to remittance senders and their beneficiaries and remittance providers, but also among regulators and policymakers. Remittance knowledge packs, particularly digital remittance tools, must be part of the emigration strategy of migrant-sending economies. Better-informed regulators can pave the way for effecting laws and guidelines on digital technology and digital remittance tools, more investments, better state of competition, and improved access to finance.

International Tourism

Tourism Recovery Should Be Matched with Greater Resilience

International tourism in Asia continues to recover lost ground, with arrivals and receipts climbing rapidly toward pre-pandemic levels. Global arrivals of 1.3 billion in 2023 herald a strong recovery globally for the second consecutive year, with total arrivals recovering around 88% of the 2019 level. This is despite continuing economic and geopolitical challenges (UNWTO 2024).[35] Among the six major regions, Europe and Latin America and the Caribbean have recovered at least 90% of pre-pandemic tourist arrivals in 2023 (Figure 5.18a). North America has recovered around 85% while Africa and the Middle East have fully recovered their pre-pandemic tourist arrivals.

Asia is the slowest region to recover, with tourist arrivals in 2023 reaching 73.2% of the 2019 numbers. This is considerable given that, during the same period in 2021 and 2022, the region recovered only 4.9% and 28.8% of its prepandemic arrivals, respectively (Figure 5.18b).

International tourism receipts have also recovered across regions, with the global total of $1.4 trillion estimated for 2023 (UNWTO 2024). Pent-up travel and the lifting of border restrictions across major destination economies boosted visitor spending and passenger transport fares and had reached $1.6 trillion in 2023, compared to $1.3 trillion in 2022. Leading the tourism receipts recovery in 2023 is the Middle East—it exceeded its pre-pandemic tourism earnings by 31.5% at $137 billion over $104 billion in 2019 (Figure 5.19). Asia, reflecting the pace of tourist arrivals, improved its tourism receipts profile in the last 2 years, but remains behind other major regions.

Various factors have contributed to Asia's laggard tourism recovery in 2023.

Many Asian destinations remained restricted to nonessential travel as late in the pandemic as 2022. Domestic policies on travel restrictions in Asia and the reopening of borders came later than in other regions, were staggered, and varied across destinations. Until the early months of 2023, the PRC's strict zero-COVID policy severely decreased visitor arrivals (ADB 2023a). Inflation also reduced purchasing power and discretionary income, making tourists more discerning in their travel plans.

---

[35] According to the United Nations World Tourism Organization (UNWTO) Panel of Tourism Experts, these economic and geopolitical challenges include the current conflict in the Middle East, the Russian invasion of Ukraine, persistent inflation, high interest rates, volatile oil prices, trade disruptions, and staffing shortages (UNWTO 2024).

Figure 5.17: Global Initiatives to Lower Remittance Costs and Enhance Cross-Border Payment Systems

2009
G8 5x5 Remittance Target

- Reduction of the global average cost of remittance service from 10% to 5% in 5 years

2011
G20 Remittance Cost Reduction Goal

- Reduction of the global cost of sending remittances by 5 percentage points

2014
G20 Plant to Facilitate Remittance Flows

- Economy-led actions in the reduction of the cost of sending remittances
- Periodic progress reviews by the GPFI

2015
UN SDGs

- Inclusion in the SDGs of a reduction to less than 3% of remittance transaction costs

2015
G20 National Remittances Plan

- National Remittances Plan finalized by G20 members
- Annual reviews and biannual updating by GPFI

2016
G20 Remittance Cost Reduction Updated Goal

- Reduction of the cost of remittances to less than 3%
- Elimination of remittance corridors with costs higher than 5% by 2023

2020
G20 Financial Inclusion Action Plan Recommendation

- Innovative payment systems development for underserved groups
- Focus on digital financial inclusion and SME finance

2021
G20 Roadmap for Cross-Border Payments

- Advancing interlinked payment systems and infrastructure
- Reduction of the average cost of remittances to below 3%

2022
G20 Roadmap for Enhancing Cross-Border Payments: Consolidated Progress Report

Three target areas:
1. Payment system interoperability
2. Regulatory frameworks
3. Cross-border data and message standards

2022
BIS CPMI Recommendations on Interlinking Payment Systems

- Framework for payment system operators and authorities
- Alternatives to correspondent banking for wholesale payments
- Benefits, challenges, and risks of interlinking arrangements

2023
CPMI Proposal on Harmonization Requirements for Cross-Border Payments

- International standards financial e-messages
- Addressing the fragmented and mixed use of payment messaging standards

BIS = Bank for International Settlements, CPMI = Committee on Payments and Market Infrastructure, G8 = Group of Eight, G20 = Group of Twenty, GPFI = Global Partnership for Financial Inclusion, SDG = Sustainable Development Goal, SMEs = small and medium-sized enterprises.

Sources: Ardic et al. (2022); BIS (2023a, 2023b); Financial Stability Board (2022); G20 Development Working Group (2021); and GPFI (2018, 2023).

Figure 5.18: International Tourist Arrivals (%)

(a) Total arrivals as share of 2019

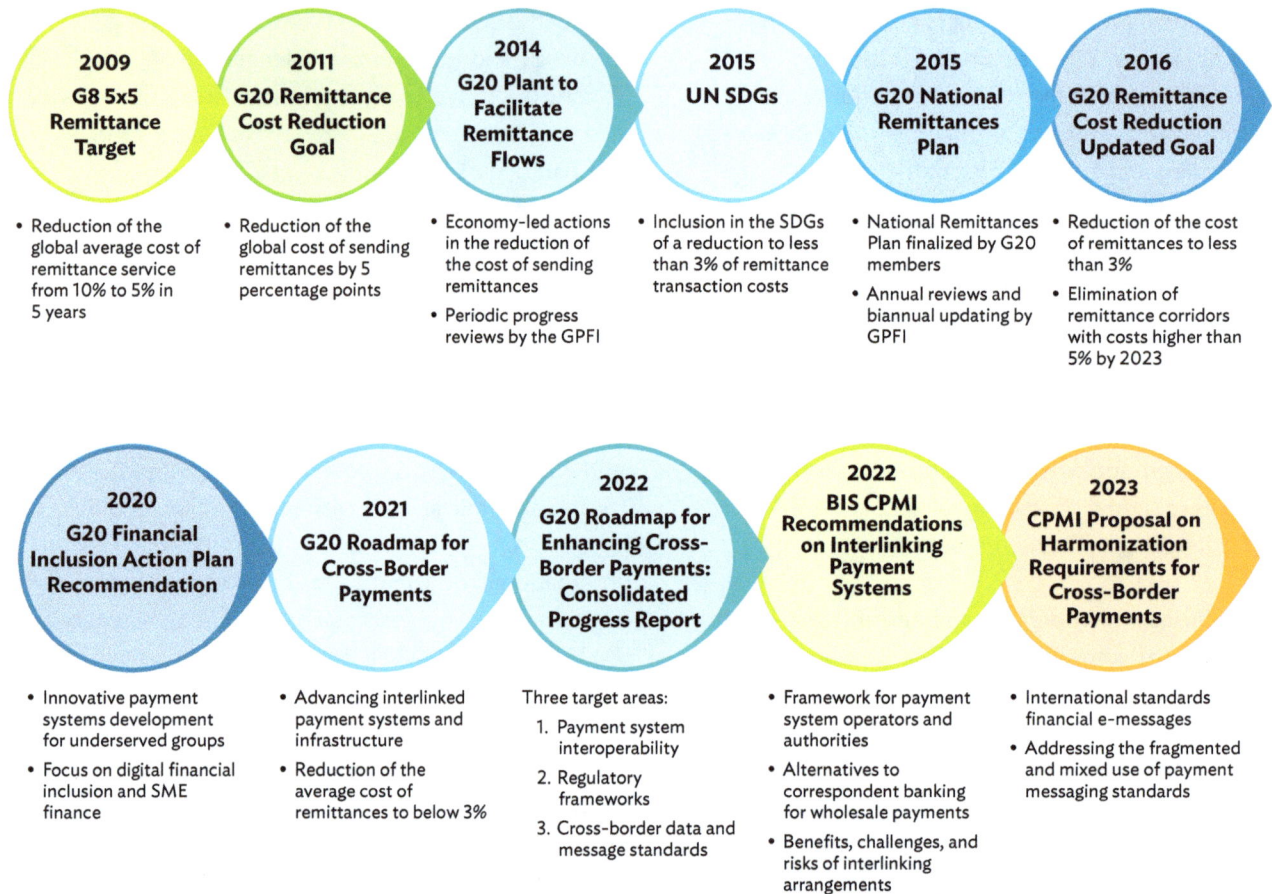

(b) Recovery rates of tourist arrivals to Asia and the Pacific
(against 2019)

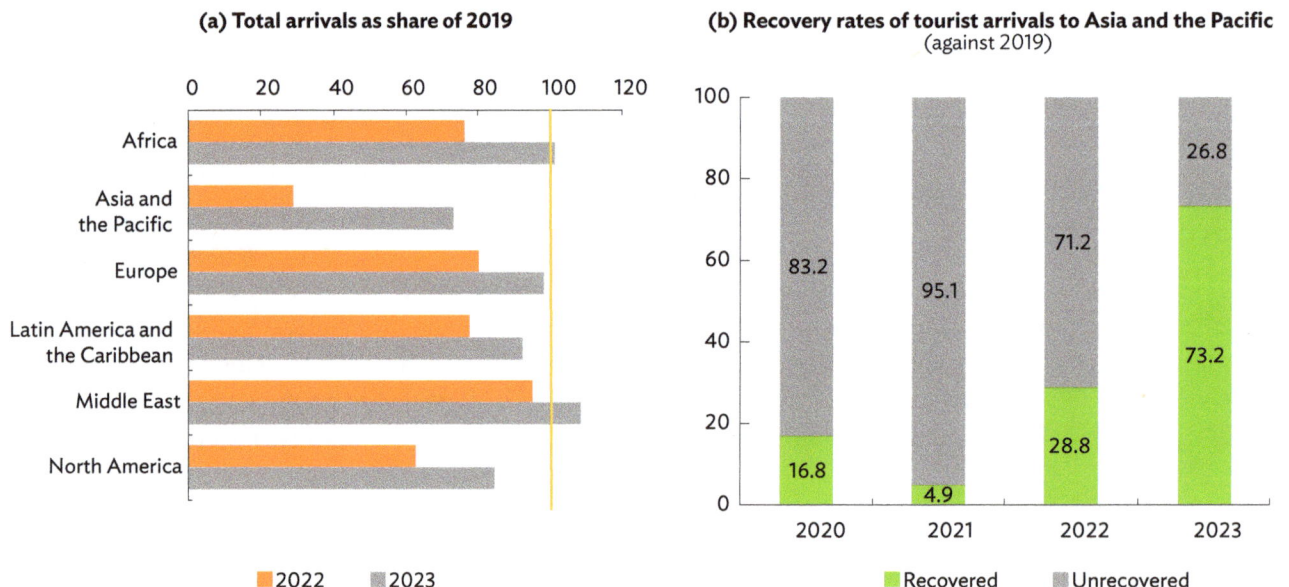

Notes: Includes economies with complete data for 2019, 2022, and 2023. The regional classification of ADB's Asian Economic Integration Report was used.

Source: ADB calculations using data from United Nations World Tourism Organization. Tourism Data Dashboard. https://www.unwto.org/tourism-data/un-tourism-tourism-dashboard (accessed January 2024).

Figure 5.19: International Tourism Receipts by Region (% of 2019)

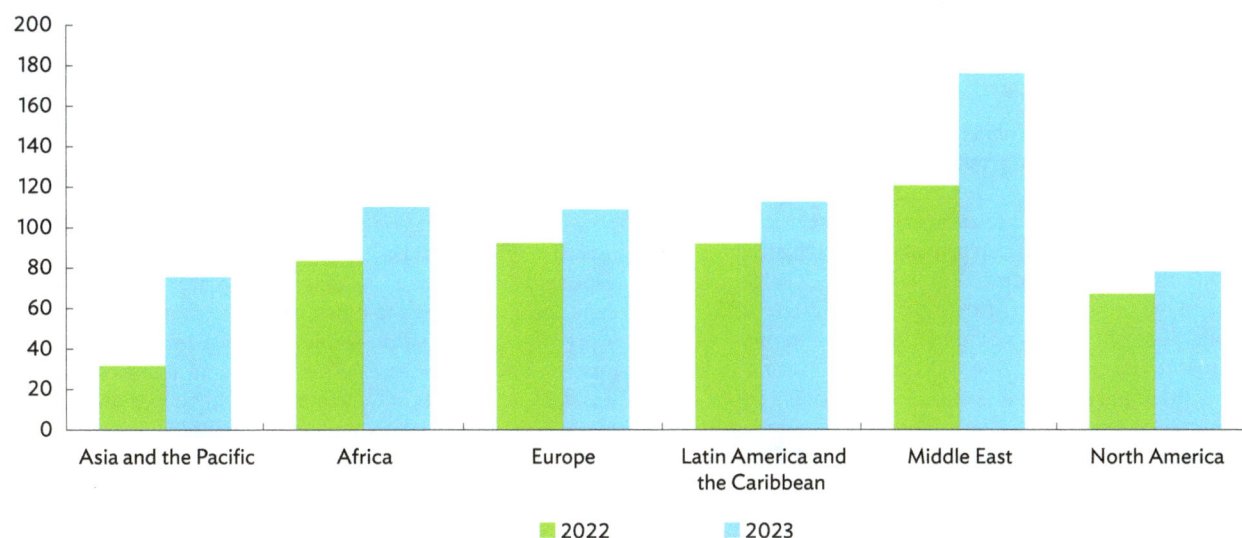

2022   2023

Note: Includes economies with complete data for 2019, 2022, and 2023. The regional classification of ADB's Asian Economic Integration Report was used.

Source: ADB calculations using data from United Nations World Tourism Organization. Tourism Data Dashboard. https://www.unwto.org/tourism-data/un-tourism-tourism-dashboard (accessed January 2024).

Even with reopened borders, the resumption of international tourism flows into the region was slowed by air connectivity issues, flight capacity challenges, and the reinstatement of visa arrangements between and among economies. International air seat capacity of Asia continues to lag behind other regions (Richter 2022). Airlines are slow in restoring capacity as fleets got retired during the pandemic and international flight seat capacity remains far below pre-pandemic levels in Asia (66% of that in 2019).[36] This is keeping air fares elevated and pushing travelers to postpone their overseas travel.

Labor and staffing issues continue to beset the air travel and tourism sectors. The COVID-19-induced exodus of tourism staff in 2020 led to 62 million job losses in travel and tourism. Staff shortages are compromising efficient airline and airport operations especially during peak travel season. In Asia, lost tourism staff has been a major impediment for tourism recovery. Thailand lost 3.9 million tourism workers in the pandemic who show little sign of returning to their old jobs. In Singapore, tourism staffing is at 78% of what it was in 2019.

More importantly, the region experienced low tourist flows from the PRC in 2021 because of travel restrictions for outbound tourists (Box 5.1).

Within Asia, variation remains among the subregions.

Recovery rates in total arrivals in 2023 were strongest for Central Asia and the Pacific—around 95% of the total arrivals in 2019—followed by South Asia and Oceania (Figure 5.20). Strong marketing and government support raised destination attractiveness for the Cook Islands, Fiji, Palau, and Samoa in the Pacific enabled the subregion to recover its 2019 tourism receipts in 2023 (Figure 5.21). During the same period, stronger arrivals to India and Nepal helped raise tourism income flows to South Asia, while vibrant receipts of Armenia, Georgia, Tajikistan, and Uzbekistan resulted in Central Asia surpassing its tourism receipts in 2023.

---

[36] United Nations World Tourism Organization. Tourism Data Dashboard. https://www.unwto.org/tourism-data/un-tourism-tourism-dashboard (accessed January 2024).

Box 5.1: Post-Pandemic Outbound Tourism from the People's Republic of China: Implications for Asian Destinations

The People's Republic of China (PRC) is a major player in global tourism. In 2019, 154.6 million outbound Chinese tourists spent $254.6 billion. On average, that is higher than those of United States tourists, and almost twice as much as German and British tourists (United Nations World Tourism Organization 2022). The zero-COVID policy and prolonged travel restrictions during 2020–2021 had kept much of the PRC's borders closed to international tourism. With the announcement of border reopening in January 2023, and even as the approach to opening travel destinations was staggered, it generated much optimism for a tourism recovery in Asia and the Pacific in 2023.

Asia accounted for about 60% of total outbound travel from the PRC from 2015 to 2019. These were most significant to East Asian economies, particularly Hong Kong, China where 67% of tourist arrivals were from the PRC (box figure 1). The resumption of PRC outbound travel was seen to stimulate demand in Asian destinations, particularly those dependent on PRC tourists.

However, the impact of outbound tourism from the PRC has been overshadowed by global macroeconomic uncertainties and inflation. A sluggish PRC economy and weaker yuan is curtailing demand for overseas travel. The revival in PRC visitors is happening at a slower pace than expected (box figure 2). Challenges in restoring flight capacity, visa processing times, and managing COVID-19-entry rules in destination economies have also dampened recovery. Although the PRC's international airline capacity was 4.8 million seats in November 2023, this was only 57% of the 2019 level (Official Airline Guide 2024).

In 2020–2022, the Asian economies most dependent on PRC visitors suffered as PRC tourism spending shrank by an estimated aggregate $145 billion per year. Palau, the Pacific economy most dependent on PRC tourists, suffered an average annual loss of $42 million (about 15% of its 2019 GDP) for 2020–2022. By Asian subregion, Southeast Asia suffered the most at 1.5% of its 2019 GDP (equivalent to $48 billion [box figure 3]).

1: Average Share of the People's Republic of China in Asian Economy's Total Tourist Arrivals, 2015–2019 (%)

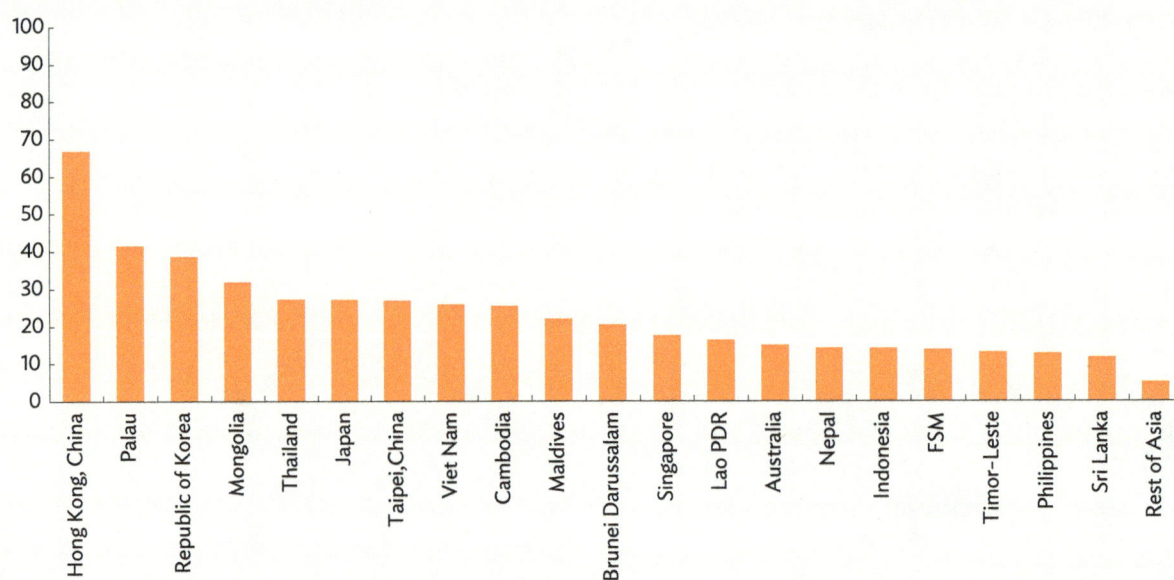

FSM = Federated States of Micronesia, Lao PDR = Lao People's Democratic Republic.

Source: ADB calculations using data from United Nations World Tourism Organization. Tourism Satellite Accounts. http://statistics.unwto.org (accessed January 2024).

continued on next page

Box 5.1 continued

Though expectations were for PRC outbound travel to pick up in the second half of 2023, the slower than anticipated recovery has led some to predict that the PRC will surpass its 2019 total in 2025 with 179 million outbound tourists (Bowerman 2023). On top of this, with the PRC economy still struggling to recover from the pandemic, PRC tourists are more conscious of spending when abroad (Martin 2023).

The attitudes of PRC outbound tourists are changing. McKinsey and Company's (2023) latest Survey of Chinese Tourist Attitudes shows that 40% of PRC tourists want to visit developed destinations in Asia such as Australia, New Zealand, and Japan. A similar survey found Australia and Thailand among top destinations for potential PRC overseas

visitors (Parulis-Cook 2023). Preferences are changing as many Chinese people choose to travel in smaller groups or more with family members. They also favor technology-assisted and/or technology-enhanced tourism. Tourism authorities and travel agencies in destination economies should consider these factors, alongside solutions to bottlenecks in tourism flows, in redesigning their strategies to attract tourists from the PRC.

2: Tourist Arrivals from the People's Republic of China to Selected Asian Economies (% of total tourist arrivals)

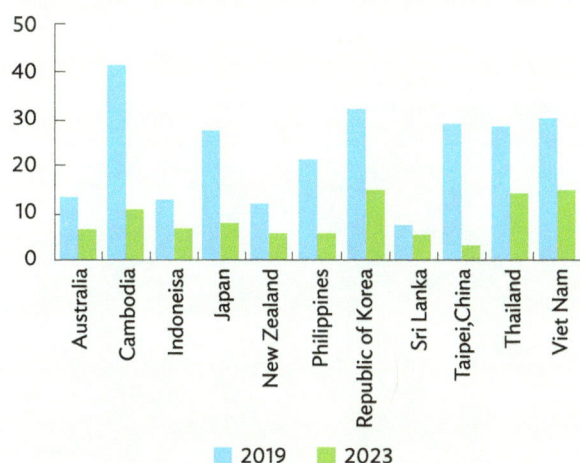

2019   2023

Source: ADB calculations using data from CEIC Data Company (accessed January 2024).

3: Estimated Decline in the Tourism Expenditure of the People's Republic of China in Asian Subregions, 2020–2022 (% of 2019 GDP)

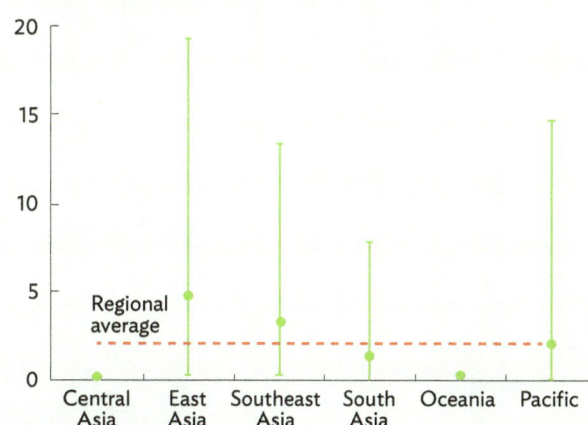

GDP = gross domestic product.

Notes: For each subregion, maximum (upper line), average (thick dot), and minimum (lower line) values are reported. The horizontal line denotes Asia's regional average of 2.1%.

Sources: ADB calculations using data from CEIC Data Company; International Monetary Fund. World Development Outlook Database. https://www.imf.org/en/Publications/WEO/weo-database/2023/October; and United Nations World Tourism Organization. Tourism Satellite Accounts. http://statistics.unwto.org (all accessed November 2023).

Sources: Bowerman (2023); CEIC Data Company; Martin (2023); McKinsey and Company (2023); Official Airline Guide (2024); Parulis-Cook (2023); United Nations World Tourism Organization (2022); and World Tourism Organization. Tourism Satellite Accounts. http://statistics.unwto.org (accessed November 2023 and January 2024).

Subregional arrivals could influence the degree of tourism cooperation within subregions.

Intraregional tourism flow is key for many ADB subregions. In 2019, intrasubregional flows (i.e., source and destination economies from same subregion) were particularly high in East Asia (72.4%) while Southeast Asia had similar intrasubregional flows (56.5%) and intersubregional flows (i.e., the source and destination

of tourists are different subregions) (Figure 5.22). This did not vanish altogether during the crisis. From 2020 to 2022, Southeast Asia had stronger intrasubregional flows (averaging 76.8%), in large part due to the efforts of ASEAN member economies to restart tourism. Strong intrasubregional ties could expedite subregional tourism strategies, while robust intersubregional ties allow for better exploration of alternative markets within the whole Asian region.

Figure 5.20: International Tourist Arrivals by Asian Subregion (% of 2019)

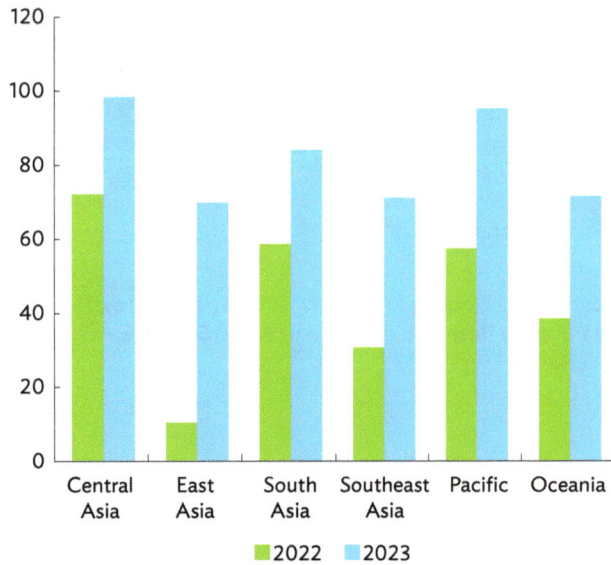

Note: Includes economies with complete data for 2019, 2022, and 2023. The regional classification of ADB's Asian Economic Integration Report was used.

Source: ADB calculations using data from United Nations World Tourism Organization. Tourism Data Dashboard. https://www.unwto.org/tourism-data/un-tourism-tourism-dashboard (accessed January 2024).

Figure 5.21: International Tourism Receipts by Asian Subregion (% of 2019)

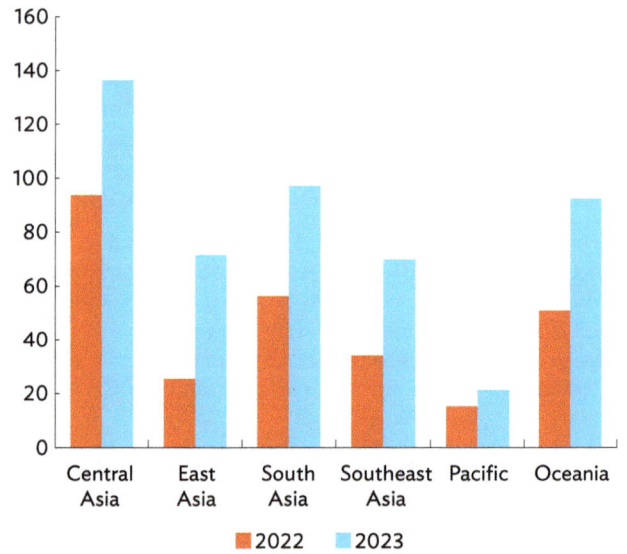

Note: Includes economies with complete data for 2019, 2022, and 2023. The regional classification of ADB's Asian Economic Integration Report was used.

Source: ADB calculations using data from United Nations World Tourism Organization. Tourism Data Dashboard. https://www.unwto.org/tourism-data/un-tourism-tourism-dashboard (accessed January 2024).

Figure 5.22: Source Markets for Tourism in Asia and the Pacific

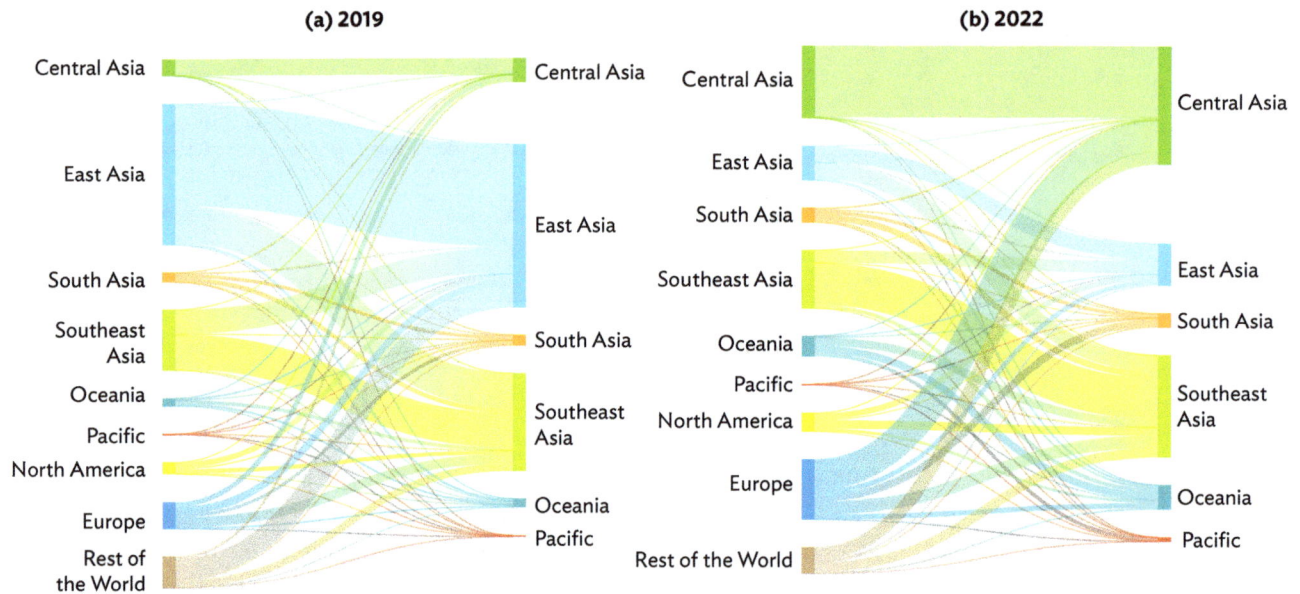

(a) 2019

(b) 2022

Source: ADB calculations using data from United Nations World Tourism Organization. Tourism Satellite Accounts. http://statistics.unwto.org (accessed January 2024).

Despite the recovery momentum in tourism activities, challenges to growth persist.

Soon after the World Health Organization declared in March 2023 that the coronavirus was no longer a public health emergency of international concern, most economies lifted their COVID-19-related restrictions. Even so, some challenges remained for the global tourism economy. According to the UNWTO Panel of Tourism Experts survey of barriers to the international tourism recovery, challenges have eased for most of the listed categories shown in Figure 5.23 between September 2022 and September 2023, except for transportation and accommodation costs. The slight uptick in consumer confidence in this period is not surprising given the limited recovery of air traffic capacity, labor shortages, and inflation.

Given the diversity of the Asian destination economies and the lingering pandemic impact, inflation, and ongoing geopolitical tensions, Asia's full return to its pre-pandemic tourism status could take until the end of 2025. Of the UNWTO Panel of Experts Survey, 41% pointed to a 2024 return while 50% believed it will take up to 2025 or later, given the comparatively slower recovery despite recent reopening of several destinations within the region (UNWTO 2023c). The UNWTO Confidence Index also indicated that 67% of tourism professionals believe that tourism will perform better in 2024 than in 2023

(UNWTO 2024). Meanwhile, the Pacific Asia Travel Association is foreseeing robust annual growth until the end of 2025 during which Asia would achieve its pre-COVID period statistics (*Travel Weekly Asia* 2023).

Digital Technology Holds Promise for Tourism Sector Recovery and Resilience

With tourism on its way to recovery, policymakers are paying attention to both short-term and long-term policy reforms. In the short-term, governments are prioritizing to get back the tourism economies and livelihoods quickly back on track to pre-pandemic level. For the long-term, governments are laying the path to "build forward better." This involves implementing recovery policies that encourage applications of digital technology to stimulate investment and behavioral changes that build resilience against future shocks. Strengthening regional cooperation in tourism has become more important than ever and is increasingly seen as being supported by digital economy cooperation.

The tourism economy was among the first sectors to digitalize on a global scale by consistently riding the waves of information and communication technology innovation and the ubiquity of internet-enabled devices. For instance, online travel agents have captured around

Figure 5.23: Barriers to the Recovery of Global Tourism

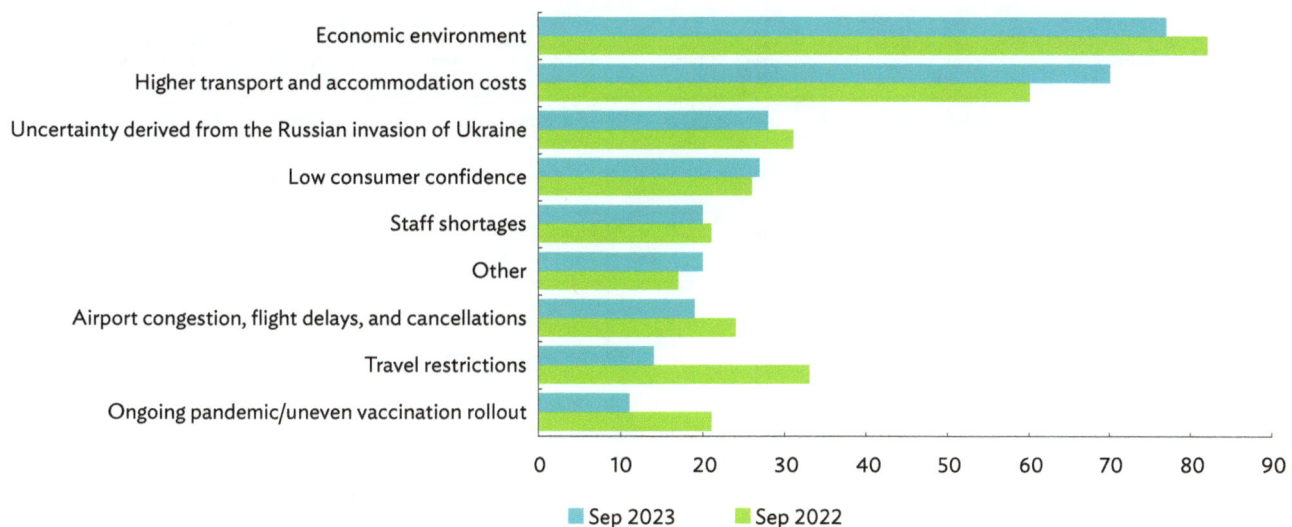

Legend: ■ Sep 2023   ■ Sep 2022

Sources: United Nations World Tourism Organization (2023a, 2023b).

40% of the global travel market (CBI 2022). From an estimated market size worth $521 billion in 2023, the online travel market is predicted to grow to $1 trillion by 2030 (Statista 2023). This exponential transformation of the tourism sector through digital innovation underscored its power to generate new business which underpin the growth, competitiveness, and sustainability of the sector. Digitalization of key aspects in aviation, travel, and tourism could generate industry profits of up to $305 billion, reallocate $100 billion of market value from traditional competitors to new players, and produce net sector and social benefits worth up to $700 billion (World Economic Forum 2017).

The imperative to transform traditional tourism into smart tourism through digitalization rests on the premise that smart tourism could help ensure the competitiveness and sustainability of current and future destinations. Australia's long-term strategy for sustainable visitor growth, THRIVE 2030, follows this premise, aiming to grow visitor spending to $230 billion by 2030. Singapore is turning one of its tourism hubs, Sentosa Island, into a hotbed for innovation and smart tourism technologies.

Given the multilayered network of the tourism economy among numerous market players and stakeholders, how much of the wide spectrum of tourism supply chains can be digitalized for efficiency and net development gains? Indeed, all smart travel facilitation and smart tourist destination activities are highly amenable to digitalization (ADB 2023c).[37] A variety of technology solutions are available (Figure 5.24). Use of these smart technology tools should help increase the flow of tourists to destinations, improve the performance of tourism businesses, enhance the tourist experience, and boost overall resource management efficiency.

However, Asian economies are not all at the same level of digital maturity to embrace digitalization of the entire value chain of tourism activities, which explains the differences in their uptake of digital technology. Transitioning to a smart tourism ecosystem requires tackling challenges beyond the digital divide. While some economies in the region are in the initial stage of building telecom infrastructure—raising internet and computer usage among its population—some are in the intermediate stage of improving digital literacy, developing regulations for cybersecurity, privacy, and

Figure 5.24: Application of Smart Tools across Tourism Value Chain

| Smart Tools | Smart Travel Facilitation | | Smart Tourist Destination | | | |
	Travel organization and booking	Transportation	Accommodation	Foods, beverages, and other shops	Tourism assets	Leisure, excursions, and tours
Smart Identity	Automated check in, smart visas, health certificates	Tourist passes, facial verification	Automated check-in and check-out	Thermal screening	Thermal screening, tourist passes	Thermal screening, tourist passes
Smart Platforms	Aggregators, marketing, chatbots, payment system	Sharing economy, aggregators, payment system	Sharing economy, aggregators, payment system	Online ordering, reservations, reviews and ratings, payment system	Information dissemination, ticket booking, payment system	Information dissemination, ticket booking, payment system
Smart Logistics	Smart baggage management	Integrated traffic management, autonomous vehicles	Smart baggage management	Food delivery systems	Crowd management	Crowd management
Smart Experience	...	...	Virtual tours	Interactive menus	Virtual tours, metaverse	Virtual tours, metaverse
Smart Devices	...	Baggage tracking, fleet management	Smart rooms	Inventory management	Smart sensors for tracking	Personalized experience

Illustrative and non-exhaustive

Source: ADB (2023c).

---

[37] Smart travel facilitation comprises of travel registration and booking; and transportation. Smart tourist destination includes accommodation; food, beverages, and other shops; tourism assets; and leisure, excursions, and tours.

building e-commerce/ e-payment systems. The final stage, the most advanced, is where most activities happen online and stakeholders are encouraged to innovate and leverage advanced technology in data analytics for business and policy decisions. Accordingly, economies vary in the extent of their intensity and level of technology and digital application for tourism services (Box 5.2).

Box 5.2: Digital Tools and Smart Tourism in Asian Economies

Economies in Asia and the Pacific are driving their pandemic recovery agendas by incorporating digital technology into smart tourism strategies. Smart tools range from identity systems such as facial verification to virtual tours promoting efficient and sustainable tourism. The Philippines in May 2023 began using the eTravel system to do away with paper-based arrival and departure cards. Cambodia is studying the use of citizen identification cards instead of passports for Thai tourists. Malaysia introduced biometrics and facial recognition technology in 2020 and the Malaysia Digital Arrival Card in October 2023 to streamline visitor arrival procedures. And Singapore has launched a new biometrics system for its citizens to clear immigration (Online Travel Evisa 2023; *Khmer Times* 2023; and Redins 2023).[a]

On a global scale, IATA (2022) reported that the International Civil Aviation Organization has obliged all its members to implement the Advance Passenger Information (API) system, which includes digital data on passengers collected by air carriers and transmitted to border control agencies before the flight. This enables border control agencies to work on security and so allows faster processing of low-risk passengers. In Asia and the Pacific, 26 economies have an API system in place. Despite its advantages, high costs and inadequate technical skills hinder some economies from implementing API.

Moving to smart destination technology, Singapore has been using facial recognition technology by providing seamless tourist/guest access to popular destinations since 2020 through contactless verification at the Universal Studios Singapore (Reuters 2020). In November 2023, Singapore also rolled out the Tourism (Attractions) Industry Digital Plan to local attractions.

Thailand has also embraced digital tools to market itself as a smart destination. The Tourism Authority of Thailand (2023) has partnerships with online platforms Agoda, Alipay, Klook, and KKday for a joint marketing initiative to revitalize tourism and promote sustainability. In 2022, Thailand launched its smart pier project featuring an intelligent passenger management system that registers tourists upon their purchase of ticket and stores the information in the marine department's cloud system (Chuenniran 2022).

Since 2020, Viet Nam has partnered with technological giants such as Facebook and Google to help promote destinations and digital transformation toward a "new normal" in tourism (Vietnam+ 2020). In transport, the economy's City Tour Hop On-Hop Off double-decker bus service in Ho Chi Minh City combines digital data on transportation and tourist preferences to design tour routes, sell tickets and accept payments virtually, provide free Wi-Fi, and multilingual narration at tourist sites (*Voice of Vietnam 2023*). Some tourism-centric villages have also started using blockchain and 3D technologies to promote history, crafts, and related information for visitors, businesses, and residents (*Vietnam Investment Review* 2023).

On the financial side, economies and digital platforms are forming partnerships to better connect local merchants with international visitors through digital payment systems. In November 2023, for instance, the Singapore Tourism Board partnered with the digital payment platform Alipay+ and the eWallet company TNG Digital to promote travel in Singapore among Malaysian visitors (Er 2023). The National Central Bank of Cambodia signed a memorandum of understanding with Alipay to give users of its "bakong" digital currency access to 83 million merchants worldwide through the Alipay network (Andersen 2023). Malaysia and the PRC also enabled cross-border digital payments for travelers with Alipay+ supported wallets from seven economies (*TTG Asia* 2023).

Incheon, billed as the Republic of Korea's first smart tourism city, introduced audio guides in English, Chinese, and Japanese through its Incheon Easy smart mobile application to help tourists navigate the city's main attractions (*Newswire* 2023).

Meanwhile, in South Asia, India's Ministry of Tourism (2022) crafted the National Digital Tourism Mission to set standards and promote cooperation in providing digital services and set up the National Integrated Database of Hospitality Industry as a platform to classify services and geotag heritage monuments.

[a] See also Online Travel Evisa. https://etravel.gov.ph/signin (accessed November 2023); and Malaysia Digital Arrival Card. https://imigresen-online.imi.gov.my/ (accessed November 2023).

Sources: ADB using Andersen (2023), Chuenniran (2022), Er (2023), Government of India, Ministry of Tourism (2022), IATA (2022), *Khmer Times* (2023), *Newswire* (2023), Redins (2023), *Reuters* (2020), Tourism Authority of Thailand (2023), TTG Asia (2023), Vietnam+ (2020), *Vietnam Investment Review* (2023), and *Voice of Vietnam* (2023).

Gaps in digitalization phases between economies add an extra layer of challenge to seeking points of convergence in devising the region's smart tourism strategies.

It also hampers the coverage and depth of regional cooperation of elements under the digital economy, which hinders sectoral efficiency and curtails improved user experience from smart tourism practices. Consider, for example, Singapore's digital agreements with some economies in the region: Digital Economy Partnership Agreement between Singapore, Chile and New Zealand; Singapore–Australia Digital Economy Agreement; and Korea–Singapore Digital Partnership Agreement (Table 5.2). However, the elements present in each of these digital economy agreements have wider coverage than the regular regional agreements like the Regional Comprehensive Economic Partnership and the Comprehensive and Progressive Trans-Pacific Partnership, which are not uniform in nature (ADB 2023c). Meanwhile, the recently concluded framework for the ASEAN Digital Economy Framework Agreement is just the kind of push the subregion needs to accelerate digital initiatives and achieve a digital economy worth $3 trillion by 2030.

Policy Recommendations

Riding on the momentum of post-pandemic tourism recovery, governments in Asia should strengthen regional cooperation and leverage digital technology for greater efficiency and resilience. Economies should seize the opportunity to "build back better" or "build forward better" by developing tourism through

Table 5.2: Digital Economy Agreements of Singapore and the Association of Southeast Asian Nations

Key Features/ Elements	Singapore			ASEAN	
	DEPA	SADEA	KSDPA	Core Target	Core Element
Artificial intelligence				Accelerate growth	Digital trade; cross-border e-commerce
Cross-border data flows					
Cryptography					
Data innovation (and regulatory sandboxes)					
Digital identities				Drive interoperability across ASEAN	Payments and e-invoicing; Digital identification and authentication
Digital inclusion					
E-invoicing					
E-payments					
E-certification				Ensure responsible digital growth	Cross-border data flows and data protection; online safety and cybersecurity
Online consumer protection					
Open government information					
Paperless trade					
Personal data protection					
Prohibiting data localization				Strengthen cooperation between economies	Cooperation on emerging topics; talent mobility and cooperation; competition policy
SMEs, cooperation					
Source code protection					
Submarine cables					
Trade facilitation					

ASEAN = Association of Southeast Asian Nations, DEPA = Digital Economy Partnership Agreement, KSDPA = Korea–Singapore Digital Partnership Agreement, SADEA = Singapore–Australia Digital Economy Agreement, SMEs = small and medium-sized enterprises.

Sources: Government of Singapore, Ministry of Trade and Industry. https://www.mti.gov.sg/Trade/Digital-Economy-Agreements (accessed November 2023); and ASEAN Secretariat (2023).

greater use of technology and digital innovation. Three key actions are involved: building digital infrastructure, strengthening regional initiatives around digital regulations, and enhancing digital skills.

Building digital infrastructure for improved availability and accessibility is key to facilitating a smart tourism ecosystem. This includes hard infrastructure (such as submarine cable, broadband, mobile and Wi-Fi networks), physical-digital infrastructure (i.e., devices and networks, and soft infrastructure (i.e., regulations around cybersecurity, privacy, and others). According to the International Telecommunications Union, Asia's digital infrastructure varies widely. The gap between high-income economies and the rest of the world when it comes to the affordability of fixed and mobile internet services is wide. Connectivity services cost nearly 10 times as much in lower-middle-income economies and nearly 30 times as much as in low-income economies, after adjusting for differences in gross national income per capita (ITU 2022). The divide needs to be narrowed for all aspects of digital infrastructure. Governments should ensure that quality internet services support videos and digital applications and that the right regulations are in place to protect consumer interests. It is important to ensure that digital participation leads to net positive development outcomes, which for tourism also translates to improved user experience and engagement.

Strengthening regional cooperation around digital regulations for safe and seamless cross-border travel is important. Aligning digital rules and standards and facilitating interoperability between digital systems need greater attention. For example, harmonizing policies and standards around data protection and privacy is paramount since international tourism deals with large amounts of data based on transactions across different tourism agents, from traveler to tour agency, airlines, hotels, governments, and others. Thales Group (2022) found that only 24% of travel consumers spend time implementing security measures. This makes it imperative that data are well protected and provided to authorized parties only on user's consent. In a similar vein, regional cooperation should facilitate a balance between security and privacy concerns while

governments should collaborate with technology companies to explore solutions that enable lawful access to encrypted data while preserving security and privacy.

Enhancing digital skills is a must to achieve the desired development outcome. This will be across all firm sizes, governments, and other stakeholders. More particularly, the small and medium-sized enterprises (SMEs) spread across multiple activities from tour operators to food and beverage and retail business face significant challenges. Many lack capacity to adopt new digital practices and they tend to digitalize general administration or marketing functions before incorporating technology in other aspects of business (OECD 2021). This implies that SMEs lack capacity in resources and skills transfer for advanced technologies such as data analytics or for broader matters like enterprise resource planning for process integration. In this scenario, to build tourism resilience and safeguard SMEs, interests, governments should help SMEs adapt to the digital ecosystem through policy interventions These include assisting with training and technology adoption; access to finance; support for targeted digital solutions; facilitation of data centers, incubators for startups and networking programs; regulatory reforms (e.g., data protection); e-government and one-stop-shops; and infrastructure investment. While many of these should be started at the economy level, expansion at the regional level will promote greater international travel with assured confidence.

In conclusion, the tourism economy requires a comprehensive approach to policymaking and governance. While technology adoption is important, so are the right safeguard policies, keeping in mind the diverse interests of consumers and businesses. Discussions of digitalization in tourism are often fragmented—digital payments, digital visa/immigration, online travel bookings—and transitioning from silos to shared and interoperable systems could optimize the cross-cutting nature of digital technologies. This shift must be accompanied by greater focus on the availability and accessibility of digital products and tools across the entire value chain of tourism activities. The amalgamation of these key elements could deliver a stronger tourism economy that is inclusive, efficient, and more resilient to shocks.

References

Andersen, D. 2023. Cambodian Digital Currency Bakong Amps Up Use Case with Alipay Agreement. *Cointelegraph*. 20 November. https://cointelegraph.com/news/cambodian-digital-currency-bakong-use-case-alipay-agreement.

Ardic, O., H. Baijal, P. Baudino, N. Y. Boakye-Adjei, J. Fishman, and R. A. Maikai. 2022. The Journey So Far: Making Cross-Border Remittances Work for Financial Inclusion. World Bank Group and Bank for International Settlements. Financial Stability Institute FSI Insights on Policy Implementation. No. 43. June. Basel.

Association of Southeast Asian Nations (ASEAN) Secretariat. 2023. ASEAN Launches World's First Regionwide Digital Economy Framework Agreement. 23 September. https://asean.org/asean-launches-worlds-first-regionwide-digital-economy-framework-agreement/.

Asian Development Bank (ADB). 2023a. *Asian Economic Integration Report 2023*. Manila.

———. 2023b. *Asian Development Outlook 2023 Special Topic*. Manila.

———. 2023c. *Promoting Smart Tourism in Asia and the Pacific Through Digital Cooperation*. Manila.

Asian Development Bank Institute (ADBI), Organisation for Economic Co-operation and Development (OECD), and the International Labour Organization (ILO). 2021. *Labour Migration in Asia: Impacts of the COVID-19 Crisis and the Post-Pandemic Future*. Tokyo, Paris, and Bangkok.

Bahia, K., M. Sanchez-Vidal, and P. Taberner. 2020. Exploring the Relationship Between Mobile Money Regulation and Usage. *TPRC48: The 48th Research Conference on Communication, Information and Internet Policy*. 10 December.

Bang, J. T., A. Mitra, and P. V. Wunnava. 2013. Financial Liberalization and Remittances: Recent Longitudinal Evidence. *IZA Discussion Papers*. No. 7497. Bonn: Institute for the Study of Labor.

Bank for International Settlements (BIS). 2022. *Interlinking Payment Systems and the Role of Application Programming Interfaces: A Framework for Cross-Border Payments*. Basel.

———. 2023a. ISO 20022 Harmonisation Requirements for Enhancing Cross-Border Payments. Basel.

———. 2023b. Interim Report to the G20: Linking Fast Payment Systems Across Borders: Considerations for Governance and Oversight. https://dwgg20.org/app/uploads/2021/09/g20-plan-to-facilitate-remittance-flows.pdf.

Bare, U. A. A., Y. Bani, N. W. Ismail, and A. Rosland. 2022. Does Financial Development Mediate the Impact of Remittances on Sustainable Human Capital Investment? New Insights from SSA Countries. *Cogent Economics & Finance*. 10 (2078460).

Bedford, C. 2023. Pacific Labour Mobility Over the Last Year: Continued Growth. *Devpolicy Blog*. 8 August. https://devpolicy.org/pacific-labour-mobility-over-the-last-year-continued-growth-20230808/.

Bowerman, G. 2023. 2023: A Vital Year for Tourism in Asia Pacific. Asia Media Centre. 3 February. https://www.asiamediacentre.org.nz/features/2023-a-vital-year-for-tourism-in-asia-pacific/.

Cambridge Centre for Alternative Finance, World Bank, and World Economic Forum. 2022. The Global COVID-19 Fintech Market Impact and Industry Resilience Report, University of Cambridge. https://www.jbs.cam.ac.uk/wp-content/uploads/2022/06/2022-global-covid19-fintech-market-study.pdf.

Centre for the Promotion of Imports from developing countries (CBI). 2022. 10 Tips to Go Digital in the Tourism Sector. 19 January. https://www.cbi.eu/market-information/tourism/tips-go-digital.

Chokossa, C. 2023. The Normalisation of Mobile Money in Sub-Saharan Africa. *Euromonitor International*. 17 March. https://www.euromonitor.com/article/the-normalisation-of-mobile-money-in-sub-saharan-africa.

Chuenniran, A. 2022. Phuket Marine Safety Goes Hi-tech with 'Smart Pier.' *Bangkok Post*. 9 June. https://www.bangkokpost.com/thailand/general/2322766/phuket-marine-safety-goes-hi-tech-with-smart-pier.

Davies, M. 2023. Correspondent Banking in the South Pacific. Reserve Bank of Australia. https://www.rba.gov.au/publications/bulletin/2023/jun/pdf/correspondent-banking-in-the-south-pacific.pdf.

De Soyres, F., M.A. Jelil, C. Cerruti, and L. Kiwara. 2018. What Kenya's Mobile Money Success Could Mean for the Arab World. *World Bank Blog*. 3 October. https://www.worldbank.org/en/news/feature/2018/10/03/what-kenya-s-mobile-money-success-could-mean-for-the-arab-world.

Er, B. P. 2023. STB Looks to Attract Malaysian Tourists with Curated Deals and Cashless Payment Options. *Marketing Interactive*. 15 November. https://www.marketing-interactive.com/stb-alipay-tng-digital-malaysian-tourism.

Evans, D. and A. Pirchio. 2015. An Empirical Examination of Why Mobile Money Schemes Ignite in Some Developing Countries but Flounder in Most. *Coase-Sandor Working Paper Series in Law and Economics*. University of Chicago Law School.

Fildes, N. 2022. Australia Raises Immigration Cap to Address Labour Shortage. *Financial Times*. 2 September. https://www.ft.com/content/4f6196d1-5dac-498f-b18b-840c2258da18.

Financial Stability Board. 2022. G20 Roadmap for Enhancing Cross-Border Payments: Priorities for the Next Phase of Work. https://www.fsb.org/2022/10/g20-roadmap-for-enhancing-cross-border-payments-priorities-for-the-next-phase-of-work/.

G20 Development Working Group. 2021. Financial Inclusion and Remittances. G20 Plan to Facilitate Remittance Flows. https://dwgg20.org/app/uploads/2021/09/g20-plan-to-facilitate-remittance-flows.pdf.

Gascon, P., G. Larramona, and M. Salvador. 2023. The Impact of Digitalization on Remittances. Evidence from El Salvador. *Telecommunications Policy*. 47 (4).

Global Partnership for Financial Inclusion (GPFI). 2018. 2018 Update to Leaders on Progress Towards the G20 Remittance Target. https://www.gpfi.org/sites/gpfi/files/documents/2018%20Update%20to%20Leaders%20on%20Progress%20Towards%20the%20G20%20Remittance%20Target.pdf.

——. 2023. 2023 Update to Leaders on Progress Towards the G20 Remittance Target. https://www.gpfi.org/sites/gpfi/files/News%20C%29%20-%202023%20Update%20to%20Leaders%20on%20Progress%20Toward%20the%20G20%20Remittance%20Target.pdf.

Global System for Mobile Communications Association (GSMA). 2021. *Status of the Industry Report on Mobile Money 2021*. https://www.gsma.com/mobilefordevelopment/wp-content/uploads/2021/03/GSMA_State-of-the-Industry-Report-on-Mobile-Money-2021_Full-report.pdf.

——. 2023a. *The State of the Industry Report on Mobile Money*. https://www.gsma.com/mobilefordevelopment/wp-content/uploads/2023/04/GSMA-SOTIR-2023_Web-1.pdf.

———. 2023b. *GSMA Mobile Gender Gap Report 2023*. https://www.gsma.com/r/wp-content/uploads/2023/07/The-Mobile-Gender-Gap-Report-2023.pdf.

Government of Australia, Department of Home Affairs. https://www.homeaffairs.gov.au/ (accessed October 2023).

Government of Australia, Department of Foreign Affairs and Trade. Pacific Engagement Visa. https://www.dfat.gov.au/geo/pacific/people-connections/people-connections-in-the-pacific/pacific-engagement-visa.

Government of Bangladesh, Bureau of Manpower, Employment, and Training. http://www.old.bmet.gov.bd/BMET/stattisticalDataAction (accessed November 2023).

Government of Canada. Temporary Residents: Temporary Foreign Worker Program (TFWP) and International Mobility Program (IMP) Work Permit Holders – Monthly IRCC Updates - Canada - International Mobility Program Work Permit Holders by Gender, Occupational Skill Level and Year in which Permit(s) Became Effective. https://open.canada.ca/data/en/dataset/360024f2-17e9-4558-bfc1-3616485d65b9 (accessed November 2023).

Government of India, Ministry of Tourism. 2022. Setting up the National Digital Tourism Mission. https://tourism.gov.in/sites/default/files/2022-09/National%20Digital%20Tourism%20Mission_2022.pdf.

Government of India, Ministry of External Affairs. Performance Smartboard. https://meadashboard.gov.in/ (accessed November 2023).

Government of Japan, Ministry of Foreign Affairs. https://www.mofa.go.jp/mofaj/ca/fna/ssw/us/ (accessed October 2023).

Government of Malaysia, Migrant Worker Protection Agency (Badan Pelindungan Pekerja Migran Indonesia). https://bp2mi.go.id/ (accessed November 2023).

Government of Nepal, Department of Foreign Employment. https://dofe.gov.np/DetailPage.aspx/id/425/lan/ne-NP (accessed November 2023).

Government of Nepal, Ministry of Labour, Employment and Social Security. 2022. Nepal Labor Migration Report 2022. https://moless.gov.np/storage/files/post_files/Nepal%20Labour%20Migration%20Report_2022.pdf.

Government of New Zealand, Immigration New Zealand. https://www.immigration.govt.nz/new-zealand-visas/visas/visa/skilled-migrant-category-resident-visa (accessed November 2023).

Government of Pakistan, Bureau of Emigration and Overseas Employment. https://beoe.gov.pk/reports-and-statistics (accessed November 2023).

Government of the Philippines, Philippine Statistical Authority. Survey of Overseas Filipinos (2020, 2021, 2022, 2023). https://psa.gov.ph/statistics/survey/labor-and-employment/survey-overseas-filipinos.

Government of Singapore, Ministry of Trade and Industry. https://www.mti.gov.sg/Trade/Digital-Economy-Agreements (accessed November 2023).

Government of Sri Lanka, Central Bank of Sri Lanka. https://www.cbsl.gov.lk/en/statistics/statistical-tables/external-sector (accessed January 2024).

Government of the United Kingdom, Home Office. https://www.gov.uk/government/organisations/home-office (accessed October 2023).

Government of the United States, Bureau of Labor Statistics. Job Openings and Labor Turnover Survey. https://www.bls.gov/jlt/ (accessed October 2023).

Government of the United States, Department of State, Bureau of Consular Affairs. https://travel.state.gov/content/travel/en/legal/visa-law0/visa-bulletin/2024/visa-bulletin-for-october-2023.html (accessed November 2023).

International Air Transport Association. 2022. Passenger Data – Air Carriers. https://www.icao.int/MID/Documents/2022/FAL%20Webinar/PPT%20 4.4%20-%20Presentation_API_PNR_ICAO-IATA.pdf.

International Labour Organization (ILO). 2021. ILO: Uncertain and Uneven Recovery Expected Following Unprecedented Labour Market Crisis. ILO Newsroom. 25 January. https://www.ilo.org/global/about-the-ilo/newsroom/news/WCMS_766949/lang--en/index.htm.

International Monetary Fund (IMF). World Development Outlook Database. https://www.imf.org/en/Publications/WEO/weo-database/2023/October (accessed October 2023).

———. Financial Development Index Database. https://data.imf.org/?sk=f8032e80-b36c-43b1-ac26-493c5b1cd33b (accessed October 2023).

International Organization for Migration (IOM). 2020. The Power of Digitalization in the Age of Physical Distancing (DISC Digest 4th Edition). https://migrationnetwork.un.org/sites/g/files/tmzbdl416/files/resources_files/disc_digest_4th_edition_digitalization_and_migrant_inclusion_final.pdf.

———. 2021. The Role of Digital Remittances. https://publications.iom.int/books/role-digital-remittances-consolidated-findings-supply-and-demand-research.

International Organization for Migration (IOM) Thailand. 2022. https://thailand.iom.int/sites/g/files/tmzbdl1371/files/documents/iom-promise-brochure_1.pdf.

International Telecommunication Union (ITU). 2022. Facts and Figures 2022. https://www.itu.int/itu-d/reports/statistics/facts-figures-2022/.

Karki, B. 2023. Singapore Upgrades Digital Solutions to Better SMEs and Tourist Experience. 8 November. https://eturbonews.com/singapore-upgrades-tourist-experience/.

Khmer Times. 2023. Cambodia Prepares for Peak Tourist Season. 5 October. https://www.khmertimeskh.com/501371744/cambodia-prepares-for-peak-tourist-season/.

Malaysia Digital Arrival Card. https://imigresen-online.imi.gov.my/ (accessed November 2023).

Martin, N. 2023. Chinese Tourists Return with an Eye on Budget, Safety. *DW.com*. 26 November. https://www.dw.com/en/chinese-tourists-return-with-an-eye-on-budget-safety/a-67407148.

Mas, I. and D. Radcliffe. 2010. Mobile Payments Go Viral: M-PESA in Kenya. World Bank. https://documents1.worldbank.org/curated/en/638851468048259219/pdf/543380WP-0M1PES1BOX0349405B01PUBLIC1.pdf.

McKinsey & Company. 2022. Mobile Wallets: Southeast Asia's New Digital Life Hacks. 25 May. https://www.mckinsey.com/industries/financial-services/our-insights/mobile-wallets-southeast-asias-new-digital-life-hack.

———. 2023. Outlook for China Tourism 2023: Light at the End of the Tunnel. 9 May. https://www.mckinsey.com/industries/travel-logistics-and-infrastructure/our-insights/outlook-for-china-tourism-2023-light-at-the-end-of-the-tunnel.

Newswire. 2023. Incheon Tourism Organization Is Promoting Smart K-Tours With 'Incheon Easy' App. 4 January. https://www.newswire.com/news/incheon-tourism-organization-is-promoting-smart-k-tours-with-incheon-21912102.

Official Airline Guide. 2024. China Outbound: Are We Nearly There Yet? 26 January. https://www.oag.com/webinars/china-outbound-are-we-nearly-there-yet-webinars-oag.

Online Travel Evisa. https://etravel.gov.ph/signin (accessed November 2023).

Organization for Economic Co-operation and Development (OECD). 2021. *The Digital Transformation of SMEs.* Paris: OECD Publishing.

Orozco, M. and J. Yansura. 2015. Remittances and Financial Inclusion: Opportunities for Central America. Inter-American Dialogue. February. https://www.thedialogue.org/wp-content/uploads/2015/06/RemitFinancialInclusion_FINAL_223.pdf.

Parulis-Cook, S. 2023. Key Developments for Chinese Tourism in 2023. *Dragon Trail International.* 22 March. https://dragontrail.com/resources/blog/must-know-developments-for-chinese-tourism-in-2023.

Peri, G. and R. Zaiour. 2022. Labor Shortages and the Immigration Shortfall. *Econofact.* 11 January. https://econofact.org/labor-shortages-and-the-immigration-shortfall.

Philippine News Agency. 2023. PBBM: ASEAN Must Address Brain Drain in Healthcare Sector. 13 April. https://www.pna.gov.ph/articles/1199385.

Redins, L. 2023. Singapore Announces Passport-Free Biometric Clearance at Borders from 2024— Updated. *BiometricUpdate.com.* 8 May. https://www.biometricupdate.com/202305/singapore-announces-passport-free-biometric-clearance-at-borders-from-2024-updated.

Reuters. 2020. Singapore's Universal Studios Deploys Facial Recognition for Entry. 3 August. https://www.reuters.com/article/us-singapore-universal-studios-idUSKBN24Z15D/.

Richter, F. 2022. This Chart Shows How Global Air Travel Is Faring. World Economic Forum. https://www.weforum.org/agenda/2022/12/this-chart-shows-how-global-air-travel-is-faring/.

Statista Market Insights. https://www.statista.com/outlook/dmo/fintech/digital-payments/digital-remittances/worldwide?currency=usd (accessed November 2023).

Statista Research Department. https://www.statista.com/ (accessed October 2023).

———. 2023. Online Travel Market Size Worldwide 2020-2030. https://www.statista.com/statistics/1179020/online-travel-agent-market-size-worldwide/.

Statistics Canada. 2022. Job Vacancies, Second Quarter 2022. https://www150.statcan.gc.ca/n1/daily-quotidien/220920/dq220920b-eng.htm?CMP=mstatcan.

Thales Group. 2022. Lack of Consumer Trust Across Industries to Protect Their Personal Data, New Research from Thales Has Revealed. 3 October. https://www.thalesgroup.com/en/countries-europe/romania/press_release/lack-consumer-trust-across-industries-protect-their-personal.

Tourism Authority of Thailand. 2023. TAT Joins Leading Online Platforms to Boost Tourism to Thailand. 28 March. https://www.tatnews.org/2023/03/tat-joins-4-leading-online-platforms-to-boost-tourism-to-thailand/.

Travel Weekly Asia. 2023. Tourism's Road to Recovery: We're Not There Yet. 1 June. https://www.travelweekly-asia.com/Travel-News/Association/Tourism-road-to-recovery-We-are-not-there-yet.

TTG Asia. 2023. Malaysia Launches Cross-Border Digital Payments. 14 November. https://www.ttgasia.com/2023/11/14/malaysia-launches-cross-border-digital-payments/.

United Nations World Tourism Organization (UNWTO). 2022. *Compendium of Tourism Statistics, Data 2016–2020, 2022 Edition.* Madrid.

———. 2023a. World Tourism Barometer. Volume 21. Issue 1. January.

———. 2023b. World Tourism Barometer. Volume 21. Issue 3. September.

———. 2023c. World Tourism Barometer. Volume 21. Issue 4. November.

———. 2024. World Tourism Barometer. Volume 22. Issue 1. January.

———. Tourism Satellite Accounts. http://statistics.unwto.org (accessed January 2024).

———. Tourism Dashboard. https://www.unwto.org/tourism-data/unwto-tourism-recovery-tracker (accessed January 2024).

Vietnam+. 2020. Digital Transformation Helps Revive Tourism Industry. 7 October. https://en.vietnamplus.vn/digital-transformation-helps-revive-tourism-industry/191116.vnp.

Vietnam Investment Review. 2023. New Digital Transformation Initiatives for the Tourism Industry. 10 November. https://vir.com.vn/new-digital-transformation-initiatives-for-the-tourism-industry-106766.html.

Visa Economic Empowerment Institute. 2022. The Economic Empowerment of Digital Remittances: How to Unlock the Benefits of Innovation and Competition. https://usa.visa.com/content/dam/VCOM/regional/na/us/sites/documents/veei-economic-empowerment-digital-remittances.pdf.

Vodafone. 2021. Milestone Cements M-Pesa as Africa's Largest Fintech Platform. 7 September. https://www.vodafone.com/news/services/M-Pesa-celebrates-reaching-50-million-customers.

Voice of Vietnam. 2023. Tourism Works to Adapt and Leverage Digital Technology. 22 October. https://english.vov.vn/en/travel/tourism-works-to-adapt-and-leverage-digital-technology-post1054252.vov.

World Bank. World Development Indicators. https://databank.worldbank.org/ (accessed October 2023).

———. 2021. *Remittance Prices Worldwide Quarterly.* Issue 40. December. https://remittanceprices.worldbank.org/sites/default/files/rpw_main_report_and_annex_q421.pdf.

———. Remittance Prices Worldwide. https://remittanceprices.worldbank.org/ (accessed July 2023).

World Bank-KNOMAD (Global Knowledge Partnership on Migration and Development). http://www.knomad.org/data/remittances (accessed December 2023).

World Economic Forum. 2017. Digital Transformation Initiative: Aviation, Travel and Tourism Industry, White Paper. Geneva. http://reports.weforum.org/digital-transformation/wp-content/blogs.dir/94/mp/files/pages/files/wef-dti-aviation-travel-and-tourism-white-paper.pdf.

6

THEME CHAPTER
Decarbonizing Global Value Chains

Introduction

Anthropogenic (human-induced) climate change is dramatically affecting the world's natural environment, its economies, and societies. The complex nature of the earth's climate system means that the overall impact of climate change remains uncertain. Yet it has myriad effects, such as higher temperatures, increased drought, water scarcity, severe fires, melting polar ice, rising sea levels, ocean warming, ocean acidification, flooding, storms, and declining biodiversity, among others. They will likely have dramatic consequences for life on earth. The direct impacts on humans include the effect on health, ability to grow food, access to fresh water and to ocean food chains, productivity, and the destruction of critical infrastructure. In turn, these effects will likely displace communities and force migration. Climate change holds the potential to weaken political, economic, and social systems, exacerbating the risk of conflict within and across nations.

Climate change and global warming have been driven by the production system developed since the First Industrial Revolution; a system based on the burning of fossil fuels for energy. This increased the concentration of heat-trapping greenhouse gases (GHGs)—particularly carbon dioxide (CO_2) and methane (CH_4)—in the earth's atmosphere. It has raised the average surface temperature of the earth, with global average temperatures in 2020 estimated to be 1.1°C above pre-industrial levels (ADB 2023a). Deforestation and land clearance both add carbon to the atmosphere and remove the earth's natural means to absorb atmospheric carbon. Significantly reducing carbon

emissions will require a fundamental change in the way humans produce and consume—particularly energy production and consumption—to rapidly move toward net zero CO_2 emissions (IPCC 2022a). Ultimately, success depends upon the speed at which production can be decarbonized.

Despite a drop in the rate of growth, GHG emissions continue to increase rapidly. According to a recent Intergovernmental Panel on Climate Change (IPCC) Assessment Report (IPCC 2022a), annual average GHG emissions during 2010–2019 were higher than in any previous decade. While the growth rate of emissions during the decade was less than the previous 10 years, the increase in the level of emissions was the highest on record. Since 1990, the largest growth in absolute emissions was in CO_2 from fossil fuels and industry, followed by CH_4, with most anthropogenic CO_2 emissions occurring in the past few decades. The PRIMAP-hist dataset indicates that half have occurred since 1990, with 85% being emitted since 1950 (Figure 6.1).

Asian economies, in particular developing economies, are highly exposed to the effects of climate change. Climate change impacts will likely fall disproportionately on developing economies, which have limited resources to mitigate and adapt to the consequences of climate change. Globally, developing Asia's population is most vulnerable to climate change (ADB 2023a), partly due to its geography and socioeconomic conditions—broad exposure to natural hazards and other climate-related risks—and partly by lower levels of economic development that limits the ability to cope with and adapt to the effects of climate change. According to the Global

Figure 6.1: Global Annual Emissions of Carbon Dioxide (million metric tons)

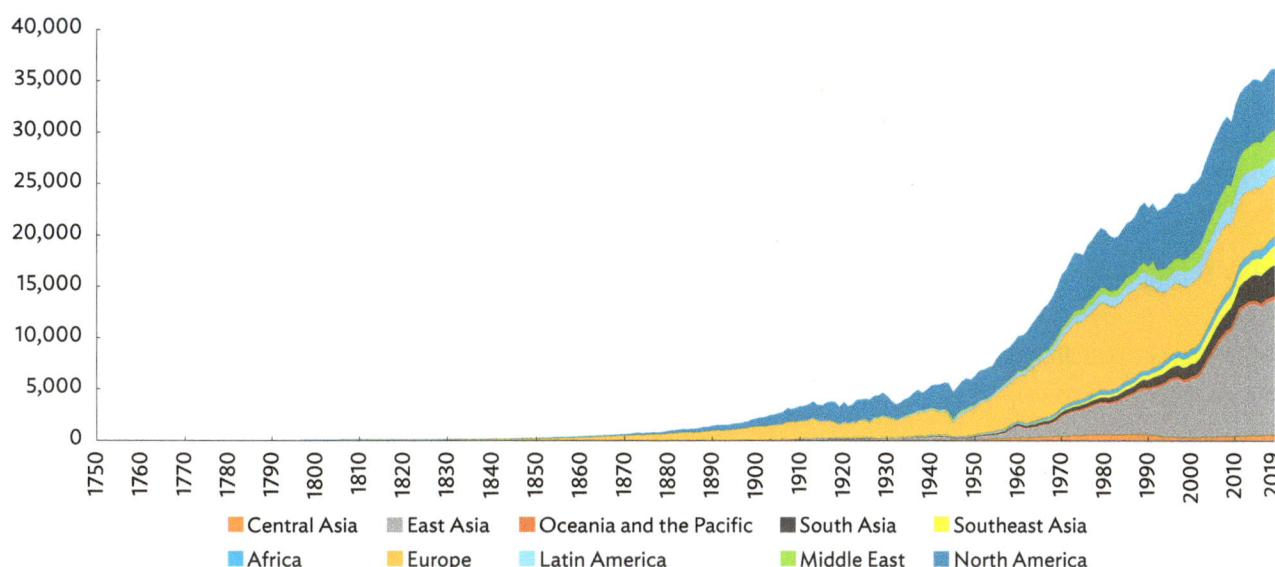

Note: Data exclude carbon dioxide emissions associated with land use, land-use change, and forestry. The regional grouping adopted is a combination of ADB and World Bank regional groupings.

Source: Gütschow (2016); and Gütschow, Günther, and Pflüger (2021).

Climate Risk Index 2021 (Ekstein, Kuenzel, and Schaefer 2021), some Asian economies (such as Bangladesh, Nepal, Pakistan, the Philippines, and Thailand) are among the top 10 economies exposed to long-term climate risk (1990–2019), while Asia accounted for more than half of all multi-hazard global average annual losses for 2000–2022 (UNESCAP 2022).

Sectoral impacts of climate change will disproportionately affect developing Asian economies. Climate change will have large negative impacts on certain sectors of the economy, including agriculture, forestry, fishing, and tourism, which many developing Asian economies depend on. Increased temperatures and drought will reduce crop yields while rising flood levels threaten food supply. Climate change alters where different crops can be grown, with severe consequences for farmers in badly affected regions. Similar effects are expected in fishing, with warmer water temperatures affecting the abundance, migratory patterns, and mortality rates of global fish stocks. The economies of fishing communities may also be affected by rising sea levels and more extreme weather events. The increased prevalence of invasive species and insect

outbreaks, along with wildfires and storms, affects the health of forests and forestry in many economies. Extreme temperatures also impact tourism. For example, poorer water quality associated with temperature rises increase toxic algae blooms, preventing recreational water activities and freshwater fishing. Rising sea levels may submerge small islands and coastal areas, with deforestation and loss of biodiversity making other tourist destinations less attractive. Climate change adds infrastructure risk, including housing and business, but also roads, railways, ports, airports, energy infrastructure, and communication systems. This adds to the large infrastructure investments needed across developing Asia to maintain growth and tackle poverty (ADB 2017).

Developing Asian economies play an increasing role as a source of emissions. Asia and the Pacific account for an increasing share of CO_2 emissions production (see Figure 6.1). Throughout the 18th and much of the 19th century, CO_2 emissions were dominated by Europe, given its leading role in the First Industrial Revolution and highlighting the role technology and structural change play in rising GHG emissions. Toward the end of the 19th century, North America began to contribute an increasing share of annual CO_2 emissions and by the mid-1920s accounted for half of all CO_2 emissions. Later in the 20th century, Asia emerged as a leading source of emissions production. By 2019, Asia accounted for 52% of global CO_2 emissions production, with East Asia (36%), South Asia (8.1%), and Southeast Asia (5.1%) accounting for the bulk of this share.[38] These changes in regional contributions to CO_2 emissions reflect a variety of factors, including changes in the structure of global production associated with falling trade costs and the rise of global value chains (GVCs), along with population and technology dynamics.

Climate Change and Global Value Chains

While international trade can alter global production patterns in ways that increase GHG emissions, it can also be an important part of the solution to climate change. Trade can be a source of low-emission goods and services, a source of green technology diffusion and, through competition, enhance production efficiency and reduce GHG emissions (WTO 2022b). To do this, however, trade policies must encourage the flow of low-emission goods, services, and knowledge, while subsidies that distort markets through carbon-intensive production or limit the adoption of green technologies or inhibit innovation should be removed (ADB 2023b). Currently, trade remains a major contributor to GHG emissions, with the rise of GVCs increasing GHG emissions as the scale of production and distance goods travel also increases. Trade has incentivized firms to move the "dirty" parts of production to economies with weak regulations, limiting how economies regulate emissions through existing domestic policies and mechanisms.

GVCs provide an opportunity for developing economies to join the global economy. GVCs split up what is needed to produce a good or service with different segments undertaken by different economies. Driven by differences in factor costs across economies, reduced transport costs and improvements in information and communication technology that help coordinate production across geographically distant locations, GVC production increased rapidly since the late 1990s and early 2000s. Expansion has come mainly through the drive for greater efficiency, particularly in multinational firms based in developed economies. This resulted in a broader global division of labor in line with comparative advantage. These changes have created opportunities for developing economies by making it easier for them to industrialize (Baldwin 2011), with some considering GVCs as a new development paradigm (Taglioni and Winkler 2016). CO_2 emissions and the GVC carbon footprint have not received much attention until recently. However, as concerns grow over the risks of climate change, the carbon content of trade facilitated by GVCs has come under increased scrutiny.

The rapid expansion of GVCs over the last few decades has led to a complex relationship between trade and GHG emissions. While GVCs contribute to development, their relationship with climate change is multidimensional and bidirectional (Box 6.1). They decouple consumption from production, with production taking place in economies and regions different from those where the final product is consumed. From an environmental perspective, one concern with this decoupling is the risk that firms in developed economies may shift production activities to developing economies where environmental regulations are weaker—the so-called pollution haven hypothesis—and where emissions efficiency may be lower. This results in higher GHG emissions for a given level of production. Driven by improved productivity, the greater

---

[38]   These data represent the flow of CO_2 emissions into the atmosphere. There is some debate as to how long emissions remain in the atmosphere (e.g., Inman 2008), creating some uncertainty as to the stock of CO_2 emissions in the atmosphere and the relative contribution of different regions to these stocks. Estimating the stock of CO_2 emissions using the CO_2 flow data from PRIMAP-hist and the Perpetual Inventory Method, Asia was estimated to account for 30.1% of CO_2 emissions in the atmosphere in 2019 under the assumption that CO_2 emissions remain in the atmosphere for 300 years and for 32.2% of CO_2 stocks if emissions remain in the atmosphere for 10,000 years. The corresponding estimates for East Asia are 20.8% and 22.1%, respectively.

scale of production within GVCs can also increase CO_2 emissions, with emission-intensive production of manufactured goods likely to be relocated to developing economies. Developing Asia, as an important GVC producer, accounts for a large and growing share of GVC emissions. Moreover, as developing Asian economies are projected to account for most global economic activity over the next several decades (Leimbach et al. 2017), their share in GVC-related emissions will doubtless continue to rise.

GVCs can weaken the efforts of policymakers to limit GHG emissions. Policymakers are increasingly interested in GVCs and the emissions embodied in GVC production. This is partly due to concerns over the carbon footprint of GVCs, but also around competitiveness and the protection of domestic industries in advanced economies that generally have more stringent environmental protections. One specific concern is that the effectiveness of efforts to reduce GHG emissions—for example,

---

Box 6.1: Understanding the Complex Relationship between Global Value Chains and Climate Change

The relationship between global value chains (GVCs) and greenhouse gas (GHG) emissions—and its resulting impact on climate change—is complex and multidirectional. GVC activity can be a significant source of carbon dioxide (CO_2) and other GHG emissions. But it can also involve more efficient production techniques and help diffuse new knowledge and technologies that reduce emissions. Conversely, climate change can impact GVCs and how they function, highlighting the costs of not adjusting climate change policies for international trade and for GVCs specifically.

Existing literature (e.g., ADB 2023b) identifies three main channels through which GVCs can affect an economy's GHG emissions: a scale effect; a structural effect; and a technological effect (ADB 2023b).

- Scale Effect: GVCs enhance productivity, which for a given technology and industry structure should increase production and emissions (Antweiler, Copeland, and Taylor 2001). This scale effect need not be linear, however. For a given technology level, increases in the level of production in an economy can potentially lead to more efficient resource use that, to some extent, can decouple the production of goods and services from the production of GHG emissions. If these economies of scale are higher in GVCs than in domestic production, the resulting emissions from production within GVCs may be less than the emissions produced if the same level of production had taken place outside of GVCs.

- Structural Effect: GVC integration can lead to changes in the economic structure of an economy, which can affect the level or intensity of its GHG emissions. Traditionally, the structural effect would be considered at the sectoral level, with some sectors considered more emission intensive than others for a given level of technology and production. Given the distributed nature of production within GVCs, however, the

contributions of individual economies to CO_2 emissions through GVC production will further depend on their specialized GVC tasks and activities, with their position in GVCs likely an important factor. Beyond tasks and activities, by shifting production toward more efficient firms, GVCs can also help reduce CO_2 emissions. Firms that trade internationally tend to be more efficient than non-trading firms. GVCs, by shifting production toward more efficient firms, can help reduce emissions if the shift also results in less emissions-intensive production (Copeland, Shapiro, and Taylor 2021).

- Technology Effect: Historically (over the past 150 years or so), a great deal of technological change resulted in higher emissions intensity, with a production structure using energy from carbon-based sources the major contributor to rising levels of CO_2 emissions. More recently, however, technological change has led to new production methods and new renewable sources of energy. As these technologies become cheaper and diffuse both within and across economies, emissions intensities may decline for a given level of production and an unchanged industrial structure. GVCs have been an important source of technological diffusion (Delera and Foster-McGregor 2023). To the extent GVCs involve the production and exchange of green products and provide access to cleaner technologies, GVCs can help reduce emissions. By creating new global markets for low carbon products, GVCs can also lower emissions by encouraging innovation in green products and technology. By promoting global competition, GVCs can also be a source of innovation, potentially opening green windows of opportunity (UNCTAD 2023). Multinational enterprises and their affiliates—that tend to be major drivers of GVCs—may also improve the environment by improving technology and management practices as well as a shift toward cleaner products (Delera 2021).

continued on next page

Box 6.1: continued

Although the three effects focus on the potential impact of GVC integration on emissions within economies, globally, impacts may differ. GVCs help reallocate production across economies, which either increases or decreases global emissions, depending on whether production is reallocated toward more emissions-efficient economies or not. In the case of the structural effect, for example, while an increase in production within GVCs may lead to a shift in production toward more efficient sectors, activities, or firms, resulting in lower emissions, if the increased GVC-related production in this economy is at the expense of production in more emission-efficient economies, global emissions could rise. While this holds for a given level of technology, in a dynamic sense, different global production structures as a result of GVCs can lead to different outcomes in terms of the production and diffusion of green technologies.

Conversely, GHG emissions and resulting climate change can have important effects on how GVCs function. Climate change policies should guarantee that GVCs can boost development in developing economies. The rise of GVCs is generally considered to have been driven by three main factors:

(i)   reductions in the costs of trade through improvements in transport technology (e.g., containerization, refrigeration) and reductions in man-made trade barriers;

(ii) improvements in information and communication technologies that help coordinate globally organized production activities within GVCs; and

(iii) differences in factor endowments and factor costs that allow activities within the value chain to be divided through careful exploitation of global comparative advantage.

Climate change risks affect these different drivers, potentially altering the extent, structure, and dynamics of production within GVCs.

By impacting transport infrastructure and costs, climate change may change the incentives for global production. Climate change is expected to impact different transport modes within transport networks. According to the Intergovernmental Panel on Climate Change (IPCC) (2022a), rising sea levels and melting ice caps will likely lead to significant damage and disruption to ports, more generally exacerbating the societal impact on coastal communities (IPCC 2022a). These concerns are not just limited to maritime transport, however, with evidence suggesting that a significant component of road and railway infrastructure is exposed to extreme flooding events (Koks et al. 2019). These potentially disrupt production, and with maritime shipping accounting for transporting up to

90% of goods and commodities (IMO 2015), there can be large economic consequences. The effects on GVC production will likely be amplified further, given the strong interdependencies between infrastructure systems in economies linked through GVCs.

Beyond the impact on natural trade costs, climate change may encourage higher man-made trade barriers. Climate change will likely reduce the availability of key natural resources, including water and food. And the transition to renewable and clean energy also relies on important yet scarce resources. This scarcity raises the possibility of rising protectionism as economies attempt to secure access. Moreover, efforts to mitigate the effects of climate change can further broaden trade barriers, with mechanisms that put a price on imported carbon resulting in higher effective average tariffs. By raising trade costs, these policy measures will likely influence the extent and geographic structure of GVC production.

The hyper-specialization that GVCs encourage can exacerbate climate change disruptions, making GVC coordination more difficult. GVCs offer the possibility of extreme specialization (Antràs 2020), with certain goods becoming highly concentrated within a few economies (Challinor, Adger, and Benton 2017). Extreme weather events linked to climate change that affect economies or regions can create bottlenecks and spill over to other regions through GVCs. The flow of goods and services may be disrupted by distant climate change events, affecting the level and volatility of production activities through supply chain disruptions in regions not directly affected by these weather events (e.g., Haraguchi and Lall 2015). This is particularly true for GVCs that rely on specialized commodities and key infrastructure (IPCC 2022a). Conversely, GVCs can also create resilience to climate change, leaving firms less reliant on domestic or regional suppliers (Lim-Camacho et al. 2017; Willner, Otto, and Levermann 2018).

An economy's comparative advantage will likely change as economies shift from fossil fuels to renewable energy sources and toward low-carbon-intensive production (IPCC 2022a). In response to climate change, certain factors—notably fossil fuels—will likely become less relevant, reducing the role economies endowed with these resources play in GVCs. Conversely, other endowments—such as those needed for clean energy production—will be more in demand, creating more GVC opportunities. Other value chains are heavily reliant on climate-sensitive inputs (e.g., food processing), with climate change potentially affecting the level and distribution of their activity. These effects will likely impact developing economies to a greater extent than advanced economies, with existing evidence suggesting that imports into the United States from developing economies are reduced by temperature

continued on next page

rises, particularly imports of agricultural products and light manufacturing (Jones and Olken 2010). This negative effect of climate change on exports from developing economies may further increase the price of goods imported by developed economies, with negative welfare effects of climate change in climate vulnerable regions being transmitted to non-vulnerable regions (Constant and Davin 2019). Over the longer term, climate change can affect the level and quality of factor endowments, shifting an economy's comparative advantage and production structure (IPCC 2022a). Extreme weather events—such as floods, drought, and extreme heat—are associated with land quality degradation, changes in the hydrological cycle and loss of land, among other impacts. Extreme weather events can also degrade physical capital, both physical infrastructure such as railways and roads as well as machinery through overheating, faster rates of depreciation and the need for longer cooling periods (IPCC 2022a). Extreme temperatures also impact

workers' ability to undertake both physical and cognitive tasks (Kjellstrom, Holmer, and Lemke 2009; Somanathan et al. 2021; UNDP 2016).

Beyond these three main drivers of GVCs, climate change can further affect the level and structure of global demand, with consequences for GVC production. The demand structure is likely affected by climate change, with changes in temperature and rainfall leading to changes in human needs. In addition to the structure of demand, levels of demand may be affected, especially in climate-vulnerable economies, which in turn can impact trade for economies strongly integrated with them (Schenker 2013; Schenker and Stephan 2014). Beyond the direct impact of climate change on demand, public awareness and concern over climate change can alter demand toward greener goods, potentially encouraging adoption of more stringent climate policies (Magnani 2000; Nordström and Vaughan 1999).

Sources: ADB using ADB (2023b); Antràs (2020); Antweiler, Copeland, and Taylor (2001); Challinor, Adger, and Benton et al. (2017); Constant and Davin (2019); Copeland, Shapiro, and Taylor (2021); Delera (2021); Delera and Foster-McGregor (2023); Haraguchi and Lall (2015); IMO (2015); IPCC (2022a); Jones and Olken (2010); Kjellstrom, Holmer, and Lemke (2009); Koks et al. (2019); Lim-Camacho et al. (2017); Magnani (2000); Nordström and Vaughan (1999); Schenker (2013); Schenker and Stephan (2014); Somanathan et al. (2021); UNCTAD (2023); UNDP (2016); and Willner, Otto, and Levermann (2018).

through domestic carbon pricing schemes—may be limited by carbon leakage through GVCs, with production activities shifting to economies where carbon pricing schemes are either weaker or nonexistent. The risk of carbon leakage and difficulty of regulating GHG emissions within GVCs—along with evidence that GVCs hold an increasing share of GHG emissions—highlight the significant challenge of GVCs in moving toward net zero emissions. These concerns are reflected in recent policy discussions, notably the development of the European Union's (EU) Carbon Border Adjustment Mechanism (CBAM), a major rationale being to prevent carbon leakage within GVCs. While evidence in favor of carbon leakage is currently limited (for example, Verde 2020), as the prevalence of carbon pricing increases and carbon prices begin to rise, then the potential for carbon leakage increases. Beyond these external pressures on developing economies, there is also self-interest involved. With climate change potentially leading to fundamental changes in production and disrupting GVCs (Box 6.1), developing economies have an incentive to decarbonize GVC activity to both use GVCs as a development tool and to position themselves better in green GVC segments.

An important challenge is how to reconcile the changes needed in the global production system to mitigate climate change with the GVC development model. Climate change mitigation requires a fundamental transition in the global production system, shifting away from a carbon-based economy toward more resource-efficient production. These changes add risk to the GVC development model, which contributes to climate change through increased energy consumption and CO_2 emissions in GVC-related transportation (Box 6.2) and production, and has shifted GHG emissions production to economies and regions with less stringent environmental policies associated with excessive waste production (Forti et al. 2020; Kaza et al. 2018). At the same time, GVCs can help reduce emissions, helping to both mitigate and adapt to climate change (Le Moigne and Ossa 2021). As the world responds to the climate challenge, there is a need to understand how government policy changes will affect GVCs, how much they can be a positive force for climate change mitigation, and how they affect the risks and vulnerabilities of the GVC model to climate change and their responses. Ultimately, the answers to these questions will depend on the extent to which GVCs contribute to CO_2 emissions, the relationship between GVC activity and CO_2 emissions, and how policy interventions to mitigate climate change will likely impact the breadth and structure of GVCs.

Box 6.2: The Role and Impact of Transportation in Carbon Dioxide Emissions

Significant amounts of greenhouse gas emissions are associated with transportation. According to the Intergovernmental Panel on Climate Change (IPCC) (2022a), transportation accounted for 15% of total net anthropogenic greenhouse gas (GHG) emissions in 2019. And unlike other sectors, there is little evidence its growth rate dropped over the previous decade. More than half the carbon dioxide (CO_2) emissions linked to transportation are due to passenger travel (Ritchie 2020). Still, transportation linked to international trade remains a significant source of emissions, with road freight accounting for 29.4% of CO_2 transportation emissions, and shipping 10.6% (Ritchie 2020). The rise of global value chains (GVCs) has been an important contributor to these rising transport-related emissions. Indeed, evidence suggests that international transport accounts for about a third of world trade-related emissions (Cristea et al. 2013). It is higher in many developed economies with substantial differences across sectors.[a] In 2015, international transport accounted for 1.14 gigatons of CO_2 emissions, accounting for 16% of value chain emissions (Wang, Wang, and Chen 2022).

GVCs increase shipping per unit of final output, increasing the average distance goods travel. One implication of GVC development is that intermediate inputs cross borders multiple times during production of final goods (Klotz and Sharma 2023). The overall distance traveled by components of a final good is thus higher than without GVCs. Much of this increase comes from maritime shipping, with the International Maritime Organization estimating that up to 90% of goods and commodities trade is through maritime shipping (IMO 2015). Recent evidence shows that, after accounting for economic growth, real transport use per unit of final consumption more than doubled from 1965 to 2020 (Ganapati and Wong 2023).

Driven by falling transportation costs, GVCs are the main factor explaining the increased distances goods travel. Despite recent price increases due to the coronavirus disease (COVID-19) pandemic, transportation costs have fallen substantially over time, with evidence suggesting that global transportation costs have declined by 33%–39% by weight and 48%–62% by value over the past half century (Ganapati and Wong 2023). The role of GVCs in increasing distances traveled by final goods is evidenced by the observation that all of the increase in global transport use by weight since 1990 can be accounted for entirely by the People's Republic of China (PRC), with trade over longer distances (more than 5,000 kilometers) accounting for most of the increase (Ganapati and Wong 2023).

Although distances traveled by goods have increased with GVCs, the impact on overall emissions is less clear. The effect of GVCs on emissions is twofold (Cristea et al. 2013). First, it leads to a reallocation of production, which can either raise or lower emissions, depending on whether production is reallocated to economies with relatively low or high emissions intensity. Second, it increases the distance traveled by goods, which raises GHG emissions. The overall effect is thus ambiguous in theory. However, evidence suggests that relative to autarky, a minority (31%) of trade flows lead to overall reduced emissions—with production in trade shifted to economies with relatively low emissions intensity, and with international transportation emissions being small relative to the differences in emissions intensities (Cristea et al. 2013).[b] Conversely, the remaining trade flows are associated with higher aggregate emissions—aggregate trade leads to higher emissions.

While GVCs may impact climate change through GHG emissions in transportation, climate change can have feedback effects on GVCs through transport as well. Climate change may change the structure of international transportation, with positive and negative consequences. One potential response could be a shift in mode of transportation (IPCC 2022a). Currently, maritime shipping is the main source of transporting goods and commodities, accounting for around 90% of world trade (IMO 2015), with other modes such as air transport being used for specific types of trade, such as time-sensitive products. As water levels in lakes and rivers drop and with the greater impact of rising sea levels and extreme weather events on port efficiency, climate change may lead to a shift to alternative modes of transportation (Koetse and Rietveld 2009; Du, Kim, and Zheng 2017). Recent concerns over the lack of rainfall at the Gatún Lake that feeds the Panama Canal, for example, resulted in a substantial fall in tonnage traveling through the canal (Arslanalp et al. 2023). Given that different forms of transport have different impacts on CO_2 emissions—with air transport the most emissions intensive, followed by road transport—a shift in transportation mode can significantly affect CO_2 emissions related to transportation. Certain changes related to climate change may also bring economic benefits and further encourage GVC development, with the melting of polar ice sheets potentially opening shorter and more profitable trade routes (Melia, Haines, and Hawkins 2016; Pizzolato et al. 2016; Ng et al. 2018; Mudryk et al. 2021). The opening of a northwest passage because of ice cap loss, for example, has been estimated to reduce maritime

continued on next page

Box 6.2: continued

shipping times and distances between Asia and Europe by up to 40% (Bekkers, Francois, Rojas-Romagosa 2018). Ultimately, the relationship between GVCs, transportation, and climate change are highly complex, with uncertainty over the net effect of GVC transportation on overall emissions and with strong feedback loops between transportation and climate change. As the IPCC (2022a)

highlighted, however, the challenges of reducing emissions in transportation are large, with scenario modeling suggesting that the sector will not reach zero emissions by 2100. This is despite possible mitigation measures including the electrification of more transport services and the use of sustainable biofuels and low-emissions hydrogen.

[a] According to the United States (US) Environmental Protection Agency (EPA), transportation accounts for about 29% of GHG emissions in the US (EPA). According to the work of Cristea et al. (2013), for example, 80% of trade-related emissions in machinery exports are from international transportation.

[b] Case study evidence on trade in cut roses shows that those produced in Kenya and shipped by air to the United Kingdom (UK) results in a reduction of emissions compared to roses produced in the UK (Williams 2007).

Sources: ADB using Arslanalp et al. (2023); Bekkers, Francois, and Rojas-Romagosa (2018); Cristea et al. (2013); Du, Kim, and Zheng (2017); Ganapati and Wong (2023); IMO (2015); IPCC (2022a); Koetse and Rietveld (2009); Klotz and Sharma (2023); Melia, Haines, and Hawkins (2016); Mudryk et al. (2021) ; Ng et al. (2018); Pizzolato et al. (2016); Ritchie (2020); and Wang, Wang, and Chen (2022).

The Contribution of Global Value Chains to Carbon Dioxide Emissions

From 1995 to 2018, global CO$_2$ emissions from all production sources rose by around 2% per year. A decomposition of CO$_2$ emissions embodied in an economy's production activities (plus direct emissions by households) shows the recent trend in global CO$_2$ emissions along with a decomposition of these emissions between different sources activity (Box 6.3).[39] The average compound annual growth rate of emissions from 1995 to 2018 was 2.1%, with the growth rate somewhat lower after 2010 (1.8%) than before (2.2%). This is consistent with the conclusion of the IPCC (2022a) that while anthropogenic carbon emissions during 2010–2019 were larger than in any other time period, the growth rate of emissions was lower than during the previous decade. According to the IPCC scenarios, efforts to limit temperature rises to 1.5°C will require peak GHG emissions to be reached by 2025 and GHG emissions to be reduced by 43% by 2030. Despite the

slowdown in the growth of CO$_2$ emissions in the most recent period, emissions continued to rise year-on-year during 1995–2019[40]—with the brief exception of the global financial crisis, indicating what is needed to achieve the goal of limiting warming to 1.5°C.

GVCs play a relatively small but increasing role in CO$_2$ emissions production. Emissions associated with domestic production for domestic consumption are by far the largest contributor to overall emissions, accounting for 64% in 2018 (Figure 6.2). Combined, traditional trade and GVCs accounted for 22% of CO$_2$ emissions in 2018, with GVCs accounting for 14% and traditional trade 8%. The average growth rate of production-based CO$_2$ emissions during 1995–2019 was smallest for household emissions (0.9% per year), compared to production for domestic consumption (2.1%), traditional trade (2.4%), and GVC trade (2.9%). Thus, the growth rate of emissions was higher for GVC production activities than for other sources of CO$_2$ emissions. Although there is some evidence of a declining growth rate of CO$_2$ emissions in GVCs, with an average annual growth rate of 3.3% for 1995–2009 and 2.3% over 2010–2018, the average

---

[39]   While commonly used in recent studies, the data used for this kind of analysis are subject to various constraints and rely on certain strong assumptions (see Box 6.2). Most notably, the approach assumes that in any given year the CO$_2$ intensity (i.e., the ratio of CO$_2$ emissions to gross output) is constant within a sector, irrespective of whether production occurs within GVCs or by domestic firms.

[40]   The Organisation for Economic Co-operation and Development (OECD) data on CO$_2$ emissions are currently not available beyond 2018, meaning that it is not possible using that data source to consider emissions during and after the COVID-19 pandemic. Data from alternative sources, however, suggest that emissions dropped substantially in 2020, with Bhanumati, de Haan, and Tebrake (2022) reporting a drop of 4.6% in 2020, although this was more than offset by the increase of 6.4% in 2021.

Box 6.3: Methodology for Measuring Emissions in Global Value Chains

The approach adopted to measure carbon dioxide (CO_2) emissions that occur within global value chains (GVCs) extends the decomposition of value-added proposed by Wang et al. (2017) to CO_2 emissions. They proposed decomposing an economy's value-added into a component that serves domestic demand, a component associated with traditional trade (e.g., the exchange of final goods) and a component associated with GVC trade. This GVC trade component was further split into two categories capturing simple and complex GVC integration, with simple GVCs involving the movement of value-added embodied in intermediate goods to an economy that uses it to produce final goods consumed in that economy, and complex GVCs involving the movement of value-added embodied in intermediate products to an economy that uses them to produce final or intermediate goods that are subsequently shipped to third economies. This approach was extended and applied to a decomposition of CO_2 emissions by, among others, Meng et al. (2018).

Under a similar decomposition, CO_2 emissions in production activities are split into three categories: (i) emissions related to domestic production for domestic consumption; (ii) emissions related to traditional trade; and (iii) emissions related to GVC trade. One further component is added to the decomposition, which is emissions that are released directly by domestic households (non-production activities such as using fuel in automobiles, heating, etc.). Box figure 1 describes the different sources into which overall emissions are decomposed.

When considering production components of the decomposition, two different perspectives are considered. The primary focus is on emissions that a sector in a particular economy produces in production activities that are then used in downstream production, either domestically or abroad. This is the standard definition of production-based CO_2 emissions from a territorial perspective, considering emissions produced within the borders of the economy. A second dimension, however, is emissions embodied in intermediate goods and services that are then used by a sector within an economy in its production activities serving either domestic demand or foreign demand through either traditional or GVC trade. This approach traces CO_2 emissions embodied in the flow of intermediate goods and services to the final product, and thus reflects a final production or use perspective, with emissions potentially being sourced both domestically and from abroad. The use perspective thus reflects CO_2 emissions received by a sector through backward linkages, while the production perspective reflects CO_2 emissions produced in a sector and supplied to other sectors and economies through forward linkages (box figure 2).

1: Decomposing Carbon Dioxide Emissions

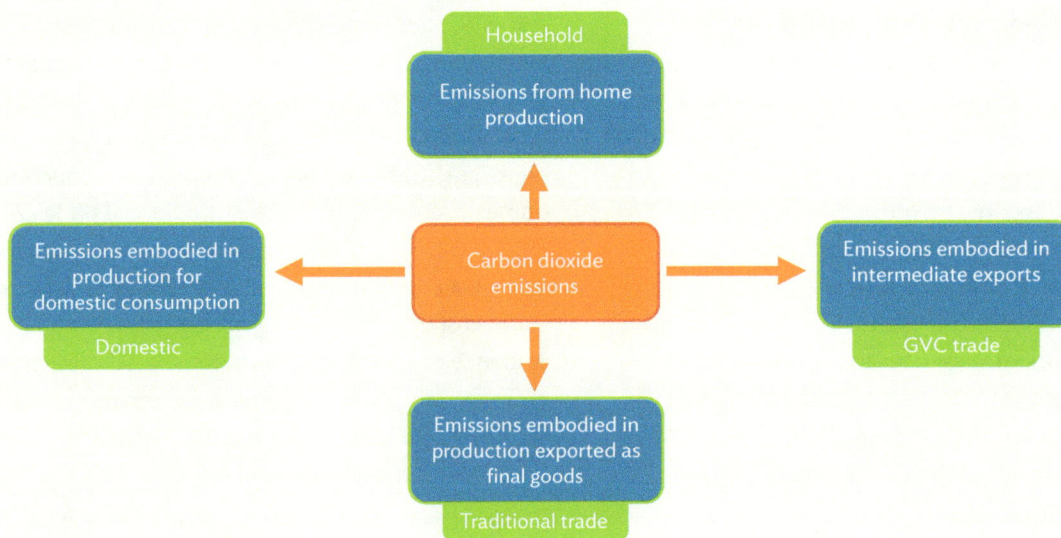

GVC = global value chain.
Source: ADB.

continued on next page

Box 6.3: continued

2: The Production and Use of Carbon Dioxide Emissions in Global Value Chains

Source: ADB.

Sources: ADB using Wang et al. (2017); and Meng et al (2018).

Figure 6.2: Decomposition of Carbon Dioxide Emissions Production (million metric tons)

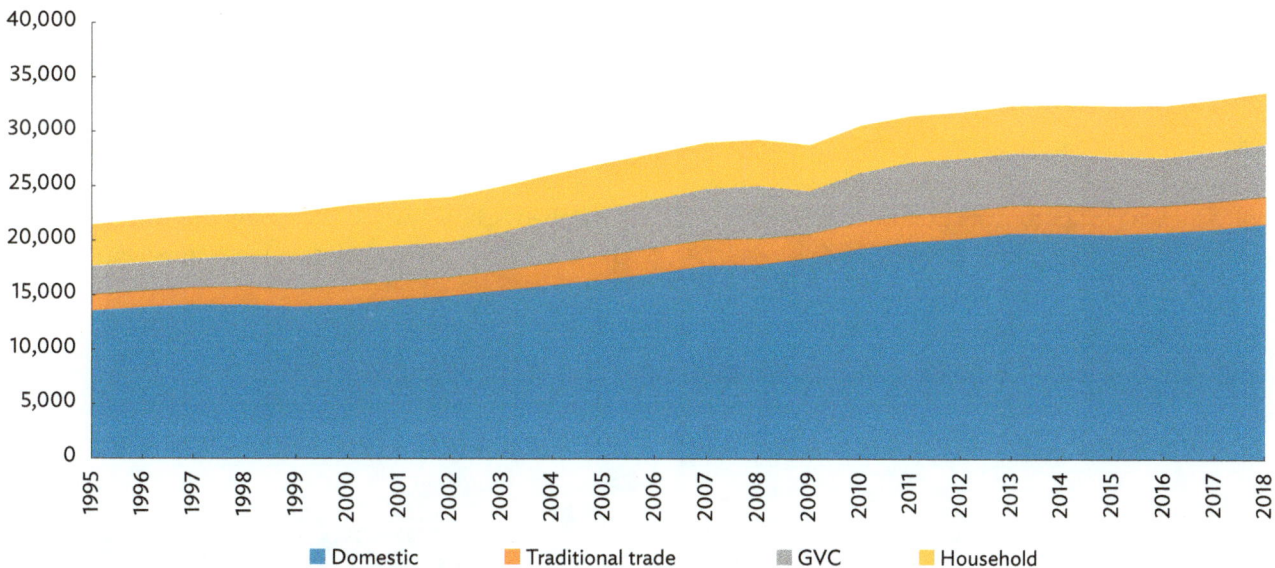

GVC = global value chain.

Note: Data on emissions are limited to carbon dioxide and include carbon dioxide emissions from the combustion of fossil fuels, but exclude emissions due to land use, land-use change, and forestry and other non-energy related industrial processes.

Sources: ADB calculations using data from Organisation for Economic Co-operation and Development (OECD). Inter-Country Input-Output Tables. https://www.oecd.org/sti/ind/inter-country-input-output-tables.htm; OECD. Carbon dioxide emissions embodied in international trade (TECO$_2$) data set. https://www.oecd.org/sti/ind/carbondioxideemissionsembodiedininternationaltrade.htm (both accessed November 2023).

growth rates of CO_2 emissions in GVCs in the latter period remain above those for the other sources of emissions (1.8% for domestic production, 1.5% for traditional trade, and 1.3% for household production). These differences in growth rates are also reflected in the changes in shares of emissions of the different sources. Combined, the two trade terms (traditional trade and GVCs) saw their share rise from 19% to 22% of total CO_2 emissions between 1995 and 2018, with the share for GVCs increasing from 12% to 14%.

Developing Asia accounts for an increasing share of GVC emissions production. Developing Asia's share in CO_2 emissions embodied in GVC production rose between 1995 and 2018 (Figure 6.3).[41] In 1995, developing Asia accounted for around 23% of overall GVC-related emissions, rising to 42% in 2018. By contrast, shares for all other regions declined. The share for developed Asia declined from 5.2% to 4.9%, and shares dropped from 23% to 15% in the EU and the United Kingdom (UK), 16% to 11% in North America, and 33% to 27% in the rest

---

41   Developing Asian economies included in the OECD databases include Brunei Darussalam; Cambodia; the PRC; Hong Kong, China; India; Indonesia; Kazakhstan; the Republic of Korea; the Lao People's Democratic Republic (Lao PDR); Malaysia; the Philippines; Singapore; Taipei,China; Thailand; and Viet Nam. Sectoral emissions data are not available for the Lao PDR in all years.

of the world.[42] These changes reflect the much higher growth rate of CO_2 emissions production in GVCs in developing Asia, with emissions growing by 238%, driven partly by inward foreign direct investment (Box 6.4). In comparison, the growth rate was 73% in developed Asia, 50% in the rest of the world, 34% in North America, and 17% in the EU and the UK.

While population growth in developing Asia accounts for part of its rising share of aggregate CO_2 emissions production, CO_2 emissions per capita are increasing while falling in other regions. In 1995, aggregate production-based CO_2 emissions per capita were lowest in developing Asia at 2.0 metric tons per capita (Figure 6.4), with emissions per capita substantially higher in North America (15.2 metric tons), the EU and the UK (8.3 metric tons), and developed Asia (7.5 metric tons). Between 1995 and 2018, emissions per capita dropped significantly in North America (to 12.3 tons per capita) along with the EU and the UK (6.8 metric tons). Conversely, developing Asia was the only region to see an increase in emissions per capita, with emissions per capita increasing from 2.0 metric tons per capita in 1995 to 4.4 metric tons in 2018.

GVCs account for the rising share of CO_2 emissions production per capita in most regions. While the share of CO_2 emissions production per capita for domestic consumption dropped in more developed regions—with shares falling by 10.7 percentage points in the EU and the UK, 6.0 percentage points in developed Asia, and 1.9 percentage points in North America—it increased by 2.2 percentage points in developing Asia. Combined with developing Asia's relatively rapid population growth, much of the increase in aggregate production-based emissions in the region was absorbed by domestic consumption. At the same time, the share of emissions per capita due to GVCs increased in the region by 1.6 percentage points between 1995 and 2018, with even larger increases elsewhere, with increases of 5.7 percentage points in developed Asia, 5.3 percentage points in the EU and the UK, and 2.2 percentage points in North America.

Figure 6.3: Carbon Dioxide Emissions Production for Global Value Chain Trade by Region (million metric tons)

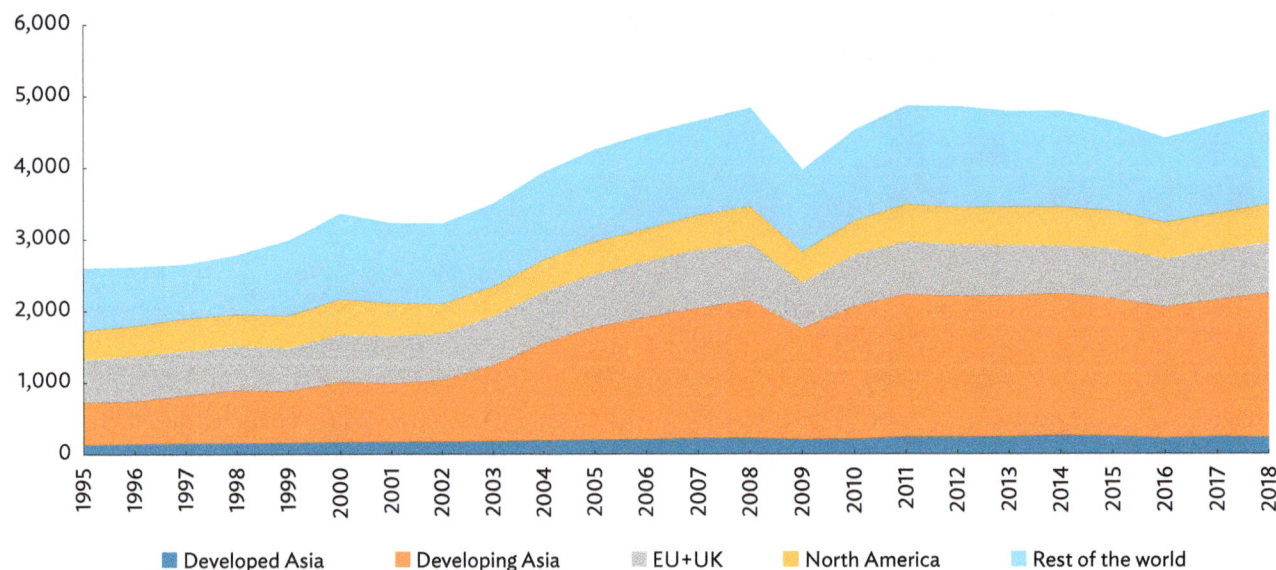

EU = European Union (27 members), UK = United Kingdom.

Note: Data on emissions are limited to carbon dioxide (CO_2) and include CO_2 emissions from the combustion of fossil fuels, but exclude emissions due to land use, land-use change, and forestry and other non-energy related industrial processes.

Sources: ADB calculations using data from Organisation for Economic Co-operation and Development (OECD). Inter-Country Input-Output Tables. https://www.oecd.org/sti/ind/inter-country-input-output-tables.htm; OECD. Carbon dioxide emissions embodied in international trade (TECO_2) data set. https://www.oecd.org/sti/ind/carbondioxideemissionsembodiedininternationaltrade.htm (both accessed November 2023).

---

[42]   Developed Asia refers to Australia, Japan, and New Zealand. The rest of the world includes Argentina, Brazil, Switzerland, Chile, Colombia, Costa Rica, Iceland, Israel, Morocco, Norway, Peru, the Russian Federation, Saudi Arabia, Tunisia, Türkiye, and South Africa, as well as an aggregate rest of the world included in OECD databases.

Box 6.4: The Contribution of Multinational Enterprises to Carbon Dioxide Emissions in Global Value Chains

Multinational enterprises (MNEs) play a major role within global value chains (GVCs) and contribute significantly to GVC carbon dioxide (CO_2) emissions. They enter host economies through foreign direct investment (FDI), combining domestic endowments (e.g., labor and resources) with foreign endowments (e.g., capital, technology, and management). They play a primary role in coordinating international trade and GVC activity. MNEs and their network of foreign affiliates account for almost two-thirds of world exports, with foreign affiliates accounting for 30% of global exports (Miroudot and Rigo 2022). Through their role in coordinating GVCs, MNEs are crucial in shaping global production patterns by allocating activities based on the host economy's resource endowments, with implications for the levels of CO_2 emissions of the economies hosting foreign affiliates. Historical evidence suggests that nearly two-thirds of industrial CO_2 and methane (CH_4) emissions from 1751 to 2010 can be attributed to 90 firms producing cement and energy (Heede 2014). A better understanding of the nexus between MNE activity and carbon emissions in GVCs can thus be critical in establishing effective cross-regional carbon governance (Wei et al. 2023; Wang, Wang, and Chen 2022).

Given their major role in GVCs, MNEs can help decarbonize GVCs. They can impose sustainability standards and

encourage the transfer of green technologies within GVCs (Thorlakson, de Zegher, and Lambin 2018). They can further use low emission-intensive suppliers and more environmentally friendly distributors within their value chains. In addition, they can also be an important source of finance for sustainable development through FDI (Steenbergen and Saurav 2023). A significant portion of overall MNE emissions transcends the boundaries of the firm and borders of their point of origin. Thus, MNEs are a major driver of an unequal exchange, with emissions production shifting from the developed to developing world, raising emissions and their associated effects on health in developing economies.

Using data from the Organisation for Economic Co-operation and Development (OECD) Activity of Multinational Enterprise (AMNE) database—which splits production activities of domestic firms and foreign affiliates—and following the approach of Li et al. (2022), the extent to which the activities of MNEs and their affiliates contribute to an economy's CO_2 emissions can be examined.[a] Including MNE activities in GVC-related emissions results in a higher share of emissions considered to be GVC-related than when using a territorial-based approach to capture GVC emissions. Using this approach, the share of emissions due to GVCs in Asia was 25.5% in 2016, with the share for all economies 26.2%.[b] The

1: Carbon Dioxide Emissions by Production Type in Asian Economies, 2016

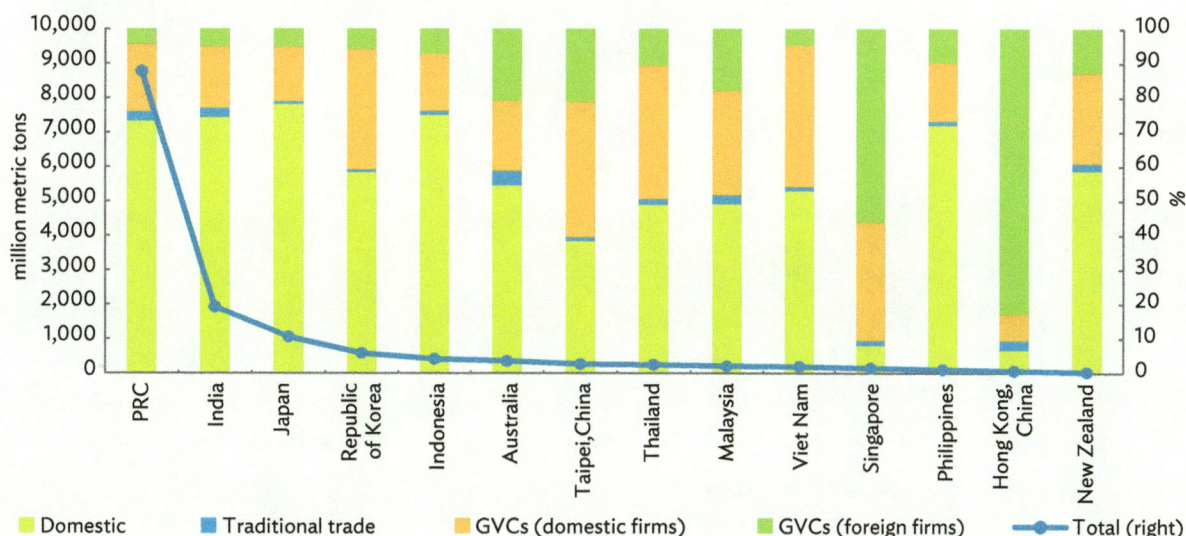

GVC = global value chain, PRC = People's Republic of China.

Note: Data on emissions are limited to carbon dioxide (CO_2) and include CO_2 emissions from the combustion of fossil fuels, but exclude emissions due to land use, land-use change, and forestry and other non-energy related industrial processes.

Sources: ADB calculations using data from Organisation for Economic Co-operation and Development (OECD). Analytical Activities of Multinational Enterprise. https://www.oecd.org/fr/sti/ind/analytical-amne-database.htm; OECD. Carbon dioxide emissions embodied in international trade (TECO$_2$) data set. https://www.oecd.org/sti/ind/carbondioxideemissionsembodiedininternationaltrade.htm (both accessed November 2023).

continued on next page

Box 6.4: continued

relative importance of MNE activity to these emissions is found to vary substantially across Asian economies. While domestic production serving domestic consumption tends to dominate in the larger economies with the highest levels of emissions, in other economies GVC activity is a major contributor to overall emissions (box figure 1). Emissions due to MNE activities within GVCs are found to be relatively important in many economies, accounting for more than 50% of GVC related emissions in Singapore; Hong Kong, China; and Australia, and for more than 30% of emissions in Indonesia; Taipei,China; Malaysia; the Philippines; and New Zealand. Conversely, the share of emissions in GVCs due to MNEs is relatively low in Viet Nam (10.4%), the Republic of Korea (14.2%), and the People's Republic of China (18%).

The contributions of GVCs and MNEs to emissions vary greatly across sectors. In Asia, GVC shares of total emissions are relatively high in typical GVC sectors like other transport equipment, electrical equipment, motor vehicles, textiles, other manufacturing, and computer and electronic products (box figure 2). Of these, other manufacturing, motor vehicles, and computer and electronic products have a higher share of emissions in GVCs due to foreign firms than to domestic firms (also for construction and publishing). For both Asian and non-Asian economies, many of the sectors with the highest share of emissions due to GVCs also have a higher share of foreign firm emissions than domestic firms. This is especially true for typical GVC sectors, highlighting the role MNEs play.

2: Sectoral Contributions to Carbon Dioxide Emissions in Asian Economies, 2016

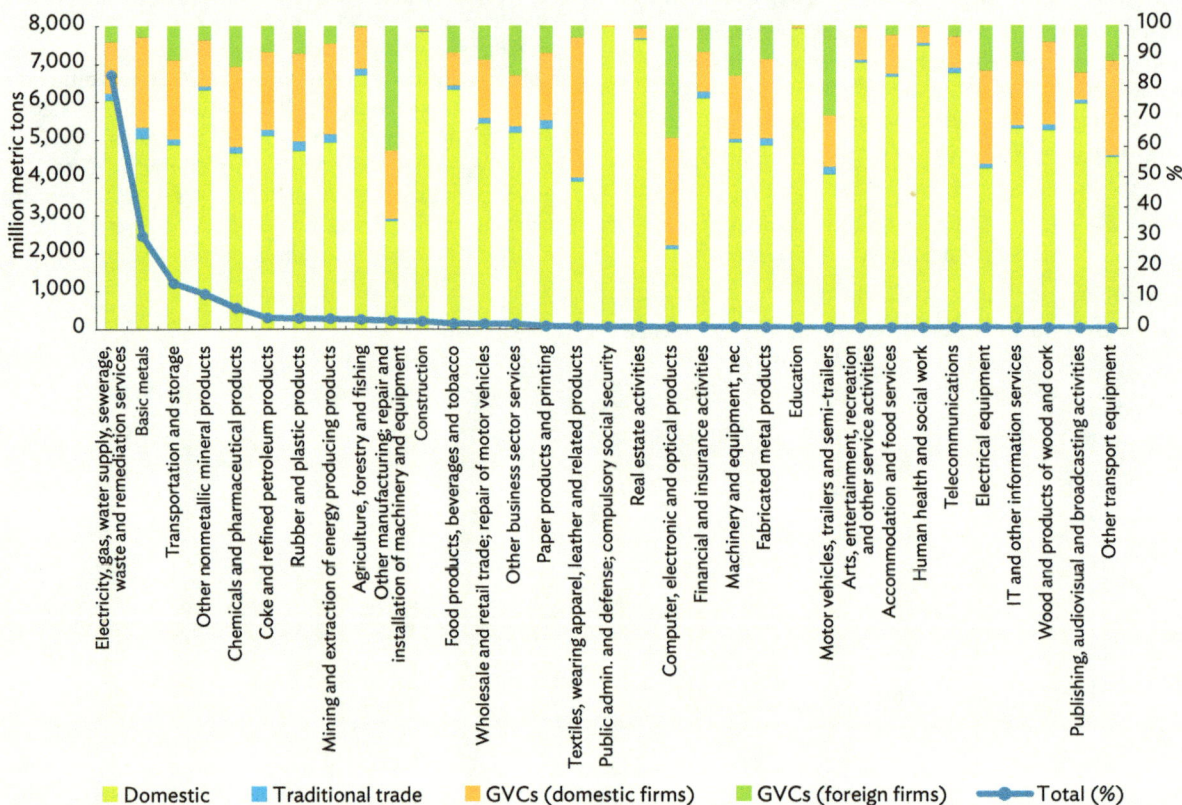

GVC = global value chain, IT = information technology, nec = not elsewhere classified.

Note: Data on emissions are limited to carbon dioxide (CO_2) and include CO_2 emissions from the combustion of fossil fuels, but exclude emissions due to land use, land-use change, and forestry and other non-energy related industrial processes.

Sources: ADB calculations using data from Organisation for Economic Co-operation and Development (OECD). Analytical Activities of Multinational Enterprise. https://www.oecd.org/fr/sti/ind/analytical-amne-database.htm; OECD. Carbon dioxide emissions embodied in international trade (TECO$_2$) data set. https://www.oecd.org/sti/ind/carbondioxideemissionsembodiedininternationaltrade.htm (both accessed November 2023).

[a]   The approach relies on similarly strong assumptions to those for estimating emissions due to GVC activity. While foreign and domestic firms are usually considered to differ in production technologies and structure due to various ownership advantages (Dunning 1988), for example, there is no separate data on CO_2 intensities for domestic and foreign firms, meaning that the same intensity is used for both domestic and foreign firms. FDI emissions intensity may also vary by type of entry or entry mode, which similarly is not captured in the data.
[b]   By comparison, the share of emissions due to GVCs in 2016 using the territorial approach is estimated at 13.6%.

Source: ADB using Li et al. (2022); Heede (2014); Miroudot and Rigo (2022); Steenbergen and Saurav (2023); Thorlakson, de Zegher, and Lambin (2018); Wei et al. (2023); and Wang, Wang, and Chen (2022).

Figure 6.4: Production Emissions per Capita by Source and Region (metric tons per capita)

Domestic in 1995 | Trade in 1995
Domestic in 2018 | Trade in 2018
GVC in 1995 | Household in 1995
GVC in 2018 | Household in 2018

EU = European Union (27 members), GVC = global value chain, UK = United Kingdom.

Note: Data on emissions are limited to carbon dioxide (CO_2) and include CO_2 emissions from the combustion of fossil fuels, but exclude emissions due to land use, land-use change, and forestry and other non-energy related industrial processes.

Sources: ADB calculations using data from Organisation for Economic Co-operation and Development (OECD). Inter-Country Input-Output Tables. https://www.oecd.org/sti/ind/inter-country-input-output-tables.htm; OECD. Carbon dioxide emissions embodied in international trade ($TECO_2$) data set. https://www.oecd.org/sti/ind/carbondioxideemissionsembodied ininternationaltrade.htm; and World Bank. World Development Indicators. https://databank.worldbank.org/source/world-development-indicators (all accessed November 2023).

The Production and Use of Embodied Carbon Dioxide Emissions in Global Value Chains

Developing Asia is a net supplier of CO_2 emissions in GVCs. Different production stages in GVCs are often done in different economies, with different economies becoming net suppliers or net recipients of emissions due to their GVC production activity. The extent to which an economy is a supplier or recipient of CO_2 emissions in GVC production depends on several factors, including its position in GVCs. An economy engaged in upstream and often energy-intensive production will likely be a net supplier of emissions, while an economy situated further downstream engaged in assembly and other activities will likely be a net recipient of the emissions embodied in imported intermediate

inputs. Previous figures reported CO_2 emissions embodied in production activities, capturing emissions in GVCs due to forward linkages or upstream production. Figure 6.5 introduces backward linkages or downstream production, reporting information on a region's emissions production in GVCs (left-hand side) and the embodied CO_2 emissions it receives through imported intermediates (right-hand side) for 2018. It shows the PRC, other developing Asia, and the rest of the world are net suppliers of GVC emissions, meaning their exports of domestically produced CO_2 embodied in intermediates exceed foreign-produced CO_2 emissions embodied in their intermediate purchases.

Figure 6.5: Regional Carbon Dioxide Emissions Production and Regional Carbon Dioxide Emissions Destinations in Global Value Chains, 2018

EU = European Union (27 members), PRC = People's Republic of China, UK = United Kingdom.

Note: Data on emissions are limited to carbon dioxide (CO_2) and include CO_2 emissions from the combustion of fossil fuels, but exclude emissions due to land use, land-use change, and forestry and other non-energy related industrial processes.

Sources: ADB calculations using data from Organisation for Economic Co-operation and Development (OECD). Inter-Country Input-Output Tables. https://www.oecd.org/sti/ind/inter-country-input-output-tables.htm; OECD. Carbon dioxide emissions embodied in international trade ($TECO_2$) data set. https://www.oecd.org/sti/ind/arbondioxideemissionsembodiedininternationaltrade.htm (both accessed November 2023).

Conversely, developed Asia, the EU and the UK, and North America receive more embodied CO_2 emissions in imported intermediate purchases within GVCs than intermediate exports. This highlights the potential challenges of GVCs for policymakers, with CO_2 emissions embodied in imported intermediate inputs—potentially not subject to a region's carbon policies—contributing substantially to CO_2 emissions embodied in a region's downstream GVC production.

Sectoral Contributions to the Production and Use of Embodied Carbon Dioxide Emissions in Global Value Chains

The production of CO_2 emissions in GVCs is concentrated in a handful of sectors, though these emissions are used across a broad range of downstream sectors. Figure 6.6 illustrates the extent of CO_2 emissions production in GVCs by sector (left-hand side) and the use of the emissions (embodied in intermediate input purchases) in GVCs (right-hand side). It underscores the strong concentration of CO_2 emissions production in a small number of sectors—electricity, chemicals, metals, mining, and transport and storage. These emissions—or the intermediates embodying these emissions—are used in downstream GVC production across a broader range of sectors, with mining, construction, agriculture, business services, and public administration accounting for higher shares. There are two dimensions to consider when looking at emissions in GVCs—the primary source of CO_2 emissions and which sectors use them. Efforts to reduce CO_2 emissions can thus focus on these two dimensions; reducing emissions in sectors where primary emissions are produced and increasing the efficiency of those that use embodied emissions in production. That the production of emissions tends to be concentrated in a small number of sectors suggests that it may be better for policymakers to pursue policies focused on production rather than use of (embodied) CO_2 emissions.

Figure 6.6: Production and Use of Carbon Dioxide Emissions in Global Value Chains by Sector, 2018

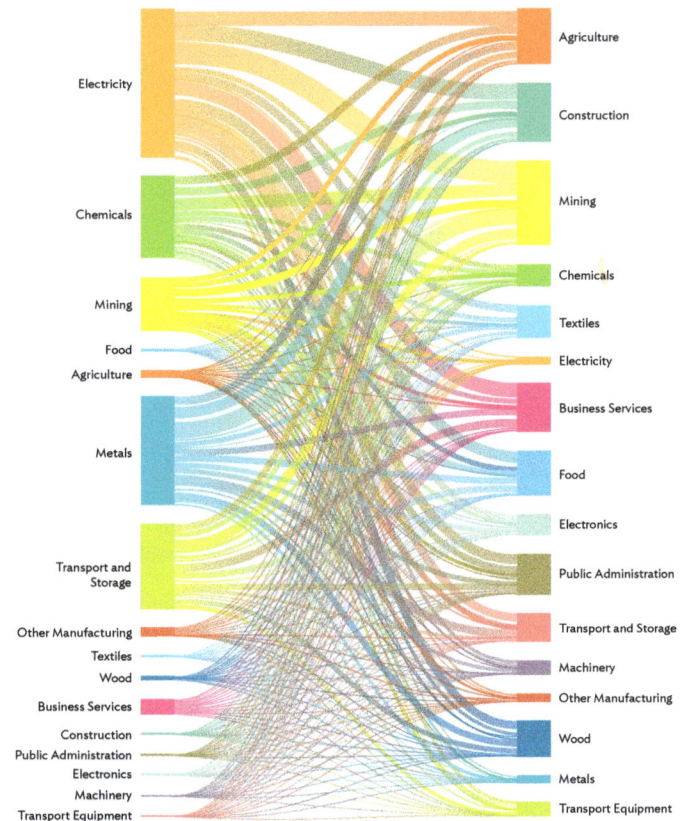

Note: Data on emissions are limited to carbon dioxide (CO_2) and include CO_2 emissions from the combustion of fossil fuels, but exclude emissions due to land use, land-use change, and forestry and other non-energy related industrial processes.

Sources: ADB calculations using data from Organisation for Economic Co-operation and Development (OECD). Inter-Country Input-Output Tables. https://www.oecd.org/sti/ind/inter-country-input-output-tables.htm; OECD. Carbon dioxide emissions embodied in international trade (TECO$_2$) data set. https://www.oecd.org/sti/ind/arbondioxideemissionsembodiedininternationaltrade.htm (both accessed November 2023).

The Relationship between Global Value Chain Activity and Carbon Dioxide Emissions

The growth rate of CO_2 emissions in developing Asia has been relatively rapid, despite a substantial drop in the emissions intensity of production. The level of CO_2 emissions in production can be decomposed into two components—one capturing CO_2 emissions intensity (e.g., the ratio of CO_2 emissions to gross output) and the other a scale effect (e.g., the level of gross output).[43] Identifying the relative importance of the two in driving aggregate emissions and of the role GVCs play in these two dimensions is crucial to understanding the impact of GVCs on CO_2 emissions. This decomposition can be used to consider the contributions of these different components to the growth rate of aggregate CO_2 emissions production. For 1995–2018, the growth rate of CO_2 emissions in developing Asia was 114% (Figure 6.7). This growth rate was substantially higher than in other regions—with the growth rate in the rest of the world 34%, developed Asia 7.7%, and North America 2.1%. Within the EU and the UK, CO_2 emissions fell by 17% over the period. The rapid growth in emissions in developing Asia was driven by the rapid growth in gross output per capita, which increased by nearly 200%, with population growth associated with a 25% increase in CO_2 emissions. These increases were partially offset by a 110% reduction in CO_2 intensity. The reduction in CO_2 intensity occurred across all regions, with the rate being largest for developing Asia. Thus, while technological and structural change have reduced CO_2 intensity in developing Asia's production, the increase in gross output per capita to satisfy both domestic and foreign demand far outweighed the reductions in CO_2 intensity, resulting in a substantial increase in emissions.[44]

Relative to their value-added contribution, GVCs account for a high share of CO_2 emissions in production. The data indicate that while there is a positive association between the share of GVCs in value-added and the share of GVCs in CO_2 emissions production, the shares of GVCs in total CO_2 emissions tend to be larger than those in value-added (Figure 6.8). As such, the sectoral structure of production in GVCs tends to be relatively emissions intensive. This confirms previous results that show international trade

Figure 6.7: Growth Rate and Decomposition of the Growth of Carbon Dioxide Emissions in Production, 1995–2018 (%)

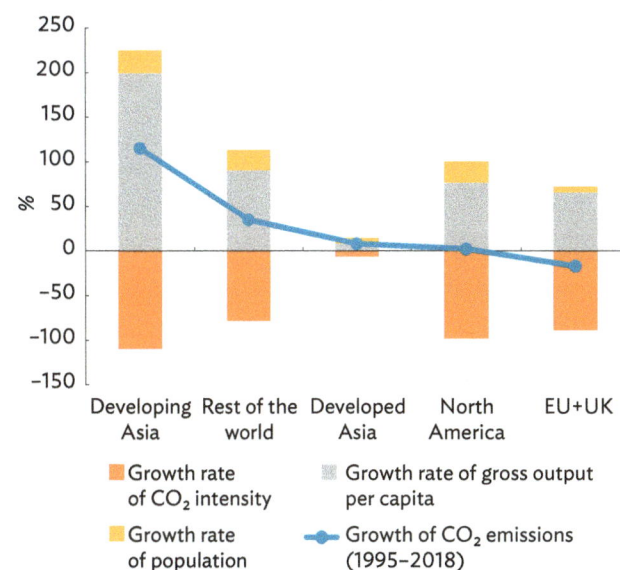

CO_2 = carbon dioxide, EU = European Union (27 members), UK = United Kingdom.

Notes: The figure decomposes the growth rate of carbon dioxide (CO_2) emissions using $\Delta \ln CO_2 = \Delta \ln \left(\frac{CO_2}{GO}\right) + \Delta \ln \left(\frac{GO}{POP}\right) + \Delta \ln POP$, where GO and POP refer to gross output and population. ln is natural logarithm, and Δ refers to the change between two time periods.

Sources: ADB calculations using data from Organisation for Economic Co-operation and Development (OECD). Inter-Country Input-Output Tables. https://www.oecd.org/sti/ind/inter-country-input-output-tables.htm; OECD. Carbon dioxide emissions embodied in international trade (TECO_2) data set. https://www.oecd.org/sti/ind/carbondioxideemissionsembodiedininternationaltrade.htm (both accessed November 2023).

is tilted toward dirty goods and sectors (Le Moigne and Ossa 2021). For GVCs, this further reflects the strong association of GVCs with manufacturing, which tends to be more emissions intensive than non-manufacturing sectors.[45]

A higher scale in GVC production does not appear to result in increased efficiency in CO_2 emissions production. While a higher level of GVC production would generally be associated with more CO_2 emissions produced in an economy, the size of the increase is theoretically

---

[43] The scale effect can further be split into a component due to the level of population and a component capturing the level of gross output per capita by writing CO_2 emissions in production as $CO_2 = \frac{CO_2}{GO} \times \frac{GO}{POP} \times POP$, with GO being gross output and POP being population. Expressing this in logs and taking the difference between two time periods, the approximate growth rate of CO_2 emissions can be decomposed into an effect due to changing CO_2 intensity and the two scale terms. This can be written as $\Delta \ln CO_2 = \Delta \ln \left(\frac{CO_2}{GO}\right) + \Delta \ln \left(\frac{GO}{POP}\right) + \Delta \ln POP$, where ln is the natural logarithm and Δ refers to the change between the two time periods.

[44] While most of the gross output per capita serves domestic demand—its share increasing from 75% to 77% during the period—the share serving GVCs remained roughly constant at around 12.5%.

[45] Since the data only report overall sectoral CO_2 intensity of production, it must be the case that it is differences in sectoral structures of GVC production relative to other forms of production that drive the differences.

ambiguous. If increases in the scale of GVC production are associated with better emissions efficiency, then a 1% higher level of GVC production would be associated with a less than 1% higher level of aggregate CO_2 emissions. Conversely, if an increase in the scale of GVC production is associated with lower emissions efficiency, then a 1% higher level of GVC production would be associated with a more than 1% increase in CO_2 emissions. Considering the cross-section of economies covered by OECD databases and the data for 2018, emissions appear to scale roughly linearly with GVC production, such that a 1% higher level of GVC production is associated with a roughly 1% higher level of CO_2 emissions.[46] So the efficiency of emissions production in GVCs does not appear to be influenced by the scale of production.

Differences in the scaling relationship exist between developed and developing economies, with a given level of GVC production associated with higher emissions in developing economies. One version of the pollution haven hypothesis is that developed economies offshore some of their emissions-intensive activities to developing economies, making those economies even more emissions-intensive in production. Thus, it may be expected that the response of CO_2 emissions to increases in GVC production may be stronger in developing economies, which increasingly rely on less emissions-efficient firms. Data for 2018 provide some limited evidence in favor of this hypothesis (Figure 6.9). While the scaling relationship for developed economies suggests constant returns to scale in emissions production due to GVC production—with a 1% increase in GVC production associated with a 1% increase in aggregate CO_2 emissions—for developing economies the relationship is above 1, such that a 1% increase in GVC production is associated with a 1.15% increase in CO_2 production.[47] Moreover, for a given level of GVC production, aggregate CO_2 emissions tend to be higher in developing economies than developed economies. This

suggests that GVC production in developing economies is more emissions-intensive than in developed economies—driven by a combination of differences in production technology and the sectoral structure of GVCs between developed and developing economies.

Figure 6.8: Scatterplot of Global Value Chain Shares in Value-Added and in Carbon Dioxide Emissions Production, 2018

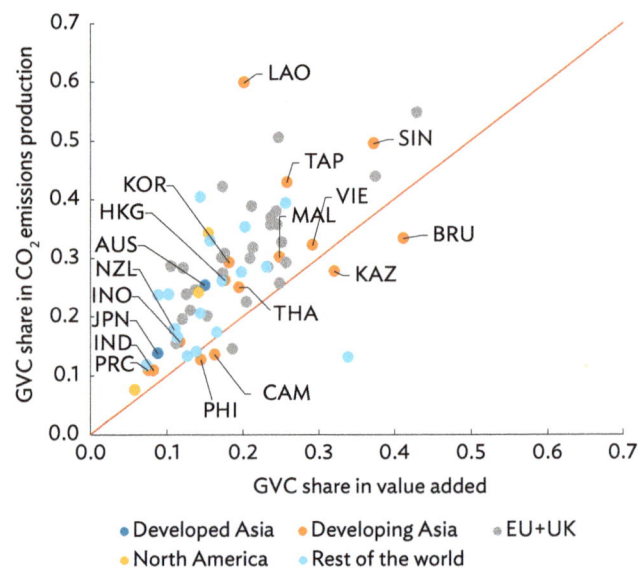

AUS = Australia; BRU = Brunei Darussalam; CAM = Cambodia; CO_2 = carbon dioxide; EU = European Union (27 members); GVC = global value chain; HKG = Hong Kong, China; IND = India; INO = Indonesia; JPN = Japan; KAZ = Kazakhstan; KOR = Republic of Korea; LAO = Lao People's Democratic Republic, MAL = Malaysia; NZL = New Zealand; PHI = Philippines; PRC = People's Republic of China; SIN = Singapore; TAP = Taipei,China; THA = Thailand; UK = United Kingdom; VIE = Viet Nam.

Note: Developed economies are defined as high-income economies according to the classification of the World Bank, while developing economies refer to all other economies. GVC shares in CO_2 emissions are calculated excluding direct household emissions to make them comparable with the production data.

Sources: ADB calculations using data from Organisation for Economic Co-operation and Development (OECD). Inter-Country Input-Output Tables. https://www.oecd.org/sti/ind/inter-country-input-output-tables.htm; OECD. Carbon dioxide emissions embodied in international trade (TECO$_2$) data set. https://www.oecd.org/sti/ind/arbondioxideemissionsembodiedininternationaltrade.htm (both accessed November 2023).

---

[46] The scaling coefficients are obtained from a regression of the log of GVC-related production-based emissions on the log of GVC-related value-added. A coefficient of 1 on the log of value-added due to GVC production indicates a proportional increase in GVC-related emissions in response to an increase in GVC-related value-added, while a value above (below) one indicates super-linear (sub-linear) scaling such that a 1% increase in GVC-related value-added is associated with a greater (less) than 1% increase in GVC-related emissions. The coefficient for GVC production is 1.02, while for domestic production it is estimated at 0.998, and for traditional trade 0.926. The coefficients are never significantly different from one, suggesting little difference in the scaling relationship between domestic production, traditional trade, and GVC trade.

[47] The statistical association is not significantly different from one in the case of developed economies but is significantly different from one for developing economies (albeit only at the 10% level).

Being more upstream in GVCs is associated with a higher level of CO$_2$ emissions. Existing evidence suggests that positioning in GVCs can affect the extent of GVC emissions.[48] Specifically, positions further upstream in the value chain—having relatively strong forward linkages—are associated with higher emissions than positions further down the chain. Evidence for 62 economies supports this hypothesis, with a moderate negative association between positioning in GVCs (measured as the relative importance of backward linkages in GVCs—from the use perspective) and their CO$_2$ emissions (Figure 6.10). The structure and positioning of an economy's GVC activity are thus relevant dimensions for its contributions to CO$_2$ emissions through GVCs, with those positioned further upstream and with relatively high forward linkages having a higher level of GVC-related emissions.

Figure 6.9: Association between Global Value Chain Production and Carbon Dioxide Emissions Production, 2018

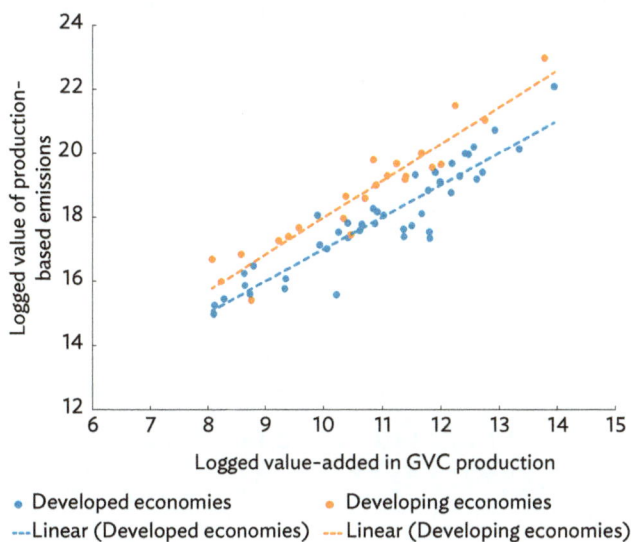

GVC = global value chain.

Note: Production-based emissions refer to those related to sectoral production activities and exclude direct emissions from households.

Sources: ADB calculations using data from Organisation for Economic Co-operation and Development (OECD). Inter-Country Input-Output Tables. https://www.oecd.org/sti/ind/inter-country-input-output-tables.htm; OECD. Carbon dioxide emissions embodied in international trade (TECO$_2$) data set. https://www.oecd.org/sti/ind/carbondioxideemissionsembodiedininternationaltrade.htm (both accessed November 2023).

Figure 6.10: Association between Global Value Chain Positioning and Carbon Dioxide Emissions in Global Value Chains, 2018

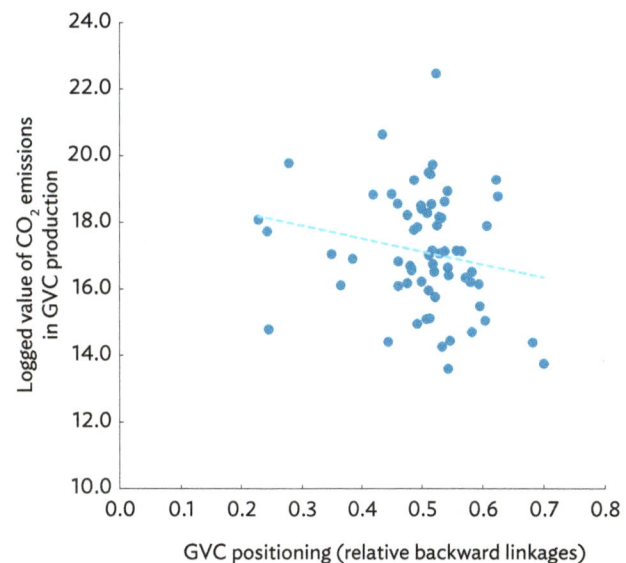

CO$_2$ = carbon dioxide, GVC = global value chain.

Notes: GVC positioning is calculated as the ratio of GVC activity from a use perspective to the sum of GVC activity from a production and use perspective. As such, the indicator captures the importance of backward relative to forward linkages in GVCs.

Sources: ADB calculations using data from Organisation for Economic Co-operation and Development (OECD). Inter-Country Input-Output Tables. https://www.oecd.org/sti/ind/inter-country-input-output-tables.htm; OECD. Carbon dioxide emissions embodied in international trade (TECO$_2$) data set. https://www.oecd.org/sti/ind/carbondioxideemissionsembodiedininternationaltrade.htm (both accessed November 2023).

CO$_2$ emissions intensity in value-added varies widely across economies, with emerging economies tending to have higher intensities. CO$_2$ intensities are particularly high in Asian economies such as Kazakhstan, the Lao PDR, Viet Nam, India, and the PRC (Figure 6.11). Based on OECD data, 6 of the top-10 economies by aggregate CO$_2$ intensity are in developing Asia. Many economies with high CO$_2$ emissions intensities—including the Russian Federation, South Africa, Saudi Arabia, and Brunei Darussalam—are heavily involved in resource extraction, highlighting again the importance of sectoral structure. Conversely, western European economies—Luxembourg, Switzerland, Sweden, France, Ireland, Austria, the UK—along with New Zealand and Costa Rica have relatively low CO$_2$ emissions intensities. In most economies, the CO$_2$ intensity associated with

---

[48]   See, for example, Huang and Zhang (2023).

GVC production in 2018 exceeds overall CO_2 intensity, the main exceptions being Saudi Arabia, Brunei Darussalam, and Kazakhstan—economies that export raw materials used in energy production elsewhere.[49]

CO_2 emissions intensities in production vary widely across sectors. The aggregate CO_2 emissions intensity of an economy depends on its sectoral structure and sectoral CO_2 emissions intensity (CO_2 emissions per unit of value-added). This represents an inverse measure of the CO_2 efficiency of production. There are wide differences in the average (across economies) CO_2 emissions intensity by sector. Electricity, water and air transport, basic metals, and nonmetallic minerals have the highest intensities with various services (such as real estate, health, publishing, and finance) showing relatively low intensities (Figure 6.12). In 2018, the CO_2 emissions intensity in electricity was 74 times that of the median sector—water transport was 44 times as large, basic metals 32 times, and air transport 26 times the median intensity.

Across many sectors, there have been substantial reductions in CO_2 emissions intensities. Between 1995 and 2018, CO_2 emissions intensities fell across nearly all sectors (except post and warehousing), with a 44% (unweighted) average decline over the period (Figure 6.12). The evidence strongly supports the view that technological change, better efficiency, and the reallocation of production through GVCs can substantially reduce the CO_2 intensity of production. Still, the drop in CO_2 intensity has not been enough to offset the increased emissions associated with the greater scale of production (see Figure 6.10). Reductions in CO_2 intensities have tended to be stronger in sectors that had initially relatively low CO_2 emissions intensities, suggesting greater challenges in bringing down emissions intensities in sectors with initially high intensities. For example, the average reduction in CO_2 emissions intensities from 1995 to 2018 for the 10 sectors with the highest initial emissions intensities was 38.6%, while the 10 with the lowest initial emissions intensities fell 50%.

Figure 6.11: Ratio of Carbon Dioxide Production to Total Value-Added, and Carbon Dioxide Production in Global Value Chains to Value-Added due to Global Value Chains, 2018

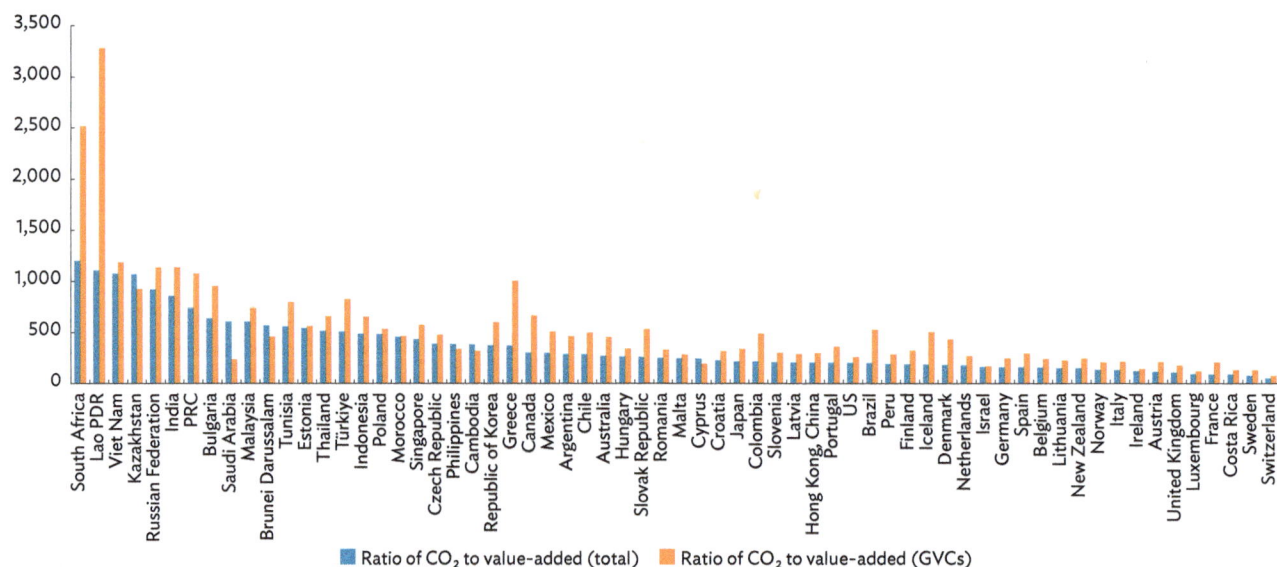

CO_2 = carbon dioxide, GVC = global value chain, Lao PDR = Lao People's Democratic Republic, PRC = People's Republic of China, US = United States.

Note: CO_2 emissions intensity is measured as the ratio of aggregated carbon dioxide emissions (in total or due to GVC production) to aggregated value-added (in total or due to GVC production), with value-added deflated using the gross domestic product deflator.

Sources: ADB calculations using data from Organisation for Economic Co-operation and Development (OECD). Inter-Country Input-Output Tables. https://www.oecd.org/sti/ind/inter-country-input-output-tables.htm; OECD. Carbon dioxide emissions embodied in international trade (TECO$_2$) data set. https://www.oecd.org/sti/ind/carbondioxideemissionsembodiedininternationaltrade.htm (both accessed November 2023).

[49] Data on sectoral CO_2 intensities by production type are not available, meaning that differences in CO_2 intensity between aggregate production and GVC production are due to differences in their sectoral structure. The OECD dataset excludes other economies heavily reliant on energy-related raw material exports such as Azerbaijan and Turkmenistan.

Figure 6.12: Log Ratio of Carbon Dioxide Emissions to Value-Added by Sector

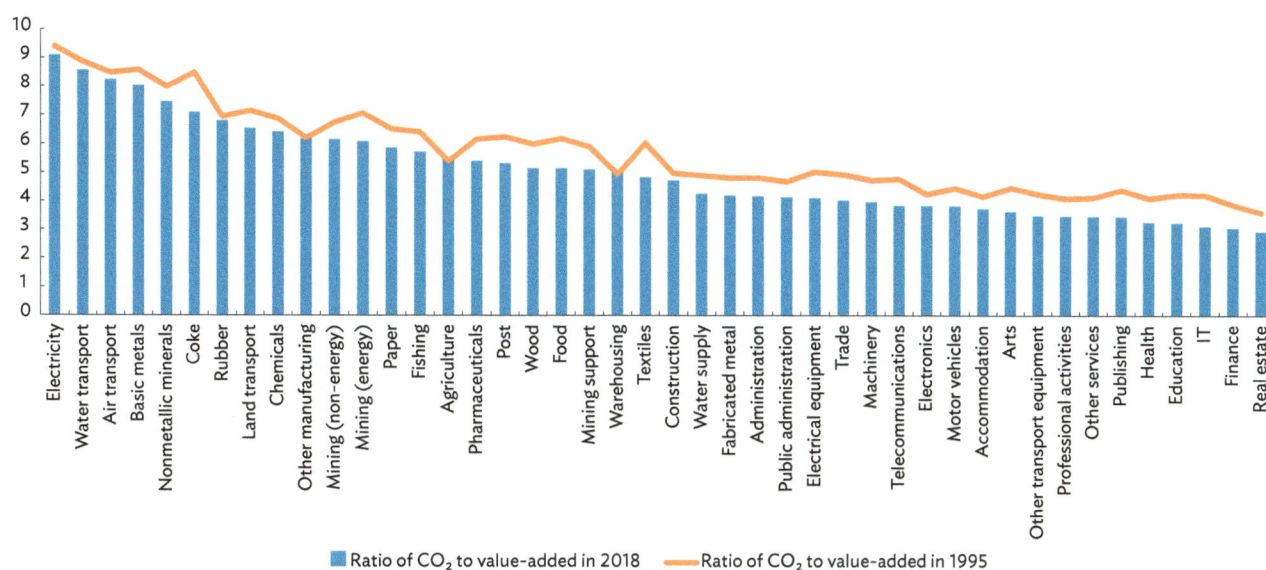

■ Ratio of CO$_2$ to value-added in 2018   —— Ratio of CO$_2$ to value-added in 1995

CO$_2$ = carbon dioxide, IT = information technology.

Note: CO$_2$ emissions intensity is measured as the ratio of sectoral CO$_2$ emissions (in production) to sectoral value-added (all aggregated across economies), with value-added deflated using the gross domestic product deflator. Data are reported in metric tons per $ million and in logs in the figure.

Sources: ADB calculations using data from Organisation for Economic Co-operation and Development (OECD). Inter-Country Input-Output Tables. https://www.oecd.org/sti/ind/inter-country-input-output-tables.htm; OECD. Carbon dioxide emissions embodied in international trade (TECO$_2$) data set. https://www.oecd.org/sti/ind/carbondioxideemissionsembodiedininternationaltrade.htm (both accessed November 2023).

Higher shares of GVC production in value-added are associated with a higher CO$_2$ emissions intensity in developing Asia and the rest of the world. A 10% increase in the share of value-added due to GVCs in an economy is associated with an increase in CO$_2$ emissions intensity of 5.7% (Figure 6.13).[50] The strength of this association differs by region, however, and is only statistically significant in developing Asia and the rest of the world. For developing Asia, a 10% increase in value-added due to GVCs is associated with a 7.0% increase in CO$_2$ emissions intensity, with a similar increase associated with a 5.7% increase in CO$_2$ emissions intensity in the rest of the world. The international division of labor is thus an important source of differences in emissions intensities across economies,

with those regions specialized in certain manufacturing sectors and in upstream GVC production having a strong positive association between GVC production shares and emissions intensities.

Structural change has played a limited role in reducing CO$_2$ emissions intensities within GVCs in developing Asia. CO$_2$ emissions intensities associated with GVC activity have dropped significantly across Asia, falling by 18% in developed Asia and by 89% in developing Asia from 1995 to 2018. These reductions have been driven entirely by reductions in CO$_2$ emissions intensities within sectors.[51] There was no shift in production activities within GVCs toward less emissions-intensive sectors in developing Asia (Figure 6.14).[52] Despite this, structural

---

[50] Replacing the GVC share in value-added with the traditional trade share gives similar results, suggesting there are few differences between different ways of providing foreign markets when considering the relationship between trade and CO$_2$ emissions intensities. Conversely, the coefficient when using the domestic production share is negative, significant, and large in absolute value, suggesting strong differences in the relationship between CO$_2$ emissions intensity and production for domestic versus foreign consumers.

[51] While the observed changes in CO$_2$ intensities were due to effects within sectors, they could still be related to external factors that lower sectoral emissions intensities. In GVCs, for example, these may include the diffusion of green technologies to the sector. They may also refer to the outsourcing of more emissions-intensive activities within the sector to other economies, though the declining intensities across all sectors and most economies suggest that in aggregate this is unlikely.

[52] The Lao PDR is excluded from the figure due to the lack of sectoral data until 2000.

Figure 6.13: Association Between the Share of Value-Added Due to Global Value Chain Production and Carbon Dioxide Emissions Intensities, 1995–2018

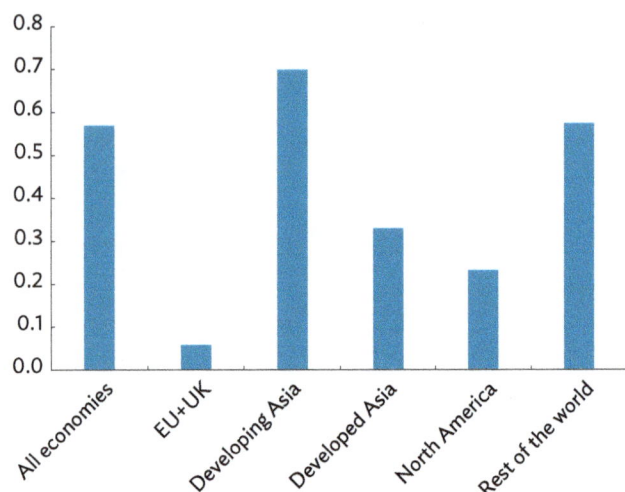

EU = European Union (27 members), UK = United Kingdom.

Notes: The figure reports the estimated coefficients on the log of the share of value-added due to global value chain (GVC) production from a regression with the log of the ratio of carbon dioxide (CO_2) emissions to value-added as dependent variable and the log of gross domestic product (GDP) per capita (and its square), the log of the share of manufacturing in value-added, the log of the urban population share, and economy, and time fixed effects. The regression model is estimated at the level of the economy, with annual data over the period 1995-2018. Since both dependent and the main explanatory variables are expressed in logs, the coefficients can be interpreted as elasticities, providing an estimate of the percentage change in the ratio of CO_2 emissions to value-added in response to a 1% change in the share of value-added due to GVC production.

Sources: ADB calculations using data from Organisation for Economic Co-operation and Development (OECD). Inter-Country Input-Output Tables. https://www.oecd.org/sti/ind/inter-country-input-output-tables.htm; OECD. Carbon dioxide emissions embodied in international trade (TECO₂) data set. https://www.oecd.org/sti/ind/carbondioxideemissionsembodiedininternationaltrade.htm; and World Bank. World Development Indicators. https://databank.worldbank.org/source/world-development-indicators (all accessed November 2023).

change has contributed to reductions in emissions intensities within GVCs for individual economies.[53] Structural change accounted for between 12% and 20% of reduced emissions intensities in India, the Republic of Korea, and Singapore, for example, and for 35% in the Philippines. In Cambodia and Hong Kong, China, structural change also helped offset some of the rise in within sector CO_2 emissions intensities.

Global Value Chains and Policies to Decarbonize Production

The Challenge of Global Cooperation for Climate Change Mitigation

Enhanced international cooperation is essential for climate change mitigation and adaptation. Despite efforts at national and subnational levels to implement carbon pricing policies, confronting the climate change crisis is a global public good. The increased interdependence of economies ultimately requires increased global coordination in dealing with the threats of climate change. GVCs, for example, deepen the interdependent links between economies and increase the potential for policies in one economy to have spillover effects on others, affecting emissions production and economic activity in other economies. As the World Trade Report 2022 (WTO 2022b) highlights, enhanced global cooperation can help deal with climate change in a variety of ways. International cooperation can create a more coherent and predictable policy environment, helping signal a commitment to decarbonization. It can increase transparency that in turn facilitates better review and monitoring of decarbonization efforts. And it can mobilize financial and technical resources to overcome capacity constraints and encourage the diffusion of green technologies across borders. Cooperation between developed and developing economies—by way of technical assistance, capacity building and knowledge exchange—can also help the spread of low-carbon technologies to developing and emerging economies.

Despite the Kyoto Protocol and Paris Agreement, for example, global coordination on climate mitigation remains weak. Recent literature examines what a global carbon pricing scheme could look like (ADB 2023a; Böhringer, Schneider, and Asane-Otoo 2021; Nordhaus 2015a; Stiglitz 2019). Proposals involve extending carbon taxes and emissions trading system (ETS) globally. A global

---

[53]   The calculations are based on a shift-share decomposition, which involves splitting the change in CO_2 emissions intensities in GVCs into two components: (i) a within-sector change in emissions intensity holding the structure of production in GVCs constant; and (ii) a between-sector or structural change effect that accounts for changes in the structure of production in GVCs while holding the sectoral CO_2 emissions intensity constant.

Figure 6.14: Rate of Change of Carbon Dioxide Emissions Intensities within Global Value Chains and the Contributions of Structural Change and Intra-Sectoral Emissions Intensities (%)

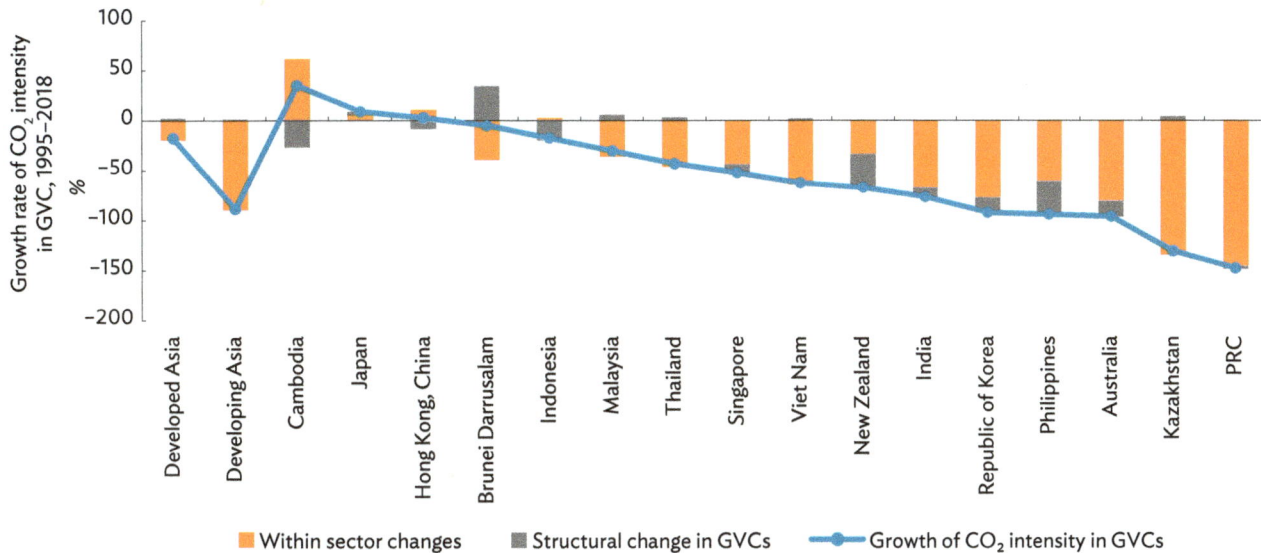

CO$_2$ = carbon dioxide, GVC = global value chain, PRC = People's Republic of China.

Note: CO$_2$ emissions intensity in GVCs is measured as the ratio of (production-based) CO$_2$ emissions due to GVC production to value-added associated with GVC production. Value-added data are deflated using the gross domestic product deflator. The contributions of structural change and intra-sectoral changes in emissions intensities are calculated using shift-share analysis.

Sources: ADB calculations using data from Organisation for Economic Co-operation and Development (OECD). Inter-Country Input-Output Tables. https://www.oecd.org/sti/ind/inter-country-input-output-tables.htm; OECD. Carbon dioxide emissions embodied in international trade (TECO$_2$) data set. https://www.oecd.org/sti/ind/carbondioxideemissionsembodiedininternationaltrade.htm (both accessed November 2023).

ETS would give economies GHG emission reduction targets and enable economies to then buy and sell surplus and deficit emission rights on the world market. A global carbon tax would involve economies applying a tax on emissions, leading to a similar reduction in emissions (Cramton et al. 2017; Nordhaus 2015b). Despite these proposals, efforts to bolster global cooperation have remained generally weak and limited. Of those that have taken place, the pledge and review mechanism of the Paris Agreement has been criticized for having limited impact on emission reduction targets (Barrett and Dannenberg 2016). Those that involve developed economies offering financial assistance to help developing economies decarbonize generally lack credibility, given the failure to meet past financial commitments (Subramanian 2022). Article 6 of the Paris Agreement provides the basis for trading GHG emission reductions, but COP28 failed to reach agreement on how to operationalize trading mechanisms.

The major challenges to coordinating carbon pricing globally stem from free-riding and fairness issues. The possibility of free riding makes carbon pricing coordination challenging, with economies and regions having an incentive not to join. This is because the benefits in setting a carbon price are shared by all economies, while the costs in terms of higher costs and lower production are incurred only by those imposing a carbon price. The issue of fairness arises as some economies—currently developed economies—have historically contributed more to global emissions than developing and industrializing economies. These differences are accounted for through the principle of common but differentiated responsibilities (CBDR), formalized during the 1992 Rio Earth Summit, which said that all jurisdictions have a responsibility to help mitigate climate change, but that they are not equally responsible.[54] A common global carbon price, therefore, may contravene the CBDR principle, while carbon

---

[54] Principle 7 of the Rio Declaration at the first Rio Earth Summit in 1992 states, "In view of the different contributions to global environmental degradation, States have common but differentiated responsibilities. The developed economies acknowledge the responsibility that they bear in the international pursuit of sustainable development in view of the pressures their societies place on the global environment and of the technologies and financial resources they command."

pricing more generally may impact certain economies disproportionately—particularly developing economies and energy producers. One solution proposed is to have different minimum international carbon prices based on an economy's development level (Parry, Black, and Roaf 2021).

Regional cooperation and related initiatives are increasingly considered alternatives to multilateral progress on decarbonization. There were past successful multilateral efforts—such as the Montreal Protocol on Substances that Deplete the Ozone Layer—that largely succeeded in phasing out

Box 6.5: Climate Clubs as Global Cooperation

In a fragmenting world with narrowing opportunities for global cooperation, climate clubs may provide a way for like-minded nations to cooperate. Reducing carbon dioxide (CO_2) and other greenhouse gas (GHG) emissions, and their associated impact on climate change, are examples of a global public good. Nordhaus (2015a, 2020) notes that international coordination and agreement on global public goods is difficult because individual economies have an incentive to defect, engaging in beggar-thy-neighbor policies. Economies thus have an incentive to free ride on others that are reducing emissions. By failing to properly acknowledge that by its very nature, climate change is a global public good with a potential for free-riding, Nordhaus argues that existing frameworks (like the Paris Accord and the earlier Kyoto Protocol) are voluntary agreements that encourage free-riding. A proposed solution is a climate club, which is based upon two main foundations: (i) members voluntarily agree to share the burden of emissions reductions; and (ii) nonmembership of the club carries certain penalties. The Carbon Border Adjustment Mechanism being implemented by the European Union is considered to hold many characteristics of a climate club.

Simple carbon club targets are needed to minimize the risk of conflict and to allow flexibility in meeting the targets. Members can agree on burden-sharing principles by undertaking harmonized emissions reductions with the aim of meeting a particular objective (e.g., keeping temperature rises below 2°C) and joining efforts to agree on a target international carbon price (and how it should rise over time) (Nordhaus 2020). This may be preferred to negotiating individual member emissions allocations—with a carbon price being simpler to work out (essentially reducing negotiations to a single price)—given the limited likelihood of success in negotiating economy level allocations. A further advantage of a carbon price target is that it leaves economies with a degree of flexibility on how they achieve the target price (e.g., either through carbon taxes or through cap-and-trade schemes).

A tariff on imports can be the most effective way of enforcing the behavior of trade partners. For the club and its related agreements to be sustainable, there needs to be some kind of sanction against nonmembers (Nordhaus 2020). This can induce economies to join the club and/or abide by club agreements. The obvious penalty would be a tariff on imports from nonparticipants, which should encourage them to enter the club and/or undertake the necessary emissions reductions (e.g., by implementing their own carbon policies). According to Nordhaus (2020), choosing a tariff is better than the alternatives, such as countervailing import duties on carbon content. There are at least two reasons for this. First, a great deal of carbon is emitted in producing non-traded goods—like electricity—which can reduce the effectiveness of the club in "correcting" behavior. Second, it is very difficult to accurately calculate the (indirect) carbon content of imports. Instead, therefore, Nordhaus argues for a uniform tariff on all imports from nonmembers.

The concept of climate clubs may also move beyond burden sharing and penalties to allow for cooperation on other ways to mitigate climate change. For example, given the potential of technology in mitigating climate change, Jakob et al. (2022) argue that climate clubs could go beyond imposing border adjustment mechanisms on nonmembers and consider broader forms of cooperation. Specifically, they argue that a club or clubs could implement common green industrial policies, including low-carbon requirements for climate-intensive globally traded basic materials—such as iron, steel, aluminum, cement, and fertilizers. The clubs could further provide support for research, development, and the diffusion of technologies and infrastructure. These mechanisms can be an incentive for joining the club, since members would gain access to markets for environmental goods.

Sources: ADB using Nordhaus (2015a, 2020) and Jakob et al. (2022).

ozone-depleting substances. Some argue that their governance and design was important for success, and that climate change efforts can learn a great deal from their experience (Sabel and Victor 2022). But in today's world, increasing geopolitical rivalry and limited progress in international fora such as the World Trade Organization increase the challenges for global cooperation on climate, with the result that global ambitions are set to accommodate the least ambitious partner (Sabel and Victor 2022). With the possibility of broad multilateral cooperation on climate change mitigation thus limited, regional cooperation is increasingly seen as a way forward. One approach uses the power of regional blocs to place conditions on trading partners, with the EU's CBAM a prime example. Another is using environmental provisions in preferential trade agreements (PTAs) to agree on a common set of standards for trade between partners. Irrespective of whether action is domestic, regional, or global, there is need for reliable and trustworthy data on CO_2 emissions and well-functioning institutions for decarbonization efforts to be effective and credible (Rosenbloom et al. 2020).

Carbon Pricing, Border Carbon Adjustment Mechanisms, and Decarbonizing Global Value Chains

There is widespread acknowledgment that carbon pricing holds the key to mitigating climate change. CO_2 emissions during production—and GHGs more generally—represent a classic negative externality, with the broader costs to society of CO_2 emissions not being internalized by those producing them. Many consider carbon pricing the most efficient way of correcting this market failure, forcing firms to pay the full (social) costs of their emissions, encouraging a reduction in emissions and a shift to cleaner forms of production. A carbon price is a market-based instrument that sets a price per metric ton (MT) of CO_2 emissions to reflect the additional costs to society. Carbon pricing generally takes two forms, a carbon tax or an ETS (or "cap and trade" system). By forcing firms to pay for their CO_2 production,

producers are encouraged to reduce their carbon intensity—by innovating or switching to alternative means of production, for example. The potentially universal nature of carbon pricing that encompasses all production and transportation can be an important force in decarbonizing GVCs and production more broadly.

While many worry over economies' slow and narrow response to the climate crisis, a wide range of carbon pricing policies are in place across a range of jurisdictions. There have been several efforts across different jurisdictions to create a carbon price through carbon taxes or ETS. According to the World Bank (2022), the number of jurisdictions with carbon pricing schemes has increased in recent years, with around 70 carbon pricing initiatives implemented in 39 jurisdictions, although only 23% of carbon emissions are covered.[55] However, only 4% of emissions are covered by carbon pricing in the range needed to prevent average global temperatures from increasing by 2°C—with this price estimated at between $50 and $100 per ton of CO_2 (Carbon Pricing Leadership Coalition 2019). As currently implemented, carbon pricing efforts also have the considerable drawback that they tend to cover relatively narrow jurisdictions (e.g., cities, states, individual economies), with the EU's ETS the major exception covering multiple economies.

The fragmented nature of carbon pricing globally leads to the risk of carbon leakage. According to the IPCC (2022a), carbon leakage can occur through three main channels (see also Dröge 2009): (i) competitiveness, (ii) the energy market, and (iii) income. Competitiveness is affected when carbon pricing in one jurisdiction pushes up production costs for firms in the jurisdiction, leading them to lose market share. The extent of the carbon leakage will depend on the extent of differences in emissions intensity between firms in the jurisdiction and trade partners, and the trade exposure of goods and services (Böhringer et al. 2022). The energy market can further play a role in carbon leakage if carbon pricing in one jurisdiction leads to lower energy demand from firms covered, which in turn lowers global demand for energy, lowering energy prices

---

and increasing energy consumption in jurisdictions not subject to carbon pricing (IPCC 2022a). Finally, the income effect occurs when carbon policies lead to changes in the terms-of-trade, which then affects the global distribution of income, consumption, and emissions (Cosbey et al. 2019). While the number of ETS and carbon tax policies has increased, this does not significantly mitigate the risk of carbon leakage. In addition to the incomplete coverage of carbon pricing policies globally, the carbon prices associated with existing schemes vary widely, creating greater opportunities for carbon leakage (Figure 6.15).

Border Carbon Adjustment Mechanisms

The lack of a globally coordinated response to climate change, combined with different rates of progress on climate action, can help encourage regions to implement border carbon adjustments. Without a globally coordinated response to climate change, economies and regions with ambitious climate targets have incentives to adopt border carbon adjustment (BCA) policies to reduce the risk of carbon leakage.

BCAs can level the playing field, ensuring that foreign producers face the same effective carbon price in export markets as domestic producers. They do this by applying fees on imported goods based on their emissions content, and possibly by exempting local firms exporting to economies with weaker domestic climate policies. BCAs align the price an importer pays with the domestic carbon price, thus removing a major incentive for production to shift to regions with a lower price and potentially reducing carbon leakage (Bellora and Fontagné 2023; Böhringer, Balistreri, and Rutherford; Branger and Quirion 2014).

While evidence of carbon leakage is limited, including that due to the EU's ETS, it could increase significantly as carbon prices begin to rise. Even though the primary aim of the EU's CBAM is to reduce the risk of carbon leakage, existing evidence suggests that carbon leakage due to the EU's ETS and other schemes has been limited (European Parliament 2020; Verde 2020; Cherniwchan and Taylor 2022). According to the World Trade Report 2022 (WTO 2022b), the lack of evidence is likely because emissions abatement costs are only a small part of a firm's total operating costs—with other costs related to capital, labor, and market proximity more important

Figure 6.15: Developments in Carbon Price under Various Carbon Pricing Initiatives ($ per metric ton)

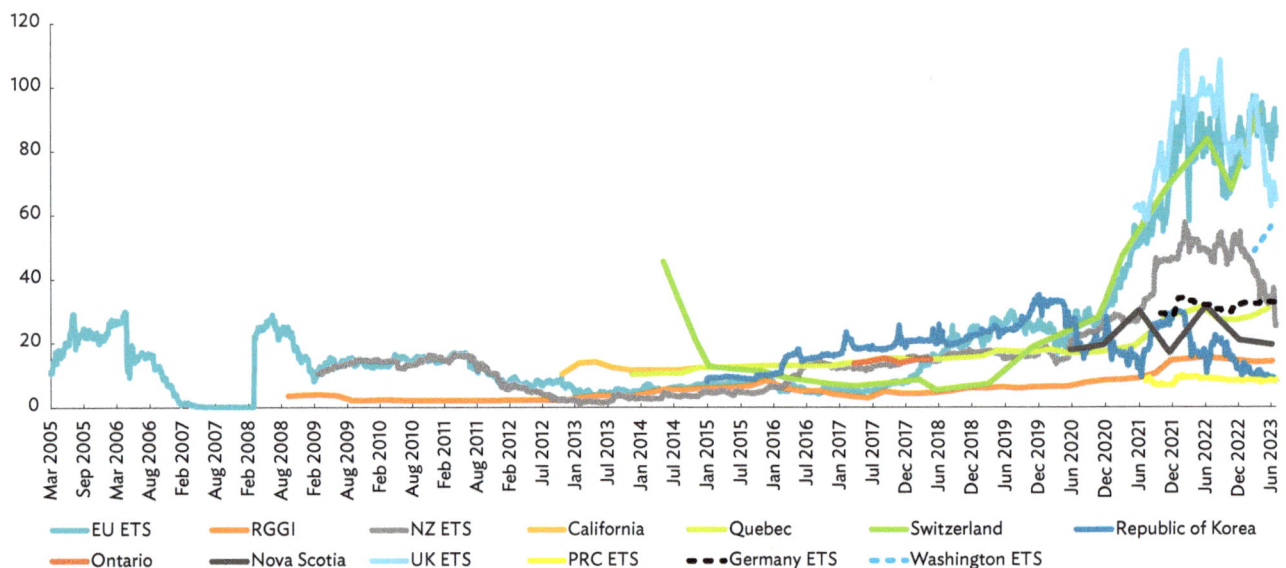

ETS = emissions trading system, EU = European Union (27 members), NZ = New Zealand, PRC = People's Republic of China, RGGI = Regional Greenhouse Gas Initiative, UK = United Kingdom.

Source: International Carbon Action Partnership Database. https://icapcarbonaction.com/en (accessed November 2023).

determinants of where a firm locates. At the same time, there is some evidence that broader carbon policies can lead to carbon leakage (European Parliament 2020), that the current lack of evidence on carbon leakage possibly due to the shielding of certain sectors is incompatible with longer-term decarbonization goals (Grubb et al. 2022), and that carbon leakage rates can be significant particularly for small open economies (Misch and Wingender 2021). Moreover, increased climate change policy ambitions will inevitably lead to rising carbon prices, which may encourage significant future carbon leakage.

While reducing carbon leakage is a major reason for implementing BCA policies, they also serve other political economy motives. BCAs can serve the dual purpose of lowering domestic opposition to carbon pricing and encouraging other economies and regions to adopt more ambitious measures. By ensuring that foreign firms pay the same price for carbon as domestic firms, BCAs can help reduce opposition by domestic firms to domestic carbon pricing and ease concerns over the potential loss of competitiveness and market share that stringent climate change policies may create. To avoid paying tariffs under BCAs, other economies are thus encouraged to increase their own ambitions in developing carbon pricing mechanisms. According to the European Parliament (2022), CBAM is intended to "incentivize non-EU economies to increase their climate ambition and ensure that the EU and global climate efforts are not undermined by production being relocated from the EU to economies with less ambitious policies."

Fairness and equity are at the heart of discussions on the impact of BCA policies. By imposing new tariffs, BCAs may reduce global demand for imported goods, driving down prices and worsening the terms of trade for those exporters covered (Bellora and Fontagné 2023; Böhringer, Fischer, and Rosendahl 2010; UNCTAD 2021). These effects will be most strongly felt by exporters in GVC supplier economies—particularly those supplying energy-intensive products—that tend to be concentrated in Asia and in developing economies (Böhringer et al. 2022). Evidence suggests that the main impact of the EU's CBAM will be on middle- and low-income economies (Beaufils et al. 2023). BCAs can also push against the CBDR principle. Adjustment mechanisms will more likely be imposed by developed economies, partially with the incentive of increasing developing economies' ambition to limit emissions, and with the requirement that firms from all regions pay the same carbon price when selling in markets covered by the mechanism (WTO 2022b). Despite these concerns, given the strong interrelationship between climate change and GVCs, and the potential for climate change to impact how GVCs function, there is an incentive for developing economies to cooperate on climate change mitigation to protect the GVC development model.

Tensions between BCA policies and World Trade Organization rules can potentially lead to trade conflict. Concerns have been raised that BCAs could amount to a form of disguised protectionism, focused more on protecting and enhancing the competitiveness of domestic firms than achieving emissions reductions. Bacchus (2021) identifies several areas for potential conflict in the context of the EU's CBAM, including the possibility that it may violate the most-favored-nation principle of the World Trade Organization (WTO), which can happen if imported products originating in different WTO members were discriminated against based on their carbon content. CBAM may also involve a charge on imports into the EU more than the "ceilings on customs duties and other charges connected with importation that have been agreed by the EU in its WTO schedule of commitments," leading to a further source of tension. Bacchus further identifies possible inconsistency with the EU's national treatment principle, with free emissions allowances to local producers continuing for some time after CBAM implementation. For some economies, it may be best to impose countermeasures to BCAs to limit their negative economic effects (Böhringer, Carbone, and Rutherford 2016). Beyond the WTO, BCAs potentially conflict with Article 3.5 of the United Nations Framework Convention on Climate Change (UNFCCC), which states that climate change mitigation measures should not serve as a "disguised restriction on international trade" or involve "arbitrary and unjustifiable discrimination."

For various legal and other reasons, BCA mechanisms will need to include default emission values that may create unwanted incentives. For CBAM, the EU has published default emissions intensities for CBAM products during the transition period (see European Commission 2023b). These rates are partly based on cross-economy evidence on CO_2 emissions intensities (e.g., Vidovic et al. 2023). A system that focuses on default intensities has drawbacks. It can lead to relatively clean producers being overcharged relative to high-carbon rivals and provides no incentive to reduce carbon intensity below the default rate (Mehling and Ritz 2023). An EU proposal to set default rates at the level of the 10% worst emitting producers is intended to remove this concern. If this were the sole metric used, however, the incentives for firms to improve their emissions efficiency would be severely diminished. Moreover, with domestic firms having to report their actual emissions and imported goods subject to default rates, there would also be the risk of BCAs being discriminatory, contrary to international trade law. On efficiency grounds and to be compatible with trade law, BCAs will therefore need to allow producers a reasonable means of demonstrating that their product's embedded emissions are below the default value. It is the responsibility of implementing jurisdictions to specify acceptable approaches for embedded emissions verification, with the current CBAM approach leaving much uncertainty.

Even with clarity on an acceptable means for emissions verification, BCA mechanisms can be seen as *de facto* discriminatory. Measurement issues within BCAs will likely be substantially more burdensome for some rather than others, with developing economies and small and medium-sized enterprises (SMEs) potentially hardest hit. In the case of CBAM, the EU's own impact assessment acknowledged the burden on SMEs would likely be substantially more than for larger firms, although no estimates of the burden or number of SMEs affected were provided (European Commission 2021b). SMEs usually do not have the resources to professionally certify CO_2 emissions in their production and supply chains, forcing them to accept what is a potentially punitive default rate (Cornago and Lowe 2021). It will be difficult for many developing economies and firms to create appropriate institutions and structures to accurately measure emissions intensities.

BCA mechanisms can provide substantial revenue, which can be used to compensate losers and help the energy transition. CBAM, for example, has been estimated to raise around €14 billion in revenue by 2030 (European Commission 2021b), with most expected to be revenue in the EU's budget (European Commission 2023). CBAM could also rebate all or part of the domestic carbon price paid by exporters to compensate them for the higher carbon price paid domestically, compared with firms in the recipient economy. Because of the border adjustment, final consumers in a jurisdiction would in principle face the same carbon tax rate on domestic and imported goods (Elliott et al. 2013). Some have proposed allocating revenues from CBAM to a carbon fund to mitigate or adapt to climate change in developing economies—to avoid claims of unfairness and to meet CBDR responsibilities (Falcao 2020).

The European Union's Carbon Border Adjustment Mechanism and Its Impact on Developing Asia

The EU's CBAM is the first BCA mechanism and remains in a transitional phase. The EU's CBAM entered into force on 1 October 2023. During the initial transition phase, importers of goods covered by CBAM need only report emissions embedded in their imports (both direct and indirect emissions), without incurring any financial cost or adjustment. Given the challenges in calculating indirect emissions, they will only be included after the transitional phase and only for some sectors (fertilizers and cement), with the methodology to construct these to be developed during the current phase. The transitional phase is thus intended to serve as a pilot and learning opportunity for different stakeholders (importers, producers, and authorities) as well as an opportunity to develop and refine methodologies for collecting information on emissions embedded in products. During the transition phase, a further review of the product scope will assess whether other products covered by the ETS should fall under CBAM. Following the transition phase, EU importers of goods covered will need to obtain CBAM certificates, which will be priced based on ETS allowances. They will then declare the emissions embedded in their imports and surrender the corresponding number of certificates. An important feature is that if an importer can prove a carbon price has already been paid on their imports during production, then the corresponding amount can be deducted.

Concerns over losing competitiveness and market share are important motivations for CBAM. The main argument put forward by the European Commission in favor of CBAM (European Commission 2021b) is that it can address some of the shortcomings of the ETS, particularly the risk of carbon leakage to economies outside the EU where no carbon price exists.[56] Despite these arguments, concerns about losing competitiveness and market share as firms following the EU's strong environmental protection regime are undercut by rivals in regions with less stringent climate policies are also serious, especially given the unease around rising energy costs for industrial competitiveness. While energy prices have been stable for many years, supply has tightened since 2021, leading to large increases in energy prices—in the aftermath of the coronavirus disease (COVID-19) pandemic, the Russian invasion of Ukraine, and ambitious environmental targets.[57] There is now greater concern that sectors heavily reliant on energy, such as iron and steel, could relocate out of the EU, potentially drawing downstream sectors with them.

Estimating the Impact of the Carbon Border Adjustment Mechanism on Emissions, Exports, and Output in Developing Asia

CBAM's impact depends a great deal on the CO_2 intensity of production in products covered. CO_2 intensity is driven by various factors, including the energy mix in production and the production technology in different economies and regions. The wide variations in CO_2 intensities across economies and regions at the aggregate level (see Figure 6.11) can also be seen when looking at specific sectors (Figure 6.16).[58] Considering the sectors covered by CBAM, regions in developing Asia and Eastern Europe often have some of the highest emissions intensities, given different production techniques and heavy reliance on coal as a source of energy across much of developing Asia.[59] Relative to the EU, CO_2 intensity in ferrous metals is found to be high in India, the PRC, and Central and West Asia, for example. These economies and subregions also have relatively high emissions intensities in nonferrous metals, with South and Southeast Asia also high in emissions intensity in this sector. Regions in developing Asia also rank high in terms of emissions intensities in mineral products and chemicals, indicating that in the sectors that are the main CBAM targets, production in developing Asia is relatively dirty, potentially raising the costs of CBAM for these subregions relative to other regions.

High CO_2 intensities imply that implicit taxes on production associated with the implementation of an ETS would be relatively high for developing Asia. Under the assumption of a carbon price of €100 per MT of CO_2, current CO_2 intensities in developing Asia would be the equivalent of a value-added tax of between 3% and 12% when considering the aggregate economy, with the rates being relatively high for India, the PRC, and Central and West Asia (Table 6.1). For individual sectors, these rates can be substantially higher. For ferrous metals, for example, the VAT equivalent rate for India would be 787% and the PRC 86%. For mineral products, VAT equivalent rates would be above 100% for Central and West Asia, South Asia, Southeast Asia, and India.

---

[56] Another perceived ETS shortcoming is that the risk of carbon leakage is managed by granting free allowances and compensation for price increases in electricity under state aid rules. Yet, as the European Commission points out (European Commission 2021b), this free allocation "weakens the price signal that the system provides for the installations receiving it compared to full auctioning," thus affecting "the incentives for investment into further abatement of GHG emissions."

[57] See, for example, European Council (2023).

[58] In the CBAM analysis, some of the larger economies (the PRC, India, Japan, and the Republic of Korea)—and thus the largest emitters—are included individually rather than as a part of any subregion. This is to avoid these economies dominating the results for subregions and because they are expected to be most impacted by CBAM. Results for subregions are thus exclusive of these large economies.

[59] The assumption throughout the modeling of CBAM is that other ETS sectors will be added to the current CBAM product list by the end of the transition phase. These include energy-intensive industries such as glass, ceramics, pulp, paper, and acids and bulk organic chemicals. Hence, these products are also considered part of CBAM in the modeling.

Figure 6.16: Carbon Intensity of Production in Selected Sectors by Economy and Region, 2017 (metric tons of carbon dioxide per $ million of value-added)

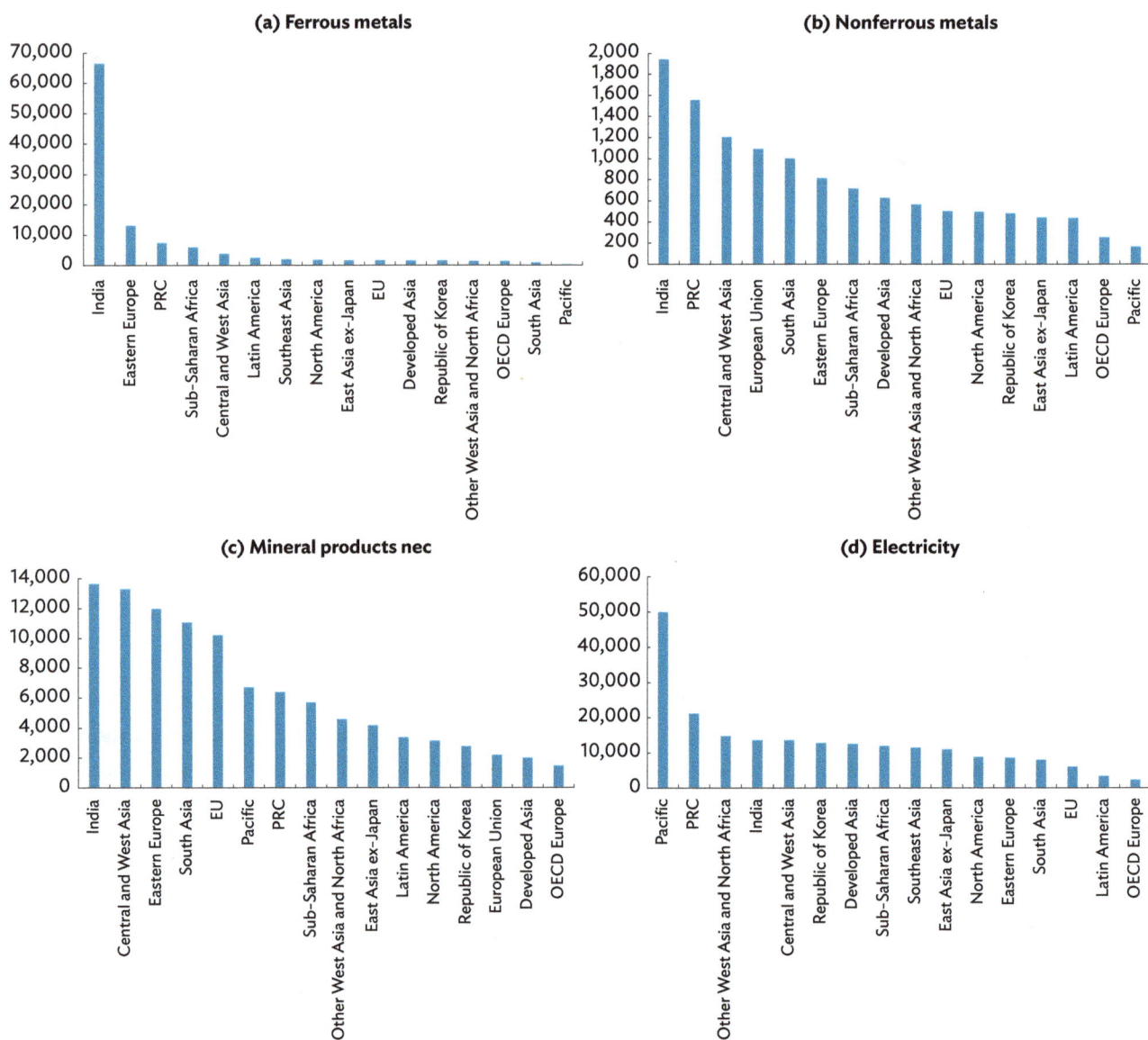

(a) Ferrous metals

(b) Nonferrous metals

(c) Mineral products nec

(d) Electricity

EU = European Union (27 members), nec = not elsewhere classified, OECD = Organisation for Economic Co-operation and Development, PRC = People's Republic of China.

Source: ADB calculations using data from Global Trade Analysis Project. GTAP 11 Data Base. https://www.gtap.agecon.purdue.edu/databases/; and International Energy Agency. Data and Statistics. https://www.iea.org/data-and-statistics (both accessed November 2023).

For electricity, which is not strongly traded, the rates are all above 100% except for South Asia. These numbers highlight the potential impact of a carbon price on the competitiveness of developing Asia given its current production technology.

CBAM's impact will also depend on the extent to which developing Asia exports the products covered to the EU. Data from UN Comtrade indicate that exports in CBAM products in 2019 were a small fraction of the region's total exports (Figure 6.17). By value, these account for less than 0.5% of exports in most regions of the world. The major exceptions are in Europe, including

Table 6.1: Value-Added Tax Equivalent of a Carbon Price of €100 per metric ton of CO_2 (%)

	Developed Asia	Central and West Asia	East Asia ex-Japan	South Asia	Southeast Asia	Pacific	PRC	India	Republic of Korea
Agriculture, forestry, and fishing	3.16	0.71	1.64	1.00	1.06	2.78	1.40	0.96	1.69
Mining	3.62	6.33	3.91	1.22	3.65	5.12	21.81	9.89	50.34
Food	1.30	1.86	1.60	0.37	1.95	1.02	3.10	1.56	1.65
Textiles	1.42	0.48	1.97	0.20	3.11	4.89	1.52	1.34	1.51
Wood	2.76	5.21	4.08	2.92	5.67	2.03	3.78	5.21	1.03
Chemicals, rubber, plastics	9.16	47.81	17.60	13.67	13.15	10.53	22.03	20.21	4.46
Pharmaceuticals	0.19	4.55	1.50	18.84	1.33	3.86	17.58	0.74	0.46
Ferrous metals	16.29	43.76	18.50	8.82	22.40	2.67	86.16	786.9	16.27
Nonferrous metals	7.39	14.24	5.18	11.84	12.91	1.89	18.41	23.00	5.62
Metal products	0.54	9.11	2.09	7.78	3.82	4.07	1.96	5.17	0.18
Mineral products nec	23.10	157.2	49.08	130.9	120.9	79.64	75.45	161.3	32.27
Computer, electronic, and optic	0.35	10.35	0.29	2.51	0.60	3.14	0.29	0.38	0.24
Machinery and equipment nec	0.22	9.19	0.29	5.79	0.96	3.10	1.32	1.93	0.22
Motor vehicles and parts	0.51	1.95	0.30	0.87	0.56	4.18	0.81	0.26	0.49
Other transport equipment	0.35	2.67	0.45	3.47	0.81	2.73	1.70	0.25	1.83
Manufactures nec	0.15	5.13	2.22	5.19	3.16	12.44	0.98	11.22	0.22
Construction	0.24	1.53	0.42	0.21	0.81	3.76	0.75	0.33	0.33
Petrochemicals, coal products	117.78	19.90	109.6	4.87	47.46	4.76	64.16	29.37	107.6
Electricity	146.01	159.13	128.5	92.75	134.04	592.0	249.0	159.7	150.1
Gas manufacture, distribution	23.27	18.72	85.85	0.03	62.92	158.2	497.6	5.60	609.7
Transport nec	10.99	16.62	20.55	9.37	27.03	48.02	16.02	21.45	22.14
Commercial services	0.17	2.14	0.15	0.14	0.32	0.11	0.46	1.00	0.29
Public services	0.19	1.68	0.35	0.31	0.24	0.07	0.68	0.43	0.24
Economy-wide	3.02	10.21	5.12	3.54	6.80	5.37	11.37	10.50	4.88

nec = not elsewhere classified, PRC = People's Republic of China.

Source: ADB calculations using data from Global Trade Analysis Project. GTAP 11 Data Base. https://www.gtap.agecon.purdue.edu/databases/; and International Energy Agency. Data and Statistics. https://www.iea.org/data-and-statistics (both accessed November 2023).

intra-EU trade, where the share in total exports of such products going to the EU is above 1.5%. Within Asia, India, Central and West Asia, and the Republic of Korea have relatively high shares when compared with other Asian regions. While the export shares are small, the exports may still represent a significant share of all exports in sectors for some economies. Moreover, there is an expectation that CBAM's scope will be expanded during the transition phase to cover other ETS sectors and potentially other products.

The EU is generally not the primary market for CBAM products originating from developing Asia, though the tariff equivalents can be large in some cases. In only a couple of cases (India and the Republic of Korea) does the EU account for more than 10% of core CBAM exports from developing Asia, suggesting that CBAM's impact on production in developing Asia may be limited (Table 6.2). Under these trade patterns, and assuming existing carbon intensities and a carbon price of €100 per MT of CO_2, the trade-weighted import tax rate equivalents of border carbon adjustments vary

Figure 6.17: Share of Total Exports of a Region Covered by the European Union's Carbon Border Adjustment Mechanism, 2017 (%)

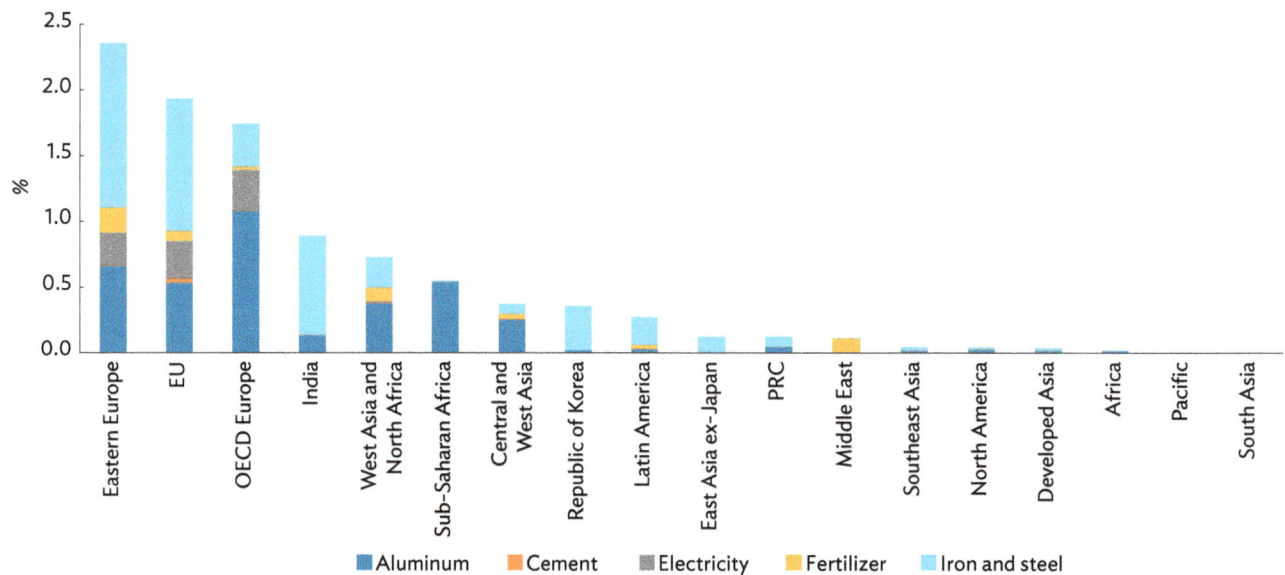

EU = European Union (27 members), OECD = Organisation for Economic Co-operation and Development, PRC = People's Republic of China.

Notes: The list of products covered by the Carbon Border Adjustment Mechanism (CBAM) is taken from European Commission (2021a). This reports information on the products covered using the Combined Nomenclature classification, which can be converted to the Harmonized System classification used by United Nations Commodity Trade Database and CEPII's Base pour l'Analyse du Commerce International (BACI) Database by removing the final two digits.

Source: Centre d'Études Prospectives et d'Informations Internationales (CEPII or the French Research Center in the International Economics). BACI Database. http://www.cepii.fr/CEPII/fr/bdd_modele/bdd_modele_item.asp?id=37; and Zignago and Gaulier (2010) (both accessed November 2023).

widely.[60] The simple average tax rate across regions of 8.1% represents a substantial cost. There are wide variations across Asian subregions, however, with the rate being relatively low in East Asia (1.7%), but higher in other regions including Central and West Asia (13.0%), South Asia (12.3%), and India (36.9%). Using the EU CO_2 intensity as the default leads to much lower trade-weighted tariffs, with tariffs less than 3% in all regions except for Central and West Asia and South Asia. The drop in tax equivalent in India to below 3% highlights the large differences in CO_2 intensities across economies and the potential impact of the choice of the default rate when implementing CBAM. When considering other ETS sectors, exports to the EU generally account for a higher share of these exports, with shares to the EU above 10% in East Asia, the PRC, India, and the Republic of Korea. The unweighted average tax rate across regions

is lower for other ETS sectors (6.7%), reflecting the lower CO_2 intensities in these other sectors, though exceptions exist, notably in the Pacific and East Asia.

Modeling CBAM's effects under various scenarios allows an examination of its potential impact on Asia.
Computable general equilibrium (CGE) models combine economic theory that identifies the structure of an economy and behavioral responses of agents (e.g., firms, households, and governments) with real-world data to model the potential effects of policies on economies (see Box 6.6). The approach involves comparing an initial baseline case with results following some change in policy, such as CBAM. By accounting for interactions between different sectors, agents, and markets, CGE models can consider the wider impact of policy interventions and quantify those effects. CGE models

---

[60]   While the CGE model accounts for existing carbon pricing efforts in Asia when calculating the predicted effects of CBAM, the trade-weighted import taxes in Table 6.2 do not adjust for existing carbon prices.

have been extensively used to estimate the effects of climate mitigation policies (Babatunde, Begum, and Said 2017). To model CBAM effects, various scenarios are compared to a baseline of the current ETS and a carbon price of €18 per MT of CO_2.[61] These scenarios include increasing the carbon price within the ETS to €100 per MT of CO_2, introducing a CBAM at a price of €100 per MT of CO_2, and increasing the price to €200 per MT of CO_2 (Table 6.3).[62]

The effects of a more stringent ETS and imposition of CBAM have ambiguous effects on emissions, output, and trade. Understanding and predicting the estimated effects of policy interventions in a CGE model—such as increases in the EU's ETS carbon price or the imposition of CBAM—is complicated by the general equilibrium nature of the model, with the direct effects of policy interventions potentially being reinforced or counteracted by indirect effects that work through changes in relative prices.

The impact of policy interventions on CO_2 emissions, output, and trade will reflect two main effects—a substitution and income effect. The substitution effect will work toward raising emissions, production, and exports of the rest of the world, while lowering these levels in the EU. A higher carbon price in the EU's ETS, for example, would involve the substitution of EU production for production in other regions, with EU firms replacing domestic intermediates with imported ones and potentially shifting downstream production out of the EU to avoid higher carbon prices for intermediates. These substitution effects are likely to be stronger in ETS sectors than in non-ETS sectors. These impacts would be expected to reduce the production of CO_2 emissions in the EU, while increasing emissions in other regions through both upstream and downstream carbon leakage. Countering these substitution effects, however, is an income effect—with the higher carbon price on intermediates for EU firms leading to cost increases for downstream producers in the EU, lowering production levels and income. Lower income levels in the EU may

in turn lower the demand for goods, particularly non-ETS goods, from other regions. As such, the income and substitution effects all work toward reducing emissions, output, and exports in the EU. For the rest of the world, however, the substitution and income effects work in opposite directions, meaning that the overall impact of a higher ETS price on CO_2 emissions, production, and exports in the rest of the world is ambiguous. Although ambiguous in theory, estimated impacts are likely to depend upon the extent of carbon leakage. If leakage from the EU to other regions is limited, then the substitution effect would likely be relatively small, with the income effect potentially dominating. Effects are also likely to differ between ETS and non-ETS products.

The effects of CBAM on emissions, output, and trade in the EU and rest of the world will also depend on the relative strengths of the substitution and income effects. With CBAM, the price of intermediates imported into the EU will become relatively higher as they are now subject to a carbon price. This can reduce the substitution effect of the ETS, with EU firms potentially substituting imported intermediates for domestic ones, raising production and emissions in the EU and reducing them in the rest of the world relative to an ETS only. Conversely, the greater cost of downstream production in the EU due to the expansion of carbon pricing to all intermediates—both domestic and foreign—may encourage firms to shift downstream production out of the EU to other regions, thus reducing output and emissions in the EU, but potentially increasing production and final product exports to the EU from other regions. As with the ETS, however, income effects are also at play. The higher carbon price of the EU would reduce output and income levels, with negative consequences for output and exports in all regions. Once again, therefore, the overall impact of CBAM on emissions, production, and trade are ambiguous. With substitution effects for intermediate and downstream production working against one another, it is perhaps more likely that income effects dominate in the case of

---

[61]   The baseline of €18 per MT of CO_2 reflects the approximate price of CO_2 in the reference year of 2017.

[62]   The revenue collected from the CBAM is assumed to go into the EU's budget in the model.

CBAM for both the EU and the rest of the world. If so, then an ETS plus CBAM is more likely to result in lower emissions, production, and exports than under an ETS only. However, that outcome would depend on carbon leakage and the extent to which downstream production moves outside the EU.

Table 6.2: Trade and Carbon Border Adjustment Mechanism Rates across Exporters

	Core CBAM Sectors			Other ETS Sectors			Carbon Intensity Relative to the EU	
	Share of Exports to EU	Trade-Weighted Import Tax at Local CO_2 Intensity, €100/MT	Trade-Weighted Import Tax Using EU Rates €100/MT	Share of Exports to EU	Trade-Weighted Import Tax at Local CO_2 Intensity, €100/MT	Trade-Weighted Import Tax Using EU Rates €100/MT	Core CBAM Products	Other ETS Products
Developed Asia	0.053	2.55%	2.10%	0.092	3.14%	2.93%	1.2	1.1
Central and West Asia	0.037	13.03%	4.16%	0.041	7.59%	4.92%	3.1	1.5
East Asia ex-Japan	0.098	1.74%	1.41%	0.121	5.01%	4.68%	1.2	1.1
South Asia	0.006	12.25%	6.02%	0.013	5.98%	4.13%	2.0	1.4
Southeast Asia	0.040	5.67%	1.97%	0.086	6.53%	3.16%	2.9	2.1
Pacific	0.085	0.85%	1.96%	0.088	14.62%	5.75%	0.4	2.5
PRC	0.086	6.52%	1.88%	0.118	5.45%	2.85%	3.5	1.9
India	0.115	36.92%	2.63%	0.163	5.99%	3.16%	14.0	1.9
Republic of Korea	0.109	2.24%	2.09%	0.178	2.89%	2.59%	1.1	1.1
European Union		7.88%	7.88%		4.13%	4.13%	1.0	1.0
OECD Europe	0.091	2.01%	3.43%	0.128	3.17%	3.20%	0.6	1.0
Eastern Europe	0.114	19.19%	4.23%	0.140	7.39%	4.25%	4.5	1.7
North America	0.045	3.54%	2.11%	0.084	6.82%	3.68%	1.7	1.9
Latin America	0.064	4.16%	2.13%	0.085	7.06%	3.86%	2.0	1.8
West Asia and North Africa	0.060	7.53%	2.38%	0.092	10.93%	4.39%	3.2	2.5
Sub-Saharan Africa	0.097	3.99%	1.75%	0.114	11.16%	4.63%	2.3	2.4

CBAM = Carbon Border Adjustment Mechanism, CO_2 = carbon dioxide, EU = European Union (27 members), ETS = emissions trading system, MT = metric ton, OECD = Organisation for Economic Co-operation and Development, PRC = People's Republic of China.

Notes: Values are output tax equivalents, weighted by exports to the EU; EU values are weighted by value of EU production rather than exports.

Source: ADB calculations using data from Global Trade Analysis Project. GTAP 11 Data Base. https://www.gtap.agecon.purdue.edu/databases/; and International Energy Agency. Data and Statistics. https://www.iea.org/data-and-statistics (both accessed November 2023).

Table 6.3: Modeling Scenarios to Consider the Impact of the European Union's Carbon Border Adjustment Mechanism on Asian Economies

Scenario	Description	Carbon Price
1	European economies impose tighter ETS carbon allocations, with a resulting €100/MT price. There is no CBAM applied at the border.	€100/MT CO_2
2	European economies impose tighter ETS carbon allocations, with a resulting €100/MT price. CBAM taxes are imposed for ETS sectors.	€100/MT CO_2
3	European economies impose tighter ETS carbon allocations, with a resulting €200/MT price. There is no CBAM applied at the border.	€200/MT CO_2
4	European economies impose tighter ETS carbon allocations, with a resulting €200/MT price. CBAM taxes are imposed for ETS sectors.	€200/MT CO_2

CBAM = carbon border adjustment mechanism, CO_2 = carbon dioxide, ETS = emissions trading system, MT = metric ton.

Notes: During the phase-in period, the CBAM regime will not apply to all ETS sectors. However, the CBAM system is expected to be expanded to all ETS sectors after the phase-in period. There is also some discussion on expanded sector coverage. These potential changes to the ETS are not modeled in this analysis. Imposing tighter ETS carbon allocations refers to reducing the supply of carbon certificates as a means of increasing the price of CO_2 emissions.

Source: ADB.

Box 6.6: Modeling the Effects of Carbon Border Adjustment Mechanism Using Computable General Equilibrium Models

A computable general equilibrium (CGE) model of global world production and trade is used to estimate the economic effects of carbon border tax scenarios. The CGE large-scale economic model translates price signals from the taxes modeled into domestic and global economic effects. The estimated effects include detailed information regarding changes in value, quantity, and price for domestic activities and associated trade flows. The general equilibrium nature of these models (meaning that sectors interact through both supply linkages and factor markets) captures complex interactions. In particular, the model simulates under different scenarios the changes in specific economic activities (sectors) that result from relative changes in cost and market access conditions. This is important, as the combined impact of policy changes across sectors will not be the same as if each sector was examined in isolation. The model has a microeconomic theoretical foundation.[a] The model uses a balanced and internally consistent global database (in this case the Global Trade Analysis Project [GTAP] version 11 database) of all trade and production across economies and industries, including trade in intermediate goods.[b]

The model can estimate the changes in GHG emissions due to changes in patterns of production and resource use. The combination of underlying baseline data and exogenous parameters (the various technical parameters in the model) determine the size and scope of these adjustments. To evaluate policy changes, the baseline (business as usual) scenario with no policy changes is compared with the counterfactual scenario that includes the changes in policy under the different scenarios. The effect of the policy change is then quantified as the difference between the two. The effects of different scenarios on CO_2 emissions can then be quantified. Data on GHG emissions and pollutants are used to compute changes in emissions resulting from this set of changes in resource allocation and production.

To illustrate the results of the modeling exercise, the figure below shows how the simulation results (the counterfactual) compare with simulated baseline values. In the right-side panel, curved line A represents the baseline trend for economic activity indicator Q (e.g., production of steel in Economy X), while line B represents the evolution of that same economic activity following the introduction of carbon taxes under the policy scenarios. The left-side panel provides a mapping from the same economic activity (in this example, production of steel in Economy X) to its environmental impact (for example, CO_2 emissions associated with different levels of steel production), represented by curved line C. The modeling results are reported as the numerical difference or percentage change from moving to B with respect to the baseline values A. In the figure, the full economic effects take time, and so the focus is on a long-run scenario. This means the benchmark economic structure is considered and compared with an alternative economic structure where investment and production patterns have had time to adjust (including longer-run capital stock changes). In this context, with T_1 as the benchmark or reference year, an alternative set of outcomes for period T_1 is examined where the changes in policy (carbon taxes) have had time to work through the economy after implementation in a prior period T_0.

Mapping Economic Effects to Their Impact on Emissions

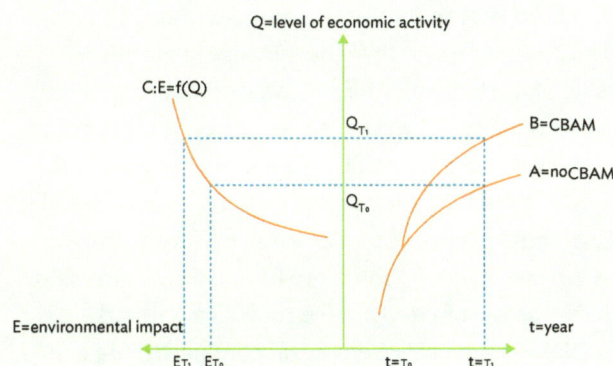

[a]   The model is based on what is known as the Eaton and Kortum model. For technical details on the model beyond the background report, see Bekkers, Francois, and Rojas-Romagosa (2018) and Bekkers et al. (2024). The model and underlying data also cover atmospheric pollution indicators, including both greenhouse gas (GHG) and non-greenhouse gas (NGHG) emissions.

[b]   The GTAP database is a global multiregional input-output (GMRIO) database containing extensive and comprehensive economic data for 140 economies/regions and 65 production sectors. It provides disaggregated data for sectoral production, consumption, taxes and subsidies, trade, government finances, labor variables for different skill levels, and data on other production factors. For documentation on the structure of the database see Aguiar et al. (2019).

Source: ADB.

CBAM is predicted to reduce carbon leakage by around half relative to an ETS with a similar carbon price. The estimated impact on CO_2 emissions of the different scenarios suggests that CBAM's direct impact on emissions will likely be limited. A shift from a price of €18 per MT to €100 per MT of CO_2 within the EU's current ETS is predicted to reduce global CO_2 emissions by a fairly modest 1%, or by 358 million MT of CO_2 (Table 6.4). Reductions in CO_2 emissions are confined to two regions, the EU itself and the Organisation for Economic Co-operation and Development (OECD), which includes several economies that are part of the EU's ETS. In the remaining economies and regions, CO_2 emissions will increase by 132.8 million MT of CO_2. The increase can provide a rough estimate of the extent of carbon leakage of the ETS, representing around 27% of the reduction in CO_2 emissions in the EU and OECD Europe.[63] The estimated reduction in emissions in the EU and OECD under CBAM at €100 per MT of CO_2 is similar to that with the ETS only at €100 per MT of CO_2 (480.6 versus 490.9 million MT of CO_2). However, the estimated carbon leakage is more than halved, from 132.8 million MT of CO_2 to 62.4 million MT of CO_2, equal to 13% of the reduction in the EU and OECD Europe under CBAM. That emissions in the EU and OECD Europe drop by a similar amount under ETS alone and ETS with CBAM, while the increase in emissions outside of the EU under CBAM is substantially smaller, suggests that CBAM will have a more negative impact on output levels outside the EU relative to a higher priced ETS only. Increasing the price of carbon to €200 per MT of CO_2 under both an ETS alone and ETS with CBAM scenario results in a further drop in global CO_2 emissions, with the drop estimated at 1.9% for ETS alone and 2.2% with CBAM, with reductions again confined to the EU and OECD Europe. The higher price is associated with somewhat higher carbon leakage rates, however—29.4% in the case of ETS alone and 13.6% in ETS with CBAM.

The estimated reduction in exports to the EU following more stringent EU carbon policies is substantial for some regions. Moving from a price of €18 per MT to €100 per MT of CO_2 within the current ETS is predicted to lead to a decline in the value of exports to the EU from all regions (Figure 6.18). Across developing Asia, the decline in exports to the EU is largest for Central and West Asia (a drop of 7.7%). In most other developing Asian subregions and economies, the estimated effects on exports to the EU are muted, with reductions of 1% or less except for South Asia (where exports drop by 1.2%). The introduction of CBAM at a price of €100 per MT of CO_2 leads to larger drops in exports to the EU for most developing Asian subregions. Estimated declines in exports to the EU are above 2% in all cases except for South Asia (1.2%) and the Republic of Korea (1.9%).[64] Interestingly, the two Asian subregions with the highest effects under the higher-priced ETS—Central and West Asia, and South Asia—do not see a further drop in exports to the EU with CBAM. A higher carbon price of €200 per MT of CO_2 within CBAM is predicted to have substantial effects on exports to the EU for many regions. Within developing Asia, reductions in exports to the EU of 4% or more are predicted for East Asia, Southeast Asia, India, the PRC, and the Republic of Korea, with the predicted decline in Central and West Asia at 14.4%.[65] This highlights the potential for more ambitious climate change targets in the EU and how they impact Asian economies.

A higher carbon price in the EU's ETS impacts upon production and exports of ETS and non-ETS sectors in the rest of the world differently. Increasing the price of carbon from €18 per MT to €100 per MT of CO_2 within the current ETS is estimated to impact on the quantity of exports to the EU differently for ETS and non-ETS sectors (Table 6.5). While exports to the EU from non-EU regions are estimated to increase in the case of ETS sectors, reflecting the substitution of domestic for imported intermediates in the EU, exports to the EU in

---

[63]   As several of the OECD Europe group are part of the EU's ETS, they are combined when calculating the reduction in emissions due to the ETS. The reduction in emissions in the EU and OECD Europe will reflect various general equilibrium effects, including the lower levels of production due to the higher carbon price and shifts of CO_2 intensive production outside the EU.

[64]   For developing Asia as a whole, exports to the EU are estimated to fall by 1.3% under an ETS at a price of €100 per MT and by 2.4% with a similar ETS and CBAM, indicating that CBAM is expected to reduce Asian exports to the EU by 1.1% at a price of €100 per MT.

[65]   Relative to an ETS at the same price of €200 per MT, CBAM is estimated to reduce developing Asia's exports to the EU by 2.1%.

Table 6.4: Change in Carbon Dioxide Emissions under Different European Union Climate Policy Scenarios (million MT of CO_2)

	ETS Only (€100/MT CO_2)	ETS and CBAM (€100/MT CO_2)	ETS Only (€200/MT CO_2)	ETS and CBAM (€200/MT CO_2)
Developed Asia	5.66	5.33	10.69	10.21
Central and West Asia	4.15	2.10	8.18	3.67
East Asia ex-Japan	2.17	1.37	3.94	2.39
South Asia	0.53	0.37	0.98	0.64
Southeast Asia	5.36	2.38	9.88	4.16
Pacific	0.10	0.03	0.20	0.05
PRC	10.70	3.72	18.70	5.46
India	11.61	7.12	23.54	14.58
Republic of Korea	2.54	1.75	4.69	3.17
European Union	-435.77	-425.38	-777.19	-759.58
OECD Europe	-55.12	-55.18	-107.91	-108.04
Eastern Europe	37.34	13.60	79.44	28.68
North America	22.74	14.50	44.01	27.89
Latin America	4.41	1.63	8.55	3.03
Other West Asia and North Africa	18.18	4.61	33.59	6.43
Sub-Saharan Africa	7.29	3.92	14.23	7.47
World	-358.10	-418.15	-624.48	-749.78
World percentage change	-1.08	-1.26	-1.88	-2.25

CBAM = carbon border adjustment mechanism, CO_2 = carbon dioxide, EU = European Union (27 members), ETS = emissions trading system, MT = metric ton, OECD = Organisation for Economic Co-operation and Development, PRC = People's Republic of China.

Sources: ADB calculations using data from Global Trade Analysis Project. GTAP 11 Data Base. https://www.gtap.agecon.purdue.edu/databases/; and International Energy Agency. Data and Statistics. https://www.iea.org/data-and-statistics (both accessed November 2023).

Figure 6.18: Percentage Change in Export Values to the European Union under Different European Union Carbon Border Adjustment Mechanism Policy Scenarios (%)

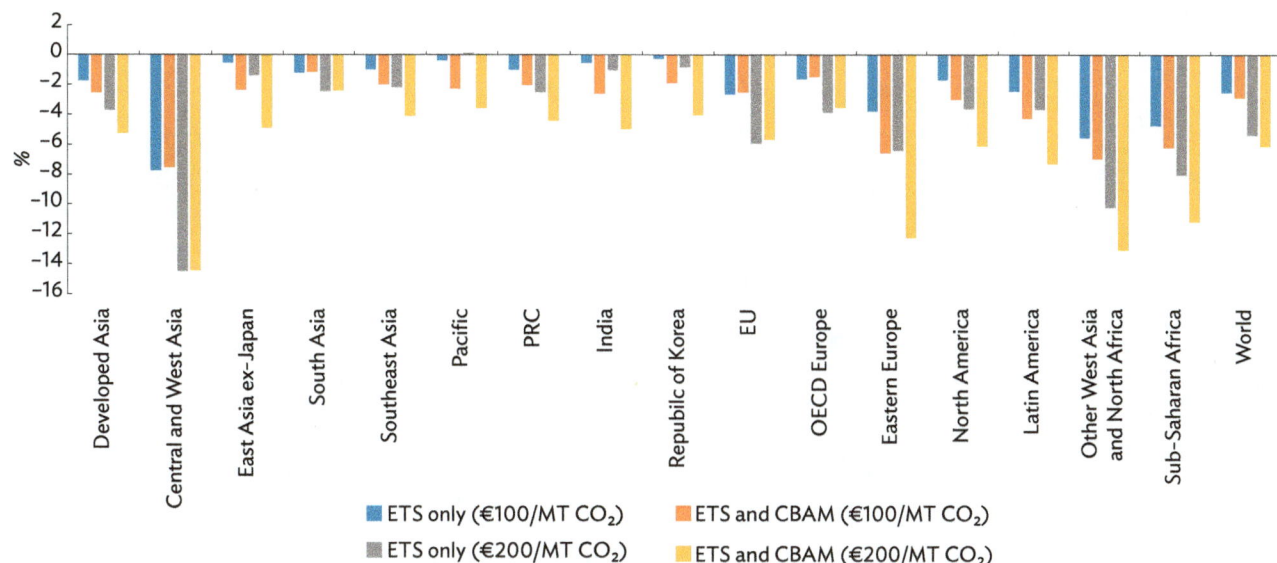

CBAM = Carbon Border Adjustment Mechanism, CO_2 = carbon dioxide, ETS = emissions trading system, EU = European Union (27 members), MT = metric ton, OECD = Organisation for Economic Co-operation and Development, PRC = People's Republic of China.

Sources: ADB calculations using data from Global Trade Analysis Project. GTAP 11 Data Base. https://www.gtap.agecon.purdue.edu/databases/; and International Energy Agency. Data and Statistics. https://www.iea.org/data-and-statistics (both accessed November 2023).

non-ETS sectors are estimated to decline across regions. Negative income effects that fall on non-ETS sectors offset the positive substitution effects in Asian regions, which given the larger share of non-ETS exports in total exports to the EU result in negative overall effects of the higher ETS. A similar pattern exists when the ETS price rises to €200 per MT of CO_2.

The introduction of CBAM in the EU redirects ETS production back toward EU producers but encourages some downstream production to shift out of the EU. Introducing CBAM at a price of €100 per MT of CO_2 is estimated to reduce exports to the EU in ETS products across non-EU regions. This reflects a second substitution effect, with intermediate demand in the EU being reoriented back toward EU suppliers relative to the higher priced ETS. The negative effects of the

ETS on exports to the EU of non-ETS products are also diminished relative to the higher priced ETS. This change likely reflects carbon leakage, with downstream producers shifting some of their production outside of the EU to avoid paying the carbon price.

Estimates of reductions in exports to the EU across Asian regions are mirrored by reductions in exports to other regions. The increase in ETS price from €18 to €100 per MT of CO_2 tends to be associated with a reduction in exports from different Asian regions to non-EU regions of between 0.5% and 1.0% (Figure 6.19). For comparison, the estimated global drop in exports to non-EU regions due to the ETS is 0.8%. While higher than that for some Asian regions, this is mainly driven by a relatively large drop in exports from the EU and OECD Europe.[66] With an ETS carbon price of €100 per MT, the imposition

Table 6.5: Percentage Change in Export Quantities of ETS and non-ETS Exports to the European Union under Different European Union Carbon Border Adjustment Mechanism Policy Scenarios (%)

	ETS Only (€100/MT CO_2)		ETS and CBAM (€100/MT CO_2)		ETS Only (€200/MT CO_2)		ETS and CBAM (€200/MT CO_2)	
	ETS Sectors	Non-ETS Sectors	ETS Sectors	Non-ETS Sectors	ETS Sectors	Non-ETS Sectors	ETS Sectors	Non-ETS Sectors
Developed Asia	7.2	-3.0	-3.2	-2.1	14.4	-6.2	-5.3	-4.6
Central and West Asia	13.4	-8.2	-4.2	-6.5	32.0	-16.1	-4.8	-12.8
East Asia ex-Japan	8.3	-2.7	-2.7	-1.9	17.8	-6.1	-3.7	-4.5
South Asia	12.1	-1.5	-4.5	-0.8	27.0	-3.1	-6.5	-1.7
Southeast Asia	7.6	-2.3	-3.0	-1.5	15.5	-4.9	-4.9	-3.3
Pacific	11.4	-2.7	-2.4	-1.9	24.9	-4.8	-2.3	-3.1
PRC	5.8	-2.3	-3.5	-1.4	11.6	-5.0	-6.0	-3.4
India	7.7	-2.7	-3.7	-1.9	16.7	-5.7	-5.3	-4.0
Republic of Korea	6.9	-2.2	-2.6	-1.4	14.5	-5.0	-4.0	-3.3
European Union	-5.7	-2.1	-4.7	-2.5	-11.9	-4.9	-10.1	-5.8
OECD Europe	-1.9	-1.6	-1.1	-1.8	-4.3	-3.9	-2.8	-4.3
Eastern Europe	9.4	-8.8	-5.1	-5.8	21.5	-17.2	-7.5	-11.9
North America	7.4	-3.3	-4.1	-2.5	15.3	-7.0	-6.7	-5.3
Latin America	9.2	-5.4	-2.4	-4.3	19.4	-9.4	-3.3	-7.4
Other West Asia and North Africa	7.0	-8.3	-5.8	-6.6	14.9	-15.7	-9.4	-12.8
Sub-Saharan Africa	10.1	-8.2	-1.7	-6.8	21.2	-15.1	-2.1	-12.4

CBAM = carbon border adjustment mechanism, CO_2 = carbon dioxide, EU = European Union (27 members), ETS = emissions trading system, MT = metric ton, OECD = Organisation for Economic Co-operation and Development, PRC = People's Republic of China.

Note: To isolate changes in production and export levels, the table reports estimated percentage changes in export quantities relative to the baseline.

Sources: ADB calculations using data from Global Trade Analysis Project. GTAP 11 Data Base. https://www.gtap.agecon.purdue.edu/databases/; and International Energy Agency. Data and Statistics. https://www.iea.org/data-and-statistics (both accessed November 2023).

---

[66]   Ignoring these two regions, only Latin America has a percentage drop (0.66%) comparable to Asia, with exports to non-EU regions increasing in Eastern Europe, West Asia and North Africa, and sub-Saharan Africa.

Figure 6.19: Percentage Change in Exports to Non-European Union Regions under Different European Union Carbon Border Adjustment Mechanism Policy Scenarios (%)

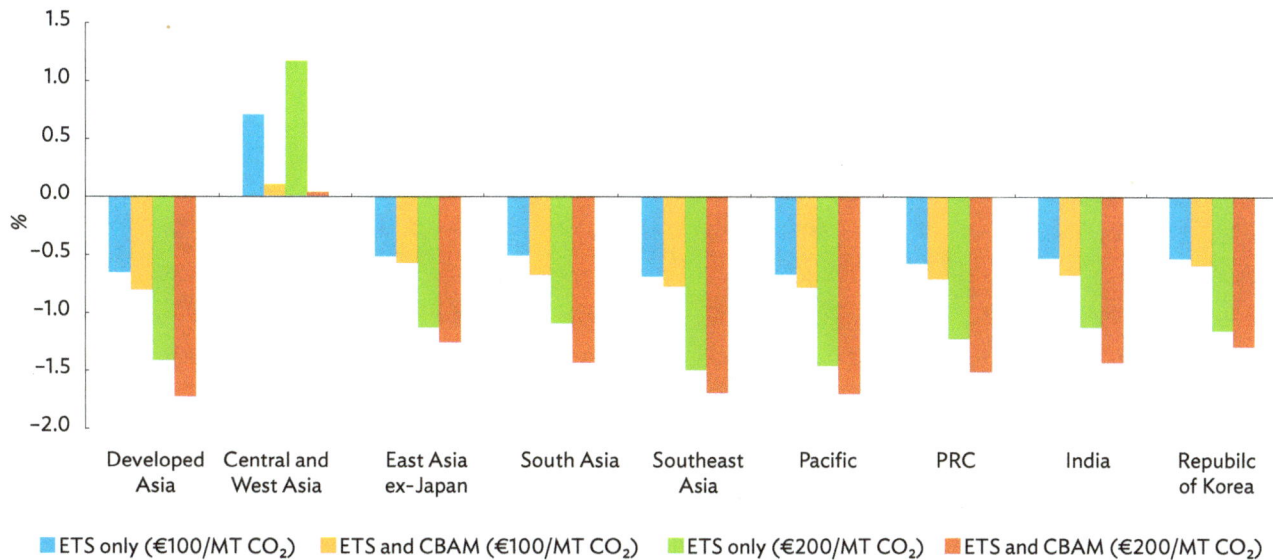

CBAM = carbon border adjustment mechanism, CO$_2$ = carbon dioxide, ETS = emissions trading system, MT = metric ton, OECD = Organisation for Economic Co-operation and Development, PRC = People's Republic of China.

Sources: ADB calculations using data from Global Trade Analysis Project. GTAP 11 Data Base. https://www.gtap.agecon.purdue.edu/databases/; and International Energy Agency. Data and Statistics. https://www.iea.org/data-and-statistics (both accessed November 2023).

of CBAM is associated with larger percentage drops in exports to non-EU regions, though still usually in the range of 0.5% to 1%. The exception in both cases is Central and West Asia, which is expected to see an increase of 0.7% in the case of the ETS alone and 0.1% with CBAM. This suggests a partial redirection of exports from the EU to other regions. Globally, the reduction in exports to non-EU regions from a CBAM with a carbon price of €100 per MT is 1.1%. Increasing the carbon price to €200 per MT of CO$_2$ significantly impacts aggregate exports from Asia. Aggregate exports are estimated to fall between 1.3% and 1.7% across subregions, again except for Central and West Asia, where exports to non-EU regions barely change from the baseline. Globally, exports are estimated to fall by around 2.4%, with the drop again relatively large from the EU, OECD Europe, and Latin America. As such, CBAM can potentially have a significant impact on trade levels, suggesting a potential trade-off between emissions reduction and trade. CBAM thus could indeed present a challenge for some economies to advance development through GVCs.

Other macroeconomic effects of more stringent climate policies in the EU on developing Asian economies are estimated to be relatively small. For instance, the estimated changes in gross domestic product (GDP) in developing Asian economies and subregions under the various scenarios are quite limited (Table 6.6). At a price of €100 per MT of CO$_2$, reductions in GDP are estimated to be less than 0.2% of GDP, with Central and West Asia, and the Pacific somewhat larger. A carbon price of €200 per MT of CO$_2$ leads to larger reductions in GDP, but still below 0.5% of GDP in all Asian subregions except Central and West Asia and the Pacific. Levels of labor displacement are also generally small, although they become more substantial as the carbon price increases (Figure 6.20). Labor displacement reflects shifts of employment across sectors and thus captures the extent of structural change in response to the EU's climate policies, possibly due to downstream leakage of production outside of the EU.[67] In comparison to the estimated global rates of labor displacement—0.14% under ETS at €100 per

---

[67] The CGE model used includes an assumption of full employment, meaning that in equilibrium the sum of labor displaced will sum to zero. The percentage of the workforce displaced is thus used to capture the extent of labor displacement across sectors.

Table 6.6: Percentage Change in Gross Domestic Product under Different European Union Carbon Border Adjustment Mechanism Modeling Scenarios (%)

	ETS Only (€100/MT CO$_2$)	ETS and CBAM (€100/MT CO$_2$)	ETS Only (€200/MT CO$_2$)	ETS and CBAM (€200/MT CO$_2$)
Developed Asia	-0.104	-0.106	-0.241	-0.246
Central and West Asia	-0.332	-0.386	-0.702	-0.818
East Asia ex-Japan	-0.112	-0.139	-0.265	-0.318
South Asia	-0.183	-0.185	-0.401	-0.408
Southeast Asia	-0.183	-0.208	-0.425	-0.475
Pacific	-0.210	-0.278	-0.420	-0.559
PRC	-0.034	-0.047	-0.097	-0.121
India	-0.029	-0.044	-0.086	-0.112
Republic of Korea	-0.088	-0.091	-0.216	-0.222
European Union	-1.844	-1.907	-4.356	-4.490
OECD Europe	-0.793	-0.853	-1.980	-2.108
Eastern Europe	-0.159	-0.365	-0.295	-0.718
North America	-0.098	-0.101	-0.223	-0.229
Latin America	-0.099	-0.125	-0.218	-0.270
Other West Asia and North Africa	-0.283	-0.390	-0.605	-0.813
Sub-Saharan Africa	-0.138	-0.195	-0.292	-0.406
World percentage change	-0.454	-0.487	-1.070	-1.137

CBAM = carbon border adjustment mechanism, CO$_2$ = carbon dioxide, ETS = emissions trading system, MT = metric ton, OECD = Organisation for Economic Co-operation and Development, PRC = People's Republic of China.

Sources: ADB calculations using data from Global Trade Analysis Project. GTAP 11 Data Base. https://www.gtap.agecon.purdue.edu/databases/; and International Energy Agency. Data and Statistics. https://www.iea.org/data-and-statistics (both accessed November 2023).

MT and 0.13% under CBAM at €100 per MT—labor displacement rates in developing Asian regions are relatively low, with only Central and West Asia having displacement rates above the global average. The extent of labor displacement is estimated to increase with increases in the carbon price to €200 per MT, though the extent of labor displacement in Asia is lower than that globally (0.3% with ETS and 0.27% with CBAM).

Reductions in production within the EU in response to CBAM are not confined to the sectors covered.
The increase in the carbon price within the ETS from €18 to €100 per MT results in relatively large reductions in production within the EU in CBAM sectors, particularly petrochemicals, electricity, and gas (Table 6.7). Reductions also occur across other sectors, with the increased costs in CBAM sectors raising the

cost and price of goods and services produced in other sectors. CBAM at a price of €100 per MT has a dual effect. On one hand, the reduction in production in CBAM sectors is generally lower than in the case of the ETS at a price of €100 per MT only, consistent with the reduction in carbon leakage from these sectors in response to CBAM. On the other hand, the reduction in production in certain downstream sectors such as textiles, pharmaceuticals, computer, electronic and optical equipment, machinery and equipment, and other transport equipment, among others, is larger under CBAM than with the ETS alone. These results are consistent with the idea of greater downstream leakage in response to CBAM, with producers substituting downstream production in the EU for production in other regions including developing Asia, to avoid paying the CBAM tariff on imports of intermediates into the EU.

Figure 6.20: Extent of Labor Displacement under Different European Union Carbon Border Adjustment Mechanism Policy Scenarios (% of workforce displaced)

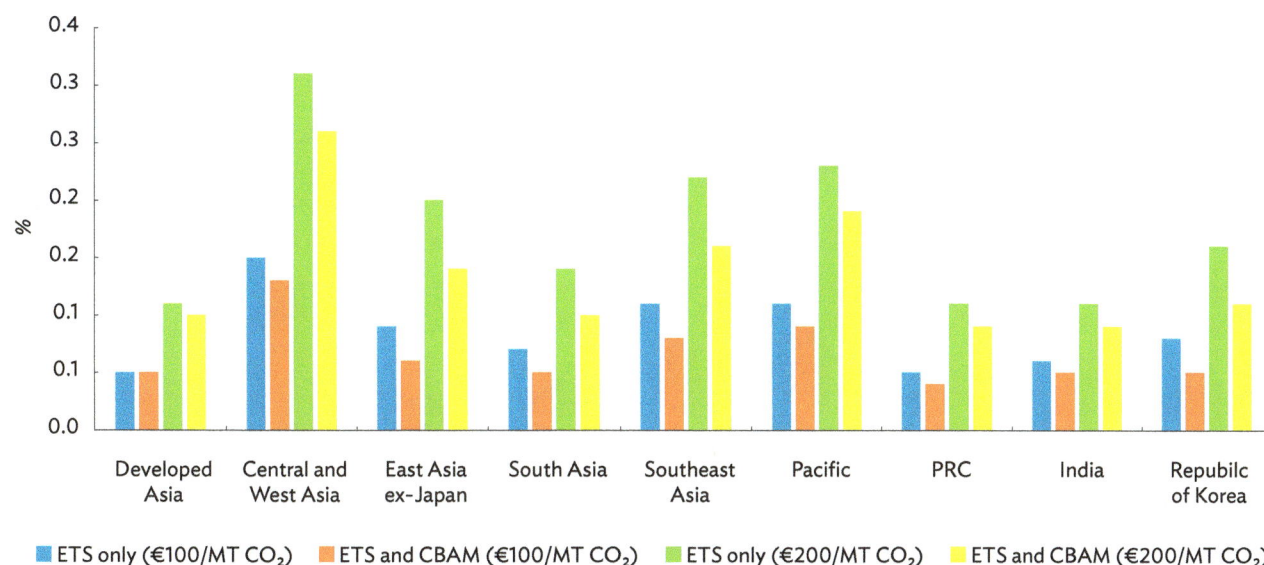

CBAM = carbon border adjustment mechanism, CO$_2$ = carbon dioxide, ETS = emissions trading system, MT = metric tons, PRC = People's Republic of China.

Sources: ADB calculations using data from Global Trade Analysis Project. GTAP 11 Data Base. https://www.gtap.agecon.purdue.edu/databases/; and International Energy Agency. Data and Statistics. https://www.iea.org/data-and-statistics (both accessed November 2023).

Table 6.7: Percentage Change in European Union Production by Sector (%)

	ETS Only (€100/MT CO$_2$)	ETS and CBAM (€100/MT CO$_2$)	ETS Only (€200/MT CO$_2$)	ETS and CBAM (€200/MT CO$_2$)
Agriculture, forestry, fishing	-0.7	-0.9	-3.2	-3.6
Mining	-3.1	-3.4	-11.2	-12.0
Food	-1.3	-1.5	-4.0	-4.4
Textiles	-1.3	-2.2	-3.5	-5.3
Wood	-3.2	-3.4	-6.9	-7.3
Chemicals, rubber, plastics	-5.8	-5.4	-11.7	-11.0
Pharmaceuticals	-1.1	-1.8	-2.5	-4.0
Ferrous metals	-7.1	-6.1	-15.5	-13.5
Nonferrous metals	-8.3	-7.9	-16.1	-15.3
Metal products	-2.7	-3.3	-5.9	-7.2
Mineral products nec	-5.8	-3.9	-12.0	-8.7
Computer, electronic and optical equipment	-1.8	-2.8	-4.1	-6.2
Machinery and equipment nec	-2.0	-2.7	-4.4	-5.9
Motor vehicles and parts	-2.0	-2.7	-4.6	-5.9
Other transport equipment	-1.4	-2.5	-3.0	-5.1
Manufactures nec	-1.3	-1.9	-2.9	-4.2
Construction	-2.6	-2.7	-6.2	-6.4
Petrochemicals, coal products	-13.2	-10.2	-26.3	-21.2
Electricity	-11.4	-10.4	-21.6	-19.5
Gas manufacture, distribution	-11.8	-9.6	-28.2	-24.1
Transport nec	-5.4	-4.9	-11.4	-10.4
Commercial Services	-1.5	-1.6	-3.7	-4.0
Public Services	-0.7	-0.6	-1.8	-1.7

CBAM = carbon border adjustment mechanism, CO$_2$ = carbon dioxide, ETS = emissions trading system, MT = metric ton, nec = not elsewhere classified, PRC = People's Republic of China.

Sources: ADB calculations using data from Global Trade Analysis Project. GTAP 11 Data Base. https://www.gtap.agecon.purdue.edu/databases/; and International Energy Agency. Data and Statistics. https://www.iea.org/data-and-statistics (both accessed November 2023).

Estimating the Impact of the Carbon Border Adjustment Mechanism Expanding into Other Regions

Whether others will follow in implementing BCA policies remains uncertain; but extending them to other regions could have larger effects on CO_2 emissions. Other economies may consider whether they should follow the EU in implementing their own version of CBAM, which would expand the coverage of exports affected. The CGE model used above can examine the impact of extending CBAM to other regions, considering scenarios in which other OECD economies (including those in Asia) implement both an ETS and a CBAM, or other ADB regional members implement both an ETS and CBAM (Table 6.8).

Extending the EU's ETS with CBAM to other OECD economies could triple the reductions in CO_2 emissions relative to a CBAM in the EU only. Extending CBAM to other OECD economies at a price of €100 per MT of CO_2 is estimated to reduce global CO_2 emissions by 1,226 million MT, or 3.7%, nearly three times the 1.3% reduction estimated for an EU CBAM (Table 6.8). Emissions in non-OECD regions are predicted to increase by 217.5 million MT, partly offsetting the 1,443.7 million MT reduced in the OECD. Notably, this implies that the rough estimate of carbon leakage of 15.1% under this scenario is slightly higher than the 13% estimate for an EU CBAM, with just over half of this leakage going to developing Asia. Increasing the carbon price to €200 per MT of CO_2 results in even larger drops in CO_2, by 6.4%, with the extent of carbon leakage also increasing to 16.9%. These results show that extending CBAM coverage and increasing its carbon price may lead to higher carbon leakage, especially in a situation with a relatively large share of global industry remaining outside any CBAM.

Including developing Asia in a CBAM can substantially reduce CO_2 emissions, while further limiting the extent of carbon leakage. Extending CBAM to cover all developing Asia is estimated to reduce global CO_2 emissions by around 8.7% at a carbon price of €100 per MT of CO_2 and by almost 15% at €200 per MT of CO_2 (Table 6.9). Moreover, the extent of carbon leakage is estimated to be much lower—7.1% at €100 per MT of CO_2 and 8.1% at €200 per MT of CO_2. This reflects the fact that as CBAMs expand to cover a predominant share of overall production, opportunities for carbon leakage decline. Compared to extending CBAM to only OECD economies, these results also highlight that the possibility for carbon leakage remains high if Asia is excluded, given the large production capability in the region.

Table 6.8: Scenarios to Consider the Impact of an Extended Carbon Border Adjustment Mechanism on Asian Economies

Scenario	Description	Carbon Price
5	All OECD economies impose tighter ETS carbon allocations, with a resulting €100/MT price. CBAM taxes are imposed for ETS sectors.	€100/MT CO_2
6	All OECD and other ADB regional members impose tighter ETS carbon allocations, with a resulting €100/MT price. CBAM taxes are imposed for ETS sectors.	€100/MT CO_2
7	All OECD economies impose tighter ETS carbon allocations, with a resulting €200/MT price. CBAM taxes are imposed for ETS sectors.	€200/MT CO_2
8	All OECD and other ADB regional members impose tighter ETS carbon allocations, with a resulting €200/MT price. CBAM taxes are imposed for ETS sectors.	€200/MT CO_2

CBAM = Carbon Border Adjustment Mechanism, CO_2 = carbon dioxide, ETS = emissions trading system, MT = metric ton, OECD = Organisation for Economic Co-operation and Development.

Notes: Given that Australia, Japan, New Zealand, and the Republic of Korea are included in the OECD, other ADB regional members refers to the remaining developing members of ADB. Imposing tighter ETS carbon allocations refers to reducing the supply of carbon certificates as a means of increasing the price of CO_2 emissions.

Source: ADB.

While extending the Carbon Border Adjustment Mechanism to other regions can lead to substantial reductions in CO_2 emissions, it can come at the cost of a significant decline in global trade. Extending CBAM to cover other OECD economies is estimated to reduce the (unweighted) average of developing Asian exports by 1.9% at a carbon price of €100 per MT of CO_2 and by 3.7% at €200 per MT of CO_2. Estimated reductions when ADB regional members are included do not have a significant additional impact on exports, with declines of 2.0% at €100 per MT of CO_2 and 3.7% at €200 per MT of CO_2 (Figure 6.21). These estimates are substantially larger than those obtained with only an EU CBAM, highlighting how extending CBAM does present risks to global trade and to the GVCs that economies have recently relied on for development.

The estimated macroeconomic effects of extending CBAM to other regions are distinct to each region. The impact on GDP of expanding ETS and CBAM to OECD and developing Asian economies varies considerably, with GDP increasing in a few developing Asian regions, particularly when considering extending CBAM to other OECD economies (Table 6.10).[68] These effects likely reflect a diversion of production away from OECD economies and toward other regions following the rise in costs within the OECD. The PRC and India are strongly affected by extending CBAM to developing Asia, likely reflecting the costs of an ETS in the context of relatively carbon-intensive production in sectors covered. While the ETS can directly impact other Asian subregions, lowering GDP, the large negative effects in India and the PRC also have negative spillover effects on other Asian subregions

Table 6.9: Change in Carbon Dioxide Emissions under Different European Union Climate Policy Scenarios (million MT of CO_2)

	ETS and CBAM for All OECD (€100/MT CO_2)	ETS and CBAM for OECD Plus ADB Members (€100/MT CO_2)	ETS and CBAM for All OECD (€200/MT CO_2)	ETS and CBAM for OECD Plus ADB Members (€200/MT CO_2)
Developed Asia	-238.13	-192.24	-410.70	-327.63
Central and West Asia	11.21	-50.97	24.02	-108.61
East Asia ex-Japan	6.34	-66.23	12.40	-116.38
South Asia	3.07	-10.16	6.19	-20.40
Southeast Asia	19.74	-147.14	39.08	-279.30
Pacific	0.01	0.26	0.08	0.65
PRC	43.25	-1429.26	88.08	-2546.10
India	30.55	-398.50	60.90	-723.82
Republic of Korea	-99.55	-80.36	-178.51	-144.30
European Union	-395.41	-334.42	-706.75	-594.83
OECD Europe	-50.83	-43.56	-100.62	-87.73
Eastern Europe	35.38	99.23	75.54	216.92
North America	-659.80	-570.42	-1240.09	-1070.53
Latin America	10.48	36.74	22.14	78.41
Other West Asia and North Africa	45.61	154.55	94.07	335.14
Sub-Saharan Africa	11.88	38.81	24.08	82.16
World	-1,226.22	-2,993.66	-2,190.10	-5,306.33
World percentage change	-3.65	-8.68	-6.43	-14.87

CBAM = carbon border adjustment mechanism, CO_2 = carbon dioxide, ETS = emissions trading system, MT = metric ton, OECD = Organisation for Economic Co-operation and Development, PRC = People's Republic of China.

Sources: ADB calculations using data from Global Trade Analysis Project. GTAP 11 Data Base. https://www.gtap.agecon.purdue.edu/databases/; and International Energy Agency. Data and Statistics. https://www.iea.org/data-and-statistics (both accessed November 2023).

[68] Unsurprisingly, the estimated effects for developed Asia and the Republic of Korea from an extension to other OECD economies are relatively large and negative.

Figure 6.21: Percentage Change in Asian Exports with an Expanded Carbon Border Adjustment Mechanism

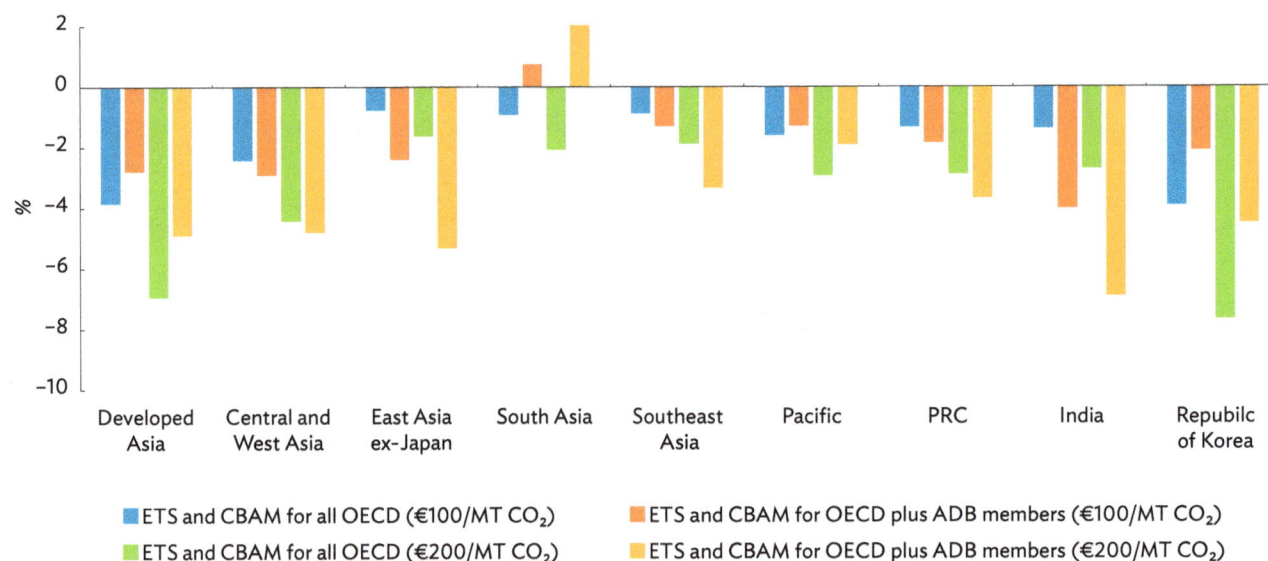

- ETS and CBAM for all OECD (€100/MT CO_2)
- ETS and CBAM for OECD plus ADB members (€100/MT CO_2)
- ETS and CBAM for all OECD (€200/MT CO_2)
- ETS and CBAM for OECD plus ADB members (€200/MT CO_2)

CBAM = carbon border adjustment mechanism, CO_2 = carbon dioxide, ETS = emissions trading system, MT = metric ton, OECD = Organisation for Economic Co-operation and Development, PRC = People's Republic of China.

Sources: ADB calculations using data from Global Trade Analysis Project. GTAP 11 Data Base. https://www.gtap.agecon.purdue.edu/databases/; and International Energy Agency. Data and Statistics. https://www.iea.org/data-and-statistics (both accessed November 2023).

Table 6.10: Percentage Change in Gross Domestic Product under Different European Union Carbon Border Adjustment Mechanism Modeling Scenarios

	ETS and CBAM for All OECD (€100/MT CO_2)	ETS and CBAM for OECD and ADB Regional Members (€100/MT CO_2)	ETS and CBAM for All OECD (€200/MT CO_2)	ETS and CBAM for OECD and ADB Regional Members (€200/MT CO_2)
Developed Asia	-1.555	0.075	-3.670	-0.178
Central and West Asia	0.522	0.984	1.323	0.799
East Asia ex-Japan	0.304	-0.669	0.685	-2.342
South Asia	0.517	0.160	1.191	-0.100
Southeast Asia	0.312	0.051	0.682	-0.675
Pacific	-0.479	0.164	-0.874	0.641
PRC	0.205	-1.882	0.400	-4.764
India	0.354	-1.921	0.726	-4.845
Republic of Korea	-2.256	-0.562	-5.027	-1.521
European Union	-1.378	0.145	-3.358	-0.115
OECD Europe	-0.643	0.054	-1.644	-0.149
Eastern Europe	0.161	1.923	0.557	4.610
North America	-0.574	0.898	-1.487	1.718
Latin America	0.239	1.483	0.578	3.357
Other West Asia and North Africa	0.236	2.383	0.713	5.759
Sub-Saharan Africa	0.214	1.450	0.563	3.399
World percentage change	-0.509	0.206	-1.261	0.137

CBAM = carbon border adjustment mechanism, CO_2 = carbon dioxide, ETS = emissions trading system, MT = metric ton, OECD = Organisation for Economic Co-operation and Development, PRC = People's Republic of China.

Sources: ADB calculations using data from Global Trade Analysis Project. GTAP 11 Data Base. https://www.gtap.agecon.purdue.edu/databases/; and International Energy Agency. Data and Statistics. https://www.iea.org/data-and-statistics (both accessed November 2023).

through supply chain linkages. These spillover effects may partially explain the relatively large reductions in GDP in East Asia and Southeast Asia. The extension of the ETS and CBAM to Asia is also estimated to lead to a relatively large amount of labor displacement, and therefore structural change, with labor displacement in developing Asian regions tending to be larger than the global average, with the exception of the Republic of Korea and Southeast Asia (Figure 6.22).

Embedded Emissions Accounting Frameworks

There is a need to develop embedded emissions accounting frameworks (EEFs) for traded products. Approaches to meeting a net zero transition—including carbon pricing and BCA mechanisms—require a consistent and accurate way to measure the emissions embodied in goods and services. Depending on the type of policy and regulation, EEFs will likely account for emissions directly associated with a certain segment of the value chain ("Scope 1" emissions), those associated with the energy produced elsewhere used in that part

of the value chain ("Scope 2" emissions), as well as emissions associated with upstream parts of the value chain (upstream "Scope 3" emissions). Accounting for embedded emissions has only recently started to attract attention. Measuring territorial GHG emissions and constructing national accounts has been a centerpiece of the United Nations Framework Convention on Climate Change (UNFCCC) from the outset. These accounts and the emissions reductions targets associated with them remain the centerpiece of climate policy in most economies. In contrast, governments are only now beginning to develop frameworks to account for emissions embedded in products.

By providing a tool for measuring, reporting, verifying, and regulating, EEFs can lay the foundation for decarbonizing GVCs in both developed and developing economies. Accurately measuring emissions in products is crucial to avoid carbon leakage in a globalized world. Indeed, one of the potential advantages of BCAs is that they can encourage transparency in emissions, with firms required to report those embodied in the products they trade. The development of EEFs can potentially support public and private efforts toward climate change mitigation and improve the efficiency and

Figure 6.22: Extent of Labor Displacement under Different European Union Carbon Border Adjustment Mechanism Modeling Scenarios (% of workforce displaced)

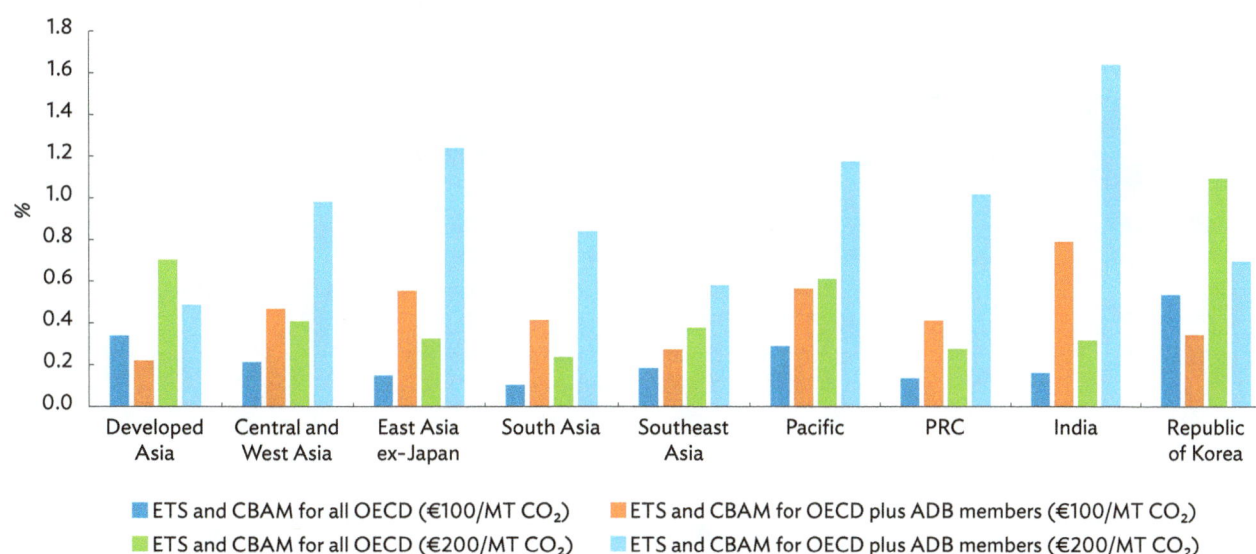

CBAM = carbon border adjustment mechanism, CO_2 = carbon dioxide, ETS = emissions trading system, MT = metric ton, OECD = Organisation for Economic Co-operation and Development, PRC = People's Republic of China.

Sources: ADB calculations using data from Global Trade Analysis Project. GTAP 11 Data Base. https://www.gtap.agecon.purdue.edu/databases/; and International Energy Agency. Data and Statistics. https://www.iea.org/data-and-statistics (both accessed November 2023).

transparency of BCAs. As the basis for firms to voluntarily disclose embodied emissions as environmental, social and governance reporting—or for domestic and eventually international efforts to identify ways to green production and GVCs—EEFs can be powerful tools to support decarbonizing GVCs. Accounting frameworks need to

be carefully designed to ensure they align with domestic frameworks and those of major trading partners. The measurement challenges are further compounded when considering the indirect emissions embodied in goods and services—Scope 2 and Scope 3 emissions.

Box 6.7: Principles of Public Embedded Emissions Accounting Frameworks

The increasing number of private emissions accounting frameworks are creating challenges for consumers and firms alike. These proliferating schemes confuse customers, leaving them unsure whether they are being "greenwashed," while firms absorb increasing costs as they obtain certification or verification from these multiple schemes to retain access to diverse markets. One solution is a public embedded emissions accounting framework (EEF). Aisbett et al. (2024) argue that an EEF should

- have one or more government principals for design, implementation, and operation;

- contribute to producing credible information about emissions embedded in products;

- help create and provide information about embedded emissions specific to products produced at a given facility, during a specified time period; and

- specify acceptable methods used in estimating embedded emissions.[a]

To succeed in supporting climate change mitigation while protecting global trade, a common set of principles is needed to facilitate the development of comparable EEFs by different jurisdictions that potentially increase the ability of independently developed public schemes to be recognized by trade partners. Clear statements of the underlying principles are ubiquitous within existing emissions accounting frameworks, including those by the

Principles Relevant to the Design of Embedded Emissions Accounting Frameworks for Achieving Both Climate Change Mitigation and Free Trade Goals

Principle Source	Definition
Accuracy (CAP and CAL)	True embedded emissions should neither be underestimated or overestimated.
Conservativeness (CAP and CAL)	Where further accuracy cannot reasonably be achieved, assumptions, default values, and alternative methods should be chosen such that the risk of reported emissions (removal) being an underestimation (overestimation) of the true values is minimized.
Monotonicity (CAL)	Embedded emissions accounting systems should not allow actors to decrease their reported emissions in a way that may increase overall emissions.
Nondiscrimination (TLL)	Embedded emissions accounting systems should not generate explicit or implicit advantage or disadvantage for like products, where "like" includes true emissions impacts.
Least restrictive means (TLL)	Embedded emissions accounting systems should be designed to meet the requirements of their intended use in the least trade-restrictive means possible.
Relevance (CAP)	Embedded emissions accounting systems should be designed to support the needs of the intended uses and users.
Subsidiarity (TLL)	Data collection and accounting should be conducted at the lowest level of aggregation and control that is consistent with meeting its intended use.
Transparency (CAP and TLL)	Information should be provided sufficient to allow stakeholders to assess robustness and reliability.

CAP = carbon accounting practice, CAL = carbon accounting literature, TLL = trade law literature.

Source: White et al. (2024).

continued on next page

Box 6.7: continued

Intergovernmental Panel on Climate Change (IPCC), the International Organisation for Standardisation (ISO), and the Greenhouse Gas (GHG) Protocol. Principles can be defined as unspecific prescriptions (Braithwaite 2002), with the box table from White et al. (2024) providing a summary of recent attempts to identify a set of principles based on trade law and carbon accounting practice. If applied to embedded emissions accounting, they could underpin a system that works toward the simultaneous goals of supporting climate change mitigation and free trade.

Principles from carbon accounting practice highlight the importance of accuracy, conservativeness, relevance, and transparency in EEFs. Achieving accuracy in EEFs requires that all emissions within agreed boundaries are counted, that double-counting is avoided, and that data sources for calculations and modeling use the best available figures. Conservativeness is an essential principle when further accuracy cannot reasonably be achieved—due to a lack of data or accounting capacity by a small organization or developing economy. This relatively recent addition to developing principles for carbon accounting arose as a means to promote developing economies' participation (Baker et al. 2010). Conservativeness is important to maintain the environmental integrity of EEFs and prevent the erosion of trust. While it may involve applying default emission factors to some locations where facility-level calculations cannot reasonably be done, appearing like those with less capacity are disadvantaged, it is a compromise between creating a prohibitive burden and actions that risk running counter to climate goals. Relevance requires that EEFs serve the needs of the user, both those reading and producing the emissions accounts. It implies that accounting should include all information necessary to inform consumers, investors, and regulators, and that it should be tied to factors that producers can account for and reasonably influence. In this sense, conservativeness and relevance both address who should be asked to bear which burdens in providing embedded emissions accounts. Finally, transparency requires that sufficient information be provided to allow stakeholders to assess robustness and reliability, and is a key principle in building trust and legitimacy in accounting schemes.

Certain principles from trade law not currently part of carbon accounting practice will be critical in developing EEFs. The principle of nondiscrimination requires that like products are treated alike, and extends to environmental attributes of products in many cases, but not yet definitively to embedded emissions (Charnovitz 2002; Bacchus 2017). There is the potential for non-discrimination to clash with other principles. For example, a system that places a higher (or lower) burden of evidence on products produced in certain locations could be viewed as discriminatory. Given that governance quality (and capacity) varies by location, however, these clauses may be necessary for accuracy or conservativeness. The least restrictive means (LRM), as articulated by the World Trade Organization, says that governments should pursue non-trade policy objectives using the least trade-restrictive means possible (Costinot 2008). For an EEF, the LRM implies minimizing the regulatory burden created by the system, including burdens of cost and time. The LRM thus requires actors to consider the capacities of reporting entities and other economies when setting accounting requirements. Finally, subsidiarity implies that counting and reporting emissions should be done at the lowest level possible while maintaining standards of accuracy. However, this should be balanced against resourcing constraints— not all facilities will have the capacity to rigorously count and report emissions. While national carbon accounting requires national aggregation, embedded emissions accounting holds the option to count distinct "modules" within the supply chain, keeping them visibly separate for traded products (White et al. 2021). This approach could support subsidiarity by allocating reporting responsibility most directly to the emitting entity, while verification and accounting could still be done nationally by public agencies.

ª Acceptable methods can be directly specified or embedded in a scheme, or acceptable externally specified methods may be referenced.

Sources: ADB using Aisbett et al. (2024); Bacchus (2017); Baker et al. (2010); Braithwaite (2002); Charnovitz (2002); Costinot (2008); and White et al. (2021, 2024).

EEFs intended to be used in conjunction with trade-related carbon policies face a larger number of design constraints than those used for other purposes. EEFs for use in trade-related carbon policies obviously need to be designed in alignment with trade rules (including those governed by the WTO). But they should also try to align with the EEFs and regulations of their trading partners. The complexity arising from the link between trade-related climate policies and EEFs can be illustrated by the example of the Australian Government's Guarantee of Origin Scheme for Hydrogen (White et al. 2021). Key drivers of the scheme were to enable export market access and attract foreign investment. In addition to providing trusted information to private markets, the scheme holds the potential to lower the regulatory burden faced by Australian firms wishing to export clean hydrogen. This can only happen, however, if it is accepted by overseas regulators. For firms wishing to export to European customers, this means it will need to be recognized by the EU as an acceptable means of calculating CBAM certificate requirements. These examples highlight how the development of EEFs in the context of international trade can quickly become prohibitively complex, especially for governments operating under tight resource constraints. These complexities will only multiply as more, and more complex products are integrated into EEFs and as the number of national EEFs increase. The only feasible and inclusive path forward is for government officials to work together to establish common basic approaches to EEF design. Without global cooperation, an overly complex regime will disadvantage smaller producers and producers from economies with bureaucracies that lack sufficient resources.

Aligning EEF methodologies to those used under an economy's carbon pricing scheme may help avoid trade disputes. Although existing national carbon accounting structures cannot support embedded emissions accounting themselves, building on these structures could be an efficient starting point (Reeve and Aisbett 2022). Firms would face lower participation costs, as existing accounting methods and experience could be used, while governments could reuse investments in policy and digital infrastructure. Economies aspiring to introduce BCAs will need to develop or identify acceptable EEFs to calculate the border adjustment required. However, international trade law requires that the imports exposed to a BCA are afforded "like treatment" to domestic products. Aligning EEF methodologies to those used under the economy's carbon pricing scheme may thus help avoid trade disputes by ensuring that accounting requirements for foreign producers are no more burdensome than those for domestic producers.

Identifying priority products to include in EEFs will determine their success in helping reduce CO$_2$ emissions. Identifying priority products will allow an assessment of products that are in the best current position to maximize utility from an EEF, as well as assessing which products need EEF support to steer them toward a net zero future. Products with relatively large emissions intensities without current decarbonization methods, for example, will uncover a green premium, potentially drawing them into a net zero position. Jackson and Aisbett (2024) identify five relevant dimensions when identifying products to include in an EEF:

(i)   **Emissions relevance.** Products with high emissions footprints and intensities, or products with the potential to displace other products with higher emitting levels should rank highly.

(ii) **Export relevance.** The development of EEFs is being driven in large part by the emergence of trade-related climate policies such as certification schemes and BCAs, highlighting the global relevance of EEFs.

(iii) **Policy relevance.** While public EEFs are being developed primarily in response to trade-related climate policies, if designed well, they can be relevant for a range of domestic and international policy and regulatory efforts. The regulatory burden of these policies will be lower if a single EEF can be used to support a wide range of policies. Thus, it is helpful to prioritize industries for which relevant policies are being developed.

(iv) **Technology readiness.** Decarbonization on a commercial level does not happen at the flick of a switch. Research and development is an integral part to this transition, which takes time and resources. This dimension evaluates the proximity to and effectiveness of low emitting production methods for a product.

(v)   **Regulatory burden.** Developing a unified and reputable EEF is full of challenges and constraints. This dimension forecasts the difficulties associated with a product's embedded emissions calculations, as well as the product's position within supply chains. If downstream, it may be able to adapt upstream input EEFs. If upstream, its EEF could prove important for many other products.

Using a single regulatory instrument across sectors and products creates substantial measurement challenges, especially in agriculture. Single regulatory instruments may apply to both agricultural and nonagricultural products. For example, the EU is increasingly talking about the risk of carbon leakage for agricultural products and the need to extend CBAM to include agriculture: "The inclusion of agricultural products in the scope of the CBAM is all the more important as the agriculture sector will be both directly and indirectly affected by the inclusion of other products, notably fertilizers, steel and aluminum" (European Parliament 2021). Coherent and consistent cross-sectoral regulatory instruments will require coherent and consistent cross-sectoral EEFs. Calculating emissions for agricultural products is more challenging and costly than for extractive and manufactured products. This stems from the importance of carbon pools for calculating carbon emissions from agriculture. There are four main types of carbon pools: above and below ground biomass, dead organic matter in or on soil, soil organic matter, and harvested products that can be further subdivided (Greenhouse Gas Protocol 2014). They act both as sources and as sinks of CO_2 and flow constantly. Carbon sequestered in carbon pools is reversible and eventually emitted back into the atmosphere. Natural variations in biological productivity and decomposition between seasons, years, and locations in the fluxes in and out of carbon pools interact with land management practices (Hurtt et al. 2020). In addition, changes in farm and land management can take decades to reach new equilibriums (Greenhouse Gas Protocol 2014).

Data on emissions due to land use and changes in land use remain fragmented and weak, increasing the measurement uncertainty in some sectors such as agriculture. Variability in calculating agricultural product emissions is much higher than for extractive and manufactured products. While calculating CO_2 emissions from fossil fuels and industrial activities can be done with relatively high confidence, accurately accounting for non-CO_2 gases and emissions in the land sector is more complicated (Luers et al. 2022). Currently, land-use emissions data are neither accurate, complete nor consistent, particularly for low- and middle-income economies (Dittmer et al. 2023; Friedlingstein et al. 2022; Grassi et al. 2021; Rosenstock and Wilkes 2021). Relative to fossil-based CO_2 emissions, emission estimates from land-use change are characterized by substantial spatial and annual variability. Historically, this has led to relatively poor accuracy in emissions accounting. It has been estimated that these uncertainties typically amount to approximately 43.8%, whereas fossil CO_2 emissions have a much lower uncertainty of 5.2% (Friedlingstein et al. 2022; Ganzenmüller et al. 2022). Some of these uncertainties stem from different terminologies and definitions, and diverse model assumptions and parameters. These uncertainties may be substantially reduced by developing uniform and widely accepted public approaches in EEFs. However, much of the uncertainty is intrinsic to the variability of biological processes and the importance of carbon pools. Resolving these sources of uncertainty will require ever increasing temporal and spatial disaggregation of measurement. This is currently happening thanks to better technology, particularly satellite imagery and analysis (Burke et al. 2021).

The rising importance of negative emissions has implications for the design of EEFs. Negative emissions technologies and services, where carbon is removed from the atmosphere and locked away in storage or a stable product, will be an important component of climate change mitigation for the rest of this century (IPCC 2022b). As with emissions attributable to a product, the absolute emissions removed from the atmosphere by CO_2 removal (as a negative emission), could be recorded transparently within EEF systems. To support rigorous accounting of negative emissions services, EEFs additionally require careful tracking and information on attributes of storage or utilization, including the type, expected timescale, and storage location (White, Aisbett, and Widnyana 2023). These aspects will be important for the integrity of EEF systems and will be a critical component of the information needed by purchasers to decide whether a given product meets their emissions requirements.

New technologies can secure the benefits of EEFs by forging trust and accountability. Even with appropriate accounting frameworks in place, trust, engagement, and transparency are issues that new technology can help alleviate. The widespread introduction of blockchain technology, for example, could potentially be an important complement to EEFs (UNFCCC 2017). The immutability and transparency blockchain technologies provide can help combat climate change in various ways, by improving the trust in tracking and monitoring GHG emissions, by transparently recording a firm's carbon footprint, and by monitoring and reporting GHG emissions reduction efforts.

Trade Policy, Preferential Trade Agreements, and the Decarbonization of Global Value Chains

Trade Policy as Climate Change Policy

Trade policy can be effective in promoting climate change mitigation and adaptation. Measures aimed at lowering tariff and nontariff barriers on climate-friendly products and services, reducing and removing subsidies and other support for carbon-intensive products and sectors, and encouraging the transfer of green technologies are some of the important ways to mitigate and adapt to the effects of climate change. These policies can help economies diversify into greener sectors and away from carbon-intensive sectors (UNFCCC 2016). Regional cooperation and integration can further encourage the decarbonization of GVCs, with environmental provisions in preferential trade agreements (PTAs) leading to greater cooperation in meeting climate commitments.

Current trade policies favor carbon-intensive imports. The IPCC (2022a) highlights that tariff and nontariff barriers tend to be lower in high-carbon-intensive sectors, with these goods traded more than low-carbon-intensive goods (Le Moigne and Ossa 2021). GVCs are important here, with trade barriers tending to be lower on upstream products, and upstream products tending to be more carbon-intensive than downstream products. Those sectors providing raw materials and intermediate goods tend to be the highest emitters of CO_2 per unit of value-added, yet they tend to face lower tariff and nontariff barriers compared with lower carbon-intensive activities (Shapiro 2021). These differences often arise for reasons unrelated to trade policy—such as lobbying activities—but can have a large impact on the structure of trade. The bias has been estimated as equivalent to a negative carbon price of $90 per MT of CO_2, with recent evidence suggesting that removing these trade policy biases could both increase global real income and reduce global carbon emissions (Shapiro 2021).

There are often strong linkages between climate mitigation policies and trade. Trade-related climate change mitigation policies raise concerns about discrimination between partners and between imported goods and domestic substitutes. Yet, these policies can also encourage trade to become greener (Fadly and Fontes 2019; Shahnazi and Shabani 2019). Trade with economies with strong environmental regulations can be a source of climate-friendly goods, services, and technology, which can help climate mitigation efforts. Trade can also raise ambitions on environmental standards and regulations, with firms exporting to highly regulated economies required to develop or adopt the higher standards that become market entry requirements. While meeting standards may increase costs for firms, they may also be an external force pressuring economies without high standards, thereby enhancing their environmental regulations (Crippa et al. 2016; Perkins and Neumayer 2012).

Carbon policies have trade implications and can be a source of trade tensions. Certain policies aimed at climate change mitigation can lead to trade tensions. One example is subsidies with local content requirements. While they may hope to encourage investment in local climate-friendly infrastructure and technology and build competitive innovation capabilities, they can also restrict trade (IPCC 2022a). These concerns have been raised with recent industrial strategies enacted by many economies. Legal challenges to subsidies have also emerged, with the EU, for example, complaining to the WTO about the UK policy of awarding subsidies for offshore wind projects (European Commission 2022).

Reducing trade policy distortions on climate-friendly goods, services, and technologies can be an important way to reduce emissions. By encouraging trade in low-carbon-intensive products, trade policy can help increase global access to clean goods and services and encourage competition in producing these goods and services. Given the non-discriminatory treatment of foreign products and the WTO's most favored nation (MFN) principle, reducing trade barriers on clean goods further broadens the spread of clean technologies. More generally, reducing trade distortions can provide appropriate incentives for economies with technological know-how to specialize in producing clean goods and services. Through these effects, trade policy can shift global demand toward low-carbon-intensive goods and services and encourage the transition toward low-carbon-intensive production. To reduce the barriers on climate-friendly goods, agreement on a set of products that are considered climate friendly would be needed, although there has been little progress since the original attempts by the Asia-Pacific Economic Cooperation (see, for example, APEC 2021). Also important will be to ensure nontariff measures are an important component of any liberalization on climate-friendly goods. Jakob et al. (2022) point out that nontariff measures can play an important role in limiting access to climate-friendly goods—as packaging and labeling requirements, technical standards and norms add substantial costs to trade in climate-friendly goods. In addition, measures related to labor market regulations—like visa and work permit requirements—can potentially limit trade in environmental services, including the sustainable management of energy, water, and forest resources.

Trade policies also play an important role in economies' strategies to decarbonize. According to WTO (2022a) and UNCTAD (2016), trade-related measures pervade the Nationally Determined Contributions (NDCs) submitted by parties to the UNFCCC. Despite this, the studies argue that NDCs do not integrate trade strategies and perspectives systematically. Environmental notifications and measures reported to the WTO are also rising. According to data from the WTO's environmental

database, the number of environmental measures and notifications reported by WTO members increased during 2009–2021 (Figure 6.23). The number of environment-related measures increased from 829 in 2009 to 2,250 in 2021, while the number of notifications increased from 480 to 931 over the same period.

Notifications to the WTO on climate change objectives have been rising over time. The WTO's environmental database also includes information on notifications directly or indirectly linked to climate change, including those on afforestation or reforestation, air pollution reduction, ozone layer protection, climate change mitigation and adaptation, energy conservation and efficiency, and alternative and renewable energy. While there is great variation in the number of notifications each year, the number of climate-related objectives have been rising over time, both in absolute terms and relative to other policies notified (WTO 2022a). The number of climate-related notifications increased from 413 in 2009 to 939 in 2021 (Figure 6.24). Considering the different subcategories, the share of notifications related to climate change mitigation and adaptation increased from 16.7% to 22.0%, while the shares related to air pollution reduction declined from 14.5% to 10.0% and alternative and renewable energy from 28.3% to 24.6%. According to the IPCC (2022a), most notifications on trade-related climate change mitigation involve support measures and technical regulations and conformity assessment procedures, such as those related to regulatory requirements to reduce use of fluorocarbons, preferential tax treatment for energy saving and new energy vehicles, and use of import licenses to regulate lighting with minimum energy performance standards (IPCC 2022a).

Preferential Trade Agreements and the Decarbonization of Global Value Chains

Given the current challenges for global cooperation on climate change issues, PTAs can play an important role in making GVCs more climate friendly. The number of PTAs has expanded rapidly since the 1990s, with their breadth also increasing. Data from the World Bank show

Figure 6.23: World Trade Organization Members' Environment-Related Notifications and Measures (number)

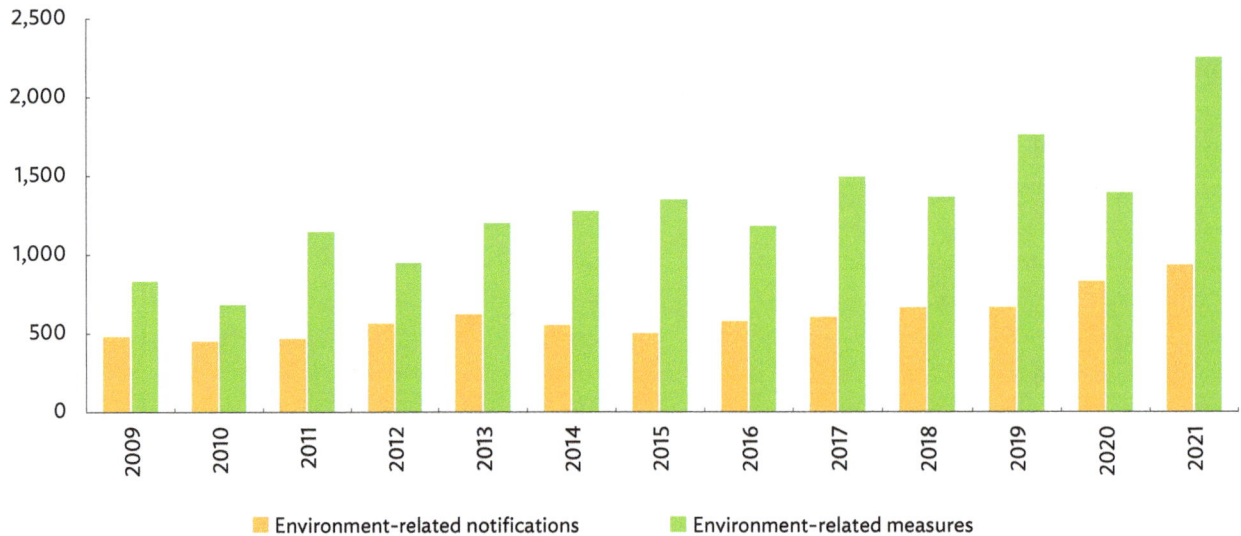

Note: Number of environment-related notifications and measures notified to the World Trade Organization, further split by category.

Source: World Trade Organization. Environmental Database. https://edb.wto.org/charts (accessed November 2023).

Figure 6.24: Number of Climate Change Objectives by Type

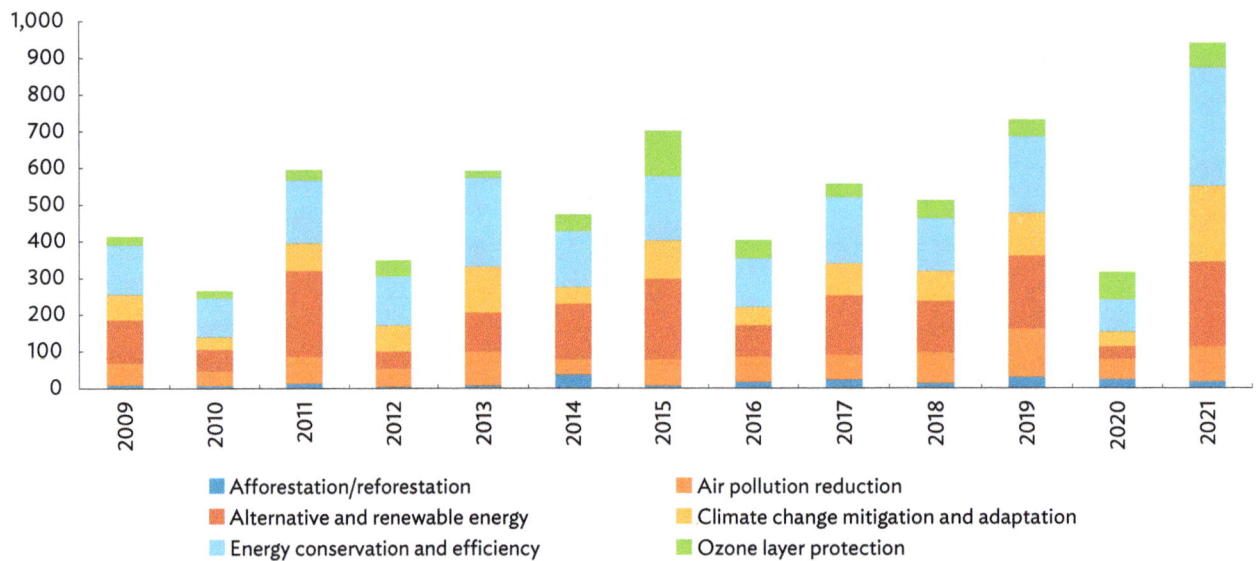

Notes: The number of objectives notified to the World Trade Organization (WTO) on six categories linked directly or indirectly to climate change: afforestation/reforestation, air pollution reduction, ozone layer protection, climate change mitigation and adaptation, energy conservation and efficiency, and alternative and renewable energy. Classification follows WTO (2022a).

Source: WTO. Environmental Database. https://edb.wto.org/charts (accessed August 2023).

the rapid rise in the number of PTAs, especially since the mid-1990s (Figure 6.25). This increase is associated with an increase in the breadth of agreements, with data showing that the average percentage of policy areas covered (from a list of 52 policy areas identified in Hofmann, Osnago, and Ruta 2017) increased from 25% in 1996 to 36% in 2015.

Figure 6.25: Number and Breadth of Preferential Trade Agreements

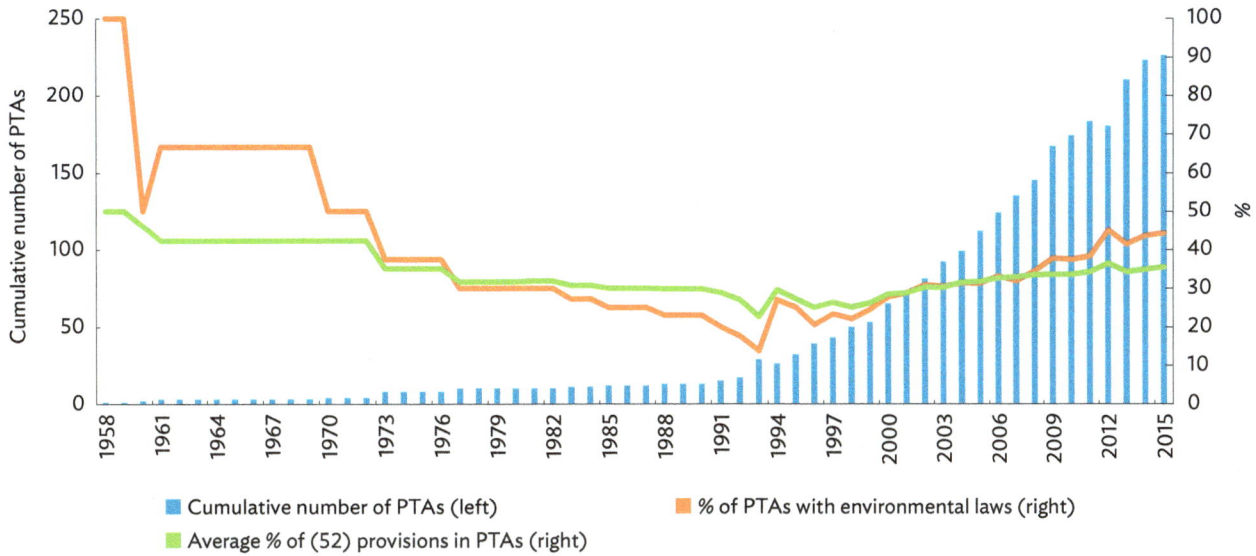

Legend:
- Cumulative number of PTAs (left)
- % of PTAs with environmental laws (right)
- Average % of (52) provisions in PTAs (right)

PTA = preferential trade agreement.

Note: The database includes information on 279 PTAs signed by 189 economies during 1958–2015, which includes all PTAs in force and notified to the World Trade Organization.

Source: Hofmann, Osnago, and Ruta (2017).

Figure 6.26: Environmental Provisions in Trade Agreements

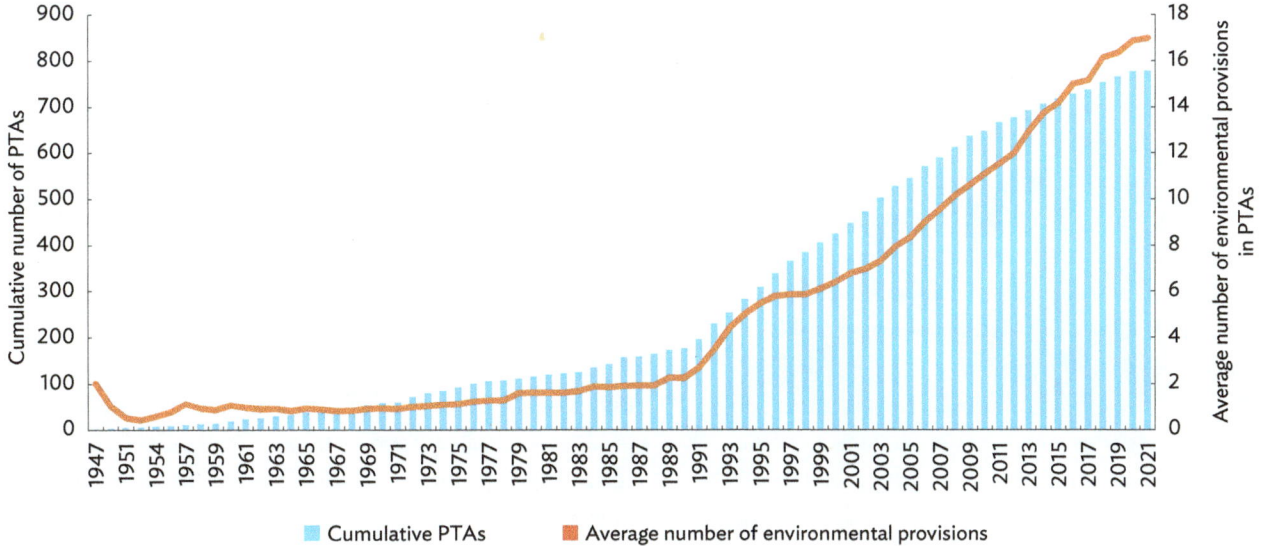

Legend:
- Cumulative PTAs
- Average number of environmental provisions

PTA = preferential trade agreement.

Note: The Trade and Environment Database (TREND) of Morin, Dür, and Lechner (2018) identifies 298 environmental provisions in a broader set of 775 trade agreements, including World Trade Organization trade facilitation agreements.

Source: Morin, Dür, and Lechne (2018).

Environmental provisions are an increasing feature of trade agreements. The share of PTAs with provisions related to environmental laws have also increased, from 21% in 1996 to 44% in 2015. Those explicitly promoting trade in environmental goods and services are increasingly incorporated into PTAs, with recent agreements further encouraging cooperation on sustainable transport (WTO 2022b). Data from the

Trade and Environment Database (Morin, Dür, and Lechne 2018) indicate that the average number of environmental provisions has increased relatively rapidly since the early 1990s (Figure 6.26) from an average of around two provisions in 1990 (out of 298 provisions) to around 17 in 2021. While 13% of agreements do not include provisions and 46% include less than five, 11% include more than 50 provisions related to the environment. These cover efforts to liberalize trade in certain goods and services (e.g., in green products) and to restrict trade by raising trade costs (e.g., for dirty products).

Environmental provisions in PTAs have ambiguous effects on GVCs and on trade in CO$_2$ emissions. By lowering the cost of trade, PTAs should enhance trade between partners. Conversely, by increasing relative trade costs for nonmembers, they can lead to trade diversion, with trade shifting from nonmembers to PTA members (Viner 1950). Also, PTAs (and especially broader PTAs) often include nondiscriminatory provisions, potentially reducing trade costs for nonmembers and creating a positive spillover or negative trade diversion effect (Mattoo, Mulabdic, and Ruta 2022; Baldwin 2014; Baldwin and Low 2009). Moreover, a proportion of the environmental provisions involve potentially higher trade costs (e.g., those regarding trade in dirty goods), which can reduce trade among PTA partners and potentially redirect trade to nonmembers. In general, therefore, the relationship between PTAs (and the provisions within PTAs) and trade, especially trade in particular types of products, remains ambiguous. This also extends to CO$_2$ emissions embodied in PTA trade. Increases in PTA trade should lead to increased emissions. But if PTAs alter the structure of trade toward green products and away from dirty goods—or if they encourage a shift to cleaner production methods—their effect on trade in CO$_2$ emissions could be negative.

By encouraging GVC trade, the presence and breadth of a PTA are positively associated with trade in CO$_2$ emissions through GVCs. Estimating the impact of the presence and breadth of a PTA on the CO$_2$ emissions

embodied in GVC trade shows that PTAs are associated with an increase in CO$_2$ emissions traded through GVCs (Figure 6.27). Specifically, the presence of a PTA is associated with an increase in CO$_2$ emissions trade through GVCs of around 6.7%, with a movement from the narrowest to the broadest PTA associated with an increase in CO$_2$ emissions trade through GVCs of 5.9%.[69] This increase in CO$_2$ emissions embodied in GVC trade is driven almost exclusively by scale effects due to an increase in the level of GVC trade (the value added that is exported through GVCs).[70] For PTA presence, the level of GVC trade accounts for 89% of the increase in CO$_2$ emissions in GVC trade, with an increase in the CO$_2$ intensity of GVC trade accounting for the remaining 11%. For PTA breadth, the impact of breadth on CO$_2$ intensity in GVCs is negative, such that the scale effect of GVC trade accounts for more than 100% (104%) of the increase in CO$_2$ emissions in GVCs.

Environmental provisions within PTAs are associated with reduced CO$_2$ emissions embodied in GVC trade between PTA partners. A higher share of environmental provisions within PTAs is found to be associated with lower levels of CO$_2$ emissions trade between PTA partners (Figure 6.28). A higher share of environmental provisions in PTAs is also associated with a reduced level of GVC trade as well as greater emissions intensity of GVC trade—which partially offsets the negative scale effect of environmental provisions. Specifically, a one standard deviation increase in the share of environmental provisions included in a PTA is associated with a reduction in CO$_2$ emissions in GVC trade of around 0.24%, with the same increase lowering GVC trade by 0.47% and increasing CO$_2$ intensity by 0.23%. Differences exist when considering trade restricting and trade liberalizing environmental provisions within PTAs. While a higher share of trade restricting provisions reduces CO$_2$ emissions in GVCs through both scale and intensity effects, trade liberalizing provisions reduce emissions through a scale effect but increase them through an intensity effect. A one standard deviation increase in the share of trade restricting environmental provisions in PTAs

---

[69]   PTA breadth is defined as the number of core provisions identified by Hofmann, Osnago, and Ruta (2017), the maximum being 18, with the variable normalized to lie between 0 and 1.

[70]   Using the identity $CO_2 = (CO_2/GVC) \times GVC$, with CO_2 being the emissions embodied in GVC exports and GVC the level of GVC exports, and rewriting as $\ln CO_2 = \ln GVC + \ln(CO_2/GVC)$, the level of CO$_2$ emissions in GVC exports can be decomposed into a scale effect (the level of GVC exports) and an intensity effect (the ratio of emissions to GVC exports).

Figure 6.27: Estimated Impact of a Preferential Trade Agreement on Global Value Chain Trade

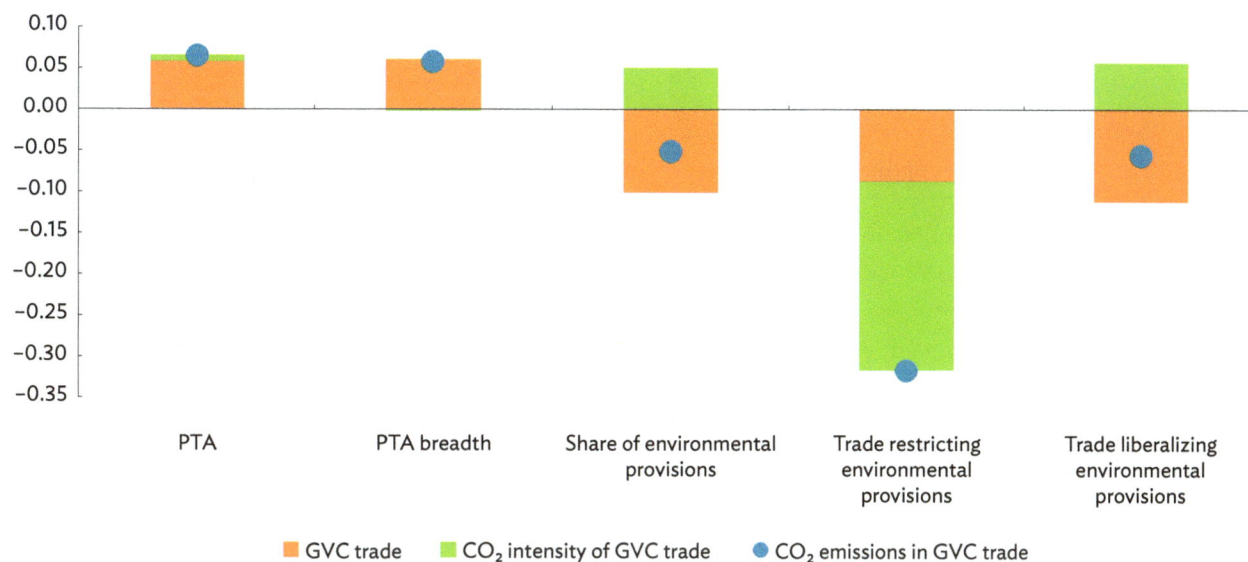

CO$_2$ = carbon dioxide, GVC = global value chain, PTA = preferential trade agreement.

Notes: The figure reports the estimated coefficient on PTA variables from a structural gravity model of (i) the log of the bilateral export of CO$_2$ emissions embodied in GVC trade, (ii) the log of the bilateral export of value-added embodied in GVC trade, and (iii) the log of the CO$_2$ intensity of GVC trade (the ratio of CO$_2$ emissions in GVCs to exports of value added in GVCs). As $\ln CO_2 = \ln GVC + \ln(CO_2/GVC)$, where GVC refers to value added embodied in GVC exports, and given that the regression method (ordinary least squares) is a linear operator, the approach allows for decomposing the effect of PTAs on CO$_2$ emissions in GVCs into a scale effect (on the level of GVC trade) and an intensity effect (on the ratio of CO$_2$ emissions to value added in GVC trade). Trade in CO$_2$ emissions in GVCs is constructed using the approach described in Box 6.3. In addition to the PTA variables, the model includes economy-pair, exporter-time, and importer-time fixed effects. In specifications where environmental provisions are included, the PTA breadth variable is also included so the results on the environmental provisions variables should be interpreted as conditional on a given level of PTA breadth. Similarly, the share of environmental provisions variable is included alongside the trade restricting and trade liberalizing variables.

Sources: ADB calculations using data from Eora Global Supply Chain Database. https://worldmrio.com/eora26/ (accessed November 2023); Hofmann, Osnago, and Ruta (2017); and Morin, Dür, and Lechne (2018).

is associated with a reduction in CO$_2$ emissions in GVCs of 1.2%, with the scale effect accounting for 0.34 percentage points and the intensity effect 0.90 percentage points. These results suggest that trade restricting provisions can reorient the structure of trade between PTA partners. A similar increase in the share of trade liberalizing provisions is associated with a reduction in emissions in GVC trade of 0.37%, with GVC trade reduced by 0.74% and emissions intensity increased by 0.37%.

In addition to PTAs, other forms of regional cooperation can also be important drivers in decarbonizing production. In 2023, for example, members of the Central Asia Regional Economic Cooperation (CAREC) Program agreed to work together to cut GHG emissions, build resilience to climate change, and help members achieve their Paris Agreement commitments. The "Regional Action on Climate: A Vision for CAREC" highlights the need to enhance collaboration and coordinate with development partners to support the

region's climate agenda. It includes the use of renewable energy sources, the energy transition, and innovative financing solutions, among others, as means of helping decarbonize the region's production. The vision further emphasizes the importance of identifying opportunities to reduce the carbon footprint of regional transport services and improving regional connectivity.

Beyond Trade Policy—Additional Ways to Decarbonize Global Value Chains

While carbon pricing and regional cooperation can drive the decarbonization of GVCs, policies involving subsidies and technology diffusion provide other opportunities, with multilateral development banks able to further support the greening of production. Without a strong expansion in geographic coverage, BCAs will unlikely be enough to reduce emissions in GVCs by the amounts needed or encourage non-participants to change their behavior. With the exception of the few economies with substantial export shares in the sectors covered, BCAs are considered unlikely to provide the necessary incentives to join a climate club (Jakob 2023). Thus, they will be limited in how much their policies can incentivize trade partners to adopt climate policies. Regional cooperation, and importantly PTAs, can encourage more ambitious climate goals, especially where the possibility of multilateral cooperation appears increasingly challenging. Regional cooperation is limited in its coverage and risks being driven by the member with the weakest climate ambitions, however. Other policies and areas also need to be considered when identifying approaches to decarbonize GVCs.

The structure of industry subsidies encourages carbon-intensive production, particularly in energy. According to the International Energy Agency (2021), fossil fuel subsidies reached $440 billion in 2021. They support carbon-intensive production and consumption, exacerbating the climate crisis, and further reduce the competitiveness of renewable energy sources. However, subsidy reforms will likely have far-reaching effects. They will likely affect trade competitiveness by raising the price of intermediate inputs in energy-intensive sectors, such as steelmaking, petrochemicals, and aluminum (Burniaux, Château, and Sauvage 2011; Cockburn, Robichaud, and Tiberti 2018; Ellis 2010; Jensen and Tarr 2003). In addition, removing subsidies may encourage firms to substitute certain energy inputs for alternative sources and improve their resource efficiency (Rentschler, Kornejew, and Bazilian 2017). Jakob et al. (2022) argue that the WTO can play an important role here, strengthening "transparency through improved notification by its members, counternotification by other members, and by addressing fossil fuel subsidy reform in the Trade Policy Review Mechanism." A new category of prohibited subsidies could be agreed upon, potentially limited to a subset of fossil fuel subsidies, based on their trade and/or environmental effects and considering the

challenges faced by developing economies in reforming subsidies. Given the WTO's current challenges, and as acknowledged by many others, subsets of economies could proceed with developing plurilateral agreements rather than waiting for all WTO members to agree on fossil fuel subsidies (Bacchus 2021).

The price of green technology, particularly for energy production, has decreased substantially, with global competition providing further opportunities for green technological change. In recent years, the price per kilowatt-hour of energy has dropped substantially across a range of green technologies, with the drop in solar power cost particularly strong in recent years (Figure 6.28). This makes green energy highly competitive in terms of price relative to energy produced by fossil fuels.[71] Moreover, recent policies such as the US Inflation Reduction Act and the EU's mission-oriented approach to innovation aim to encourage research and development in renewable energy along with climate adaptation and mitigation. These initiatives offer an opportunity to encourage competition in developing new climate-related technologies that can help mitigate climate change using technology-based solutions (Mattoo and Subramianian 2013). If these technologies, including low-cost batteries and carbon capture and storage techniques, are more easily spread to developing economies, economies may be able to meet their energy needs without increasing CO_2 emissions. The possibility of opening green windows of opportunity in developing economies (UNCTAD 2023) through technological change, along with changes to public institutions and markets, may allow developing economies to quickly catch up and potentially leapfrog in applying green technologies, avoiding development of a carbon-based production system. GVCs, particularly the approaches of lead MNEs, can be important in decarbonizing GVCs and production more broadly through technology diffusion and adoption. Given the sectoral structure of developing Asian economies in GVCs, shifting to green energy sources can be an important source of GVCs emission efficiency.

---

[71]   While the price of green energy is highly competitive, energy produced through green sources remains relatively small. Scaling up these technologies to meet total energy needs may involve substantial costs and challenges.

Figure 6.28: Levelized Cost of Energy of Alternative Renewable Energy Sources ($/kWh)

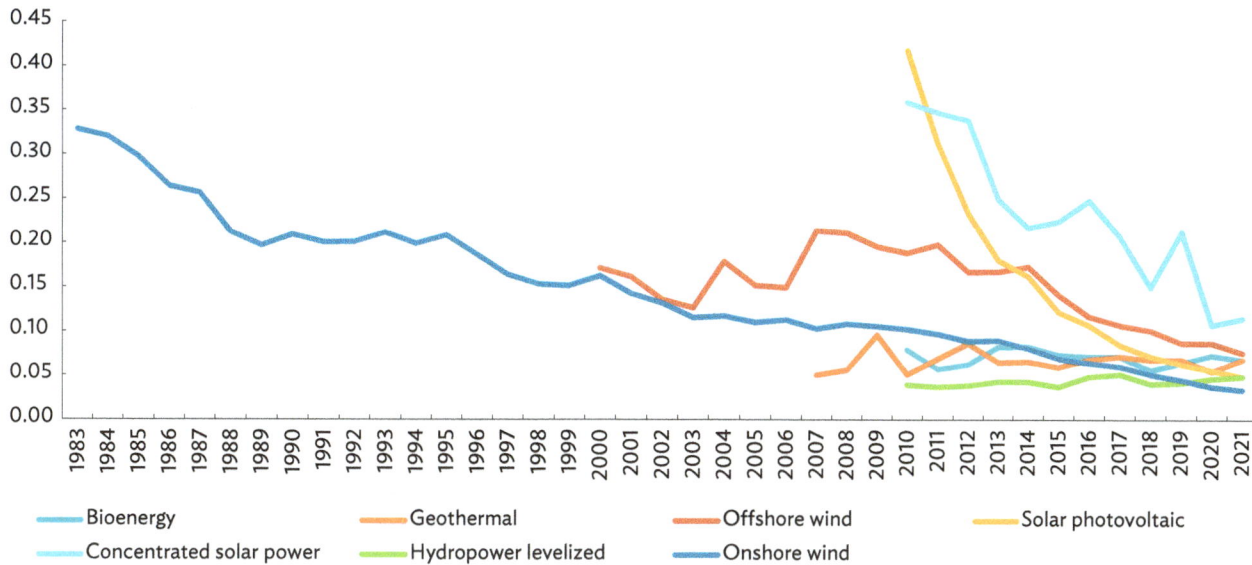

kWh = kilowatt-hour.

Notes: Data on the average cost per unit of energy generated across the lifetime of a new power plant. Data are expressed in constant 2021 United States dollars.

Source: Our World in Data. Levelized Cost of Energy by Technology. https://ourworldindata.org/grapher/levelized-cost-of-energy.

The diffusion of technology that improves CO_2 emissions intensities can also help reduce global emissions, while stimulating international trade in the process. Adopting the CGE model used to consider the impacts of CBAM, it is further possible to study the effects of a convergence in CO_2 emissions intensities across economies. Specifically, the effect of allowing for a partial convergence of the emissions intensity of these economies toward the average OECD CO_2 intensity (50% convergence)—in the policy scenario that extends CBAM to the rest of the OECD and to ADB regional members at a carbon price of €200 per MT—is examined. With the exceptions of developed Asia and the Republic of Korea, both included in the OECD group, and relative to the baseline, GDP is estimated to increase across the different Asian regions, with relatively large increases in Central and West Asia, India, the PRC, and Southeast Asia (Table 6.11). These changes reflect the relatively high CO_2 emissions intensities in these regions, with a convergence to 50% of the OECD level implying a significant decline in emissions intensity. Compared to the baseline, exports are also found to increase in most Asian regions, with the exceptions of developed Asia and the Pacific. Relative to the earlier scenarios, the extent of labor displacement is also found to be large when allowing for a convergence in emissions

intensities, suggesting that the convergence could lead to substantial structural changes. Finally, in terms of global CO_2 emissions, while the extended CBAM with a carbon price of €200 per MT is predicted to lower global emissions by 14.9%, when a partial convergence in emissions intensity is also allowed for, global emissions are predicted to drop by 17.2%. These results highlight the importance of technology diffusion and other means of improving emissions intensities. While the effects of CBAM often involve a trade-off between emissions reduction and trade and GVC activity, this exercise suggests that improvements in emissions intensities could mitigate this trade-off, making it possible for both emissions to fall and exports to rise in response to emissions intensity convergence.

Multilateral development banks are an important source of finance for climate change mitigation and adaptation, though current financing falls short of what is needed. Perhaps the worst bottleneck in decarbonizing production is finance, with the climate finance gap particularly pronounced in developing economies. Multilateral development banks (MDBs) already play an important role in providing climate finance, using their ability to mobilize finance cheaply on capital markets. They accounted for $51 billion in climate finance to low and middle-income economies in 2021 (EIB 2022). Initiatives such as ADB's commitment for at least 75% of its operations to support climate change by 2030 (ADB 2023c) further signal the importance of climate change and climate finance in MDB activities. Innovative financing mechanisms such as ADB's Innovative Finance Facility for Climate Asia and the Pacific, which will use partner guarantees for leverage, could accelerate billions of dollars in much-needed climate change funding.

In addition to increasing the value of climate change funds, MDBs will need to ensure they are deployed more efficiently and effectively. To use resources effectively, MDBs need to direct these resources toward sustainable activities, which requires them to appropriately define sustainable activities and assess and track the impact of their investments (St George and Marten 2023). Various challenges must be addressed, including a lack of capacity to evaluate the returns to green technologies and projects. This reflects both a lack of knowledge on the environmental impact of the technology and appropriate ways to measure the return on investments, the increased risk associated

with new business models serving climate-friendly growth, and on choosing the most appropriate financial instruments. MDBs will need to develop innovative tools to evaluate potential projects. This will allow them to build a pipeline of climate-related projects, develop a knowledge-base on successful projects (for capacity building within MDBs and governments in developing economies), de-risk climate projects to attract private investment, and explore new and innovative financing options to support investment in new and innovative climate technologies. MDBs can also help mitigate the financial risks associated with climate projects, potentially crowding-in private sector investment. An important component will be developing robust monitoring and evaluation systems, using common standards to monitor and evaluate projects, such as those for climate mitigation finance tracking (ADB 2021).

Beyond climate finance, MDBs can be an important source of technical support, capacity building, and policy advice, ensuring that developing economies are investing in green infrastructure. MDBs can assist economies to build the capacity to design, implement, and

Table 6.11: Predicted Changes in Macroeconomic Variables in Response to Carbon Dioxide Emissions Intensity

	Change in GDP (%)	Change in Exports (%)	Labor Force Displacement (% of workforce displacement)
Developed Asia	-1.29	-4.31	0.86
Central and West Asia	12.07	6.38	2.76
East Asia ex-Japan	0.69	-1.04	1.42
South Asia	1.18	7.67	1.36
Southeast Asia	5.20	2.67	1.50
Pacific	3.62	-4.98	1.63
PRC	6.33	0.27	1.41
India	7.68	0.40	2.57
Republic of Korea	-0.86	-2.23	1.25
European Union	-1.16	-1.54	0.91
OECD Europe	-0.74	-2.47	0.73
Eastern Europe	15.91	9.70	3.37
North America	1.90	-0.65	0.47
Latin America	1.71	-4.04	0.92
Other West Asia and North Africa	2.83	-6.15	1.75
Sub-Saharan Africa	1.38	-7.48	1.16
World percentage change	2.30	-3.48	1.08

GDP = gross domestic product, OECD = Organisation for Economic Co-operation and Development, PRC = People's Republic of China.

Sources: ADB calculations using data from Global Trade Analysis Project. GTAP 11 Data Base. https://www.gtap.agecon.purdue.edu/databases/; and International Energy Agency. Data and Statistics. https://www.iea.org/data-and-statistics (both accessed November 2023).

monitor climate change mitigation projects, and provide training and technical support to ensure effective project management and sustainable outcomes. By assisting in the design and implementation of climate-related projects, MDBs can help economies develop projects that both reduce emissions and enhance socioeconomic development. MDBs also have an important role to play in offering policy advice that helps economies create and implement effective climate change mitigation policies. MDBs can also use their convening power as a platform for exchanging knowledge and best practices among economies.

Technology transfer, especially in the context of GVCs, is another area where MDBs can play a role. Access to green infrastructure will become increasingly important for lead firms in GVCs, both in response to more aggressive climate policies of different economies and to the increasing relevance of environmental, social, and governance commitments. MDBs can help facilitate sustainable investments along value chains, assist with the spread of green technologies and ensure appropriate standards are in place (UNEP 2022). Adopting common principles for accounting and tracking climate finance by MDBs can be useful in ensuring climate finance is targeted appropriately (ADB 2021). They can also help ensure transparency and traceability of CO_2 emissions in GVCs. One important challenge in developing EEFs, for example, is the difficulty in ensuring alignment with trade rules and with those of diverse trade partners. MDBs can work to help create an alignment mechanism through their capacity-building activities in green trade facilitation, with the strong potential to help in decarbonizing GVCs. By doing this, MDBs can play a role both in decarbonizing GVCs and cementing their continued role as development escalator for developing economies.

References

Asian Development Bank (ADB). 2017. *Meeting Asia's Infrastructure Needs*. Manila.

———. 2021. *Common Principles for Climate Mitigation Finance Tracking*. Manila.

———. 2023a. *Asia in the Global Transition to Net Zero: Asian Development Outlook 2023 Thematic Report*. Manila.

———. 2023b. *Asian Economic Integration Report 2023: Trade, Investment, and Climate Change in Asia and the Pacific*. Manila.

———. 2023c. *Climate Change Action Plan 2023–2030*. Manila.

Aguiar, A., M. Chepeliev, E. Corong, R. McDougall, and D. van der Mensbrugghe. 2019. The GTAP Data Base: Version 10. *Journal of Global Economic Analysis*. 4 (1). pp. 1–27.

Aisbett, A., H. Aslam, J. Borevitz, S. Burkitbayeva, C. Jackson, J. McQueen, O. Pearce, and L. White. 2024. Public Embedded Emissions Accounting Frameworks to Support the Asian Net Zero Transition. Background Paper for the *Asian Economic Integration Report 2024* Theme Chapter on "Decarbonizing Global Value Chains." Manuscript.

Antràs, P. 2020. Conceptual Aspects of Global Value Chains. *World Bank Economic Review*. 34 (3). pp. 551–574.

Antweiler, W., B. Copeland, and M.S. Taylor. 2001. Is Free Trade Good for the Environment? *American Economic Review*. 91 (4). pp. 877–908.

Asia-Pacific Economic Cooperation (APEC). 2021. A Review of the APEC List of Environmental Goods. *APEC Policy Support Unit Policy Brief*. No. 41. Singapore.

Arslanalp, S., R. Koepke, A. Sozzi, and J. Verschuur. 2023. Climate Change is Disrupting Global Trade. *International Monetary Fund Blog*. 15 November. https://www.imf.org/en/Blogs/Articles/2023/11/15/climate-change-is-disrupting-global-trade.

Bacchus, J. 2017. *The Case for a WTO Climate Waiver: Special Report*. Waterloo: Centre for International Governance Innovation.

———. 2021. Legal Issues with the European Carbon Border Adjustment Mechanism. Briefing Paper. No. 125. 9 August. San Francisco: CATO Institute.

Baker, D.J., G. Richards, A. Grainger, P. Gonzalez, S. Brown, R. DeFries, A. Held, J. Kellndorfer, P. Ndunda, D. Ojima, P.E. Skrovseth, C.J. Souza, and F. Stolle. 2010. Achieving Forest Carbon Information with Higher Certainty: A Five-Part Plan. *Environmental Science and Policy*. 13 (3). pp. 249–260.

Baldwin, R. 2011. Trade and Industrialisation after Globalisation's 2nd Unbundling: How Building and Joining a Supply Chain are Different and Why It Matters. *National Bureau for Economic Research Working Paper*. No. 17716. Cambridge: NBER.

Baldwin, R.E. 2014. *Multilateralising 21st Century Regionalism*. Global Forum on Trade: Reconciling Regionalism and Multilateralism in a Post-Bali World. Paris: OECD Conference Centre.

Baldwin, R.E. and P. Low. 2009. *Multilateralizing Regionalism: Challenges for the Global Trading System*. Geneva: World Trade Organization.

Barrett, S. and A. Dannenberg. 2016. An Experiment Investigation into 'Pledge and Review' in Climate Negotiations. *Climatic Change*. 138 (1). pp. 339-351.

Babatunde, K.A., A.A. Begum, and F.F. Said. 2017. Application of Computable General Equilibrium (CGE) to Climate Change Mitigation Policy: A Systemic Review. *Renewable and Sustainable Energy Reviews*. 78. pp. 61–71.

Beaufils, T., H. Ward, M. Jakob, and L. Wenz. 2023. Assessing Different European Carbon Border Adjustment Mechanism Implementations and Their Impact on Trade Partners. Communications Earth and Environment. 4 (131). pp. 1–9.

Bekkers, E., J.F. Francois, and H. Rojas-Romagosa. 2018. Melting Ice Caps and the Economic Impact of Opening the Northern Sea Route. *The Economic Journal*. 128 (610). pp. 1095–1127.

Bekkers, E., E. Corong, J.F. Francois, and H. Rojas-Romagosa. 2023. A Ricardian Trade Structure in CGE: Modeling Eaton-Kortum Based Trade with GTAP. *Journal of Global Economic Analysis*. 8 (2). pp. 1–59.

Bellora, C. and L. Fontagné. 2023. EU in Search of a Carbon Border Adjustment Mechanism. *Energy Economics*. 123. 106673.

Bhanumati, P., M. de Haan, and J.W. Tebrake. 2022. Greenhouse Emissions Rise to Record, Erasing Drop During Pandemic. *International Monetary Blog*. 30 June. https://www.imf.org/en/Blogs/Articles/2022/06/30/greenhouse-emissions-rise-to-record-erasing-drop-during-pandemic.

Böhringer, C., C. Fischer, and K.E. Rosendahl. 2010. The Global Effects of Subglobal Climate Policies. *B.E. Journal of Economic Analysis and Policy*. 10 (2). pp. 1–35.

Böhringer, C., C. Fischer, K.E. Rosendahl, and T.F. Rutheford. 2022. Potential Impacts and Challenges of Border Carbon Adjustments. *Nature Climate Change*. 12. pp. 22–29.

Böhringer, C., E.J. Balistreri, and T.F. Rutherford. 2012. The Role of Border Carbon Adjustment in Unilateral Climate Policy: Overview of an Energy Modeling Forum Study (EMF 29). *Energy Economics*. 34 (s2). pp. S97–S110.

Böhringer, C., J. Carbone, and R. Rutherford. 2016. The Strategic Value of Carbon Tariffs. *American Economic Journal: Economic Policy*. 8 (1). pp. 28–51.

Böhringer, C., J. Schneider, and E. Asane-Otoo. 2021. Trade in Carbon and Carbon Tariffs. *Environmental and Resource Economics*. 78. pp. 669–708.

Braithwaite, J. 2002. Rules and Principles: A Theory of Legal Certainty. *Australasian Journal of Legal Philosophy*. 27. pp. 1–46.

Branger, F. and P. Quirion. 2014. Would Border Carbon Adjustments Prevent Carbon Leakage and Heavy Industry Competitiveness Losses? Insights from a Meta-Analysis of Recent Economic Studies. *Ecological Economics*. 99. pp. 29–39.

Burke, M., A. Driscoll, D.B. Lobell, and S. Ermon. 2021. Using Satellite Imagery to Understand and Promote Sustainable Development. *Science*. 371 (6535). pp. 1–12.

Burniaux, J., J. Château, and J. Sauvage. 2011. The Trade Effects of Phasing Out Fossil-Fuel Consumption Subsidies. *OECD Trade and Environment Working Papers*. No. 2011/05. Paris: OECD.

Carbon Pricing Leadership Coalition. 2019. *Report of the High-Level Commission on Carbon Pricing and Competitiveness*. Washington, DC: The World Bank.

Centre d'Études Prospectives et d'Informations Internationales. Base pour l'Analyse du Commerce International (BACI) Database. http://www.cepii.fr/CEPII/fr/bdd_modele/bdd_modele_item.asp?id=37 (accessed November 2023).

Challinor, A., W. Adger, and T. Benton. 2017. Climate Risks Across Borders and Scales. *Nature Climate Change*. 7. pp. 621–623.

Charnovitz, S. 2002. The Law of Environmental PPMs in the WTO: Debunking the Myth of Illegality. *Yale Journal of International Law.* 27 (1). pp. 59–110.

Cherniwchan, J. and M.S. Taylor. 2022. International Trade and the Environment: Three Remaining Empirical Challenges. *NBER Working Paper.* No. 30020. Cambridge, MA: National Bureau of Economic Research.

Cockburn, J., V. Robichaud, and L. Tiberti. 2018. Energy Subsidy Reform and Poverty in Arab Countries: A Comparative CGE-Microsimulation Analysis of Egypt and Jordan. *The Review of Income and Wealth.* 64 (s1). pp. S249–S273.

Copeland, B.R., J.S .Shapiro, and M.S. Taylor. 2021. Globalization and the Environment. *NBER Working Paper.* 28797. Cambridge, MA: National Bureau of Economic Research.

Constant, K. and M. Davin. 2019. Unequal Vulnerability to Climate Change and the Transmission of Adverse Effects through International Trade. *Environmental Resource Economics.* 74. pp. 727–759.

Cornago, E. and S. Lowe. 2021. Avoiding the Pitfalls of an EU Carbon Border Adjustment Mechanism, Centre for European Reform. *Centre for European Reform Insight.* 5 July. https://www.cer.eu/insights/avoiding-pitfalls-eu-carbon-border-adjustment-mechanism.

Cosbey, A., S. Droege, C. Fischer, and C. Munnings. 2019. Developing Guidance for Implementing Border Carbon Adjustment: Lessons, Cautions, and Research Needs from the Literature. *Review of Environmental Economics and Policy.* 13 (1). pp. 3–22.

Costinot, A. 2008. A Comparative Institutional Analysis of Agreements on Product Standards. *Journal of International Economics.* 75 (1). pp. 197–213.

Cramton, P., D.J.C. MacKay, A. Ockenfels, and S. Stoft. 2017. *Global Carbon Pricing: The Path to Climate Cooperation.* Cambridge: The Massachusetts Institute of Technology Press.

Crippa, M., G. Janssens-Maenhout, F. Dentener, D. Guizzardi, K. Sindelarova, M. Muntean, R. Van Dingenen, and C. Granier. 2016. Forty Years of Improvements in European Air Quality: Regional Policy-Industry Interactions with Global Impacts. *Atmospheric Chemistry and Physics.* 16 (6). pp. 3825–3841.

Cristea, A., D. Hummels, L. Puzzello, and M. Avetisyan. 2013. Trade and the Greenhouse Gas Emissions from International Freight Transport. *Journal of Environmental Economics and Management.* 65 (1). pp. 153–173.

Delera, M. 2021. Is Production in Global Value Chains (GVCs) Sustainable? A Review of the Empirical Evidence on Social and Environmental Sustainability in GVCs. *Poverty Reduction, Equity and Growth Network (PEGNet) Policy Studies.* 04/2020. Kiel: Kiel Institute for the World Economy, PEGNet.

Delera, M. and N. Foster-McGregor. 2023. Revisiting International Knowledge Spillovers: The Role of GVCs. *Industrial and Corporate Change.* 32 (5). pp. 1163–1191.

Dittmer, K.M., E. Wollenberg, M. Cohen, and C. Egler. 2023. How Good Is the Data for Tracking Countries' Agricultural Greenhouse Gas Emissions? Making Use of Multiple National Greenhouse Gas Inventories. *Frontiers in Sustainable Food Systems.* 7. pp. 1–7.

Dröge, S. 2009. *Tackling Leakage in a World of Unequal Carbon Prices.* Cambridge: Climate Strategies.

Du, Q., A.M. Kim, and Q. Zheng. 2017. Modeling Multimodal Freight Transportation Scenarios in Northern Canada under Climate Change Impacts. *Research in Transportation Business and Management.* 23. pp. 86–96.

Dunning, J. 1988. The Eclectic Paradigm of International Production: A Restatement and Some Possible Extensions. *Journal of International Business Studies*. 19. pp. 1–31.

Ekstein, D., V. Kuenzel, and L. Schaefer. 2021. Global Climate Risk Index 2021: Who Suffers Most from Extreme Weather Events? Weather-Related Loss Events in 2019 and 2000-2019. *Germanwatch: Briefing Paper*. Bonn, Germany: Germanwatch.

Elliott, J., I. Foster, S. Kortum, G.K. Jush, T. Munson, and D. Weisbach. 2013. Unilateral Carbon Taxes, Border Tax Adjustments and Carbon Leakage. *Theoretical Inquiries in Law*. 14 (1). pp. 207–244.

Ellis, J. 2010. *The Effects of Fossil-Fuel Subsidy Reform: A Review of Modelling and Empirical Studies*. Geneva: Global Subsidies Initiative of the International Institute for Sustainable Development.

Eora. Eora26. https://worldmrio.com/eora26/ (accessed November 2023).

European Commission. 2021a. Annexes to the Regulation of the European Parliament and of the Council on the Establishment of a Carbon Border Adjustment Mechanism (CBAM). https://www.euractiv.com/wp-content/uploads/sites/2/2021/06/CBAM-regulation-ANNNEXES-Draft.pdf

——. 2021b. Impact Assessment Report: Proposal for a Regulation of the European Parliament and of the council Establishing a Carbon Border Adjustment Mechanism. *European Commission Staff Working Document*. Brussels: European Commission.

——. 2022. EU Challenges Discriminatory Practices of UK's Green Energy Subsidy Scheme at WTO. News Article. 28 March. Brussels: Directorate-General for Trade. https://policy.trade.ec.europa.eu/news/eu-challenges-discriminatory-practices-uks-green-energy-subsidy-scheme-wto-2022-03-28_en (accessed November 2023).

——. 2023a. Brussels: Default Values for the Transitional Period of the CBAM Between 1 October 2023 and 31 December 2025. *Directorate-General Taxation and Customs Union*.

——. 2023b. Questions and Answers: An Adjusted Package for the Next Generation of Own Resources. Press Corner: Questions and Answers. 20 June. https://ec.europa.eu/commission/presscorner/detail/en/qanda_23_3329 (accessed November 2023).

European Council. 2023. Infographic - Energy Price Rise Since 2021. https://www.consilium.europa.eu/en/infographics/energy-prices-2021 (accessed November 2023).

European Investment Bank (EIB). 2022. *Multilateral Development Banks' Climate Finance in Low and Middle-Income Countries Reaches $51 Billion in 2021*. Luxembourg.

European Parliament. 2020. Economic Assessment of Carbon Leakage and Carbon Border Adjustment. Briefing. Policy Department, Directorate-General for External Policies.

——. 2021. *Draft Opinion of the Committee on Agriculture and Rural Development for the Committee on the Environment, Public Health and Food Safety on the Proposal for a Regulation of the European Parliament and of the Council Establishing a Carbon Boder Adjustment Mechanism*. Brussels. https://www.europarl.europa.eu/doceo/document/AGRI-PA-699239_EN.pdf (accessed November 2023).

——. 2022. Deal Reached on New Carbon Leakage Instrument to Raise Global Climate Ambition. Press Release. 13 December. https://www.europarl.europa.eu/news/en/press-room/20221212IPR64509/deal-reached-on-new-carbon-leakage-instrument-to-raise-global-climate-ambition (accessed November 2023).

Fadly, D. and F. Fontes. 2019. Geographical Proximity and Renewable Energy Diffusion: An Empirical Approach. *Energy Policy*. 129. pp. 422–435.

Falcao, T. 2020. Toward Carbon Tax Internationalism: The EU Border Carbon Adjustment Proposal. *Tax Notes International*. 98 (9). pp. 1047–1054

Forti, V., C.P. Baldé, R. Kuehr and B. Garam. 2020. *The Global E-Waste Monitor 2020: Quantities, Flows and the Circular Economy Potential*. Bonn: United Nations University, Institute for Training and Research, Geneva: International Telecommunications Union, Rotterdam: International Solid Waste Association.

Friedlingstein, P. et al. 2022. Global Carbon Budget 2022. *Earth System Science Data*. 14 (11). pp. 4811–4900.

Ganapati, S. and W.F. Wong. 2023. How Far Goods Travel: Global Transport and Supply Chains from 1965-2020. *Journal of Economic Perspectives*. 37 (3). pp. 3–30.

Ganzenmüller, R., S. Bultan, K. Winkler, R. Fuchs, F. Zabel, and J. Pongratz. 2022. Land-Use Change Emissions Based on High-Resolution Activity Data Substantially Lower than Previously Estimated. *Environmental Research Letters*. 17. 064050.

Gaulier, G. and S. Zignago. 2010. BACI: International Trade Database at the Product-Level. The 1994-2007 Version. *Centre d'Études Prospectives et d'Informations Internationales Working Paper*. No. 2010-23. Paris: CEPII.

Greenhouse Gas Protocol. 2014. *GHG Protocol Agricultural Guidance: Interpreting the Corporate Accounting and Reporting Standard for the Agricultural Sector*. Washington, DC.

Global Trade Analysis Project. GTAP 11 Data Base. https://www.gtap.agecon.purdue.edu/databases/v11/ (accessed November 2023).

Grassi, G. et al. 2021. Critical Adjustment of Land Mitigation Pathways for Assessing Countries' Climate Progress. *Nature Climate Change*. 11. pp. 425–434.

Grubb, M., N.D. Jordan, E. Hertwich, K. Neuhoff, K. Das, K.R. Bandyopadhyay, H. van Asselt, M. Sato, R. Wang, W.A. Pizer, and H. Oh. 2022. Carbon Leakage, Consumption, and Trade. *Annual Review of Environment and Resources*. 47. pp. 753–795.

Gütschow, J., A. Günther, and M. Pflüger. 2021. The PRIMAP-hist National Historical Emissions Time Series (1750-2019). Version 2.3.1. Zenodo.

Gütschow, J., L. Jeffery, R. Gieseke, R. Gebel, D. Stevens, M. Krapp, and M. Rocha. 2016. The PRIMAP-hist National Historical Emissions Time Series. *Earth System Science Data*. 8. pp. 571–603.

Haraguchi, M. and U. Lall. 2015. Flood Risks and Impacts: A Case Study of Thailand's Floods in 2011 and Research Questions for Supply Chain Decision Making. *International Journal of Disaster Risk Reduction*. 14 (3). pp. 256–272.

Heede, R. 2014. Tracing Anthropogenic Carbon Dioxide and Methane Emissions to Fossil Fuel and Cement Producers, 1854–2010. *Climatic Change*. 122. pp. 229–241.

Hofmann, C., A. Osnago, and M. Ruta. 2017. Horizontal Depth: A New Database on the Content of Preferential Trade Agreements. *World Bank Policy Research Working Paper*. No. 7981. Washington, DC: The World Bank.

Huang, Y. and Y. Zhang. 2023. Digitalization, Positioning in Global Value Chain and Carbon Emissions Embodied in Exports: Evidence from Global Manufacturing Production-Based Emission. *Ecological Economics*. 205. 107674.

Hurtt, G. C., L. Chini, R. Sahajpal, S. Frolking, B.L. Bodirsky, K. Calvin, J.C. Doelman 2020. Harmonization of Global Land Use Change and Management for the Period 850–2100 (LUH2) for CMIP6. *Geoscientific Model Development*. 13 (11). pp. 5425–5464.

Inman, M. 2008. Carbon Is Forever. *Nature Climate Change*. 1. pp. 156–158.

International Energy Agency (IEA). Data and Statistics. https://www.iea.org/data-and-statistics (accessed November 2023).

———. 2021. *World Energy Outlook 2021*. Paris.

International Carbon Action Partnership. International Carbon Action Partnership Database. https://icapcarbonaction.com/en (accessed November 2023).

International Maritime Organization (IMO). 2015. "Shipping: Indispensable to the World" Selected as World Maritime Day theme for 2016. Press Briefing. London.

Intergovernmental Panel on Climate Change (IPCC). 2022a. Climate Change 2022: Impacts, Adaptation and Vulnerability. Contribution of Working Group II to the Sixth Assessment Report of the Intergovernmental Panel on Climate Change. Cambridge and New York: Cambridge University Press.

———. 2022b. Climate Change 2022: Mitigation of Climate Change. Working Group III Contribution to the Sixth Assessment Report of the Intergovernmental Panel on Climate Change. Cambridge and New York: Cambridge University Press.

Jackson, C. and E. Aisbett. 2024. Multi-Criteria Analysis for Green Industrial Policy: Methodology for Application to Australia's Guarantee of Origin Scheme? *ZCEAP Working Paper*. No. ZCWP 01-24.

Jakob, M. 2023. The Political Economy of Carbon Border Adjustment in the EU. *Oxford Review of Economic Policy*. 39 (1). pp. 134–146.

Jakob, M., S. Afionis, M. Åhman, A. Anotci, M. Arenes, F. Ascensäo, H. Van Asselt 2022. How Trade Policy Can Support the Climate Agenda: Ensure Open Markets for Clean Technologies and Products. *Science*. 376. pp. 1401–1403.

Jensen, J. and D. Tarr. 2003. Trade, Exchange Rate, and Energy Pricing Reform in Iran: Potentially Large Efficiency Effects and Gains to the Poor. *Review of Development Economics*. 7 (4). pp. 543–562.

Jones, B.F. and B.A. Olken. 2010. Climate Shocks and Exports. *American Economic Review*. 100 (2). pp. 454–459.

Kaza, S., L.C. Yao, P. Bhada-Tata, and V.W. Frank. 2018. What a Waste 2.0: A Global Snapshot of Solid Waste Management to 2050. *Urban Development Series*. Washington, DC: The World Bank.

Kjellstrom, T., I. Holmer, and B. Lemke. 2009. Workplace Heat Stress, Health and Productivity – An Increasing Challenge for Low and Middle-Income Countries During Climate Change. *Global Health Action*. 2. pp. 1–6.

Klotz, R. and R. Sharma. 2023. Trade Barriers and CO_2. *Journal of International Economics*. 141. 103726. Hamilton, New York: Colgate University.

Koetse, M.J. and P. Rietveld. 2009. The Impact of Climate Change and Weather on Transport: An Overview of Empirical Findings. *Transportation Research Part D: Transport and Environment*. 14 (3). pp. 205–221.

Koks, E.E., J. Rozenberg, C. Zorn, M. Tariverdi, M. Vousdoukas, S.A. Fraser, J.W. Hall, and S. Hallegatte. 2019. A Global Multi-Hazard Risk Analysis of Road and Railway Infrastructure Assets. *Nature Communications*. 10. 2677.

Le Moigne, M. and R. Ossa. 2021. Buy Green Not Local: How International Trade Can Help Save Our Planet. Kühne Center *Impact Series*. No. 03. Zurich: University of Zurich.

Leimbach, M., E. Kriegler, N. Roming, and J. Schwanitz. 2017. Future Growth Paths of World Regions: A GDP Scenario Approach. *Global Environmental Change*. 42. pp. 215–225.

Li, M., B. Meng, Y. Gao, Z. Wang, Z. Zhang, and Y. Sun. 2022. Tracing CO_2 Emissions in Global Value Chains: Multinationals vs. Domestically-owned Firms. *Sustainable Global Supply Chains Discussion Papers*. No. 2. Bonn: Research Network Sustainable Global Supply Chains.

Lim-Camacho, L., E.E. Plagányi, S. Crimp, J.H. Hodgkinson, A.J. Hobday, S.M. Howden, and B. Loechel. 2017. Complex Resource Supply Chains Display Higher Resilience to Simulated Climate Shocks. *Global Environmental Change*. 46. pp. 126–138.

Luers, A. L. Yona, C.B. Field, R.B. Jackson, K.J. Mach, B.W. Cashore, C. Elliott, L. Gifford, C. Honigsberg 2022. Make Greenhouse-Gas Accounting Reliable - Build Interoperable Systems. Comment. *Nature*. 607 (7920). pp. 653–656.

Magnani, E. 2000. The Environmental Kuznet's Curve, Environmental Protection Policy and Income Distribution. *Ecological Economics*. 32 (3). pp. 431–443.

Mattoo, A., A. Mulabdic, and M. Ruta. 2022. Trade Creation and Trade Diversion in Deep Agreements. *Canadian Journal of Economics*. 55 (3). pp. 1598–1637.

Mattoo, A. and A. Subramanian. 2013. *Greenprint: A New Approach to Cooperation on Climate Change*, Washington, DC: Center for Global Development.

Mehling, M.A. and R.A. Ritz. 2023. From Theory to Practice: Determining Emissions in Traded Goods under a Border Carbon Adjustment. *Oxford Review of Economic Policy*. 39 (1). pp. 123–133.

Melia, N., K. Haines, and E. Hawkins. 2016. Sea Ice Decline and 21st Century Trans-Arctic Shipping Routes. *Geophysical Research Letters*. 43 (18). pp. 9720–9728.

Meng, B., G.P. Peters, Z. Wang, and M. Li. 2018. Tracing CO_2 Emissions in Global Value Chains. *Energy Economics*. 73. pp. 24–42.

Miroudot, S. and D. Rigo. 2022. Multinational Production and Investment Provisions in Preferential Trade Agreements. *Journal of Economic Geography*. 22 (6). pp. 1275–1308.

Misch, F. and P. Wingender. 2021. Revisiting Carbon Leakage. *International Monetary Fund Working Paper*. No. 2021/207. Washington, DC: IMF.

Morin, J-F., A. Dür, and L. Lechner. 2018. Mapping the Trade and Environment Nexus: Insights from a New Data Set. *Global Environmental Politics*. 18 (1). pp. 122–139.

Mudryk, L.R., J. Dawson, S.E. Howell, C. Derksen, T.A. Zagon, and M. Brady. 2021. Impact of 1, 2 and 4 °C of Global Warming on Ship Navigation in the Canadian Arctic. *Nature Climate Change*. 11. pp. 673–679.

Ng, A.K.Y., J. Andrews, D. Babb, Y. Lin, and A. Becker. 2018. Implications of Climate Change for Shipping: Opening the Arctic Seas. *Wiley Interdisciplinary Reviews (WIREs) Climate Change*. 9 (2).

Nordhaus, W. 2015a. Climate Clubs: Overcoming Free-rising in International Climate Policy. *American Economic Review*. 105 (4). pp. 1339–1370.

———. 2015b. *The Climate Casino: Risk, Uncertainty, and Economics for a Warming World*. New Haven: Yale University Press.

————. 2020. The Climate Club: How to Fix a Failing Global Effort. *Foreign Affairs.* May/June 2020. https://www.foreignaffairs.com/articles/united-states/2020-04-10/climate-club.

Nordström, H. and S. Vaughan. 1999. Trade and Environment. *World Trade Organization Special Studies.* 4. Geneva: WTO.

Our World in Data. Levelized Cost of Energy by Technology, World. https://ourworldindata.org/grapher/levelized-cost-of-energy (accessed November 2023).

Organisation for Economic Co-operation and Development (OECD). Inter-Country Input-Output (ICIO) Tables. https://www.oecd.org/sti/ind/inter-country-input-output-tables.htm (accessed November 2023).

————. Carbon Dioxide Emissions Embodied in International Trade (TECO$_2$) data set. https://www.oecd.org/sti/ind/carbondioxideemissionsembodiedininternationaltrade.htm (accessed November 2023).

————. The Analytical AMNE Database - Multinational Enterprises and Global Value Chains. https://www.oecd.org/fr/sti/ind/analytical-amne-database.htm (accessed November 2023).

Parry, I.W.H., S. Black, and J. Roaf. 2021. Proposal for an International Carbon Price Floor Among Large Emitters. *International Monetary Fund Staff Climate Note.* No. 2021/001. Washington: IMF.

Perkins, R. and E. Neumayer. 2012. Does the 'California Effect' Operate across Borders? Trading- and Investing-Up in Automobile Emission Standards. *Journal of European Public Policy.* 19 (2). pp. 217–237.

Pizzolato, L., S.E.L. Howell, J. Dawson, F. Laliberté, and L. Copland. 2016. The Influence of Declining Sea Ice on Shipping Activity in the Canadian Arctic. *Geophysical Research Letters.* 43 (23). pp. 12146–12154.

Reeve, A. and E. Aisbett. 2022. National Accounting Systems as a Foundation for Embedded Emissions Accounting in Trade-Related Climate Policies. *Journal of Cleaner Production.* 371. 133678.

Rentschler, J., M. Kornejew, and M. Bazilian. 2017. Fossil Fuel Subsidy Reforms and Their Impact on Firms. *Energy Policy.* 108. pp. 617–623.

Ritchie, H. 2020. Cars, Planes, Trains: Where Do CO$_2$ Emissions from Transport Come from? *Our World in Data.* https://ourworldindata.org/co2-emissions-from-transport (accessed November 2023).

Rosenbloom, D., J. Markard, F.W. Geels, and L. Fuenfschilling. 2020. Why Carbon Pricing Is Not Sufficient to Mitigate Climate Change – and How "Sustainability Sransition Policy" Can Help. *Proceedings of the National Academy of Sciences.* 117 (16). pp. 8664–8668.

Rosenstock, T.S. and A. Wilkes. 2021. Reorienting Emissions Research to Catalyse African Agricultural Development. *Nature Climate Change.* 11 (6). pp. 463–465.

Sabel, C.F. and D.G. Victor. 2022. *Fixing the Climate: Strategies for an Uncertain World.* New Jersey: Princeton University Press.

Schenker, O. 2013. Exchanging Goods and Damages: The Role of Trade on the Distribution of Climate Change Costs. *Environmental Resource Economics.* 54. pp. 261–282.

Schenker, O. and G. Stephan. 2014. Give and Take: How the Funding of Adaptation to Climate Change can Improve the Donor's Terms-of-Trade. *Ecological Economics.* 106. pp. 44–55.

Shahnazi, R. and Z.D. Shabani. 2019. The Effects of Spatial Spillover Information and Communications Technology on Carbon Dioxide Emissions in Iran. *Environmental Science and Pollution Research.* 23 (23). pp. 24198–24212.

Shapiro, J.S. 2021. The Environmental Bias of Trade Policy. *Quarterly Journal of Economics*. 136 (2). pp. 831–886.

Somanathan, E., R. Somanathan, A. Sudarshan, and M. Tewari. 2021. The Impact of Temperature on Productivity and Labor Supply: Evidence from Indian Manufacturing. *Journal of Political Economy*. 129 (6). pp. 1–66.

St George, C. and D. Marten. 2023. How Can Multilateral Development Banks Collaborate to Accelerate Climate Finance? *Carbon Trust: Insights*. 4 December. https://www.carbontrust.com/news-and-insights/insights/how-can-multilateral-development-banks-collaborate-to-accelerate-climate-finance.

Steenbergen, V. and A. Saurav. 2023. *The Effect of Multinational Enterprises on Climate Change: Supply Chain Emissions, Green Technology Transfers, and Corporate Commitments*. Washington, DC: The World Bank.

Stiglitz, J.E. 2019. Addressing Climate Change through Price and Non-Price Interventions. *European Economic Review*. 119. pp. 594–612.

Subramanian, A. 2022. Global Cooperation Is Not Necessary to Fight Climate Change. *Project Syndicate*. 10 November. https://www.project-syndicate.org/commentary/multilateral-cooperation-climate-change-unnecessary-inflation-reduction-act-by-arvind-subramanian-2022-11.

Taglioni, D. and D. Winkler. 2016. *Making Global Value Chains Work for Development: Trade and Development*. Washington, DC: World Bank.

Thorlakson, T., J.F. de Zegher, and E.F. Lambin. 2018. Companies' Contribution to Sustainability through Global Supply Chains. *Proceedings of the National Academy of Sciences*. 115 (9). pp. 2072–2077.

United Nations Conference on Trade and Development (UNCTAD). 2016. *UNFCCC Nationally Determined Contributions: Climate Change and Trade*. Geneva.

———. 2021. *A European Union Carbon Border Adjustment Mechanism: Implications for Developing Countries*. Geneva.

———. 2023. *Technology and Innovation Report 2023: Opening Green Windows: Technological Opportunities for a Low-Carbon World*. Geneva.

United Nations Development Programme (UNDP). 2016. *Climate Change and Labour: Impacts of Heat in the Workplace*. New York.

United Nations Environment Programme (UNEP). 2022. Technology Transfer for Climate Mitigation and Adaptation: Analysing Needs and Development Assistance Support in Technology Transfer Processes. *Policy Brief*. Copenhagen: UNEP.

United Nations Economic and Social Commission for Asian and the Pacific (UNESCAP). 2022. *2022 Review of Climate Ambition in Asia and the Pacific: Raising NDC Targets with Enhanced Nature-Based Solutions with a Special Feature on Engagement of Children and Youth in Raising National Climate Ambition*. New York: United Nations.

United Nations Framework Convention on Climate Change (UNFCCC). 2016. *The Concept of Economic Diversification in the Context of Response Measures*. Technical Paper. Bonn.

———. 2017. *How Blockchain Technology Could Boost Climate Action*. News. Bonn. https://unfccc.int/news/how-blockchain-technology-could-boost-climate-action (accessed November 2023).

United States Environmental Protection Agency (US EPA). 2023. *Carbon Pollution from Transportation*. Transportation, Air Pollution, and Climate Change. https://www.epa.gov/transportation-air-pollution-and-climate-change/carbon-pollution-transportation (accessed November 2023).

Verde, S. 2020. The Impact of the EU Emissions Trading System on Competitiveness and Carbon Leakage: The Econometric Evidence. *Journal of Economic Surveys.* 34 (2). pp. 320-343.

Vidovic, D., A. Marmier, L. Zore, and J. Moya. 2023. *Greenhouse Gas Emission Intensities of the Steel, Fertilisers, Aluminium and Cement Industries in the EU and Its Main Trading Partners.* Luxembourg: Publications Office of the European Union.

Viner, J. 1950. *The Customs Union Issue.* New York: Carnegie Endowment for International Peace.

Wang, S., X. Wang, and S. Chen. 2022. Global Value Chains and Carbon Emission Reduction in Developing Countries: Does Industrial Upgrading Matter? *Environmental Impact Assessment Review.* 97. 106895.

Wang, Z., S.J. Wei, X. Yu, and K. Zhu. 2017. Measures of Participation in Global Value Chains and Global Business Cycles. *National Bureau of Economic Research Working Paper.* No. 23222. Cambridge: NBER.

Wei, G., M. Bi, X. Liu, Z. Zhang, and B.J. He. 2023. Investigating the Impact of Multi-Dimensional Urbanization and FDI on Carbon Emissions in the Belt and Road Initiative Region: Direct and Spillover Effects. *Journal of Cleaner Production.* 384. No. 35608.

White, L.V., R. Fazeli, W. Cheng, E. Aisbett, F.J. Beck, K.G.H. Baldwin, P. Howarth, and L. Neill. 2021. Towards Emissions Certification Systems for International Trade in Hydrogen: The Policy Challenge of Defining Boundaries for Emissions Accounting. *Energy.* 215. pp. 119139–119139.

White, L., E. Aisbett, and J. Widnyana. 2023. Treatment of Negative Emissions within Embedded Emissions Accounting. *ZCEAP Policy Brief.* https://iceds.anu.edu.au/files/NES policy brief_oct2023.pdf.

White, L., E. Aisbett, O. Pearce, and W. Cheng. 2024. Principles for Embedded Emissions Accounting to Support Trade-Related Climate Policy. *ZCEAP Working Paper.* No. 02-24.

Williams, A. 2007. Comparative Study of Cut Roses for the British Market Produced in Kenya and the Netherlands. *Precis Report for World Flowers.* Cranfield, Bedford: Cranfield University.

Willner, S.N., C. Otto, and A. Levermann. 2018. Global Economic Response to River Floods. *Nature Climate Change.* 8. pp. 594–598.

World Bank. Carbon Pricing Dashboard. https://carbonpricingdashboard.worldbank.org/ (accessed November 2023).

———. World Development Indicators. https://databank.worldbank.org/source/world-development-indicators (accessed November 2023).

———. 2022. *State and Trends of Carbon Pricing 2022.* Washington, DC.

World Trade Organization (WTO). Environmental Database. https://edb.wto.org/charts (accessed November 2023).

———. 2022a. Trade and Climate Change: Information of Trade Policies Adopted to Address Climate Change. *Information Brief.* Geneva.

———. 2022b. *World Trade Report 2022: Climate Change and International Trade.* Geneva.

7 Statistical Appendix

The statistical appendix comprises 10 tables of selected indicators on economic integration for the Asian Development Bank's (ADB) 49 members from Asia and the Pacific. The succeeding notes describe the economy groupings and the calculation procedures undertaken.

Regional Groupings

- Asia and the Pacific refers to the 49 regional members of ADB.
- Developing Asia refers to Asia excluding Australia, Japan, and New Zealand.
- The European Union consists of Austria, Belgium, Bulgaria, Croatia, Cyprus, Czechia, Denmark, Estonia, Finland, France, Germany, Greece, Hungary, Ireland, Italy, Latvia, Lithuania, Luxembourg, Malta, the Netherlands, Poland, Portugal, Romania, Slovakia, Slovenia, Spain, and Sweden.

Table Descriptions

Table A1: Asia-Pacific Regional Cooperation and Integration Index

The Asia-Pacific Regional Cooperation and Integration Index (ARCII) is a composite index that measures the degree of regional cooperation and integration in Asia and the Pacific. It comprises eight dimensional indexes based on 41 indicators to capture the contributions of eight different aspects of regional integration: (i) trade and investment, (ii) money and finance, (iii) regional value chains, (iv) infrastructure and connectivity, (v) people and social integration, (vi) institutional arrangements, (vii) technology and digital connectivity, and (viii) environmental cooperation. The construction of ARCII follows two steps: first, the 41 indicators have been weight-averaged in each of the eight dimensions to produce eight composite dimensional indexes; second, these eight dimensional indexes are weight-averaged to generate an overall index of regional integration. In each step, the weights are determined based on principal component analysis. For more details on the methodology and to download the data, please see Asia-Pacific Regional Cooperation and Integration Index Database. https://aric.adb.org/database/arcii.

Table A2: Regional Integration Indicators—Asia and the Pacific (% of total)

The table provides a summary of regional integration indicators for three areas: movement in trade and investment, movement in capital, and people movement (migration, remittances, and tourism); for Asian subregions, including the Association of Southeast Asian Nations (ASEAN) plus 3 (including Hong Kong, China). Cross-border flows within and across subregions are shown, as well as total flows with Asia and the rest of the world. Table descriptions of Tables A3 and A7 (movement in trade and investment); Tables A5 and A6 (movement in capital); and Tables A8, A9, and A10 (people movement) provide additional description for each indicator.

Table A3: Trade Share—Asia and the Pacific (% of total trade)

It is calculated as $T_{ij}/T_{iw} \cdot 100$, where T_{ij} is the total trade of economy "i" with economy "j", and T_{iw} is the total trade of economy "i" with the world. A higher share indicates a higher degree of regional trade integration.

Table A4: Free Trade Agreement Status—Asia and the Pacific

It is the number and status of bilateral and plurilateral free trade agreements (FTAs) with at least one of the Asian economies as signatory. FTAs only proposed are excluded. It covers FTAs with the following status: framework agreement signed—the parties initially negotiate the contents of a framework agreement, which serves as a framework for future negotiations; negotiations launched—the parties, through the relevant ministries, declare the official launch of negotiations or set the date for such, or start the first round of negotiations; signed but not yet in effect—parties sign the agreement after negotiations have been completed, however, the agreement has yet to be implemented; and signed and in effect—provisions of the FTA come into force, after legislative or executive ratification.

Table A5: Cross-Border Portfolio Equity Holdings Share—Asia and the Pacific (% of total cross-border portfolio equity holdings)

It is calculated as $E_{ij}/E_{iw} \cdot 100$ where E_{ij} is portfolio equity holdings of economy "i" issued by economy "j", and E_{iw} is the total global cross-border portfolio equity holdings of economy "i". Calculations are based solely on available data in the Coordinated Portfolio Investment Survey (CPIS) database of the International Monetary Fund (IMF). Rest of the world (ROW) includes equity securities issued by international organizations defined in the CPIS database and "not specified (including confidential) category." A higher share indicates a higher degree of regional integration.

Table A6: Cross-Border Portfolio Debt Holdings Share—Asia and the Pacific (% of total cross-border portfolio debt holdings)

It is calculated as $D_{ij}/D_{iw} \cdot 100$ where D_{ij} is portfolio debt holdings of economy "i" issued by economy "j", and D_{iw} is the total global cross-border portfolio debt holdings of economy "i". Calculations are based solely on available data in the CPIS database of the IMF. ROW includes debt securities issued by international organizations defined in the CPIS database and "not specified (including confidential) category." A higher share indicates a higher degree of regional integration.

Table A7: Foreign Direct Investment Inflow Share—Asia and the Pacific (% of total FDI inflows)

It is calculated as $F_{ij}/F_{iw} \cdot 100$ where F_{ij} is the foreign direct investment (FDI) received by economy "i" from economy "j", and F_{iw} is the FDI received by economy "i" from the world. Figures are based on net FDI inflow data. A higher share indicates a higher degree of regional integration. The bilateral FDI database was constructed using data from the United Nations Conference on Trade and Development, ASEAN Secretariat, Eurostat, and domestic sources. For missing data in recent years, bilateral FDI estimates derived from a gravity model are used. All bilateral data available from previous years were utilized to estimate the following gravity equation:

$$lnFDI_{ijt} = \alpha + \beta1 lnGDP_{it} + \beta2 lnGDP_{jt} + \gamma X_{ijt} + \delta_i F_i + \delta_j F_j + \delta_t F_t + v_{ijt}$$

where FDI_{ijt} is the FDI from economy "j" (home) to economy "i" (host) in year t, GDP_{it} is the gross domestic product (GDP) of economy "i" in year t, GDP_{jt} is the GDP of economy "j" at year t, X_{ijt} are the usual gravity variables (distance, contiguity, common language, colonial relationship) between economies "i" and "j", and $F_i, F_j, F_t,$ are home, host, and year fixed effects, respectively, and v_{ijt} is the error term. Data on distance, contiguity, common language, colonial relationship are from the Centre d'Études Prospectives et d'Informations Internationales (the French Research Center in International Economics) and data on GDP are from the World Development Indicators of the World Bank. For more details on methodology and data sources, please see Asian Economic Integration Report 2018 online Annex 1: http://aric.adb.org/pdf/aeir2018_ onlineannex1.pdf.

Table A8: Remittance Inflows Share—Asia and the Pacific
(% of total remittance inflows)

It is calculated as $R_{ij}/R_{iw} \cdot 100$ where R_{ij} is the remittance received by economy "i" from partner "j", and R_{iw} is the remittance received by economy "i" from the world. Remittances refer to the sum of the following: (i) workers' remittances which are recorded as current transfers under the current account of the IMF's Balance of Payments (BOP); (ii) compensation of employees which includes wages, salaries, and other benefits of border, seasonal, and other nonresident workers and which are recorded under the "income" subcategory of the current account; and (iii) migrants' transfers which are reported under capital transfers in the BOP's capital account. Transfers through informal channels are excluded.

Table A9: Outbound Migration Share—Asia and the Pacific
(% of total outbound migrants)

It is calculated as $M_{ij}/M_{iw} \cdot 100$ where M_{ij} is the number of migrants of economy "i" residing in economy "j" and M_{iw} is the number of all migrants of economy "i" residing overseas. This definition excludes those traveling abroad on a temporary basis. A higher share indicates a higher degree of regional integration.

Table A10a: Inbound Tourism Share—Asia and the Pacific
(% of total inbound tourists)

It is calculated as $V_{ij}/V_{iw} \cdot 100$ where V_{ij} is the number of individuals from economy "i" that have arrived as tourists in destination "j" and V_{iw} is the total number of individuals from economy "i" that have arrived as tourists in all international destinations. A higher share indicates a higher degree of regional integration.

Table A10b: Outbound Tourism Share—Asia and the Pacific
(% of total outbound tourists)

It is calculated as $V_{ij}/V_{iw} \cdot 100$ where V_{ij} is the number of individuals from economy "i" that have traveled as tourists in destination "j" and V_{iw} is the total number of individuals from economy "i" that have traveled as tourists abroad. A higher share indicates a higher degree of regional integration.

Table A1: Asia-Pacific Regional Cooperation and Integration Index

(a) Overall Asia-Pacific Regional Cooperation and Integration Index and Dimensional Subindexes—Asia and the Pacific

Year	Overall Index	Trade and Investment Integration	Money and Finance Integration	Regional Value Chain	Infrastructure and Connectivity	People and Social Integration	Institutional Arrangements	Technology and Digital Connectivity	Environmental Cooperation
2006	0.419	0.411	0.354	0.547	0.454	0.573	0.211	0.361	0.327
2007	0.421	0.370	0.347	0.551	0.455	0.577	0.215	0.374	0.332
2008	0.422	0.383	0.346	0.541	0.463	0.566	0.222	0.384	0.332
2009	0.437	0.414	0.360	0.532	0.474	0.573	0.228	0.386	0.342
2010	0.437	0.416	0.380	0.538	0.477	0.580	0.231	0.413	0.338
2011	0.427	0.431	0.330	0.534	0.479	0.581	0.232	0.430	0.339
2012	0.431	0.438	0.341	0.538	0.481	0.589	0.235	0.429	0.336
2013	0.445	0.400	0.407	0.543	0.482	0.573	0.236	0.460	0.338
2014	0.438	0.404	0.380	0.536	0.479	0.575	0.238	0.460	0.338
2015	0.451	0.457	0.405	0.538	0.481	0.572	0.241	0.481	0.344
2016	0.448	0.423	0.370	0.537	0.479	0.568	0.242	0.476	0.342
2017	0.448	0.444	0.371	0.534	0.481	0.570	0.245	0.495	0.345
2018	0.457	0.479	0.372	0.522	0.489	0.578	0.246	0.523	0.347
2019	0.458	0.409	0.368	0.542	0.508	0.588	0.246	0.528	0.345
2020	0.456	0.414	0.383	0.548	0.503	0.576	0.246	0.545	0.345
2021	0.457	0.391	0.377	0.553	0.498	0.549	0.244	0.568	0.367

(b) Overall Asia-Pacific Regional Cooperation and Integration Index—Asian Subregions and Subregional Initiatives

	Central Asia	East Asia	Southeast Asia	South Asia	Oceania	ASEAN	CAREC	GMS	SASEC	IMT-GT	BIMP-EAGA	SAARC	BIMSTEC
2006	0.352	0.475	0.407	0.339	0.452	0.418	0.320	0.405	0.307	0.400	0.375	0.338	0.360
2007	0.353	0.475	0.398	0.321	0.445	0.409	0.330	0.360	0.302	0.383	0.369	0.321	0.341
2008	0.357	0.476	0.401	0.313	0.450	0.411	0.336	0.360	0.302	0.399	0.373	0.313	0.340
2009	0.390	0.491	0.406	0.320	0.459	0.416	0.358	0.381	0.309	0.403	0.381	0.320	0.340
2010	0.363	0.489	0.412	0.315	0.466	0.421	0.353	0.386	0.306	0.403	0.382	0.315	0.345
2011	0.356	0.471	0.397	0.332	0.448	0.406	0.348	0.383	0.323	0.401	0.378	0.332	0.361
2012	0.364	0.475	0.409	0.330	0.458	0.416	0.354	0.379	0.320	0.387	0.373	0.330	0.352
2013	0.360	0.482	0.440	0.322	0.464	0.447	0.368	0.431	0.316	0.414	0.388	0.322	0.350
2014	0.360	0.485	0.420	0.316	0.448	0.428	0.364	0.427	0.309	0.404	0.383	0.316	0.347
2015	0.364	0.487	0.443	0.332	0.451	0.450	0.378	0.455	0.308	0.401	0.386	0.332	0.369
2016	0.366	0.498	0.427	0.326	0.453	0.435	0.364	0.451	0.306	0.399	0.382	0.326	0.357
2017	0.370	0.489	0.415	0.313	0.444	0.423	0.381	0.425	0.299	0.401	0.387	0.314	0.337
2018	0.376	0.490	0.427	0.318	0.437	0.435	0.384	0.452	0.301	0.409	0.394	0.318	0.354
2019	0.391	0.487	0.421	0.320	0.435	0.429	0.400	0.436	0.300	0.407	0.393	0.320	0.354
2020	0.402	0.470	0.444	0.322	0.452	0.451	0.390	0.447	0.314	0.417	0.395	0.322	0.362
2021	0.403	0.481	0.429	0.331	0.447	0.436	0.396	0.405	0.319	0.410	0.397	0.336	0.377

(c) Regional Integration Index — Asia and the Pacific and Other Regions

	Asia and the Pacific	European Union	Latin America	Africa	Middle East	North America
2006	0.419	0.597	0.379	0.335	0.370	0.484
2007	0.421	0.595	0.372	0.334	0.368	0.497
2008	0.422	0.587	0.374	0.331	0.373	0.505
2009	0.437	0.591	0.378	0.324	0.375	0.510
2010	0.437	0.591	0.390	0.348	0.384	0.508
2011	0.427	0.590	0.380	0.348	0.390	0.506
2012	0.431	0.590	0.392	0.355	0.394	0.510
2013	0.445	0.596	0.399	0.349	0.394	0.509
2014	0.438	0.594	0.387	0.368	0.393	0.510
2015	0.451	0.599	0.383	0.373	0.394	0.507
2016	0.448	0.603	0.377	0.367	0.396	0.507
2017	0.448	0.607	0.386	0.356	0.398	0.502
2018	0.457	0.602	0.386	0.369	0.412	0.494
2019	0.458	0.597	0.385	0.382	0.413	0.503
2020	0.456	0.609	0.393	0.372	0.415	0.490
2021	0.457	0.610	0.388	0.379	0.419	0.505

ASEAN = Association of Southeast Asian Nations, BIMP-EAGA = Brunei Darussalam-Indonesia-Malaysia-Philippines East ASEAN Growth Area , BIMSTEC = Bay of Bengal Initiative for Multi-Sectoral Technical and Economic Cooperation, CAREC = Central Asia Regional Economic Cooperation, GMS = Greater Mekong Subregion, IMT-GT = Indonesia-Malaysia-Thailand Growth Triangle, SAARC = South Asian Association for Regional Cooperation, SASEC = South Asia Subregional Economic Cooperation.

Notes:
(i)   The Asia-Pacific Regional Cooperation and Integration Index (ARCII) for each subregion (subregional initiative) for each year is calculated by averaging the ARCII scores for all the economies in each subregion (member economies in each subregional initiative).
(ii) The economy coverage for subregions and subregional initiatives includes Central Asia (Armenia, Azerbaijan, Georgia, Kazakhstan, the Kyrgyz Republic, Tajikistan, Turkmenistan, and Uzbekistan); East Asia (the People's Republic of China [PRC]; Hong Kong, China; Japan; the Republic of Korea; Mongolia; and Taipei,China); Southeast Asia (Brunei Darussalam, Cambodia, Indonesia, the Lao People's Democratic Republic [Lao PDR], Malaysia, Myanmar, the Philippines, Singapore, Thailand, Timor-Leste, and Viet Nam); South Asia (Afghanistan, Bangladesh , Bhutan, India, Maldives, Nepal, Pakistan, and Sri Lanka); the Pacific (Cook Islands, Fiji, Kiribati, Marshall Islands, Federated States of Micronesia, Nauru, Palau, Papua New Guinea, Samoa, Solomon Islands, Tonga, Tuvalu, Vanuatu, and Niue); Oceania (Australia and New Zealand); ASEAN (Brunei Darussalam, Cambodia, Indonesia, the Lao PDR, Malaysia, the Philippines, Singapore, Thailand, and Viet Nam); CAREC (Afghanistan, Azerbaijan, the PRC, Georgia, Kazakhstan, the Kyrgyz Republic, Mongolia, Pakistan, Tajikistan, Turkmenistan, and Uzbekistan); GMS (Cambodia, the PRC, the Lao PDR, Myanmar, Thailand, and Viet Nam); SASEC (Bangladesh, Bhutan, India, Maldives, Myanmar, Nepal, and Sri Lanka); IMT-GT (Indonesia, Malaysia, and Thailand); BIMP-EAGA (Brunei Darussalam, Indonesia, Malaysia, and the Philippines); SAARC (Afghanistan, Bangladesh, Bhutan, India, Maldives, Nepal, Pakistan, and Sri Lanka); BIMSTEC (Bangladesh, Bhutan, India, Myanmar, Nepal, Sri Lanka, and Thailand).
(iii) The regional integration index for each region (Table A1c) is calculated in the same method as ARCII but is based on worldwide normalization, i.e., normalizing raw indicator values using global minimum and maximum values.
(iv) Estimates for the Asian subregions and subregional initiatives represent intra-subregional and intra-subregional initiative integration, respectively.
(v)   Remittance data used in Indicator V-c (Proportion of intraregional remittances to total remittances) were changed to outward remittances.
(vi) Indicator VIII-c (environmental health score) is revised in the current estimation to ensure compatibility of values across time. It was recomputed using the time series data published by the Environmental Performance Index (EPI) team. Issue categories under the environmental health policy objective which do not have good data coverage from 2006 to 2020 were excluded from the computation (e.g., waste management).

Sources: ADB. Asia Regional Integration Center. Asia-Pacific Regional Cooperation and Integration Index Database. https://aric.adb.org/database/arcii (accessed October 2019); and methodology from C. Y. Park and R. Claveria. 2018. Constructing the Asia-Pacific Regional Integration Index: A Panel Approach. *ADB Economics Working Papers*. No. 544. Manila: ADB; H. Huh and C. Y. Park. 2018. Asia-Pacific Regional Integration Index: Construction, Interpretation, and Comparison. *Journal of Asian Economics*. 54. pp. 22–38; and H. Huh and C.Y. Park. 2017. Asia-Pacific Regional Integration Index: Construction, Interpretation, and Comparison. *ADB Economics Working Papers*. No. 511. Manila: ADB.

Table A2: Regional Integration Indicators—Asia and the Pacific (% of total)

	Movement in Trade and Investment		Movement in Capital		People Movement		
	Trade (%)	FDI (%)	Equity Holdings (%)	Bond Holdings (%)	Migration (%)	Tourism (%)	Remittances (%)
	2022	2022	2022	2022	2020	2022	2021
Within Subregions							
ASEAN+3 (including HKG)ᵃ	44.4 ▼	46.1 ▼	19.6 ▲	17.6 ▲	36.8 ▼	42.1 ▲	30.3 ▲
Central Asia	8.6 ▼	4.6 ▲	0.0 ▲	0.2 ▲	8.8 ▼	46.4 ▼	3.1 ▼
East Asia	32.1 ▼	46.7 ▼	16.7 ▲	11.4 ▲	33.6 ▲	15.4 ▲	32.8 ▲
South Asia	5.4 ▼	0.3 ▲	0.3 ▼	0.0 —	19.5 ▼	5.2 ▼	6.7 ▼
Southeast Asia	22.4 ▲	9.7 ▲	6.9 ▲	7.5 ▲	30.1 ▼	47.8 ▲	10.8 ▼
Oceania and the Pacific	4.4 ▼	5.5 ▼	3.9 ▲	4.5 ▲	53.8 ▼	25.5 ▼	42.5 ▲
Across Subregions							
ASEAN+3 (including HKG)ᵃ	13.0 ▲	2.9 ▼	3.5 ▲	5.3 ▲	13.2 ▲	6.2 ▲	8.7 ▲
Central Asia	27.3 ▲	65.6 ▼	7.6 ▲	25.9 ▲	0.7 ▲	0.5 ▼	0.2 ▼
East Asia	22.8 ▲	7.4 ▲	2.5 ▲	7.5 ▲	16.2 ▲	19.1 ▲	15.6 ▲
South Asia	31.8 ▼	39.5 ▲	12.1 ▲	10.2 ▼	7.5 ▲	17.5 ▲	8.9 ▲
Southeast Asia	47.0 ▼	28.6 ▲	30.0 ▼	33.6 ▲	20.2 ▲	19.5 ▲	20.2 ▲
Oceania and the Pacific	71.3 ▼	3.1 ▼	10.2 ▼	16.1 ▲	4.6 ▼	21.8 ▲	5.1 ▼
TOTAL (within and across subregions)							
Asia and the Pacific	**57.2 ▼**	**44.0 ▼**	**21.8 ▲**	**22.8 ▲**	**35.1 ▼**	**4.7 ▲**	**25.5 ▼**
ASEAN+3 (including HKG)ᵃ	57.4 ▼	48.9 ▼	23.1 ▲	22.9 ▲	50.0 ▲	48.3 ▲	39.0 ▲
Central Asia	35.9 ▼	70.2 ▼	7.6 ▲	26.0 ▲	9.5 ▼	46.9 ▼	3.2 ▼
East Asia	54.9 ▼	54.1 ▼	19.2 ▲	18.8 ▲	49.8 ▲	34.6 ▲	48.4 ▲
South Asia	37.2 ▼	39.8 ▲	12.4 ▲	10.2 ▼	27.0 ▼	22.7 ▲	15.6 ▲
Southeast Asia	69.3 ▲	38.3 ▲	36.9 ▲	41.1 ▲	50.2 ▲	67.3 ▲	31.0 ▲
Oceania and the Pacific	75.7 ▼	8.6 ▼	14.1 ▼	20.6 ▲	58.4 ▲	47.2 ▲	47.6 ▲
With the rest of the world							
Asia and the Pacific	**42.8 ▲**	**56.0 ▲**	**78.2 ▼**	**77.2 ▼**	**64.9 ▲**	**95.3 ▼**	**74.5 ▲**
ASEAN+3 (including HKG)ᵃ	42.6 ▲	51.1 ▲	76.9 ▼	77.1 ▼	50.0 ▼	51.7 ▲	61.0 ▼
Central Asia	64.1 ▲	29.8 ▲	92.4 ▼	74.0 ▼	9.5 ▼	53.1 ▲	96.8 ▲
East Asia	45.1 ▲	45.9 ▲	80.8 ▼	81.2 ▼	49.8 ▲	65.4 ▲	51.6 ▲
South Asia	62.8 ▲	60.2 ▼	87.6 ▲	89.8 ▲	73.0 ▲	77.3 ▲	84.4 ▲
Southeast Asia	30.7 ▼	61.7 ▼	63.1 ▼	58.9 ▼	49.8 ▼	32.7 ▲	69.0 ▼
Oceania and the Pacific	24.3 ▲	91.4 ▲	85.9 ▲	79.4 ▼	41.6 ▲	52.8 ▼	52.4 ▼

— = unchanged from previous period; ▲ = increase from previous period; ▼ = decrease from previous period.

ASEAN = Association of Southeast Asian Nations; FDI = foreign direct investment; HKG = Hong Kong, China.

ᵃ Includes ASEAN (Brunei Darussalam, Cambodia, Indonesia, the Lao People's Democratic Republic, Malaysia, Myanmar, the Philippines, Singapore, Thailand, and Viet Nam) plus Hong Kong, China; Japan; the People's Republic of China; and the Republic of Korea.

Trade—no data available on the Cook Islands and Niue.

Equity and Bond Holdings—based on investment from Australia; Bangladesh; Hong Kong, China; India; Indonesia; Japan; Kazakhstan; Malaysia; Mongolia; New Zealand; Pakistan; Palau; the People's Republic of China; the Philippines; the Republic of Korea; Singapore; and Thailand.

Migration—share of migrant stock to total migrants in 2020 (compared with 2015).

Tourism—share of outbound tourists to total tourists in 2022 (compared with 2021).

Remittances—share of inward remittances to total remittances in 2021 (compared with 2019).

Sources: ADB calculations using data from ASEAN Secretariat. ASEANstats Database. https://www.aseanstats.org (accessed July 2019); CEIC Data Company; Eurostat. Balance of Payments. http://ec.europa.eu/eurostat/web/balance-of-payments/data/database (accessed November 2023); International Monetary Fund (IMF). Coordinated Portfolio Investment Survey. https://data.imf.org/CPIS (accessed September 2023); IMF. Direction of Trade Statistics. https://data.imf.org/DOT (accessed December 2023); United Nations. Department of Economic and Social Affairs, Population Division. International Migrant Stock 2020. http://www.un.org/en/development/desa/population/migration/data/index.shtml (accessed May 2023); United Nations Conference on Trade and Development. World Investment Report. https://unctad.org/topic/investment/world-investment-report (accessed August 2023); United Nations World Tourism Organization. Tourism Satellite Accounts. https://www.e-unwto.org/toc/unwtotfb/current (accessed January 2024); and World Bank. Global Knowledge Partnership for Migration and Development. Bilateral Remittance staff estimates (December 2022). https://knomad.org/data/remittances (accessed August 2023)..

Table A3: Trade Shares—Asia and the Pacific, 2022 (% of total trade)

Reporter	Asia and the Pacific	of which		EU+UK	US	ROW
		PRC	Japan			
Central Asia	**35.9**	**17.7**	**1.1**	**28.1**	**2.0**	**34.0**
Armenia	22.9	12.4	1.4	16.5	3.3	57.3
Azerbaijan	17.2	4.1	0.6	53.8	1.1	27.9
Georgia	31.7	9.7	1.7	21.1	6.7	40.5
Kazakhstan	35.0	17.5	1.6	32.3	2.1	30.6
Kyrgyz Republic	55.5	35.0	0.8	5.4	2.1	37.1
Tajikistan	48.5	12.3	0.7	5.6	2.4	43.5
Turkmenistan	76.8	64.6	0.3	7.0	0.6	15.6
Uzbekistan	44.3	18.8	0.6	9.2	0.8	45.7
East Asia	**54.9**	**13.6**	**5.0**	**12.4**	**11.8**	**21.0**
China, People's Republic of	45.5	0.0	5.7	15.1	12.1	27.4
Hong Kong, China	80.7	48.4	3.8	7.1	5.2	7.1
Japan	57.5	20.3	0.0	10.7	14.0	17.8
Korea, Republic of	56.9	21.9	6.0	10.5	13.6	19.0
Mongolia	74.9	64.0	3.2	4.8	1.3	19.0
Taipei,China	71.8	29.1	8.2	8.8	12.3	7.1
South Asia	**37.2**	**11.2**	**1.9**	**13.7**	**10.7**	**38.3**
Afghanistan	65.9	17.9	2.8	3.7	0.8	29.6
Bangladesh	48.4	15.9	2.9	23.5	9.7	18.5
Bhutan	97.9	5.3	0.2	1.3	0.1	0.6
India	34.6	9.9	1.8	12.6	11.1	41.7
Maldives	55.1	10.4	1.1	9.5	2.5	33.0
Nepal	85.5	13.6	0.4	2.7	3.5	8.3
Pakistan	37.4	18.7	1.9	16.2	9.2	37.2
Sri Lanka	49.3	13.8	1.8	18.6	12.8	19.4
Southeast Asia	**69.3**	**18.5**	**7.0**	**8.6**	**11.0**	**11.1**
Brunei Darussalam	79.2	11.8	14.6	1.6	2.7	16.5
Cambodia	61.1	21.3	3.6	10.4	16.9	11.6
Indonesia	72.8	22.8	7.9	6.6	7.8	12.8
Lao People's Democratic Republic	93.2	30.8	1.6	3.4	1.6	1.7
Malaysia	72.1	17.1	6.4	8.3	9.4	10.2
Myanmar	81.2	29.1	4.6	13.6	2.0	3.2
Philippines	74.7	18.0	10.7	8.5	9.8	7.0
Singapore	69.9	12.8	4.8	9.5	9.8	10.8
Thailand	64.5	17.9	10.1	8.0	11.1	16.4
Timor-Leste	90.3	24.7	3.3	2.4	2.1	5.2
Viet Nam	64.7	24.4	6.6	9.5	17.1	8.6
Pacific	**85.5**	**18.6**	**10.4**	**8.5**	**2.2**	**3.9**
Fiji	80.9	12.3	2.9	3.4	7.6	8.2
Kiribati	91.0	3.8	3.6	2.5	1.5	5.1
Marshall Islands	77.7	19.9	7.2	15.7	1.6	5.0
Micronesia, Federated States of	39.1	4.2	4.3	0.4	15.9	44.7
Nauru	80.8	4.4	4.0	1.2	1.1	17.0
Palau	50.3	25.1	6.3	6.7	23.3	19.8
Papua New Guinea	93.8	19.2	14.7	4.9	0.8	0.5
Samoa	78.6	8.0	3.9	4.2	10.4	6.8
Solomon Islands	86.7	41.3	1.4	9.3	1.8	2.3
Tonga	79.4	11.8	3.8	5.1	11.0	4.6
Tuvalu	68.4	0.8	3.1	14.5	1.7	15.4
Vanuatu	88.9	8.7	12.3	2.8	1.8	6.6
Oceania	**75.0**	**27.9**	**12.6**	**9.9**	**6.7**	**8.4**
Australia	76.0	28.2	13.6	9.5	6.3	8.2
New Zealand	68.0	25.4	6.1	12.4	9.9	9.7
Asia and the Pacific	**57.2**	**15.1**	**5.4**	**11.9**	**11.1**	**19.9**
Developing Asia	**56.2**	**13.9**	**5.6**	**12.1**	**11.0**	**20.7**

EU = European Union (27 members), ROW = rest of the world, UK = United Kingdom, US = United States.

Source: ADB calculations using data from International Monetary Fund. Direction of Trade Statistics. http://data.imf.org/dot (accessed December 2023).

Table A4: Free Trade Agreement Status—Asia and the Pacific, as of November 2023

Economy	Under Negotiation		Signed But Not Yet In Effect	Signed and In Effect	Total
	Framework Agreement Signed	Negotiations Launched			
Armenia	0	5	2	13	20
Australia	0	4	1	21	26
Azerbaijan	0	1	1	10	12
Bangladesh	0	3	0	5	8
Bhutan	0	1	0	3	4
Brunei Darussalam	0	1	0	11	12
Cambodia	0	1	1	10	12
China, People's Republic of	0	9	4	21	34
Cook Islands	0	0	0	4	4
Fiji	0	0	0	6	6
Georgia	0	0	1	14	15
Hong Kong, China	0	2	0	8	10
India	0	20	0	17	37
Indonesia	0	10	1	17	28
Japan	0	6	0	21	27
Kazakhstan	0	7	2	13	22
Kiribati	0	0	0	4	4
Korea, Republic of	0	11	4	23	38
Kyrgyz Republic	0	5	2	13	20
Lao People's Democratic Republic	0	1	0	10	11
Malaysia	0	8	0	18	26
Maldives	0	1	1	2	4
Marshall Islands	0	0	0	5	5
Micronesia, Federated States of	0	0	0	5	5
Mongolia	0	1	0	2	3
Nauru	0	0	0	4	4
Nepal	0	1	0	2	3
New Zealand	0	2	2	15	19
Niue	0	0	0	4	4
Pakistan	0	6	2	11	19
Palau	0	0	0	4	4
Papua New Guinea	0	0	0	7	7
Philippines	0	3	1	10	14
Samoa	0	0	0	5	5
Singapore	0	7	4	31	42
Solomon Islands	0	0	0	6	6
Sri Lanka	0	5	0	6	11
Taipei,China	1	2	2	4	9
Tajikistan	0	0	0	8	8
Thailand	1	9	0	15	25
Tonga	0	0	0	4	4
Turkmenistan	0	0	1	5	6
Tuvalu	0	0	0	4	4
Uzbekistan	0	1	0	11	12
Vanuatu	0	0	1	5	6
Viet Nam	0	2	1	15	18

Notes:
(i)   Framework agreement signed: The parties initially negotiate the contents of a framework agreement, which serves as a framework for future negotiations.
(ii) Negotiations launched: The parties, through the relevant ministries, declare the official launch of negotiations or set the date for such, or start the first round of negotiations.
(iii) Signed but not yet in effect: Parties sign the agreement after negotiations have been completed. However, the agreement has yet to be implemented.
(iv) Signed and in effect: Provisions of free trade agreement come into force, after legislative or executive ratification.

Source: ADB. Asia Regional Integation Center. https://aric.adb.org (accessed November 2023).

Table A5: Cross-Border Portfolio Equity Holdings—Asia and the Pacific, 2022 (% of total cross-border portfolio equity holdings)

Reporter	Partner					
	Asia and the Pacific	of which		EU+UK	US	ROW
		PRC	Japan			
Central Asia	**7.6**	**0.0**	**5.5**	**21.3**	**64.5**	**6.6**
Armenia	—	—	—	—	—	—
Azerbaijan	—	—	—	—	—	—
Georgia	—	—	—	—	—	—
Kazakhstan	7.6	0.0	5.5	21.3	64.5	6.6
Kyrgyz Republic	—	—	—	—	—	—
Tajikistan	—	—	—	—	—	—
Turkmenistan	—	—	—	—	—	—
Uzbekistan	—	—	—	—	—	—
East Asia	**19.2**	**6.5**	**1.1**	**13.0**	**29.2**	**38.5**
China, People's Republic of	56.7	—	1.0	7.5	20.1	15.7
Hong Kong, China	26.9	21.2	2.2	10.6	5.7	56.9
Japan	4.7	0.5	—	14.7	38.0	42.6
Korea, Republic of	11.1	2.6	3.0	18.7	61.1	9.2
Mongolia	53.9	1.2	0.9	13.1	24.7	8.3
Taipei,China	—	—	—	—	—	—
South Asia	**12.4**	**2.9**	**0.7**	**33.6**	**48.2**	**5.8**
Bangladesh	100.0	—	—	—	—	0.0
Bhutan	—	—	—	—	—	—
India	12.6	2.9	0.7	34.5	49.3	3.6
Maldives	—	—	—	—	—	—
Nepal	—	—	—	—	—	—
Pakistan	—	—	—	1.0	1.3	97.7
Sri Lanka	—	—	—	—	—	—
Southeast Asia	**36.9**	**11.1**	**3.7**	**13.6**	**24.9**	**24.7**
Brunei Darussalam	—	—	—	—	—	—
Cambodia	—	—	—	—	—	—
Indonesia	98.7	0.1	0.4	0.0	—	1.3
Lao People's Democratic Republic	—	—	—	—	—	—
Malaysia	47.1	6.9	3.7	20.3	24.1	8.4
Philippines	18.6	0.1	0.3	58.2	21.7	1.6
Singapore	36.2	12.4	3.9	11.9	25.1	26.8
Thailand	15.2	0.7	0.9	29.1	27.9	27.8
Timor-Leste	—	—	—	—	—	—
Viet Nam	—	—	—	—	—	—
Oceania and the Pacific	**14.1**	**1.8**	**4.1**	**9.8**	**51.6**	**24.5**
Australia	12.3	1.9	4.3	9.8	52.2	25.7
Cook Islands	—	—	—	—	—	—
Fiji	—	—	—	—	—	—
Kiribati	—	—	—	—	—	—
Marshall Islands	—	—	—	—	—	—
Micronesia, Federated States of	—	—	—	—	—	—
Nauru	—	—	—	—	—	—
New Zealand	28.2	0.7	3.0	10.1	47.0	14.7
Niue	—	—	—	—	—	—
Palau	—	—	—	—	—	—
Papua New Guinea	—	—	—	—	—	—
Samoa	—	—	—	—	—	—
Solomon Islands	—	—	—	—	—	—
Tonga	—	—	—	—	—	—
Tuvalu	—	—	—	—	—	—
Vanuatu	—	—	—	—	—	—
Asia and the Pacific	**21.8**	**6.7**	**2.0**	**12.7**	**31.6**	**33.9**
Developing Asia	**32.7**	**11.0**	**2.6**	**12.3**	**23.9**	**31.1**

— = unavailable, EU = European Union (27 members), ROW = rest of the world, UK = United Kingdom, US = United States.

Source: ADB calculations using data from International Monetary Fund. Coordinated Portfolio Investment Survey. https://data.imf.org/cpis (accessed September 2023).

Table A6: Cross-Border Portfolio Debt Holdings—Asia and the Pacific, 2022 (% of total cross-border portfolio debt holdings)

Reporter	Asia and the Pacific	of which PRC	of which Japan	EU+UK	US	ROW
Central Asia	**26.0**	**16.9**	**2.5**	**12.7**	**37.1**	**24.1**
Armenia	—	—	—	—	—	—
Azerbaijan	—	—	—	—	—	—
Georgia	—	—	—	—	—	—
Kazakhstan	26.0	16.9	2.5	12.7	37.1	24.1
Kyrgyz Republic	—	—	—	—	—	—
Tajikistan	—	—	—	—	—	—
Turkmenistan	—	—	—	—	—	—
Uzbekistan	—	—	—	—	—	—
East Asia	**18.8**	**4.9**	**2.0**	**23.8**	**39.6**	**17.8**
China, People's Republic of	35.8	—	4.1	11.8	22.4	30.0
Hong Kong, China	43.5	22.5	6.6	13.4	27.5	15.6
Japan	8.3	0.7	—	29.6	46.0	16.1
Korea, Republic of	13.6	2.7	3.1	21.6	47.9	16.9
Mongolia	67.3	6.7	0.1	6.8	22.4	3.5
Taipei,China	—	—	—	—	—	—
South Asia	**10.2**	**—**	**—**	**34.6**	**52.6**	**2.5**
Bangladesh	—	—	—	—	—	—
Bhutan	—	—	—	—	—	—
India	10.2	—	—	35.6	54.1	0.0
Maldives	—	—	—	—	—	—
Nepal	—	—	—	—	—	—
Pakistan	8.3	—	—	—	—	91.7
Sri Lanka	—	—	—	—	—	—
Southeast Asia	**41.1**	**8.2**	**12.2**	**4.3**	**35.9**	**18.7**
Brunei Darussalam	—	—	—	—	—	—
Cambodia	—	—	—	—	—	—
Indonesia	78.3	1.7	0.0	0.8	16.7	4.2
Lao People's Democratic Republic	—	—	—	—	—	—
Malaysia	42.0	9.0	2.6	12.9	19.2	25.9
Philippines	36.4	3.5	0.7	4.2	38.5	20.9
Singapore	39.4	8.6	12.9	4.0	37.6	18.9
Thailand	61.1	4.6	18.3	7.1	15.1	16.7
Timor-Leste	—	—	—	—	—	—
Viet Nam	—	—	—	—	—	—
Oceania and the Pacific	**20.6**	**2.8**	**6.2**	**19.9**	**30.1**	**29.3**
Australia	20.9	3.3	7.2	21.4	29.3	28.4
Cook Islands	—	—	—	—	—	—
Fiji	—	—	—	—	—	—
Kiribati	—	—	—	—	—	—
Marshall Islands	—	—	—	—	—	—
Micronesia, Federated States of	—	—	—	—	—	—
Nauru	—	—	—	—	—	—
New Zealand	18.6	—	—	9.9	35.6	35.9
Niue	—	—	—	—	—	—
Palau	—	—	—	—	—	—
Papua New Guinea	—	—	—	—	—	—
Samoa	—	—	—	—	—	—
Solomon Islands	—	—	—	—	—	—
Tonga	—	—	—	—	—	—
Tuvalu	—	—	—	—	—	—
Vanuatu	—	—	—	—	—	—
Asia and the Pacific	**22.8**	**5.5**	**4.0**	**20.1**	**38.3**	**18.8**
Developing Asia	**37.2**	**10.3**	**7.5**	**10.6**	**32.0**	**20.2**

— = unavailable, EU = European Union (27 members), ROW = rest of the world, UK = United Kingdom, US = United States.

Source: ADB calculations using data from International Monetary Fund. Coordinated Portfolio Investment Survey. https://data.imf.org/cpis (accessed September 2023).

Table A7: Foreign Direct Investment Inflow Share—Asia and the Pacific, 2022 (% of total FDI inflows)

Reporter	Asia and the Pacific	PRC	Japan	EU+UK	US	ROW
Central Asia	**70.2**	**22.3**	**8.1**	**200.4**	**65.0**	**(235.6)**
Armenia	1.3	0.6	0.0	(0.9)	0.9	98.8
Azerbaijan	(9.2)	(0.2)	(6.2)	(62.6)	(6.2)	178.0
Georgia	11.8	5.4	3.4	64.4	8.2	15.6
Kazakhstan	64.9	23.5	5.5	208.8	83.6	(257.3)
Kyrgyz Republic	152.9	112.1	2.6	69.3	3.7	(125.9)
Tajikistan	11.2	3.5	1.4	12.3	3.1	73.4
Turkmenistan	89.5	0.9	0.0	6.0	0.0	4.5
Uzbekistan	3.4	0.4	0.1	2.1	(0.4)	94.8
East Asia	**54.1**	**2.9**	**2.2**	**9.8**	**6.3**	**29.9**
China, People's Republic of	85.8	0.0	2.4	6.2	1.2	6.9
Hong Kong, China	15.0	6.9	1.5	4.1	2.1	78.8
Japan	47.2	3.9	0.0	32.4	29.9	(9.5)
Korea, Republic of	17.3	4.7	8.5	35.7	48.3	-1.3
Mongolia	22.2	7.7	3.0	103.5	3.7	(29.4)
Taipei,China	12.3	3.0	2.8	1.0	0.6	86.2
South Asia	**39.8**	**1.3**	**3.9**	**20.6**	**15.2**	**24.4**
Bangladesh	40.1	5.4	3.0	34.2	10.2	15.5
Bhutan	69.9	0.0	0.0	11.2	0.0	18.9
India	40.3	0.0	4.0	19.8	16.1	23.9
Maldives	3.1	1.0	0.9	5.5	0.0	91.4
Nepal	19.8	15.1	0.0	14.6	8.5	57.1
Pakistan	62.8	38.2	6.3	33.8	11.2	-7.8
Sri Lanka	9.3	1.5	0.9	7.7	1.6	81.4
Southeast Asia	**38.3**	**5.4**	**10.3**	**13.8**	**16.1**	**31.8**
Brunei Darussalam	(14.4)	(1.7)	(1.3)	(5.8)	(1.2)	121.5
Cambodia	3.1	0.3	0.2	0.8	0.2	95.9
Indonesia	83.6	16.3	8.2	7.4	8.9	0.1
Lao People's Democratic Republic	5.5	1.0	0.4	1.4	0.4	92.7
Malaysia	49.3	4.8	12.9	(4.4)	50.8	4.4
Philippines	14.1	0.2	6.5	0.6	2.7	82.6
Singapore	35.1	4.8	12.0	19.7	17.1	28.1
Thailand	69.8	8.2	14.0	16.8	9.4	4.0
Timor-Leste	0.0	0.0	0.0	0.1	0.0	99.9
Viet Nam	1.9	0.4	0.2	0.6	0.1	97.4
Oceania and the Pacific	**8.6**	**(2.7)**	**1.7**	**20.9**	**2.6**	**67.9**
Australia	1.5	(3.2)	1.2	23.2	2.3	73.0
Cook Islands	—	—	—	—	—	—
Fiji	11.0	2.0	2.1	6.9	8.5	73.6
Kiribati	—	—	—	—	—	—
Marshall Islands	—	—	—	—	—	—
Micronesia, Federated States of	—	—	—	—	—	—
Nauru	—	—	—	—	—	—
New Zealand	39.9	0.0	3.5	(0.2)	5.6	54.7
Niue	—	—	—	—	—	—
Palau	6.4	1.3	3.8	0.0	5.4	88.2
Papua New Guinea	517.7	3.9	1.3	19.4	0.0	(437.1)
Samoa	—	—	—	—	—	—
Solomon Islands	22.2	2.2	2.5	10.6	6.5	60.7
Tonga	—	—	—	—	—	—
Tuvalu	—	—	—	—	—	—
Vanuatu	(468.1)	(70.3)	(75.9)	(340.0)	0.0	908.1
Asia and the Pacific	**44.0**	**3.3**	**4.9**	**15.1**	**10.3**	**30.5**
Developing Asia	**48.1**	**3.9**	**5.5**	**13.6**	**10.2**	**28.1**

( ) = negative, — = unavailable, EU = European Union (27 members), FDI = foreign direct investment, ROW = rest of the world, UK = United Kingdom, US = United States.

Sources: ADB calculations using data from Association of Southeast Asian Nations Secretariat; CEIC Data Company; Eurostat. Balance of Payments; Organisation for Economic Co-operation and Development; and United Nations Conference on Trade and Development. Bilateral FDI Statistics. http://unctad.org/en/Pages/Home.aspx (accessed November 2023).

Table A8: Remittance Inflows Share—Asia and the Pacific, 2021 (% of total remittance inflows)

Reporter	Asia and the Pacific	Middle East	EU+UK	US	ROW
Central Asia	**3.2**	**2.1**	**7.8**	**2.2**	**84.7**
Armenia	4.3	0.5	14.8	12.3	68.1
Azerbaijan	7.3	9.9	5.6	3.1	74.1
Georgia	9.8	4.3	21.9	5.0	59.0
Kazakhstan	1.3	1.2	30.0	0.9	66.7
Kyrgyz Republic	2.9	4.3	15.2	1.4	76.2
Tajikistan	5.2	1.3	7.5	1.5	84.5
Turkmenistan	—	—	—	—	100.0
Uzbekistan	—	—	—	—	100.0
East Asia	**48.4**	**0.3**	**11.1**	**28.1**	**12.0**
China, People's Republic of	52.8	0.4	11.1	23.9	11.8
Hong Kong, China	39.0	0.0	12.7	22.9	25.3
Japan	23.0	0.3	16.3	44.0	16.4
Korea, Republic of	37.1	0.2	5.7	48.3	8.7
Mongolia	39.2	1.7	35.4	—	23.7
Taipei,China	—	—	—	—	—
South Asia	**15.6**	**56.6**	**10.6**	**12.8**	**4.5**
Bangladesh	34.7	52.4	7.2	4.2	1.4
Bhutan	85.6	—	4.1	—	10.3
India	9.9	58.2	9.1	17.7	5.1
Maldives	73.3	0.8	18.6	—	7.3
Nepal	49.5	36.6	4.7	8.3	0.9
Pakistan	8.1	62.1	17.1	8.0	4.8
Sri Lanka	21.2	46.8	19.1	2.9	10.0
Southeast Asia	**31.0**	**19.5**	**11.1**	**30.1**	**8.3**
Brunei Darussalam	—	—	—	—	—
Cambodia	69.5	0.0	8.9	18.5	3.1
Indonesia	41.3	51.3	3.9	2.5	1.0
Lao People's Democratic Republic	76.0	—	5.1	17.3	1.6
Malaysia	88.8	0.1	4.7	4.2	2.3
Philippines	16.5	27.5	9.0	35.0	12.1
Singapore	—	—	—	—	—
Timor-Leste	41.4	2.1	25.6	24.1	6.8
Thailand	85.2	—	14.5	—	0.3
Viet Nam	35.7	0.0	13.6	43.7	7.0
Oceania and the Pacific	**47.6**	**0.7**	**22.5**	**19.8**	**9.4**
Australia	27.9	1.6	46.4	16.2	7.9
Cook Islands	—	—	—	—	—
Fiji	63.5	—	3.1	21.6	11.8
Kiribati	90.5	—	7.5	—	2.0
Marshall Islands	0.8	—	0.1	97.4	1.6
Micronesia, Federated States of	—	—	—	—	—
Nauru	—	—	—	—	—
New Zealand	78.3	0.0	12.4	6.7	2.5
Niue	—	—	—	—	—
Palau	13.1	—	8.2	—	78.7
Papua New Guinea	93.8	—	4.7	—	1.5
Samoa	68.5	—	0.8	22.5	8.2
Solomon Islands	87.1	—	12.3	—	0.6
Tonga	57.0	—	0.7	40.0	2.2
Tuvalu	—	—	—	—	—
Vanuatu	56.9	—	16.5	—	26.6
Asia and the Pacific	**25.5**	**32.2**	**10.7**	**19.5**	**12.2**
Developing Asia	**25.5**	**32.8**	**10.5**	**19.1**	**12.1**

— = unavailable, EU = European Union (27 members), ROW = rest of the world, UK = United Kingdom, US = United States.

Source: ADB calculations using data from World Bank. Global Knowledge Partnership for Migration and Development. Bilateral Remittance staff estimates (December 2022). https://knomad.org/data/remittances (accessed August 2023).

Table A9: Outbound Migration Share—Asia and the Pacific, 2020 (% of total outbound migrants)

Reporter	Asia and the Pacific	of which PRC	of which Japan	EU+UK	US	ROW
Central Asia	**9.5**	**—**	**—**	**16.4**	**2.6**	**71.5**
Armenia	18.9	—	—	10.3	9.1	61.6
Azerbaijan	14.5	—	—	4.5	2.7	78.3
Georgia	11.0	—	—	20.9	4.6	63.5
Kazakhstan	1.4	—	—	28.8	0.9	69.0
Kyrgyz Republic	3.7	—	—	13.4	1.1	81.7
Tajikistan	6.2	—	—	6.2	1.2	86.3
Turkmenistan	2.5	—	—	4.6	1.4	91.5
Uzbekistan	22.5	—	—	3.9	3.1	70.4
East Asia	**49.8**	**2.5**	**8.5**	**10.8**	**25.9**	**13.5**
China, People's Republic of	55.2	—	7.4	10.9	20.9	13.0
Hong Kong, China	39.2	20.8	—	12.6	22.9	25.3
Japan	24.0	0.7	—	19.5	39.6	16.9
Korea, Republic of	38.4	6.6	20.7	5.6	47.1	8.9
Mongolia	42.6	—	—	27.6	—	29.8
Taipei,China	—	—	—	—	—	—
South Asia	**27.0**	**0.0**	**0.2**	**9.1**	**8.9**	**54.9**
Bangladesh	42.2	0.0	0.2	6.1	3.5	48.1
Bhutan	86.8	—	—	3.5	—	9.7
India	18.3	0.0	0.2	7.9	15.2	58.6
Maldives	78.8	—	—	13.6	—	7.5
Nepal	58.2	—	—	3.0	6.8	32.0
Pakistan	20.5	0.1	0.3	14.6	6.5	58.4
Sri Lanka	22.4	0.2	1.3	19.1	2.6	55.8
Southeast Asia	**50.2**	**1.7**	**3.1**	**7.5**	**18.7**	**23.5**
Brunei Darussalam	75.0	—	—	13.5	—	11.5
Cambodia	75.8	—	0.4	7.5	14.0	2.6
Indonesia	42.7	0.7	1.2	3.8	2.3	51.2
Lao People's Democratic Republic	80.8	—	—	4.4	13.4	1.5
Malaysia	88.0	0.3	0.6	5.6	4.0	2.4
Philippines	17.0	0.9	4.5	8.8	33.8	40.4
Singapore	64.7	—	0.9	20.1	9.6	5.6
Timor-Leste	43.4	1.1	4.9	24.6	23.6	8.5
Thailand	86.9	—	—	12.9	—	0.2
Viet Nam	38.5	8.9	9.9	13.1	41.4	7.1
Oceania and the Pacific	**58.4**	**0.2**	**0.8**	**19.8**	**14.6**	**7.3**
Australia	28.1	0.7	1.9	45.5	17.3	9.1
Cook Islands	99.9	—	—	0.0	—	0.0
Fiji	63.4	—	—	3.0	22.0	11.6
Kiribati	92.9	—	—	4.8	—	2.3
Marshall Islands	1.3	—	—	0.0	95.9	2.7
Micronesia, Federated States of	2.8	—	—	0.6	47.0	49.6
Nauru	97.0	—	—	0.9	—	2.1
New Zealand	79.0	—	0.4	12.4	6.2	2.5
Niue	99.5	—	—	—	—	0.5
Palau	12.1	—	—	7.6	—	80.3
Papua New Guinea	48.9	—	—	38.7	—	12.4
Samoa	67.3	—	—	0.7	20.0	12.0
Solomon Islands	88.2	—	—	11.0	—	0.7
Tonga	57.8	—	—	0.7	38.3	3.2
Tuvalu	81.1	—	—	1.6	—	17.2
Vanuatu	26.9	—	—	16.1	—	57.0
Asia and the Pacific	**35.1**	**0.8**	**2.2**	**10.0**	**13.5**	**41.4**
Developing Asia	**34.9**	**0.9**	**2.3**	**9.7**	**13.3**	**42.2**

— = unavailable, EU = European Union (27 members), ROW = rest of the world, UK = United Kingdom, US = United States.

Source: ADB calculations using data from United Nations. Department of Economic and Social Affairs, Population Division. International Migrant Stock 2020. http://www.un.org/en/development/desa/population/migration/data/index.shtml (accessed May 2023).

Table A10a: Inbound Tourism Share—Asia and the Pacific, 2022 (% of total inbound visitors)

Destination	Asia and the Pacific	of which PRC	EU+UK	US	ROW
Central Asia	**62.4**	**0.2**	**2.9**	**0.6**	**34.0**
Armenia	26.8	0.3	7.8	3.2	62.3
Azerbaijan	18.2	0.2	4.6	0.8	76.4
Georgia	27.7	0.2	6.2	0.8	65.3
Kazakhstan	58.9	0.4	2.6	0.4	38.1
Kyrgyz Republic	88.9	0.1	0.6	0.2	10.3
Tajikistan	—	—	—	—	—
Turkmenistan	—	—	—	—	—
Uzbekistan	—	—	—	—	—
East Asia	**72.8**	**9.2**	**7.7**	**11.3**	**8.2**
China, People's Republic of	—	—	—	—	—
Hong Kong, China	84.5	62.7	5.6	4.3	5.6
Japan	80.5	4.9	7.0	8.4	4.1
Korea, Republic of	63.7	7.2	9.9	17.2	9.2
Mongolia	34.4	3.9	4.9	3.0	57.7
Taipei,China	76.8	2.7	5.4	9.9	7.9
South Asia	**34.0**	**0.9**	**36.7**	**6.0**	**23.3**
Bangladesh	—	—	—	—	—
Bhutan	71.0	0.8	12.4	11.6	5.0
India	—	—	—	—	—
Maldives	26.9	0.8	41.5	4.8	26.8
Nepal	56.1	1.6	22.2	12.6	9.1
Pakistan	—	—	—	—	—
Sri Lanka	—	—	—	—	—
Southeast Asia	**70.5**	**2.8**	**10.7**	**6.7**	**12.1**
Brunei Darussalam	—	—	—	—	—
Cambodia	84.7	4.7	8.4	4.1	2.7
Indonesia	76.3	3.0	14.7	3.3	5.7
Lao People's Democratic Republic	—	—	—	—	—
Malaysia	—	—	—	—	—
Philippines	42.0	1.4	10.7	20.1	27.2
Singapore	78.6	2.1	9.7	5.1	6.6
Thailand	—	—	—	—	—
Timor-Leste	—	—	—	—	—
Viet Nam	58.2	3.0	8.8	7.5	25.5
Oceania and the Pacific	**66.9**	**2.0**	**16.2**	**8.7**	**8.3**
Australia	59.6	2.4	21.1	8.8	10.4
Cook Islands	99.1	—	0.0	0.5	0.4
Fiji	84.3	1.0	2.3	11.6	1.8
Kiribati	82.2	8.2	2.5	15.3	0.0
Marshall Islands	—	—	—	—	—
Micronesia, Federated States of	—	—	—	—	—
Nauru	—	—	—	—	—
New Zealand	73.9	1.2	11.9	7.9	6.3
Niue	—	—	—	—	—
Palau	—	—	—	—	—
Papua New Guinea	86.5	6.2	5.4	5.7	2.3
Samoa	80.6	2.1	0.8	8.3	10.3
Solomon Islands	—	—	—	—	—
Tonga	84.9	1.7	1.4	13.2	0.6
Tuvalu	86.7	9.3	5.8	4.4	3.1
Vanuatu	87.2	1.6	0.0	0.0	12.8
Asia and the Pacific	**65.6**	**2.5**	**9.1**	**5.1**	**20.2**
Developing Asia	**64.8**	**2.4**	**8.3**	**4.6**	**22.3**

— = unavailable, EU = European Union (27 members), ROW = rest of the world, UK = United Kingdom, US = United States.

Source: ADB calculations using data from United Nations World Tourism Organization. Tourism Satellite Accounts. http:/ statistics.unwto.org/ (accessed January 2024).

Table A10b: Outbound Tourism Share—Asia and the Pacific, 2022 (% of total outbound visitors)

Reporter	Asia and the Pacific	of which PRC	EU+UK	US	ROW
Central Asia	**46.9**	**–**	**31.2**	**0.2**	**21.7**
Armenia	53.6	–	3.3	0.7	42.4
Azerbaijan	2.2	–	88.6	0.0	9.2
Georgia	13.3	–	12.1	0.4	74.2
Kazakhstan	63.5	–	1.9	0.4	34.3
Kyrgyz Republic	87.9	–	0.6	0.2	11.3
Tajikistan	87.8	–	4.0	0.1	8.1
Turkmenistan	18.8	–	41.9	0.6	38.7
Uzbekistan	83.8	–	0.2	0.1	15.9
East Asia	**34.6**	**–**	**14.7**	**10.0**	**40.7**
China, People's Republic of	17.1	–	10.3	4.0	68.6
Hong Kong, China	42.0	–	10.6	3.1	44.3
Japan	36.6	–	28.4	21.1	13.9
Korea, Republic of	52.8	–	16.8	15.6	14.7
Mongolia	65.1	–	1.4	5.9	27.6
Taipei,China	63.0	–	13.1	11.8	12.0
South Asia	**22.7**	**–**	**12.4**	**10.8**	**54.1**
Afghanistan	1.1	–	0.8	0.3	97.8
Bangladesh	23.7	–	3.7	4.8	67.9
Bhutan	–	–	–	–	–
India	28.0	–	16.7	15.3	40.1
Maldives	46.9	–	15.4	0.9	36.9
Nepal	52.0	–	19.6	10.0	18.4
Pakistan	6.7	–	5.6	3.3	84.4
Sri Lanka	44.8	–	5.7	4.7	44.8
Southeast Asia	**67.3**	**–**	**5.6**	**3.2**	**23.9**
Brunei Darussalam	78.4	–	0.8	1.2	19.6
Cambodia	94.9	–	0.5	2.9	1.7
Indonesia	45.5	–	2.7	2.1	49.8
Lao People's Democratic Republic	97.0	–	1.7	0.8	0.5
Malaysia	71.9	–	4.9	1.2	22.0
Myanmar	83.8	–	0.7	1.5	14.0
Philippines	41.6	–	8.8	7.2	42.4
Singapore	71.2	–	13.1	4.9	10.8
Thailand	82.7	–	5.8	2.4	9.1
Timor-Leste	99.7	–	0.2	0.0	0.1
Viet Nam	91.0	–	1.4	4.2	3.3
Oceania and the Pacific	**47.2**	**–**	**26.6**	**8.5**	**17.7**
Australia	41.4	–	30.4	8.7	19.6
Cook Islands	91.7	–	3.5	0.8	4.1
Fiji	82.1	–	0.8	12.2	4.9
Kiribati	86.7	–	2.4	4.6	6.3
Marshall Islands	18.2	–	51.9	4.3	25.7
Micronesia, Federated States of	8.5	–	1.1	4.5	85.8
Nauru	93.0	–	3.9	1.0	2.1
New Zealand	68.5	–	12.7	8.1	10.6
Niue	84.9	–	3.0	0.9	11.2
Palau	24.2	–	2.9	4.0	68.8
Papua New Guinea	96.3	–	1.5	1.2	1.0
Samoa	87.7	–	0.6	7.5	4.3
Solomon Islands	87.9	–	2.8	3.6	5.8
Tonga	87.4	–	2.4	8.6	1.6
Tuvalu	74.7	–	3.3	8.3	13.8
Vanuatu	84.9	–	2.3	1.1	11.7
Asia and the Pacific	**44.7**	**–**	**19.4**	**5.3**	**30.6**
Developing Asia	**44.8**	**–**	**18.3**	**4.4**	**32.6**

— = unavailable, EU = European Union (27 members), ROW = rest of the world, UK = United Kingdom, US = United States.

Source: ADB calculations using data from United Nations World Tourism Organization. Tourism Satellite Accounts. http://statistics.unwto.org/ (accessed January 2024).

www.ingramcontent.com/pod-product-compliance
Lightning Source LLC
Chambersburg PA
CBHW050242220326
41598CB00048B/7486